Science Fiction

collectibles

Identification &
Price Guide

Stuart W. Wells III

Science Fiction
Collectibles

Identification and Price Guide

by Stuart W. Wells III

CONTENTS

ACKNOWLEDGMENTS

The author extends his heartfelt thanks to Rob Rintoul, Brian Brick, Tim Frederick, Morgan McClain, Jim Main, and Rich Maurizio for their assistance and for permitting their collections to be photographed for this work. Thanks also to Alex Maurizio and to Debby and Marty Krim for some of the photographs used in the book.

Many manufacturers of items supplied information, catalogs or photographs. Thanks to: Don Post Studios, Alan Payne at Icons, Don Schmidt at Tiger Electronics, Tracy at Illusive Originals, Chaz Fitzhugh at Applause, Jim Schneider at Star Jars, Joshua Izzo at Topps, and Matt Mariani at Decipher, Inc.

Several local retailers were kind enough to let me photograph inventory in their stores. Thanks to:

Todd Testa and Larry Russo at Castle Comics, Milford, Conn.
(Comics, Toys, Model Kits and Statues) (203) 877-3610, Website: www.castlecomics.com

David Kruseski and Steven Bryant at Heroes Comics & Cards, Norwalk, Conn.
(Comics and CCGs) (203) 750-0505

Jeff Kubarych at Route 7 Comics & Collectibles, Ridgefield, Conn.
(Comics, Action Figures and Star Wars collectibles) (203) 894-1499

Pat Callanan at Cave Comics, Newtown, Conn. (Comics)

INTRODUCTION

Science fiction is largely a 20th century phenomena, and for most of the century it has been divided into two quite separate worlds — The Book World and The Media World. Readers reside in the Book World. They collect books, pulp magazines and science fiction cover art and go to conventions where they can meet their favorite authors and artists. They consider themselves to be much superior to the movie and TV fans who inhabit the Media World. Fans collect movie memorabilia, action figures and other toys, comic books and trading cards. They go to shows where they can get autographs from major and minor stars of Star Wars, Star Trek and their other favorite TV shows and movies. Fans generally don't care about Readers one way or the other, which is too bad, because nothing is more infuriating to Readers than indifference.

There are other differences between these two races. For one, Readers largely created their own world. Science fiction was published mostly in pulp magazines in the 1930s and 1940s and no respectable book publisher would touch it. A few enterprising readers started their own specialty book publishing operations and printed the first books by authors such as Isaac Asimov, Ray Bradbury, Arthur C. Clarke and Robert A. Heinlein, among others. Readers created and have always run their own conventions. Media fans have to wait for Hollywood to produce movies and TV shows and for the toy companies to produce collectibles, while their shows are generally run on a "for profit" basis by show promoters.

Despite these cultural differences, there is considerable crossover between these two worlds. Readers go to the movies and watch *Star Trek*, *Babylon-5* and other TV shows, while most media fans read some science fiction books in addition to the latest *Star Trek* and *Star Wars* novels. In addition, both Readers and Fans are collectors; however, they know little or nothing about each other's collectibles. This book is designed to bridge the gap and cover the collectibles of both worlds.

This book covers the whole range of science fiction collectibles from both worlds. In order to fit the information within the covers of a single volume, I have included almost exclusively science fiction with a space theme and omitted fantasy and horror collectibles, as well as comic book superheroes.

This book is divided into six sections: Action Figures, Books, Comics, Models & Statues, Toys, and Trading Cards.

The Action Figure section includes series from *Aliens* to *The X-Files* and includes extensive listings of the many *Star Trek* and *Star Wars* action figures.

The Books section covers publishers, authors, media books and pulp magazines.

The Comics section covers a wide variety of science fiction comic books, including those based on TV shows and movies as well as original series such as *Mystery in Space*.

The Models & Statues section includes model kits and the increasingly popular statues and fine replicas.

The Toys section includes all types of collectibles not covered in the other sections, including dolls and figures, ray guns, robots, space ships and toys based on movies and TV shows.

The Trading cards sections covers cards from all of your favorite TV shows and movies plus the many series of cards reproducing paintings by science fiction and fantasy artists.

Grading

Most collectible items are graded on a 10 point scale from C-10 (the best) down to C-1. Hardly anything old qualifies as a C-10 and nobody admits that anything they are trying to sell is a C-1, so the actual number of categories is probably less than 10. Prices in this book are for items in their original packaging in "near mint" condition, which corresponds to about C-9 or C-9.5. The occasional extra-ordinary item that is actually "mint" i.e. C-10 commands a slightly higher price. How much higher depends on how much better than an ordinary near mint copy it actually is. Mint means the same thing, regardless of age and type of product. It is not the same thing as "new." Many, probably most new action figures header cards are not mint. They have been handled when they were put in the shipping box, taken out of the box and hung on a rack, maybe dropped on the floor, handled by the check-out clerk, etc. This leaves an item which is a defect-free collectible, acceptable anywhere at the near-mint price. The figure inside is most likely mint, but rarely the package. "Near mint" does vary somewhat with the type of product. Some kinds of things are simply more durable than others and do not normally show any wear from normal handling. For those things, there is very little difference between the ordinary, i.e. near mint and the extra-ordinary, i.e. mint and probably very little difference in price. Unless the listed item is described as "loose," the price includes all packaging and in-pack premiums such as trading cards.

ACTION FIGURES

Action figures began as an attempt to sell dolls to boys and the earliest action figures were 12" tall and wore clothes, just like Barbie. Captain Action was more or less a space hero since he carried a ray gun and fought Dr. Evil, a non-human. Two of his many costumes were the traditional space heroes Buck Rogers and Flash Gordon. Mego dominated this market in the 1970s and among its many popular characters were lines from *Star Trek*, *Planet of the Apes*, *The Black Hole* and *Buck Rogers*. Then *Star Wars* came along in 1978 and changed the market forever. Action figures became a lot smaller and had molded-on outfits. These are the items listed as action figures in this section. Don't worry, these popular collectibles are still covered in the book, they are just listed later in the TOYS section along with other figures (die-cast, PVC, bendable, etc.).

Vehicles, both for dolls and action figures, are also covered in the TOYS section, grouped with replica spaceships and similar items. These ships are more important in science

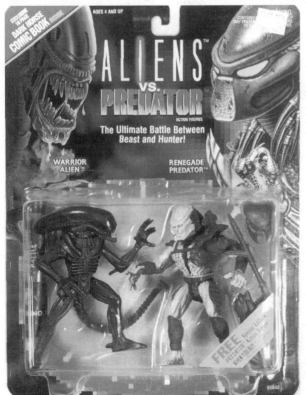

Aliens vs. Predator: Warrior Alien & Renegade Predator
(Kenner 1993)

fiction and space collectibles than they are in superhero and similar collectibles because Spider-Man and Superman can get along perfectly well without cars and other vehicles but Han Solo and Captain Kirk would be nothing without theirs. The only exception among the superheroes is Batman, who has a similar relationship which his cars, planes and boats as science fiction heroes do.

Action figures have become one of the predominate collectibles in the 1990s and, on average, about two new ones arrive every day at your local toy store. As with many categories covered in this book, *Star Trek* and *Star Wars* action figures are especially plentiful. However, a number of other popular science fiction shows and movies have produced figures as well. The *Stargate*, *ID-4 Independence Day*, *Lost in Space*, *Mars Attacks*, *Starship Troopers* and *X-Files* movies have all had action figure series produced in the last few years and the *Babylon 5* television show has finally yielded some action figures as well. New figures were made for two old shows — *Battlestar Galactica* and *Terminator 2*, while both *Aliens* and *Predator* figures have appeared regularly for the last several years with little or no actual movie backup. Don't get lost in all the activity surrounding 1999's new *Star Wars* movie and neglect these series.

Action figure collecting is driven by female figures, villainous aliens and variations. Among action figures, heroes tend to be produced in great abundance because the humans for whom they are actually designed — about half your height and one-quarter your weight — like the heroes. Often that makes the aliens, villains, rogues and other disreputable characters, and especially the females, relatively scarce. If you don't know which character from a new series is going to be the most collectible, the female figure is always a good choice; there is rarely more than one produced and often she is short-packed. And, while you can't exactly expect a toy company to produce a figure from the shower scene from *Starship Troopers*, sometimes the female is even attractively, and lightly, dressed. It didn't take a genius to figure that the first Seven of Nine doll would be popular with collectors.

Variations are obviously harder to pick out, because they rarely occur in the same shipment. You have to have an eagle eye to spot a variation even when you have both figures together to make the comparison and it's ten times as difficult if you have to remember exactly what the original looked like. Collectors have to keep both their eyes and ears open to learn about a variation before it gets published in one of the action figure collector magazines. By the time you read about it, you can bet that the scarce variation will be very scarce indeed. Still, many can be found with some careful searching at several stores. This is still a lot cheaper than buying a variation figure from a dealer. Variations always draw high prices when they are first discovered. Usually you can do a lot better by waiting and looking. Out of ten allegedly scarce variations, five will usually turn out to be easy to find and four more can be located at retail with a little effort. Even if you pay triple original retail after waiting, when you could have paid double by buying it from the first dealer who had it, you will still be way ahead of the game.

ALIENS
Kenner (1992–98)

The Aliens line from Kenner is based on the *Aliens* and *Aliens vs. Predator* comic books from Dark Horse and on *Aliens*, the excellent second movie in the series, which was released in 1986.

4¾" Space Marines, with mini comic book
Bishop (Android) (#65770, 1992) $12.00
Corp. Hicks (#65760, 1992) 10.00
Drake (#65750, 1992) 10.00
Lt. Ripley (#65790, 1992) 15.00
Lt. Ripley reissue "Real Flame Action" (#65790) 12.00
Sgt. Apone (#65780, 1992) 10.00

"Special Deluxe Marine" without mini comic book
Space Marine ATAX (#65711, 1993) 12.00

Aliens vs. Marine 10th Anniv. Two-Packs
Corp. Hicks vs. King Alien (#27819, 1996) 12.00
Drake vs. Alien Arachnid (#27818, 1996) 12.00
Hudson vs. Scorpion Alien (#27823, 1996) 12.00
O'Malley vs. Queen Face Hugger (#27824, 1996) 12.00

Vasquez vs. Night Cougar Alien (#27820, 1996) 15.00

Aliens (1992)
Alien Queen (#65710) 15.00
    Foreign issue (#83570) with trading card 10.00
Bull Alien with Face Hugger (#65740) 12.00
Gorilla Alien with Face Hugger (#65720) 13.00
Scorpion Alien with Face Hugger (#65730) 10.00

Aliens (1993)
Flying Alien Queen (#65712) 10.00
Killer Crab Alien (#65705) .10.00
Mantis Alien (#65721) 10.00
Panther Alien (#65707) 9.00
Queen Face Hugger (#65701) 9.00
Rhino Alien (#65741) 10.00
Snake Alien (#65702) 10.00

Aliens (1994–95)
Alien Arachnid (#65714) 10.00
King Alien (Deluxe Alien Leader) (#65726) 15.00
Night Cougar Alien (#65728) 8.00
Wild Boar Alien (#65715) 10.00
Swarm Alien, Electronic (1995) 20.00

Aliens (1997)
Bull Alien (#27884) 5.00
Gorilla Alien (#27887) 5.00
Mantis Alien (#27889) 5.00
Rhino Alien (#27895) 5.00
Snake Alien (#27888) 5.00
Warrior Alien (#27886) 5.00

Aliens Hive Wars (1998)
Acid Alien (#57003) 5.00
Hive Warrior Alien (#57004) 5.00
Integer 3 (#57005) 5.00
Corporal Hicks (#57006) 5.00

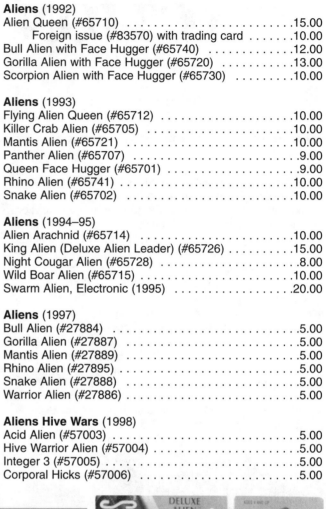

Lt. Ripley, Queen Face Hugger, & Deluxe Alien Leader (Kenner 1992–94)

Aliens: Drake vs. Alien Arachnid (Kenner 1996) Alien Resurrection: Warrior Drone (Hasbro 1998)
& Babylon 5: Ambassador Kosh Naranek (Exclusive Premiere 1998)

Night Recon Predator (#57001) 5.00
Warrior Predator (#57002) 5.00
Two-Pack
Warrior Alien (vs.) Renegade Predator 2-pack
    (#65840, 1993) with comic book 20.00
    Foreign issue (#247149, 1994) 10.00
Note: The foreign issue Alien vs. Predator 2-pack was distrib-
uted in U.S. by Kay-Bee/Toy Works in late 1996.

Oversize Two-Pack Figures
Aliens vs. Predator, The Ultimate Battle, 10" figures
    in window box (#27790, 1996) 35.00
Aliens vs. Corp. Hicks, 12" figures (#27759, 1997)
    KayBee special 40.00

ALIEN RESURRECTION
Hasbro (1998)

These figures are based on the 1997 movie starring
Sigourney Weaver (again) and Winona Ryder as Call. Call
was a store special and Ripley disappeared very early. The
aliens are still in the stores, waiting for red tags.

Deluxe Assortment, 6" (#74000, Feb. 1998) window box
Aqua Alien (#74007) $10.00
Battle Scarred Alien 10.00
Call (#74002) 15.00
Newborn Alien (#74006) 10.00
Ripley (#74001) 15.00
Warrior Alien (#74004) 10.00

12" Alien, Hasbro Signature Series
Warrior Drone (#27900) 20.00

Alien Hatchling Assortment, tubed (#27890, 1998)
Alien Face Hugger (#27891) 10.00
Alien Offspring 10.00

ARMAGEDDON
Mattel (1998)

From the 1998 Disney disaster movie starring Bruce
Willis, Ben Affleck and several other oil drilling characters
turned unlikely heroes. The movie was high on special effects
but very low on plausibility; nevertheless, it was emotionally
gripping. See also the TOYS section.

8" Special Collector Figure in Mattel Wheels package,
    with Hot Wheels Logo
A. J. Frost (#19413) $12.00
Harry Stamper (#19412) 12.00

BABYLON 5
Exclusive Premiere (1997–98)

In early 1998, *Babylon 5* moved to TNT for both reruns
and new shows, and got its first action figures. This very fine
show has been short on toy collectibles in first four years and
it's about time a few were made. The dolls from this series are
listed in the TOYS section.

6" figures Toys "R" Us and Diamond exclusives
Ambassador Delenn, with hair (#20014) $6.00
    Diamond variant version, bald 10.00
Ambassador Londo Mollari (#20016) 6.00
Captain John Sheridan (#20013) 6.00
G'Kar (#20015) 6.00
    Diamond variant version, repaint 10.00

2nd Series (1998)
Kosh Naranek (#20027) 7.00
Marcus Cole (#20029) 7.00
Susan Ivanova (#20026) 7.00
Vir Coto (#20028) 7.00

BATTLESTAR GALACTICA
Mattel (1978–79)

From the late 1970s ABC television series starring Lorne Green as Adama, John Colicos as Baltar, Richard Hatch as Apollo and Dirk Benedict as Lt. Starbuck.

3¾" Figures (1978)
Commander Adama (#2868) $45.00
Cylon Centurian (#2870), silver 40.00
Daggit (#2873), brown 35.00
Daggit (#2873), tan 35.00
Imperious Leader (#2869) 25.00
Lt. Starbuck (#2871) 45.00
Ovion (#2872) 25.00

Second Batch
Baltar (#1161) 85.00
Boray (#1163) 80.00
Cylon Commander (#1162), gold 100.00
Lucifer (#1164) 90.00

Boxed Sets
Three-figure boxed set (Gold Cylon, Baltar and Lucifer) 90.00
Four-figure boxed set (Daggit, Ovion, Imperious Leader and Silver Cylon) 75.00
Six Figure Gift Set (Ovion, Imperious Leader, Cylon Centurian, Daggit, Commander Adama and Lt. Starbuck) (#1154, 1979) 150.00

Large Figures
Colonial Warrior 12" Figure (#2536, 1979) 85.00
Cylon Centurian 12" Figure (#2537, 1979) 80.00

BATTLESTAR GALACTICA
Trendmasters (1997)

"In the farthest corners of the galaxy, the thousand-year war rages on. In a battle of right against might, the elite Blue Squadron takes on the treacherous Cylon attackers in a clash of cosmic proportions. Join the heroic Colonial Warriors as they blast through the dreaded Cylon starfleet. It's the ultimate galactic adventure!" If you *are* going to produce figures from this almost 20-year old show, why not make them in

Battlestar Galactica: Cylon Centurian (Mattel 1978)
& Starbuck (Trendmasters 1997)

Bionic Six: Madame-O (LGN 1986)
& Buck Rogers: Ardella (Mego 1979)

Star Wars–size. The show had a large cast and plenty of vehicles, providing many toy possibilities.

6" Figures (Early 1997)
Cylon Centurion (silver) (#06903) $7.00
Cylon Commander (gold) (#06904) 10.00
Imperious Leader (#06913) 7.00
Starbuck (#06905) 9.00

BIONIC SIX
LJN (1986)

The *Bionic Six* was a science fiction animated series from the mid 1980s. The series pitted the Bennett family against Dr. Scarab and his evil minions of destruction. LJN produced this extensive line of plastic and die-cast metal figures along with vehicles and accessories in 1986. You could still find a few around at discount in the early 1990s.

3¾" Bennett Family Figures
Bunji $20.00
Eric 12.00
F.L.U.F.F.I. 25.00
Helen 12.00
Jack 12.00
J.D. 12.00
Meg 12.00

Dr. Scarab's Evil Minions of Destruction
Chopper 12.00
Dr. Scarab 12.00
Glove 12.00
Klunk 12.00
Madame-O 12.00
Mechanic 12.00

THE BLACK HOLE
Mego (1979–80)

From the Walt Disney science fiction movie starring Maximillian Schell as Dr. Reinhardt, Anthony Perkins as Dr. Durant, Robert Forster, Joseph Bottoms, Yvette Mimieux and Ernest Borgnine as Harry Booth.

3¾" Figures
Captain Dan Holland $22.00
Dr. Hans Reinhardt 20.00
Dr. Durant 22.00

Captain Power: Corporal Pilot Chase (Mattel 1987)
Captain Scarlet: Destiny Angel (Vivid Imaginations 1993)

Dr. Kate McCrae 22.00
Harry Booth 22.00
Maximillian 60.00
Pizer 35.00
V.I.N.Cent 50.00

Later Figures (1980)
Sentry Robot 65.00

Overseas Figures
Humanoid 750.00
Old B.O.B. 175.00
S.T.A.R. 300.00

BUCK ROGERS
IN THE 25th CENTURY
Mego (1979)

From the television show starring Gil Gerard as Buck Rogers, Erin Gray as Wilma Deering, Tim O'Connor as Dr. Huer and Pamela Hensley as Ardella.

3¾" Figures
Ardella $35.00
Buck Rogers 55.00
Draco 20.00
Draconian Guard 20.00
Dr. Huer 20.00
Killer Kane 25.00
Tiger Man 20.00
Twiki 40.00
Wilma Deering 60.00

CAPTAIN POWER AND THE
SOLDIERS OF THE FUTURE
Mattel (1987)

"Bio Dreads—monstrous computer creatures—now rule earth and Lord Dread wants to eliminate all biological life forms. Humanity's only hope lies with Captain Power and the Soldiers of the Future!"

This was an attempt by Mattel to cash in on the interactive television game market, which wasn't as successful as all the hype had made it seem. Some of the toys themselves had devices that would interact during various segments of the television program that was aired during the time the toys were on the market.

3¾" Figures
Blastarr Ground Guardian $10.00
Captain Power 10.00
Lt. Tank Ellis 10.00
Lord Dread 10.00
Major Hawk Masterson 10.00
Soaron Sky Sentry 10.00

Second Series (1988)
Col. Stingray Johnson 25.00
Corporal Pilot Chase 15.00
Dread Trooper 60.00
Dread Commander 60.00
Sergeant Scout Baker 12.00
Tritor 30.00

CAPTAIN SCARLET
AND THE MYSTERONS
Vivid Imaginations (1993–94)

The British television series, from Gerry Anderson, occasionally aired on the Sci-Fi Channel. As with many of Anderson's programs, it involved his "Super-Marionation" process, with high-tech marionettes.

4" Figures
Captain Black $10.00
Captain Blue 10.00
Captain Scarlet 10.00
Colonel White 10.00
Destiny Angel 15.00
Lieutenant Green 10.00

DEFENDERS OF THE EARTH
Galoob (1985)

This series included Flash Gordon and Ming, along with other King Features Syndicate's popular comic strip characters Mandrake the Magician, Lothar and The Phantom.

Defenders of the Earth: Flash Gordon (Galoob 1985)
Doctor Who: Mel (Dapol 1988)

Talking Dalek (Palitoy 1976)

5½" Figures, with Battle Action Knobs (Asst. #5100)
Flash Gordon, Swashbuckling Space Hero $20.00
Garax, Ultimate Evil Robot 25.00
Ming, the Merciless 18.00

DOCTOR WHO
Denys Fisher (1976)

Doctor Who is the long-running B.B.C. television show that was also quite popular in the United States when it was shown here in syndication. United States fans are most familiar with Tom Baker, the fourth Doctor, in his trademark scarf, battling a variety of villains with the aid of K-9, his trusty robot dog. This series of action figures is from that era. The most famous of the villains were the Daleks, wheeled robots that first appeared in 1963, and their creator/leader Davros.

Figures
Cyberman $250.00
Dalek 200.00
Doctor Who (4th) 200.00
Giant Robot 225.00
K-9 . . . . .250.00
Leela 225.00

Talking Figure
Talking Dalek (Palitoy) 225.00

DOCTOR WHO
Dapol (1988–95)

Doctor Who was still popular in the late 1980s and early 1990s when Dapol got the license to produce action figures. The series celebrated its 25th season in 1988—it's a few years older than *Star Trek* and was in continuous production for the 25 years. By then the show was on its seventh Doctor, played by Sylvester McCoy. There was no shortage of Daleks in this toy series.

4" Figures
Ace $10.00
Cyberman 15.00
Davros with left hand (error) 20.00
Davros, no left hand (correct) 15.00
Ice Warrior 15.00

K-9, gray 10.00
Mel, blue shirt 15.00
Mel, pink shirt 18.00
The 7th Doctor, brown coat .18.00
The Tetrap 15.00

4" Daleks
White with gold spots 10.00
Black with gold spots 10.00
Black with silver spots 10.00
Gray with blue spots 10.00
Red with black spots 10.00
Red with silver spots 10.00
Red with gold spots 10.00
Gray with black spots 10.00

4½" Daleks using Louis Marx tools, with friction drives
Red Dalek 15.00
Silver Dalek 15.00
Black Dalek 15.00
Gray Dalek 15.00
White Dalek 15.00

6" Daleks from Louis Marx molds, with tricky-action drives
Silver finish special Dalek .20.00
Gold finish special Dalek 20.00

Sets and Playsets
Doctor Who 25th Anniversary Commemorative Set,
 with Mel, K-9, 7th Doctor, red Dalek,
 Cyberman, Tardis and battery-operated
 console 125.00
Gift Set with Mel, K-9, 7th Doctor, red Dalek,
 Cyberman and Tardis 100.00
The Dalek Army including seven 4" Daleks plus
 Davros, in box 100.00

DUNE
LJN (1984)

Dune, by Frank Herbert, is one of the most highly regarded science fiction novels ever published. Unfortunately, the same cannot be said for the movie, which starred Kyle MacLachlan as Paul, Sting as Feyd and included Jurgen Prochnow as Duke Leto, Max Von Sydow, José Ferrer as the Emperor and Patrick Stewart. It's a complicated story which is much easier to understand in the 45-minute-longer video tape release than in the original theatrical release. The figures owe their popularity to the fame of the source material. There were a number of sequels to the novel, but none to the movie.

6" Figures with "Battle-Matic" Action
Baron Harkonnen $30.00
Feyd 30.00
Paul Atreides 30.00
Rabban 30.00
Sardaukar Warrior 45.00
Stilgar the Freman 30.00

E.T. THE EXTRA-TERRESTRIAL
LJN (1982–83)

From one of the most entertaining (and top grossing) movies of all time, directed by Steven Spielberg.

Dune: Feyd (LJN 1984)
& Exo-Squad Jumptroops: Colleen O'Reilly (Playmates 1994)

Figures
Action figure, glowing heart $12.00
Action figure, scarf with Speak & Spell 12.00
Action figure, dress and hat 12.00
Action figure, robe 12.00
E.T. & Elliott-powered Bicycle 15.00
Talking figure 30.00
Talking figure, dressed 30.00
Walking figure, glowing heart 20.00
Walking figure, scarf 20.00
Walking figure, dress and hat 20.00
Walking figure, robe 20.00

EXOSQUAD
Playmates (1993–95)

The ExoSquad figures feature Shawn Napier and his Police Enforcer E-Frames battling to save the earth from Neosapien oppressors. They are based on the animated television series from Universal. The series was set in the 22nd century. The human figures are small, while the E-Frames vary in size from tiny to gigantic. Original retail prices varied with size from $3.00 for the smallest figures to $30.00 or more for the largest. You can still find a lot of them around at discount prices.

General Purpose 5" E-Frame with 3" Figures (Asst. #6300, 1993) in window box with fold-over flap
Alec DeLeon (Field Communications) $20.00
    Reissue in hanging window box (1995) 12.00
J.T. Marsh (Aerial Attack) .20.00
    Reissue in hanging window box (1995) 12.00
Phaeton (Command) 20.00
    Reissue in hanging window box (1995) 12.00
Typhonus (High Speed Stealth) 20.00
    Reissue in hanging window box (1995) 12.00

General Purpose 5" E-Frame with 3" Figures (Asst. #6300, 1994) in window box with fold-over flap
Nara Burnes (Reconnaissance) 20.00
    Reissue in hanging window box (1995) 12.00
Rita Torres (Field Sergeant) 20.00
    Reissue in hanging window box (1995) 12.00
Sean Napier (Police Enforcer) 20.00
    Reissue in hanging window box (1995) 12.00
Wolf Bronski (Ground Assault) 20.00

    Reissue in hanging window box (1995) 12.00

General Purpose 5" E-Frame with 3" Figures (Asst. #6300, 1995) in hanging window box
General Draconis (Interrogator) 12.00
Jinx Madison (Fire Warrior) 12.00
Jonas Simbacca (Pirate Captain) 12.00
Marsala (Sub-Sonic Scout) 12.00
Peter Tanaka (Samurai) 12.00

Light Attack 8" E-Frames with 3" Figure (Asst. #6320, 1993–94) battery powered in large try-me box
General Shiva (Amphibious Assault) (1993) 28.00
Livanus (Troop Transport) (1994) Neosapien 28.00
Maggie Weston (Field Repair) (1994) 28.00
Marsala (Rapid Assault) (1993) 28.00

Jumptroops with Ultralight E-Frame Battle Machines (Asst. #6380, 1994–95) on header card
Captain Avery F. Butler (Command) 10.00
Gunnery Sergeant Ramon Lightfeather (Heavy Gravity) 10.00
Lance Corporal Vince Pellegrino (Fireboss) 10.00
Second Lieutenant Colleen O'Reilly (Rapid Recon) . . .10.00

Special Mission 5" E-Frames (1995) in box with flap
Alec DeLeon (All-Terrain) .14.00
J.T. Marsh (Deep Space) .14.00
Typhonus (Deep Submergence) 14.00
Wolf Bronski (Subterranean) 14.00

Neosapien Warriors (1995) on header card
Neo Cat 10.00
Neo Lord 10.00

Exoconverting E-Frame in box with hanging flap
J.T. Marsh 15.00

Real Walking Series (1995) in huge cubical box
Livia (Neo Sapien Walking) 28.00
Marsala (Exowalking) 22.00

Exo Squad: Alec DeLeon (Field Communications) E-Frame
(Playmates 1993)

Exo Squad Robotech, Spartan Battloid (Playmates 1995) Flash Gordon: Dale Arden (Playmates 1996)
ID4 (Independence Day): Steven Hiller (Trendmasters 1996)

Mini Exo-Command Assortment (1996)
Alec DeLeon and Phaeton with Vesta Space Port
    Battleset 7.00
J.T. Marsh and Typhonus with Resolute II Hangar
    Battleset 7.00
Phaeton and J.T. Marsh with Olympus Mons
    Command Ship Bridge Battleset 7.00

Space Series E-Frames, in large cubical box
Kaz Takagi (Exo-fighter) 28.00
Thrax (Neo-fighter) 28.00

EXOSQUAD ROBOTECH SERIES
Playmates (1995)

In 1995, Robotech Defense Force war machines have come to reinforce mankind's final hope, the ExoSquad! They get there through a space fold, since they have different backgrounds. The two series don't really mesh all that well.

3" Attack Mecha Figures (1995)
Excaliber MK VI Battloid Tactical Corps Assignment . . .$5.00
Gladiator Battloid Tactical Corps Assignment 5.00
Raidar X Battloid Tactical Corps Assignment 5.00
Spartan Battloid Tactical Corps Assignment 5.00
Excaliber MK VI Battloid Civil Defense Unit 5.00
Gladiator Battloid Civil Defense Unit 5.00
Raider X Battloid Civil Defense Unit 5.00
Spartan Battloid Civil Defense Unit 5.00

7" Robotech Defense Force Attack Mecha (1995)
Excaliber MK VI Destroid 9.00
Gladiator Destroid 9.00
Raidar X Destroid 9.00
Spartan Destroid 9.00

7" Invid and Zentraedi Attack Mecha (1995)
Bioroid Invid Fighter 9.00
Invid Scout Ship 9.00
Zentraedi Power Armor Botoru Battalion 9.00

Zentraedi Power Armor Quadrona Battalion 9.00

Battlepod Class E-Frames (1995) on header card
Invid Shock Trooper 18.00
Officer's Battlepod 18.00
Zentraedi Tactical Battlepod 18.00

FLASH GORDON
Mattel (1979)

Based on the animated television series, not the lousy live-action film from 1980. Flash Gordon remains one of the classics of early adventure science fiction to this day.

3¾" Figures
Beastman $40.00
Captain Arak 100.00
Dr. Zarkov 35.00
Flash Gordon 20.00
Lizard Woman 30.00
Ming 20.00
Thun, the Lion Man 25.00
Vultan 100.00

FLASH GORDON
Playmates (1996)

The figures are from an updated animated television series. Nothing can save Mongo except Flash Gordon, in this version "a hip, flip skateboardin' teenager with an attitude." We don't know about you, but we'd put our money on Ming. Both the characters and figures looked like teenagers and didn't appeal to collectors. They bought the babes—Dale Arden and Princess Thundar—but had no interest in the other figures.

5" Figures (Aug. 1996)
Dale Arden $12.00
Flash Gordon in Flight Suit .6.00
Flash Gordon in Mongo Outfit 6.00

General Lynch 6.00
Kobalt the Mercenary 6.00
Ming the Merciless 6.00
Prince Talon 6.00
Princess Thundar 15.00

ID 4 (INDEPENDENCE DAY)
Trendmasters (1996)

This movie, starring Will Smith, Jeff Goldblum and Bill Pullman, opened on July 3, 1996. Most collectors prefer Trendmaster's *Mars Attacks* figures, even though they liked this movie better.

6" Figure (1996) with one of 11 Mission Disks.
Captain Steven Hiller $8.00
President Thomas J. Whitmore 8.00
Technical Expert David Levinson 8.00

8" Aliens (1996) with Host
Alien Attacker Pilot 10.00
Alien Science Officer 10.00
Alien Shock Trooper 10.00
Alien Weapons Expert 10.00
Alien Zero Gravity 10.00

Large Alien Figures
Alien Supreme Commander with Host and motion
     sensor, in window box 20.00
Alien Supreme Commander with Bio-Containment
     Chamber 15.00

LOST IN SPACE
Trendmasters (1998)

The movie version of this classic 1960s TV show opened in March 1998. Predictably, the Judy Robinson figure has drawn the most collector interest and seems to be quite scarce. The Future Smith robot has also proven to be a winner.

The Movie Series
Battle Armor Major Don West $6.00
Cryo-Chamber Will Robinson 6.00
Cryo-Suit Dr. Judy Robinson 12.00
Proteus Armor Dr. Smith 6.00
Proteus Armor Prof. John Robinson 6.00

ID4 (Independence Day): Attacker Pilot (Trendmasters 1996)
Lost in Space: Judy Robinson (Trendmasters 1998)

Mars Attacks: Martian Spy Girl & Martian Trooper
(Trendmasters 1996)

Sabotage Action Dr. Smith 6.00

Movie Series Robots
Battle Ravaged Robot 12.00
Future Smith, with movie sounds 25.00
Robot with Blazing Lights and Battle Sounds 20.00
Rocket Launcher Robot 12.00

Classic Series Robot
Robot B-9 in open box 20.00

MARS ATTACKS
Trendmasters (1996)

From the movie directed by Tim Burton starring Jack Nicholson and the rest of Hollywood. Originally based on the Topps trading card set, with art by Norm Saunders, who wasn't credited in the movie or the action figures. The figures are faithful to the movie and comic book series. Most of them have voice chips and come in "Try-Me" packs, but The Kay-Bee/Toy Works chain got ones without the chip, in regular packs. Comic book–based figures come on purple header cards, while those based on the movie come on red header cards. The scarce Martian Spy Girl has attained the best collector price.

5" Comic Book Figures on purple header card
Supreme Commander (#6692) with voice chip $7.00
     Version without voice chip (#6695) 9.00
Paeec Overlord (#6693) 7.00
     Version without voice chip (#6696) 9.00
Martian Trooper (#6694) 7.00
     Version without voice chip (#6697) 9.00

Smaller Figures with computer disk
B.A.D.A.A.M.A. (#6702) 7.00
Doom Robot (#6703) 7.00

5" Movie Figures on red header card
Martian Ambassador (#6979) 8.00
     Version without voice chip (#7518) 9.00
Martian Trooper (#6980) 8.00
     Version without voice chip (#7519) 9.00
Martian Leader (#6981) 8.00
     Version without voice chip (#7520) 9.00

Men in Black: Street Striker Kay (Galoob 1997) Predator: Scavage & Deluxe Predator (Clan) Leader (Kenner 1994)

Martian Spy Girl (#6985) 35.00
    Version without voice chip (#7517) 40.00

Large Figures with Throbbing Brain, Evil Voice and
    Flashing Lights
Martian Supreme Commander (#6683) 30.00
Supreme Martian Ambassador (#6994) 30.00

MEN IN BLACK
Galoob (1997)

Men in Black was a summer 1997 movie spoof which starred Tommy Lee Jones and Will Smith as super secret government agents "saving the world from the scum of the universe." It opened during Roswell, New Mexico's 50th anniversary celebration of the famous alien crash landing, so its timing couldn't have been better, although the figures could have been. They were readily available as red tag specials in 1998.

5" Figures, carded
Alien-Ambush Jay vs. Tree Trunk Alien 7.00
Flame-Bustin' Jay vs. Scorched Alien 7.00
Street-Striker Kay vs. Manhole Alien 7.00
Slime-Fightin' Kay vs. Edgar the Alien 7.00
Alien-Attack Edgar 7.00

5" Figures, window box
Mikey with "Exploding Body" 10.00
Jeebs with "Regenerating Heads" 10.00
Jay vs. Alien Perp (#76225) 10.00

Large Figure, window box
Alien Terrorist Edgar 19.00

PREDATOR
Kenner (1994, 1997)

There have been two *Predator* movies. The first starred Arnold Schwartzenegger and the second starred Danny Glover. The figures are also based on the Dark Horse Comics series "Aliens vs. Predators" and these figures were marketed with the Aliens figures. The popular Alien and Predator two-packs are listed under Alien. There was a mail-in offer for a free special edition Predator when you buy any three Aliens or Predators. It was sort of a problem for collectors because you had to "cut out the purchase seals" from the package, making them less collectible, but it has proven to be a good value.

4¾" Figures (1994)
Cracked Tusk (Predator) $9.00
Scavage Predator, dark green 11.00
    Light green 25.00
Spiked Tail 9.00
Stalker Predator 9.00
Nightstorm Predator 9.00
Lasershot Predator, Electronic 22.00
Lava Planet Predator 9.00
Deluxe Predator (Clan) Leader 14.00
Ambush Predator, clear plastic, with 4 pieces of
    armor and small instruction sheet, mail-in figure . .35.00

Large Figure (1995)
Ultimate Predator, 10" 18.00

Figures (1997) on shrink bubble header card
Scavage 6.00
Stalker Predator 6.00
Renegade Predator 6.00
Spiked Tail Predator 6.00

ROBOTECH
Matchbox (1986)

Robotech was a very popular Americanized Japanese animated space saga. A damaged alien spaceship lands on Earth containing advanced technology. The evil Zentraedi want the ship and the Robotech Defense Force of young warriors is determined to keep it for Earth. There are several related comic book series listed in the COMICS section.

The Zentraedi figures are a lot bigger than the Robotech figures. Miriya was enlarged when she defected to the Zentraedi and a Zentraedi warrior was micronized in an attempt to infiltrate the Robotech Defense Force. The series included versions of these characters in both sizes. The figures have generated significant collector interest.

3¾" Robotech Defense Force Figures
Dana Sterling (#7213) $25.00
Lisa Hayes (#7212) 16.00
Rand (#7214) 9.00
Rick Hunter (#7210) 18.00
Scott Bernard (#7211) 30.00

Second Batch
Lunk (#7221) 22.00
Max Sterling (#7222) 17.00
Miriya (#7225)(red outfit) 20.00
Miriya (black outfit) 60.00
Rook Bartley (#7223?) 50.00
Roy Fokker (#7220) 16.00

Robotech Masters Enemy Figures
Bioroid Terminator (#7217) .15.00
Corg, Invid Enemy (#7218) .12.00
Micronized Zentraedi Warrior (#7216) 12.00
Robotech Master (#7215) 10.00
Zor Prime (#7219) 8.00

6" Zentraedi Figures
Armoured Zentraedi Warrior (#7265) 18.00
Breetai (#7261) 18.00
Dolza (#7264) 18.00
Exedore (#7262) 18.00
Khyron (#7263) 18.00
Miriya (#7266) 22.00

7" Robotech Defense Force Attack Mecha
Excaliber MkVI 35.00
Gladiator 35.00
Raidar X 40.00
Spartan 40.00

7" Zentraedi Attack Mecha
Invid Bioroid Fighter 30.00
Invid Scout Ship 30.00
Zentraedi Power Armour Botoru Batallion 45.00
Zentraedi Power Armour Quadrono Batallion 45.00

ROBOTECH
Harmony Gold (1991–94)

Harmony Gold reissued the *Robotech* figures, along with Lynn Minmei, which was never produced by Matchbox in the 3¾" size. After 1994, the action figures were licensed to Playmates and incorporated into their Exo-Squad action figure series, despite some logical inconsistences. The two series had similar armored walking "vehicles" but completely different story lines.

3¾" Robotech Defense Force, reissues
Dana Sterling $18.00
Lisa Hayes 12.50
Lunk 15.00
Lynn Minmei 18.00
Max Sterling 12.50
Miriya (black outfit) 10.00
Miriya (purple outfit) 10.00
Miriya (red outfit) 12.00
Rand 10.00
Rick Hunter 10.00
Rook Bartley 18.00
Roy Fokker 10.00
Scott Bernard 10.00

Robotech Masters Enemy Figures
Bioroid Terminator 10.00
Corg 10.00
Robotech Master 10.00

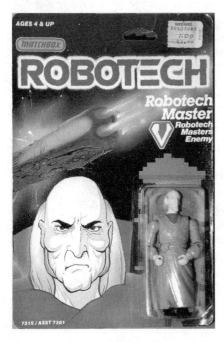  

Robotech: Robotech Master (Matchbox 1986) Robotech: Lisa Hayes & Rand (Harmony Gold 1991)

StarGate: Ra & Daniel (Hasbro 1994) & Starship Troopers: Carmen Ibanez (Galoob 1997)

Micronized Zentraedi Warrior	12.50
Zor Prime	10.00

SPACE ACADEMY
Hasbro (1977)

A Woolworth stores exclusive, based on a CBS television series set at a training school for space explorers. *Lost in Space's* Jonathan Harris was Issac Gampu, the three-hundred-year-old head of the Space Academy. The series starred Ric Carrott as Chris, Brian Tochi as Tee Gai and Eric Greene as Loki, all cadets at the Academy.

Figures

Issac Gampu	$45.00
Chris	.45.00
Tee Gai	.45.00
Loki	.45.00

STARGATE
Hasbro (1994)

From the summer 1994 "blockbuster" movie starring Kurt Russell as O'Neil, Jaye Davidson as Ra and James Spader as Daniel. The movie was okay, but not as big as its hype, and all of the figures and vehicles were discounted in due course.

The *Stargate SG-1* series on cable television has explored more of the universe implicit in the Stargate concept and is quite a good show. That probably means it won't last long enough to revive the action figure line.

3¾" Figures

Daniel (Archaeologist)	$5.00
Ra (Ruler of Abydos)	.5.00
Horus (Attack Pilot)	.5.00
Skaara (Rebel Leader)	.5.00
Anubis (Chief Guard)	.5.00
Horus (Palace Guard)	.5.00
Lt. Kowalsky (Weapons Expert)	.5.00

STARSHIP TROOPERS
Galoob (1997)

This movie was based on the Robert Heinlein Hugo Award–winning novel originally published in 1959. The movie featured legions of computer generated bugs vs. a batallion of good looking but relatively unknown young actors. The bugs ripped off a lot of human arms and legs and the humans kicked a lot of bug butt. Among the humans, your chances of survival depended largely on your looks — the better you looked in a shower scene, the better your chances. The movie was popular with teenagers, just as the book was 40 years ago. Those who read the book 40 years ago wished they had filmed one of Heinlein's adult classics, like *The Moon is a Harsh Mistress* or *Stranger in a Strange Land*.

5" Figures (Sept. 1997)

Mega Marauder Johnny Rico	.5.00
Bug Thrasher Carmen Ibanez	.5.00
Toxic Raider Ace Levy	.5.00
Firestorm Johnny Rico	.5.00
Jetpack Ace Levy	.5.00
Cyber Commando Sugar Watkins	.5.00

STAR TREK
Mego Figures: See Dolls

STAR TREK: THE MOTION PICTURE
Mego (1979)

In addition to dolls, Mego produced 3¾" figures of the crew from this movie and six unrelated aliens. These later were sold mostly overseas.

3¾" Crew figures (1979)

Capt. Kirk	$25.00
Mr. Spock	.30.00
Decker	.30.00
Ilia	.30.00
Scotty	.25.00
Dr. McCoy	.30.00

Alien figures (1979)
Klingon 75.00
Zaranite 150.00
Betelgeusian 150.00
Arcturian 125.00
Megarite 150.00
Rigellian 140.00

STAR TREK III
Ertl (1984)

In 1984, Ertl produced 3¾" action figures of Kirk, Spock, Scotty and the Klingon Kruge (along with his dog) based on *Star Trek III: The Search For Spock*.

3¾" Die-Cast Figures
Kirk $35.00
Spock 40.00
Scotty 35.00
Klingon Leader 45.00

STAR TREK: THE NEXT GENERATION
Galoob (1988)

Star Trek returned to television in the form of *The Next Generation* and Galoob made a total of 10 action figures in 1988. Data was the most popular character and a variation in his figure has increased collector interest. The Tasha Yar figure was also scarce. Galoob quit making *Next Generation* action figures and there were no more produced for four long years.

3¾" Figures (Asst. #5340)
Captain Jean-Luc Picard $15.00
Commander William Riker 15.00
Lieutenant Geordi LaForge 18.00
Lieutenant Worf 18.00
Lieutenant Tasha Yar 25.00
Lieutenant Commander Data, speckled face 30.00
    Variation with blue face 150.00
Q 75.00
Ferengi 75.00
Selay 75.00
Antican 75.00

Riker & Borg, loose (Playmates 1992)

Star Trek, The Next Generation: Tasha Yar (Galoob 1988) & Gowron the Klingon (Playmates 1992)

STAR TREK: THE NEXT GENERATION
Playmates (1992–96)

Playmates, flush with cash from the success of their Teenage Mutant Ninja Turtles figures, acquired the *Star Trek* figures license in 1992. Their figures are 5" tall and are extremely well detailed, with weapons and accessories plus a logo base. There are several variations in the first year's figures. The most significant is the Geordi LaForge figure, which originally came with a removable visor. The package back of the original version of this figure shows Geordi with his visor removed. The later, more common and less valuable version has a non-removable visor figure and the picture on the back shows LaForge with his visor on. The only way to tell the difference, without removing the figure and destroying its value, is to look for this picture.

5" Figures, 1992 Series, no trading card or Space Cap
Captain Jean-Luc Picard (#6011) $20.00
Lieutenant Commander Data (#6012) 20.00
Lieutenant Worf (#6013) 20.00
Commander William Riker (#6014) 20.00
Lieutenant Commander Geordi LaForge (#6015)
    original version, with removable visor 40.00
    Variation without removable visor (#6015) 20.00
Lieutenant Commander Deanna Troi (#6016) 20.00
Romulan (#6051) 25.00
Ferengi (#6052) 25.00
    Variation with no black on boots (#6052) 45.00
Gowron (#6053) 20.00
    Variation without gold trim (#6053) 40.00
Borg (#6055) 20.00
    Variation with reversed photo on back 45.00

Playmates second batch of figures came with a special edition SkyBox Trading Card. Then all 23 figures were reissued in 1994 with Space Caps, under the same product numbers and with only slight packaging changes. Many of these are scarce and more valuable than the original versions.

5" Figures, 1993 Series with 3½" SkyBox trading card, **Reissue Figures** (1994) with Space Cap
Dr. Beverly Crusher (#6019) with card 15.00
    Reissue (#6019) with Space Cap 20.00
Guinan (#6020) with card 15.00
    Reissue (#6020) with Space Cap 30.00
Cadet Wesley Crusher (#6021) with card 15.00
    Reissue (#6021) with Space Cap 25.00

Star Trek, The Next Generation: K'Ehleyr, Q & Lore (Playmates 1993)

Locutus, Captain Jean-Luc Picard as a Borg (#6023)
    with card 15.00
    Reissue (#6023) with Space Cap 30.00
Klingon Warrior Worf (#6024) with card 15.00
    Reissue (#6024) with Space Cap 25.00
Lt. Commander Geordi LaForge, in Dress Uniform
    (#6026) with card .12.00
    Reissue (#6026) with Space Cap 25.00
Mordock the Benzite (#6057) with card 18.00
    Reissue (#6057) with Space Cap 30.00
(Ambassador) K'Ehleyr (#6059) with card 12.00
    Reissue (#6059) with Space Cap 20.00
Captain Jean-Luc Picard, in First Season Uniform
    (#6071) with card .12.00
    Reissue (#6071) with Space Cap 30.00
Lieutenant Commander Data, in First Season
    Uniform (#6072) with card 15.00
    Reissue (#6072) with Space Cap 30.00
Lieutenant (JG) Worf, in First Season Uniform
    (#6073) with card .12.00
    Reissue (#6073) with Space Cap 25.00
Commander William T. Riker, in Second Season
    Uniform (#6074) with card 15.00
    Reissue (#6074) with Space Cap 35.00
Lieutenant (J.G.) Geordi LaForge, in First Season
    Uniform (#6075) with card 12.00
    Reissue (#6075) with Space Cap 30.00
Counselor Deanna Troi, in Second Season Uniform
    (#6076) with card .12.00
    Reissue (#6076) with Space Cap 20.00
Borg (#6077) with card 12.00
    Reissue (#6077) with Space Cap 30.00

1993 Series, Second Batch with 3½" trading card
Ambassador Spock (#6027) with card 12.00
    Reissue (#6027) with Space Cap 12.00
Admiral (Leonard H.) McCoy (#6028) with card 10.00
    Reissue (#6028) with Space Cap 12.00
Captain (Montgomery) Scott (#6029) with card 10.00
    Reissue (#6029) with Space Cap 12.00
Commander Sela (#6056) with card 12.00
    Reissue (#6056) with Space Cap 15.00

"Q" (Mischievous Omniscient Being) (#6058) with
    card 12.00
    Reissue (#6058) with Space Cap 15.00
(Captain) Dathon, A Tamarian Captain (#6060) with
    card 12.00
    Reissue (#6060) with Space Cap 200.00
Vorgon, A Mysterious Alien Race From the Future
    (#6061) with card .12.00
    Reissue (#6061) with Space Cap 40.00
Lore, Data's Evil Twin Brother (#6022) with card 12.00
    Reissue (#6022) with Space Cap 15.00

Most of Playmates 1994 figures came with a special "SkyCap." The Space Cap frame was supposed to list the figures in the assortment, but this changed throughout the year. Originally, only the 23 reissue figures were listed. Most of the later figures have a Space Cap frame that lists 40 figures, but eventually Picard as Dixon Hill was listed for a total of 41 figures. Not all of these figures were actually produced and some others that did appear did not have Space Caps, so the frame does not work well as a checklist. Some of the figures were extremely rare, leading to collector prices that were quite high.

5" Figures, 1994 Series with Space Cap
Lieutenant Commander Data as a Romulan (#6031) . .10.00
Captain Picard as a Romulan (#6032) 10.00
LaForge as a Tarchannen III Alien (#6033) 10.00
Commander Riker as a Malcorian (#6034) 10.00
Lieutenant Commander Deana Troi, in 6th Season
    Uniform (#6035) 12.00
Lieutenant Worf, in Starfleet Rescue Outfit (#6036) . . .15.00
Hugh Borg (#6037) 15.00
Lieutenant Barclay (#6045) 12.00

1994 Series, Second Batch without Space Cap or card
Lieutenant Commander Data in Dress Uniform
    (#6941) 15.00
Captain Picard in Duty Uniform (#6942) 10.00
Ensign Wesley Crusher (#6943) 10.00
Gowron in Ritual Klingon Attire (#6945) 50.00

Lieutenant Thomas Riker (#6946) 150.00
Lieutenant Commander Data, from *"Redemption"*
   (#6947) 300.00

1994 Series, Third Batch with Space Cap
Dr. Noonian Soong (#6038) 15.00
Q in Judge's Robe (#6042) 20.00
Ensign Ro Laren (#6044) 25.00
Esoqq (#6049) 80.00
Captain Jean-Luc Picard as Dixon Hill (#6050) 15.00
Note: Canadian release figures come on a generic blister card
with no figure name. The name appears only on a strip,
in blue, on the plastic bubble which covers the figure.
Ambassador Sarek, Canada release 175.00
Lwaxana Troi, Canada release 175.00

In 1995, Playmates came out with another new group of figures, along with a new package design, and a different style of trading card. Many of the packages have a "7th Season" sticker, but many figures can be found both with and without this sticker.

Playmates kept changing the packaging on its figures. It started with *Star Trek: The Next Generation* packaging, added Episode and Series designations, then changed to generic *Star Trek* packaging and finally dropped the Episode and Series designations. There is no completely satisfactory way to group these figures.

5" Figures, 1995 Series with 3½" trading card
Lt. Cmdr. Geordi LaForge in Movie Uniform (#6960) . .10.00
Dr. Beverly Crusher in Starfleet Duty Uniform
   (#6961) 10.00
Lt. Cmdr. Data, in Movie Uniform (#6962) 10.00
Lieutenant Natasha Yar (#6965) 10.00
Lwaxana Troi (#6967) 10.00
Ambassador Sarek (#6968) 10.00
The Nausicaan ("Tapestry!") (#6969) 10.00
Ensign Ro Laren, reissue (#6981) 10.00
Dr. Noonian Soong, reissue (#6982) 10.00
Jean-Luc Picard, Retired Starfleet ("All Good Things"
   Series) (#6974) 18.00

Lieutenant Worf in Ritual Klingon Attire ("Holodeck"
   Series) (#6985) 25.00
Captain Jean-Luc Picard as Locutus ("Holodeck"
   Series) (#6986) 25.00
Lieutenant Commander Data in 1940s' Attire
   ("Holodeck" Series) (#6979) 20.00

5" Figures (1995) on generic Star Trek header card
   with Next Generation trading card
Sheriff Worf in Western Attire ("A Fist Full of Datas")
   (#6434) 12.00
Dr. Beverly Crusher in 1940s' Attire ("The Big
   Goodbye") (#6435) 10.00
Counselor Deanna Troi as Durango in Western Attire
   ("A Fist Full of Datas") (#6438) 15.00

5" Figures (1995) on generic Star Trek header card
   with no trading card
Borg ("Interstellar Action" Series) (#6441) 22.00
Lieutenant (J.G.) Geordi LaForge ("Interstellar
   Action" Series) (#6443) 22.00

5" Figures (1995–96) on generic Star Trek header card,
   with 3½" The Next Generation trading card
Dr. Katherine Pulaski (#6428, 1995) 12.00
Vash (#6429) 25.00
Captain Picard as Galen ("The Gambit") (#6432) 8.00
Geordi LaForge, Retired Starfleet Officer and
   Journalist ("All Good Things") (#6433) 10.00
The Traveler (#6436) 13.00
(Governor) Worf, Governor of H'Atoria (#6437,
   1996) 10.00

1996 Series with 4" "30th Anniversary" Star Trek:
   The Next Generation trading card
Admiral William T. Riker ("All Good Things")
   (#16034) 8.00

ORIGINAL STAR TREK SERIES
Playmates (1996)

It took Playmates about four years to produce action figures based on the original series. By then, Spock, McCoy

Star Trek, The Next Generation: Captain Picard as a Romulan & Esoqq (Playmates 1994)
& Interstellar Action Series: Borg (Playmates 1995)

Star Trek: Vina as Orion Animal Woman & Lt. Reginald Barclay limited edition (Playmates 1996)
& Classic Star Trek Movie Series Commander Spock (Playmates 1995)

and Scott had already appeared in *The Next Generation* line-up, based on their cameo roles. Vina is one of four figures from the original pilot episode for *Star Trek*. She disappeared from the toy stores quickly as hot-blooded collectors grabbed her just as quickly as Captain Pike did in the original show.

5" Figures (1996) on generic Star Trek header card,
    with 4" "30th Anniversary" Star Trek trading card
(Nurse) Christine Chapel (#6447) 8.00
Captain Christopher Pike ("The Cage") (#6448) 8.00
(Yeoman) Janice Rand (#6449) 8.00
Captain James T. Kirk, Captain's Casual Attire
    (#16031) 8.00
Mister Spock ("The Cage") (#16038) 8.00
The Talosian Keeper ("The Cage") (#16039) 13.00
Vina as Orion Animal Woman ("The Cage") (#16040) . .25.00

LIMITED EDITION FIGURES

In 1996, Playmates issued three limited edition figures. The figures were limited to such a small number that they never reached the display racks in toy stores because the stock boys bought them first. The stock boys made a killing and most collectors couldn't afford the figures. Many collectors were so mad that they gave up on the series. In 1998, Playmates reissued the figures together in a three-pack, but collectors remained unimpressed. Most of them waited for the item to become a red tag special before even considering buying it.

Limited (1,701 of Each Figure) (1996) no trading card
Captain Jean-Luc Picard ("Tapestry") (#6442) with
    limited edition sticker 400.00
Tasha Yar ("Yesterday's Enterprise") (#16043) no
    limited edition sticker 300.00

Limited (3,000 of Each Figure) (1996) no trading card
Lt. Reginald Barclay (PADD) ("Projections")
    (#16044) with limited edition sticker 175.00

CLASSIC STAR TREK — MOVIE SERIES
Playmates (1995)

5" Figures with 4½" trading card
Admiral Kirk (Star Trek: The Motion Picture) (#6451) . .$8.00
Commander Spock (*Star Trek: The Motion Picture*)
    (#6452) no trading card 8.00
Dr. McCoy (*Star Trek: The Motion Picture*) (#6453) 8.00
Lt. Sulu (*Star Trek: The Motion Picture*) (#6454) 8.00
Lt. Uhura (*Star Trek: The Motion Picture*) (#6455) 9.00
Khan (*The Wrath of Khan* (#6456) 12.00
Martia (*The Undiscovered Country*) (#6457) 10.00
General Chang (*The Undiscovered Country*) (#6458) . .10.00
Commander Kruge (*The Search for Spock*) (#6459) . . .10.00
Lt. Saavik (*The Wrath of Khan*) (#6460) 12.00

STAR TREK: GENERATIONS
Playmates (1994)

This series, including the first figures of B'Etor and Lursa (in Klingon outfits showing a lot of cleavage) and the first separate action figure of Chekov, although he was included in the Classic (Bridge) figure set from 1993. Walter Koenig, who played Chekov, may now actually be better known as Bester, from *Babylon 5*.

5" Figures
Admiral James T. Kirk (#6911) $20.00
Montgomery Scott (#6914) 35.00
Pavel A. Chekov (#6916) 40.00
Captain Jean-Luc Picard (#6918) 10.00
Lieutenant Commander William Riker (#6919) 12.00
Commander Deanna Troi (#6920) 15.00
Lieutenant Commander Data (#6921) 12.00
Lieutenant Commander Worf (#6922) 10.00
Lieutenant Commander Geordi LaForge (#6923) 15.00
Doctor Beverly Crusher (#6924) 18.00
Guinan (#6927) 15.00
Dr. Soran (#6925) 13.00
B'Etor (#6928) 18.00
Lursa (#6929) 18.00
Captain James T. Kirk in Space Suit (#6930) 15.00
Lt. Commander Worf in 19th-Century Outfit (#6931) . . .12.00

STAR TREK: FIRST CONTACT
Playmates (1996)

These movie figures included Zephram Cochrane and Lilly, but some were still available in toy stores two years later, so their prices have remained modest.

6" Figures (Oct. 1996) with mini poster
Captain Jean-Luc Picard (#16101) $7.00
Commander William T. Riker (#16102) 7.00
Lt. Cmdr. Geordi LaForge (#16103) 7.00
Lt. Commander Data (#16104) 7.00
Lt. Commander Worf (#16105) 7.00
Commander Deanna Troi (#16106) 9.00
Dr. Beverly Crusher (#16107) 8.00
The Borg (#16108) 8.00
Zephram Cochrane (#16109) 8.00
Lily (#16110) 9.00
Picard in Starfleet Space Suit (#16115) 9.00

STAR TREK: DEEP SPACE NINE
Playmates (1994–96)

The first Deep Space Nine figure series included all the regular cast plus everybody's favorite villain, Gul Dukat. The only other character who wasn't drawn from the regular cast was Quark's favorite barfly, Morn.

5" Figures First Series (1994) with 3½" trading card
Commander Benjamin Sisko (#6201) $9.00
(Security Chief) Odo (#6202) 15.00
Quark (#6203) 15.00
Chief Miles O'Brien (#6204) 15.00
Lieutenant Jadzia Dax (#6205) 20.00
Major Kira Nerys (#6206) .15.00
Commander Gul Dukat (#6207) 20.00
Dr. Julian Bashir (#6208) .30.00
Morn (#6210) 20.00

Second Series (1995) with Space Cap
Commander Benjamin Sisko in Starfleet Dress
    Uniform (#6220) 8.00
Chief Miles O'Brien in Starfleet Dress Uniform (#6226) . .8.00
Jake Sisko (#6235) 12.00
Vedek Bareil (#6236) 20.00
(The) Tosk (#6237) 15.00
Rom (#6241) 15.00

*Star Trek: Deep Space Nine: Odo & Lt. Thomas Riker
(Playmates 1995)*

Lt. Jadzia Dax in Starfleet Duty Uniform (#6242) 12.00
Dr. Julian Bashir in Starfleet Duty Uniform (#6243) 12.00
Chief Miles O'Brien in Starfleet Duty Uniform (#6244) .10.00
Captain Picard in Deep Space Nine Uniform (#6245) . . .8.00
Lieutenant Thomas Riker in Deep Space Nine
    Uniform (#6246) 15.00
Q in Deep Space Nine Uniform (#6247) 12.00

In 1995, figures from all the television series (except "Voyager") began appearing on generic *Star Trek* header cards. The only distinction between the three series is in the Space Cap or trading card premium and the listing on the package back.

Third Series (1995–96) on generic Star Trek header card with
    Deep Space Nine Space Cap
The Hunter of Tosk (#6439, 1995) 12.00
Lieutenant Jadzia Dax from "Blood Oath" in Ritual
    Klingon Attire (#6440, 1995) 15.00
Grand Nagus Zek (#6444, 1996) 10.00
Commander Benjamin Sisko from "Crossover"
    (#6445, 1996) 8.00
Security Chief Odo from "Necessary Evil" (#6446,
    1996) 10.00

Fourth Series (1996) on generic Star Trek header card, with
    4" "30th Anniversary" Deep Space Nine trading card
The Jem'Hadar (#16032) 10.00
Lt. Commander Worf (#16033) 10.00
Elim Garak (#16035) 9.00

STAR TREK VOYAGER
Playmates (1995–96)

Figures from the *Voyager* series began appearing on their own separate style of header card in late 1995. The second series of *Voyager* figures included villains such as the Vidiian, a Kazon and the Cardassian spy/traitor Ensign Seska.

5" Figures First Series (1995) with 3½" Voyager trading card
Captain Kathryn Janeway (#6481) $20.00
Lieutenant B'Elanna Torres (#6485) 20.00
The Doctor (#6486) 15.00
Lieutenant Tuvok (#6487) .15.00
Neelix the Talaxian (#6489) 15.00
Commander Chakotay (#6482) 15.00
Lieutenant Tom Paris (#6483) 15.00
Ensign Harry Kim (#6484) .15.00
Kes the Ocampa (#6488) 25.00

*Star Trek Generations: Scotty (Playmates 1994)
& Star Trek First Contact: Lily (Playmates 1996)*

Star Trek Deep Space Nine: Jadzia Dax (Playmates 1996) Star Trek Voyager: Neelix The Talaxian (Playmates 1995)
& Star Trek Space Talk Series: Riker (Playmates 1995)

Second Series (1996) with 3½" Voyager trading card
Ensign Seska (#16460) 10.00
Lt. Carey (#16461) 6.00
The Kazon (#16462) 9.00
Vidiian (#16463) 9.00
B'Elanna Torres the Klingon, from "Faces" (#16465) . . .9.00
Chakotay The Maquis (#16466) 6.00

STAR TREK SPACE TALK
Playmates (1995)

Space Talk figures are larger than the normal *Star Trek* action figures and say three phrases each. There is also a *U.S.S. Enterprise NCC 1701-D* in this series and it says over 100 phrases.

7" Figures, with Adventure Booklet
Captain Jean-Luc Picard (#6081) $10.00
Commander William Riker (#6082) 10.00
(Hugh) Borg (#6085) 25.00
Q (#6086) 15.00

STARFLEET ACADEMY
Playmates (Sept. 1996)

Starfleet Academy figures came with a CD-Rom adventure, which can't be removed without destroying the mint-in-package value of the figure. I wonder what's on it.

5" Figures with CD-Rom
Cadet Jean-Luc Picard (#16001) $7.00
Cadet William Riker (#16002) 7.00
Cadet Geordi LaForge (#16004) 7.00
Cadet Worf (#16005) 7.00

MULTI-PACKS
Playmates (1993–94)

The Classic Figure set included the first Playmates action figures from the original *Star Trek* series. The Officers set was a Toys "R" Us exclusive. Both were eventually discounted but they have now become more valuable.

5" Figures in window box
Classic Star Trek Classic Collector Figure Set, 7
    original crew in window box (#6090, 1993) $40.00
Star Fleet Officers Collectors' Set, 6 officers in
    window box, (#6190, 1994) 25.00

STAR TREK
Playmates (1997)

The two *Deep Space Nine* and two *Voyager* figures shipped in quantity (at least in our area) and were all readily available for almost all of 1997 and into 1998 at discount. However, the original series figures and Professor Data were never available in our area until they appeared at discount in November 1997 at Kay-Bee stores.

5" figures (Mar. 1997) with 4" trading card
Captain Kurn (#16020) 7.00
Captain Benjamin Sisko (#16021) 7.00
Seska as a Kardassian (#16022) 7.00
Tom Paris Mutated (#16023) .7.00

5" Star Trek The Original Series figures (Asst. #6430)
Gorn Captain (#16041) 10.00
The Mugatu (#16042) with 4" trading card 15.00
Dr. McCoy in Dress Uniform .35.00
Captain Kirk in Environmental Suit (#16048) with 4"
    trading card 12.00
Harry Mudd (#16154) 12.00

5" Star Trek The Next Generation figures (Asst. #6430)
Professor Data (#16152) with 4" trading card 10.00
Dr. Beverly Crusher (#16047, 1997) limited to
    10,000 figures (from *Star Trek Generations*) 30.00

Spencer Gifts exclusives (1996) no trading card,
    limited to 10,000 figures
Lt. Commander Montgomery Scott (#16045) 40.00
Lt. Hikaru Sulu (#16046) 40.00
Spencer Gifts exclusives (Christmas 1997)
Lt. Commander Jadzia Dax (#65268) 17.00
Security Officer Neelix (#65269) 17.00

STAR TREK WARP SERIES
Playmates (1997–98)

Playmates revised the packaging on its *Star Trek* line with the "Warp Factor" figures which appeared beginning in the fall of 1997. The header cards were re-designed and each batch was clearly distinguished by being a different warp factor. However, each group included figures from two or more of the shows or movies. I have followed this system in the listings below. Six inch figures were also produced in the same packaging style, in their own warp factor groups. They are listed immediately following the five inch figures.

5" Warp Factor 1 series (Asst. #65100, Sept. 1997)
Chief Miles O'Brien (#65106) $20.00
Captain Benjamin Sisko (#65107) 7.00
Lt. Commander Jadzia Dax (#65108) 7.00
Constable Odo (#65109) 7.00
Dr. Julian Bashir (#65110) .7.00
Captain Koloth (#65111) 7.00

5" Warp Factor 2 series (Asst. #65100, Oct., 1997)
Sisko as a Klingon (#65101) 7.00
Ilia Probe (#65102) 7.00
Leeta the Dabo Girl (#65103) 7.00
Swarm Alien (#65104) 7.00
Captain Beverly Picard (#65112) 7.00

5" Warp Factor 3 series (Asst. #65100, Nov., 1997)
Edith Keeler (#65114) 7.00
Cadet Data (#65116) 7.00
Cadet Beverly Howard Crusher (#65117) 7.00
Cadet Deanna Troi (#65115) 7.00
Mr. Spock (#65105) 7.00

5" Warp Factor 4 series (Asst. #65140, March 1998)
Andorian (#65120) 7.00
Keiko O'Brien (#65121) 7.00
Trelane (#65122) 7.00
Kang (#65123) 7.00
Intendant Kira (#65124) 40.00

5" Warp Factor 5 series (August 1998)
Kirk (from "City on the Edge of Forever") 7.00
Spock (from "City on the Edge of Forever") 7.00
Borg Queen 7.00
Seven of Nine 7.00

1701 series 3-Pack (Feb. 1998)
1701 Collector Series: Captain Jean-Luc Picard from
    "Tapestry," Lt. Natasha Tasha Yar from
    "Yesterday's Enterprise", Lt. Reginald Barclay
    from "Projections" with identical equipment to
    original limited edition figures (#16122) 25.00

Twin Pack Assortment
Batch I (Asst. #65180, July 1998)
Captain Jean-Luc Picard as Dixon Hill and Guinan
    as Gloria (from "Clues") (#65181) 15.00
Captain James Kirk with Balok and Balok's Puppet
    (from "The Corbomite Maneuver") (#65182) 15-.00

Transporter Figure Series
Batch I (June 1998) with lights and sound effects
Captain James Kirk (#65401) 12.00
Mr. Spock (#65402) 12.00
Dr. McCoy (#65403) 12.00
Lt. Uhura (#65404) 12.00
Chief Engineer Montgomery Scott (#65405) 12.00

6" Warp Factor I Figures (Asst. #16250, Feb. 1998)
Captain Jean-Luc Picard (#16251) 8.00
Commander William Riker (#16252) 8.00
Lt. Commander Worf (#16253) 8.00
Borg (#16254) 8.00
Q (#16255) 8.00

6" Warp Factor 2 Figures (June 1998)
Cardassian Soldier (#16256) 10.00
Jem'Hadar Soldier (#16257) 10.00
Captain Benjamin Sisko (#16258) 10.00
Chief Miles O'Brien (#16266) 10.00
Lt. Commander Jadzia Dax (#16260) 10.00

Star Trek: Gorn Captain; Star Trek Warp Factor 2:Leeta the Dabo Girl & Star Trek Warp Factor 3: Cadet Deanna Troi (Playmates 1997

*Star Trek Twin Pack: Captain James Kirk with Balok and Balok's Puppet (Playmates 1998)
& Star Wars: Greedo (Kenner 1978)*

STAR WARS
Kenner (1977–1986)

All *Star Wars* action figure prices are volatile and generally increasing. This will almost certainly continue with the forthcoming release of another movie in the series. As this book is going to press, the last few action figures from the original movies are just appearing and there is much speculation (but no figures) from the new movies. Toy stores will want to make room for the flood of new figures when they arrive, which should make it an excellent time to buy figures from the last few years at discount.

The very first *Star Wars* action figures arrived in 1978, in the mail, if you bought the famous Early Bird Package. The figures came in a white plastic tray in a white mailer box. In the very earliest packages, Chewbacca has a dark green plastic rifle instead of the later black plastic and Luke has a telescoping lightsaber which not only extends out of his arm, it telescopes out of the middle of the blade and almost reaches the floor. This version lightsaber can occasionally be found on carded Luke Skywalker and also Darth Vader and Ben (Obi-Wan) Kenobi figures.

Early Bird "Figures" (Early 1978)
Early Bird figures R2-D2, Luke Skywalker, Princess
      Leia and Chewbacca, in tray and box 500.00

Packaging Variations — Header Cards
Star Wars action figures are heavily collected, and every tiny variation in the figure or the packaging makes a difference in the price. The chief packaging variation is the changed movie logo from *Star Wars* to *The Empire Strikes Back* and then to *Return of the Jedi* as each of those new movies premiered. After the movies, figures were issued on *Power of the Force* header cards with a collectible coin as a premium. Most of the figures were also available in the

United States on foreign "Tri-Logo" header cards which had *Return of the Jedi* movie logos in three languages. There are variations among Tri-Logo header cards as well, but all are lumped together for pricing purposes.

Packaging variations — Card Backs
The cards for the first 12 figures, which includes all the major characters, have a picture and list on the back which shows just these original 12 figures. They are called 12-backs and command the highest prices. When eight new figures were added, the card back was changed to reflect this, becoming 20-backs. The original 12 figures also appeared on these cards. The 21st figure was the regular Boba-Fett figure and it got a 21-back card. Most collectors treat 20 and 21-back figures as part of the same series, without distinction or price difference. They are listed as 20/21 backs in this book.

The first Empire Strikes Back figures appeared on 31-back cards, but the earlier 21 figures were re-released on 21-back cards with the Empire Strikes Back Logo. Many other variations exist with figures being added to the list on the back along with various mail-in offers. Most of these have little effect on value, but individual collectors might want to acquire a particular back that they do not have. There are two slightly different 12-backs, eight different 20-backs, and two or more versions of most of the others, for a total of 45 different U.S. header cards. The only ones with any extra collector value are the 48-back cards which contain a *Revenge of the Jedi* offer.

Figure Variations
The most significant of the figure variations was with the Jawa, where the original version had a vinyl cape. This was quickly changed to cloth, which was used for all the rest of the figures. The few vinyl-caped Jawas are the most valuable of all the *Star Wars* figures and currently sell in the $1,500 range, with loose figures going for $250.00 to $300.

Care in buying is essential, because a loose Jawa in cloth cape is only worth $15 and a fake vinyl cape is not hard to make.

STAR WARS SERIES
Kenner (1978–79)

First series, 12-back cards (1978)
Artoo-Detoo (R2-D2) (#38200) 150.00
Ben (Obi-Wan) Kenobi (#38250) **gray hair** 225.00
Ben (Obi-Wan) Kenobi (#38250) **white hair** 225.00
Chewbacca (#38210) 300.00
Darth Vader (#38230) 200.00
Death Squad Commander (#38290) 200.00
Han Solo (#38260) **large head**, dark brown hair 575.00
Han Solo (#38260)**small head**, brown hair 500.00
Jawa (#38270) **vinyl cape** 3,000.00
Jawa (#38270) **cloth cape** 200.00
Luke Skywalker (#38180) **blond hair** 375.00
Princess Leia Organa (#38190) 300.00
Sand People (#38280) 225.00
See-Threepio (C-3PO) (#38220) 150.00
Stormtrooper (#38240) 225.00

Second Series, New Figures on 20/21-back cards
Boba Fett (#39250) 850.00
Death Star Droid (#39080) 150.00
Greedo (#39020) 150.00
Hammerhead (#39030) 4" figure 140.00
Luke Skywalker X-Wing Pilot (#39060) 150.00
Power Droid (#39090) 2¼" figure 135.00
R5-D4 (#39070) 2½" figure 135.00
Snaggletooth (#39040) **red**, 2¾" figure 125.00

Star Wars: Princess Leia Organa (Kenner 1978)

Walrus Man (#39050) 135.00

Reissue Figures on 20/21-back cards
Artoo-Detoo (R2-D2) (#38200) 100.00
Ben (Obi-Wan) Kenobi (#38250) **gray hair** 125.00
Ben (Obi-Wan) Kenobi (#38250) **white hair** 150.00
Chewbacca (#38210) 100.00
Darth Vader (#38230) 100.00
Death Squad Commander (#38290) 100.00
Han Solo (#38260) **large head**, dark brown hair 600.00
Han Solo (#38260) **small head**, brown hair 500.00
Jawa (#38270) **cloth cape** 90.00
Luke Skywalker (#38180) **blond hair** 250.00
Princess Leia Organa (#38190) 250.00
Sand People (#38280) 150.00
See-Threepio (C-3PO) (#38220) 100.00
Stormtrooper (#38240) 150.00

THE EMPIRE STRIKES BACK SERIES
Kenner (1980–82)

Third Series, New Figures (1980)
Bespin Security Guard (#39810) **white** 65.00
Bossk (Bounty Hunter) (#39760) 125.00
FX-7 (Medical Droid) (#39730) 50.00
Han Solo (Hoth Outfit) (#39790) 90.00
IG-88 (Bounty Hunter) (#39770) 95.00
Imperial Stormtrooper (Hoth Battle Gear) (#39740) . . .60.00
Lando Calrissian (#39800) **no teeth** 60.00
Lando Calrissian (#39800) **white teeth** 65.00
Leia Organa (Bespin Gown) (#39720) **crew neck** . . .175.00
Leia Organa (Bespin Gown) (#39720) **crew neck,**
    new package 150.00
Leia Organa (Bespin Gown) (#39720) **turtle neck** . . .175.00
Leia Organa (Bespin Gown) (#39720) **turtle neck,**
    new package 150.00
Luke Skywalker (Bespin Fatigues) (#39780) 185.00
Luke Skywalker (Bespin Fatigues) **new package** 145.00
Rebel Soldier (Hoth Battle Gear) (#39750) 50.00

Fourth Series, New Figures (1981)
AT-AT Driver (#39379) 80.00
Dengar (#39329) 60.00
Han Solo (Bespin Outfit) (#39339) 125.00
Imperial Commander (#39389) 45.00
Leia Organa (Hoth Outfit) (#39359) 125.00
Lobot (#39349) 45.00
Rebel Commander (#39369) 40.00
2-1B (#39399) 75.00
Ugnaught (#39319) 45.00
Yoda (#38310) **brown snake** 80.00
Yoda (#38310) **orange snake** 75.00

Fifth Series, New Figures (1982)
Artoo-Detoo (R2-D2) (with Sensorscope) (#69590) . . .50.00
AT-AT Commander (#69620) 40.00
Bespin Security Guard (#69640) **black** 50.00
Cloud Car Pilot (Twin Pod) (#69630) 60.00
C-3PO (Removable Limbs) (#69600) 60.00
4-LOM (#70010) 150.00
Imperial Tie Fighter Pilot (#70030) 100.00
Luke Skywalker (Hoth Battle Gear) (#69610) 75.00
Zuckuss (#70020) 75.00

Reissue Figures on *Empire Strikes Back* header cards
Artoo-Detoo (R2-D2) (#38200) 50.00
Ben (Obi-Wan) Kenobi (#38250) **gray hair** 90.00
Ben (Obi-Wan) Kenobi (#38250) **white hair** 90.00

The Empire Strikes Back: IG-88 & Lando Calrissian
(Kenner 1980)

Boba Fett (#39250) 275.00
Chewbacca (#38210) 85.00
Darth Vader (#38230) 75.00
Death Star Droid (#39080) 130.00
Greedo (#39020) 125.00
Hammerhead (#39030) 4" figure 115.00
Han Solo (#38260) **large head**, dark brown hair 250.00
Han Solo (#38260) **small head**, brown hair 300.00
Jawa (#38270) **cloth cape** .75.00
Luke Skywalker (#38180) **blond hair** 200.00
Luke Skywalker (#38180) **brown hair** 225.00
Luke Skywalker (X-Wing Pilot) (#39060) 115.00
Power Droid (#39090) 2¼" figure 125.00
Princess Leia Organa (#38190) 295.00
R5-D4 (#39070) 2½" figure 125.00
Sandpeople (#38280) 115.00
See-Threepio (C-3PO) (#38220) 60.00
Snaggletooth (#39040) **red**, 2¾" figure 100.00
Star Destroyer Commander (#38290) 100.00
Stormtrooper (#38240) 80.00
Walrus Man (#39050) 125.00

RETURN OF THE JEDI
Kenner (1983–84)

There were a lot of *Return of the Jedi* figures produced and a number of them, particularly figures from the sixth series, were still available wholesale to comic shops and similar outlets in the early 1990s.

Sixth Series, New Figures (1983)
Admiral Ackbar (#70310) .30.00
Bib Fortuna (#70790) 30.00
Biker Scout (#70820) 35.00
Chief Chirpa (#70690) 30.00
Emperor's Royal Guard (#70680) 40.00
Gamorrean Guard (#70670) 25.00
General Madine (#70780) .30.00
Klaatu (#70730) **tan arms** or **gray arms** 30.00
Lando Calrissian (Skiff Guard) (#70830) 45.00
Logray (Ewok Medicine Man) (#70710) 30.00
Luke Skywalker (Jedi Knight) (#70650) with **green
    lightsaber** 100.00
Luke Skywalker (Jedi Knight) (#70650) with **blue
    lightsaber** 175.00
Nien Nunb (#70840) 35.00
Princess Leia Organa (Boushh Disguise) (#70660) . . .50.00

Rebel Commando (#70740) 30.00
Ree-Yees (#70800) 30.00
Squid Head (#70770) 30.00
Weequay (#70760) 30.00

Seventh Series, New Figures (1984)
AT-ST Driver (#71330) 30.00
B-Wing Pilot (#71280) 30.00
8D8 (#71210) 30.00
The Emperor (#71240) 35.00
Han Solo (Trench Coat) (#71300) 50.00
Klaatu (Skiff Guard) (#71290) 30.00
Lumat (#93670) 40.00
Nikto (#71190) 30.00
Paploo (#93680) 40.00
Princess Leia Organa (Combat Poncho) (#71220) 60.00
Prune Face (#71320) 30.00
Rancor Keeper (#71350) .30.00
Teebo (#71310) 40.00
Wicket W. Warrick (#71230) 50.00

Reissue Figures on Return of the Jedi header cards
Artoo-Detoo (R2-D2) (with Sensorscope) (#69420) . . .35.00
AT-AT Commander (#69620) 35.00
AT-AT Driver (#39379) 35.00
Ben (Obi-Wan) Kenobi (#38250) **gray hair** 50.00
Ben (Obi-Wan) Kenobi (#38250) **gray hair** new
    package 50.00
Ben (Obi-Wan) Kenobi (#38250) **white hair** 50.00
Bespin Security Guard (#39810) **white** 30.00
Bespin Security Guard (#69640) **black** 45.00
Boba Fett (#39250) 300.00
Boba Fett (#39250) new package 275.00
Bossk (Bounty Hunter) (#39760) 75.00
Chewbacca (#38210) 50.00
Chewbacca (#38210) new package 45.00
Cloud Car Pilot (Twin Pod) (#69630) 40.00
Darth Vader (#38230) 50.00
Darth Vader (#38230) new package 45.00
Death Squad Commander (#38290) 65.00
Death Star Droid (#39080) 70.00
Dengar (#39329) 35.00
4-LOM (#70010) 30.00
FX-7 (Medical Droid) (#39730) 40.00
Greedo (#39020) 55.00
Hammerhead (#39030) 75.00
Han Solo (Bespin Outfit) (#39339) 75.00

Return of the Jedi: Prune Face & Obi-Wan Kenobi (Kenner 1983)

Star Wars Power of the Force: Yak Face; Artoo-Detoo (R2-D2) & Gamorrean Guard (Kenner 1985)

Han Solo (Hoth Outfit) (#39790) 75.00
Han Solo (#38260) **large head**, dark brown hair,
    new package 200.00
Han Solo (#38260) **small head**, brown hair 175.00
Han Solo (#38260) **small head**, brown hair new
    package 185.00
IG-88 (Bounty Hunter) (#39770) 75.00
Imperial Commander (#39389) 35.00
Imperial Stormtrooper (Hoth Battle Gear) (#39740) . . .50.00
Imperial Tie Fighter Pilot (#70030) 55.00
Jawa (#38270) **cloth cape** 45.00
Lando Calrissian (#39800) **white teeth** 45.00
Leia Organa (Bespin Gown) (#39720) **turtle neck** . .150.00
Leia Organa (Bespin Gown) (#39720) **crew neck** . . .125.00
Lobot (#39349) 35.00
Luke Skywalker (#38180) **blond hair** 175.00
Luke Skywalker (#38180) **blond hair**, new package . .165.00
Luke Skywalker (#38180) **brown hair** 160.00
Luke Skywalker (#38180) **brown hair,** new package .150.00
Luke Skywalker (Bespin Fatigues) (#39780) new
    package, **yellow hair** 140.00
Luke Skywalker (Bespin Fatigues) (#39780) new
    package, **brown hair** 90.00
Luke Skywalker (Hoth Battle Gear) (#69610) 40.00
Luke Skywalker (X-Wing Fighter Pilot) (#39060) 50.00
Power Droid (#39090) 2¼" figure 55.00
Princess Leia Organa (#38190) 425.00
Princess Leia Organa (Hoth Outfit) (#39359) 100.00
Princess Leia Organa (Hoth Outfit) (#39359) new
    package 75.00
R5-D4 (#39070) 60.00
Rebel Commander (#39369) 30.00
Rebel Soldier (Hoth Battle Gear) (#39750) 35.00
See-Threepio (C-3PO) (Removable Limbs) (#69430) . .35.00
Snaggletooth (#39040) **red** 55.00
Stormtrooper (#38240) 50.00
Too-Onebee (2-1B) (#71600) 40.00
Tusken Raider (Sand People) (#38280) 75.00
Ugnaught (#39319) 35.00

Walrus Man (#39050) 60.00
Yoda The Jedi Master (#38310) **brown snake** 60.00
Yoda (#38310) **brown snake** 65.00
Zuckuss (#70020) 35.00

THE POWER OF THE FORCE
Kenner (1985)

The Power of the Force figures were produced after all three movies had come and gone. Kenner added silver colored aluminum coins as an in-package premium. Without a new movie to pump-up sales, less of these figures were ordered and many that were scheduled were never made. Now they are among the most valuable of *Star Wars* figures. Several were released only overseas.

There were 15 new figures and 22 figures which were reissued in this series. All of them came with coins, making a total of 37 figures that came with coins. However, two of the foreign release figures (AT-AT Driver and Nikto) came with coins from other figures, so only 35 different coins came with these 37 figures. However, coins were also available as a mail-in premium with a proof of purchase from some prior *The Empire Strikes Back* and *Return of the Jedi* figures and so there are actually 62 coins in the series to collect. They are covered in the TOY section of this book.

Eighth Series, New Figures (1985) with silver coin
A-Wing Pilot (#93830) 100.00
Amanaman (#93740) 250.00
Anakin Skywalker (#93790) foreign release 1,750.00
Artoo-Detoo (R2-D2) Pop-up Lightsaber (#93720) . . .150.00
Barada (#93750) 100.00
EV-9D9 (#93800) 160.00
Han Solo (Carbonite Chamber) (#93770) 225.00
Imperial Dignitary (#93850) 75.00
Imperial Gunner (#93760) 150.00
Lando Calrissian (General Pilot) (#93820) 110.00
Luke Skywalker (Battle Poncho) (#93710) 100.00

Luke Skywalker, Stormtrooper Outfit (#93780) 425.00
Romba (#93730) 50.00
Warok (#93810) 50.00
Yak Face (#93840) foreign release 1,750.00

Reissue Figures on Power of the Force header cards
AT-AT Driver (#39379) foreign release only 350.00
AT-ST Driver (#71330) 60.00
B-Wing Pilot (#71280) 30.00
Ben (Obi-Wan) Kenobi (#38250) **white hair** 100.00
Ben (Obi-Wan) Kenobi (#38250) **gray hair** 125.00
Biker Scout (#70820) 80.00
Chewbacca (#38210) 100.00
Darth Vader (#38230) 90.00
The Emperor (#71240) 75.00
Gamorrean Guard (#70670) foreign release only 150.00
Han Solo (Trench Coat) (#71300) 500.00
Imperial Stormtrooper (#38240) 250.00
Jawa (#38270) **cloth cape** 75.00
Luke Skywalker (Jedi Knight) (#70650) with **green
    lightsaber** 175.00
Luke Skywalker (X-Wing Fighter Pilot) (#39060) 100.00
Lumat (#93670) 50.00
Nikto (#71190) foreign release only 350.00
Paploo (#93680) 45.00
Princess Leia Organa (Combat Poncho) (#71220) . . .100.00
See-Threepio (C-3PO) Removable Limbs (#69430) . .75.00
Teebo (#71310) 200.00
Wicket W. Warrick (#71230) 200.00
Yoda (with **brown snake**) (#38310) 400.00

TRI-LOGO (RETURN OF THE JEDI)
Kenner (1984–86)

Tri-Logo is just the universally used collector's short-hand name for figures on header cards with *Return of the Jedi* logos in three languages. Different Tri-Logo cards were made for different countries, but collectors generally ignore such differences and all such cards for a given figure have the same value — generally a lower value than the same figure on any other type of card. Tri-Logo figures are often in lesser condition than those from other series, which further reduces their value. Figures on beat-up cards are often worth little more than the corresponding loose figure.

*Tri-Logo: Han Solo in Carbonite & Anakin Skywalker
(Kenner 1985)*

Bib Fortuna & Squid Head, loose (Kenner 1980–85)

Reissue Figures on Tri-Logo header card
Admiral Ackbar (#70310) 15.00
Amanaman (#93740) 150.00
Anakin Skywalker (#93790) foreign release 125.00
Artoo-Detoo (R2-D2) (#38200) 35.00
Artoo-Detoo (R2-D2) (with Sensorscope) (#69590) . . .28.00
Artoo-Detoo (R2-D2) with Pop-up Lightsaber
    (#93720) 100.00
AT-AT Commander (#69620) 25.00
AT-AT Driver (#39379) 25.00
AT-ST Driver (#71330) 14.00
A-Wing Pilot (#93830) 60.00
B-Wing Pilot (#71280) 12.00
Barada (#93750) 60.00
Ben (Obi-Wan) Kenobi (#38250) **gray hair** 50.00
Ben (Obi-Wan) Kenobi (#38250) **white hair** 50.00
Bespin Security Guard (#39810) **white** 25.00
Bespin Security Guard (#69640) **black** 25.00
Bib Fortuna (#70790) 15.00
Biker Scout (#70820) 15.00
Boba Fett (#39250) 250.00
Bossk (Bounty Hunter) (#39760) 55.00
C-3PO (Removable Limbs) (#69600) 25.00
Chewbacca (#38210) 35.00
Chief Chirpa (#70690) 17.00
Cloud Car Pilot (Twin Pod) (#69630) 30.00
Darth Vader (#38230) 40.00
Death Squad Commander (#38290) 65.00
Death Star Droid (#39080) .70.00
Dengar (#39329) 25.00
8D8 (#71210) 15.00
The Emperor (#71240) 15.00
Emperor's Royal Guard (#70680) 20.00
EV-9D9 (#93800) 100.00
4-LOM (#70010) 25.00
FX-7 (Medical Droid) (#39730) 60.00
Gamorrean Guard (#70670) 18.00
General Madine (#70780) 15.00
Greedo (#39020) 70.00
Hammerhead (#39030) 70.00
Han Solo (#38260) **large head**, dark brown hair 150.00
Han Solo (Bespin Outfit) (#39339) 40.00
Han Solo (Hoth Outfit) (#39790) 40.00
Han Solo (in Carbonite Chamber) (#93770) 175.00
Han Solo (in Trench Coat) (#71300) 25.00
IG-88 (#39770) 75.00
Imperial Commander (#39389) 25.00

Tri-Logo: Lumat (Kenner 1984); Ewoks: King Gorneesh (Kenner 1985) & Chief Chirpa, loose (Kenner 1983)

Imperial Dignitary (#93850) 45.00
Imperial Gunner (#93760) 125.00
Imperial Stormtrooper (Hoth Battle Gear) (#39740) . . .50.00
Imperial Stormtrooper(#38240) new package 60.00
Imperial Tie Fighter Pilot (#70030) 55.00
Jawa (#38270) **cloth cape** .65.00
Klaatu (#70730) with **tan arms** or **gray arms** 15.00
Klaatu (in Skiff Guard Outfit) (#71290) 15.00
Lando Calrissian (#39800) **white teeth** 45.00
Lando Calrissian (General Pilot) (#93820) 70.00
Lando Calrissian (Skiff Guard Disguise) (#70830) . . .20.00
Leia Organa (Bespin Gown) (#39720) **turtle neck** . . .125.00
Leia Organa (Hoth Outfit) (#39359) 60.00
Lobot (#39349) 25.00
Logray (Ewok Medicine Man) (#70710) 15.00
Luke Skywalker (#38180) **blond hair** 125.00
Luke Skywalker (#38180) **brown hair** 135.00
Luke Skywalker (Bespin Fatigues) (#39780) **yellow
   hair** 125.00
Luke Skywalker (Bespin Fatigues) (#39780) **brown
   hair** 125.00
Luke Skywalker (Hoth Battle Gear) (#69610) 35.00
Luke Skywalker (in Battle Poncho) (#93710) 60.00
Luke Skywalker (Jedi Knight) (#70650) **blue
   lightsaber** (#70650) 90.00
Luke Skywalker (Jedi Knight) (#70650) **green
   lightsaber** 60.00
Luke Skywalker (X-Wing Fighter Pilot) (#39060) 80.00
Luke Skywalker, Stormtrooper Outfit (#93780) 225.00
Lumat (#93670) 25.00
Nien Nunb (#70840) 20.00
Nikto (#71190) 15.00
Paploo (#93680) 25.00
Power Droid (#39090) 70.00
Princess Leia Organa (#38190) 150.00
Princess Leia Organa (Boushh Disguise) (#70660) . . .25.00
Princess Leia Organa (Combat Poncho) (#71220) 25.00
Prune Face (#71320) 15.00
R5-D4 (#39070) 70.00

Rancor Keeper (#71350) 15.00
Rebel Commander (#39369) 25.00
Rebel Commando (#70740) .15.00
Rebel Soldier (Hoth Battle Gear) (#39750) 25.00
Ree-Yees (#70800) 15.00
Romba (#93730) 30.00
See-Threepio (C-3PO) (#38220) 45.00
Snaggletooth (**red**) (#39040) 70.00
Squid Head (#70770) 15.00
Teebo (#71310) 20.00
Tusken Raider (Sand People) (#38280) 65.00
2-1B (#39399) 40.00
Ugnaught (#39319) 25.00
Walrus Man (#39050) 60.00
Warok (#93810) 30.00
Weequay (#70760) 15.00
Wicket W. Warrick (#71230) 25.00
Yak Face (#93840) foreign release 325.00
Yoda (with **brown snake**) (#38310) 50.00
Zuckuss (#70020) 25.00

(STAR WARS
TV ANIMATED SERIES)
DROIDS
Kenner (1985)

A couple of Ewok movies (*The Ewok Adventure* and *Ewoks: The Battle For Endor*) were produced, along with both an Ewoks and a Droids animated ABC television series. No collector I know will admit to having a video tape of any of them and the figures haven't attained much of a collector following. This may be undeserved, because, judged on their own, the figures are not too bad.

Two of the Droids figures are collected — the A-Wing Pilot and Boba Fett — but only because they are popular figures from the previous lines. The greatest collector interest in the rest of the Droids and Ewoks may well be in the coins,

Sy Snootles and the Rebo Band (Kenner 1984)

rather than the figures. They form their own sets and sell for between $5 and $8 each. This is a significant fraction of the value of the carded figures.

3¾" Figures (1985) with copper or gold colored coin
Artoo-Detoo R2-D2 (#71780) with pop-up lightsaber . .100.00
A-Wing Pilot (#93830) Reissue on *DROIDS* header
    card 175.00
Boba Fett (#39260) 700.00
Jann Tosh (#71840) 20.00
Jord Dusat (#71810) 20.00
Kea Moll (#71800) 20.00
Kez-Iban (#71850) 20.00
See-Threepio C-3PO (#71770) 125.00
Sise Fromm (#71820) 100.00
Thall Joben (#71790) 20.00
Tig Fromm (#71830) 90.00
Uncle Gundy (#71880) 15.00

EWOKS
Kenner (1985)

3¾" Figures (1985) with copper or gold colored coin
Dulok Shaman (#71150) 15.00
Dulok Scout (#71160) 15.00
King Gorneesh (#71180) 15.00
Logray (Ewok medicine man) (#71260) 15.00
Urgah Lady Gorneesh (#71170) 15.00
Wicket W. Warrick (#71250) 20.00

MAIL-INS

Mail-Ins
Boba Fett with Rocket Launcher (mail-in offer)
    unpainted blue/gray with red missile, with
    mailer box and letter $200.00
Bossk, Boba Fett, Darth Vader, IG-88, in plastic
    bags with Kenner logo, plus white mailer box
    listing the figures (#38871, 1980) 200.00
Bossk (1980) 25.00
4-LOM (1982) 25.00
Admiral Ackbar (1983) 20.00
Nien Nunb (1983) 20.00
The Emperor (1984) 20.00
Anakin Skywalker (1985) .40.00

SY SNOOTLES AND THE REBO BAND
Sy Snootles and the Rebo Band (#71360, 1984)
    Original *Return of the Jedi* header card 150.00
    Reissue on Tri-Logo header card 95.00
    Loose, each 15.00

STAR WARS (NEW):
THE POWER OF THE FORCE
Kenner (1995–98)

Kenner reintroduced the *Star Wars* figures starting in 1995. The first item to appear was the Classic Edition 4-Pack and, in some ways, it is the functional equivalent of the Early Bird Figures from the original series — an initial four figures which are not on their own header cards.

Star Wars Power of the Force Classic Edition 4-
    Pack, with 4 promo cards (#69595 1995) 55.00

The reintroduction of *Star Wars* action figures was a resounding success and hooked many collectors who had played with *Star Wars* figures as kids when they first came out. Collector interest in the original figures—always strong—got even stronger.

Packaging Variations
The most significant packaging changes in the new series is in the color of the header card. The 1995 and 1996 header cards have a red or orange laser blast running diagonally across them, while the 1997 cards have a green laser blast. Shadows of the Empire figures, from late 1996 are on purple laser blast cards. In 1998, the cards remain green, but all figures have a "Freeze Frame Action Slide." Most 1997 green cards have a holographic picture sticker, but limited quantities of many of the figures were issued without this sticker. All green cards, and late 1996 red cards for some figures, have collection numbers at the top. In 1998, the collection numbers are at the bottom and the cards are color coded by collection. Hopefully, the following information will help you sort all of these changes out.

Package printing numbers
All of Kenner's 1995–1998 action figures have a small printed number on the back, at the bottom, which can be used to distinguish earlier packages from later ones. The first six digits of the number are unique to the particular figure and do not change even if the UPC code or the figure's name are changed. However, it's the two digits after the decimal point that collectors look at. These are package revision numbers. The first version of each package is numbered ".00" and each

Star Wars Red Cards: Yoda & Obi-Wan Kenobi (Kenner 1995)

Star Wars Red Cards: Boba Fett, Luke Skywalker & Han Solo in Carbonite (Kenner 1995–96)

time there is a printing change this number is increased, so that if there have been three changes, the number will read ".03" and so on. Many of the figures have had printing changes on their header cards. The one you want is the one with the lower revision code, usually ".00". However, this number only works for *printing* changes, not for variations in the figure itself. Through out this section, these numbers are reported in [brackets] so as to distinguish them from UPC codes, which are listed in (parentheses).

Collection Numbers

The idea of the "Collection number" was to sort the action figures into groups so that "Collection 1" would be the Rebel Alliance, "Collection 3" would be the Galactic Empire and "Collection 2" would be the various non-aligned aliens. The idea was that the boxes shipped to the stores would indicate which collection was in the box and so the store would have to devote space for all three collections and there would always be a wide variety for sale — plenty of Rebels, plenty of Aliens and plenty of Imperial forces.

Unfortunately, there weren't equal numbers of each type, and new figures were not added at uniform rates in each group, but all boxes have to contain 16 figures. The result has been that a lot of figures came out in the "wrong" collection and later in the "right" collection. The five most important, i.e. valuable, collection "errors" are Grand Moff Tarkin, Ponda Baba, Weequay Skiff Guard, Yoda and Rebel Fleet Trooper, all of whom came out first in Collection 2, but were soon switched to other collections. All of these are quite difficult to find in the error collection and are worth about three to four times as much as they are with the correct number.

Other Variations

A holo sticker picture was added to the header cards about the time that they switched from red/orange to green. and in early 1998 a number of the figures could be found without stickers, so many figures are available both with and without the sticker. The peg holes used for hanging the figure were widened in mid-1997 and the bubble was changed so that the carded figure would stand up. None of these changes has had much effect on value, but the difference in holo stickers might be significant someday.

Basically, you can never go wrong with a package having printing number ".00."

Figure Variations

In addition to the packaging variations, there are several important variations in the figures. The one that affects the most figures is the change from the ridiculously long early lightsabers to shorter lightsabers. This yielded variations for Darth Vader, Luke Skywalker and Ben (Obi-Wan) Kenobi. The later figure also had a packaging change with his original head photo being replaced by a full-figure photo. If short lightsabers were not enough, some figures were found with short lightsabers in the plastic slots designed for long sabers. Luke Skywalker (Jedi Knight) originally came with a brown vest, but this was switched to black, matching the rest of his costume. Boba Fett now comes with a black circle on the back of each hand. Originally he had a bar across this circle, forming two "half-circles." These variations have had the most significant effect on price. Late in 1997 a variation occurred in Han Solo in Endor Gear. His pants changed color from Navy blue (almost black) to brown.

(NEW) POWER OF THE FORCE
RED CARD SERIES
Kenner (1995–96)

3¾" Figures (Asst. #69570, 1995)
Ben (Obi-Wan) Kenobi (#69576) head photo, long
  lightsaber $45.00
  Full-figure photo, long lightsaber 50.00
  Full-figure photo, short lightsaber 7.50

Chewbacca (#69578) 6.00
C-3PO (#69573) 10.00
Darth Vader (#69572) with long lightsaber [.00] 25.00
    Short lightsaber, long slot 40.00
    Short lightsaber .7.50
Han Solo (#69577) 9.00
Luke Skywalker (#69571) long lightsaber 40.00
    Short lightsaber .10.00
Princess Leia Organa (#69579) [.00] 10.00
R2-D2 (#69574) 6.00
Stormtrooper (#69575) .8.00

Second Batch (Asst. #69570, March 1996)
Boba Fett (#69582) with half circle on hand [.00] 50.00
    Full circles on hand [.01] 8.00
Han Solo in Hoth Gear (#69587) closed hand 6.00
    Open hand 25.00
Lando Calrissian (#69583) [.00] 10.00
Luke Skywalker in Dagobah Fatigues (#69588)
    long lightsaber .30.00
    Short lightsaber in long slot 25.00
    Short lightsaber .20.00
Luke Skywalker in X-Wing Fighter Pilot Gear
    (#69581) long lightsaber 25.00
    Short lightsaber in long slot 20.00
    Short lightsaber .15.00
TIE Fighter Pilot (#69584) warning on sticker 30.00
    Warning on card .6.00
TIE Fighter Pilot (#69673) [.02] 5.00
Yoda (#69586) [.00] 7.50
Yoda (#69672) [.01] 6.00

Third Batch (Sept. 1996 with Shadows of the Empire figures)
Han Solo in Carbonite "Carbonite Freezing
    Chamber" (#69613) [.00] 15.00
    "Carbonite Block" (#69613) 7.50
Jedi Knight Luke Skywalker (#69596) brown vest 75.00
    Black vest [.00] .8.00

SHADOWS OF THE EMPIRE

Shadows of the Empire figures appeared in September 1996. They are based on the book series, not any of the movies. One package variation did show up in the two-packs. Boba Fett vs. IG-88 packages with printing code ".01" stated on the back that Boba Fett's "Vehicle of Choice:" was the

Princess Leia in Boushh Disguise & Dash Rendar (Kenner 1996)

"*Slave I.*" This was the final line in his description, after "Weapon of Choice" Earlier packages, with printing code ".00" omitted the phrase "Vehicle of Choice:" but did include the words "*Slave I.*"

PURPLE CARD SERIES
Kenner (1996)

3¾" Figures (Sept. 1996)
Chewbacca (Bounty Hunter) (#69562) [.00] 7.00
Dash Rendar (#69561) [.00] 7.00
Leia (Boushh Disguise) (#69602) [.00] 8.00
Leia (Boushh Disguise) Collection 1 (#69818) [.01] . .150.00
Luke Skywalker (Imperial Guard) (#69566) [.00] 7.00
Prince Xizor (#69594) [.00] 7.00

Two-Packs, with special comic book
Boba Fett vs. IG-88 (#69568, Sept. 1996) [.00]
    without "Vehicle of Choice" on data card 15.00
    with "Vehicle of Choice: Slave I" [.01] 12.00
Darth Vader vs. Prince Xizor (#69567, 1996) 12.00

POWER OF THE FORCE 1996–97

The fourth batch of Power of the Force figures appeared in December 1996 with the captions "Collection 1" or "Collection 2" at the top. The two collections appeared at the same time, and the earliest versions came on a header card with an orange laser blast, the same color used on the other new "Power of the Force" figures from 1995–96.

These proved to be quite scarce, as the header cards were all quickly changed to a green laser blast design. Just as collectors were digesting these changes, holographic sticker pictures were added to the cards.

TRANSITION — RED "COLLECTION" CARDS
Kenner (1996)

Fourth Batch (Dec. 1996)
Collection 1 Figures (Asst. #69570, Dec. 1996)
Death Star Gunner (#69608) [.00] 25.00
Greedo (#69606) [.00] .25.00
Tatooine Stormtrooper (#69601) [.00] 25.00

Collection 2 Figures (Asst. #69605, Dec. 1996)
Jawas (#69607) [.00] 20.00
Luke Skywalker "Stormtrooper Disguise" (#69604) [.00] .20.00
Momaw Nadon "Hammerhead" (#69629) [.00] 20.00
R5-D4 (#69598) no small parts warning [.00] 20.00
    With small parts warning 15.00
Tusken Raider (#69603) [.00] 20.00

All of the interest focused on the year's most popular figure, Princess Leia as Jabba's Prisoner. This scantily clad number initially sold for $15 to $20 as all of the early ones were grabbed by eager collectors or dealers. However, more appeared and the price started to fall. As still more arrived and the figure became common, the price fell to the same as the other figures.

GREEN CARD SERIES
Kenner (1997)

Reissue of Collection 1 Transition Figures
Death Star Gunner (#69608) 8.00
Death Star Gunner (#69608) with holo picture 6.00

Tusken Raider (Kenner 1996) Princess Leia Organa as Jabba's Prisoner & Luke Skywalker in Ceremonial Outfit (Kenner 1997)

Greedo (#69606) 10.00
Greedo (#69606) with holo picture 6.00
Sandtrooper (prev. Tatooine Stormtrooper) (#69601) . .8.00
Sandtrooper (#69601) with holo picture 6.00

Collection 1, Second Batch (Asst. #69570, April 1997)
Bib Fortuna (#69634) 10.00
Emperor Palpatine (#69633) 10.00
Han Solo in Endor Gear (#69621) **blue pants** 6.00
Lando Calrissian as Skiff Guard (#69622) 6.00

Collection 1, Reissues (Asst. #69570, April–Aug. 1997)
Ben (Obi-Wan) Kenobi (#69576) 5.00
Boba Fett (#69582) 18.00
C-3PO (#69573) 5.00
Chewbacca (#69578) 5.00
Han Solo (#69577) 5.00
Jedi Knight Luke Skywalker (#69816) 5.00
Lando Clarissian 40.00
Luke Skywalker (Stormtrooper Disguise) (#69819) 5.00
Luke Skywalker (X-wing Fighter Pilot) (#69581) 5.00
Princess Leia Organa (#69579) 5.00
Princess Leia (Boushh Disguise) (#69818) 7.00
R2-D2 (#69574) 5.00
Yoda (#69586) 5.00

Collection 1, Third Batch (Asst. #69570, July 1997)
Bespin Han Solo (#69719) 5.00
Darth Vader (#69572) 10.00
Hoth Rebel Soldier (#69821) 5.00
Luke Skywalker (Hoth Gear) (#69822) 5.00
Rebel Fleet Trooper (#69696) 5.00

Collection 1, Fourth Batch (Asst. #69570, Oct. 1997)
Han Solo (Endor Gear) (#69621) **brown pants** 25.00
Han Solo in Carbonite (#69613) 5.00
Luke Skywalker (Ceremonial Outfit) (#69691) 12.00
Princess Leia Organa (Jabba's Prisoner) (#69683) 10.00

Reissue of Collection 2 Transition Figures (Early 1997)
Jawas (#69607) 6.00
Jawas (#69607) with holo picture 6.00
Luke Skywalker in "Stormtrooper Disguise" 12.00
Luke Skywalker in "Stormtrooper Disguise" with holo
    picture 10.00
Momaw Nadon "Hammerhead" (#69629) 6.00
Momaw Nadon "Hammerhead" (#69629) with holo
    picture 6.00
R5-D4 (#69598) with warning 6.00
R5-D4 (#69598) with holo picture, with warning 6.00
Tusken Raider (#69603) closed hand 25.00
Tusken Raider (#69603) open hand 6.00
Tusken Raider (#69603) with holo picture 6.00

Collection 2, Second Batch (Asst. #69605, March 1997)
AT-ST Driver (#69623) 7.00
Bossk (#69617) 5.00
Hoth Rebel Soldier (#69631) 10.00
Luke Skywalker in Hoth Gear (#69619) 10.00
2-1B Medic Droid (#69618) 5.00

Collection 2, Third Batch (Asst. #69605, July-Aug. 1997)
Bib Fortuna (#69812) 5.00
Jedi Knight Luke Skywalker (#69816) 10.00
Ponda Baba (#69708) 20.00
Rebel Fleet Trooper (#69696) 20.00
TIE Fighter Pilot (#69673) 10.00
Weequay Skiff Guard (#69707) 20.00
Yoda (#69672) 10.00

Collection 2, Fourth Batch (Asst. #69605, Sept. 1997)
Admiral Ackbar (#69686) 5.00
ASP-7 Droid (#69704) 5.00
Dengar (#69687) 9.00
4-Lom (#69688) 9.00
Grand Moff Tarkin (#69702) 35.00
Luke Skywalker (Ceremonial Outfit) (#69691) 40.00

Collection 2, Fifth Batch (Asst. #69605, Nov. 1997)
EV-9D9 (#69722) 5.00
Gamorrean Guard (#69693) .5.00
Han Solo in Carbonite (#69613) 7.00
Malakili (Rancor Keeper) (#69723) 5.00
Nien Nunb (#69694) 5.00
Saelt-Marae (Yak Face) (#69721) 5.00

Collection 3 (Asst. #69705, July 1997)
Darth Vader (#69802) 5.00
Darth Vader (#69802) SOTE figure 50.00
Death Star Gunner (#69809) 5.00
Emperor Palpatine (#69811) .5.00
Ponda Baba (#69708) 5.00
Sandtrooper (#69808) 5.00
Stormtrooper (#69803) 5.00
TIE Fighter Pilot (#69806) 5.00
Weequay Skiff Guard (#69707) 5.00

Collection 3, 2nd Batch (Asst. #69705 1997)
AT-ST Driver (#69823) 5.00
Boba Fett (#69804) 5.00
Emperor's Royal Guard (#69717) 5.00
Garindan (Long Snout) (#69706) 5.00
Grand Moff Tarkin (#69702) .5.00
Snowtrooper (#69632) 5.00

Specials
Four figure set of Han Solo in Endor Gear, Lando
    Calrissian as Skiff Guard, AT-ST driver and
    Darth Vader (J.C. Penney catalog 1997) 20.00

POWER OF THE FORCE 1998

The new header card packaging for 1998 adds a 35mm "Freeze Frame Action Slide" as an in-package premium and color codes the "Collection Number" (Red for Collection 1, Yellow for Collection 2 and Blue for Collection 3) on a strip at the bottom of the package.

The high points of this year's new figures include the first Biggs Darklighter figure, Darth Vader in removable hel-met, with his finely sculpted head revealed, Captain Piett and Expanded Universe figures Mara Jade and Grand Admiral Thrawn (from Heir to the Empire) and Kyle Katarn (from the Dark Forces Video Game and Comic).

The first batch of "Freeze Frame Action Slide" "Collection 1" figures arrived on schedule in February 1998. Happily or unhappily, they all had a printing error and so corrected versions, with new printing numbers arrived quickly as well. The error is on the back of the header card, under the picture of Jabba and Han, where weary collectors are advised to "Collect all these *Star Wars* Action Figures." In the list that follows, "Saelt-Marae" is misspelled as "Sealt-Marie" — two errors in just 10 letters. The error is the same on all packages and the corrected version has the higher printing number.

GREEN CARD—FREEZE FRAME SERIES
Kenner (1998)

1998 Figures With Freeze Frame Action Slide
Collection 1 (1st half, 1998)
Endor Rebel Soldier (#69716) [.00] 15.00
Endor Rebel Soldier (#69716) [.01] 7.50
Lando Calrissian (General's Gear) (#69756) [.00] 15.00
Lando Calrissian (General's Gear) (#69756) [.01] 7.00
Princess Leia Organa (Ewok Celebration Outfit)
    (#69714) [.00] 15.00
Princess Leia Organa (Ewok Celebration Outfit)
    (#69714) [.01] 7.00

Reissues
Bespin Han Solo (#69719) [.01] 9.00
Bespin Han Solo (#69719) [.02] 6.50
Han Solo 6.50
Han Solo in Carbonite (#69817) [.04] 9.00
Han Solo in Carbonite (#69817) [.05] 6.50
Han Solo in Endor Gear (#69621) [.01] 9.00
Han Solo in Endor Gear (#69621) [.02] 5.00
Hoth Rebel Soldier (#69821) [.02] 9.00
Hoth Rebel Soldier (#69821) [.03] 6.50
Lando Calrissian (Skiff Guard) (#69622) [.01] 9.00
Lando Calrissian (Skiff Guard) (#69622) [.02] 6.50

Freeze Frame: Zuckuss, Ugnaughts & Biggs Darklighter (Kenner 1998)

Flash Back Photo: Luke Skywalker and Hoth Chewbacca & 3-D PlayScene Grand Admiral Thrawn (Kenner 1998)

Luke Skywalker (Stormtrooper) (#69819) [.03] 10.00
Luke Skywalker (Stormtrooper) (#69819) [.04] 6.50
Luke Skywalker (Ceremonial Gear) 6.50
Ben Obi Wan Kenobi [.03] 9.00
Ben Obi Wan Kenobi [.04] 6.50
Princess Leia (Jabba's Prisoner) (#69683) [.01] 9.00
Princess Leia (Jabba's Prisoner) (#69683) [.02] 6.50
Rebel Fleet Trooper (#69696) [.01] 9.00
Rebel Fleet Trooper (#69696) [.01 sticker] 6.50
Rebel Fleet Trooper (#69696) [.02] 6.50

Collection 2 (1st half, 1998)
Biggs Darklighter (#69758) [.00] 8.00
Ewoks: Wicket & Logray (#69711) [.00] 9.00
Lak Sivrak (#69753) [.00] 8.00
Reissues
Admiral Ackbar (#69696) [.01] 6.50
EV-9D9 (#69722) [.01] 6.50
Gamorrean Guard (#69693) [.01] 6.50
Malakilli (#69723) [.01] 6.50
Nien Nunb (#69694) [.01] 6.50
Saelt-Marae (Yak Face) (#69721) [.01] 6.50

Collection 3 (1st half, 1998)
Captain Piett (#69757) [.00] 7.00
Darth Vader with removable helmet (#69836) [.00] 10.00
Ishi Tib (#69754) [.00] 7.00
Zuckuss (#69747) [.00] 7.00
Reissues
Boba Fett (#69803) [.04] 6.50
Darth Vader (#69802) [.03] 6.50
Emperor Palpatine (#69811) [.02] 6.50
Emperor's Royal Guard (#69717) [.01] 6.50
Garindan (#69706) [.01] 6.50
Grand Moff Tarkin (#69702) [.02] 6.50
Snowtrooper (#69632) [.02] .6.50
Stormtrooper (#69803) [.02] .6.50
TIE Fighter Pilot (#69806) [.05] 6.50
Sandtrooper 6.50

Collection 1 (2nd half, 1998)
Bespin Luke Skywalker (#69713) [.00] 30.00
Bespin Luke Skywalker (#69713) [.01] 15.00
Princess Leia (New Likeness) (#69824) 6.50
Princess Leia (Hoth Gear) 6.50
R2-D2 with Periscope 6.50
C-3PO (Captured) 7.50
Lobot (#69856) 6.50
Luke Skywalker (New Likeness) (#69881) 6.50
Chewbacca as Boushh's Bounty (#69882) 6.50
Mon Mothma (#69859) 7.50
Orrimaarko (Prune Face) (#69858) 6.50

Collections 2 & 3 (2nd half, 1998)
Ugnaughts (#69837) 2-pack 6.50
8D8 (#69834) 6.50
Death Star Trooper (#69838) .6.50
Ree-Yees 6.50
AT-AT Driver 6.50
AT-ST Driver 6.50
Death Star Droid 6.50
Pote Snitkin 6.50
Weequay 6.50

Collection 2: Expanded Universe: 3-D PlayScene
Clone Emperor Palpatine (#69886) 6.50
Dark Trooper (#69894) 6.50
Grand Admiral Thrawn (#69888) 10.00
Imperial Sentinel (#69887) 6.50
Kyle Katarn (#69893) 6.50
Luke Skywalker (in Black Cloak) (#69883) 6.50
Mara Jade (#69891) 10.00
Princess Leia in Black Cloak (#69884) 6.50
Spacetrooper (#69892) 6.50

Flash Back Photo (Episode I)
Ben (Obi-Wan) Kenobi (#84037) 6.50
Darth Vader (#84046) 6.50
Emperor Palpatine (#84042) .6.50

Hoth Chewbacca (#84051) 6.50
Luke Skywalker (#84036) 6.50
Princess Leia in Ceremonial Dress (#84038) 6.50
R2-D2 (#84043) 6.50
Yoda (#894039) 6.50

MAIL-IN AND EXCLUSIVE FIGURES

There have been quite a few mail-in and exclusive figures in the new series. The first to be offered was the Froot Loops mail-in Han Solo in Stormtrooper disguise. Both the cereal box and the figure are collectible. Since this offer was not tied to any *Star Wars* event or product, many collectors missed it. By contrast, the Spirit of Obi-Wan Kenobi mail-in from Frito Lay was tied to the theater release of the Special Editions of the movies in early 1997. Hardly anyone was unaware of it. The figure can not truly be said to be an action figure as it is not articulated, but Kenner treats it as one on its website and collectors have generally considered it so as well.

The theater edition Jedi Knight Luke Skywalker is the most valuable of the exclusive figures. It was given away during the first showing of the Special Edition of *Star Wars, A New Hope* on January 31, 1997. There was no prior announcement, not all theaters got the figure and there was no sign of any such figure when I saw the picture at 7:00 p.m. that day. A number of alert movie theater ushers and ticket takers did quite well for themselves by taking home a supply. The figure is identical to the common version sold in stores—only the header card is different.

Many of the *Star Wars* vehicles came with exclusive figures. This practice will continue in 1998, when it will be hard to find a vehicle without an exclusive figure. If you want all the figures you will have to collect vehicles too. The most interesting of these exclusives is the Wedge Antilles error figure. The first batches of the *Millennium Falcon* carry case came with a Wedge Antilles with a white stripe down each arm. This was clearly visible as the figure can be seen in the gun turret of the ship. Later batches of these carry cases corrected the figure. Locally, the original carry case with the error figure was available for quite a while after news of the error appeared in collector magazines. While the error figure

is still the more desirable version, the price difference is not particularly large. New shipments of the carry case, with the correct figure, appeared in local Toys "R" Us stores in March 1998. This new supply will keep the overall price of the figure within reason, but may lead to a greater price differential between the error and corrected versions.

Mail-in Figures
Mail-in Han Solo in Stormtrooper disguise, in plastic
 bag, (Froot Loops offer) with mailer box 30.00
Spirit of Obi-Wan Kenobi, with box (Frito Lay offer,
 1997) 10.00
Cantina Band Member, Official Star Wars Fan Club
 exclusive, in plastic bag, with five musical
 instruments (#69734, 1997) in white mailer
 box 15.00
Cantina Band Set, five figures: (All five figures are
 the same as above. Only the instruments are
 different.) Official Star Wars Fan Club 50.00
 Loose: Doikk N'ats with Fizzz Instrument 10.00
 Loose: Figrin D'an with Kloo Horn Instrument . . .10.00
 Loose: Ickabel with Fanfars Instrument 10.00
 Loose: Nalan with Bandfill Instrument 10.00
 Loose: Techn with Omnibox Instrument 10.00
B'Omarr Monk, Hasbro Internet Website offer, in
 plastic bag, with instruction sheet (#69718,
 1997–98) in white mailer box 12.00
Oola and Salacious Crumb, Official Star Wars Fan
 Club exclusive (May 1998) in window box 20.00

Give-away figure
Jedi Knight Luke Skywalker, Exclusive Star Wars
 Trilogy Edition, carded, movie theater (1997) . . .100.00

DELUXE FIGURES

Deluxe figures have met with a decidedly mixed reviews among collectors and in collector publications. None of the weapons/accessories in these packages appeared in the movie. Only a few of the deluxe figures have been created, and they follow the basic concept behind the Mini-Rigs from the original series which was to sell weapons and accessories that fit in with the ones featured in the film and could be envisioned as "just off camera."

Star Wars Fan Club: Oola and Salacious Crumb (Kenner 1998) Deluxe Probe Droid (Kenner 1997)
& B'Omar Monk mail-in figure, loose (Kenner 1998)

Epic Force: Boba Fett; Electronic Power F/X: Ben (Obi-Wan) Kenobi & Millennium Minted Coin: Han Solo, loose (Kenner 1998)

DELUXE FIGURES
Kenner (1995–97)

1st Wave (Asst. #69610, 1996) (on red header card)
Deluxe Crowd Control Stormtrooper (#69609, 1996)
  with 2 warning stickers [.00] 30.00
  Variation, with 1 warning sticker? 8.00
  Reissue, printed warnings [.01] 7.00
Deluxe Han Solo with Smuggler Flight Pack
  (#69612, 1996) [.00] .10.00
Deluxe Luke Skywalker's Desert Sport Skiff (#69611,
  1996) [.00] 11.00

2nd Wave (on green header cards)
Deluxe Boba Fett (#69638, 1997) [.00] card says
  "Weaponry: Photon Torpedo" 12.00
  Variation [.01] says "Weaponry: Proton
  Torpedo" 11.00
Deluxe Probe Droid (#69677, 1997) [.00] card with
  red color scheme back picturing figures from
  the Shadows of the Empire series 25.00
  Variation [.01] 8.00
  Variation [.02] green color scheme 6.00

Third Wave (green header card)
Deluxe Hoth Rebel Soldier (#69744, 1997) [.00] 9.00
Deluxe Snowtrooper (#69724, 1997) [.00] 9.00

ELECTRONIC POWER F/X
Kenner (1997)

Electronic Power F/X (Asst. #69615) green header cards
Ben (Obi-Wan) Kenobi (#69643, 1997) [.00] 9.00
Darth Vader (#69644, 1997) [.00] 9.00
Luke Skywalker (#69746, 1997) [.00] 9.00
R2-D2 (Artoo-Detoo) (#69646, 1997) [.00] 9.00
  Variation [.01] blue UPC code bars 8.00
  Variation [.02] black UPC code bars 8.00
Emperor Palpatine (#69726, 1997) [.00] energy bolts
  pictured pointing up 10.00

Variation [.01] energy bolts pictured
  pointing down 8.00

EPIC FORCE

These 5" figures were introduced at the 1998 Toy Fair. Other than the size, the gimmick is the rotating base, which lets the collector see all sides of the figure without removing it from the package.

5" Epic Force Figures with in-package rotating base.
Darth Vader (#69761) [.00] .15.00
Bespin Luke Skywalker (#69762) [.00] 15.00
Boba Fett (#69763) [.00] 15.00
C-3PO 15.00
Han Solo Stormtrooper 15.00
Stormtrooper 15.00
Princess Leia 15.00
Obi-Wan 15.00
Chewbacca 15.00

MILLENNIUM MINTED COIN COLLECTION

The original Power of the Force coins are a popular collectible and Kenner is bringing them back in 1998 in the Millennium Minted Coin Collection series. Each figure in the series comes with a gold-colored coin mounted on a display pedestal. Figures and coins are packaged in a window box which has a back window so you can see the back of the coin. The back of the coin is different from the back of the original coins, so even someone who doesn't notice that the original coins are silver-colored should still be able to tell them apart. The initial boxes appeared in early April and included just three different figures. The combination costs about $10, which is about $3 to $4 more than the figure alone. This seems about right, but a lot of collectors are reluctant to buy still another version of a character that they already own.

4" figures with gold coin (Asst. #69675, April 1998) in box
Bespin Han Solo (#84022) [.00] 10.00
Chewbacca (#84023) [.00] .10.00
Snowtrooper (#84028) [.00] 10.00
Emperor Palpatine 10.00
Luke Skywalker in Endor Gear 10.00
Princess Leia in Endor Gear 10.00
Princess Leia 10.00
C-3PO 10.00

MULTI-PACKS

The Cinema Scenes three-packs first appeared in June 1997 with the "Death Star Escape" group. Although Kenner calls them "Cinema Scenes" packs, this phrase doesn't appear anywhere on the package. However the back of the package contains a scene from the movie, with sprocket holes down each side to look like a piece of 70mm film. They are collected, in part, because each one contains at least one figure that is not otherwise available.

The Death Star Escape was a Toys "R" Us exclusive and included a Han Solo Stormtrooper figure which had only been released as the Froot Loops mail-in. The Cantina Showdown was a WalMart exclusive, at least at first, and included the never-before released Dr. Evazan. At the beginning of 1998, two more appeared. The Purchase of the Droids featured Uncle Owen Lars and the Final Jedi Duel had the Emperor seated on his throne/chair. The third group includes the first-ever versions of Jabba's Dancers and collectors are already drooling. There's just nothing quite like a sexy alien female to get a collector's blood boiling.

Three-packs are produced in much smaller quantities than carded figures, contain at least one exclusive figure and retail for the same price as three figures, making them a pretty good deal.

"CINEMA SCENES"
Kenner (1997–98)

Cinema Scenes Three-Packs in green *New Power of the Force* window boxes
Death Star Escape with Chewbacca plus Han Solo

and Luke Skywalker as Stormtroopers
(#69737) [.00] 15.00
Cantina Showdown with Dr. Evazan, Ponda Baba
and Obi-Wan Kenobi (#69738) [.00] 15.00

Second Batch (1998)
Final Jedi Duel with Emperor Palpatine, Darth Vader
and Luke Skywalker (#69783) [.00] 19.00
Variation [.01] box 18.00
Purchase of the Droids with Uncle Owen Lars, C-
3PO and Luke Skywalker (#69778) [.00] 19.00
Variation [.01] box 18.00

Third Batch (1998)
Jabba's Dancers with Rustall, Greeta and Lyn Me
(#69849) [.00] 20.00
Cantina Aliens with Labria, Nabrun Leids and
Takeel (#84059) 20.00

TWO-PACKS
PRINCESS LEIA COLLECTION

Princess Leia Collection (Feb. 1998) on header card
Princess Leia and R2-D2 (#66936) [.00] 15.00
Princess Leia (Medal Ceremony) and Luke
Skywalker (#66937, 1998) [.00] 15.00
Princess Leia (Bespin) and Han Solo (#66938) [.00] . .15.00
Princess Leia (Endor Celebration) and Wicket the
Ewok (#66939) [.00] 15.00

STINGRAY
Matchbox (1992)

This is a very good line of figures which adapts the Gerry Anderson syndicated television series to G.I. Joe and *Star Wars* size. Marina and Phones are highly collectible.

3¾" Figures
Commander Sam Shore $10.00
Captain Troy Tempest 10.00
Marina 20.00
Phones 35.00
Titan 10.00

Cinema Scenes: Jabba The Hutt's Dancers & Princess Leia Collection: Princess Leia and Wickett the Ewok (Kenner 1998)

Stingray: Marina (Matchbox 1992), Tarzan: The Epic Adventures: Tars Tarkas & Tarzan of Mars (Trendmasters 1995)

TARZAN: THE EPIC ADVENTURES
Trendmasters (1995–96)

Edgar Rice Burroughs' Mars series actually saw print earlier than his Tarzan series. (*Under the Moons of Mars*, All Story Magazine, beginning Feb. 1912; *Tarzan of the Apes*, All Story Magazine, beginning Oct. 1912) Tarzan was the more popular by far, with many novels and movies, but there are 11 Mars books and several comic book adaptations. Burroughs also wrote the Pellucidar series and Tarzan got there in *Tarzan at the Earth's Core*. He never made it to Mars in the novels. Trendmasters gets him to Mars though, to join John Carter, Dejah Thoris, Tars Tarkas and the other Martians. All the figures in this series are listed below, even though Tarzan would not qualify as space/science fiction on his own. There are also bendie figures listed in the TOY section.

6" Tarzan, Lord of the Jungle Figures, with badge
Numa the Golden Lion, with riding harness (#06053) .$10.00
Tarzan, Lord of the Jungle 6.00
Tarzan City of Gold (#06029) 6.00
Tarzan the Hunter, with bow and snake (#06239) 6.00

6" Tarzan at the Earth's Core Figures, with badge
Horib the Snakeman (#06051) 6.00
Tarzan Dino Armored (#06241) 6.00

6" Tarzan, Conqueror of Mars Figures, with badge
Nolach the Kaldane (#06052) 6.00
Tars Tarkas, The Green Martian (#06028) 6.00
Tarzan of Mars (#06050) 6.00

6" Talking Figures, in window box
Horib the Snakeman (#06055) 10.00
Tars Tarkas, The Green Martian (#06032) 10.00
Tarzan City of Gold (#06033) 10.00
Tarzan the Warrior (#06232) 10.00
Tarzan Dino Armored (#06235) 10.00
14" Figures, with CDS Light Motion Sensor & computer disk

City of Gold Armor Tarzan (#06125) 20.00
Jungle King Armor Tarzan (#06118) 20.00
Kerchak (#06243) 20.00

TERMINATOR 2
Kenner (1991–92)

From the movie starring Arnold Schwarzenegger, Linda Hamilton, Robert Patrick and Joe Morton. The movie had excellent special effects and a good story. Both it and its predecessor are rated among the top science fiction movies of all time by *Cinescape* magazine.

5" Figures (Dec. 1991)
Battle Damage Terminator (#56410, 1992) $12.00
Power Arm Terminator (#56420, 1992) 12.00
Techno-Punch Terminator (#56430, 1992) 12.00
Blaster T-1000 (#56440, 1992) 12.00

Second Batch (Summer 1992)
Secret Weapon Terminator (#56480, 1992) 15.00
Exploding T-1000 (#56490, 1992) 15.00

Third Batch (Fall 1992)
John Connor, with Motorcycle (#56550, 1992) 25.00
Meltdown Terminator (#60202) 20.00
Endoglow Terminator (#60203) 20.00
White Hot T-1000 (#60204) with White missile 20.00
    Reissue, with red missile 20.00

Fourth Batch (Nov. 1992)
Damage Repair Terminator (#60205) 17.00
Cyber Grip with "Crushing Claw Action" (#60206?) 17.00

Oversize Figure (1992)
Ultimate Terminator, 13½" figure with Battle Noises
    and Light-Up Eyes (#56530) 35.00

TERMINATOR 2: FUTURE WAR
Kenner (1993)

Kromium is a skull-faced villain who "Grows into a Towering Foe!" He also seems to have large horns on his head, wear body armor and be a Cyborg. We guess the idea is to make Arnold handsome by comparison. Cyber-Grip Villain was recycled from the Cyber Grip tail-end figure from the previous series. This has led to some confusion in magazine price listings.

5" Figures (1993)
Battle Ready Terminator (#60208) $6.00
Hidden Power Terminator (#60209) 6.00
Kromium (#60210) 6.00
Metal-Mash Terminator (#60213) 10.00
Hot Blast Terminator (#60214) 6.00
Rapid Repair Terminator (#60215) 10.00
Cyber-Grip Villain (#60216) .6.00
3-Strike Terminator (#60217) 6.00

TERMINATOR 2 JUDGMENT DAY
Toy Island (1995–97)

Toy Island continued both this series and the Robocop series when Kenner was done with them. The figures are cheaper looking than those from the major toy companies and designed to sell at a modest price. They are not really collected in themselves, but fans of the two series will probably want one if they can find one cheap.

4" Figures
Endoskeleton (#50106) $7.00
T-1000 (#50107) 7.00

15" figures (1997)
Endoskeleton T2 in window box (#50104) 20.00

TERMINATOR 2 3-D
Kenner (1997)

Kenner took another turn with the Terminator line in 1997. Collectors either haven't noticed or don't care, but I think the large figure will make a nice collectible when it becomes available at red tag prices.

Terminator 2 Future War: Rapid Repare Terminator (Kenner 1993)
& Terminatro 2 3-D: John Connor (Kenner 1997)

The X-Files: Agent Dana Scully & Attack Alien on variant header card (McFarlane 1998)

5" figures (Asst. #27172, Nov. 1997)
John Connor with Motorcycle (#27173) 5.00
Exploding T-1000 (#27174) .5.00
Techno-Punch Terminator (#27175) 5.00
Power Arm Terminator (#27176) 5.00
Hot Blast Terminator (#27177) 5.00
Battle-Ready Terminator (#27178) 5.00

12" figure (Oct. 1997)
T-800 figure, box with flap (#27179) 20.00

X-FILES MOVIE
McFarlane Toys (1998)

Based on the 1998 summer movie staring David Duchovny and Gillian Anderson, created by Chris Carter. The story begins with the mysterious bombing of a Dallas office building and leads to the antarctic and alien monsters. The Lone Gunmen put in a brief appearance while the usual suspects, CSM and WGM (Cigarette Smoking Man and Well-Groomed Man) have significant parts. The black oil, bees and corn fields provide sinister, but familiar plot elements.

The figures did not arrive until after the movie had opened. The sculpts capture the two stars very well, which is a good thing, because four versions of each star were issued with the same series of accessories. All of the figures also come on two different header cards—one is completely rectangular and the other has the left upper corner cut out. Both are shown above.

Figures (Asst. #61000, June 1998)
Agent Fox Mulder with Cryo-Pod (#16101) $12.00
Agent Fox Mulder with shrouded figure (#16101) 12.00
Agent Dana Scully with Cryo-Pod (#16102) 12.00
Agent Dana Scully with shrouded figure (#16102) 12.00
Agent Mulder with Alien (#16111) 12.00
Agent Mulder with Victim (#16111) 12.00
Agent Scully with Alien (#16112) 12.00
Agent Scully with Victim (#16112) 12.00
Fireman with bio hazard carrier (#16113) 15.00
Attack Alien, two figures (#16114) 15.00

BOOKS

Collecting Science Fiction Books

In the beginning, a little over 100 years ago, science fiction was H.G. Wells and Jules Verne and not much else. Then in 1913, Edgar Rice Burroughs came along. His first published story was about John Carter of Mars, but some jungle hero he created (I forget his name) achieved greater popularity. Burroughs produced 11 John Carter books over the years, plus others set on Venus and the center of the Earth. Books by Verne and Wells, plus *Brave New World*, by Aldous Huxley and later *Nineteen Eighty-Four*, by George Orwell were all important in the evolution of modern science fiction, but they were, and are, published as part of main stream fiction. First editions of these works rarely fall into the hands of book dealers who specialize in science fiction. They are largely collected by persons specializing in literature and modern first editions, while Burroughs books are mostly collected by fans of Burroughs.

The books that now grace the shelves in the science fiction and fantasy section of most book stores did not evolve directly from Verne, Wells, Orwell or even Burroughs. They could have, and maybe they would have, if it had not been for the Depression, but they didn't. Instead, they derive from the pulp magazines of the 1920s to 1940s and from the comic strips of the 1930s. The name science fiction wasn't even invented until the late 1920s—by the acknowledged father of science fiction, Hugo Gernsbach, editor of *Amazing Stories*. His magazine, and the others that sprang up in the 1930s were the primary places that science fiction was published for almost 25 years.

Spaceships, Rayguns and the other mainstays of early science fiction became popular in the 1930s with Buck Rogers and Flash Gordon. They were originally comic strips and were adapted to movie serials. It was all highly popular, but it meant that the public at large viewed science fiction as the stuff of lurid pulps and comic strips. For the first 25 years after the name science fiction was invented you couldn't get the literary establishment to publish any of it in a book — not even a paperback.

While paperbacks were published beginning in 1939, the war years 1942–45 restricted paper supplies. In any event, the number of true science fiction paperbacks published in the

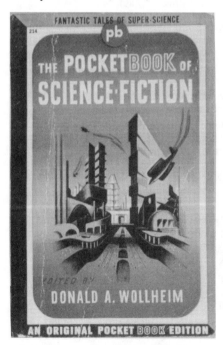 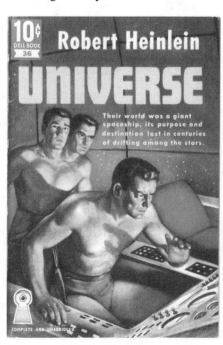 

Collectible early paperbacks: The Pocket Book of Science-Fiction *edited by Donald A. Wollheim (Pocket Books 1943);* Universe, *by Robert Heinlein (Dell Books 1951) and* The First Men in the Moon *by H. G. Wells (Dell Books 1947)*

Time Trap *and* Worlds Within *by Rog Phillips (Century 1949 & 1950) and* The Dying Earth *by Jack Vance (Hillman 1950)*

entire 1940s doesn't reach **ten** unless you count a few digest-sized, very magazine looking, science fiction "books." Part of the reason is that most early paperbacks were reprints of hardcovers and the regular hardcover publishers weren't producing science fiction books. 1950–52 saw some publishers starting to publish science fiction, but it really didn't get going in paperbacks until Ace and Ballantine got into the act in 1953.

1940s paperback science fiction books
Don Wollheim, ed. *The Pocket Book of Science Fiction*, Pocket #214, 1943
H.G. Wells *The First Men in the Moon*, Dell #201, 1947
H.G. Wells *The Invisible Man*, Dell #269, 1948
Pat Frank, *Mr. Adam*, Pocket #498, 1948
C.S. Lewis *Out of the Silent Planet*, Avon #195, 1949
Orson Welles, ed. *Invasion From Mars*, Dell #305, 1949
Rog Phillips *Time Trap*, Century #116, 1949

1950
Curt Siodmak *Donovan's Brain*, Bantam #819
Fredric Brown *What Mad Universe*, Bantam #835
Stanton Coblentz *Into Plutonian Depths*, Avon #281
Ralph Milne Farley *An Earth Man on Venus*, Avon #285
George Orwell *1984*, Signet #798
Edmond Hamilton *Beyond the Moon*, Signet #812
C.S. Lewis, *Perelandra*, Avon #277
Rog Phillips *Worlds Within*, Century #124
Ray Cummings *The Princess of the Atom*, Avon #FN1
Jack Williamson *The Green Girl*, Avon #FN2
Jack Vance *The Dying Earth*, Hillman Periodicals #41, 1950

1951
Robert A. Heinlein *Universe*, Dell 10¢ Edition #36
Robert A. Heinlein *The Man Who Sold the Moon*, Signet #847
Robert A. Heinlein *The Day After Tomorrow*, Signet #882
Ray Bradbury, *The Martian Chronicles*, Bantam #886

1952
L. Sprague de Camp *Rogue Queen*, Dell #600

Wylie & Balmer *When Worlds Collide*, Dell #627
A.E. Van Vogt *Mission: Interplanetary*, Signet #914
A.E. Van Vogt *Away and Beyond*, Avon #548
Robert A. Heinlein *The Green Hills of Earth*, Signet #943
Robert A. Heinlein *The Puppet Masters*, Signet #980
Raymond Healy, ed. *New Tales of Space and Time*, Pocket #908
Ray Bradbury, *The Illustrated Man*, Bantam #991
Ray Bradbury, ed. *Timeless Stories for Today and Tomorrow*, Bantam #A944
John Wyndham *Revolt of the Triffids*, Popular #411
Jack Williamson *Dragon's Island*, Popular #447

1940s and early 1950s digest size science fiction "books"
Curt Siodmak *Donovan's Brain*, Mercury Mystery #87, 1942
Herold M. Sherman *The Green Man*, Century #104, 1949
Murray Leinster *Fight For Life*, Crestwood Prize #10, 1949
Manly Wade Wellman *Sojarr of Titan*, Crestwood Prize #11, 1949
George O. Smith *Operation Interstellar*, Century #B10, 1950
Rog Phillips *World of If*, Century Merit #B13, 1951
see also Galaxy Science Fiction Novels

Hardcover specialty publishers

In the late 1940s and into the early 1950s, science fiction was published by specialty publishers — fans, really — who put out hardcover versions of novels which had appeared in the pulps. These included early books by giants such as Asimov, Heinlein, Bradbury, etc. The only famous science fiction author who had books published by a regular commercial publisher in the 1940s was Heinlein — but only his juveniles. Every other famous science fiction book from this era was produced by a specialty publisher. Many of these, like Isaac Asimov's Foundation trilogy, voted the best science fiction series of all time, remain classics to this day. One good thing about specialty publishing is that virtually all of the books were sold to fans, so most of them are still around. Fantasy Press, Gnome Press, Arkham House, Don Grant

Foundation and Empire *and* Second Foundation, *by Isaac Asimov (Gnome Press 1952 & 1953)*
Second and third volumes in the Foundation trilogy, voted science fiction's best series.

(Buffalo Book Company, etc.) virtually created the science fiction book category by themselves.

Unfortunately, all of them were under severe financial pressure by the mid 1950s. Essentially they were the victims of their own success. They paved the way for the acceptance of science fiction as a legitimate category of book publishing, and the much better funded regular book publishers took it over. They could sell their books to libraries and book stores, as well as fans, and afford to pay the authors more. By the end of the 1950s, specialty publishing was almost dead, but collectors have not forgotten this golden age of specialty publishing. Books published by Fantasy Press, Gnome Press, Don Grant and the others are still collected as much by publisher as by author. Of course, the more famous authors are worth a lot more than the hacks.

The era of the specialty publisher started to change in 1950 when Doubleday started its science fiction program. This eventually killed the specialty publishers, but it brought science fiction books to a lot more people. Doubleday hardcover books were sold primarily to libraries. Doubleday's science fiction book club, started in 1953, went to ordinary people. About the same time, Ballantine Books and Ace Books started publishing paperback science fiction books. Other publishers followed suit.

Paradoxically, while more science fiction books were being produced, less first edition hardcovers from the 1950s are in circulation in the hands of collectors. Doubleday hard-

covers (but not book club editions nor ex-library copies) are quite scarce. These include such famous titles as *The Martian Chronicles* and *The Illustrated Man* by Ray Bradbury, Asimov's Trantorian novels and *Mission of Gravity* by Hal Clement. Starting in 1953, Ballantine Books produced a limited number of hardcover versions of its early paperbacks and these are even rarer. These include *Fahrenheit 451* and *The October Country* by Bradbury, *Childhood's End* and *Earthlight* by Arthur C. Clarke plus *To Live Forever* by Jack Vance and *The Green Odyssey* by Philip José Farmer.

SF Paperbacks—the 1950s

Ballantine was the leader in publishing science fiction in paperbacks in the early 1950s. Their program started in 1953 and included books by Arthur C. Clarke, Ray Bradbury, Theodore Sturgeon, John Wyndham, Frederik Pohl and others. Almost all of the early covers were painted by Richard Powers and his surreal style came to represent the science fiction genre for many people. Their line was considered more serious and literary while the other publishers, with their spaceship and raygun action covers were more in the pulp magazine mold. None of these characteristics were firm rules; there were always exceptions and editors generally published the best science fiction stories they could get their hands on, even if they were packaged to look like the others in their line.

Avon, Signet and other publishers had science fiction lines and many excellent novels and interesting examples of science fiction art appeared from them. While these novels continue to be reprinted, these particular paperbacks are not as well known as those from Ballantine and Ace and tend to be collected by author rather than by imprint.

The pulps died off by the early 1950s and gave way to science fiction digest magazines. A lot of important fiction was first published in these magazines, and some still continue to this day. Several famous novels were also published in this format in the early 1950s before science fiction paperback publishing became established. The most famous of these are the Galaxy science fiction novels. These started in 1950 and included Arthur C. Clarke's first published book *Prelude to Space* as well as *Pebble in the Sky* by Isaac Asimov, *Fear* by L. Ron Hubbard (yes, that L. Ron Hubbard) and books by Jack Williamson, Clifford D. Simak, James Blish and C.L. Moore, among others.

Science fiction is a genre best suited to short stories or novel trilogies. Think of it as *The Twilight Zone* or *Babylon 5*. It is very difficult to tell a great science fiction story at the inbetween length of one novel or one movie. Every science fiction tale is set in some imaginary world that is different from our own. The short story focuses on one aspect of this world and lets the reader fill in all the background. In a novel, the author reveals the background of this different world and it becomes a major character in the story. But if this different world is at all imaginative, it cries out for more stories that illuminated all the differences and tell us what happens next and what happened before. This is all in addition to our usual interest in reading or seeing another adventure starring our favorite heroes.

Science fiction specialty hardcover publishing just about died off in the 1950s but it was revived in the 1970s and continues to this day. Donald M. Grant was still in business.

He published beautiful editions of just about every work by Robert E. Howard and is best known for publishing collector editions of Stephen King's *The Dark Tower* series.

Phantasia published a number of first and special collector editions of many well known authors. Usually these are small print run editions, authographed and slipcased. Underwood Miller specialized in the works of Jack Vance, although that was not their original plan. His specialty is science fantasy, sort of a combination of science fiction and fantasy, and many of his stories are adventure tales without any startling new scientific concepts. But his aliens and humans are more colorful, quirky and exotic than anyone else's. However Chuck Miller and Tim Underwood chose him, he remains one of my favorite authors.

As with earlier incarnations of specialty publishing, all of the books end up in the hands of collectors and dealers and most of the collectors who want one already have one. This, plus the number of different titles produced has meant that price increases have often been modest, at best.

One interesting sideline collectible has been the ocassional non-genre book produced by famous science fiction authors. In our society, nothing quite grips our interests as the purient, so it is not suprising that the most collectible of all these works has been the soft or hard-core porno novel, often written under a psuedonym. Collectors have been quite astute at uncovering these lurid items and identifying the true authors. Among the most famous of the hard-core variety are *The Image of the Beast*, *A Feast Unknown* and *Blown* by Philip José Farmer — never one to shy away from the topic. They were published by Essex House in 1968–69 and are worth between $150 and $250 each, in part because they feature characters from his other novels. Another famous title, *The Tides of Lust* by Samuel R. Delaney, was published by

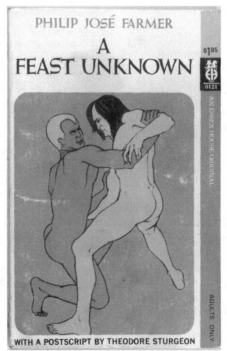
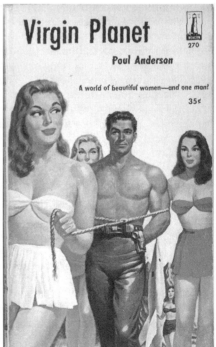

The Image of the Beast, *and* A Feast Unknown, *by Philip José Farmer (Essex House 1968–69)*
and Virgin Planet *by Poul Anderson (Galaxy Beacon 1959)*

Astounding, Oct. 1939 issue; pulp magazine featuring Grey
Lensman *by E.E. "Doc" Smith, later published by Fantasy Press*

Lancer Books in 1973 in two slightly different (but, sadly,
non-pictorial) covers. It sells for about $150 in either version.
The most collectible of the soft-core variety were the 11 science fiction books published by Galaxy Beacon paperbacks
from 1959 to 1961. Most of these were regular science fiction
stories which had been "sexed up" a bit for the edition,
although there was no need to do this for the two by Philip
José Farmer. Brian Aldiss, Poul Anderson and A.E. Van Vogt
also had books in this series. They are notable by how mild
the then-racy sex scenes seem today — not nearly racy
enough to embarass a politician. The best part of collecting
these titles comes in getting them autographed at a show.

In order to be worth collecting, any hardcover book
must be in near-mint condition, with dust jacket in similar
shape. The only defect in a dust jacket that does not significantly reduce value is "price-clipping," where a small portion
of the inside front flap of the dust jacket is cut to remove the
original price. This was commonly done to books given as
gifts and by some used book dealers who wanted to charge
more than original price. It is a pointless practice today,
because the price is also printed on the bar code box in back.

COLLECTING HARDCOVER PUBLISHERS

ARKHAM HOUSE

Arkham House started in 1939 to publish the works of
H.P. Lovecraft and other masters of horror fiction. In this
field, it is unsurpassed. While Lovecraft was its primary
focus, Arkham also published first books by Ray Bradbury
and Fritz Leiber. It is also famous in the field of heroic fantasy field for keeping the work of Robert E. Howard alive with
the publication of *Skull-Face and Others* in 1946. It is the
first, and most famous of the specialty publishers, but its con-
tribution to early science fiction publishing was modest, con-
sisting primarily of *Slan* by A. E. Van Vogt. Primarily, it
paved the way for Don Grant, Fantasy Press and Gnome
Press.

Selected science fiction and associational titles
Van Vogt, A. E., *Slan*, 1946, 4,051 copies $350.00
Howard, Robert E., *Skull-Face and Others*, 1946,
    3,004 copies, Hannes Bok cover art 850.00
Long, Frank Belknap, *The Hounds of Tindalos*,
    1946, 2,602 copies, Hannes Bok cover art 250.00
Bradbury, Ray, *Dark Carnival*, 1947, 3,112 copies 950.00
Leiber, Fritz, *Night's Black Agents*, 1947, 3,084
    copies 200.00
Wright, S. Fowler, *The Throne of Saturn*, 1949,

Slan, by A.E. Van Vogt (Arkham House 1946)

3,062 copies 100.00
Howard, Robert E., *The Dark Man and Others*,
  1963, 2,029 copies 200.00
Long, Frank Belknap, *The Horror From the Hills*,
  1963, 1,997 copies 150.00
Wellman, Manly Wade, *Who Fears the Devil?*,
  1963, 2,058 copies, Lee Brown Coye cover   . . .250.00

AVALON

Avalon published 136 science fiction novels from August 1956 to August 1968, about one every month. The books were designed for the library market. They are all the same size, have a similar look, and the great majority are undistinguished titles which were available for many years at one or two dollars each. They aren't much more valuable today. However, particularly in the 1950s, a number of books by more famous authors were included, and these are much more valuable. The challenge for collectors was to complete a whole set and hopefully to find some of the valuable titles mixed in with the cheap titles at a second hand book store somewhere that didn't know any better. This was made easier by the fact that several of the better authors were published under pseudonyms.

Collecting has picked up on this publisher. The last set that I saw offered was for $9,000.

Collectors should note that many of these books had library-style plastic wrappers for the dust jackets, with black edges that leave a residue on the jacket. This substantially reduces the book's value.

Selected titles
Russell, Eric Frank, *Three to Conquer*, 1956, Ed
  Emshwiller cover art (first Avalon science
  fiction title) $125.00
van Lhin, Eric (Del Rey, Lester), *Police Your Planet*,

1956, Ed Emshwiller cover art 40.00
Anderson, Poul, *Star Ways*, 1956, Ed Emshwiller
  cover 175.00
Vance, Jack, *Big Planet*, 1957, Ed Emshwiller
  cover art 300.00
de Camp, L. Sprague, *Solomon's Stone*, 1957,
  Ric Binkley cover art .100.00
de Camp, L. Sprague, *The Tower of Zanid*, 1958,
  Ric Binkley cover art .100.00
Vance, Jack, *The Languages of Pao*, 1958, Ric
  Binkley cover art 450.00
Del Rey, Lester, *Day of the Giants*, 1959, Ed
  Emshwiller cover art 40.00
Anderson, Poul, *Virgin Planet*, 1959, Ed Emshwiller
  cover art 125.00
de Camp, L. Sprague, *The Glory That Was*, 1960,
  Ed Emshwiller cover art 60.00
de Camp, L. Sprague & Pratt, Fletcher, *Wall of
  Serpents*, 1960, Ed Emshwiller cover art 175.00
de Camp, L. Sprague, *The Search of Zei*, 1962,
  Ed Emshwiller cover art 65.00
de Camp, L. Sprague, *The Hand of Zei*, 1963, Ed
  Emshwiller cover art 65.00

BALLANTINE BOOKS

Ballantine Books started its paperback science fiction publishing program in 1953. Publisher Ian Ballantine packaged the books as literature rather than as pulp fiction. Since literature was typically published in hardcover books and paperbacks were reprints, many of the early paperback originals were also bound in hardcover; but very few of them were actually produced. This makes early Ballantine hardcover books among the most difficult to find books in the field. The high quality of the fiction and the fame of the authors makes them expensive. About half of the hardcovers were bound from the same pages as the paperbacks and are listed as "small size" below. The other half are regular sized books.

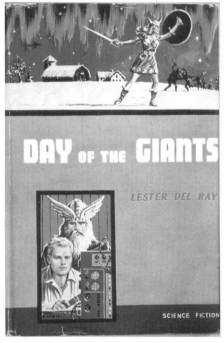

Day of the Giants by Lester Del Rey (Avalon Press 1959), The Space Merchants *by Frederik Pohl and C. M. Kornbluth (Ballantine 1953)
& The Green Odyssey by Philip José Farmer (Ballantine 1957)*

For the first couple of years they had full color dust jackets with the same cover art as the paperbacks, but starting in 1954 cheaper one or two color art was used.

Ray Bradbury had a number of copies of his two titles bound in hardcover for himself and friends and these are especially highly sought editions, but the most famous version is the special signed and numbered asbestos binding of *Fahrenheit 451*.

Other highly prized editions include Arthur C. Clarke's *Childhood's End*, *Earthlight*, *Reach for Tomorrow* and *Expedition to Earth*, John Wyndham's *Out of the Deeps*, *Re-Birth* and *The Midwich Cuckoos*, Philip José Farmer's *The Green Odyssey* and Jack Vance's *To Live Forever*. A total of about 40 produced. Collectors also look for three associational titles by famous science fiction authors: *I, Libertine* by Theodore Sturgeon (writing as Frederick Ewing) and a *A Town is Drowning* and *Presidential Year* by Frederik Pohl and Cyril Kornbluth.

Selected hardcover titles

Pohl, Frederik ed., *Star Science Fiction Stories*, 1953, small size, Richard Powers cover $200.00
Pohl, Frederik & Kornbluth, Cyril, *The Space Merchants*, 1953, small size, Richard Powers cover 250.00
Pratt, Fletcher, *The Undying Fire*, 1953, Richard Powers cover 50.00
Kersh, Gerald, *The Secret Masters*, 1953, Richard Powers cover 50.00
Kuttner, Henry, (with Moore, C. L.), *Ahead of Time*, 1953, Richard Powers cover 250.00
Clarke, Arthur C., *Childhood's End*, 1953, Richard Powers cover 850.00
Bradbury, Ray, *Fahrenheit 451*, 1953, Joseph Mugnaini illustrations and cover
  Red cloth binding with gold print (author's copies) 3,250.00
  Red boards with gold print 1,000.00
  Red boards with yellow print 900.00
  Asbestos binding, signed & numbered (200 made) no dust jacket 4,500.00
Pohl, Frederik ed., *Star Science Fiction Stories No. 2*, 1953, Richard Powers cover 200.00
Duncan, David, *Dark Dominion*, 1954 . . . . .50.00
Pohl, Frederik & Kornbluth, Cyril, *Search the Sky*, 1954, Richard Powers cover 350.00
Crane, Robert, *Hero's Walk*, 1954 . . . . .35.00
Sheckley, Robert, *Untouched by Human Hands*, 1954 . . . . .100.00
Pohl, Frederik ed., *Star Short Novels*, 1954, small size 250.00
Pohl, Frederik ed., *Star Science Fiction Stories No. 3*, 1955, small size, Richard Powers cover .600.00
Clarke, Arthur C., *Earthlight*, 1955, Richard Powers cover 600.00
Duncan, David, *Beyond Eden*, 1955, small size, Richard Powers cover .50.00
Boucher, Anthony, *Far and Away*, 1955, small size, Richard Powers cover .50.00
Wilson, Richard, *The Girls From Planet 5*, 1955, small size, Richard Powers cover 50.00
Clarke, Arthur C., *Reach for Tomorrow*, 1956, Richard Powers; sideways 500.00
Bradbury, Ray, *The October Country*, 1956, Joseph Mugnaini cover

  Red cloth binding with gold print (author's copies) 2,500.00
  Dull red cloth, black print "BB" upside down . .1,000.00
  Red boards with black paint 500.00
Mead, Harold, *The Bright Phoenix*, 1956, small size Richard Powers cover 35.00
Vance, Jack, *To Live Forever*, 1956, dark blue or light blue binding 600.00
Farmer, Philip José, *The Green Odyssey*, 1957 . . . .1,250.00

DOUBLEDAY

Doubleday began publishing science fiction as a category in 1950. It certainly started out well, with classics by Isaac Asimov, Ray Bradbury, Hal Clement and Robert A. Heinlein. It continued to publish books by Isaac Asimov for the next 40 years and commemorated this with a special 40th anniversary reprint edition in 1990. However, for much of this period, Doubleday concentrated on the library market and new authors, who managed to establish their reputations at Doubleday, moved on to better-paying publishers. Since most of Doubleday's print runs went to libraries, trade editions are generally scarce, making its early titles, and the best of its later titles, quite valuable. Ex-library copies are neither scarce, nor valuable, but can be a useful source for missing dust jackets.

Early Doubleday

Huxley, Aldous, *Brave New World*, see HUXLEY
Ehrlich, Max, *The Big Eye*, 1949 . . . .$75.00

Pebble in the Sky *by Isaac Asimov (Doubleday 1950)*

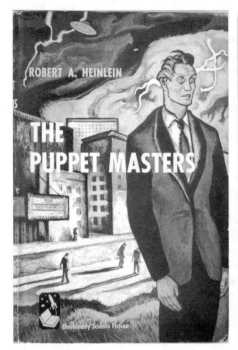

The Puppet Masters *by Robert A. Heinlein (Doubleday 1951),* Mission of Gravity *by Hal Clement (Doubleday 1954)* & The Black Star Passes *by John W. Campbell, Jr. (Fantasy Press 1953)*

Doubleday Science Fiction Library

Asimov, Isaac, *Pebble in the Sky*, 1950, Richard
    Powers cover art 750.00
    same, "Young Moderns" edition 75.00
Bradbury, Ray, *The Martian Chronicles*, 1950 . . . . . . .850.00
    Reprint, Doubleday 1958 . . . . .100.00
Clement, Hal, *Needle*, 1950 .200.00
    same, "Young Moderns" edition 50.00
Heinlein, Robert A., *Waldo and Magic, Inc.*, 1950 . . . .300.00
Bond, Nelson S., *Lancelot Biggs: Spaceman*, 1950. . . .100.00
    "Young Moderns" edition 50.00
Asimov, Isaac, *The Stars, Like Dust*, 1951 . . . . .250.00
Bradbury, Ray, *The Illustrated Man*, 1951 . . . . .500.00
    Reprint, Doubleday 1958 . . . . .100.00
DuBois, Theodora, *Solution T-25*, 1951, Richard
    Powers cover art 50.00
Heinlein, Robert A., *The Puppet Masters*, 1951 . . . . . .500.00
Asimov, Isaac, *The Currents of Space*, 1952 . . . . . . .175.00
Bradbury, Ray, *The Golden Apples of the Sun*,
    1953, Joseph Mugnaini cover art 300.00
Gallico, Paul, *The Foolish Immortals*, 1953 . . . . .50.00
Asimov, Isaac, *The Caves of Steel*, 1954 . . . . .500.00
Clement, Hal, *Mission of Gravity*, 1954, Joe
    Mugnaini cover art 500.00
Nearing, Homer Jr., *The Sinister Researches of*
    C. P. Ransom, 1954, Edward Gorey cover art . . .40.00
Asimov, Isaac, *The End of Eternity*, 1955, Mel
    Hunter cover art 350.00
Herbert, Frank, *The Dragon in the Sea*, 1956,
    Mel Hunter cover art 450.00
Asimov, Isaac, *The Naked Sun*, 1957 . . . . .650.00
Asimov, Isaac, *Earth is Room Enough*, 1957 . . . . . . .250.00
Heinlein, Robert A., *The Door Into Summer*, 1958,
    Mel Hunter cover art .1,000.00
Charbonneau, Louis, *No Place on Earth*, 1958, Joe
    Mugnaini cover art 40.00

FANTASY PRESS

Fantasy Press published 46 titles between 1947 and the late 1950s. Publisher Lloyd Eshbach included one of his own in the series plus a short non-fiction book. He had better luck with the Lensmen series by E. E. "Doc" Smith, and the fine novels by Jack Williamson, Robert A. Heinlein, John W. Campbell, Jr. and others that he published. Just about all of his titles had a limited edition of from 300 to 500 copies which were numbered and signed on a separate plate, in addition to the regular trade edition. That feature, plus the generally high quality of the book production, especially in contrast to Gnome Press, has made Fantasy Press one of the most sought-after publishers. As with all of the specialty publishers, most Fantasy Press books went to fans and not libraries so they are still around in the hands of collectors and dealers. It is actually possible to look for the signed, numbered editions and collect them without going bankrupt. One notable exception is *The History of Civilization* which consists of the six volumes in the Lensman series, bound in half leather. There were only 75 sets made and they are very expensive. It's considered to be a special, separate reprint set, highly desirable on its own, but not necessary to having, say, a complete set of signed, numbered Fantasy Press editions.

The three "Golden Science Fiction Library" trade paperbacks are also noteworthy. They have all gold covers with black printing and originally sold for $1 each. They date from 1956, but were bound from pages left over from the original print runs of the books from 1950, 1951 and 1954 respectively. They were not initially sold directly to fans and collectors so they can be harder to find than the limited hardcover editions.

Collectors should note that Don Grant obtained leftover unbound sheets for many of these titles and bound them. He made sure that they could be distinguished from the originals, but not everyone is quite so careful. They make very handsome copies, but they are not worth a whole lot to collectors.

Selected titles

Smith, E. E. "Doc", *Spacehounds of IPC*, 1947, #300, A. J. Donnell cover art $350.00
Trade edition, 2,008 copies 150.00
Williamson, Jack, *The Legion of Space*, 1947, #500, A. J. Donnell cover art 200.00
Trade edition, 2,970 copies 100.00
Taine, John, *The Forbidden Garden*, 1947, #500, A. J. Donnell cover art 125.00
Trade edition, 3,029 copies 60.00
Eshbach, Lloyd, *Of Worlds Beyond*, 1947, non-fiction trade edition only 75.00
Van Vogt, A. E., *The Book of Ptath*, 1947, #500, A. J. Donnell cover art 200.00
Trade edition, 3,021 copies 100.00
Weinbaum, Stanley G., *The Black Flame*, 1948, #500, A. J. Donnell cover art 250.00
Trade edition, 3,246 copies 100.00
Smith, E. E. "Doc", *Triplanetary*, 1948, #500, A. J. Donnell cover art 300.00
Trade edition, 4,941 copies 125.00
Heinlein, Robert A., *Beyond This Horizon*, 1948, #500, A. J. Donnell cover art 1,250.00
Trade edition, 3,502 copies 300.00
Zagat, A. L., *Seven Out of Time*, 1949, #500, A. J. Donnell cover art .75.00
Trade edition, 3,037 copies 25.00
Smith, E. E. "Doc", *First Lensman*, Press 1950, #500, A. J. Donnell cover art 300.00
Trade edition, 5,885 copies 125.00
Verrill, A. Hyatt, *The Bridge of Light*, 1950, #300, Edd Cartier cover art 75.00
Trade edition, 2,556 copies 25.00
Smith, E. E. "Doc", *Galactic Patrol*, 1950, #500, Ric Binkley cover art 350.00
Trade edition, 6,628 copies 200.00

Carr, Robert S., *Beyond Infinity*, 1951, #350, Hannes Bok cover art .60.00
Trade edition, 3,109 copies 30.00
Smith, E. E. "Doc", *Gray Lensman*, 1951, #500, Hubert Rogers cover art 350.00
Trade edition, 5,096 copies 150.00
Miller, P. Schuyler, *The Titan*, 1952, #350, Hannes Bok cover art 200.00
Trade edition, 3,042 copies 100.00
Smith, E. E. "Doc", *Second Stage Lensman*, 1953, #500, Ric Binkley cover art 250.00
Trade edition, 4,962 copies 150.00
Heinlein, Robert A., *Assignment in Eternity*, 1954, #500, Ric Binkley cover art 750.00
Trade edition, 4,026 copies 250.00
McClary, Thomas C., *Three Thousand Years*, 1954, #300, Brooks cover art 125.00
Trade edition, 3,153 copies 50.00
Smith, E. E. "Doc", *Children of the Lens*, 1954, #500, Ric Binkley cover art 300.00
Trade edition, 5,042 copies 125.00
Smith, E. E. "Doc", *The History of Civilization*, 1954, 6 volumes in Lensman series, 75 sets bound in half-leather, acetate dust jackets, with original box 6,000.00
Eshbach, Lloyd Arthur, *Tyrant of Time*, 1955, #500, Ric Binkley cover art 75.00
Trade edition, 3,051 copies 25.00
Coblentz, Stanton A., *Under the Triple Suns*, 1955, #300, Hannes Bok cover art 60.00
Trade edition, 3,121 copies 25.00

Golden Science Fiction Library, Trade paperbacks

Smith, E. E. "Doc", *Galactic Patrol*, #1, 1956, 500 copies 60.00
Campbell, John W. Jr., *The Moon is Hell!*, #2, 1956, 500 copies 50.00
Leinster, Murray, *Operation: Outer Space*, #3, 1956, 500 copies 50.00

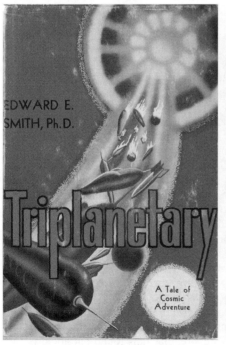

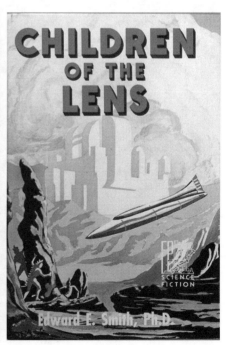

Triplanetary, First Lensman *and* Children of the Lens, *by E.E. "Doc" Smith (Fantasy Press 1948, 1950 & 1954)*

GNOME PRESS

Gnome Press published about 85 books its 13-year existence. In the science fiction field, it is best known for the Foundation trilogy and Robot books by Isaac Asimov, several Robert A. Heinlein and Arthur C. Clarke titles plus important works by Clifford Simak, Hal Clement, Andre Norton (as Andrew North) and others. Between 1950 and 1957, Gnome Press also published seven Conan books by Robert E. Howard, with help from L. Sprague de Camp and Bjorn Nyberg. These are scarce and valuable ($900 to $1,000 for the set) but they are in the sword and sorcery genre, and therefore beyond the scope of this book. Collectors in both fields know Gnome Press for high acid content paper and generally less than stellar production values. Publisher Martin Greenberg's business practices were also reportedly less than stellar.

Selected titles

de Camp, L. Sprague & Pratt, Fletcher, *The Carnelian Cube*, 1948, David Kyle cover art . . .$100.00
Owen, Frank, *The Porcelain Magician*, 1948, Dunn cover art 40.00
Heinlein, Robert A., *Sixth Column*, 1949, Edd Cartier cover art 500.00
Bond, Nelson S., *The Thirty-First of February*, 1949, James Gibson cover art 60.00
Bond, Nelson S., *The Thirty-First of February*, 1949, #112 copies, signed 400.00
Asimov, Isaac, *I, Robot*, 1950, Edd Cartier cover art .1,250.00
Beyer, William Gray, *Minions of the Moon*, 1950,

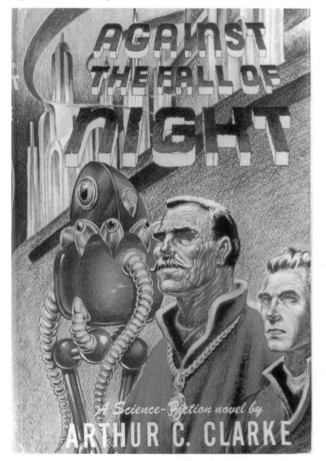

Against the Fall of Night *by Arthur C. Clarke (Gnome Press 1953)*

Edd Cartier cover art 40.00
Simak, Clifford D., *Cosmic Engineers*, 1950, Edd Cartier cover art 150.00
Asimov, Isaac, *Foundation*, 1951, cloth binding, David Kyle cover art 1,000.00
boards, 2nd printing 400.00
Asimov, Isaac, *Foundation and Empire*, 1952, red boards, Edd Cartier cover art 800.00
2nd binding 200.00
Simak, Clifford D., *City*, 1952, Kelly Freas cover art . . .600.00
Asimov, Isaac, *Second Foundation*, blue boards, 1953, Ric Binkley cover art 700.00
Schachner, Nat, *Space Lawyer*, 1953, Ric Binkley cover art 50.00
Shiras, Wilmar H., *Children of the Atom*, 1953, Kelly Freas cover art .125.00
Elliott, H. Chandler, *Reprieve From Paradise*, 1955, Mel Hunter cover art 30.00
Wallace, F. L., *Address: Centauri*, 1955, Ed Emshwiller cover art 25.00
Barnes, Arthur K., *Interplanetary Hunter*, 1956, Ed Emshwiller cover art 25.00
West, Wallace, *The Bird of Time*, 1958 . . . . .30.00
Godwin, Tom, *The Survivors*, 1958 . . . . .50.00
Heinlein, Robert A., *Methusalah's Children*, 1958, Leo & Diane Dillon cover art 300.00
Smith, E. E. "Doc", *Gray Lensman*, 1961 . . . . .50.00
Cole, Everett B., *The Philosophical Corps*, 1961, W. I. Van der Poel cover art 35.00

Gnome Trade paperbacks

Asimov, Isaac, *I, Robot*, 1, Robot, 1950 . . . . .50.00
Bond, Nelson S., *The Thirty-First of February*, 1950 . . .30.00
Simak, Clifford D., *Cosmic Engineers*, 1950, ...50.00
Smith, E. E. "Doc", *The Vortex Blaster*, 1960?, ...50.00
Smith, George O., *Pattern for Conquest*, 1959? 30.00

Gnome Science Fiction Book Club editions

Asimov, Isaac, *Second Foundation*, 1953 . . . . .12.00
Van Vogt, A. E., *The Mixed Men*, 1953 . . . . .10.00
Clarke, Arthur C., *Sands of Mars*, 1953 . . . . .12.00

DON GRANT

In the world of specialty publishing, Don Grant has tried the hardest for the longest. He started just after the war, with Thomas Hadley as Grant Hadley Enterprises, publishing *Rhode Island on Lovecraft*, a pamphlet. Grant was drafted, and Hadley continued with Ken Krueger as the Buffalo Book Company and later under his own name when Krueger left. Grant was not financially involved but had a hand in editorial matters. It was Grant who continued in specialty publishing, but for most of his publishing career he has concentrated on fantasy and horror. After a stint as the Grandon Company, he settled in as Donald M. Grant, Publisher and produced quality illustrated editions of Robert E. Howard's Conan stories, plus other fantasy, horror and non-fiction along with some science fiction. His most famous recent books are Stephen King's *The Dark Tower* series, which are science fiction and different from King's better known horror titles. The first *Dark Tower* book was distributed primarily to the science fiction trade and I bought one of the limited-edition copies for only a modest premium above its original retail price. It shot up in value when King's regular fans found out about it, but the best part of the deal came later. The publisher gave a pref-

The Skylark of Space by E. E. "Doc" Smith (Buffalo Book 1946); The Weapon Makers by A. E. Van Vogt (Hadley 1946) and The Ringworld Engineers by Larry Niven (Phantasia 1979)

erence on the limited-edition copies of the second *Dark Tower* book to collectors who owned a copy of the first title. Everyone else went into a lottery. When the third and fourth titles appeared, the rules were the same. Buying that first title allowed me to purchase all of the others at a good price, too!

Buffalo Book
Taine, John, *The Time Stream*, 1946 . . . .$300.00
Smith, E.E. "Doc", *The Skylark of Space*, 1946 . . . . .500.00

Hadley, selected title
Van Vogt, A.E., The Weapon Makers 1946 . . . . .200.00

Grandon Company
Kline, Otis Adelbert, *The Port of Peril*, 1949, ...50.00
Browne, Howard, *The Return of Tharn*, 1956 . . . . . .200.00
Munn, H. Warner, *The Werewolf of Ponkert*, 1958 . . .150.00

Donald M. Grant
Howard, Robert E. (numerous titles, mostly heroic fantasy, including the Conan series)
Resnick, Michael, *A Goddess of Ganymede*, 1967, Neal McDonald cover art 50.00
King, Stephen, *The Dark Tower: The Gunslinger*, 1982, #500, Michael Whelan dust jacket in cloth slipcase 1,500.00
One of 35, signed, lettered 3,000.00
Trade edition 500.00
Second printing 200.00
King, Stephen, *The Dark Tower II: The Drawing of the Three*, 1987, #850 copies, Phil Hale illustrations and dust jacket, in cloth slipcase . . .750.00
Trade edition 100.00
King, Stephen, *The Dark Tower III: The Waste-lands*, 1991, #1,250 copies, illustrated and dust jacket by Ned Dameron, in cloth slipcase . .400.00
Trade edition 50.00
King, Stephen, *The Dark Tower IV: Wizard and Glass*, 1997, #, 2 volumes in cloth slipcase 400.00

PHANTASIA

Phantasia started with high quality reprints of classic science fiction and moved on to high quality limited editions of new work by high quality authors including *Startide Rising* and *The Uplift War* by David Brin and *Firestarter* by Stephen King. Some of these have been very popular with collectors, but some of the reprints have not done as well as I would have predicted.

Selected titles
de Camp, L. Sprague & Pratt, Fletcher, *Wall of Serpents*, 1978, #200, George Barr cover art . . .$60.00
trade edition, 1,800 copies 35.00
Williamson, Jack, *The Reign of Wizardry*, 1979, #175, Stephen Fabian cover art 65.00
trade edition, 1,500 copies 40.00
Niven, Larry, *The Ringworld Engineers*, 1979, #500, Paul Lehr cover art 100.00
Farmer, Philip José, *The Magic Labyrinth*, 1980, #500, Alex Schomburg cover art 75.00
Farmer, Philip José, *The Maker of Universes*, 1980, #200 copies 60.00
trade edition, 1,200 copies 25.00
Farmer, Philip José, *The Gates of Creation*, 192pp, 1981, #250, George Barr cover art 50.00
trade edition, 1,000 copies 20.00
Farmer, Philip José, *A Private Cosmos*, 1981, #250, Eric Ladd cover art 50.00
trade edition, 1,000 copies 20.00
Farmer, Philip José, *Behind the Walls of Terra*, 1982, #250 copies 50.00
trade edition, 1,000 copies 20.00
Ellison, Harlan, *Stalking the Nightmare*, 1982, #700 copies 95.00
trade edition, 3,200 copies 35.00
trade edition, 2nd printing 15.00
Farmer, Philip José, *The Lavalite World*, 1983, #250 copies 50.00

trade edition, 1,000 copies 20.00
Farmer, Philip José, *Gods of Riverworld*, 1983,
    #650, Kevin E. Johnson cover art 50.00
Asimov, Isaac, *The Robots of Dawn*, 1983, #750,
    Barclay Shaw cover art 75.00
Farmer, Philip José, *River of Eternity*, 1983, #500
    copies 40.00
    trade edition, 3,000 copies 15.00
Asimov, Isaac, *Robots and Empire*, 1985, #650 copies .65.00
Brin, David, *Startide Rising*, 1985, #375, David
    Cherry cover art 300.00
    trade edition, 1,125 copies 175.00
Brin, David, *The Uplift War*, 1987, #475, Wayne
    Barlowe cover art 175.00
    One of 26, signed, special binding 500.00
    trade edition 75.00
Shatner, William, *TekWar*, 1989, #475, David Cherry
    cover art 125.00

SHASTA

Shasta was a Chicago publisher famous for publishing *The Checklist of Fantastic Literature* by Everett F. Bleiler, a non-fiction classic; and for not publishing *River of Eternity* by Philip José Farmer after it won its contest as best novel— it later became the basis of Farmer's award-winning Riverworld series and finally saw publication in its original form from Phantasia press in 1983.

It did produced 19 science fiction books, many of which are highly sought by collectors for their dust jackets by

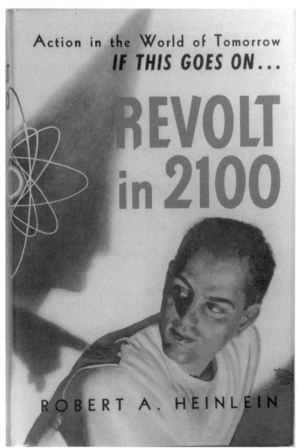

Revolt in 2100 *by Robert A. Heinlein (Shasta 1953)*

Hannes Bok or for the signed subscriber's editions by Robert A. Heinlein, Alfred Bester, Murray Leinster and others. They also published *Slaves of Sleep* by L. Ron Hubbard, who became famous (or infamous, depending on your point of view) in other, non-science fictional (or possibly science fictional, again, depending on your point of view) pursuits.

Selected titles
Hubbard, L. Ron, *Slaves of Sleep*, 1948, Hannes
    Bok cover art, signed subscriber copy $1,000.00
    Trade edition 350.00
Campbell, John W. Jr., *Who Goes There?*, 1948,
    Hannes Bok cover art, signed subscriber copy . . .400.00
    Trade edition 250.00
Wright, S. Fowler, *The World Below*, 1949, Sidney
    Boss cover art, signed subscriber copy 75.00
    Trade edition 25.00
Heinlein, Robert A., *The Man Who Sold the Moon*,
    1950, Hubert Rogers cover art, signed
    subscriber copy 750.00
    Trade edition 350.00
Campbell, John W. Jr., *Who Goes There?*, 1951,
    cover art, movie tie-in edition 100.00
Heinlein, Robert A., *The Green Hills of Earth*, 1951,
    Hubert Rogers cover art, signed subscriber
    copy 600.00
    Trade edition 300.00
Mullen, Stanley, *Kinsmen of the Dragon*, 1951,
    Hannes Bok cover art, signed subscriber copy . . .125.00
    Trade edition 35.00
Gray, Curme, *Murder in Millennium VI*, 1952 . . . . .50.00
Campbell, John W. Jr., *Cloak of Aesir*, 1952, signed
    subscriber copy 400.00
    Trade edition 75.00
Bester, Alfred, *The Demolished Man*, 1953, signed
    subscriber copy 400.00
    Trade edition 300.00
Heinlein, Robert A., *Revolt in 2100*, 1953, Hubert
    Rogers cover art, signed subscriber copy 500.00
    Trade edition 250.00
Brown, Fredric & Reynolds, Mack eds., *Science-
Fiction Carnival*, 1953, Ardri Ames cover art 75.00

UNDERWOOD MILLER

Although it was not its original intention, Underwood Miller published mostly hardcover reprints of science fantasy by Jack Vance. These were all high-quality books, with a limited, signed edition plus a trade edition. They sold much better than anyone expected because of the quality and because the idosyncratic style of Jack Vance had a number of devoted fans, myself among them.

Along the way, Tim Underwood and Chuck Miller published books by Roger Zelazny, Harlan Ellison, Robert Silverberg, Stephen Donaldson and Anne McCaffrey, while working their way through just about everything Jack Vance wrote. Their and Jack's most famous book was their first.

First title
Vance, Jack, *The Dying Earth*, 1976, numbered
    and signed, limited to 111 copies, George
    Barr illustrations and dust jacket $500.00
    Trade edition 150.00

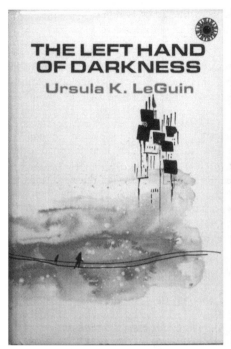
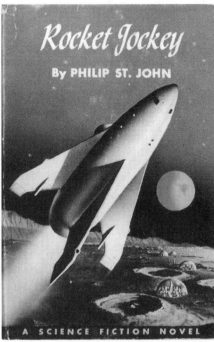
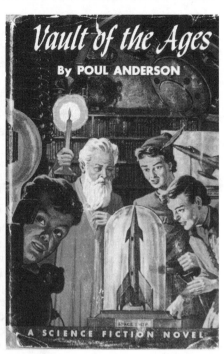

The Left Hand of Darkness *by Ursula K. LeGuin (Walker 1969);* Rocket Jockey *by Philip St. John (actually by Lester Del Rey)*
& Vault of the Ages *by Poul Anderson (Winston 1952–53)*

WALKER

Walker is primarily known for producing first hardcover editions of several of the 1960s more famous novels. Its less famous titles were easy to find, but the good ones were very scarce. This made Walker editions desirable to collectors — more desirable than any other reprint publisher.

Selected titles
McCaffrey, Anne, *Dragonflight*, 1969, ...$500.00
LeGuin, Ursula K., *The Left Hand of Darkness*,
    1969, Jack Gaughan cover art 500.00
McCaffrey, Anne, *The Ship Who Sang*, 1969,
    Jack Gaughan cover art 450.00
Zelazny, Roger, *Jack of Shadows*, 1971 . . . . .350.00
Leiber, Fritz, *The Wanderer*, 1970, Jack Gaughan
    cover art 350.00
Niven, Larry, *A Gift From Earth*, 1970, Jack
    Gaughan cover art 30000

WINSTON

The John C. Winston Company published 34 juvenile science fiction/space adventure books from 1952 to 1960. Teenager boys bought them, read them and dreamed about space travel. In addition to good stories, they featured a distinctive rocket ship inside a circle logo on the dust jacket and exciting endpapers by Alex Schomburg. Poul Anderson, Arthur C. Clarke and Jack Vance contributed to the series and Lester del Rey wrote eight of them, using his own name and a couple of pseudonyms. All the books were reprinted regularly and sold well over the years. The company became part of Holt Rinehart & Winston, which continued to reprint. The result of this is that first editions in near mint dust jackets are few and far between. The only other significant publisher of juvenile science fiction at this time was Charles Scribner's Sons, which published all 12 of Robert A. Heinlein's juveniles, but no one else's.

Selected titles
Jones, Raymond F., *Son of the Stars*, 1952, Alex
    Schomburg cover art $150.00
del Rey, Lester, *Marooned on Mars*, 1952, Paul
    Orban cover art 50.00
Anderson, Poul, *Vault of the Ages*, 1952, blue
    binding, black letters, Paul Orban cover art 200.00
Clarke, Arthur C., *Islands in the Sky*, 1952, Alex
    Schomburg cover art 200.00
Oliver, Chad, *Mists of Dawn*, 1952, Alex
    Schomburg cover art 75.00
Vance, Jack, *Vandals of the Void*, 1953, Alex
    Schomburg cover art 200.00

SCIENCE FICTION BOOK CLUB

Doubleday started its Science Fiction Book Club in early 1953. In order to have a supply of books to offer with the first flyer (along with its first two monthly selections), it made a special purchase of 19 trade books. The two anthologies were purchased from other regular publishers and were offered at $1.90 each. *The Sands of Mars* and *The Mixed Men* were purchased from Gnome Press and these books plus the other 15, which were purchased from themselves, sold for $1. These, and most of its other 1953 offerings can be distinguished from other Science Fiction Book Club titles because they are slightly shorter that the standard size. This makes them an interesting and not well known collectible subset.

Beginning in 1958, a printer's code appears in the gutter of the last signature of almost all of Doubleday's book club printings (and its regular hardcovers too, for that matter). The code can be use to distinguish between initial and later book club printings. In the code, the letter identifies the year and the number identifies the week, so, for example, "C13" means the 13th week of 1961.

However, collectors mostly disdain *all* book club editions and don't care about first and later book club printings. The only time it matters is on those very few books where the book club edition is the true first edition because there was no prior hardcover or paperback edition. See discussion below.

Mostly collectors want to identify book club editions so they can avoid buying them. There are several identifying charactistics and it is easy to tell the difference between the regular trade edition and the book club edition if you have both in your hand, but it's not so easy if you have only one. Of course, if the copyright page says "First Edition," it's a trade edition and not a book club edition, but not all publishers identify their editions this way.

The dust jacket: The best place to look is the dust jacket, if it is complete. A trade book has a price, usually at top of the inside flap, while a book club edition says "Book Club Edition," usually at the bottom of this flap. The price was often clipped on a trade book which was given as a gift and if the top and bottom corners of the flap are both missing, it is not as easy to distinguish between book club and trade edition dust jackets. In this case, look at the back of the dust jacket. Most trade books have either an advertisement for other books from the publisher or jacket copy praising this book. Book club editions omit this. They also omit bar codes, but they often have a number code which corresponds to the monthly catalog number. Early book club editions had text on

the back which begins with "Today's Fiction—Tomorrow's Facts" in bold. No trade edition used this text.

The binding: Book club bindings were traditionally cheaper than the bindings on trade editions. Boards were used instead of cloth, but some trade editions also had cheap bindings. Book club editions have improved in quality in the 1990s so this doesn't work as well as it used to.

The listing below is not meant to encourage you to acquire these book club editions. Rather, it is designed to let you compare these prices with the corresponding trade editions. Reputable dealers will rarely deal in these editions at all, and if they do, they will clearly identify a book club edition, but who knows what you can find on the shelf of some used book store somewhere. You might get lucky, but most of the time it will be one of these editions.

Special Purchase Books
Asimov, Isaac, *The Stars, Like Dust*, Doubleday
  1953 . . . .$15.00
Bond, Nelson S., *Lancelot Biggs: Spaceman*,
  Doubleday 1953 . . . . .15.00
Bradbury, Ray, *The Martian Chronicles*, Doubleday
  1953 . . . . .15.00
Bradbury, Ray, *The Illustrated Man*, Doubleday 1953 . .15.00
Campbell, John ed., *The Astounding Science Fiction
  Anthology*, Simon & Schuster 1953 . . . . .15.00
Clarke, Arthur C., *Sands of Mars*, Gnome 1953 . . . . . .15.00
Clement, Hal, *Needle*, Doubleday 1953 . . . . .15.00
Conklin, Groff ed., *Omnibus of Science Fiction*, Crown 1953 . .15.00
de Camp, L. Sprague, *Rogue Queen*, Doubleday
  1953 . . . . .15.00
DuBois, Theodora, *Solution T-25*, Doubleday 1953 . . .15.00
Heinlein, Robert A., *The Puppet Masters*, Doubleday
  #536-A, 1953 . . . . .15.00
Kornbluth, C. M., *Takeoff*, Doubleday 1953 . . . . .15.00
Merwin, Sam Jr., *The House of Many Worlds*,
  Doubleday 1953 . . . . .15.00
Merwin, Sam Jr., *The White Widows*, Doubleday
  1953 . . . . .15.00
Nearing, Homer Jr., *The Sinister Researches of C.
  P. Ransom*, Doubleday 1954, Edward Gorey 15.00
Pratt, Fletcher, *Double in Space*, Doubleday 1953 . . . .15.00
Pratt, Fletcher, *Double Jeopardy*, Doubleday 1953 . . . .15.00
Van Vogt, A.E., *The Mixed Men*, Gnome 1953 . . . . . . .15.00
Wyndham, John, *The Day of the Triffids*, Doubleday
  1953 . . . . .15.00

There are a few important early book club editions where the trade publisher and the Science Fiction Book Club both published the same book. Torquil, distributed by Dodd Mead, published the true first editions and the book club used the same print run for their copies. The only way to tell the two apart is the dust jacket. The trade edition has a price of $2.95 to $3.50 and the back cover of the dust jacket is different. The trade editions are very scarce. Collectors want only the first printings, with code numbers as given. Some of the copies on the market are probably the result of taking a dust-jacket from an ex-library copy and putting it on a good condition book club edition. There is no way to tell, but you can at least look for the correct printing code.

Torquil Book Club editions
Hamilton, Edmond, *The Star of Life*, 1959, code 4 . . .$15.00
Hamilton, Edmond, *The Haunted Stars*, 1960, B3 . . . .15.00

*Things to Come, advertising flyer (Science Fiction Book Club,
September–October 1953)*

Hamilton, Edmond, *Battle for the Stars*, 1961, C42 . . . .15.00
Anderson, Poul, *Twilight World*, 1961, code B49 . . . . .15.00
Russell, Eric Frank, *The Great Explosion*, 1962, D29 . . .15.00
Schmitz, James H., *A Tale of Two Clocks*, 1962, D6 . . .15.00

In 1968, the science fiction book club started buying some books that had no prior hardcover printing, just a paperback printing. This makes the book club edition the first hardcover edition and makes it somewhat more valuable than other book clubs. A collector can usually identify these titles easily by the use of a paperback publishers imprint such as Ace, Ballantine, Berkley, Daw, or Signet, etc. The important thing when collecting them is to look for the printing code in the last signature. If you know the correct code, you can identify the first printing. The copyright page does not identify printings and the book club reprints frequently. First hardcover editions of authors like Philip K. Dick are usually very valuable, but when they are issued from the book club their value is a lot less.

Book Club is first hardcover edition
Wyndham, John, *Chocky*, 1968, code 40J $25.00
Anthony, Piers, *Omnivore*, 1969, code 20K 25.00
Schmitz, James H., *The Demon Breed*, 1969, 24K 25.00
Brunner, John, *The Jagged Orbit*, Ace 1969, 40K 25.00
Dick, Philip K., *The Preserving Machine*, 1969, 48K 25.00
Dick, Philip K., *Galactic Pot-Healer*, 1970, 08L 25.00
Moorcock, Michael, *The Black Corridor*, 1970, 16L 25.00
Dick, Philip K., *Our Friends from Frolix 8*, 1971, B3 . . . .25.00

The really interesting book club editions are the few that are true "first editions." The first of those to appear was *Triad* by A. E. Van Vogt, but it's really just a first combined edition, since all three of the included titles had seen previous publication. The book club started this practice again in the 1970s and it has as produced a lot of these 3-in-one editions in the last 25 years. They are not particularly valuable. The second book listed below is *A Princess of Mars*, by Edgar Rice Burroughs. It's hardly a first edition, since the book was originally published in 1917, but the book club bought new Frank Frazetta art for the cover. It must have sold well, because it issued the rest of the series in two-in-one volumes, also with new Frazetta art, in subsequent years.

Down in the Black Gang *by Philip José Farmer,* & The Last
Hurrah of the Golden Horde *by Norman Spinrad (Science Fiction
Book Club 1971 & 1970)*

Since there was no corresponding hardcover and no paperback publisher involved either, the book club put *A Princess of Mars* out under the "Nelson Doubleday" imprint. This was the first time this imprint was used for one of its books, but it was hardly the last. A number of true first editions followed, some of them with Frazetta art as well. Well known authors such as Piers Anthony, Samuel R. Delaney, Philip José Farmer, Frank Herbert and Robert Silverberg had first editions published by the Science Fiction Book Club. Silverberg's *A Time of Changes* won the Nebula award and C. J. Cherryh's *Downbelow Station* won the Hugo award. Although these first editions are worth a lot more than other book clubs, they still haven't proved to be worth any where near as much as trade editions would have been. Make sure to check the printing codes, because later printings are priced just like ordinary book club editions — cheap.

Book Club is first edition, selected titles
Van Vogt, A. E., *Triad*, Simon and Schuster 1959,
    code A13 . . . .$30.00
Burroughs, Edgar Rice, A Princess of Mars, Nelson
    Doubleday 1970, with code 20L, Frazetta
    cover art (1st use of this art) 25.00
Silverberg, Robert, *Downward to the Earth*, Nelson
    Doubleday 1970, with code 28L (Frazetta art) . . .30.00
Spinrad, Norman, *The Last Hurrah of the Golden
    Horde*, Nelson Doubleday 1970, with code
    27L 30.00
Farmer, Philip José, *Down in the Black Gang*,
    Nelson Doubleday 1971, with code 18M 30.00
Silverberg, Robert, *A Time of Changes*, Nelson
    Doubleday 1971, with code 22M (Nebula
    award) 35.00
Delany, Samuel R., *Driftglass*, Nelson Doubleday
    1971, with code 24M 30.00
Anderson, Poul, *The Dancer From Atlantis*, Nelson
    Doubleday 1971, with code 29M (Frazetta
    art) 30.00
Herbert, Frank, *Hellstrom's Hive*, Nelson Doubleday
    1973, with code 42P 30.00
Anthony, Piers, *Orn*, Nelson Doubleday 1971, with
    code B37 (Frazetta art) 25.00
Anthony, Piers, *Ox*, Nelson Doubleday 1976, with
    code G3 . . . . .25.00
Cherryh, C. J., *Downbelow Station*, Nelson
    Doubleday 1981, with code L10 (Hugo
    award) 30.00

COLLECTING PAPERBACK PUBLISHERS

ARMED FORCES EDITIONS

Paper was in short supply during World War II but our boys in the service were not completely cut off from literature. A number of famous books were re-printed in armed forces editions for the troops. These were usually bound sideways and designed to fit in a soldier's uniform pocket. Covers were black, usually with a black and white picture of the hardcover plus the title. A number of famous science fiction, fantasy and horror titles were included and some survive in collector's hands. Most titles were already classics, with many reprintings in cheap hardcovers and even paperbacks already available. Thus armed-forces editions are rarely any

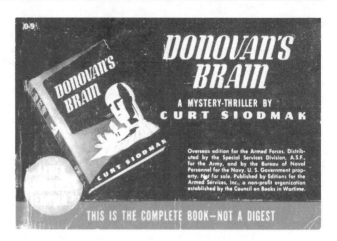

When Worlds Collide *by Edwin Balmer and Philip Wylie;* Donovan's Brain *by Curt Siodmak (Armed Services Editions 1945 & 1944)*

kind of "first" edition, but they are appealing for what they were and for their relative scarcity.

Selected science fiction and associational titles

Burroughs, Edgar Rice, *Tarzan of the Apes*, #M-16, 1944 . . . .$250.00

Burroughs, Edgar Rice, *The Return of Tarzan*, #O-22, 1944, photo of HC 250.00

Frank, Pat, *Mr. Adam*, #1217, 1947 . . . . .30.00

Haggard, H. Rider, *King Solomon's Mines*, #795, 1945 . .25.00

Haggard, H. Rider, *She*, #881, 1946 . . . . .25.00

Shelley, Mary W., *Frankenstein; or, The Modern Prometheus*, #909, 1946 . . . . .75.00

Siodmak, Curt, *Donovan's Brain*, #O-9, 1944 . . . . . . .40.00

Stevenson, Robert Louis, *The Strange Case of Dr. Jekyll & Mr. Hyde*, #885, 1946 . . . . .100.00

Stoker, Bram, *Dracula*, #L-25, 1944 . . . . .100.00

Stoker, Bram, *Dracula*, #851, 1946 . . . . .50.00

Twain, Mark, *A Connecticut Yankee in King Arthur's Court*, #E-139, 1944 . . . . .15.00

Wells, H. G., *The Food of the Gods*, #958, 1946 . . . . .40.00

Wells, H. G., *The Island of Dr. Moreau*, 698, 1945 . . . .40.00

Wells, H. G., *The Time Machine*, #T-2, 1945 . . . . .50.00

Wells, H. G., *The War of the Worlds*, #745, 1945 . . . . .50.00

Wells, H. G., *The War of the Worlds*, #1091, 1946 . . . .30.00

Wylie, Philip, & Balmer, Edwin, *When Worlds Collide*, #801, 1945 . . . . .30.00

ACE BOOKS

While all the paperbacks from the 1950s are interesting, most science fiction collectors have a special place in their hearts for the Ace Double. For 35¢ or so, you could get two novels, each with its own front cover. When you were done with one, you could just flip it over and start on the second one. Ace's other genre fiction was published in the same way, and in the same numbering system, but the genres had different spine colors. The price was indicated by an initial letter ("D" 35¢, "F" 40¢, "M" 45¢, "G" 50¢, etc.) The doubles started in 1954 and inflation finally caught up with the original 35¢ price about the end of the 1950s. Isaac Asimov, Gordon Dickson, Philip K. Dick, Poul Anderson, Jack Vance, Philip José Farmer and A.E. Van Vogt all appeared in early Ace doubles. Authors and purists often note the annoying tendency of editors to cut a few chapters from any novel which was a little too long to fit into the format. This had not reduced collector interest, but anyone wishing to read these

stories should probably look for a more recent edition.

The "F" series of 40¢ doubles started in 1961, but the "D" price and number series continued as singles. "F" series doubles gave way to "M" series in about 1964.

"F" was never a very pure doubles series anyway, because the great Edgar Rice Burroughs paperback publishing spree began in 1962 and these were all "F" series singles. Burroughs had produced over 50 very popular novels, but they had never been available in paperback. When they were all given paperback editions in the space of a couple of years (Tarzan by Ballantine Books and science fiction plus some Tarzan by Ace) they ended up representing a significant fraction of all the paperback books (of all kinds) printed during the period.

Early Ace: "D" series Doubles and selected singles

Van Vogt, A. E., *The World of Null-A* **and** *The Universe Maker*, Ace-Double #D-31, 1953, ...$35.00

Howard, Robert E., *Conan the Conqueror* **and** Brackett, Leigh, *The Sword of Rhiannon*, Ace-Double #D-36, 1953 . . . . .50.00

Russell, Eric Frank, *Sentinels From Space* **and** Wollheim, Donald ed., *The Ultimate Invader and Other Science Fiction*, Ace-Double #D-44, 1954 . . . . .20.00

Leinster, Murray, *Gateway to Elsewhere* **and** Van Vogt, A. E., *The Weapon Shops of Isher*, Ace-Double #D-53, 1954 . . . . .25.00

de Camp, L. Sprague, *Cosmic Manhunt* **and** Simak, Clifford D., *Ring Around the Sun*, Ace-Double #D-61, 1954 . . . . .25.00

Hubbard, L. Ron, *Return to Tomorrow*, Ace #S-66, 1954 . . . . .40.00

Norton, Andre, *Daybreak — 2250 A.D.* **and** Padgett, Lewis, *Beyond Earth's Gate*, Ace-Double #D-69, 1954 . . . . .20.00

Wollheim, Donald ed., *Tales of Outer Space* **and** *Adventures in the Far Future*, Ace-Double #D-73, 1954 . . . . .15.00

Leinster, Murray, *The Brain-Stealers* **and** Bellamy, Francis R., *Atta*, Ace-Double #D-79, 1954 . . . . . .15.00

Dee, Roger, *An Earth Gone Mad* **and** Asimov, Isaac, *The Rebellious Stars*, Ace-Double #D-84, 1954 . . . . .25.00

Williams, Robert Moore, *The Chaos Fighters*, Ace #S-90, 1955 . . . . .15.00

Leinster, Murray, *The Other Side of Here* **and** Van Vogt, A. E., *One Against Eternity*, Ace-Double #D-94, 1955 . . . . .25.00

Nourse, Alan E., *A Man Obsessed* **and** Norton, Andre, *The Last Planet*, Ace-Double #D-96, 1955 . . . . .25.00

Williams, Robert Moore, *Conquest of the Space Sea* **and** Brackett, Leigh, *The Galactic Breed*, Ace-Double #D-99, 1955 . . . . .25.00

Dick, Philip K., *Solar Lottery* **and** Brackett, Leigh, *The Big Jump*, Ace-Double #D-103, 1955 . . . . . .75.00

Asimov, Isaac, *The 1,000-Year Plan* **and** Anderson, Poul, *No World of Their Own*, Ace-Double #D-110, 1955 . . . . .20.00

Williamson, Jack, *Dome Around America* **and** Harness, Charles L., *The Paradox Men*, Ace-Double #D-118, 1955 . . . . .15.00

Merwin, Sam Jr., *Three Faces of Time* **and** Norton, Andre, *The Stars are Ours!*, Ace-Double #D-121, 1955 . . . . .20.00

Asimov, Isaac, *The Man Who Upset the Universe*, Ace #D-125, 1955 . . . . .20.00

Wollheim, Donald ed., *Adventures on Other Planets*, Ace #S-133, 1955 . . . . .15.00

Williams, Nick Bodie, *The Atom Curtain* **and** Dickson, Gordon R., *Alien From Arcturus*, Ace-Double #D-139, 1956 . . . . .15.00

Correy, Lee, *Contraband Rocket* **and** Leinster, Murray, *The Forgotten Planet*, Ace-Double #D-146, 1956 . . . . .15.00

St. Clair, Margaret, *Agent of the Unknown* **and** Dick, Philip K., *The World Jones Made*, Ace-Double #D-150, 1956 . . . . .50.00

Dickson, Gordon R., *Mankind on the Run* **and** Norton, Andre, *The Crossroads of Time*, Ace-Double #D-164, 1956 . . . . .25.00

Williamson, Jack & Gunn, James, *Star Bridge*, Ace #D-169, 1956 . . . . .15.00

Van Vogt, A. E., *The Pawns of Null-A*, Ace #D-187, 1956 . . . . .12.00

Dick, Philip K., *The Man Who Japed*, Ed Emshwiller cover **and** Tubb, E. C., *The Space-Born*, Ace-Double #D-193, 1956 . . . . .50.00

Anderson, Poul, *Planet of No Return* **and** Norton, Andre, *Star Guard*, Ed Emshwiller cover, Ace-Double #D-199, 1956 . . . . .20.00

Dick, Philip K., *Eye in the Sky*, Ace #D-211, 1957 . . . .50.00

Gunn, James E., *This Fortress World*, Ed Emshwiller cover **and** Silverberg, Robert, *The 13th Immortal*, Ace-Double #D-223, 1957 . . . . .15.00

Merril, Judith & Kornbluth, Cyril, as "Judd, Cyril," *Gunner Cade* **and** Piper, H. Beam & McGuire, J. J., *Crisis in 2140*, Ed Emshwiller cover, Ace-Double #D-227, 1957 . . . . .15.00

Silverberg, Robert, *Master of Life and Death*, Ed Emshwiller cover **and** White, James, *The Secret Visitors*, Ace-Double #D-237, 1957 . . . . . .15.00

Long, Frank Belknap, *Space Station # 1*, Ed Emshwiller cover **and** Van Vogt, A. E., *Empire of the Atom*, Ace-Double #D-242, 1957 . .15.00

Norton, Andre, as "North, Andrew," *Sargasso of Space*, Ed Emshwiller cover **and** Dick, Philip K., *The Cosmic Puppets*, Ace-Double #D-249, 1957 . . . . .50.00

Anderson, Poul, *Star Ways*, Ed Emshwiller cover **and** Bulmer, Kenneth, *City Under the Sea*, Ace-Double #D-255, 1957 . . . . .15.00

Dick, Philip K., *The Variable Man and Other Stories*, Ace #D-261, 1957, Ed Emshwiller cover 40.00

Bloch, Robert, *Terror in the Night and Other Stories* **and** *The Shooting Star*, Ace-Double #D-265, 1958 . . . . .75.00

Vance, Jack, *Slaves of the Klau*, Ed Emshwiller cover **and** *Big Planet*, Ed Emshwiller cover, Ace-Double #D-295, 1958 . . . . .25.00

Anderson, Poul, *War of the Wing-Men*, Ed Emshwiller cover **and** *The Snows of Ganymede*, Ace-Double #D-303, 1958 . . . . .15.00

Russell, Eric Frank, *The Space Willies* **and** *Six Worlds Yonder*, Ed Emshwiller cover,

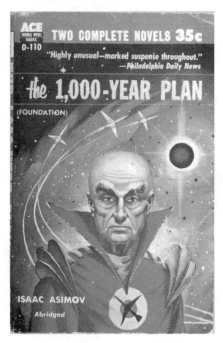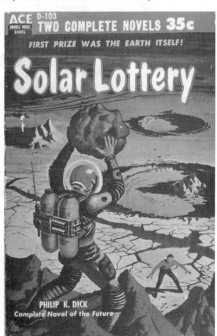

The 1,000-Year Plan *by Isaac Asimov (Ace double 1955);* The Genetic General *by Gordon R. Dickson (Ace double 1960)* & Solar Lottery *by Philip K. Dick (Ace double 1955)*

Ace-Double #D-315, 1958 . . . . .15.00

Anderson, Poul, *The War of Two Worlds* **and** Brunner, John, *Threshold of Eternity*, Ed Emshwiller cover, Ace-Double #D-335, 1959 . . . .12.00

Simak, Clifford D., *Ring Around the Sun*, Ace #D-339, 1959, 1st Single 15.00

Dick, Philip K., *Solar Lottery*, Ace #D-340, 1959, 1st Single 15.00

Norton, Andre, as, "North, Andrew," *Voodoo Planet*, Ed Emshwiller cover **and** *Plague Ship*, Ace-Double #D-345, 1959 . . . . .15.00

Asimov, Isaac, *The 1,000-Year Plan*, Ace-1X, D-110, 1959, 1st Single 20.00

Norton, Andre, *The Last Planet*, Ace-1X, D-96, 1959, 1st Single 20.00

Norton, Andre, *The Stars are Ours!*, Ace-1X, D-121, 1959, 1st Single 20.00

Leinster, Murray, *The Forgotten Planet*, Ace-1X, D-146, 1959, 1st Single 20.00

Ellison, Harlan, *A Touch of Infinity* **and** *The Man With Nine Lives*, Ed Emshwiller cover, Ace-Double #D-413, 1960 . . . . .50.00

Dick, Philip K., *Dr. Futurity* **and** Brunner, John, *Slavers of Space*, Ed Emshwiller cover, Ace-Double #D-421, 1960 . . . . .40.00

Dickson, Gordon R., *The Genetic General* **and** *Time to Teleport*, Ed Emshwiller cover, Ace-Double #D-449, 1960 . . . . .15.00

Brunner, John, *The Skynappers* **and** Dick, Philip K., *Vulcan's Hammer*, Ace-Double #D-457, 1960 . . .40.00

Leiber, Fritz, *The Big Time* **and** *The Mind Spider and Other Stories*, Ace-Double #D-491, 1961 . . .35.00

Ace Doubles, selected from other series

Bradley, Marion Zimmer, *The Door Through Space* **and** Chandler, A. Bertram, *Rendezvous on a Lost World*, Ace-Double #F-117, 1961 . . . . .10.00

Dickson, Gordon R., *Spacial Delivery* **and** *Delusion World*, Ace-Double #F-119, 1961 . . . . .10.00

Bradley, Marion Zimmer, *Seven From the Stars* **and** Laumer, Keith, *Worlds of the Imperium*, Ace-Double #F-127, 1962 . . . . .10.00

Chandler, A. Bertram, *The Rim of Space* **and** Brunner, John, *Secret Agent of Terra*, Ace-Double #F-133, 1962 . . . . .10.00

Anderson, Poul, *The Makeshift Rocket* **and** *Un-man & Other Novellas*, Ace-Double #F-139, 1962 . . . .10.00

Silverberg, Robert, *Next Stop the Stars* **and** *The Seed of Earth*, Ace-Double #F-145, 1962 . . . . . .10.00

Norton, Andre, *Sea Siege* **and** *Eye of the Monster*, Ace-Double #F-147, 1962 . . . . .10.00

Bradley, Marion Zimmer, *The Sword of Aldones* **and** *The Planet Savers*, Ace-Double #F-153, 1962 . . .12.00

Farmer, Philip José, *Cache From Outer Space* **and** *The Celestial Blueprint*, Ace-Double #F-165, 1962 . . . . .12.00

White, James, *Second Ending* **and** Delany, Samuel R., *The Jewels of Aptor*, Jack Gaughan cover, Ace-Double #F-173, 1962 . . . . .15.00

Vance, Jack, *The Five Gold Bands* **and** *The Dragon Masters*, Jack Gaughan cover, Ace-Double #F-185, 1963 . . . . .20.00

Delany, Samuel R., *Captives of the Flame*, Jack Gaughan cover **and** Brunner, John, as "Woodcott, Keith," *The Psionic Menace*, Ace #F-199, 1963 . . . . .15.00

Van Vogt, A. E., *The Twisted Men* **and** Silverberg, Robert, as "Knox, Calvin M.," *One of Our Asteroids Is Missing*, Ace-Double #F-253, 1964 . .10.00

Delany, Samuel R., *The Towers of Toron* **and** Williams, Robert Moore, *The Lunar Eye*, Ace-Double #F-261, 1964 . . . . .15.00

Vance, Jack, *The Houses of Iszm* **and** *Son of the Tree*, Ace-Double #F-265, 1964 . . . . .15.00

Delany, Samuel R., *The Ballad of Beta-2* **and** Petaja, Emil, *Alpha Yes, Terra No!*, Ace-Double #M-121, 1965 . . . . .10.00

Delany, Samuel R., *Empire Star* **and** Purdom, Tom, *The Tree Lord of Imeten*, Ace-Double #M-139, 1966 . . . . .10.00

Vance, Jack, *The Brains of Earth* **and** *The Many Worlds of Magnus Ridolph*, Ace-Double #M-141, 1966 . . . . .10.00

Dick, Philip K., *The Unteleported Man* **and** Cory, Howard L., *The Mind Monsters*, Ace-Double #G-602, 1966 . . . . .20.00

Vance, Jack, *The Last Castle* **and** Wayman, Tony Russell, *World of the Sleeper*, Ace-Double #H-21, 1967 . . . . .10.00

Petaja, Emil, *Tramontane* **and** Moorcock, Michael, *The Wrecks of Time*, Ace-Double #H-36, 1967 . . . . .8.00

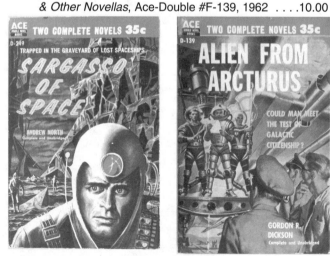

Sargasso of Space *by Andrew North (Andre Norton)* & Alien from Arcturus *by Gordon R. Dickson (Ace doubles 1957 and 1956)*

Return to Tomorrow *by L. Ron Hubbard* & The Weapon Shops of Isher *by A. E. Van Vogt (Ace singles 1954 and 1960)*

AVON

Avon's earliest books of interest to science fiction collectors are there several associational horror titles by A. Merritt (*Seven Footprints to Satan*, *Burn Witch, Burn!*, *Creep Shadow, Creep!* and *The Fox Woman* plus H.P. Lovecraft's *The Lurking Fear and Other Stories*. Much of the appeal of these titles and of their early science fiction is in the covers, which were marvelous.

Early Avon (Small size, 25¢ cover price)
Lewis, C.S. *Out of the Silent Planet*, Avon #195, 1949 (religious SF) $50.00
Wylie, Philip, *Gladiator*, Avon #216, 1949 . . . . .20.00
Lewis, C.S. *Perelandra*, Avon #277, 1950 (religious SF) 45.00
Cummings, Ray, *The Princess of the Atom*, Avon #FN1, 1950 . . . . .35.00
Williamson, Jack, *The Green Girl*, Avon #FN2, 1950 . .75.00
Coblentz, Stanton, *Into Plutonian Depths*, Avon #281, 1950 . . . . .60.00
Farley, Ralph Milne, *An Earth Man on Venus*, Avon #285, 1950 . . . . .75.00
Huxley, Aldous, *After Many a Summer Dies the Swan*, Avon #AT435, 1952 (cover price = 35¢. This book was previously advertised as code #388, but that edition was never published) 20.00
Van Vogt, A.E., *Away and Beyond*, Avon #548, 1952 . .15.00

Early Avon (Associational horror, small size, 25¢ cover price)
Merritt, A., *Seven Footprints to Satan*, Avon #26, 1943 . . . . .60.00
Merritt, A., *Burn Witch, Burn!*, Avon #43, 1944 . . . . . .50.00
Merritt, A., *Creep, Shadow Creep!*, Avon #117, 1947 . .50.00
Lovecraft, H.P., *The Lurking Fear and Other Stories*, Avon #136, 1947 . . . . .60.00
Merritt, A., *The Fox Woman*, Avon #214, 1949 . . . . . .60.00

Merritt, A., *Seven Footprints to Satan*, Avon 235, 1950 (2nd edition) 30.00
Merritt, A., *The Metal Monster*, Avon #315, 1951 . . . . .40.00
Merritt, A., *The Ship of Ishtar*, Avon #324, 1951 . . . . . .40.00
Merritt, A., *The Moon Pool*, Avon #370, 1951 . . . . .40.00
Merritt, A., *Burn Witch, Burn!*, Avon #392, 1951 (2nd edition) 25.00
Merritt, A., *Dwellers in the Mirage*, Avon #413, 1952 . .35.00

1950s Avon (small size, 35¢ cover price)
Huxley, Aldous, *After Many a Summer Dies the Swan*, Avon #T75, 1954 (large; 2nd edition) 5.00
Bond, Nelson, *No Time Like the Future*, Avon #T80, 1954 (large) 10.00
Herbert, Frank, *21st Century Sub*, Avon #T146, 1956 . .7.00
Tucker, Wilson, *Tomorrow Plus X*, Avon #T168, 1957 . . . . .5.00
Clement, Hal, *From Outer Space*, Avon #T175, 1957 . . .7.00
Smith, George O., *Space Plague*, Avon #T180, 1957 . . .5.00
Sohl, Jerry, *The Time Dissolver*, Avon #T186, 1957 . . . .5.00
Blish, James, *Year 2018!*, Avon #T193, 1957 . . . . .6.00
Lewis, C.S., *The Tortured Planet*, Avon #T211, 1958 . .10.00
Shiras, Wilmar H., *Children of the Atom*, Avon #T221, 1958 . . . . .5.00
Blish, James, *Earthman, Come Home*, Avon #T225, 1958 . . . . .6.00
Asimov, Isaac, *2nd Foundation, Galactic Empire*, Avon #T232, 1958 . . . . .10.00
Blish, James, *Vor*, Avon #T238, 1958 . . . . .5.00
McIntosh, J.T., *Worlds Apart*, Avon #T249, 1958 . . . . . .5.00
Van Vogt, A.E., *The Mind Cage*, Avon #T252, 1958 . . . .5.00
Heinlein, Robert A., *Waldo: Genius in Orbit*, Avon #T261, 1958 . . . . .8.00
Blish, James, *ESPer*, Avon #T268, 1958 . . . . .5.00
Kuttner, Henry, *Destination: Infinity*, Avon #T275, 1958 . . . . .5.00
Blish, James, *The Triumph of Time*, Avon #T279, 1958 . . . . .8.00
Moore, C. L., *Doomsday Morning*, Avon #T297, 1959 . .7.00

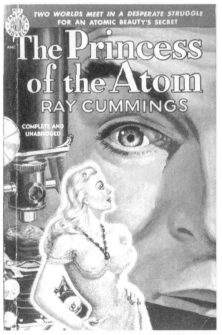
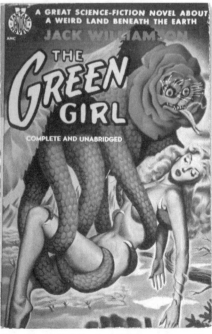

The Princess of Mars *by Ray Cummiings;* The Green Girl *by Jack Williamson; and* Into Plutonian Depths *by Stanton A. Coblentz (Avon 1950) A girl on the never cover never hurts sales*

BALLANTINE BOOKS

Early Ballantine

Pohl, Frederik ed., *Star Science Fiction*, Ballantine #16, 1953, Richard Powers cover $15.00

Pohl, Frederik & Kornbluth, Cyril, *The Space Merchants*, Ballantine #21, 1953, Richard Powers cover 15.00

Pratt, Fletcher, *The Undying Fire*, Ballantine #25, 1953, Richard Powers cover 15.00

Kersh, Gerald, *The Secret Masters*, Ballantine #28, 1953, Richard Powers cover 15.00

Kuttner, Henry, with Moore, C. L., *Ahead of Time*, Ballantine #30, 1953, Richard Powers cover 15.00

Clarke, Arthur C., *Childhood's End*, Ballantine #33, 1953, 1st, Richard Powers cover 40.00

Moore, Ward, *Bring the Jubilee*, Ballantine #38, 1953, Richard Powers cover 15.00

Bradbury, Ray, *Fahrenheit 451*, Ballantine #41, 1953, Joseph Mugnaini cover 50.00

Sturgeon, Theodore, *More Than Human*, Ballantine #46, 1953, Richard Powers cover 20.00

Wyndham, John, *Out of the Deeps*, Ballantine #50, 1953, Richard Powers cover 15.00

Clarke, Arthur C., *Expedition to Earth*, Ballantine #52, 1953, Richard Powers cover 20.00

Pohl, Frederik ed., *Star Science Fiction Stories #2*, Ballantine #55, 1954, Richard Powers cover 10.00

Duncan, David, *Dark Dominion*, Ballantine #56, 1954, Richard Powers cover 10.00

Siodmak, Curt, from Smith, R., *Riders to the Stars*, Ballantine #58, 1954, Richard Powers cover 10.00

Clarke, Arthur C., *Prelude to Space*, Ballantine #68, 1954, Richard Powers cover 15.00

Sheckley, Robert, *Untouched by Human Hands*, Ballantine #73, 1954, Richard Powers cover 10.00

Anderson, Poul, *Brain Wave*, Ballantine #80, 1954, Richard Powers cover .15.00

Pohl, Frederik ed., *Star Short Novels*, Ballantine #89, 1954, Richard Powers cover 10.00

Oliver, Chad, *Shadows in the Sun*, Ballantine #91, 1954 . . . . .10.00

Vidal, Gore, *Messiah*, Ballantine #94, 1954, Richard Powers cover 15.00

Pohl, Frederik ed., *Star Science Fiction Stories #3*, Ballantine #96, 1955, Richard Powers cover 8.00

Clarke, Arthur C., *Earthlight*, Ballantine #97, 1955, Richard Powers cover .50.00

Tenn, William, *Of All Possible Worlds*, Ballantine #99, 1955, Richard Powers cover 15.00

Wyndham, John, *Re-Birth*, Ballantine #104, 1955, Richard Powers cover .15.00

Pohl, Frederik & Kornbluth, Cyril, *Gladiator-At-Law*, Ballantine #107, 1955, Richard Powers cover . . .15.00

Oliver, Chad, *Another Kind*, Ballantine #113, 1955, Richard Powers cover .10.00

Wilson, Richard, *The Girls From Planet 5*, Ballantine #117, 1955, Richard Powers cover 15.00

Sturgeon, Theodore, *Caviar*, Ballantine #119, 1955, Richard Powers cover .15.00

Kuttner, Henry & Moore, C. L., *No Boundaries*, Ballantine #122, 1955, Richard Powers cover . . .15.00

Sheckley, Robert, *Citizen in Space*, Ballantine #126, 1955, Richard Powers cover 10.00

Clarke, Arthur C., *Reach for Tomorrow*, Ballantine #135, 1956, Richard Powers cover 20.00

Bradbury, Ray, *The October Country*, Ballantine #F139, 1956, Joseph Mugnaini cover 35.00

Vance, Jack, *To Live Forever*, Ballantine #167, 1956, Richard Powers cover 25.00

Clement, Hal, *Cycle of Fire*, Ballantine #200, 1957, Richard Powers cover .10.00

Farmer, Philip José, *The Green Odyssey*, Ballantine #210, 1957, Richard Powers cover 40.00

Wyndham, John, *The Midwich Cuckoos*, Ballantine #299K, 1959 . . . . .15.00

  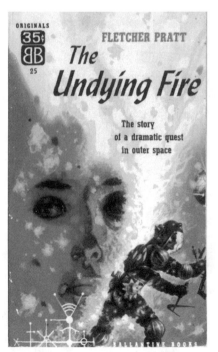

The Space Merchants, *by Frederik Pohl & C. M. Kornbluth;* Star Science Fiction Stories No. 2, *edited by Frederik Pohl; &* The Undying Fire *by Fletcher Pratt (Ballantine Books 1953, 1954 & 1953) A completely different approach to covers than Avon.*

BANTAM

Early Bantam (Small size, 25¢, "A" 35¢ cover price)
Siodmak, Curt, *Donovan's Brain*, Bantam #819, 1950 .$25.00
Brown, Fredric, *What Mad Universe*, Bantam #835, 1950 . .25.00
Bradbury, Ray, *The Martian Chronicles*, Bantam
#886, 1951 . . . . .25.00
Bradbury, Ray, *The Illustrated Man*, Bantam
#991, 1952 . . . . .25.00
Bradbury, Ray, ed., *Timeless Stories for Today
and Tomorrow*, Bantam #A944, 1952 . . . . .35.00
Huxley, Aldous, *Brave New World*, Bantam
#A1071, 1953 . . . . .15.00
Brown, Fredric, *Space on My Hands*, Bantam
#1077, 1953 . . . . .20.00
Collier, John, *Fancies and Goodnights*, Bantam
#A1106, 1953 . . . . .15.00
Bradbury, Ray, *The Golden Apples of the
Sun*, Bantam #A1241, 1954 . . . . .15.00
Padgett, Lewis, *Line to Tomorrow and Other
Stories*, Bantam #1251, 1954 . . . . .20.00
Brown, Fredric, *What Mad Universe*, Bantam
#1253, 1954 (2nd edition) 12.00
Bradbury, Ray, *The Martian Chronicles*, Bantam
#1261, 1954 (2nd edition) 15.00
Vonnegut, Kurt, *Utopia 14*, Bantam #A1262, 1954 . . . .30.00
Sohl, Jerry, *Costigan's Needle*, Bantam #1278,
1954 . . . . .15.00
Bradbury, Ray, *The Illustrated Man*, Bantam
#1282, 1954 (2nd edition) 15.00
Brown, Fredric, *The Lights in the Sky are Stars*,
Bantam #1285, 1955 .15.00
Kapek, Karel, *War With the Newts*, Bantam
#A1292, 1955 . . . . .12.00
Matheson, Richard, *Third From the Sun*, Bantam
#1294, 1955 . . . . .35.00

DELL

Dell was one of the early publishers of paperbacks. Its earliest books are called "map backs" because each edition had (surprise) a map on the back. In edition to the science fiction books listed, Edgar Rice Burroughs' *The Cave Girl* and *Tarzan and the Lost Empire*, along with H. Rider Haggard's *She* and *King Solomon's Mines* are popular with collectors.

The scarcest early Dell edition is *Universe* by Robert A. Heinlein. This is 64 page story and was published in a spine-stapled booklet as a "Dell 10 cent Edition" in 1951. Dell is also noted for the first book edition of *The Sirens of Titan* by Kurt Vonnegut, which appeared in 1959. Dell remained the publisher of Vonnegut's novels in paperback for many years.

Early Dell (Small size, Map Backs, 25¢ cover price)
Wells, H.G., *The First Men in the Moon*, Dell #201,
1947 . . . .$25.00
Wells, H.G., *The Invisible Man*, Dell #269, 1948 . . . . . .25.00
Welles, Orson, ed., *Invasion From Mars*, Dell #305,
1949 . . . . .25.00

Early Dell (Associational)
Burroughs, Edgar Rice, *The Cave Girl*, Dell #320,
1949 . . . . .50.00
Haggard, H. Rider, *She*, Dell #339, 1949 . . . . .25.00
Haggard, H. Rider, *King Solomon's Mines*, Dell
#433, 1950 (Movie photo cover) 25.00
Burroughs, Edgar Rice, *Tarzan and the Lost Empire*,
Dell #536, 1951 . . . . .45.00

Dell 10¢ Edition (Small size booklet)
Robert A. Heinlein *Universe*, Dell 10¢ Edition #36,
1951 . . . . .125.00

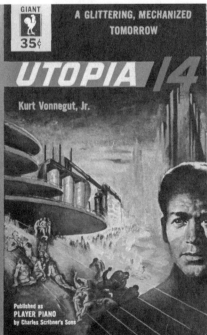
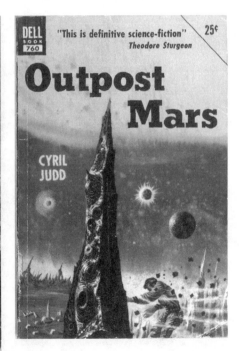

Brave New World *by Aldous Huxley and* Utopia 14 *by Kurt Vonnegut, Jr (Bantam 1953 & 1954).*
and Outpost Mars, *by Cyril Judd (Dell 1954)*

Dell 25¢ Edition (Small size)

de Camp, L. Sprague, *Rogue Queen*, Dell #600,
  1952 . . . . .35.00

Wylie & Balmer, *When Worlds Collide*, Dell #627,
  1952 . . . . .20.00

Simak, Clifford D., *First He Died*, Dell #680, 1953 . . . .20.00

Van Vogt, A.E., *Slan*, Dell #696, 1953 . . . . .15.00

Judd, Cyril, *Outpost Mars*, Dell #760, 1954 . . . . .15.00

Carr, Robert S., *Beyond Infinity*, Dell #781, 1954 . . . . .10.00

Tucker, Wilson, *The Long Loud Silence*, Dell #791,
  1954 . . . . .10.00

Dell 35¢ Edition (Small size)

Conklin, Groff, ed., *Six Great Short Novels of
  Science Fiction*, Dell #D-9, 1954 . . . . .5.00

Campbell, John W., *Who Goes There? and Other
  Stories*, Dell #D150, 1955 . . . . .25.00

Pangborn, Edgar, *A Mirror For Observers*, Dell
  #D246, 1958 . . . . .5.00

Finney, Jack, *The Third Level*, Dell #D274, 1958 . . . . .10.00

Dell First Editions (Small size, 25¢; "B" code 35¢ cover price)

Crossen, Kendell, *Year of Consent*, Dell #32, 1954 . . . .5.00

Finney, Jack, *The Body Snatchers*, Dell #42, 1955 . . . .25.00

Merril, Judith, ed., *S-F: The Year's Greatest Science
  Fiction and Fantasy*, Dell #B103, 1956 . . . . .10.00

Merril, Judith, ed., *S-F: The Year's Greatest Science
  Fiction and Fantasy, 2nd Annual Volume*,
  Dell #B110, 1957 . . . . .10.00

Merril, Judith, ed., *S-F: The Year's Greatest Science
  Fiction and Fantasy, 3rd Annual Volume*, Dell
  #B119, 1958 . . . . .10.00

Sturgeon, Theodore, *The Cosmic Rape*, Dell #B120,
  1958 . . . . .40.00

Merril, Judith, ed., *S-F: The Year's Greatest Science
  Fiction and Fantasy, 4th Annual Volume*, Dell
  #B129, 1959 . . . . .10.00

Vonnegut, Kurt, *The Sirens of Titan*, Dell #B138,
  1959 . . . . .40.00

FAWCETT

Gold Medal

Matheson, Richard, *I Am Legend*, Fawcett
  Gold Medal #417, 1954 . . . .$150.00

Matheson, Richard, *The Shrinking Man*,
  Fawcett Gold Medal #s577, 1956 . . . . .125.00

Marguilies, Leo, ed. *Three Time Infinity*,
  Fawcett Gold Medal #726, 1958 . . . . .15.00

Vonnegut, Kurt, *Canary in a Cat House*,
  Fawcett Gold Medal #s1153, 1961 . . . . .125.00

Crest

McIntosh, J.T., *The Rule of the Pagbeasts*,
  Fawcett Crest #150, 1956 . . . . .15.00

Hamilton, Edmond, *City at World's End*, Fawcett
  Crest #s184, 1957 . . . . .10.00

Dikty, T.E., ed., *5 Tales of Tomorrow*, Fawcett
  Crest #s197, 1957 . . . . .10.00

Mantly, John, *The 27th Day*, Fawcett Crest
  #s209, 1958 . . . . .10.00

Verne, Jules, *From the Earth to the Moon and A
  Trip Around It*, Fawcett Crest #s216, 1958 . . . . . . .5.00

Gernsbach, Hugo, *Ralph 124C41+*, Fawcett Crest
  #s226, 1958 . . . . .20.00

POCKET

Early Pocket

Wollheim, Don, ed. *The Pocket Book of Science
  Fiction*, Pocket #214, 1943 . . . .$50.00

Frank, Pat, *Mr. Adam*, Pocket #498, 1948 . . . . .10.00

Healy, Raymond, ed. *New Tales of Space and Time*,
  Pocket #908, 1952 . . . . .10.00

Leinster, Murray, *Space Platform*, Pocket #920, 1953 . .15.00

MacDonald, John D., *Planet of the Dreamers*,
  Pocket #943, 1953 . . . . .20.00

Wells, H.G., *The War of the Worlds*, Pocket #947,
  1953 . . . . .20.00

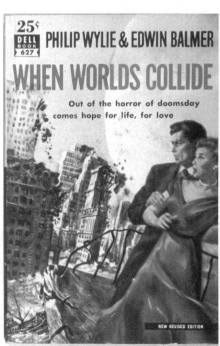

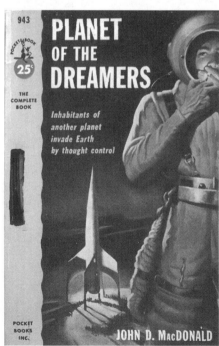

When Worlds Collide *by Philip Wylie & Edwin Balmer (Dell 1952),* Ralph 124C 41+ *by Hugo Gernsback (Crest 1958)
and* Planet of the Dreamers *by John D. MacDonald (Pocket 1953)*

Clarke, Arthur C., *Sands of Mars*, Pocket #989, 1954 . .20.00
Margulies & Friend, ed., *My Best Science Fiction Story*, Pocket #1007, 1954 . . . . .15.00
Leinster, Murray, *Space Tug*, Pocket #1037, 1955 . . . .15.00
Conklin, Groff, ed., *Science Fiction Terror Tales*, Pocket #1045, 1955 . . . . .15.00
Conklin, Groff, ed., *Invaders of Earth*, Pocket #1074, 1955 . . . . .15.00
Wells, H.G., *The Invisible Man*, Pocket #1140, 1957 . . .15.00
Christopher, *No Blade of Grass*, Pocket #1183, 1958 . .20.00
Oliver, Chad, *The Winds of Time*, Pocket #1222, 1959 . . . . .15.00

Early Pocket (Associational)
Swift, Jonathan, *Gulliver's Travels*, Pocket #34, 1939 . .30.00
Stoker, Bram, *Dracula*, Pocket #452, 1947 . . . . .30.00

POPULAR LIBRARY

Early Popular Library (Small size, 25¢ cover price)
Ehrlich, Max, *The Big Eye*, Popular #273, 1950 . . . . .$25.00
Wyndham, John, *Revolt of the Triffids*, Popular #411, 1952 . . . . .35.00
Williamson, Jack, *Dragon's Island*, Popular #447, 1952 . . . . .25.00

SIGNET

Early Signet (Large size, 25¢ cover price)
Orwell, George *1984*, Signet #798, 1950 . . . .$25.00
Hamilton, Edmond *Beyond the Moon*, Signet #812, 1950 . . . . .15.00
Heinlein, Robert A., *The Man Who Sold the Moon*, Signet #847, 1951 . . . . .25.00
Heinlein, Robert A., *The Day After Tomorrow*, Signet #882, 1951 . . . . .15.00
Van Vogt, A.E., *Mission: Interplanetary*, Signet #914, 1952 . . . . .15.00
Heinlein, Robert A., *The Green Hills of Earth*, Signet #943, 1952 . . . . .20.00
Heinlein, Robert A., *The Puppet Masters*, Signet #980, 1952 . . . . .20.00
Van Vogt, A.E., *Destination: Universe!*, Signet #1007, 1953 . . . . .15.00
Heinlein, Robert A. ed., *Tomorrow, The Stars*, Signet #1044, 1953 . . . . .15.00
Asimov, Isaac, *The Currents of Space*, Signet #1082, 1953 . . . . .15.00
Bester, Alfred, *The Demolished Man*, Signet #1105, 1954 . . . . .15.00
Tucker, Wilson, *The Time Masters*, Signet #1127, 1954 . . . . .10.00
Heinlein, Robert A., *Assignment in Eternity*, Signet #1161, 1954 . . . . .15.00
Heinlein, Robert A., *Revolt in 2100*, Signet #1194, 1955 . . . . .15.00
Vernon, Roger Lee, *The Space Frontiers*, Signet #1224, 1955 . . . . .10.00
Asimov, Isaac, *The Caves of Steel*, Signet #S1240, 1955 . . . . .15.00
Asimov, Isaac, *I, Robot*, Signet #S1282, 1956 . . . . . .20.00
Leinster, Murray, *Operation: Outer Space*, Signet #S1346, 1957 . . . . .10.00
Bester, Alfred, *The Stars My Destination*, Signet #S1389, 1957 . . . . .15.00
Asimov, Isaac, *The Martian Way and Other Stories*, Signet #S1433, 1957 . . . . .10.00
Heinlein, Robert A., *Double Star*, Signet #S1444, 1957 . . . . .10.00
Clarke, Arthur C., *The City and the Stars*, Signet #S1464, 1957 . . . . .10.00
Asimov, Isaac, *The End of Eternity*, Signet #S1493, 1958 . . . . .10.00
Bester, Alfred, *Starburst*, Signet #S1524, 1958 . . . . . .10.00

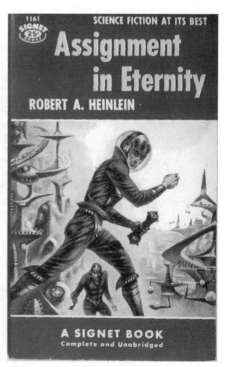

The Big Eye *by Max Ehrlich (Popular Library 1950),*
The Currents of Space *by Isaac Asimov &* Assignment in Eternity *by Robert A. Heinlein (Signet 1953 & 1954)*

GALAXY

Galaxy Science Fiction Novels (Digest magazine size and paper, 25¢ cover price; 35¢ #6 and on)
World Editions, Inc.
Russell, Eric Frank, *Sinister Barrier*, Galaxy #1, 1950 .$15.00
Williamson, Jack, *The Legion of Space*, Galaxy #2, 1950 ....15.00
Clarke, Arthur C., *Prelude to Space*, Galaxy #3, 1951 ....25.00
Wright, S. Fowler, *The Amphibians*, Galaxy #4, 1951 ..15.00
Wright, S. Fowler, *The World Below*, Galaxy #5, 1951 ....15.00
Jones, Raymond, *The Alien*, Galaxy #6, 1951 ....15.00
Simak, Clifford D., *Empire*, Galaxy #7, 1951 ....20.00

Galaxy Publish Corp.
Stapledon, Olaf, *Odd John*, Galaxy #8, 1952 ....20.00
Temple, William F., *Four Sided Triangle*, Galaxy #9, 1952 ....15.00
Franklin, Jay, *Rat Race*, Galaxy #10, 1952 ....12.00
Tucker, Wilson, *The City in the Sea*, Galaxy #11, 1952 ....15.00
Merwin, Sam Jr., *The House of Many Worlds*, Galaxy #12, 1952 ....18.00
Taine, John, *Seeds of Life*, Galaxy #13, 1952 ....12.00
Asimov, Isaac, *Pebble in the Sky*, Galaxy #14, 1953 .20.00
Mitchell, J. Leslie, *Three Go Back*, Galaxy #15, 1953 .15.00
Blish, James, *The Warriors of Day*, Galaxy #16, 1953 ....15.00
Padgett, Lewis, *Well of the Worlds*, Galaxy #17, 1953 ....15.00
Hamilton, Edmond, *City at World's End*, Galaxy #18, 1953 ....15.00
Blish, James, *Jack of Eagles*, Galaxy #19, 1953 .....15.00
Leinster, Murray, *The Black Galaxy*, Galaxy #20, 1954 ....15.00
Williamson, Jack, *The Humanoids*, Galaxy #21, 1954 .15.00

Merwin, Sam Jr., *Killer to Come*, Galaxy #22, 1954 ...15.00
Reed, David V., *Murder in Space*, Galaxy #23, 1954 ..15.00
de Camp, L. Sprague, *Lest Darkness Fall*, Galaxy #24, 1955 ....18.00
Leinster, Murray, *The Last Spaceship*, Galaxy #25, 1955 ....18.00
Padgett, Lewis, *Chessboard Planet*, Galaxy #26, 1956 ....18.00
Jameson, Malcolm, *Tarnished Utopia*, Galaxy #27, 1956 ....15.00
Leiber, Fritz, *Destiny Times Three*, Galaxy #28, 1957 .25.00
Hubbard, L. Ron, *Fear*, Galaxy #29, 1957 ....35.00
Pratt, Fletcher, *Double Jeopardy*, Galaxy #30, 1957 ...25.00
Moore, C. L., *Shambleau*, Galaxy #31, 1957 ....25.00

Galaxy S.F. Novels (small size, 35¢ cover price, Wally Wood Covers)
Wallace, F. L., *Address: Centauri*, Galaxy #32, 1957 ..25.00
Clement, Hal, *Mission of Gravity*, Galaxy #33, 1957 ...30.00
Wellman, Manly Wade, *Twice in Time*, Galaxy #34, 1958 ....25.00
Clifton & Riley, *The Forever Machine*, Galaxy #35, 1958 ....25.00

Galaxy Beacon (large size, 35¢ cover price)
Stapledon, Olaf, *Odd John*, Beacon #236, 1959 ......50.00
Jones, Raymond F., *The Deviates*, Beacon #242, 1959 .40.00
Smith, George O., *Troubled Star*, Beacon #256, 1959 .40.00
Garrett & Harris, *Pagan Passions*, Beacon #263, 1959 .40.00
Anderson, Poul, *Virgin Planet*, Beacon #270, 1960 .....50.00
Farmer, Philip José, *Flesh*, Beacon #277, 1960 .....75.00
Merwin, Sam Jr., *The Sex War*, Beacon #284, 1960 ...45.00
Farmer, Philip José, *A Woman A Day*, Beacon #291, 1960 ....75.00
Van Vogt, A. E., *The Mating Cry*, Beacon #298, 1960 .60.00
Aldiss, Brian W., *The Male Response*, Beacon #305, 1961 ....50.00
Judd, Cyril, *Sin in Space*, Beacon #312, 1961 ....50.00

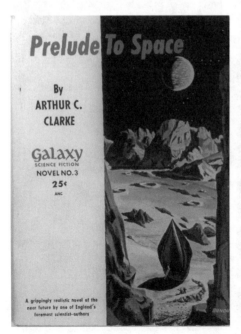

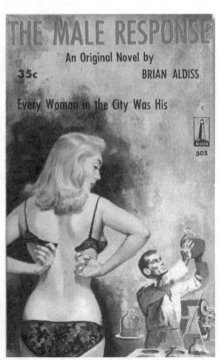

Prelude to Space *by Arthur C. Clarke (Galaxy 1951);* The Forever Machine *by Mark Clifton and Frank Riley (Galaxy 1958); and* The Male Response *by Brian W. Aldiss (Galaxy Beacon 1961) When magazine size and paperback size didn't sell, Galaxy went back to sex.*

COLLECTING AUTHORS

As science fiction books have become an established category, science fiction book collecting has come to mirror general book collecting. First-edition hardcovers of the first book by an author who later becomes famous have seen the greatest collector interest. If that book happens to have been published by one of the more collectible publishers, its price will be a lot higher.

First-edition paperbacks of author's first books are a lot more valuable than reprint paperbacks, but they are still paperbacks and do not generally become incredibly valuable. In addition to prejudices against paperbacks in general, paperback print runs are about 10 times as large as hardcover print runs, which means that they are rarely very scarce. Several prominent authors had many of their books published first in paperback. Collector interest is fairly high in books by Dean R. Koontz, who wrote a lot of science fiction before he became famous in the horror genre. Most of Philip K. Dick's early science fiction appeared as paperback originals, often in Ace doubles and they now rank among the most valuable of 1950s and 1960s paperbacks.

Book dealers rarely find it profitable to list paperbacks in their catalogs because the cost of printing the catalog, accepting the order, and shipping the book is too high relative to the value of the item. If you are looking for a particular paperback science fiction book for your collection, try used book stores and especially book dealers at science fiction conventions.

As discussed above, just about every book published by the Science Fiction Book Club is a reprint and worth very lit-tle as a collectible. Most dealers will not list them in their cat-alogs and don't really want them in their stock at all. The few book clubs that are actually first editions suffer from this stig-ma. Some of these books have even won awards and if they had been published by anyone else, they would be worth a lot of money, but they are book club editions, so they are cheap. You can collect them if you want to. Maybe things will change. You can also collect second or third printings if you like. In many cases, these print runs were low and since most dealers won't touch them, a second printing can be very hard to find. Maybe someday everyone will want to collect scarce book-club first-editions and hardcover second printings. Maybe, but don't hold your breath. The flying saucers will land in your back yard to talk to your pet Yeti much sooner than that.

The listing below is highly selective because there are far, far too many science fiction books to list them all here. I have tried to include author's first books, award winners and titles with considerable collector interest, i.e. those that have significantly increased in value. Most books do not have a lot of collector interest and do not increase in value. The list would also be substantially different if literary value alone were the criterion. Blockbuster new novels by well estab-lished authors have large print runs and so their first trade edi-tions are not scarce and not particularly valuable. In fact, most can be found one or two years after publication in remainder piles at large book stores and at stores specializing in remainders. This is a great place to pick up collectibles for about one quarter of original cover price — about the same as the paperback reprint. It's hard to go wrong at that price, and you can read a hardcover book, if you do it carefully, without destroying its value.

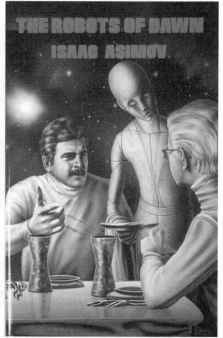

Stranger in a Strange Land by Robert A. Heinlein (Putnam 1961) Dune *by Frank Herbert (Chilton 1965)*
& The Robots of Dawn by Isaac Asimov (Phantasia 1983)

*Brain Wave by Poul Anderson (Ballantine 1954) & Omnivore by
Piers Anthony (SFBC 1968)*

ADAMS, DOUGLAS

Hitchhiker Series
The Hitchhikers Guide to the Galaxy, Crown
    Harmony 1980 . . . .$60.00
The Restaurant at the End of the Universe, Crown
    Harmony 1981 .25.00
Life, The Universe and Everything, Crown Harmony
    1982 . . . . .25.00

ALDISS, BRIAN W.

Greybeard, Doubleday 1964 . . . . .150.00
The Primal Urge, Ballantine #F555, 1961, Richard
    Powers cover 10.00
Starship, Criterion 1959 . . . . .150.00
See also GALAXY BEACON publisher

ANDERSON, POUL

After Doomsday, Ballantine #579, 1962, Ralph
    Brillhart cover .10.00
The Enemy Stars, Lippincott 1959 . . . . .300.00
Guardians of Time, Ballantine #422K, 1960, Richard
    Powers cover 10.00
The High Crusade, Doubleday 1960 . . . . .350.00
Orion Shall Rise, Phantasia 1983, #600, Darrell
    Sweet cover art 50.00
Strangers From Earth, Ballantine #483K, 1961 . . . . . .10.00
Tau Zero, Doubleday 1970 . . . . .200.00
Three Hearts and Three Lions, Doubleday 1961 . . .350.00
Trader to the Stars, Doubleday 1964 . . . . .300.00
Twilight World, Torquil 1961 . . . . .250.00
See also AVALON & WINSTON publishers

Flandry Series
Agent of the Terran Empire, Chilton 1965 . . . . .75.00
Ensign Flandry, Chilton 1966 . . . . .50.00
Flandry of Terra, Chilton 1965 . . . . .40.00

with Dickson, Gordon R.
Earthman's Burden, Gnome 1957, Edd Cartier cover
    art 150.00

ANTHONY, PIERS

(pseudonym of Piers A. D. Jacob)
Chthon, Ballantine U6107, 1967 (Author's First
    Book) 25.00
Omnivore, Ballantine #72014, 1968 . . . . .10.00

Macroscope, Avon #W166, 1969 . . . . .15.00
    HC: Gregg 1985 .75.00
SOS The Rope, Pyramid X1890, 1968 . . . . .15.00
A Spell for Chameleon, Ballantine Del Rey #25855,
    1977 (first Xanth book) 10.00
On a Pale Horse, Del Rey 1983 (first Incarnations
    book) 50.00

with Margroff, Robert
The Ring, Ace A-19, 1968, Leo & Diane Dillon cover . . .7.00

ASIMOV, ISAAC

Fantastic Voyage, Houghton Mifflin 1966 . . . . .200.00
Fantastic Voyage II: Destination Brain, Doubleday
    1987 . . . . .25.00
    Limited edition: Doubleday 1987, signed,
        #450 copies 150.00
The Gods Themselves, Doubleday 1972 (Hugo &
    Nebula awards) 250.00
The Martian Way and Other Stories, Doubleday
    1955 . . . . .250.00
Nemesis, Doubleday 1989, limited, signed 250.00
    Trade edition 25.00
Pebble in the Sky, see DOUBLEDAY
    40th anniversary reprint, Doubleday 1990,
        signed, in slipcase 150.00
Triangle, Doubleday 1961, trade edition 150.00
See also DOUBLEDAY publisher

Foundation Series (Hugo award, All-time series)
    see GNOME
Foundations Edge, Doubleday 1982 (Hugo award)
    1st edition has code M36 on page 365 . . . . .75.00
    Limited edition: Whispers 1982, signed
        numbered .100.00
Foundation and Earth, Doubleday 1986, signed,
    limited to #299 copies, boxed, no dustjacket . . .150.00
    Trade edition 25.00

Robot Stories
I, Robot, see GNOME
    Grosset & Dunlap 1952, reprint edition 25.00
The Caves of Steel & *The Naked Sun*, see DOUBLEDAY
The Robots of Dawn, *Robots and Empire*, see
    PHANTASIA
    Trade Editions: Doubleday 1983 & 1985,
        each 25.00

*Lucky Starr and the Moons of Jupiter & Lucky Starr and the Rings
of Saturn by Paul French i.e. Isaac Asimov (Doubleday 1957–58)*

*No Enemy But Time by Michael Bishop (Timescape 1982)
& Earthman Come Home by James Blish (Putnam 1955)*

The Rest of the Robots, Doubleday 1964 . . . . .200.00

as French, Paul:
David Starr — Space Ranger, Doubleday 1952 . . . . .300.00
Lucky Starr and the Pirates of the Asteroids,
    Doubleday 1953, Richard Powers cover art 275.00
Lucky Starr and the Oceans of Venus, Doubleday
    1954, Richard Powers cover art 250.00
Lucky Starr and the Big Sun Mercury, Doubleday
    1956 . . . . .200.00
Lucky Starr and the Moons of Jupiter, Doubleday
    1957 . . . . .150.00
Lucky Starr and the Rings of Saturn, Doubleday
    1958 . . . . .125.00

ASPRIN, ROBERT
The Cold Cash War, St. Martins 1977 . . . . .60.00

ATTANASIO, A. A.
Radix, Morrow 1981 . . . . .200.00
    TPB: Morrow Quill #508, 1981 . . . . .30.00

BALLARD, J.G.
Chronopolis, Putnam 1971 . . . . .100.00
The Drowned World and The Wind From Nowhere,
    Doubleday 1965 . . . . .150.00
The Wind From Nowhere, Berkley #F600, 1962 (first
    book) 15.00
Memories of the Space Age, Arkham House 1988 . . . .20.00

BEAR, GREG
Blood Music, Arbor House 1985 . . . . .100.00
Hegira, Dell #13473, 1979 (first book) 50.00
Queen of Angels, Warner 1990 . . . . .75.00
    Limited edition: Easton 1989, signed 100.00
Moving Mars, Tor 1993 (Nebula award) 35.00
The Wind From a Burning Woman, Arkham House
    1983, Vincent DiFate cover art 40.00
    Author's copies: #250 copies, signed by
    author 300.00

BENFORD, GREG
Timescape, Simon & Schuster 1980 (Nebula award) .100.00
Deeper Than the Darkness, Ace #14215, 1970 (first
    book) 15.00

BESTER, ALFRED
The Demolished Man, see SHASTA (Hugo award)
The Stars My Destination, Signet #S1389, 1956 . . . . .12.00

BISHOP, MICHAEL
No Enemy But Time, Timescape 1982 (Nebula
    award) 125.00
A Funeral For the Eyes of Fire, Ballantine #24350,
    1975 (first book) 10.00

BLISH, JAMES
A Case of Conscience, Ballantine #256, 1958 (Hugo
    award) 40.00
Earthman, Come Home, Putnam 1955 (Cities in
    Flight series) 150.00
The Frozen Year, Ballantine 1957, Richard Powers . .150.00
Jack of Eagles, Greenberg 1952 . . . . .150.00
Mission to the Heart Stars, Putnam 1965 (Juvenile) . . .75.00
The Seedling Stars, Gnome 1957, Leo & Diane
    Dillon cover art 25.00
So Close to Home, Ballantine #465K, 1961 . . . . .10.00

BOULLE, PIERRE
Planet of the Apes, Vanguard 1963 . . . . .125.00

BOVA, BEN
Star Conquerors, Winston 1959 (first book) 200.00

with Lucas, George
THX 1138, Paperback Library #64-624, 1971 . . . . . . .25.00

BRACKETT, LEIGH
The Big Jump, Ace-Double #D-103, 1955 . . . . .75.00
The Long Tomorrow, Doubleday 1955 . . . . .300.00
The Starmen, Gnome 1952 . . . . .125.00

BRADBURY, RAY
Fahrenheit 451, see BALLANTINE HC
    PB: Ballantine #41 (true 1st edition) 60.00
The Illustrated Man, The Martian Chronicles, see
    DOUBLEDAY
The Machineries of Joy, Simon & Schuster 1964 . . . .200.00
The Martian Chronicles, Doubleday 1950, green
    binding 850.00
    Reprint, Doubleday 1958 . . . . .100.00

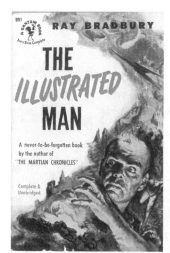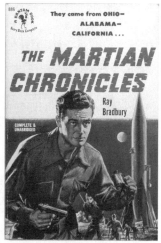

*The Illustrated Man & The Martian Chronicles
both by Ray Bradbury (Bantam 1952 & 1951)*

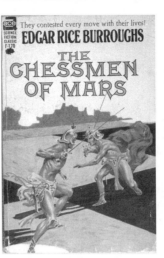
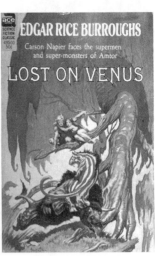

Fahrenheit 451 *by Ray Bradbury (Ballantine 1953)*
& The Uplift War *by David Brin (Phantasia 1987)*

A Medicine for Melancholy, Doubleday 1958 . . . . . . .300.00
The October Country, see BALLANTINE HC
    PB: Ballantine #F139, 1955 . . . . .25.00

BRADLEY, MARION ZIMMER

The Door Through Space, Ace-Double #F-117, 1961 . .10.00
The Planet Savers & The Sword of Aldones,
    Ace-Double #F-153, 1962 (Darkover novels) 10.00

BRIN, DAVID

Startide Rising, Bantam #23495, 1983 (Hugo and
    Nebula awards) 15.00
    Limited edition, see PHANTASIA
The Uplift War, see PHANTASIA (Hugo award)
Sundiver, Bantam #13312, 1980 (first book) 15.00
The Postman, Bantam 1985 . . . . .50.00

BROWN, FREDRIC

And the Gods Laughed, Phantasia 1987, #475,
    Kelly Freas cover art 00
    Trade edition 00
Martians, Go Home, Dutton 1955 . . . . .300.00
Rogue in Space, Dutton 1957 . . . . .400.00
Space on My Hands, Shasta 1951 . . . . .150.00
What Mad Universe, Dutton 1949 . . . . .450.00

BROWNE, HOWARD

Warroir of the Dawn, Reilly & Lee 1943 . . . . .100.00

BRUNNER, JOHN

Stand on Zanzibar, Doubleday 1968 (Hugo award) . .250.00
    PB: Ballantine #01713, 1969, 1st 10.00
Double, Double, Ballantine #72019, 1969 . . . . .8.00
Out of My Mind, Ballantine #U5064, 1967 . . . . .5.00

BUDRYS, ALGIS

False Night, Lion 230, 1954 . . . . .50.00
The Unexpected Dimension, Ballantine #388K, 1960 . .10.00

BUJOLD, LOIS McMASTER

Barrayar, Baen #72083-X, 1990 (Hugo award) 25.00
    HC: Easton Press 1991, limited edition 150.00
The Vor Game, Baen #72014-7, 1990 (Hugo award) . .25.00
Falling Free, Baen #65398-9, 1988 (Nebula award) . . .25.00

The Chessmen of Mars & Lost On Venus
both by Edgar Rice Burroughs (Ace 1962 & 1963)

BURGESS, ANTHONY

(pseudonym of John A. B. Wilson)
A Clockwork Orange, Norton 1962 . . . . .400.00
    PB: Ballantine #U5032, 1965, 1st 20.00

BURROUGHS, EDGAR RICE

John Carter series
A Princess of Mars, McClurg 1917, without dust
    jacket 750.00
    1st edition, **with** dust jacket 10,000.00
    PB: Ballantine #F701, 1963 . . . . .10.00
Note: All other Burroughs hardcovers omitted.
The Gods of Mars, Ballantine #F702, 1963 . . . . .10.00
The Warlord of Mars, Ballantine #F711, 1963 . . . . . . .10.00
Swords of Mars, Ballantine #F728, 1963 . . . . .10.00
Synthetic Men of Mars, Ballantine #F739, 1963 . . . . . .8.00
Llana of Gathol, Ballantine #F762, 1963 . . . . .8.00
Thuvia, Maid of Mars, Ace #F-168, 1962, Roy
    Krenkel cover 10.00
    Ballantine #F770, 1963 .8.00
The Chessmen of Mars, Ace #F-170, 1962, Roy
    Krenkel cover 10.00
    Ballantine #F776, 1963 .8.00
The Mastermind of Mars, Ace #F-181, 1963, Roy
    Krenkel cover 10.00
    Ballantine #U2036, 1963 . . . . .8.00
A Fighting Man of Mars, Ace #F-190, 1963, Roy
    Krenkel & Frazetta cover 15.00
    Ballantine #U2037, 1964 . . . . .8.00
John Carter of Mars, Ballantine #U2041, 1965 . . . . . .10.00

Carson Napier series
Pirates of Venus, Ace #F-179, 1963, Roy Krenkel
    cover 10.00
Lost on Venus, Ace #F-221, 1963, Frank Frazetta
    cover 15.00
Carson of Venus, Ace #F-247, 1963, Frank Frazetta
    cover 15.00
Escape on Venus, Ace #F-268, 1964, Roy Krenkel
    cover 10.00
The Wizard of Venus, Ace #90190, 1970 . . . . .5.00

Moon Maid series
The Moon Maid, Ace #F-157, 1962, Roy Krenkel
    cover 10.00
The Moon Men, Ace #F-159, 1962 . . . . .10.00

Pellucidar series

At the Earth's Core, Ace #F-156, 1962, Roy Krenkel
cover 10.00
Pellucidar, Ace #F-158, 1962, Roy Krenkel cover 10.00
Tanar of Pellucidar, Ace #F-171, 1962, Roy Krenkel
cover 10.00
Tarzan at the Earth's Core, Ace #F-180, 1963, Frank
Frazetta cover 15.00
Back to the Stone Age, Ace #F-245, 1963, Krenkel &
Frazetta cover 15.00
Land of Terror, Ace #F-256, 1964, Frank Frazetta
cover 15.00
Savage Pellucidar, Ace #F-280, 1964, Frank
Frazetta cover 15.00

BUTLER, OCTAVIA

Patternmaster, Doubleday 1976 . . . . .250.00

CAIDIN, MARTIN

Cyborg, Arbor 1972 (first Steve Austin) 300.00

CAMPBELL, JOHN W. JR.

The Black Star Passes, Fantasy Press 1953, #500 . .250.00
Trade edition: 2,994 copies 125.00
Cloak of Aesir, see SHASTA
The Incredible Planet, Fantasy Press 1949, #250
signed 250.00
Same, numbered, but not signed, #250 . . . . . .150.00
Trade edition: 3,998 copies 100.00
Invaders From the Infinite, Gnome 1960 . . . . .50.00
Also: Fantasy Press 1961, 112 copies, no
DJ 400.00
Islands of Space, Fantasy Press 1956, #50 signed . .400.00
Trade edition: 3,000 copies 100.00
The Mightiest Machine, Hadley 1947 . . . . .250.00
The Moon is Hell!, Fantasy Press 1951, #500,
Hannes Bok cover art 250.00
Trade edition: 3,706 copies 125.00
Who Goes There?, see SHASTA (filmed as *The Thing*)

CARD, ORSON SCOTT

Ender's Game, Tor 1985 (Hugo and Nebula award) . .750.00
The Folk of the Fringe, Phantasia 1989, #475, Carl
Lundgren cover art .125.00
Trade edition: 3,000 copies 30.00

A Planet Called Treason, St. Martins 1969 . . . . .100.00
Speaker For the Dead, Tor 1986 (Hugo and Nebula
award) 150.00

CHERRYH, C. J.

Cuckoo's Egg, Phantasia 1985, #350, Randall
Asplund cover art 50.00
Trade edition: 2,400 copies 25.00
Cyteen, Warner 1988 (Hugo award) 125.00
Downbelow Station, SFBC edition, 1981, with code
L10 on page 438 (Hugo award) 25.00
PB: Daw #420, 1981 . . . . .10.00
Forty Thousand in Gehenna, Phantasia 1983, #350,
Phil Parks cover art .50.00
Trade edition: 2,350 copies 30.00
The Kif Strike Back, Phantasia 1985, #350, David
Cherry cover art 50.00
Trade edition: 2,000 copies 30.00
Visible Light, Phantasia 1986, #300, David Cherry
cover art 40.00
Trade edition: 1,500 copies 20.00

Chanur series

Chanur's Venture, Phantasia 1984, #350, Victoria
Poyser cover art 40.00
Trade edition: 2,400 copies 25.00
Chanur's Homecoming, Phantasia 1986, #350,
David Cherry cover art 40.00
Trade edition 20.00
The Pride of Chanur, Phantasia 1987, #350, David
Cherry cover art 40.00
Trade edition 20.00

CLARKE, ARTHUR C.

Against the Fall of Night, Gnome 1953, Kelly Freas
cover art 250.00
Childhood's End see BALLANTINE
Earthlight, Ballantine HC 1955 . . . . .1,000.00
Expedition to Earth, Ballantine HC, 1953, Richard
Powers cover 200.00
PB: Ballantine #52, 1953 . . . . .20.00
A Fall of Moondust, Harcourt, Brace & World 1961 . . .200.00
The Fountains of Paradise, Harcourt 1979 (Hugo
and Nebula awards) .25.00
Imperial Earth, Harcourt Brace & Jovanovich 1976 . . . .50.00
Islands in the Sky, see WINSTON

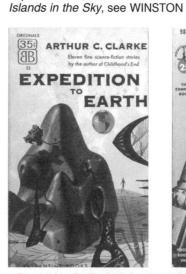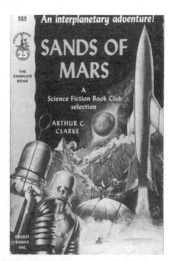

Who Goes There? & The Incredible Planet *both by John W.
Campbell, Jr. (Shasta 1948) and (Fantasy Press 1949)*

Expedition To Earth & Sands of Mars *both by Arthur C. Clarke
(Ballantine 1953 & Pocket 1954)*

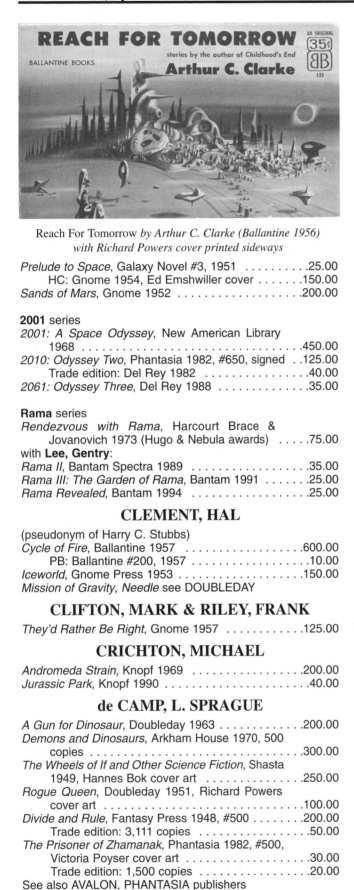

Reach For Tomorrow *by Arthur C. Clarke (Ballantine 1956)*
with Richard Powers cover printed sideways

Prelude to Space, Galaxy Novel #3, 1951 . . . . .25.00
    HC: Gnome 1954, Ed Emshwiller cover 150.00
Sands of Mars, Gnome 1952 . . . . .200.00

2001 series
2001: A Space Odyssey, New American Library
    1968 . . . . .450.00
2010: Odyssey Two, Phantasia 1982, #650, signed . .125.00
    Trade edition: Del Rey 1982 . . . . .40.00
2061: Odyssey Three, Del Rey 1988 . . . . .35.00

Rama series
Rendezvous with Rama, Harcourt Brace &
    Jovanovich 1973 (Hugo & Nebula awards) 75.00
with **Lee, Gentry**:
Rama II, Bantam Spectra 1989 . . . . .35.00
Rama III: The Garden of Rama, Bantam 1991 . . . . . .25.00
Rama Revealed, Bantam 1994 . . . . .25.00

CLEMENT, HAL

(pseudonym of Harry C. Stubbs)
Cycle of Fire, Ballantine 1957 . . . . .600.00
    PB: Ballantine #200, 1957 . . . . .10.00
Iceworld, Gnome Press 1953 . . . . .150.00
Mission of Gravity, *Needle* see DOUBLEDAY

CLIFTON, MARK & RILEY, FRANK

They'd Rather Be Right, Gnome 1957 . . . . .125.00

CRICHTON, MICHAEL

Andromeda Strain, Knopf 1969 . . . . .200.00
Jurassic Park, Knopf 1990 . . . . .40.00

de CAMP, L. SPRAGUE

A Gun for Dinosaur, Doubleday 1963 . . . . .200.00
Demons and Dinosaurs, Arkham House 1970, 500
    copies 300.00
The Wheels of If and Other Science Fiction, Shasta
    1949, Hannes Bok cover art 250.00
Rogue Queen, Doubleday 1951, Richard Powers
    cover art 100.00
Divide and Rule, Fantasy Press 1948, #500 . . . . . . .200.00
    Trade edition: 3,111 copies 50.00
The Prisoner of Zhamanak, Phantasia 1982, #500,
    Victoria Poyser cover art 30.00
    Trade edition: 1,500 copies 20.00
See also AVALON, PHANTASIA publishers

with **de Camp, Catherine**
The Bones of Zora, Phantasia 1983, #300, Victoria
    Poyser cover art 30.00
    Trade edition: 2,000 copies 20.00
The Incorporated Knight, Phantasia 1987, #275,
    Victoria Poyser cover art 35.00
    Trade edition 20.00

with **Miller, P. Schuyler**
Genus Homo, Fantasy Press 1950, #500, Edd
    Cartier cover art 350.00
    Trade edition: 2,999 copies 150.00

with **Pratt, Fletcher**
Land of Unreason, Holt 1942 . . . . .250.00
The Castle of Iron, Gnome 1950, Hannes Bok cover
    art 75.00
See AVALON, GNOME publishers

DELANY, SAMUEL R.

Captives of the Flame, Ace-Double #F-199, 1963 . . . .12.50
The Towers of Toron, Ace-Double #F-261, 1964 . . . . .12.50
City of a Thousand Suns, Ace #F-322, 1965 . . . . . . .12.50
    All three as: *The Fall of the Towers*, Ace
    #22640, 1970 . . . . .25.00
Babel-17, Ace #F-388, 1966 (Nebula award) 30.00
Dhalgren, Bantam #Y8554, 1975 . . . . .35.00
The Einstein Intersection, Ace #F-427, 1967 (Nebula
    award) 20.00
The Jewels of Aptor, Ace-Double #F-173, 1962 . . . . . .40.00
    Ace #G-706, 1968, 1st Single 5.00
Nova, Doubleday 1968 .125.00

DEL REY, LESTER

Moon of Mutiny, Holt Rinehart Winston 1961 . . . . . . .125.00
Nerves, Ballantine 1956, small size 150.00
See also AVALON, WINSTON publishers

DICK, PHILLIP K.

Clans of the Alphane Moon, Ace #F-309, 1964 . . . . . .30.00
The Crack in Space, Ace #F-377, 1966, Jerome
    Podwil cover 25.00
*Dr. Bloodmoney, or How We Got Along After the
    Bomb*, Ace #F-337, 1965 . . . . .30.00
    HC: Gregg 1977 . . . . .400.00
Do Androids Dream of Electric Sheep, Doubleday

The Wheels of If *&* The Tower of Zanid
both by L. Sprague de Camp (Shasta 1949 & Avalon 1958)

1968 (filmed as *Blade Runner*) 1,250.00
The Game-Players of Titan, Ace #F-251, 1963, Jack
    Gaughan cover 35.00
    HC: Gregg Press 1979 . . . . .75.00
Martian Time-Slip, Ballantine #U2191, 1964 . . . . .25.00
The Man in the High Castle, Putnam 1963 (Hugo
    award) code D36 on page 239 . . . . .850.00
A Maze of Death, Doubleday 1970 . . . . .700.00
Now Wait For Last Year, Doubleday 1974 . . . . .225.00
The Preserving Machine, Ace #67500, 1969 . . . . . .18.00
A Scanner Darkley, Doubleday 1977 . . . . .400.00
The Simulacra, Ace #F-301, 1964 . . . . .35.00
The Three Stigmata of Palmer Eldritch, Doubleday
    1965 . . . . .1,500.00
Time Out of Joint, Lippincot 1959 . . . . .500.00
Solar Lottery, Ace-Double #D-103, 1955 (first book) . . .75.00
    PB: Ace #D-340, 1959, 1st single 15.00
Ubik, Doubleday 1969
    . . . . .700.00
The World Jones Made, Ace-Double #D-150, 1956 . . .50.00
    PB: Ace #F-429, 1967, 1st Single 15.00

with **Nelson, Ray**
The Ganymede Takeover, Ace #G-637, 1967 . . . . . . .15.00

DICKSON, GORDON R.

The Genetic General, Ace-Double #D-449, 1960 . . . . .15.00
Alien From Arcturus, Ace-Double #D-139, 1956 . . . . . .15.00

DISCH, THOMAS

The Genocides, Berkley F1170, 1965 (first book) 50.00
    HC: Gregg Press 1978 .65.00
Camp Concentration, Doubleday 1969 . . . . .150.00

EISENSTEIN, PHYLLIS

Born to Exile, Arkham House 1978, 4,148 copies,
    Stephen Fabian cover art 25.00

ELLISON, HARLAN

Alone Against Tomorrow, Macmillan 1971 . . . . .150.00
Approaching Oblivion, Walker 1974 . . . . .50.00
Doomsman, Belmont Double #B50-779, 1967 . . . . . . .25.00
Signed copy: Impossible. Author will not sign; prefers to buy your
    book and rip it in half. Don't sell! The more he destroys,
    the more yours will be worth!
The Man With Nine Lives/ A Touch of Infinity,
    Ace-Double #D-413, 1959 . . . . .50.00

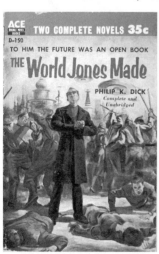
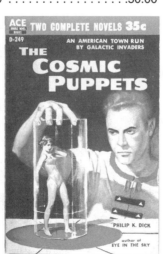

The World Jones Made & The Cosmic Puppets
both by Philip K. Dick (Ace doubles 1956 & 1957)

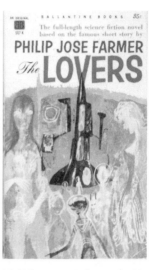

Doomsman *by Harlan Ellison (with* Telepower, *Belmont double
1967) &* The Lovers *by Philip José Farmer (Ballantine 1961)*

Stalking The Nightmare, Phantasia 1982, #40
    lettered copies in wood box designed by
    Steven Kirk 2,000.00
Strange Wine, Harper & Row 1978 . . . . .100.00
See also PHANTASIA publisher

EVANS, E. EVERRETT

Man of Many Minds, Fantasy Press 1953, #300 . . . . .125.00
    Trade edition: 4,098 copies 40.00
Alien Minds, Fantasy Press 1955, #300, Hannes Bok
    cover art 100.00
    Trade edition: 2,988 copies 30.00

FARMER, PHILIP JOSÉ

The Alley God, Ballantine #F588, 1962, Richard
    Powers cover 15.00
A Barnstormer in Oz, Phantasia #600, Alex Ebel
    cover art 60.00
Dare, Ballantine #U2193, 1965 . . . . .12.00
Flesh, Galaxy #277, 1960 . . . . .75.00
    HC: Doubleday 1968 .300.00
The Green Odyssey, see BALLANTINE HC
    PB: Ballantine 210, 1956 . . . . .50.00
Inside, Outside, Ballantine #U2192, 1964, ...12.00
    HC: Gregg Press 1980 .75.00
The Lovers, Ballantine #507K, 1961 . . . . .25.00
Strange Relations, Ballantine #391K, 1960 . . . . .25.00

Riverworld Series
To Your Scattered Bodies Go, Putnam 1971 (Hugo
    award) 500.00
The Fabulous Riverboat, Putnam 1971 . . . . .200.00
See also PHANTASIA publisher

Tier World Series
The Maker of Universes, Ace #F-367, 1965 . . . . .15.00
The Gates of Creation, Ace #F-412, 1966, Gray
    Morrow cover 15.00
A Private Cosmos, Ace #G-724, 1968 . . . . .10.00
Behind the Walls of Terra, Ace #71135, 1970 . . . . . . .10.00
see also PHANTASIA publisher

FOSTER, ALAN DEAN

Spellsinger at the Gate, Phantasia 1983,
    #450, Kevin E. Johnson cover art 65.00

The Day of the Dissonance, Phantasia 1984,
    #375, Kirk Reinert cover art 50.00
    Trade edition: 2,375 copies 20.00
The Moment of the Magician, Phantasia 1984,
    #375, Romas Kukalis cover art 45.00
    Trade edition: 2,375 copies 20.00
The Paths of the Perambulator, Phantasia 1985,
    #300, Kevin E. Johnson cover art 40.00
    Trade edition: 1,500 copies 20.00
The Time of the Transference, Phantasia 1986,
    #300, Kevin E. Johnson cover art 40.00
    Trade edition 20.00

FRANK, PAT

Mr. Adam, Lippincott 1946 . . . . .50.00
Alas, Babylon, Lippincott 1959 . . . . .300.00

GERNSBACH, HUGO

Ralph 124C 41+, Stratford 1925 . . . . .1,500.00
    Also: Fell 1950 . . . . .75.00

GIBSON, WILLIAM

Neuromancer, Ace #56956, 1984 (Hugo and Nebula
    awards) 100.00
    Limited HC: Phantasia 1986, #375 copies,
    new introduction, Barclay Shaw cover art 350.00
    Trade edition 150.00

GUNN, JAMES E.

This Fortress World, Gnome 1955 . . . . .50.00

HALDEMAN, JOE

The Forever War, St. Martins 1975 (Hugo & Nebula
    awards) 500.00
War Year, Holt 1972 (war adventure) 100.00

HALL, AUSTIN

People of the Comet, Griffin 1948 . . . . .35.00

HAMILTON, EDMUND

Battle for the Stars, Torquil 1961 (trade edition) code
    C42 . . . . .100.00
City at World's End, Fell 1951 . . . . .75.00
The Haunted Stars, Torquil 1960 (trade edition) code
    B3 . . . . .150.00
The Star of Life, Torquil 1959, (trade edition) code 4 .200.00

The Star Kings, Fell 1949 . . . . .150.00

HARRISON, HARRY

The Stainless Steel Rat, Berkley #F-672, 1961 . . . . .10.00
Make Room!, Make Room!, Doubleday 1966 . . . . . .200.00
Bill, The Galactic Hero, Doubleday 1965 . . . . .150.00

HARRISON, WILLIAM

Roller Ball Murder, Morrow 1974 . . . . .35.00

HEINLEIN, ROBERT A.

Assignment in Eternity, Fantasy Press 1953,
    signed on plate 750.00
    Trade edition: 1st printing 250.00
Beyond This Horizon, see FANTASY PRESS
Double Star, Doubleday 1956 (Hugo award) 1,250.00
Farnham's Freehold, Putnam 1964 . . . . .700.00
The Menace From Earth, Gnome 1959 . . . . .250.00
The Man Who Sold the Moon, *The Green Hills of
    Earth*, *Revolt in 2100*, see SHASTA
The Moon is a Harsh Mistress, Putnam 1966 (Hugo
    award) 1,500.00
Orphans of the Sky, Putnam 1964 . . . . .250.00
Starship Troopers, Putnam 1959 (Hugo award) 1,250.00
Stranger in a Strange Land, Putnam 1961 (Hugo
    award) code C22 page 408 . . . . .1,500.00
The Unpleasant Profession of Jonathan Hoag,
    Gnome 1959 . . . . .150.00
See also DOUBLEDAY publisher

Juveniles
Rocket Ship Galilleo, Scribners 1947 . . . . .1,000.00
Space Cadet, Scribners 1948 . . . . .500.00
Red Planet, Scribners 1949 . . . . .300.00
Farmer in the Sky, Scribners 1950 . . . . .250.00
Starman Jones, Scribners 1953 . . . . .350.00

HENDERSON, ZENNA

Pilgrimage: The Book of the People, Doubleday
    1961 . . . . .350.00
The People: No Different Flesh, Doubleday 1967 . . . .250.00

HERBERT, FRANK

The Green Brain, Ace #F-379, 1966, Gerald
    McConnell cover 8.00
See also DOUBLEDAY publisher

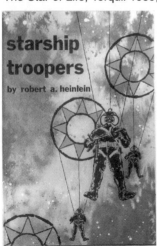

*Starship Troopers & The Moon is a Harsh Mistress
both by Robert A. Heinlein (Putnam 1959 & 1956)*

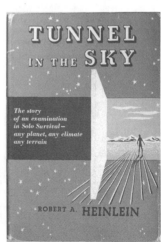

*Rocket Ship Galileo & Tunnel in the Sky,
both by Robert A. Heinlein (Scribners 1947 & 1955)*

Dune series
Dune, Chilton 1965 (Hugo and Nebula awards) 1,500.00
　　　PB: Ace N-3, 1967, John Schoenherr cover 15.00
Dune Messiah, Putnam 1969 . . . . .350.00
Children of Dune, Putnam 1976 . . . . .175.00
God Emperor of Dune, Berkley/Putnam 1981, limited
　　　to #750 copies, signed, slipcase, no dust jacket .125.00
　　　Trade edition: 1981 . . . . .50.00
Heretics of Dune, Putnam 1984, limited to #1,500
　　　copies, signed, slipcase, no dust jacket 100.00
　　　Trade edition: 1984 . . . . .40.00
Chapterhouse Dune, Putnam 1985, limited to #750
　　　copies, signed, slipcase, no dust jacket 100.00
　　　Trade edition: 1985 . . . . .25.00

HUBBARD, L. RON

Death's Deputy, FPCI 1948 . . . . .225.00
Final Blackout, Hadley 1948 . . . . .400.00
The Kingslayer, FPCI 1949 . . . . .300.00
Slaves of Sleep, see SHASTA
Typewriter in the Sky & Fear, Gnome 1951 . . . . . . .300.00
Triton, FPCI 1949 . . . . .300.00

HUXLEY, ALDOUS

Brave New World, Doubleday 1932, #250 copies,
　　　signed 1,500.00
　　　Trade edition 300.00

JAKES, JOHN

When the Star Kings Die, Ace #G-656, 1967 . . . . . . .10.00
The Planet Wizard, Ace #67060, 1969 . . . . .7.00
Tonight We Steal the Stars, Ace-Double #81680,
　　　1969 . . . . .7.00

JONES, RAYMOND F.

Renaissance, Gnome 1951 . . . . .40.00
This Island Earth, Shasta 1952 (filmed as This
　　　Island Earth, basis of the Metaluna Monster,
　　　film used again in Mystery Science Theater
　　　3,000 movie) 175.00

KING, STEPHEN

The Gunslinger series, See DONALD M. GRANT
Firestarter, Phantasia 1980, signed, limited to #725
　　　copies, in slipcase .750.00
　　　Limited edition: 1/26 copies, special binding . .7,500.00

Slaves of Sleep & The Kingslayer *both by L. Ron Hubbard*
(Shasta 1948) and (FPCI 1949)

Takeoff *by C. M. Kornbluth (Pennant 1953)*
& Ahead of Time by Henry Kuttner (Ballantine 1953)

　　　Trade edition: Viking 1980 . . . . .35.00
The Stand, Doubleday 1978 . . . . .350.00
　　　Uncut edition: Doubleday 1990 . . . . .25.00

as **Bachman, Richard**
The Long Walk, Signet #J8754, 1979 . . . . .100.00
The Running Man, Signet #AE1508, 1982 . . . . .75.00
Roadwork, Signet pb 1981 . . . . .100.00
Rage, Signet #J7654, 1977 . . . . .125.00
Thinner, New American Library 1984 . . . . .125.00

KNIGHT, DAMON

Masters of Evolution, Ace-Double #D-375, 1959 . . . . .12.00

KOONTZ, DEAN R.

Anti-Man, Paperback Library #63-384, 1970 . . . . .35.00
Beastchild, Lancer #74719, 1970 . . . . .40.00
The Dark Symphony, Lancer #74621, 1970 . . . . .35.00
Dark of the Woods, Ace-Double #12793, 1970 . . . . . . .35.00
The Fall of the Dream Machine, Ace-Double
　　　#22600, 1969 . . . . .30.00
Fear That Man, Ace-Double #23140, 1969 . . . . .30.00
Hell's Gate, Lancer #74656, 1970 . . . . .35.00
Nightmare Journey, Berkley Putnam 1975 . . . . .250.00
Starquest, Ace-Double #H-70, 1968 . . . . .35.00
Time Thieves, Ace-Double #00990, 1972 . . . . .30.00
A Werewolf Among Us, Ballantine #3055, 1973 . . . . . .35.00

KORNBLUTH, C. M.

A Mile Beyond the Moon, Doubleday 1958 . . . . .35.00
Takeoff, Doubleday 1952 . . . . .35.00
The Syndic, Doubleday 1953 . . . . .75.00
Not This August, Doubleday 1955 . . . . .35.00

KOTZWINKLE, WILLIAM

E.T.: The Extra-Terrestrial, Putnam 1982 . . . . .65.00

KUTTNER, HENRY

Fury, Grosset & Dunlap 1950 . . . . .75.00

with **Moore, C. L.**
Bypass to Otherness, Ballantine #497K, 1961 . . . . . . .10.00
No Boundaries, Ballantine 1955, small size,
　　　Richard Powers cover 300.00

Line to Tomorrow *by Lewis Padgett (Henry Kuttner) (Bantam 1954)* & Retief of the CDT *by Keith Laumer (Doubleday 1971)*

as **Padgett, Lewis**:
A Gnome There Was, Simon & Schuster 1950 . . . . . .200.00
Robots Have No Tails, Gnome 1952 . . . . .200.00
Mutant, Gnome 1953 . . . . .250.00
Tomorrow and Tomorrow & The Fairy Chessmen,
    Gnome 1951 . . . . .200.00

LAUMER, KEITH

Envoy to New Worlds, Ace-Double #F-223, 1963
    (first Retief book) 8.00
Galactic Diplomat, Doubleday 1965 . . . . .100.00
Retief's War, Doubleday 1966 . . . . .60.00
Retief and the Warlords, Doubleday 1968 . . . . .50.00
Retief: Ambassador to Space, Doubleday 1969 . . . . .40.00
Retief of the CDT, Doubleday 1971 . . . . .35.00
Retief's Ransom, Putnam 1971 . . . . .30.00

LE GUIN, URSULA K.

The Left Hand of Darkness, Ace #47800, 1969
    (Hugo & Nebula awards) 50.00
    HC: Walker 1969 . . . . .750.00
City of Illusions, Ace #G-626, 1967 . . . . .7.00
The Dispossessed, Harper & Row 1974 (Hugo &
    Nebula awards) 350.00
The Lathe of Heaven, Scribners 1971 . . . . .300.00
Rocannon's World, Ace-Double #G-574, 1966 . . . . . . .7.00
    HC: Garland, 1975 no dustjacket 150.00

Earthsea series
A Wizard of Earthsea, Parnassus 1968 . . . . .1,500.00
The Tombs of Atuan, Atheneum 1971 . . . . .300.00
The Farthest Shore, Atheneum 1972 . . . . .200.00
Tehanu: The Last Book of Earthsea, Atheneum 1990
    (Nebula award) 100.00

LEE, TANITH

Dreams of Dark and Light, Arkham House 1986 . . . . . .35.00
The Dragon Horde, Farrar Strauss & Girouix 1971
    (first book) 75.00

LEIBER, FRITZ

The Big Time, Ace-Double #D-491, 1961 (Hugo
    award) 35.00
    Ace #G-627, 1967, 1st Single 5.00
    HC: Gregg 1976 . . . . .400.00
Gather Darkness, Pellegrini & Cudahy 1950 . . . . . . .200.00

The Wanderer *by Fritz Leiber (Walker 1970)*
& Sideways in Time *by Murray Leinster (Shasta 1950)*

Nights Black Agents, see ARKHAM HOUSE (first
    book)
Our Lady of Darkness, Berkley Putnam 1977
    (World Fantasy Award) 125.00
The Wanderer, Ballantine #U6010, 1964 (Hugo
    award) 10.00
    HC: Walker, 1970 . . . . .250.00

LEINSTER, MURRAY

(pseudonym of Will F. Jenkins)
City on the Moon, Avalon 1957, Ed Emshwiller cover . .50.00
Colonial Survey, Gnome 1957, Wallace A. Wood
    cover art 175.00
The Forgotten Planet, Gnome 1954, Ed Emshwiller
    cover art 75.00
The Last Spaceship, Fell 1949 . . . . .75.00
Operation: Outer Space, Fantasy Press 1954, #300 . .250.00
    Trade edition: 3,523 copies 75.00
Out of This World, Avalon 1958, Ric Binkley cover
    art 45.00
Sidewise in Time, Shasta 1950, Hannes Bok cover
    art, signed subscriber copy 200.00
    Trade edition 125.00
Space Platform, Shasta 1953, signed subscriber
    copy 200.00
    Trade edition 125.00
Space Tug, Shasta 1953, signed subscriber copy 200.00
    Trade edition 125.00

LONG, FRANK BELKNAP

John Carstairs: Space Detective, Fell 1949 . . . . .100.00
The Rim of the Unknown, Arkham House 1972,
    3,650 copies 40.00

LUSTBADER, ERIC VAN

The Sunset Warrior, Doubleday 1977 . . . . .35.00
Shallows of Night, Doubleday 1978 . . . . .25.00
Dai-San, Doubleday 1978 .20.00
Beneath an Opal Moon, Doubleday 1980 . . . . .20.00

MALZBERG, BARRY

Beyond Apollo, Random House 1972 . . . . .100.00
Phase IV, Pocket #77710, 1973 . . . . .10.00

MARTIN, GEORGE R. R.

Dying of the Light, Simon & Schuster 1977 . . . . .60.00

 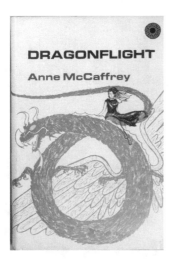

Third From The Sun *by Richard Matheson (Bantam Books 1955)*
& Dragonflight *by Anne McCaffrey (Walker 1969)*

MATHESON, RICHARD

Bid Time Return, Viking 1975 (World Fantasy
　　award) 400.00
　　PB: as *Somewhere in Time*, Ballantine
　　#28900, 1980 (movie tie-in) 15.00
Born of Man and Woman, Chamberlain 1954 (first
　　book)..................................400.00
I Am Legend, Fawcett Gold Medal #417, 1954
　　(filmed as *The Omega Man*) 15.00
　　HC: Walker 1970 ....225.00
　　PB: Berkley #S2041, 1971 (Movie tie-in) 10.00
The Shrinking Man, Fawcett Gold Medal #s577,
　　1956 (filmed as *The Incredible Shrinking
　　Man*) 100.00
A Stir of Echoes, Lippincott 1958 ....250.00
What Dreams May Come, Putnam 1978 (filmed) 100.00

McCAFFREY, ANNE

Decision at Doona, Ballantine #01576, 1969 ....10.00
Restoree, Ballantine #U6108, 1967 ....40.00
The Ship Who Sang, Ballantine #1881, 1969 ....12.00
　　HC: Walker 1969 ....250.00

Dragonriders of Pern series
Dragonflight, Ballantine #U6124, 1968 (first
　　Dragonriders of Pern book) 15.00
　　HC: Walker 1969 ....400.00
Dragonquest, Ballantine #2245 ....15.00
The White Dragon, Ballantine Del Rey 1978 ....50.00

MCINTOSH, J. T.

World Out of Mind, Doubleday 1953, Richard
　　Powers cover art 35.00
The Fittest, Doubleday 1955 ....35.00
One in Three Hundred, Doubleday 1954 00
Born Leader, Doubleday 1954, Richard Powers
　　cover art 30.00

McINTYRE, VONDA N.

Dreamsnake, Houghton Mifflin 1978 (Hugo and
　　Nebula award) 200.00

MERLE, ROBERT

The Day of the Dolphin, Simon & Schuster 1969 .....75.00

MERRIL, JUDITH

Shadow on the Hearth, Doubleday 1950 ....50.00

with **Cyril Kornbluth**, as **Cyril Judd**
Outpost Mars, Abelard 1952 ....100.00

MERWIN, SAM JR.

The White Widows, Doubleday 1953 ....35.00
The House of Many Worlds, Doubleday 1951 ....40.00

MILLER, WALTER M. JR.

A Canticle for Liebowitz, Lippencott 1960, (Hugo
　　award) 1,000.00

MOORCOCK, MICHAEL

The Wrecks of Time, Ace-Double #H-36, 1966 ....7.00

MOORE, C. L.

Black God's Shadow, Grant 1977, signed, #150
　　copies, boxed 150.00
Doomsday Morning, Doubleday 1957 ....125.00
Judgment Night, Gnome 1952, Kelly Freas cover art .150.00
Northwest of Earth, Gnome 1954 ....200.00
Shambleau and Others, Gnome 1953 ....225.00

MURPHY, PAT

The Falling Woman, Tor 1986 (Nebula award) 100.00

NIVEN, LARRY

A Gift From Earth, Ballantine #72113, 1968 ....12.00
　　HC: Walker 1970 ....100.00
Neutron Star, Ballantine #U6120, 1968 ....12.00
Ringworld, Ballantine #2046, 1970 (Hugo & Nebula
　　awards) 30.00
　　HC: Holt, Rinehart & Winston 1977 ....50.00
The Shape of Space, Ballantine #01712, 1969 ....10.00
World of Ptavvs, Ballantine #U2328, 1966 (first
　　Known Space book) 30.00

with **Barnes, Steve**
Dream Park, 434pp, Phantasia 1981, #600, Rowena
　　Morrill cover art 75.00

with **Pournelle, Jerry**
Luciver's Hammer, Playboy Press 1977 ....75.00

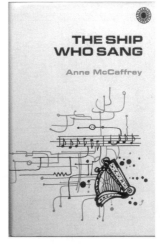 

The Ship Who Sang *by Anne McCaffrey (Walker 1969)* &
A Canticle for Leibowitz *by Walter M. Miller Jr. (Lippencott 1960)*

The Mote in God's Eye, Simon & Schuster 1974 . . . .150.00
Oath of Fealty, Phantasia 1981, #750 . . . . .75.00

NOLAN, WILLIAM F.

with **Johnson, George Clayton**
Logan's Run, Dial 1967 . . . . .250.00
Logan's World, Bantam 11418, 1977 . . . . .6.00
Logan's Search, Bantam 13805, 1980 . . . . .5.00

NORTON, ANDRE

Star Rangers, Harcourt Brace 1953 . . . . .275.00
Star Guard, Harcourt Brace 1955 . . . . .200.00
The Stars Are Ours, World 1954 . . . . .200.00
Star Born, World 1957 . . . . .175.00
Starman's Son, Harcourt Brace 1952 . . . . .250.00

as **North, Andrew**
Plague Ship, Gnome 1956, Ed Emshwiller cover art . .350.00
Sargasso of Space, Gnome 1955, Ed Emshwiller
    cover art 350.00
Starman's Son 2250 AD, Harcourt Brace 1952 . . . . .600.00

OLIVER, CHAD

Another Kind, Ballantine 1955, small size, Richard
    Powers cover, tan cloth, red cloth or light
    blue cloth binding 150.00
Shadows in the Sun, Ballantine 1954, tan cloth,
    blue cloth or green cloth binding 100.00
The Winds of Time, Doubleday 1957 . . . . .100.00

ORWELL, GEORGE

Nineteen Eighty-four, Harcourt 1949, red dust jacket .500.00
    Same, in blue dust jacket 200.00

PANGBORN, EDGAR

A Mirror for Observers, Doubleday 1954
    (International Fantasy award) 300.00
West of the Sun, Doubleday 1953, Richard Powers
    cover art 75.00

PANSHIN, ALEXEI

Rite of Passage, Ace #A-16, 1968 (Nebula award) 15.00

POHL, FREDERICK

Alternating Currents, Ballantine 1956, small size
    Richard Powers cover .500.00

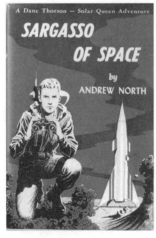
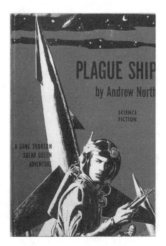

Sargasso of Space & Plague Ship *both by Andrew North*
i.e. Andre Norton (Gnome 1955 & 1956)

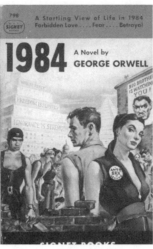
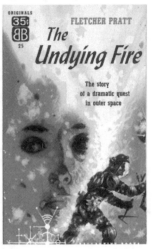

1984 *by George Orwell (Signet 1949)* & The Undying Fire *by*
Fletcher Pratt (Ballantine 1953)

    PB: Ballantine #130, 1956 . . . . .35.00
Drunkard's Walk, Gnome 1960 . . . . .75.00
    PB: Ballantine #439K, 1960 . . . . .10.00
Gateway, St. Martins 1977 (Hugo award) 300.00
Man Plus, Random House 1976 (Nebula award) 150.00
The Man Who Ate the World, Ballantine #397K,
    1960 . . . . .10.00
Slave Ship, Ballantine HC 1957 regular size Richard
    Powers 350.00
    PB: Ballantine #192, 1957 . . . . .15.00

with **Kornbluth, Cyril**
The Space Merchants, see BALLANTINE
Gladiator-At-Law, Ballantine 1955, small size,
    Richard Powers cover 400.00
    PB: Ballantine #107, 1955 . . . . .15.00
Search The Sky, see BALLANTINE

with **Williamson, Jack**
Undersea Quest, Gnome 1954, Ed Emshwiller cover
    art 125.00
Undersea Fleet, Gnome 1956, Ed Emshwiller cover
    art 100.00
Undersea City, Gnome 1958, Wallace A. Wood
    cover art 50.00

PRATT, FLETCHER

Double Jeopardy, Doubleday 1952 . . . . .50.00
Double in Space, Doubleday 1951, Richard Powers
    cover art 50.00

RESNICK, MICHAEL

Eros Ascending, Phantasia 1984, #300, Kevin E.
    Johnson cover art 40.00
    Trade edition: 1,500 copies 25.00
Eros at Zenith, Phantasia 1984, #300, Kevin E.
    Johnson cover art 40.00
    Trade edition: 1,500 copies 25.00

ROBINSON, FRANK M.

The Power, Lippincott 1956 . . . . .350.00

ROBINSON, KIM STANLEY

Red Mars, Harper Collins TPB 1992 (Nebula award) . .30.00
    Limited HC: Easton 1993, no dustjacket 100.00

ROBINSON, SPIDER

Callahan and Company, Phantasia 1988, #300,
   David Cherry cover art 100.00
   Trade edition 35.00

RODDENBERRY, GENE

Star Trek: The Motion Picture, Simon & Schuster
   1978, limited edition, in slipcase, signed &
   numbered x/#500 . . . . .250.00
   Trade edition 25.00

RUSS, JOANNA

The Zanzibar Cat, Arkham House 1983 . . . . .100.00

RUSSELL, ERIC FRANK

Sinister Barrier, Fantasy Press 1948, #500 . . . . .350.00
   Trade edition: 3,918 copies 150.00
Dreadful Sanctuary, Fantasy Press 1951, #350,
   Edd Cartier cover art 250.00
   Trade edition: 2,975 copies 125.00
Deep Space, Fantasy Press 1954, #300 . . . . .250.00
   Trade edition: 2,986 copies 100.00
The Great Explosion, Torquil 1962 (trade edition)
   code D29 . . . . .200.00

SCARBOROUGH, ELIZABETH ANN

The Healer's War, Doubleday 1988 (Nebula award) . . .75.00

SCHMITZ, JAMES

Agent of Vega, Gnome 1960 . . . . .40.00
A Tale of Two Clocks, Torquil 1962 (trade edition)
   code D6 . . . . .200.00
The Witches of Karres, Chilton 1966 . . . . .600.00
   PB: Ace A-13, 1968, Leo & Diane Dillon
     cover 8.00

SHEA, MICHAEL

Polyphemus, Arkham House 1987 . . . . .20.00

SHECKLEY, ROBERT

Citizen in Space, Ballantine 1955, small size,
   Richard Powers cover 150.00
Immortality Delivered, Avalon 1958, Ric Binkley
   cover art 150.00
The 10th Victim, Ballantine #U5050, 1965, 1st 15.00

SHEPARD, LUCIUS

The Jaguar Hunter, Arkham House 1987 . . . . .75.00
The Ends of the Earth, Arkham House 1991 . . . . . . .40.00

SHUTE, NEVIL

On the Beach, Morrow 1957 . . . . .50.00

SILVERBERG, ROBERT

Colission Course, Avalon 1961, Ed Emshwiller
   cover art 40.00
Homefaring, Phantasia 1983, #450, Alex Ebel
   cover art 50.00
Lord Valentine's Castle, Harper & Row 1980 . . . . . . .40.00
Starman's Quest, Gnome 1958 . . . . .75.00
The Thirteenth Immortal, Ace-Double #D-223, 1957 . . .15.00
A Time of Changes, SFBC 1971 (Nebula award) 30.00
   PB: Signet Q4729, 1971 . . . . .10.00

as David Osborne
Aliens from Space, Avalon 1958, Ric Binkley cover
   art 60.00
Invisible Barriers, Avalon 1958, Ric Binkley cover art . .20.00

as Ivar Jorgenson
Starhaven, Avalon 1958, Ric Binkley cover art 60.00

with Garrett, Randall as Robert Randall
The Dawning Light, Gnome 1958 . . . . .30.00
The Shrouded Planet, Gnome 1957 . . . . .40.00

SIMAK, CLIFFORD

All Flesh is Grass, Doubleday 1965 . . . . .125.00
City (International Fantasy Award) see GNOME
Cosmic Engineers, see GNOME
   TPB: Gnome Trade paperback (1950) 100.00
The Creator, Crawford (booklet) 1946 (story) 500.00
Time and Again, Simon & Schuster 1951 . . . . .125.00
Way Station, Doubleday 1963 (Hugo award) 600.00

SIMMONS, DAN

Hyperion, Doubleday Foundation 1989 (Hugo award) .300.00
The Fall of Hyperion, Doubleday Foundation 1990 . . .125.00
Song of Kali, Bluejay 1985 (World Fantasy award)
   (1st book) 200.00

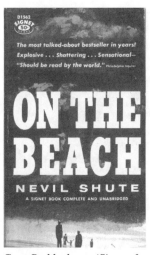

Star Trek, The Motion Picture by Gene Roddenberry (Simon & Schuster 1978) & On the Beach by Nevil Shute (Signet 1958)

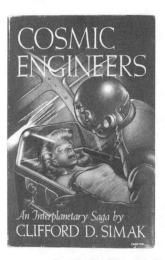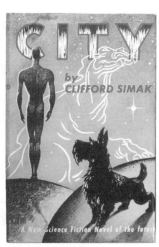

Cosmic Engineers & City both by Clifford Simak (Gnome 1950 & 1952)

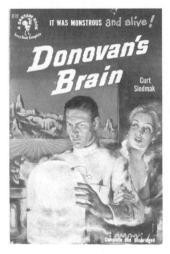

Donovan's Brain *by Curt Siodmak (Bantam 1950)*
& More Than Human *by Theodore Sturgeon (Ballantine 1954)*

SIODMAK, CURT

Donovan's Brain, Knopf 1942 . . . . .400.00

SMITH, E.E. "DOC"

The Vortex Blaster, Fantasy Press 1960, 341
   copies, Edd Cartier cover art 500.00
The Vortex Blaster, Gnome 1960 . . . . .40.00
   TPB: Gnome Trade paperback (1960) 25.00

Skylark series
The Skylark of Space (with Garby, Lee Hawkins)
   Buffalo 1946 . . . . .500.00
   Also: Hadley 75.00
   Also: FFF 75.00
Skylark Three, Fantasy Press 1948, #500 . . . . .200.00
   Trade edition: 4,017 copies 00
Skylark of Valeron, Fantasy Press 1949, #500 . . . . .250.00
   Trade edition: 4,958 copies 100.00
Lensmen series: see FANTASY PRESS

SMITH, GEORGE O.

Pattern for Conquest, Gnome 1949, Edd Cartier
   cover art 30.00
Highways in Hiding, Gnome 1956, Ed Emshwiller
   cover art 100.00
The Path of Unreason, Gnome 1958 . . . . .40.00

STAPLEDON, OLAF

Odd John, Dutton 1936 . . . . .150.00

STERLING, BRUCE

Crystal Express, Arkham House 1989, ...65.00

STEWART, GEORGE R.

Earth Abides, Random House 1949 (International
   Fantasy award) 350.00
   PB: Ace K-154, 1962 . . . . .5.00

STUART, W. J.

Forbidden Planet, Farrar, Straus & Cudahy 1956 . . . .250.00
   PB: Bantam #A-1443, 1956 . . . . .25.00

STURGEON, THEODORE

Caviar, Ballantine 1955, small size, Richard Powers
   cover 400.00

The Dreaming Jewels, Greenberg 1950 . . . . .150.00
It, Prime pb 1948 (story) 50.00
More Than Human, Farrar Straus & Young 1953
   (International Fantasy Award) 350.00
   PB: Ballantine #46, 1954 . . . . .50.00
A Touch of Strange, Doubleday 1958 . . . . .150.00
Without Sorcery, Prime 1948 . . . . .300.00
   Slipcase edition: signed 1,750.00
Not Without Sorcery, Ballantine #506K, 1961 . . . . . . .15.00
Some of Your Blood, Ballantine #458K, 1961 . . . . . . .30.00

SWANWICK, MICHAEL

Stations of the Tide, Morrow 1991 (Nebula award) . . .150.00

TAINE, JOHN

Seeds of Life, Fantasy Press 1951, #300 . . . . .200.00
   Trade edition: 4,273 copies 50.00
The Crystal Horde, Fantasy Press 1952, #300,
   Hannes Bok cover art 175.00
   Trade edition: 2,976 copies 50.00
G.O.G. 666, Fantasy Press 1954, #300 . . . . .150.00
   Trade edition: 3,042 copies 40.00
See also FANTASY PRESS, BUFFALO BOOK publishers

TIPTREE, JAMES, JR.

Her Smoke Rose Up Forever, Arkham House 1990 . . .25.00
Tales of the Quintana Roo, Arkham House 1986 . . . . .12.00

TUCKER, WILSON

The City in the Sea, Rinehart 1951 . . . . .75.00
The Long Loud Silence, Rinehart 1952 . . . . .75.00
The Time Masters, Rinehart 1953 . . . . .75.00

VAN VOGT, A.E.

Empire of the Atom, Shasta 1957 . . . . .100.00
Masters of Time, Fantasy Press 1950, #500, Edd
   Cartier cover art 250.00
   Trade edition: 4,064 copies 100.00
The Mixed Men, Gnome 1952 . . . . .150.00
Out of the Unknown, FPCI 1948 . . . . .250.00
Slan, see ARKHAM HOUSE
The Voyage of the Space Beagle, Simon & Schuster
   1950 . . . . .100.00
The Weapon Makers, Hadley 1946 . . . . .200.00
The Weapon Shops of Isher, Greenberg 1951 . . . . . .100.00
The Wizard of Linn, Ace #F-154, 1962 . . . . .8.00

E Pluribus Unicorn *by Theodore Sturgeon (Ballantine 1956)*
& Slan *by A. E. Van Vogt (Dell 1953)*

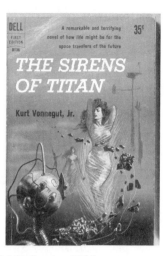

Vandals of the Void & To Live Forever
both by Jack Vance (Winston 1953 & Ballantine 1956)

The World of Null-A, Simon & Schuster 1948 . . . . . . .100.00
    HC rep: Grosset & Dunlap 1950 . . . . .35.00
See also FANTASY PRESS publisher

VANCE, JACK

The Dying Earth, Hillman #41, 1950 . . . . .200.00
    HC: see UNDERWOOD MILLER
The Blue World, Ballantine #U2169, 1966 . . . . .10.00
City of the Chasch, Ace #G-688, 1968, Jeff Jones
    cover 5.00
The Dragon Masters, Ace-Double #F-185, 1963 . . . . .25.00
Eight Fantasms and Magics, Macmillan 1969 . . . . . . .250.00
The Eyes of the Overworld, Ace #M-149, 1966 . . . . . .10.00
    HC: Gregg Press 1977 . . . . .150.00
Emphyrio, Doubleday 1969 . . . . .500.00
The Languages of Pao see AVALON
    PB: Ace #F-390, 1966, Gray Morrow cover 10.00
The Last Castle, Ace-Double #H-21, 1967 . . . . .15.00
The Space Pirate, Toby pb 1953 . . . . .60.00
To Live Forever, see BALLANTINE HC
    PB: Ballantine #167, 1956 . . . . .12.00
Vandals of the Void, see WINSTON

VARLEY, JOHN

Titan, Berkley Putnam 1979 . . . . .75.00
Wizard, Berkley Putnam 1980 . . . . .85.00
Demon, Putnam 1984 . . . . .75.00
Millennium, Berkley TPB #6250, 1983 . . . . .35.00

VIDAL, GORE

Messiah, Dutton 1954 . . . . .500.00

VINGE, JOAN

The Snow Queen, Dial 1980 (Hugo award) 100.00
World's End, Bluejay 1984 . . . . .20.00
The Dune Storybook, Putnam 1984 (movie tie-in) 25.00

VONNEGUT, KURT

Player Piano, Scribners 1952 (first book) 1,000.00
Cat's Cradle, Holt Rinehart Winston 1963 . . . . .750.00
Slaughterhouse-Five, Delacorte 1969 . . . . .500.00
The Sirens of Titan, Dell B138, 1959 . . . . .100.00
    HC: Houghton Mifflin 1961 . . . . .1,500.00

Messiah *by Gore Vidal (Ballantine 1954)*
& The Sirens of Titan *by Kurk Vonnegut, Jr. (Dell 1959)*

WEINBAUM, STANLEY G.

A Martian Odyssey and Others, Fantasy Press 1949,
    #500 art 250.00
    Trade edition: 3,158 copies 100.00
The Red Peri, Fantasy Press 1952, #300 . . . . .200.00
    Trade edition: 3,185 copies 75.00

WELLMAN, MANLY WADE

The Invading Asteroid, Stellar #15, 1932 . . . . .50.00
Twice in Time, Avalon 1957, Ric Binkley cover art 25.00
The Dark Destroyers, Avalon 1959, Ed Emshwiller
    cover art 75.00
Giants from Eternity, Avalon 1959, Ed Emshwiller
    cover art 25.00
Island in the Sky, Avalon 1961, Ed Emshwiller cover art .75.00
See also ARKHAM HOUSE publisher

WELLS, H. G.

The Time Machine, Holt 1895 . . . . .750.00
The War of the Worlds, Harper 1898 . . . . .300.00

WILHELM, KATE

Where Late the Sweet Birds Sang, Harper & Row
    1976 (Hugo award) 150.00
The Mile Long Spaceship, Berkley F862, 1963 . . . . . . .5.00
    HC: Gregg Press 1980 . . . . .50.00
The Killer Thing, Doubleday 1967 . . . . .35.00

WILLIAMSON, JACK

The Legion of Space see FANTASY PRESS
The Cometeers, Fantasy Press 1950, #500, Edd
    Cartier cover art 400.00
    Trade edition: 3,192 copies 100.00
Darker Than You Think, Fantasy Press 1948, #500 . .425.00
    Trade edition: 4,351 copies 100.00
Dragon's Island, Simon & Schuster 1951 . . . . .80.00
The Legion of Time, Fantasy Press 1952, #350 . . . . .200.00
    Trade edition: 4,604 copies 25.00
The Humanoids, Simon & Schuster 1949 . . . . .75.00
    HC rep.: Grosset & Dunlap 1950 . . . . .25.00
The Humanoid Touch, Phantasia 1980, #500 . . . . . . .50.00

as **Stewart, Will:**
Seetee Shock, Simon & Schuster 1949 . . . . .100.00
Seetee Ship, Gnome 1951, Edd Cartier cover art 150.00

with **Breuer, M. J.**: *The Girl From Mars*, Steller #1,
    1930 . . . . .100.00

with **Gunn, James**
Star Bridge, Gnome 1955 . . . . .35.00

WILLIS, CONNIE

Doomsday Book, Bantam 1992 (Nebula award) 300.00
Fire Watch, Bluejay 1985 (first book) 200.00
Lincoln's Dreams, Bantam 1987 . . . . .100.00

WILSON, COLIN

The Space Vampires, Random House 1976 . . . . .65.00
The Mind Parasites, Arkham House 1967, 3,045
    copies 85.00

WOLFE, GENE

Operation Ares, Berkley S1858, 1970 (first book) 35.00

The Book of the New Sun Series:
The Shadow of the Torturer, Simon & Schuster 1980 .150.00
The Claw of the Conciliator, Timescape 1981
    (Nebula Award) 85.00
The Sword of the Lichtor, Timescape 1982 . . . . .60.00
The Citadel of the Autarch, Timescape 1983 . . . . . . .60.00

WOLLHEIM, DONALD A.

as **Grinnell, David**
Edge of Time, Avalon 1958, Ric Binkley cover art 25.00
Destiny's Orbit, Avalon 1961, Ed Emshwiller cover art .20.00
Across Time, Avalon 1956, Ed Emshwiller cover art . .35.00
The Martian Missile, Avalon 1959, Ed Emshwiller
    cover art 20.00
Destination Saturn, Avalon 1967, Ed Emshwiller
    cover art 20.00

WYLIE, PHILIP

The Disappearance, Rinehart 1951 . . . . .100.00
Gladiator, Knopf 1930 . . . . .300.00
    PB: Avon #216 . . . . .20.00
Tomorrow, Rinehart 1954 .50.00

with **Balmer, E.**
When Worlds Collide, Stokes 1933 . . . . .200.00
After Worlds Collide, Stokes 1934 . . . . .175.00

WYNDHAM, JOHN

(pseudonym of John Beynon Harris)
The Day of the Triffids, Doubleday 1951 . . . . .450.00
Out of the Deeps, Ballantine 1953 . . . . .250.00
    PB: Ballantine #50, 1953 . . . . .12.00
The Midwich Cuckoos, Ballantine 1958, Powers 100.00
    PB: Ballantine #299K, 1953 . . . . .15.00
    PB: as *Village of the Damned*, Ballantine
        453K, 1960 (movie tie-in) 10.00
Re-Birth, Ballantine 1955, small size, Richard
    Powers cover 150.00
    PB: Ballantine #104, 1955 . . . . .5.00
Trouble With Lichen, Ballantine #449K, 1960,
    Richard Powers cover 10.00
The Infinite Moment, Ballantine #546, 1961, Richard
    Powers cover 15.00

ZELAZNY, ROGER

Creatures of Light and Darkness, Doubleday 1969 . . .400.00
Damnation Alley, Putnam 1969 . . . . .150.00
The Doors of His Face, The Lamps of His Mouth,
    Doubleday 1971 . . . . .300.00
The Dream Master, Ace #F-403, 1966, Kelly Freas
    cover 30.00
Jack of Shadows, see WALKER
Lord of Light, Doubleday 1967 (Hugo award) 1,250.00
Madwand, Phantasia 1981, #15, Rowena Morrill
    cover art 75.00
    Also: Phantasia 1981, #750, Rowena Morrill
        cover art 25.00
This Immortal, Ace #F-393, 1966 (Hugo award) 50.00

Amber Series
Nine Princes in Amber, Doubleday 1970 . . . . .100.00
The Guns of Avalon, Doubleday 1972 . . . . .400.00
Sign of the Unicorn, Doubleday 1975 . . . . .75.00
The Hand of Oberon, Doublday 1976 . . . . .75.00
The Courts of Chaos, Doubleday 1978 . . . . .50.00
Trumps of Doom, Arbor House 1985 . . . . .40.00
    Limited edition: Underwood Miller 1985,
        #500 copies 100.00
Blood of Amber, Arbor House 1986 . . . . .35.00
    Limited edition: Underwood Miller 1986,
        #400 copies 75.00

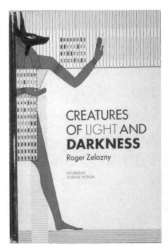

Out of the Deeps & Trouble With Lichen *both by John Wyndham*
(Ballantine 1953 & 1960)

Creatures of Light and Darkness & Sign of the Unicorn
both by Roger Zelazny (Doubleday 1969 & 1975)

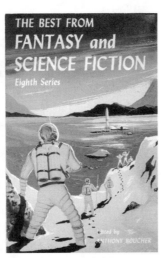

Dangerous Visions edited by Harlan Ellison (Doubleday 1967) & The Best From Fantasy & Science Fiction, Eighth Series edited by Anthony Boucher (Doubleday 1959)

ANTHOLOGIES

A good anthology will either reprint the "best of" the stories that the editor could get the rights to, or the best new stories that the editor could coax out of authors who were within his budget. The list below is a sampling of noted anthologies from the 1940s and 1950s, many from the same specialty publishers as the most valuable novels published in the science fiction field. The sad fact is that there are very few collectors who are interested in anthologies and so prices are relatively low. Almost the only exceptions of note are the two *Dangerous Visions* anthologies edited by Harlan Ellison, which have developed a sort of cult following because of the quality of the stories. There are many excellent anthology available, but you should buy one to read the stories — don't expect to turn a fancy profit on the book in the future.

BOUCHER, ANTHONY, ed.

The Best From Fantasy & Science Fiction, Third Series, Doubleday 1954, Bonestell cover 25.00
The Best From Fantasy & Science Fiction, Fourth Series, Doubleday 1955 . . . . .20.00
The Best From Fantasy & Science Fiction, Fifth Series, Doubleday 1956 . . . . .20.00
The Best From Fantasy & Science Fiction, Sixth Series, Doubleday 1957 . . . . .18.00
The Best From Fantasy & Science Fiction, Seventh Series, Doubleday 1958 . . . . .18.00
The Best From Fantasy & Science Fiction, Eighth Series, Doubleday 1959 . . . . .18.00

CONKLIN, GROFF, ed.

Science-Fiction Terror Tales, Gnome 1955 . . . . .35.00
A Treasury of Science Fiction, Crown 1948 . . . . .45.00
The Best of Science Fiction, Crown 1946 . . . . .50.00
The Big Book of Science Fiction, Crown 1950 . . . . . .40.00
The Omnibus of Science Fiction, Crown 1952 . . . . . .35.00

ELLISON, HARLAN, ed.

Dangerous Visions, Doubleday 1967 . . . . .350.00
Again, Dangerous Visions, Doubleday 1972 . . . . . . .200.00
Medea: Harlan's World, Phantasia 1985, #475, Kelly Freas cover 250.00

Trade edition: 1,500 copies 75.00

GREENBERG, MARTIN, ed.

Men Against the Stars, Gnome 1950 . . . . .100.00
Journey to Infinity, Gnome 1951 . . . . .35.00
Travelers of Space, Gnome 1951 . . . . .25.00
Five Science Fiction Novels, Gnome 1952 . . . . .25.00
The Robot and the Man, Gnome 1953 . . . . .35.00
All About the Future, Gnome 1955 . . . . .35.00
Coming Attractions, Gnome 1957 . . . . .20.00

HEINLEIN, ROBERT A., ed.

Tomorrow, the Stars, Doubleday 1951, Richard Powers cover 125.00

MERRIL, JUDITH, ed.

SF: The Year's Greatest Science Fiction and Fantasy, Gnome 1956 .25.00
SF: '57 The Year's Greatest Science Fiction, Gnome 1957 . . . . .25.00
SF: '58 The Year's Greatest Science Fiction, Gnome 1958 . . . . .25.00
SF: '59 The Year's Greatest Science Fiction, Gnome 1959 . . . . .25.00

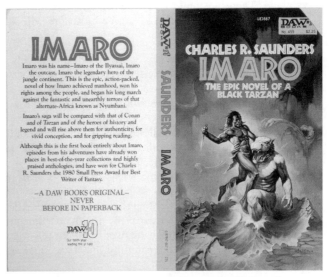

Original cover proof for Imaro *by Charles R. Saunders. Reference to Tarzan was eliminated prior to publication.*

COVER PROOFS

This is an esoteric area of collecting if there ever was one. Cover proofs are issued for most paperbacks to enable book store purchasers to gage the sales appeal of the book. Most are thrown away, but some are kept by artists, who use them for artistic ideas and inspiration and, of course, by a few collectors. Age, and fame of the book have the greatest effect on their value, but most are worth less than $1. A very few become quite interesting because the book never gets published or the art or text is changed in some significant way (merely replacing solicitation art with the final art isn't usually significant). In the two examples shown above, *Blood's a Rover* by Harlan Ellison (a sequel to *A Boy and His Dog*, with art by Richard Corben, was never published, while the cover for *Imaro* by Charles R. Saunders. was changed before publication to omit reference to "The Black Tarzan" because of objections by the Edgar Rice Burroughs estate.

MEDIA BOOKS

MOVIE/TV TIE-INS

Generally movie and TV novelizations and tie-in books are collected by fans of the movie or series, but not by science fiction fans. The exceptions are those by the better known authors. Novelizations of early movies are fairly scarce, but just about every current movie has a novelization and these are issued in fairly large quantity, so they are rarely scarce or valuable. There are quite a few of these novels being produced these days, as any trip to a large bookstore will show you.

There is a regular cottage industry of tie-in novels for *Star Trek* and *Star Wars*. These sell well and are popular with the general public; some even make the best sellers lists. Other popular shows like the *X-Files* have been trying the route, with some success. Science Fiction book sellers report that any new novelization will sell well for the first month it is available, but very slowly thereafter. This means that fans read the latest book, but collectors do not seem to look for missing titles. In any event, the books have large print runs and are not scarce. If you wish to collect these books you will be able to do quite well by waiting for them to be remaindered in about one and one-half years after initial hardcover publication. You can then buy the hardcover for about the price of the paperback version, read it carefully, and have a nice addition to your collection.

Alien & Aliens, *movie novelizations by Alan Dean Foster (Science Fiction Book Club 1979 & 1986)*

ALIEN NATION

Movie Novel
Foster, Alan Dean, *Alien Nation*, Warner #35264-0, 1988 . . . . .7.00

ALIENS

Movie Novels
Foster, Alan Dean, *Alien*, Warner #82-977, 1979 . . . . .10.00
    SFBC: Warner 4008-9, 1979, code J27 . . . . .15.00
Foster, Alan Dean, *Aliens*, Warner #30139-6, 1986 . . .10.00
    SFBC: Warner #10324-2, 1986, code Q34 . . . . . .12.00

Series Novels
1. Perry, Steve, *Earth Hive*, Bantam #56120-0, 1992 . . .7.50
2. Perry, Steve, *Nightmare Asylum*, Bantam #56158-8, 1993 . . . . .6.00
3. Perry, Steve, *The Female War*, Bantam #56159-6, 1993 . . . . .6.00
4. Bischoff, David, *Genocide*, Bantam #56371-8, 1994 . . . . .6.00
5. Sheckley, Robert, *Alien Harvest*, Bantam #56441-2, 1995 . . . . .6.00
6. Scofield, Sandy, *Rogue*, Bantam #56442-0, 1995 . . .6.00
7. Perry, Steve, *Labyrinth*, Bantam #57491-4, 1996 . . .6.00
8. Navarro, Yvonne, *Music of the Spears*, Bantam #57492-2, 1996 . . . . .6.00

Perry, S. D., *Aliens: Berserker*, Bantam Spectra #57731-X, 1998 . . . . .6.00

ALIENS VS. PREDATOR

Bischoff, David, *Hunter's Planet*, Bantam #56556, 1994 . . . . .5.00
Perry, Steve, *Prey*, Bantam #56555-9, 1994 . . . . .5.00

BABYLON 5

Novels
1. Vornholt, John, *Voices*, Dell #, 1995 . . . . .5.50
2. Tilton, Lois, *Accusations*, Dell #22058-0, 1995 . . . . .5.50
3. Vornholt, John, *Blood Oath*, Dell #22059-9, 1995 . . . .5.50
4. Mortimore, Jim, *Clark's Law*, Dell #22229-X, 1996 . . .5.50
5. Barrett Jr., Neal, *The Touch of Your Shadow, The Whisper of Your Name*, Dell #22230-3, 1996 . . . . .5.50
6. Sterling, S.M., *Betrayals*, Dell #22234-6, 1996 . . . . . .5.50
7. Cavelos, Jeanne, *The Shadow Within*, Dell #22348-2, 1997 . . . . .5.50
8. Sarrantonio, Al, *Personal Agendas*, Dell #22351-2, 1997 . . . . .5.50
9. Drennan, Kathrynn, *To Dream in the City of Sorrows*, Dell #22354-7, 1997 . . . . .5.50
Navarro, Yvonne, *The River of Souls*, Dell #, 1998 . . . . .5.50

Babylon 5: In the Beginning *by Peter David (Dell 1998)*
& The A–Z Guide to Babylon 5 *by David Bassom (Dell 1997)*

David, Peter, *In the Beginning*, Dell #42252-2, 1998 . . . .5.50
David, Peter, *Thirdspace*, Dell #, 1998 . . . . .5.50

Season by Season Guide
1. Killick, Jane, *Signs and Portens*, Del Rey TPB #,
   1998 . . . . .11.00
2. Killick, Jane, *The Coming of Shadows*, Del Rey
   TPB #, 1998 . . . . .11.00
3. Killick, Jane, *Point of No Return*, Del Rey TPB
   #42449-2, 1998 . . . . .11.00
4. Killick, Jane, *No Surrender, No Retreat*, Del Rey
   TPB #, 1998 . . . . .11.00

Keyes, J. Gregory, *Dark Genesis: The Birth of Psi
   Corps*, Dell #, 1998 . . . . .6.00
Jurasik, Peter & Keith, William H., *Diplomatic Act*,
   Baen Starline 1998 . . . . .22.00

Non-Fiction
Bassom, David, *The A–Z Guide to Babylon 5*, Dell
   #22385-7, 1997. . . . . .7.00
Lane, Andy, *The Babylon File*, Virgin Books #0049-3,
   1997. . . . . .6.00
Bassom, David, *Creating Babylon 5*, Del Rey TPB
   #41452, 1997 . . . . .18.00
Mortimore, Jim, *Babylon 5 Security Manual* 20.00

BATTLESTAR GALACTICA

TV Show Novels
1. Larson, Glen A. & Thurston, Robert, *Battlestar
   Galactica*, Berkley, 03958-7, 1978 . . . . .15.00
   SFBC: 1978, printing code I47 . . . . .15.00
2. Larson, Glen A. & Thurston, Robert, *The Cylon
   Death Machine*, Berkley, 04080-1, 1979,
   Frank Frazetta cover 12.00
3. Larson, Glen A. & Thurston, Robert, *The Tombs
   of Kobol*, Berkley, 04267-7, 1979 . . . . .12.00
4. Larson, Glen A. & Thurston, Robert, *The Young
   Warriors*, Berkley, 04655-9, 1980 . . . . .12.00
5. Larson, Glen A. & Resnick, Michael, *Galactica
   Discovers Earth*, Berkley, 04744-X, 1980 . . . . . . .10.00
6. Larson, Glen A. & Yermakov, Nicholas, *The Living
   Legend*, Berkley, 05249-4, 1982 . . . . .10.00
7. Larson, Glen A. & Yermakov, Nicholas, *War of the
   Gods*, Berkley, 05660-0, 1982 . . . . .10.00

Battlestar Galactica & *The Cylon Death Machine, by Glen A.
Larson & Robert Thurston (Berkley 1978–79)*

8. Larson, Glen A. & Goulart, Ron, *Greetings From
   Earth*, Berkley, 06047-0, 1983 . . . . .10.00
9. Larson, Glen A. & Goulart, Ron, *Experiment in
   Terra*, Berkley, 06418-2, 1984 . . . . .10.00
10. Larson, Glen A. & Goulart, Ron, *The Long
    Patrol*, Berkley, 07105-7, 1984 . . . . .10.00
11. Larson, Glen A. & Thurston, Robert, *The
    Nightmare Machine*, Berkley, 08618-6, 1985,
    James Warhola 10.00
12. Larson, Glen A. & Thurston, Robert, *'Die,
    Chameleon!'*, Berkley, 09095-7, 1986, James
    Warhola cover 10.00
13. Larson, Glen A. & Thurston, Robert, *Apollo's
    War*, Berkley, 09476-6, 1987, James Warhola
    cover 10.00
14. Larson, Glen A. & Thurston, Robert, *Surrender
    the Galactica!*, Ace(Berkley), 05104-9, 1988 . . . .10.00
Reprints of any of the above, each 5.00

Photostory Movie Adaptation
Larson, Glen A. & Anobile, Richard J., *Battlestar
   Galactica: The Photostory*, Berkley, 4139-5,
   1979 . . . . .20.00
Comics Adaptation
also, McKenzie, Stan Lee, *Battlestar Galactica
   (Comics Version)*, Ace Tempo, 04876, 1978 . . . .15.00

Hatch, Richard & Golden, Christopher, *Battlestar
   Galactica: Armageddon*, ...20.00
   PB: 7.00
Hatch, Richard & Golden, Christopher, *Battlestar
   Galactica: Warhawk*, ...20.00

THE BLACK HOLE

Movie Novel
Foster, Alan Dean, *The Black Hole*, Ballantine-Del
   Rey #28538-7, 1979 . . . . .10.00
   SFBC: Del Rey 3705-1, 1980 . . . . .7.00

BLADE RUNNER

Movie Novels
Dick, Philip K., *Blade Runner*, Ballantine Del Rey
   #30129, 1982 . . . . .15.00
Jeter, K. W., *The Edge of Human*, Bantam #57570-
   8, 1996 . . . . .6.00

Jeter, K. W., *Reluctant Night*, Bantam #57775-1,
1997 . . . . .6.00

BLAKE'S 7

1. Hoyle, Trevor, Terry Nation's *Blake's 7: Scorpio
Attack*, Citadel, 1082-X, 1988 . . . . .10.00
2. Hoyle, Trevor, Terry Nation's *Blake's 7: Project
Avalon*, Citadel, 1102-8, 1988, Burroughs 10.00
3. Hoyle, Trevor, Terry Nation's *Blake's 7: Their
First Adventure*, Citadel, 1103-6, 1988 . . . . .10.00
4. Hoyle, Trevor, Terry Nation's *Blake's 7: Scorpio
Attack*, Citadel, 1082-X, 1988 . . . . .10.00
also, Darrow, Paul, Avon: *A Terrible Aspect*,
LyleStuCitad, 1112-5, 1989 . . . . .10.00

BUCK ROGERS

*The Collected Works of Buck Rogers in the 25th
Century*, ed. by Robert C. Dille, Dick Culkins
art, written by Nowlan and others, stories
from 1929 to 1943, HC (Chelsea House 1969) . .75.00
Nowlan, Philip Francis, *Armageddon 2419 A.D.*
originally published in Amazing Stories, Aug. 1928
HC: Avalon 1962 . . . . .40.00
PB: Ace #F-188, 1963 .10.00
reprints 5.00
Revised by Robinson, Spider, *Armageddon 2419
A.D.*, Ace #02939-6, 1978 . . . . .7.00
Sequels
Holmes, John Eric, *Mordred*, Ace #54220-4, 1980 . . . .8.00
Silbersack, John, *Rogers' Rangers*, Ace #73380-8,
1983 . . . . .6.00

TV Show novels
Steele, Addison E., *Buck Rogers in the 25th
Century*, Dell 10843, 1978, film adaptation 10.00
Steele, Addison E., *That Man on Beta*, Dell 10948,
1979 . . . . .8.00

Buck Rogers: Martian War
0. (Anon.) ed., *Buck Rogers: Arrival*, TSR, 582-0,
1989 . . . . .10.00
1. Murdock, M. S., *Buck Rogers: Rebellion 2456*,
TSR, 728-9, 1989 . . . . .8.00
2. Murdock, M. S., *Buck Rogers: Hammer of Mars*,
TSR, 751-3, 1989 . . . . .8.00

Blade Runner, *comics adaptation (Marvel 1982)*
Buck Rogers: First Power Play *by John Miller (TSR 1990)*

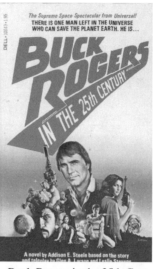 

Buck Rogers in the 25th Century *by Addison Steele (Dell 1978)*
& Dark Star *by Alan Dean Foster (Ballantine 1974)*

3. Murdock, M. S., *Buck Rogers: Armageddon Off
Vestra*, TSR, 761-0, 1989 . . . . .8.00

Buck Rogers: Inner Planets
1. Miller, John, *Buck Rogers: First Power Play*, TSR,
840-4, 1990 . . . . .8.00
2. Murdock, M. S., *Buck Rogers: Prime Squared*,
TSR, 863-3, 1990 . . . . .8.00

CLOSE ENCOUNTERS
OF THE THIRD KIND

Close Encounters of the Third Kind, Fotonovel, Dell
#10979, 1978 . . . . .25.00

DARK STAR

Movie Novel
Foster, Alan Dean, *Dark Star*, Ballantine #24267-X,
1974 . . . . .15.00

DOCTOR WHO

Whitaker, David, *Doctor Who in an Exciting
Adventure with the Daleks*, Avon G1322,
1967, photo 10.00
Bentham, *Doctor Who: The Early Years*, 1980s 15.00
Dicks, Terrance, *The Further Adventures of Doctor
Who*, Nelson Doubleday 1986 . . . . .7.00
Haining, Peter, *Dr. Who A Celebration*, 1980s 12.00
Haining, Peter, *Dr. Who File*, 1980s 10.00
Haining, Peter, *Dr. Who Key to Time* 1980s 12.00
Haining, Peter, *Dr. Who Time Travellers*, Grosset &
Dunlap 1980s 10.00
Strandring, *Dr. Who Illus A to Z*, 1980s 10.00
Harris, *Dr. Who Technical Manual*, 1980s 15.00
Nathan, T, *Dr. Who The Tardis Inside*, 1980s 10.00
Nathan, T, *Dr. Who The Companions*, 1980s 10.00

**Doctor Who books, Target, more than 160
produced from 1973 to 1990, each** **4.00**

Doctor Who (intro by Harlan Ellison
1. Dicks, Terrance, *Doctor Who and the Day of the
Daleks*, Pinnacle #40565-0, 1979 . . . . .6.00
2. Hulke, Malcolm, *Doctor Who and the Doomsday
Weapon*, Pinnacle #40566-9, 1979 . . . . .5.00

3. Hulke, Malcolm, *Doctor Who and the Dinosaur Invasion*, Pinnacle #40606-1, 1979 . . . . .5.00
4. Dicks, Terrance, *Doctor Who and the Genesis of the Daleks*, Pinnacle #40608-8, 1979 . . . . .5.00
5. Dicks, Terrance, *Doctor Who and the Revenge of the Cybermen*, Pinnacle #40611-8, 1979 . . . . . . .5.00
6. Dicks, Terrance, *Doctor Who and the Loch Ness Monster*, Pinnacle #40609-6, 1979 . . . . .5.00
7. Dicks, Terrance, *Doctor Who and the Talons of Weng-Chaing*, Pinnacle #40638-X, 1979 . . . . . . .5.00
8. Hinchcliffe, Philip, *Doctor Who and the Masque of Mandragora*, Pinnacle #40646-0, 1979 . . . . . .5.00
9. Dicks, Terrance, *Doctor Who and the Android Invasion*, Pinnacle #40641-X, 1980 . . . . .5.00
10. Hinchcliffe, Philip, *Doctor Who and the Seeds of Doom*, Pinnacle #41620-2, 1981 . . . . .5.00

ENEMY MINE

Movie Novel
Longyear, Barry, *Enemy Mine*, Charter-Berkley #20672-7, 1985 . . . . .10.00

FLASH GORDON

Adaptations from Alex Raymond's original stories
Flash Gordon #1: The Lion Men of Mongo, adapted by Ron Goulart, Avon 18515, 1974 . . . . .5.00
Flash Gordon #2: The Plague of Sound, adapted by Ron Goulart, Avon 19166, 1974 . . . . .5.00
Flash Gordon #3: The Space Circus, adapted by Ron Goulart, Avon 19695, 1974 . . . . .5.00
Flash Gordon #4: The Time Trap of Ming XIII, adapted by Carson Bingham, Avon 20446, 1974 . . . . .5.00
Flash Gordon #5: The Witch Queen of Mongo, adapted by Carson Bingham, Avon 21378, 1974 . . . . .5.00
Flash Gordon #6: The War of the Cybernauts, adapted by Carson Bingham, Avon 22335, 1975 . . . . .5.00

Flash Gordon Comics
The Amazing Adventures of Flash Gordon, Vol. 1, Ace-Tempo 17349, 1980 . . . . .5.00
The Amazing Adventures of Flash Gordon, Vol. 2, Ace-Tempo 17348, 1980 . . . . .5.00

Flash Gordon: #3 The Space Circus by Ron Goulart & #4 The Time Trap of Ming XIII by Carson Bingham (Avon 1974)

The Amazing Adventures of Flash Gordon, Vol 2: War of the Citadels & Vol 6: Citadels on Earth (Ace-Tempo 1980)

The Amazing Adventures of Flash Gordon, Vol. 3, Ace-Tempo 17347, 1980 . . . . .5.00
The Amazing Adventures of Flash Gordon, Vol. 4, Ace-Tempo 17154, 1980, Boris Vallejo cover 7.50
The Amazing Adventures of Flash Gordon, Vol. 5, Ace-Tempo 17208, 1980 . . . . .6.00
The Amazing Adventures of Flash Gordon, Vol. 6, Ace-Tempo 17245, 1980 . . . . .6.00

Flash Gordon, reprints of the original Alex Raymond Sunday color comic strips:
Volume 1: *"Mongo, The Planet of Doom,"* from 1934–35, Kitchen Sink 1990 . . . . .34.95
  Softcover 19.95
Volume 2: *"Three Against Ming,"* from 1935–37, Kitchen Sink 1991 .34.95
  Softcover (0-87816-139-2) 19.95
Volume 3: *"The Tides of Battle,"* from 1937–39, Kitchen Sink 1992 .34.95
  Softcover (0-87816-162-7) 21.95
Volume 4: *"The Fall of Ming,"* from 1939–41, Kitchen Sink 1993 . . . . .34.95
  Softcover (0-87816-168-6) 21.95
Volume 5: *"Between Worlds at War,"* from 1941–43, Kitchen Sink 1993 . . . . .34.95
  Softcover (0-87816-177-5) 21.95
Volume 6: *"Triumph in Tropica"* from 1943–44, Kitchen Sink 1994 . . . . .34.95
  Softcover (0-87816-199-6) 21.95
Flash Gordon, reprints of the original Austin Briggs daily black-and-white comic strips:
The Dailies, Volume 1, strips from 1940–42, Kitchen Kitchen Sink 1993 Softcover (0-87816-172-4) . . .10.95
The Dailies, Volume 2, strips from 1941, Kitchen Sink 1993 Softcover (0-87816-187-2) 10.95
Flash Gordon, The Daily Strip, 1951, reprinting the original strips from 1951–53 by Dan Barry, Harvey Kurtzman and Frank Frazetta, black and white, Kitchen Sink 1988 Hardcover, signed .25.00
  Also Trade Paperback (1988) 12.00
  Reprint 1991 (0-87816-134-5) 10.00

Flash Gordon
1. (Anon.), *Massacre in the 22nd Century*, Tempo, 12963-9, 1980, Boris Vallejo cover 7.00

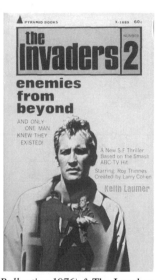

Futureworld *by John Ryder Hall (Ballantine 1976) &* The Invaders *#2: Enemies From Beyond by Keith Laumer (Pyramid 1967)*

2. (Anon.), *War of the Citadels*, Tempo, 17215-1,
   1980, Boris Vallejo cover 7.00
3. (Anon.), *Crises on Citadel II*, Tempo, 17231-3,
   1980, Boris Vallejo cover 7.00
4. (Anon.), *Forces From the Federation*, Tempo,
   17233-X, 1981, Boris Vallejo cover 7.00
5. (Anon.), *Citadels Under Attack*, Tempo, 17234-8,
   1981. . . . . .5.00
6. (Anon.), *Citadels on Earth*, Tempo, 17254-2, 1981 . . .5.00

FUTURE WORLD

Movie Novelization
Hall, John Ryder, *Futureworld*, Ballantine #25559,
   1976 . . . . .8.00

INVADERS

TV Show novels
1. Laumer, Keith, *The Invaders*, Pyramid, R-1664,
   1967 . . . . .10.00
2.. Laumer, Keith, *Enemies From Beyond*, Pyramid,
   X-1689, 1967 . . . . .10.00
3.. Bernard, Rafe, *Army of the Undead*, Pyramid,
   R-1711, 1967 . . . . .10.00

LAND OF THE GIANTS

TV Show novels
1. Leinster, Murray, *Land of the Giants*, Pyramid,
   X-1846, 1968 . . . . .10.00
2. Leinster, Murray, *The Hot Spot*, Pyramid, X-1921,
   1969 . . . . .10.00
3. Leinster, Murray, *Unknown Danger*, Pyramid,
   X-2105, 1969 . . . . .10.00
Rathjen, Carl Henry, *Flight of Fear*, Whitman, 1516,
   1969 . . . . .20.00

THE LAST STARFIGHTER

Movie Novel
Foster, Alan Dean, *The Last Starfighter*, Berkley
   #07255-X, 1984 . . . . .10.00

MARS ATTACKS

Movie tie-in
Archer, Nathan, *Martian Deathtrap*, Ballantine Del
   Rey #40953-1, 1997 . . . . .5.00
Murill, Ray W., *War Dogs of the Golden Horde*

HC: Del Rey 1996 . . . . .20.00
PB: Ballantine Del Rey #40954-X, 1997 . . . . .5.00

MEN IN BLACK

Movie tie-in
Perry, Steve, *Men in Black*, Bantam #57756-5, 1997 . . .6.00

OUTLAND

Movie tie-in
Foster, Alan Dean, *Outland*, Warner #95829-8, 1981 . .15.00

PLANET OF THE APES

Movie tie-in books
Boulle, Piere, *Planet of the Apes*
Avallone, Michael, *Beneath the Planet of the Apes*,
   Bantam #S5674, 1970 . . . . .12.00
Gerrold, David, *Battle for the Planet of the Apes*,
   Award, AN1139, 1973. . . . . .10.00
Pournelle, Jerry, *Escape from the Planet of the
   Apes*, Award, AN1240, 1974 . . . . .10.00
Jakes, John, *Conquest of the Planet of the Apes*,
   Award, AN1241, 1974, photo cover 10.00
Reprints, any 5.00

TV Show Tie-ins
1. Effinger, George Alec, *Man the Fugitive*, Award,
   AN1373, 1974, photo 10.00
2. Effinger, George Alec, *Escape to Tomorrow*,
   Award, AN1407, 1975, photo 10.00
3. Effinger, George Alec, *Journey into Terror*,
   Award, AN1436, 1975, photo 10.00
4. Effinger, George Alec, *Lord of the Apes*, Award,
   AN1488, 1975, photo 10.00

Return to the Planet of the Apes
1. Arrow, William (Rotsler, William) *Visions from
   Nowhere*, Ballantine, 25122-9, 1976, ...10.00
2. Arrow, William (Pfeil, Don) *Escape from Terror
   Lagoon*, Ballantine, 25167-9, 1976 . . . . .10.00
3. Arrow, William, *Man, the Hunted Animal*,
   Ballantine, 25211-X, 1976 . . . . .10.00

PREDATOR

Archer, Nathan, *Predator: Concrete Jungle*, Bantam
   Spectra #56557-5, 1995 . . . . .5.00

Land of the Giants *by Murray Leinster (Pyramid 1968) &* Escape from the Planet of the Apes *by Jerry Pournelle (Award 1974)*

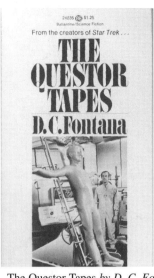   

The Questor Tapes by D. C. Fontana (Ballantine 1974) & Space:
1999, The Space Guardians by Brian Ball (Pocket 1975)

Robotech Genesis promo booklet & Sentinels #1: The Devil's
Hand by Jack McKinney (Ballantine Del Rey 1987 & 1988)

Archer, Nathan, *Predator: Cold War*, Bantam
   Spectra #57493-0, 1997 . . . . .5.00

THE QUESTOR TAPES

TV Show pilot novelization
Fontana, D. C., *The Questor Tapes*, Ballantine
   #24236, 1974 . . . . .15.00

ROBOTECH

Robotech 1st, (actually by Brain Daley & James Luceno)
1. McKinney, Jack, *Genesis*, Waldenbooks, 1987,
   David Schleinkofer 10.00
   PB: BB-Del Rey, 34133-3, 1987 . . . . .8.00
2. McKinney, Jack, *Battle Cry*, BB-Del Rey, 34134-1,
   1987 . . . . .8.00
3. McKinney, Jack, *Homecoming*, BB-Del Rey,
   34136-8, 1987 . . . . .8.00
4. McKinney, Jack, *Battlehymn*, BB-Del Rey,
   34137-6, 1987 . . . . .8.00
5. McKinney, Jack, *Force of Arms*, BB-Del Rey,
   34138-4, 1987 . . . . .8.00
6. McKinney, Jack, *Doomsday*, BB-Del Rey,
   34139-2, 1987 . . . . .8.00
Robotech 2nd
7. McKinney, Jack, *Southern Cross*, BB-Del Rey,
   34140-6, 1987 . . . . .8.00
8. McKinney, Jack, *Metal Fire*, BB-Del Rey, 34141-4,
   1987 . . . . .8.00
9. McKinney, Jack, *The Final Nightmare*, BB-Del
   Rey, 34142-2, 1987 . . . . .8.00
Robotech 3rd
10. McKinney, Jack, *Invid Invasion*, BB-Del Rey,
    34143-0, 1987 . . . . .7.00
11. McKinney, Jack, *Metamorphosis*, BB-Del Rey,
    34144-9, 1987 . . . . .7.00
12. McKinney, Jack, *Symphony of Light*, BB-Del
    Rey, 34145-7, 1987 . . . . .7.00
Robotech: Sentinels
13. McKinney, Jack, *The Sentinels #1: Devil's Hand*,
    BB-Del Rey, 35300-5, 1988 . . . . .7.00
14. McKinney, Jack, *The Sentinels #2: Dark Powers*,
    BB-Del Rey, 35301-3, 1988 . . . . .7.00
15. McKinney, Jack, *The Sentinels #3: Death Dance*,
    BB-Del Rey, 35302-1, 1988 . . . . .7.00
16. McKinney, Jack, *The Sentinels #4: World Killers*,

BB-Del Rey, 35304-8, 1988 . . . . .7.00
17. McKinney, Jack, *The Sentinels #5: Rubicon*,
    BB-Del Rey, 35305-6, 1988 . . . . .7.00
Robotech-end, 18, McKinney, Jack, *The End of the
   Circle*, BB-Del Rey, 36311-6, 1990 . . . . .7.00
Reprints of any of the above, each 5.00

SPACE: 1999

TV Show novels
1. Tubb, E. C. *Space 1999 #1: Breakaway*
   PB: Pocket #80184-8, 1975 . . . . .10.00
   HC: Aeonian, 671, 1976 . . . . .20.00
2. Rankine, John, *Space 1999 #2: Moon Odyssey*
   PB: Pocket #80185-6, 1975 . . . . .10.00
   HC: Aeonian, 672, 1976 . . . . .20.00
3. Ball, Brian N., *Space 1999 #3: The Space
   Guardians*
   PB: Pocket #80198-8, 1975 . . . . .10.00
   HC: Aeonian, 673, 1976 . . . . .20.00
4. Tubb, E. C., *Space 1999 #4: Collision Course*
   PB: Pocket #80274-7, 1976 . . . . .10.00
   HC: Aeonian, 674, 1976 . . . . .20.00
5. Rankine, John, *Space 1999 #5: Lunar Attack*
   PB: Pocket #80305-0, 1976 . . . . .10.00
   HC: Aeonian, 675, 1976 . . . . .20.00
6. Rankine, John, *Astral Quest*, Pocket #80392-1,
   1976 . . . . .10.00
7. Tubb, E. C., *Alien Seed*, Pocket #80520-7, 1976 . . . .9.00
8. Rankine, John, *Android Planet*, Pocket #80706-4,
   1976 . . . . .9.00
9. Tubb, E. C., *Rogue Planet*, Pocket #80710-2,
   1976 . . . . .9.00
10. Rankine, John, *Phoenix of Megaron*, Pocket
    #80764-1, 1976 . . . . .9.00
Space 1999, 2nd series
1. Butterworth, Michael, *Planets of Peril*, Warner,
   88341-7, 1977 . . . . .9.00
2. Butterworth, Michael, *Mind-Breaks of Space*,
   Warner, 88342-5, 1977 . . . . .9.00
3. Butterworth, Michael, *The Space-Jackers*, Warner,
   88343-3, 1977 . . . . .9.00
4. Butterworth, Michael, *The Psychomorph*, Warner,
   88344-1, 1977 . . . . .9.00
5. Butterworth, Michael, *The Time Fighters*, Warner,
   88345-X, 1977 . . . . .9.00

6. Butterworth, Michael, *The Edge of the Infinite*,
    Warner, 88346-8, 1977 . . . . .9.00

STARGATE

Novels based on Movie
McCay, Bill, *Rebellion*, Roc #45502-9, 1995 . . . . .6.00
McCay, Bill, *Retaliation*, Roc #45516-9, 1996 . . . . .6.00
McCay, Bill, *Retribution*, Roc #45556-8, 1997 . . . . .6.00
McCay, Bill, *Reconnaissance*, Roc #45663-7, 1998 . . . .6.00

STARMAN

Movie Novel
Foster, Alan Dean, *Starman*, Warner #32598-8, 1984 . . .7.00

STAR TREK

The first *Star Trek* books were produced while the show was still in its first season on television — and most of them are still in print! The earliest books were episode adaptations, but today most *Star Trek* stories are original novels. There are over 200 novels in existence, and all four of the TV shows have ongoing novel series. Book collectors always look for first editions and these will always be more valuable than reprints.

Books about *Star Trek* also date back to the 1960s. Many of the creators of the TV shows and movies, from Gene Roddenberry to artist Rick Sternbach, as well as all the original cast members, have written books about the show.

Reference works about the show and the episodes, plus the starships and the equipment used in the original TV series were largely produced by fans in the 1970s. Many of these books have gone on to see legitimate editions from major publishers. Collectors have to choose between the usually more valuable first editions and the much more useful corrected, updated and expanded later editions.

There are also a number of books which can best be described as "fictional reference" books, because information on Starfleet and alien technology, institutions, worlds, languages and races is created to fill in portions of the *Star Trek* universe which the shows barely mention.

Star Trek & Star Trek 2, *episodes adapted by James Blish*
(Bantam 1967 & 1968)

Star Trek Fotonovel *#1 (Bantam 1977)* & Mission to Horatius *by*
Mack Reynolds (Whitman 1968)

Small Press
Before there was a professional market for original *Star Trek* novels, several would-be authors wrote and published their own amateur editions. Some of these authors have gone on to publish professional *Star Trek* novels and other science fiction books. These unauthorized novels are scarce, and not well known to *Star Trek* collectors.

Lorrah, Jean, *The Night of the Twin Moons*, Lorrah,
    none, 1976 . . . . .15.00
Bartel, Martin M., *Secret Agent Enterprise*, TK
    Graphics, none, 1977 .10.00
Steiner, D. T., *Spock Enslaved!*, Love Child, 1974 . . . .15.00
Gross, Edward, *Trek: The Lost Years*, Pioneer,
    220-8, 1989 . . . . .12.00

Juvenile
The first professional and first authorized novelization of *Star Trek* was a juvenile by Mack Reynolds, a popular adventure science fiction author in his day. He died in early 1983, just prior to a scheduled appearance as guest of honor at a major science fiction convention. *Star Trek* juvenile novels are still being published today, but collectors ignore them.

Star Trek, Mission to Horatius, by Mack Reynolds,
    pictorial cover juvenile, Whitman 1968 . . . . .50.00
Star Trek, The Prisoner of Vega, by Sharon Lerner
    and Christopher Cerf, pictorial cover juvenile,
    Random House 1977 .35.00

Star Trek TV episode adaptations
1. Blish, James, *Star Trek*, Bantam F3459, 1967,
    1st, James Bama cover .10.00
2. Blish, James, *Star Trek 2*, Bantam F3439, 1968 . . . . .9.00
3. Blish, James, *Star Trek 3*, Bantam F4371, 1969 . . . . .9.00
4. Blish, James, *Star Trek 4*, Bantam S7009, 1971 . . . . .9.00
5. Blish, James, *Star Trek 5*, Bantam S7300, 1972 . . . . .8.00
6. Blish, James, *Star Trek 6*, Bantam S7364, 1972 . . . . .8.00
7. Blish, James, *Star Trek 7*, Bantam N8610, 1975 . . . .8.00
8. Blish, James, *Star Trek 8*, Bantam SP7550, 1972 . . .8.00
9. Blish, James, *Star Trek 9*, Bantam SP7808, 1973 . . .8.00
10. Blish, James, *Star Trek 10*, Bantam N8401,
    1974 . . . . .8.00
11. Blish, James, *Star Trek 11*, Bantam Q8717,
    1975 . . . . .8.00

*Star Trek Log One & Star Trek Log Two by Alan Dean Foster
(Ballantine 1974)*

12. Blish, James & Lawrence, J. A., *Star Trek 12*,
Bantam 11382-8, 1977. . . . . .8.00
Blish, James, *Spock Must Die!*, Bantam H5515, 1970 .10.00
Reprints of any of the above, each 5.00

Hardcover reprints
Blish, James, *The Star Trek Reader*, Dutton, 1976 . . . .25.00
Blish, James, *The Star Trek Reader II*, Dutton, 1977 . .20.00
Blish, James, *The Star Trek Reader III*, Dutton, 1977 . .20.00
Blish, James, *The Star Trek Reader IV*, Dutton, 1978 . .20.00

Star Trek Logs

Alan Dean Foster adapted episodes from the *Star Trek* animated TV series and these were published by Ballantine Books as *Star Trek Log One* through *Star Trek Log 10*. These books are still in print from Ballantine under its Del Rey books imprint. The first editions of these books are dated from 1974 to 1978 and can be determined by the "First Printing" statement on the copyright page.

1. Foster, Alan Dean, *Star Trek Log One*, Ballantine,
24014-6, 1974 . . . . .15.00
2. Foster, Alan Dean, *Star Trek Log Two*, Ballantine,
24184-3, 1974 . . . . .15.00
3. Foster, Alan Dean, *Star Trek Log Three*,
Ballantine, 24260-2, 1975 . . . . .15.00
4. Foster, Alan Dean, *Star Trek Log Four*, Ballantine,
24435-4, 1975 . . . . .15.00
5. Foster, Alan Dean, *Star Trek Log Five*, Ballantine,
24532-6, 1975. . . . . .12.00
6. Foster, Alan Dean, *Star Trek Log Six*, Ballantine,
24655-1, 1976. . . . . .12.00
7. Foster, Alan Dean, *Star Trek Log Seven*,
Ballantine, 24965-8, 1976. . . . . .12.00
8. Foster, Alan Dean, *Star Trek Log Eight*,
Ballantine, 25141-5, 1976. . . . . .12.00
9. Foster, Alan Dean, *Star Trek Log Nine*, Ballantine,
25557-7, 1977 . . . . .10.00
10. Foster, Alan Dean, *Star Trek Log Ten*, BB-Del
Rey, 27212-9, 1978 . . . . .10.00
Reprints of any of the above, each 5.00

Some of the best of the classic TV series episodes were adapted to book form as FotoNovels between 1977 and 1978. Full-color pictures from the shows were used with word bal-

loons to tell the episode story in comic book style. These are desirable as collectibles.

Star Trek FotoNovels
1. (Anon.), from script by Ellison, Harlan, *The City on
the Edge of Forever*, Bantam 11345-3, 1977 . . . .30.00
2. (Anon.), from script by Peeples, Samuel A.,
Where No Man Has Gone Before, Bantam
11346-1, 1977 . . . . .25.00
3. (Anon.), from script by Gerrold, David, *The
Trouble With Tribbles*, Bantam 11347-X, 1977 . . . .30.00
4. (Anon.), from script by Hamner, Robert, *A Taste
of Armageddon*, Bantam 11348-8, 1978 . . . . .25.00
5. (Anon.), from script by Coon, Gene L.,
Metamorphosis, Bantam 11349-6, 1978 . . . . .25.00
6. (Anon.), from script by Aroeste, Jean A., *All Our
Yesterdays*, Bantam 11350-X, 1978 . . . . .25.00
Reprints of any of the above, each 15.00
7. (Anon.), from script by Crawford, Oliver, *The
Galileo 7*, Bantam 12041-7, 1978 . . . . .15.00
8. (Anon.), from script by Harmon, David P., *A
Piece of the Action*, Bantam 12022-0, 1978 . . . .20.00
9. (Anon.), from script by Coon, Gene L., *The Devil
in the Dark*, Bantam 12021-2, 1978 . . . . .20.00
10. (Anon.), from script by Bixby, David P., *Day of
the Dove*, Bantam 12017-4, 1978 . . . . .15.00
11. (Anon.), from script by Hamon, David P., *The
Deadly Years*, Bantam 12028-X, 1978 . . . . .15.00
12. (Anon.), from script by Sturgeon, Theodore,
Amok Time, Bantam 12012-3, 1978 . . . . .20.00

Movie Foto Novels
M1. Anobile, Richard ed., *Star Trek: The Motion
Picture Photostory*, Pocket #83089-9, 1980 . . . . .15.00
M2. Anobile, Richard ed., *Star Trek II: The Wrath of
Kahn Photostory*, Pocket #83089-9, 1980 . . . . . .15.00

Movie Novelizations

When the *Star Trek* movies started in 1979, a collectors hardcover edition was produced, but, for the next five movies, there were no hardcover trade editions, only paperback adaptations. For several of these, a book-club edition appeared a month or two before the corresponding paperback, making them the true first editions. Book-club editions have a printing code in the gutter on one the last few pages of the book. These codes can be used to distinguish first printings from

*Star Trek II: The Wrath of Khan & Star Trek III: The Search For
Spock by Vonda N. McIntyre (Science Fiction Book Club 1982–84)*

Mudd's Angels *by J. A. Lawrence &* Vulcan *by Kathleen Sky*
(Bantam 1978)

reprintings, which are not usually acknowledged on the copyright page.

Roddenberry, Gene, *Star Trek, The Motion Picture*,
Limited edition hardcover, no DJ, 1979 . . . . . . .150.00
PB: Pocket #83088-0, 1979 . . . . .7.00
Trade HC: Simon & Schuster 1980 . . . . .50.00
SFBC: Pocket 3830-7, 1980 . . . . .5.00
McIntyre, Vonda N., *Star Trek II: The Wrath of Kahn*,
SFBC edition, Pocket 3119-5 1982, code
M44 . . . . .15.00
PB: Pocket #45610-5, 1982 . . . . .7.00
HC: Gregg 1984, reprint 20.00
McIntyre, Vonda N., *Star Trek III: The Search For
Spock*, SFBC edition, Pocket 3722-6, July
1984, code O23 on page 218 . . . . .15.00
PB: Pocket #49500-3, 1984 . . . . .7.00
HC: Gregg 1984, reprint 20.00
McIntyre, Vonda N., *Star Trek IV: The Voyage
Home*, Pocket #63266-3, 1986 . . . . .5.00
SFBC: Pocket #10630-2; 1987, code R10
on page 187 . . . . .9.00
Dillard, J. M., *Star Trek V: The Final Frontier*, Pocket
#68008-0, 1989 . . . . .5.00
SFBC: Pocket 15600-0 1990 . . . . .9.00
Dillard, J. M., *Star Trek VI: The Undiscovered
Country*, Pocket #75883-7, 1991 . . . . .5.50
Dillard, J. M., *Star Trek Generations*, Pocket Books
51742-2, 1994, hardcover 20.00
PB: Pocket #53753-9, 1994 . . . . .6.00
Dillard, J. M., *Star Trek First Contact*, Pocket
#00316-X, 1996 . . . . .20.00
PB: Pocket #, 1996 . . . . .6.00

Star Trek Novels from Bantam Books

In the late 1970s and early 1980s, *Star Trek* books were produced by Bantam Books. The books by Joe Haldeman — *Planet of Judgment* and *World Without End* — are the most highly sought of these early novels. He's the Hugo and Nebula award-winning author of *The Forever War*. It was highly unusual for a famous author to write a TV or movie adaptation at this time. Usually they were authored by younger and less famous authors as a lower rung on their career ladders. This has changed in the 1990s, as *Star Trek*,

Star Wars and *The X-Files* books have been published in hardcover and even become bestsellers. Now there is enough money in it to interest a first-rank author.

Cogswell, Theodore R. & Spano, Charles A. Jr.,
Spock, Messiah! A Star Trek Novel, Bantam
#10159-5, 1976 . . . . .15.00
Eklund, Gordon, *The Starless World*, Bantam
#12371-8, 1978 . . . . .12.00
Eklund, Gordon, *Devil World*, Bantam #13297-0,
1979 . . . . .12.00
Gerrold, David, *The Galactic Whirlpool*, Bantam
#14242-9, 1980 . . . . .15.00
Goldin, Stephen, *Trek to Madworld*, Bantam
#12618-0, 1979 . . . . .12.00
Haldeman, Jack C. II, *Perry's Planet*, Bantam
#13580-5, 1980 . . . . .15.00
Haldeman, Joe, *Planet of Judgment*, Bantam
#11145-0, 1977 . . . . .20.00
Haldeman, Joe, *World Without End*, Bantam
#12583-4, 1979 . . . . .20.00
Lawrence, J. A., *Mudd's Angels*, Bantam #11802-1,
1978 . . . . .12.00
Marshak, Sondra & Culbreath, Myrna eds., *Star
Trek: the New Voyages*, Bantam #02719-0,
1976 . . . . .10.00
Marshak, Sondra & Culbreath, Myrna eds., *Star
Trek: the New Voyages 2*, Bantam #11392-5,
1978 . . . . .10.00
Marshak, Sondra & Culbreath, Myrna, *The Price of
the Phoenix*, Bantam #10978-2, 1977 . . . . .12.00
Marshak, Sondra & Culbreath, Myrna, *The Fate of
the Phoenix*, Bantam #12779-9, 1979 . . . . .12.00
Sky, Kathleen, *Vulcan!*, Bantam #12137-5, 1978 . . . . .12.00
Sky, Kathleen, *Death's Angel*, Bantam #14703-X,
1981 . . . . .12.00
Reprints of any of the above, each 5.00

Star Trek Novels from Pocket Books

In the early 1980s, Pocket Books published *Star Trek* novels under the "Timescape" imprint which it used on science fiction books. It's from a book of the same name by Gregory Benford. Rowena Morrill and Boris Vallejo, two well-known science fiction cover artists provided many of the covers in the early years. In researching this book, I met an avid fan of these books. She reported that she had looked for

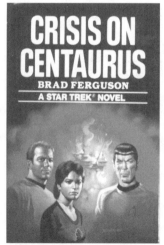 

Crisis on Centaurus *by Brad Ferguson &* Yesterday's Son *by A. E Crispin (Science Fiction Book Club 1986 & 1983)*

The Tears of the Singers *by Melinda Snodgrass* & Deep Domain
by Howard Weinstein (Pocket 1984 & 1987)

one particular early book in this series for several years. When she found it, she was able to buy it at half price. Even though a particular title may be elusive, none of these books has attained much of a collector's value. Most of the buyers are just fans looking for a title they have not read, so factors like first edition, cover artist, author fame and mint condition do not matter much.

Numbered

0. McIntyre, Vonda N., *Enterprise: The First Adventure*, Pocket #62581-0, 1986 . . . . .10.00
1. *Star Trek, The Motion Picture*, see above
2. McIntyre, Vonda N., *The Entropy Effect*, Pocket Timescape #83692-7, 1981 . . . . .12.00
3. Vardeman, Robert E., *The Klingon Gambit*, Pocket Timescape #83276-X, 1981 . . . . .12.00
4. Weinstein, Howard, *The Covenant of the Crown*, Pocket Timescape #83307-3, 1981 . . . . .10.00
5. Marshak, Sondra & Culbreath, Myrna, *The Prometheus Design*, Pocket Timescape #83398-7, 1982, Rowena Morrill cover 10.00
6. Correy, Lee, *The Abode of Life*, Pocket Timescape #83297-2, 1982, Rowena cover 10.00
7. *Star Trek II: The Wrath of Khan*, see above
8. Cooper, Sonni, *Black Fire*, Pocket Timescape #83632-3, 1983, Boris Vallejo cover 10.00
9. Marshak, Sondra & Culbreath, Myrna, *Triangle*, Pocket Timescape #83399-5, 1983, Boris Vallejo cover 10.00
10. Murdock, M. S., *Web of the Romulans*, Pocket Timescape #46479-5, 1983, Boris cover 10.00
11. Crispin, A. C., *Yesterday's Son*, Pocket Timescape #47315-8, 1983, Boris Vallejo cover 10.00
12. Vardeman, Robert E., *Mutiny on the Enterprise*, Pocket Timescape #46541-4, 1983, Boris Vallejo cover 12.00
13. Duane, Diane, *The Wounded Sky*, Pocket Timescape #47389-1, 1983, Boris Vallejo cover 10.00
14. Dvorkin, David, *The Trellisane Confrontation*, Pocket Timescape #46543-0, 1984, Rowena Morrill cover 10.00
15. Bear, Greg, *Corona*, Pocket #47390-5, 1984, Boris Vallejo cover .12.00
16. Ford, John M., *The Final Reflection*, Pocket

#47388-3, 1984, Boris Vallejo cover 12.00
17. *Star Trek III: The Search for Spock*, see above
18. Duane, Diane, *My Enemy, My Ally*, Pocket #50285-9, 1984, Boris Vallejo cover 8.00
19. Snodgrass, Melinda, *The Tears of the Singers*, Pocket #50284-0, 1984, Boris Vallejo cover 8.00
20. Lorrah, Jean, *The Vulcan Academy Murders*, Pocket #50054-6, 1984, Boris Vallejo cover 8.00
21. Kagan, Janet, *Uhura's Song*, Pocket #54730-5, 1985, Boris Vallejo cover .8.00
22. Yep, Laurence, *Shadow Lord*, Pocket #47392-1, 1985, Boris Vallejo cover .8.00
23. Hambly, Barbara, *Ishmael*, Pocket #55427-1, 1985, Boris Vallejo cover .8.00
24. Van Hise, Della, *Killing Time*, Pocket #52488-7, 1985, Boris Vallejo cover .7.00
25. Bonanno, Margaret W., *Dwellers in the Crucible*, Pocket #60373-6, 1985, Boris Vallejo cover 7.00
26. Larson, Majliss, *Pawns and Symbols*, Pocket #55425-5, 1985, Boris Vallejo cover 7.00
27. Dillard, J. M., *Mindshadow*, Pocket #60756-1, 1986, Boris Vallejo cover 7.00
28. Ferguson, Brad, *Crisis on Centaurus*, Pocket #61115-1, 1986, Boris Vallejo cover 7.00
29. Carey, Diane, *Dreadnought!*, Pocket #61873-3, 1986, Boris Vallejo cover 7.00
30. Dillard, J. M., *Demons*, Pocket #62524-1, 1986, Boris Vallejo cover 6.00
31. Carey, Diane, *Battlestations!*, Pocket #63267-1, 1986, Boris Vallejo cover? 6.00
32. DeWeese, Gene, *Chain of Attack*, Pocket #63269-8, 1987 . . . . .6.00
33. Weinstein, Howard, *Deep Domain*, Pocket #63329-5, 1987 . . . . .6.00
34. Carter, Carmen, *Dreams of the Raven*, Pocket #64500-5, 1987 . . . . .6.00
35. Duane, Diane & Morwood, Peter, *The Romulan Way*, Pocket #63498-4, 1987 . . . . .6.00
36. Ford, John M., *How Much for Just the Planet?*, Pocket #62998-0, 1987 . . . . .6.00
37. Dillard, J. M., *Bloodthirst*, Pocket #64489-0, 1987 . .6.00
38. Lorrah, Jean, *The Idic Epidemic*, Pocket #63574-3, 1988 . . . . .6.00
38. Bonanno, Margaret W., *Star Trek: Strangers From the Sky*, Pocket #64049-6, 1987, Boris

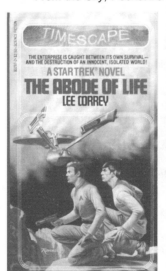

The Abode of Life *by Lee Correy* & The Prometheus Design *by Sondra Marshak & Myrna Culbreath (Pocket Timescape 1982)*

Battlestations! by Diane Carey & Time For Yesterday by A. C. Crispin (Pocket 1986 & 1988)

Vallejo fold-out cover 7.00
39. Crispin, A. C., *Time for Yesterday*, Pocket #60371-X, 1988, Boris Vallejo cover 6.00
40. Dvorkin, David, *Time Trap*, Pocket #64870-5, 1988 . . . . .6.00
41. Paul, Barbara, *The Three-Minute Universe*, Pocket #65816-6, 1988 . . . . .6.00
42. Reeves-Stevens, Garfield & Reeves-Stevens, Judith, *Memory Prime*, Pocket #65813-1, 1988 . . .6.00
43. DeWeese, Gene, *The Final Nexus*, Pocket #66018-7, 1988 . . . . .6.00
44. Fontana, D. C., *Vulcan's Glory*, Pocket #65667-8, 1989 . . . . .5.00
45. Friedman, Michael Jan, *Double, Double*, Pocket #66130-2, 1989 . . . . .5.00
46. Klass, Judy, *The Cry of the Onlies*, Pocket #68167-2, 1989 . . . . .5.00
47. Ecklar, Julia, *The Kobayashi Maru*, Pocket #65817-4, 1989 . . . . .5.00
48. Morwood, Peter, *Rules of Engagement*, Pocket #66129-9, 1990 .5.00
49. Clowes, Carolyn, *The Pandora Principle*, Pocket #65815-8, 1990 . . . . .5.00
50. Duane, Diane, *Doctor's Orders*, Pocket #66189-2, 1990 . . . . .5.00
51. Mitchell, V. E., *Enemy Unseen*, Pocket #68403-5, 1990 . . . . .5.00
52. Kramer-Rolls, Dana, *Home is the Hunter*, Pocket #66662-2 1990 . . . . .5.00
53. Hambly, Barbara, *Ghost-Walker*, Pocket #64398-8, 1991 . . . . .5.00
54. Ferguson, Brad, *A Flag Full of Stars*, Pocket #73918-2, 1991 . . . . .5.00
55. DeWeese, Gene, *Renegade*, Pocket #65814-X, 1991 . . . . .5.00
56. Friedman, Michael Jan, *Legacy*, Pocket #74468-2, 1991 . . . . .5.00
57. David, Peter, *Rift*, Pocket #74796-7, 1991 . . . . . . .6.00
58. Friedman, Michael Jan, *Faces of Fire*, Pocket #74992-7, 1992 . . . . .5.50
59. David, Peter & Michael Jan Friedman & Robert Greenberger, *The Disinherited*, Pocket #77958-3, 1992 . . . . .5.00
60. Graf, L. A., *Ice Trap*, Pocket #78068-9, 1992 . . . . . .5.00
61. Vornholt, John, *Sanctuary*, Pocket #76994-4, 1992 . .5.00

62. Graf, L. A., *Death Count*, Pocket #79322-5, 1992 . . .5.00
63. Grandall, Melissa, *Shell Game*, Pocket #79572-4, 1993 . . . . .5.50
64. Gilden, Mel, *The Starship Trap*, Pocket #79324-1, 1993 . . . . .5.50
65. Mitchell, V. E., *Windows of a Lost World*, Pocket #79512-0, 1993 . . . . .5.50
66. Milan, Victor, *From the Depths*, Pocket #86911-6, 1993 . . . . .5.50
67. Carey, Diane, *The Great Starship Race*, Pocket #87250-8, 1993 . . . . .6.00
68. Graf, L. A., *Firestorm*, Pocket #86588-9, 1993 . . . . .5.50
69. Hawke, Simon, *The Patrian Transgression*, Pocket #88044-6, 1994 . . . . .5.50
70. Graf, L. A., *Traitor Winds*, Pocket #86913-2 . . . . . .5.50
71. Hambly, Barbara, *Crossroad*, Pocket #79323-3, 1994 . .6.00
72. Weinstein, Howard, *The Better Man*, Pocket #86912-4, 1994 . . . . .5.50
73. Dillard, J. M., *Recovery*, Pocket #88342-9, 1995 . . .5.50
74. Flinn, Denny Martin, *The Fearful Summons*, Pocket #89007-7, 1995 . . . . .6.00
75. Carey, Diane & Dr. James I. Kirkland, *First Frontier*, Pocket #52045-8, 1995 . . . . .6.00
76. David, Peter, *The Captain's Daughter*, Pocket #52047-4, 1995 . . . . .6.00
77. Oltion, Jerry, *Twilight's End*, Pocket #53873-X, 1996 . .6.00
78. Smith, Dean Wesley & Kristine Kathryn Rusch, *The Rings of Tautee*, Pocket 00171-X, 1996 . . . . .6.00
79. Carey, Diane, *Invasion #1: First Strike*, Pocket #54002-5, 1996 . . . . .6.50
80. Gunn, James & Sturgeon, Theodore, *The Joy Machine*, Pocket #00221-S, 1996 . . . . .6.00
81. Oltion, Jerry, *Mudd in Your Eye*, Pocket #00260-0, 1996 . . . . .6.00
82. Vornholt, John, *Mind Meld*, Pocket #00258-9, 1997 . .6.00
83. Sargent, Pamela & Zebrowski, George, *Heart of the Sun*, Pocket #00237-6, 1997 . . . . .6.00
84. Cox, Greg, *Assignment: Eternity*, Pocket #00117-5, 1998 . . . . .6.00

Unnumbered

A number of *Star Trek* books have been published in hardcover in recent years. This is in addition to the numbered paperback originals which are regularly added to the four on-going series. Some of the hardcovers have made it on to best-sellers lists for a couple of months, which is extraordinary for a genre novel. Unfortunately, this works against the book becoming a valued collectible, because Pocket's print runs are correspondingly large. Books by Shatner would have the best chance of being collectible, but they have the largest print runs and nobody thinks he did much of the writing anyway. The best way to collect these books is to wait for them to be remaindered and buy them for about $5 each. You can't go wrong that way.

Bonanno, Margaret Wander, *Strangers from the Sky*, Pocket #73481-4, 1990 .6.00
Bonanno, Margaret Wander, *Probe*, Pocket #79065-X, 1992 . . . . .6.00
Carey, Diane, *Best Destiny*, Pocket #79588-0, 1993 . . . .6.00
Carey, Diane, *Final Frontier*, Pocket #64752-0, 1988 . . . .7.00
Crispin, A.C., *Sarek*, Pocket #79561-9, 1994 . . . . . . .25.00
    PB: Pocket #79562-7, 1995 . . . . .6.00
Dillard, J. M., *The Lost Years*, Pocket #68293-8, 1989 . .5.00
    SFBC: Pocket 15783-4, 1990 . . . . .5.00
Duane, Diane, *Spock's World*, Pocket #66851-X, 1988 . .5.00

Friedman, Michael Jan, *Shadows on the Sun*,
     Pocket 1993 . . . . .22.00
     PB: Pocket #86910-8, 1994 . . . . .6.00
Reeves-Stevens, Judith & Garfield, *Star Trek: Prime
     Directive*, Pocket #70772-8, 1990 . . . . .20.00
     SFBC: Pocket 17774-1, 1990 . . . . .7.50
     PB: Pocket 74466-6, 1991 . . . . .6.00
Reeves-Stevens, Judity & Garfield, *Federation*,
     Pocket #89422-6, 1994 . . . . .25.00
     PB: Pocket #89423-4, 1994 . . . . .6.50
Shatner, William & Reeves-Stevens, Judith & Garfield,
     The Ashes of Eden, Pocket #52035-0, 1995 . . . .30.00
     PB: Pocket #52036-9, 1995 . . . . .6.50
Shatner, William & Reeves-Stevens, Judith &
     Garfield, *The Return*, Pocket #52610-3, 1996 . . .25.00
     PB: Pocket #52609-X, 1997 . . . . .6.50
Shatner, William & Reeves-Stevens, Judith &
     Garfield, *Avenger*, Pocket #52132-9, 1997 . . . . .23.00
     PB: 6.50
Shatner, William, *Spectre*, Pocket #00878-1, 1998 . . . .23.00
Shatner, William, *Dark Victory*, Pocket #00882-X, 1999 . .23.00
Sherman, Josepha & Shwartz, Susan, *Vulcan's
     Forge*, Pocket #00926-5, 1997 . . . . .23.00
     PB: Pocket #00927-3, 1998 . . . . .6.50
Reprints of any of the above, each 5.00

STAR TREK: THE NEXT GENERATION

Pocket Books has been just as successful selling novels based on *The Next Generation* as with those based on the original *Star Trek* series. Over 40 novels have been published to date based on this series. None of these novels has attracted serious collector interest, as yet, and so they are worth about cover price, unless someone has read them. It's almost impossible to read a paperback without bending the spine and cover, and books in this condition are worth only a few dollars as reading copies.

Numbered

1. Carey, Diane, *Ghost Ship*, Pocket #66579-0, 1988 . . .8.00
2. DeWeese, Gene, *The Peacekeepers*, Pocket
     #66929-X, 1988 . . . . .7.00
3. Carter, Carmen, *The Children of Hamlin*, Pocket
     #67319-X, 1988 . . . . .6.00
4. Lorrah, Jean, *Survivors*, Pocket #67438-2, 1989 . . . .6.00
5. David, Peter, *Strike Zone*, Pocket #67940-6, 1989 . . .6.00
6. Weinstein, Howard, *Power Hungry*, Pocket

The Return *by William Shatner* & All Good Things *by Michael
Jan Friedman (Pocket 1997 & 1995)*

Imzadi *by Peter David &* Dark Mirror *by Diane Duane
(Pocket (1993 & 1994)*

     #67714-4, 1989 . . . . .5.00
7. Vornholt, John, *Masks*, Pocket #67980-5, 1989 . . . . .5.00
8. Dvorkin, Daniel & Dvorkin, David, *The Captain's
     Honor*, Pocket #68487-6, 1989 . . . . .5.00
9. Friedman, Michael Jan, *A Call to Darkness*,
     Pocket #68708-5, 1989 . . . . .5.00
10. David, Peter, *A Rock and a Hard Place*, Pocket
     #69364-6, 1990 . . . . .6.00
11. Sharee, Keith, *Gulliver's Fugitives*, Pocket
     #70130-4, 1990 . . . . .5.00
12. Carter, Carmen & Peter David & Friedman,
     Michael Jan, *Doomsday World*, Pocket
     #70237-8, 1990 . . . . .5.00
13. Crispin, Ann, *The Eyes of the Beholder*, Pocket
     #70010-3, 1990 . . . . .5.00
14. Weinstein, Howard, *Exiles*, Pocket #70560-1, 1990 . .5.00
15. Friedman, Michael Jan, *Fortune's Light*, Pocket
     #70836-8, 1991 . . . . .5.00
16. Vornholt, John, *Contamination*, Pocket #70561-
     X, 1991 . . . . .5.00
17. Gilden, Mel, *Boogeyman*, Pocket #70970-4, 1991 . .5.00
18. David, Peter, *Q-In-Law*, Pocket #73389-3, 1991 . . . .6.00
19. Weinstein, Howard, *Perchance To Dream*,
     Pocket #70837-6, 1992 . . . . .5.00
20. Mancour, T. L., *Spartacus*, Pocket #76051-X, 1992 . . .5.00
21. McCay, A. W. & Flood, E. L., *Chains of
     Command*, Pocket #74264-7, 1992 . . . . .5.00
22. Mitchell, V. E., *Imbalance*, Pocket #77571-5, 1992 . . .5.00
23. Vornhold, John, *War Drums*, Pocket #79236-9, 1992 . .5.00
24. Hamilton, Laurell, *Nightshade*, Pocket #79566-X, 1992 .5.00
25. Bischoff, David, *Grounded*, Pocket #79747-6, 1993 . .6.00
26. Hawke, Simon, *The Romulan Prize*, Pocket
     #79746-8, 1993 . . . . .5.00
27. Vornholt, John, *Guises of the Mind*, Pocket
     #79236-9, 1993 . . . . .5.00
28. Peel, John, *Here There Be Dragons*, Pocket
     #86571-4, 1993 . . . . .5.00
29. Wright, Susan, *Sins of Commission*, Pocket
     #79704-2, 1993 . . . . .5.00
30. Thompson, W. R., *Debtors' Planet*, Pocket
     #88341-0, 1994; 5.00
31. Galanter, David & Brodeur, Greg, *Foreign Foes*,
     Pocket #88414-X, 1994 . . . . .5.00
32. Friedman, John & Ryan, Kevin, *Requiem*, Pocket
     #79576-8, 1995 . . . . .5.00
33. ab Hugh, Dafydd, *Balance of Power*, Pocket
     #52003-2, 1995 . . . . .5.00

34. Hawke, Simon, *Glaze of Glory*, Pocket #88045-4, 1995 .5.00
35. Greenberger, Robert, *The Romulan Strategem*, Pocket #87997-9, 1995 . . . . .5.00
36. DeWeese, Gene, *Into the Nebula*, Pocket #89453-6, 1995 . . . . .5.00
37. Ferguson, Brad, *The Last Stand*, Pocket #50105-4, 1995 . . . . .5.00
38. Johnson, J. S. & Cox, Greg, *Dragon's Honor*, Pocket #50107-0 1996 . . . . .5.00
39. Vorn Holt, John, *Rogue Saucer*, Pocket #54197-0, 1996 . . . . .5.00
40. Dillard, J. M. & O'Malley, Kathleen, *Possession*, Pocket #86485-8; 1996 . . . . .5.00
41. Smith, Dean Wesley & Rusch, Kristine Kathryn, *Invasion 2: The Soldier of Fear*, Pocket #54174-9, 1996 . . . . .5.00
42. Thompson, W. R., *Infiltrator*, Pocket #56831-0, 1996 ..5.00
43. Sargent, Pamela & Zebrowski, George, *A Fury Scorned*, Pocket #52703-7, 1996 . . . . .6.00
44. Peel, John, *The Death of Princes*, Pocket #56808-6, 1996 . . . . .5.00
45. Duane, Diane, *Intellivore*, Pocket #56832-9, 1997 ..6.00
46. Friesner, Esther, *To Storm Haven*, Pocket #56838-8, 1997 . . . . .6.00
47. Cox, Greg, *The Q Continuum: Q-Space*, Pocket #01915-5, 1997 . . . . .6.00
48. Cox, Greg, *The Q Continuum: Q-Zone*, Pocket #01921-X, 1997 . . . . .6.00
49. Cox, Greg, *The Q Continuum: Q-Strike*, Pocket #01922-8, 1998 . . . . .6.00

Unnumbered
Carey, Diane, *Ship of the Line*, Pocket #00924-9, 1997 . . . . .22.00
    PB: 5.00
Carey, Diane, *Descent*, Pocket #88267-8, 1993 . . . . . .6.00
Carter, Carmen, *The Devil's Heart*, Pocket #79426-4, 1994 .6.00
David, Peter, *Q-Squared*, Pocket #89152-9, 1994 . . .22.00
    PB: Pocket #89151-0, 1995 . . . . .6.00
David, Peter, *Imzadi*, Pocket 1993 . . . . .22.00
    PB: Pocket #86729-6, 1993 . . . . .6.00
    PB: Pocket #02610-0, 1998 . . . . .4.00
David, Peter, *Imzadi II, Triangle*, Pocket #02532-5, 1998 .23.00
David, Peter, *Vendetta*, Pocket #74145-4, 1991 . . . . . . .6.00
Duane, Diane, *Dark Mirror*, Pocket #79438-8, 1994 . . . .6.00
Friedman, Michael Jan, *All Good Things*, Pocket #50014-7 1995 . . . . .20.00
    PB: Pocket #52148-9, 1995 . . . . .6.00
Friedman, Michael Jan, *Crossover*, Pocket #89677-6, 1995 . . . . .23.00
    PB: Pocket #89676-8, 1996 . . . . .6.00
Friedman, Michael Jan, *Kahless*, Pocket #54779-8, 1996 . . . . .23.00
    PB: Pocket #00887-0, 1997 . . . . .6.00
Friedman, Michael Jan, *Relics*, Pocket #86476-9, 1992 .6.00
Friedman, Michael Jan, *Reunion*, Pocket #78755-1, 1994 .6.00
Friedman, Michael Jan, *Planet X*, Pocket #99994-3, 1996 (X-Men crossover) 6.00
Gerrold, David, *Encounter at Farpoint*, Pocket #65241-9, 1987 . . . . .6.00
Lorrah, Jean, *Metamorphosis*, Pocket #68402-7, 1990 . . .6.00
Smith, Dean Wesley & Rusch, Kristine Kathryn, *Star Trek: Klingon*, Pocket #00257-0, 1996 . . . . .6.00
Taylor, Jeri, *Unification*, Pocket #77056-X, 1991 . . . . . . .6.00
Vornholt, John, *The Dominion War #1*, Pocket #02499-X, 1996 . . . . .6.00
Wright, Susan, *Sins of Commission*, Pocket #79704-

2, 1994 . . . . .6.00
Wright, Susan, *The Best and the Brightest*, Pocket #01549-4, 1998 . . . . .6.50

STAR TREK DEEP SPACE NINE

Pocket Books sells novels based on *Deep Space Nine* and *Star Trek Voyager*, as well as the other two TV series. None of them has become a high-priced collectible, but they have proved to be just as popular with readers as the classic *Star Trek* and *The Next Generation* series.

Numbered
1. Dillard, J. M., *Emissary*, Pocket #79858-8, 1993 . . . .6.00
2. David, Peter, *The Seige*, Pocket #87083-1, 1993 . . . .6.00
3. Jeter, K. W., *Bloodletter*, Pocket #87275-3, 1993 . . . .6.00
4. Schofield, Sandy, *The Big Game*, Pocket #88030-6, 1993 . . . . .6.00
5. ab Hugh, Dafydd, *Fallen Heroes*, Pocket #88459-X, 1994 . . . . .6.00
6. Tilton, Lois, *Betrayal*, Pocket #88177-5, 1994 . . . . . .6.00
7. Friesner, Esther, *Warchild*, Pocket #88116-7, 1994 . . .6.00
8. Vornholt, John, *Antimatter*, Pocket #88560-X, 1994 . . .6.00
9. Scott, Melissa, *Proud Helios*, Pocket #88390-9, 1995 .6.00
10. Archer, Nathan, *Valhalla*, Pocket #88115-9, 1995 . . .6.00
11. Cox, Greg & Betancourt, John Gregory, *Devil in the Sky*, Pocket #88114-0, 1995 . . . . .6.00
12. Sheckley, Robert, *The Laertian Gamble*, Pocket #88690-8, 1995 . . . . .6.00
13. Carey, Diane, *Station Rage*, Pocket #88561-8, 1995 ..6.00
14. Smith Dean Wesley & Rausch, Kristine Kathryn, *The Long Night*, Pocket #55165-5, 1996 . . . . .6.00
15. Peel, John, *Objective Bajor*, Pocket #56811-6, 1996 ..6.00
16. Graf, L. A., *Invasion 3: Time's Enemy*, Pocket #54150-1, 1996 . . . . .6.00
17. Betancourt, John Gregory, *The Heart of the Warrior*, Pocket #00239-2, 1996 . . . . .6.00
18. Friedman, Michael Jan, *Saratoga*, Pocket #56897-3, 1996 . . . . .6.00
19. Wright, Susan, *The Tempest*, Pocket #00227-9, 1997 . . . . .6.00
20. David, Peter & Friedman, Michael Jan, *Wrath of the Prophets*, Pocket #53817-9, 1997 . . . . .6.00
21. Garland, Mark A., *Trial By Error*, Pocket #00251-1, 1997 . . . . .6.00
22. ab Hugh, Dafydd, *Vengeance*, Pocket #00468-9, 1998 .6.00

Star Trek: Deep Space Nine: Warped *by K. W. Jeter & The Laertian Gamble by Robert Sheckley & (Pocket 1995)*

 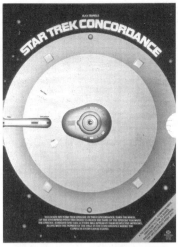 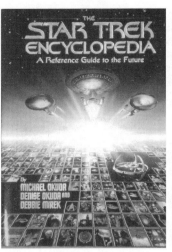 

Star Trek Voyager: The Garden *by Melissa Scott (Pocket 1997),* Star Trek Concordance *by Bjo Trimble (Ballantine 1976),* The Star Trek Encyclopedia *by Okuda, Okuda & Mirek (Pocket 1994) &* The Making of Star Trek *by Whitfield & Roddenberry (Ballantine 1968)*

Unnumbered

Barnes, Steve, *Far Beyond the Stars*, Pocket
#02430-2, 1998 . . . . .6.50
Carey, Diane, *The Search*, Pocket #50604-8, 1994 . . . .5.50
Carey, Diane, *Trials and Tribble-ations*, Pocket
#00902-8, 1996 . . . . .4.00
Carey, Diane, *The Way of the Warrior*, Pocket
#56813-2, 1995 . . . . .6.00
Carey, Diane, *The Dominion War #2*, Pocket
#02497-3, 1998 . . . . .6.50
Jeter, K. W., *Warped*, Pocket #87252-4, 1995. . . . . . .22.00
PB: Pocket #56781-0, 1996 . . . . .6.00

STAR TREK VOYAGER

Numbered

1. Graf, L. A., *Caretaker*, Pocket #51914-X, 1995 . . . . . .6.00
2. Smith, Dean Wesley & Kristine Kathryn Rusch:
The Escape, Pocket #52096-2 1995 . . . . .6.00
3. Archer, Nathan, *Ragnarok*, Pocket #52044-X, 1995 . . .6.00
4. Wright, Susan, *Violations*, Pocket #52046-6, 1995 . . .6.00
5. Betancourt, John Gregory, *Incident at Arbuk*,
Pocket #52048-5, 1995 .6.00
6. Golden, Christie, *The Murdered Sun*, Pocket
#53783-0, 1996 . . . . .6.00
7. Garland, Mark A. & Charles G. McGraw, *Ghost of
a Chance*, Pocket #56798-5, 1996 . . . . .6.00
8. Lewitt, S. N., *Cybersong*, Pocket #56783-7, 1996 . . . .6.00
9. ab Hugh, Dafydd, *Invasion 4: The Final Fury*,
Pocket #54181-1, 1996 .6.00
10. Haber, Karen, *Bless the Beasts*, Pocket #56780-
2, 1996 . . . . .6.00
11. Scott, Melissa, *The Garden*, Pocket #56799-3, 1997 .6.00
12. Wilson, David Niall, *Chrysalis*, Pocket #00150-7, 1997 .6.00
13. Cox, Greg, *The Black Shore*, Pocket #56061-1, 1997 .6.00
14. Golden, Christie, *Marooned*, Pocket #01423-4, 1997 . .6.00
15. Smith, Dean Wesley, Rusch, Kristine Kathryn &
Hoffman, Nina Kiriki, *Echoes*, Pocket
#00200-7, 1998 . . . . .6.00
16. Golden, Christie, *Seven of Nine*, Pocket #02491-
4, 1998 . . . . .6.00

Unnumbered

Braga, Brannon & Carey, Diane L., *Flashback*,
Pocket #00383-6, 1996 .6.00
Taylor, Jeri, *Mosaic*, Pocket #56311-4, 1996 . . . . .22.00
PB: Pocket #56312-2, 1997 . . . . .6.00
Taylor, Jeri, *Pathways*, Pocket #00346-1, 1998 . . . . . .23.00

CROSSOVERS
Day of Honor

1. Friedman, Michael Jan & Taylor, Jeri, *Day of
Honor: The Television Episode, A Novel*,
Pocket #01981-3, 1997 (Voyager) 6.00
2. Graf, L. A., *Armageddon Sky*, Pocket #00675-4
(Deep Space Nine) 6.00
3. Friedman, Michael Jan, *Her Klingon Soul*, Pocket
#00240-6, 1997 (Voyager) 6.00
4. Smith, Dean Wesley & Rusch, Kristine Kathryn,
Treaty's Law, Pocket #00424-7, 1997 (Classic) . . .6.00

The Captains Table

1. Graf, L. A. *War Dragons*, Pocket #01463-3, 1998
(Classic) 6.50
2. Friedman, Michael Jan, *Dujonian's Hoard*, Pocket
#01465-X, 1998 (The Next Generation) 6.50
3. Smith, Dean Wesley & Rusch, Kristine Kathryn,
The Mist, Pocket #01471-4, 1998 (Deep
Space Nine) 6.50
4. Carey, Diane, *Fire Ship*, Pocket #01467-6, 1998
(Star Trek Voyager) 6.50
5. David, Peter, *One Burned*, Pocket #02078-1,
1998 (New Frontier) 6.50
6. Oltion, Jerry, *Where Sea Meets Sky*, Pocket
#02400-0, 1998 . . . . .6.50

New Frontier

1. David, Peter, *Book 1: House of Cards*, Pocket
#01395-5, 1998 . . . . .4.00
2. David, Peter, *Book 2: Into The Void*, Pocket
#01396-3, 1998 . . . . .4.00
3. David, Peter, *Book 3: The Two Front War*, Pocket
#01397-1, 1998 . . . . .4.00
4. David, Peter, *Book 4: End Game*, Pocket #01398-
X, 1998 . . . . .4.00
5. David, Peter, *Book 5: Martyr*, Pocket #02936-6,
1998 . . . . .4.00
6. David, Peter, *Book 6: Fire on High*, Pocket
#02037-4, 1998 . . . . .6.00
David, Peter, *New Frontier*, Pocket HC #01978-3
(paperback size) rep. #1–#4 . . . . .15.00

Star Trek Voyager: Starfleet Academy

1. Weiss, Bobbi J. G. & Weiss, David Cody, *Lifeline*,
Pocket Minstrel #00845-5, 1997 . . . . .4.00
Turtleback 10.00

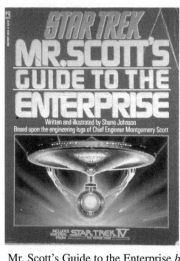
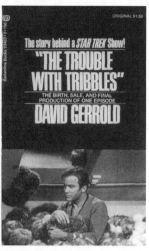

Mr. Scott's Guide to the Enterprise *by Shane Johnson (Pocket 1987)* & The Trouble With Tribbles *by David Gerrold (Ballantine 1973)*

2. Gallagher, Diana G. & Burke, Martin G., *The Chance Factor*, Pocket Minstrel, 00732-7, 1997 . . .5.00
   Turtleback 10.00
3. Barnes-Svarney, Patricia L., *Quarantine*, 1997 . . . . . .5.00
   Turtleback 10.00

Star Trek Non-Fiction
Art Books
Reeves-Stevens, Judity & Garfield, *The Art of Star Trek*, Pocket 1995 . . . . .55.00

Cast Memoirs
Shatner, William & Shatner, Lisbeth, *The Captain's Log: William Shatner's Personal Account*, Pocket #68652-6, 1989 . . . . .25.00
Beyond Uhura, Star Trek & Other Memories by Nichelle Nichols, Putnam 1994, photo cover. . . .20.00
Koenig, Walter, *Star Trek: Chekov's Enterprise*, Pocket 1980 . . . . .25.00

Other Non-fiction
Johnson, Shane, *Star Trek: The Worlds of the Federation*, Pocket TPB #66989-3, 1989 . . . . . . .13.00
Asherman, Allan, *The Star Trek Compendium*, Pocket TPB #68440-X, 1989 . . . . .15.00
Asherman, Allan, *The Star Trek Interview Book*, Pocket #61794-X, 1988 . . . . .15.00
Gerrold, David, *The Trouble With Tribbles*, Ballantine Books #23402-2, 1973, illustrations by Tim Kirk and 32 pages of black & white photos. 15.00
Whitfield, Stephen & Roddenberry, Gene, *The Making of Star Trek*, Ballantine Books #73004, 1968, with 64 pages of photos 25.00
Gross, Edward, *The Making of the Next Generation*, Pioneer #219-4, 1989 .20.00
Johnson, Shane, *Mr. Scott's Guide to the Enterprise*, illustrated by Shane Johnson, Pocket TPB #63576-X, 1987 . . . . .15.00
Trimble, Bjo, *Star Trek Concordance*, Ballantine Books TPB #25137, 1976 . . . . .50.00
Okuda, Michael, Okuda, Denise & Mirek, Debbie, *The Star Trek Encyclopedia*, Pocket #88689-3, 1994 . . . . .50.00
Peel, John, *The Trek Encyclopedia Second Edition*, Pioneer Books TPB #350-6, 1992, includes all 6 movies. 20.00

Sternback, Rick & Okuda, Michael, *Star Trek, The Next Generation Technical Manual*, Pocket Books TPB #70427-3, 1991 . . . . .15.00
Dillard, J. M., *Star Trek Where No One Has Gone Before, A History in Pictures*, Pocket Books 1994 . . . . .50.00
Van Hise, James & Schuster, Hal, *Unauthorized and Uncensored Trek Crew Companion*, Pioneer Books TPB345-X, 1994, covers all four series 20.00
Gerrold, David, *The World of Star Trek*, revised edition including information from Star Trek III, Bluejay Books TPB #94463-2, 1984 . . . . . . .20.00
The Physics of Star Trek, by Lawrence M. Krauss, Basic Books 1995 . . . . .20.00

Trek Magazine
1. Irwin & Love ed., *The Best of Trek*, Signet #08030-0, 1978 . . . . .10.00
2. Irwin & Love ed., *The Best of Trek #2*, Signet #13466-4, 1979 . . . . .8.00
3. Irwin & Love ed., *The Best of Trek #3*, Signet #13092-8, 1980 . . . . .8.00
4. Irwin & Love ed., *The Best of Trek #4*, Signet #11221-0, 1981, Eddie Jones 8.00
5. Irwin & Love ed., *The Best of Trek #5*, Signet #11751-4, 1982 . . . . .8.00
6. Irwin & Love ed., *The Best of Trek #6*, Signet #12493-6, 1983, Paul Alexander 8.00
7. Irwin & Love ed., *The Best of Trek #7*, Signet #12977-6, 1984, Eddie Jones 8.00
8. Irwin & Love ed., *The Best of Trek #8*, Signet #13488-5, 1985, Paul Alexander 8.00
9. Irwin & Love ed., *The Best of Trek #9*, Signet #13816-3, 1985 . . . . .8.00
10. Irwin & Love ed., *The Best of Trek #10*, Signet #14311-6, 1986 . . . . .8.00
11. Irwin & Love ed., *The Best of Trek #11*, Signet #14576-3, 1986, Paul Alexander 8.00
12. Irwin & Love ed., *The Best of Trek #12*, Signet #14935-1, 1987 . . . . .8.00
13. Irwin, Walter & Love, G. B. eds., *The Best of Trek #13*, Signet #15325-1, 1988 . . . . .8.00
14. Irwin, Walter, *The Best of Trek #14*, Signet #15614-5, 1988 . . . . .8.00
15. Irwin, Walter & Love, G. B. eds., *The Best of Trek #15*, Roc #45015-9, 1990 . . . . .8.00

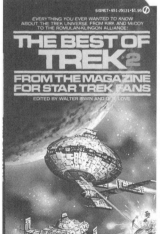
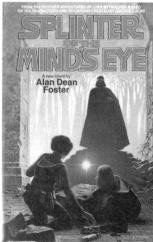

The Best of Trek #2 *by Irwin & Love, ed. (Signet 1979)* & Splinter of the Mind's Eye *by Alan Dean Foster (Ballantine Del Rey 1978)*

Star Wars *by George Lucas &* The Empire Strikes Back *by Donald Glut (Science Fiction Book Club 1978 & 1980)*

STAR WARS

The very first mass market *Star Wars* item produced was the movie novelization paperback book which appeared in late November 1976, seven months before the movie opened. No one knew how big the movie would be and the book had a very normal first print run. The first edition can be identified by the line "First Edition: December 1976" at the bottom, on the copyright page. The paperback was reprinted many times and none of these are scarce, or valuable.

The novel appeared in hardcover in the fall of 1977. The trade hardcover is scarce and valuable. It has a gold dust jacket, and says "Hardbound Ballantine Books Edition: October 1977/First Edition: December 1976" in two lines on the copyright page.

While the first paperback edition and the hardcover edition enjoy cross-over collector interest from persons who are not primarily *Star Wars* fans, book club editions have no collector following whatsoever apart from die-hard *Star Wars* fans. Consequently, the book-club edition of the original *Star Wars* novel, and for that matter, any *Star Wars novel*, is not valuable. The one exception might be the very first printing of the book-club edition of *Star Wars*. This can be identified by the printing code "S27" in the gutter on page 183. It appeared before the trade hardcover, making it the first hardcover edition of the book.

After the other movies were novelized and a few original novels were published, there was a slack time, but in mid 1991, *Star Wars* novels returned with Timothy Zahn's *Heir to the Empire*. This book made it to the top of the *New York Times* bestseller lists. In the 1990s, the books (and the comics) have overall continuity. This makes these novels important in the *Star Wars* universe, because there are only about six hours of actual films.

Movie Novelizations

Star Wars, by Alan Dean Foster (uncredited ghost
    writer) from screenplay by George Lucas,
    Ballantine #26061-9, Dec. 1976 . . . . .25.00
    Ballantine-Del Rey #26079-1, Aug. 1977,
      Movie tie-in 10.00
    SFBC: Del Rey #2403-4, 1977, with 16 pages

of color photos from the movie, printing
    code S27 . . . . .15.00
    HC: Del Rey 1977, with movie photos 60.00
    Paperback reprints 4.00

The Empire Strikes Back, by Donald F. Glut,
    Ballantine-Del Rey #28392-9, May 1980 . . . . . . .15.00
    SFBC: Del Rey #3863-8, 1980, code K29 . . . . . .10.00
    HC: Ballantine-Del Rey 1994 . . . . .16.00
    Paperback reprints 4.00

Return of the Jedi, by James Kahn, Ballantine-
    Del Rey #30767-4, June 1983 . . . . .10.00
    SFBC: Del Rey #2144-4, 1983, code N31 . . . . . .12.00
    HC: Ballantine-Del Rey 1994 . . . . .16.00
    Paperback reprints 4.00

Star Wars Trilogy by George Lucas, Donald F.
    Glut & James Kahn, Del Rey TPB #34806-0,
    1987 . . . . .10.00

Movie Novelizations: Illustrated Editions
The Empire Strikes Back: The Illustrated Edition,
    by Donald F. Glut, Del Rey #28831-9, 1980,
    Ralph McQuarrie illustrations and cover 10.00
Return of the Jedi Illustrated Edition, by James
    Kahn, Del Rey #30960-X, June 1983 . . . . .10.00

Novels (1978–89)
Splinter of the Mind's Eye, by Alan Dean Foster,
    Del Rey 1978 . . . . .20.00
    SFBC: Del Rey 2597-3, 1978 . . . . .5.00
    PB: Ballantine-Del Rey #26062-7, 1978 . . . . .6.00
    Paperback reprints 5.00

Han Solo Series, by Brian Daley
Han Solo at Stars' End, Del Rey 1979 . . . . .20.00
    SFBC: Del Rey 3356-3, 1979 . . . . .5.00
    PB: Ballantine-Del Rey #29664-8, 1979 . . . . .5.00
    Paperback reprints 5.00
Han Solo's Revenge, Del Rey 1979 . . . . .20.00
    SFBC: Del Rey #3670-7, 1980 . . . . .5.00
    PB: Ballantine-Del Rey #28840-8, 1980 . . . . .5.00
    Paperback reprints 5.00
Han Solo and the Lost Legacy, Ballantine-Del Rey
    #28710-X, 1980 . . . . .10.00
    SFBC: Del Rey #3398-5, Dec. 1980 . . . . .7.50

Han Solo at Stars' End *&* Han Solo's Revenge
by Brian Daley (Del Rey 1979)

Paperback reprints 5.00
Combined edition: *The Han Solo Adventures*,
   Del Rey #37980-2, 1992 . . . . .6.00

Lando Calrissian Series, by L. Neil Smith
Lando Calrissian and the Mindharp of Sharu,
   Ballantine-Del Rey #31158-2, 1983 . . . . .15.00
   SFBC: Del Rey #3639-2, 1984 . . . . .5.00
Lando Calrissian and the Flamewind of Oseon,
   Ballantine-Del Rey #31163-9, 1983 . . . . .15.00
   SFBC: Del Rey #3588-1, 1984 . . . . .5.00
Lando Calrissian and the Starcave of ThonBoka,
   Ballantine-Del Rey #31164-7, 1983 . . . . .15.00
   SFBC: none
Classic Star Wars: The Lando Calrissian Adven-
   tures, Del Rey #39110-1, 1994 . . . . .6.00

Novels (1990–98)
   Timothy Zahn's *Heir to the Empire* launched the current
phase of *Star Wars* publishing. It appeared about six months
before the first Dark Horse Comic — *Dark Empire* and it
reached #1 on the *New York Times* bestseller's list. As the first
collectible of the 1990s, after the 1985 to 1990 dark ages, this
book is highly collectible.

   The novels and story collections are listed below in their
approximate order of appearance, based on the first book in
the series. Titles first published in hardcover appear first, followed by paperback series.

   Now that publication of new *Star Wars* novels is in full
swing, print runs are large and price appreciation is unlikely.
The best way to collect is to wait until the hardcover book you
want is available for half price or less on the remainder tables
at your favorite book store; and then look through all of them
to find a first edition. You can accumulate a handsome hardcover collection this way, at reasonable prices.

Novels and Story Collections (1990–98)
Hardcover originals:
Grand Admiral Thrawn series by Timothy Zahn
Heir to the Empire, Bantam Spectra 1991 . . . . .30.00
   Limited Ed. HC: Bantam 1991, signed, in
      slipcase 150.00

SFBC: Bantam #18382-2, 1991 . . . . .5.00
PB: Bantam Spectra #29612-4, 1992 . . . . .6.00
Dark Force Rising, Bantam Spectra 1992 . . . . .25.00
   Limited Ed. HC: Bantam June 1992, signed,
      in slipcase 140.00
   SFBC: Bantam #19949-7, 1992 . . . . .7.00
   PB: Bantam Spectra #56071-9, 1993 . . . . .5.00
The Last Command, Bantam Spectra 1993 . . . . .25.00
   Limited Ed. HC: not seen 140.00
   SFBC: Bantam #00913, 1993 . . . . .7.00
   PB: Bantam Spectra #56492-7, 1994 . . . . .5.00

Other Novels
The Truce At Bakura, by Kathleen Tyers, Bantam
   Spectra 1994 . . . . .25.00
   SFBC: Bantam #02501, 1994 . . . . .7.00
   PB: Bantam Spectra #56872-8, 1994 . . . . .5.00
The Courtship Of Princess Leia, by Dave Wolverton,
   Bantam Spectra 1994 . . . . .25.00
   SFBC: Bantam #03409, 1994 . . . . .7.00
   PB: Bantam Spectra #56937-6, 1995 . . . . .5.00
The Crystal Star, by Vonda N. McIntyre, Bantam
   Spectra 1994 . . . . .25.00
   SFBC: Bantam #06637, 1995 . . . . .7.00
   PB: Bantam Spectra #57174-5 1995 . . . . .5.00
Children of the Jedi, Barbara Hambly, Bantam
   Spectra 1995 . . . . .25.00
   SFBC: Bantam #07692, 1995 . . . . .8.00
   PB: Bantam Spectra #57293-8, 1996 . . . . .5.00
Star Wars Darksaber, by Kevin J. Anderson, Bantam
   Spectra 1995 . . . . .25.00
   SFBC: Bantam 1995 . . . . .8.00
   PB: Bantam Spectra #56611-9, 1996 . . . . .5.00
Shadows Of The Empire, by Steve Perry, Bantam
   Spectra 1996 . . . . .25.00
   SFBC: Bantam 1996 . . . . .8.00
   PB: Bantam Spectra #57413-2, 1997 . . . . .5.00
The New Rebellion, by Kristine Kathryn Rusch,
   Bantam Spectra 1996 . . . . .25.00
   SFBC: Bantam #14441, 1997 . . . . .8.00
   PB: Bantam Spectra #57414-0, 1997 . . . . .5.00
Planet of Twilight, by Barbara Hambly, Bantam
   Spectra 1997 . . . . .25.00
   SFBC: Bantam 1997 . . . . .8.00
   PB: Bantam Spectra #57517-1, 1998 . . . . .6.00

*The second and third Lando Calrissian novels by L. Neil Smith
(Ballantine Del Rey 1983)*

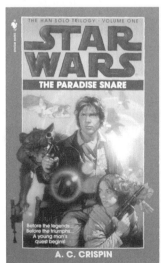

The Han Solo Trilogy: The Paradise Snare & Rebel Dawn *by A. C.
Crispin (Bantam 1997 & 1998)*

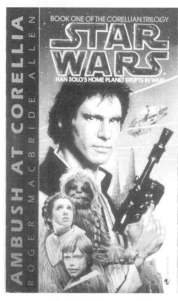  

Ambush at Corellia *by Roger MacBride Allen (Bantam 1995)* Star Wars: The Essential Guide to Characters *by Andy Mangels*
(Del Rey 1995) & The Art of Dave Dorman *edited by Stephen D. Smith & Lurene Haines (Friedlander 1996)*

Specter of the Past, by Timothy Zahn, Bantam
    Spectra 1997 . . . . .24.00
    SFBC: Bantam 1997 .8.00
    PB: Bantam Spectra #29804-6, 1998 . . . . .6.00
I, Jedi, by Michael Stackpole, Bantam Spectra 1998 . .24.00
Vision of the Future, Bantam Spectra 1998 . . . . .24.00

Paperback originals:
The Jedi Academy Trilogy by Kevin J. Anderson
1. *Jedi Search*, Bantam Spectra #29798-8, 1994 . . . . . .6.00
2. *Dark Apprentice*, Bantam Spectra #29799-6, 1994 . . .5.00
3. *Champions of the Force*, Bantam Spectra
    #29802-X, 1994 . . . . .5.00
The Jedi Academy Trilogy, combined edition,
    SFBC: $14.98, Bantam #0562 . . . . .10.00

The Corellian Trilogy by Roger McBride Allen
1. *Ambush At Corellia*, Bantam Spectra #29803-8,
    1995 . . . . .5.00
2. *Assault At Selonia*, Bantam Spectra #29805-4,
    1995 . . . . .5.00
3. *Showdown At Centerpoint*, Bantam Spectra
    #29806-2, 1995 . . . . .5.00
The Corellian Trilogy, combined edition
    SFBC: Bantam 10.00

Star Wars Tales edited by Kevin J. Anderson
Star Wars: Tales from the Mos Eisley Cantina,
    Bantam Spectra #56468-4, 1995 . . . . .5.00
Star Wars Tales From Jabba's Palace, Bantam
    Spectra #56815-9, 1996 . . . . .5.00
Star Wars: Tales of the Bounty Hunters, Bantam
    Spectra #56816-7, 1996, ...5.00

Black Fleet Crisis by Michael Kube-McDowell
1. *Before The Storm*, Bantam Spectra #57273-3, 1996 . .6.00
2. *Shield of Lies*, Bantam Spectra #57277-6, 1996 . . . . .6.00
3. *Tyrant's Test*, Bantam Spectra #57275-X, 1997 . . . . .6.00
Black Fleet Crisis, combined edition, SFBC, Bantam
    #15119 . . . . .10.00

X-Wing series, by Michael A. Stackpole
1. *Rogue Squadron*, Bantam Spectra #56801-9, 1996 . . .6.00

2. *Wedge's Gamble*, Bantam Spectra #56802-7, 1996 . . .6.00
3. *The Krytos Trap*, Bantam Spectra #56803-5, 1996 . . .6.00
4. *The Bacta War*, Bantam Spectra #56804-3, 1997 . . . .6.00
by Aaron Allston
5. *Wraith Squadron*, Bantam Spectra #57894-4, 1998 . . .6.00
6. *Iron Fist*, Bantam Spectra #57897-9, 1998 . . . . .6.00

Han Solo Trilogy by A.C. Crispin
1. *Star Wars The Paradise Snare*, Bantam Spectra
    #57415-7, 1997 . . . . .6.00
2. *Star Wars The Hutt Gambit*, Bantam Spectra
    #57416-7, 1997 . . . . .6.00
3. *Rebel Dawn*, Bantam Spectra #57417-5, 1998 . . . . . .6.00

Bounty Hunter Wars by K. W. Jeter
1. *The Mandalorian Armor*, Bantam Spectra #57885-
    5, 1998 . . . . .6.00
2. *Slave Ship*, Bantam Spectra #57888-X, 1998 . . . . . . .6.00

Schweighofer, Peter ed.: *Star Wars: Tales from the
    Empire*, Bantam Spectra #57876-6, 1997 . . . . . .5.00

NON-FICTION

Star Wars books come in every conceivable category of
non-fiction. There are art books, sketch books, making of the
movie books, reference books, humor books and even fictional non-fiction books. Many books include elements of
several categories, making organization of the following lists
problematic. You may have to search a little for the title you
are interested in.

Art of... Books
The Art of Star Wars, edited by Carol Titelman,
    Ballantine Books 1979 . . . . .25.00
    TPB: Ballantine #27666-3, 1979 . . . . .15.00
    SFBC: Ballantine #3823-2, Summer 1980 . . . . . .15.00
Retitled: *The Art of Star Wars, Episode IV, A New
    Hope*, Del Rey TPB #39202-7, 1994 . . . . .20.00
Revised as: *Second Edition of The Art of Star Wars:
    A New Hope*, by Carol Titelman & George
    Lucas, Del Rey TPB #39202-7, 1997 . . . . .19.00
The Art of the Empire Strikes Back, edited by

The Time Tunnel & Timeslip! *by Murray Leinster (Pyramid 1967)*

Deborah Call Del Rey, 1980 . . . . .25.00
SFBC: Del Rey 5579-8, 1981 . . . . .15.00
TPB: Ballantine #28833-5, 1980 . . . . .15.00
Retitled: *The Art of Star Wars, Episode V, The
    Empire Strikes Back*, Ballantine/Del Rey TPB
    #39203-5, 1994, repackaged 20.00
Revised as: *Second Edition of The Art of Star Wars:
    The Empire Strikes Back*, edited by Deborah
    Call, Del Rey TPB #39203-5, 1997 . . . . .19.00
The Art of Return of the Jedi, including the film script
    by Lawrence Kasdan and George Lucas, Del
    Rey, Nov. 1983 . . . . .25.00
SFBC: Del Rey 5393-4, 1984 . . . . .15.00
Retitled: *The Art of Star Wars, Episode VI, Return of
    the Jedi*, Del Rey TPB #39204-3, 1994 . . . . . . .20.00
Revised as: *Second Edition of The Art of Star Wars:
    Return of the Jedi*, Del Rey TPB #39204-3,
    1997, adds material from the special edition 19.00
The Art of Star Wars Galaxy edited by Gary Cerani,
    Topps TPB #01-5, 1993 . . . . .20.00
    HC: Underwood Miller 1994, limited to
        1,000 copies, boxed, signed 150.00
The Art of Star Wars Galaxy, Volume Two by C.
    Cerani and Gary Cerani, Topps TPB #03-1,
    1994 . . . . .20.00
Star Wars: The Art of the Brothers Hildebrandt, by
    Bob Woods, Ballantine TPB #42301-1, 1997 . . . .25.00
Star Wars: The Art of Dave Dorman, edited by
    Stephen D. Smith and Lurene Haines,
    Friedlander 1996, signed, 2,500 copies 75.00
    TPB: Friedlander #37-5, Dec. 1996 . . . . .25.00
The Illustrated Star Wars Universe, edited by Martha
    Banta, Bantam 1995 .20.00
The Illustrated Star Wars Universe, by Kevin J.
    Anderson, Bantam Spectra, 1995 . . . . .35.00
    TPB, Bantam 37484-2, 1997 . . . . .18.00
Industrial Light & Magic: The Art of Special Effects,
    by Thomas G. Smith, Del Rey 1986 . . . . .25.00
Illustrated Screenplays
Star Wars: A New Hope Illustrated Screenplay
    Ballantine TPB #42069-7, 1998 . . . . .12.00
*Star Wars: The Empire Strikes Back Illustrated
    Screenplay* Ballantine TPB #42070-5, 1998 . . . .12.00
Star Wars: Return of the Jedi Illustrated Screenplay
    Ballantine TPB #42079-9, 1998 . . . . .12.00

Guide to
A Guide to the Star Wars Universe, by Raymond L.
    Velasco, Ballantine-Del Rey #31920-6, 1984 . . . . .7.50
*A Guide to the Star Wars Universe, Second Edition,
    Revised & Expanded*, by Bill Slavicsek, Del
    Rey TPB #38625-6, 1996 . . . . .10.00
Star Wars: The Essential Guide To Characters, by
    Andy Mangels, Del Rey TPB #39535-2, 1995 . . .18.00
*Star Wars: The Essential Guide To Vehicles and
    Vessels*, by Bill Smith, Del Rey TPB #39299-
    X, 1996 . . . . .18.00
*Star Wars: The Essential Guide to Weapons and
    Technology*, by Bill Smith, Del Rey TPB
    #41413-6, 1997 . . . . .18.00
Star Wars Technical Journal, by Shane Johnson, Del
    Rey 1995 . . . . .35.00
The Secrets of Star Wars: Shadows of the Empire,
    by Mark Cotta Vaz, Del Rey TPB #40236-7,
    1996 . . . . .15.00

Sketchbook
The Star Wars Sketchbook, by Joe Johnston,
    Ballantine TPB #27380, 1977 . . . . .25.00
The Empire Strikes Back Sketchbook, by Joe
    Johnston & Rodis Jamero, Ballantine TPB
    #28836-X, July 1980 .35.00
Return of the Jedi Sketchbook, by Joe Johnston,
    Ballantine TPB, 1983 .25.00

Smithsonian
*Star Wars: The Magic of Myth: Companion to the
    Exhibition at the National Air and Space
    Museum, Smithsonian Institution*, by Mary
    Henderson, Bantam Broadway 1997 . . . . .50.00
    TPB: Bantam Broadway #37810-4, 1997 . . . . . . .25.00

Comic
The Marvel Comics Illustrated Version of Star Wars,
    by Roy Thomas, Ballantine-Del Rey #27492-
    X, 1977, Howard Chaykin art 10.00
The Empire Strikes Back, by Archie Goodwin, & Al
    Williamson, Marvel Comics #02114, 1980 . . . . . . .5.00

THE THING

Movie Novels
Campbell, John W., Jr. *Who Goes There* (Basis of
    1950s classic film) see under SHASTA

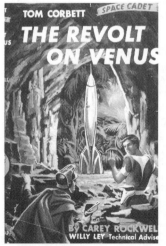

Tom Corbett Space Cadet: The Revolt on Venus & Stand By For
Mars! *by Carey Rockwell (Grosset & Dunlap 1952–54)*

20 Million Miles to Earth *by Henry Sleasar (Amazing 1957)*
& Whirlwind by Charles Grant (Harper 1995)

Foster, Alan Dean, *The Thing*, Bantam #20477-7,
  1982 (John Carpenter movie tie-in) 10.00
  SFBC: Bantam #4790-2, 1982 . . . . .10.00

TIME TUNNEL

TV Show novels
Leinster, Murray, *The Time Tunnel*, Pyramid,
  R-1522, 1967, Jack Gaughan cover art 10.00
Leinster, Murray, *Timeslip!*, Pyramid, R-1680, 1967,
  photo cover 10.00

TOM CORBETT

1. Rockwell, Carey, *Stand By for Mars!*, Grosset &
    Dunlap 1952 00
2. Rockwell, Carey, *Danger in Deep Space*,
    Grosset & Dunlap 1953 00
3. Rockwell, Carey, *On the Trail of the Space
    Pirates*, Grosset & Dunlap 1953 00
4. Rockwell, Carey, *The Space Pioneers*, Grosset
    & Dunlap, 1954 00
5. Rockwell, Carey, *The Revolt on Venus*, Grosset
    & Dunlap 1954 00
6. Rockwell, Carey, *Treachery in Outer Space*,
    Grosset & Dunlap 1954 00
7. Rockwell, Carey, *Sabotage in Space*, Grosset &
    Dunlap 1955 00
8. Rockwell, Carey, *The Robot Rocket*, Grosset &
    Dunlap 1956 00

20 MILLION MILES TO EARTH

Sleasar, Henry, *20 Million Miles to Earth*, Amazing
  Story magazine size 1957 . . . . .150.00

V

TV Show novels
1. Crispin, A. C., *V*, Pinnacle, 42237-7, 1984 . . . . . .15.00
2. Weinstein, Howard & Crispin, A. C., *V: East Coast
    Crisis*, Pinnacle, 42259-8, 1984 . . . . .10.00
3. Wold, Allen L., *V: The Pursuit of Diana*, Pinnacle,
    42401-9, 1984 . . . . .10.00
4. Proctor, George W., *V: The Chicago Conversion*,
    Pinnacle, 42429-9, 1985 . . . . .10.00
5. Sullivan, Timothy, *V: The Florida Project*,
    Pinnacle, 42430-2, 1985 . . . . .10.00
6. Weinstein, Howard, *V: Prisoners and Pawns*,

Pinnacle, 42439-6, 1985 . . . . .10.00
7. Sucharitkul, Somtow, *V: The Alien Swordmaster*,
    Pinnacle, 42441-8, 1985 . . . . .12.00
8. Wold, Allen L., *V: The Crivit Experiment*, Pin-
    nacle 42466-3, 1985 . . . . .10.00
9. Sullivan, Timothy, *V: The New England Resis-
    tance,* Pinnacle, 42467-1, 1985 . . . . .10.00
10. Crispin, A. C. & Marshall, *V: Death Tide*, Pinnacle,
    42469-8, 1985 . . . . .10.00
11. Proctor, George W., *V: The Texas Run*,
    Pinnacle, 42470-1, 1985 . . . . .10.00
12. Weinstein, Howard, *V: Path to Conquest*, Tor,
    55725-5, 1987 . . . . .12.00
13. Sullivan, Timothy, *V: To Conquer the Throne*,
    Tor, 55727-1, 1987 . . . . .10.00
14. Tannehill, Jayne, *V: The Oregon Invasion*, Tor,
    55729-8, 1988 . . . . .10.00
15. Wold, Allen, *V: Below the Threshold*, Tor,
    55732-8, 1988 . . . . .10.00
16. Sucharitkul, Somtow, *V: Symphony of Terror*,
    Tor, 55482-5, 1988 . . . . .12.00
Reprints of any of the above, each 5.00

WAR OF THE WORLDS

Dillard, J. M., *War of the Worlds: The Resurrection*,
  Pocket #67304-1, 1988 . . . . .10.00
Anderson, Kevin J., *War of the Worlds: Global
  Dispatches*, Bantam Spectra #57598-8, 1997 . . . .6.00

X-FILES

TV Show novels
Anderson, Kevin J., *Antibodies*, Harper Prism 1997 . . .22.00
  PB: Harper Prism #105624-3, 1998 . . . . .6.50
Anderson, Kevin J., *Ground Zero*, Harper Prism
  1995 . . . . .22.00
  PB: Harper Prism #105677-4, 1998 . . . . .6.50
Anderson, Kevin J., *Ruins*, Harper Prism 1996 00
  PB: Harper Prism #105736-3, 1998 . . . . .6.50
Hand, Elizabeth & Carter, Chris, *The X-Files: Fight
  the Future*, 1998 . . . . .23.00
  PB 1998 . . . . .6.00
Mezrich, Ben, *Skin*, ...6.00
Grant, Charles L., *The X-Files: Goblins*, 1994 . . . . . . .6.00
Grant, Charles L., *The X-Files: Whirlwind*, Harper
  Prism #105415-1, 1995 .6.00
Grant, Charles L., *The X-Files: Hunter*, 1995 . . . . . . .6.00
Grant, Charles L., *The X-Files*, 1995 . . . . .6.00
Grant, Charles L., Goblins/Whirlwind, Harper TPB
  #105347-3, 1996 . . . . .12.00

1. Martin, Les & & Carter, Chris *X Marks the Spot*,
    1995 . . . . .5.00
2. Martin, Les, *Darkness Falls*, 1995 . . . . .5.00
3. Martin, Les, *Tiger, Tiger*, 1995 . . . . .5.00
4. Steiber, Ellen, *Squeeze*, 1996 . . . . .5.00
5. Martin, Les, *Humbug*, 1996 . . . . .5.00
6. Steiber, Ellen, *Shapes*, 1996 . . . . .5.00
7. Martin, Les, *Fear*, 1996 .5.00
8. Royce, Easton & Martin, Les, *Voltage*, 1996 . . . . . .5.00
9. Martin, Les & Royce, Easton *E.B.E.*, 1997 . . . . .5.00
10. Martin, Les, *Die, Bug, Die*, 1997 . . . . .5.00
11. Martin, Les, *Ghost in the Machine*, 1997 . . . . . . .5.00

ZARDOZ

Boorman, John & Stair, Bill, *Zardoz*, Signet #Q5830,
  1974 . . . . .10.00

  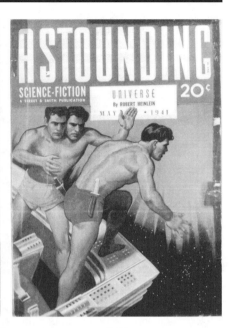

Amazing Stories (April 1932); Amazing Stories (May 1931) Astounding Science Fiction (May 1941)

PULP MAGAZINES

Pulp magazines were the dominant form of science fiction publishing from 1926 to the late 1940s. Covers were exciting and sometimes titilating and some of the stories were even good. Initially these stories had to find their audience because science fiction was new (the word had hardly even been coined). Then came the Depression and then a world war and paper shortages. It's hardly surprising that authors and publishers were struggling for this whole period. Magazine covers had to be as lurid as possible to survive and this gave science fiction somewhat of a bad reputation with the literary elite. Hardcover publishers would hardly touch the stuff until the early 1950s.

There is nothing quite like a lurid picture of a sweet young girl about to be ravished by a bug-eyed monster to get a true collector's blood flowing and thus pulp magazines have always been popular. The problem is condition. Pulp magazines were made with pulp paper — newspaper stock basically and its high acid content is eating away at the remaining pulps. While you read this page, a couple more have crumbled into dust. Most of the collectors were kids who loved these magazines in their youth and that makes them at least 60 years old today, so pretty soon they will crumble into dust too. While they have money, pulp prices will remain high, but when the last survivor dies happy, after finally assembling a complete collection, who will his heirs sell it to?

Books from the 1930s to 1950s have somewhat the same problem, but they have held up better. Books before about 1930 were printed on paper with a high cloth content and they do not suffer from this problem and many recent books are printed on acid-free paper so they will last a long time as well.

Pricing

Most pulp magazines are in very good condition or less and I have used "very good" as the basis for the prices listed below. The very occassionally encountered pulp magazine in fine condition is worth **twice** the price given and one in near fine condition is worth **50% more** than the price given. Prices for issues in a given year or period are based on an issue with average quality stories for the magazine in question. Stories by certain famous authors increase the price over the price given: Isaac Asimov, Ray Bradbury, Edgar Rice Burroughs, H. P. Lovecraft or Robert A. Heinlein stories add about **50%** to the value of an issue as does a story featuring Buck Rogers. L. Ron Hubbard stories **double** the price of an issue — due more to collecting by his followers and disciples than to the litterary merits of the stories. In *Weird Tales*, a Robert E. Howard story adds 25% to an issue's value, 50% if it is a Conan story. The length and significance of the author's story would also be a factor.

There were, of course, a lot more magazines than the ones listed and pulp magazines included adventure and horror titles, all of which published the occasional fantastic story.

AMAZING STORIES

Amazing Stories (Apr. 1926–) Initially large size, edited for the first three years by the legendary Hugo Gernsback.

Vol 1: #1 thru #9 (1926–27)	75.00
Vol 2: #1 thru #12 (1927–28)	50.00
Vol 3: #1 thru #12 (1928–29)	25.00
Vol 4: #1 thru #12 (1929–30)	20.00
Vol 5: #1 thru #12 (1930–31)	20.00
Vol 6: #1 thru #12 (1931–32)	17.00
Vol 7: #1 thru #12 (1932–33)	17.00
Becomes standard Pulp size on Oct. 1933	
Vol 8: #1 thru #12 (1933–34)	17.00
Vol 9: #1 thru #11 (1934–35)	15.00
Vol 10: #1 thru #13 (1935–36)	15.00
Vol 11: #1 thru #6 (1937)	15.00
Vol 12: #1 thru #7 (1938)	15.00
Vol 13 thru Vol 16: #1 thru #12 (1939–42)	15.00
Vol 17: #1 thru #10 (1943)	15.00
Vol 18: #1 thru #5 (1944)	15.00

Vol 19: #1 thru #4 (1945) 10.00
Vol 20: #1 thru #9 (1946) 10.00
Vol 21: #1 thru #12 (1947) 10.00
Vol 22: #1 thru #12 (1948) 7.00
Vol 23: #1 thru #12 (1949) 7.00
Vol 24: #1 thru #12 (1950) 5.00
Vol 25: #1 thru #12 (1951) 5.00
Vol 26: #1 thru #12 (1952) 5.00

Becomes digest size magazine (Apr.–May 1953)
Vol 27: #1 thru #8 (1953) 5.00
Vol 28: #1 thru #5 (1954) 3.00
Vol 29: #1 thru #7 (1955) 3.00
Vol 30: #1 thru #12 (1956) 3.00
Vol 31: #1 thru #12 (1957) 3.00
Becomes: Amazing Science Fiction (Feb. 1958)
Becomes: Amazing Science Fiction Stories (May 1958)
Vol 32 and Vol 33: #1 thru #12 (1958–59) 3.00
Becomes: Amazing Stories (Oct. 1960)
Vol 34 thru Vol. 38: #1 thru #12 (1960–64) 3.00
Vol 39: #1 thru #6 (1965) 3.00
Vol 40: #1 thru #10 (1965–67) 3.00

Amazing Stories Annual
1 issue (1927) 60.00
Amazing Stories Quarterly
Vol 1: #1 thru #4 (1928) 30.00
Vol 2: #1 thru #4 (1929) 30.00
Vol 3: #1 thru #4 (1930) 25.00
Vol 4: #1 thru #4 (1931) 25.00
Vol 5: #1 thru #3 (1932) 25.00
Vol 6: #4 (1933) 20.00
Vol 7: #1 and #2 (1934) 20.00

ASTOUNDING/ANALOG

As a pulp magazine, the title was always *Astounding...* but in 1960 the title became *Analog Science Fiction — Science Fact.* It switched from pulp size to digest size in 1943. In the early years, it is famous for publishing E.E. "Doc" Smith's *Skylark* and *Lensmen* series and other science fiction adventure stories. The magazine is also famous for the editorship of John W. Campbell, Jr. from Nov. 1937 onwards. He brought in stories by Isaac Asimov, Robert A. Heinlein, A.E. Van Vogt, Hal Clement, Theodore Sturgeon, Poul Anderson and Clifford Simak, keeping it as science fiction's leading magazine for many years and winning many Hugo awards. Frank Herbert's *Dune* and Anne McCaffrey's *Dragonflight* made their first appearances here.

Astounding Stories of Super-Science (1930–31, 33)
Astounding Stories (1931–32, 1933–38)
Astounding Science Fiction (1938–60)
Vol 1: #1 thru #3 (1930) 500.00
Vol 2: #1 thru #3 (1930) 200.00
Vol 3: #1 thru #3 (1930) 100.00
Vol 4: #1 thru #3 (1930) 75.00
Vol 5 thru Vol 11: #1 thru #3 (1931–33) 50.00
Vol 12 thru Vol 16: #1 thru #6 (1933–36) 35.00
Vol 17 thru Vol 19: #1 thru #6 (1936–37) 25.00
Vol 20 thru Vol 22: #1 thru #6 (1937–39) 20.00
Vol 23 thru Vol 25: #1 thru #6 (1939–40) 17.00
Vol 26 thru Vol 29: #1 thru #6 (1940–42) 15.00
Vol 30 thru Vol 32: #1 thru #6 (1942–43) 12.00

digest size
Vol 32: #3 thru #6 (1943–44) 12.00
Vol 33: #1 thru #6 (1944) 12.00
Vol 34 and Vol 35: #1 thru #6 (1944–45) 10.00
Vol 36 and Vol 37: #1 thru #6 (1945–46) 9.00
Vol 38 and Vol 39: #1 thru #6 (1946–47) 8.00
Vol 40 and Vol 41: #1 thru #6 (1947–48) 7.00
Vol 42 and Vol 43: #1 thru #6 (1948–49) 6.00
Vol 44 and Vol 45: #1 thru #6 (1949–50) 5.00
Vol 46 thru Vol 49: #1 thru #6 (1950–52) 4.00
Vol 50 thru Vol 64: #1 thru #6 (1952–60) 3.00

Becomes: Analog
Vol 64 thru end 3.00

PLANET STORIES

This magazine was famous for a number of stories by Ray Bradbury as well as numorous novelettes by Leigh Brackett and early fiction by Poul Anderson, not to mention

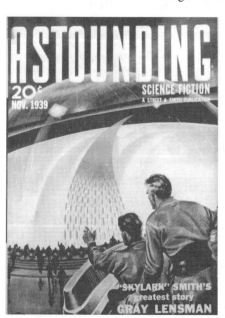

Astounding Science Fiction (Nov. 1939 & Oct. 1937) Planet Stories (Nov. 1953)

Planet Stories (Fall 1940) Startling Stories (Nov 1939) Thrilling Wonder Stories (Fall 1945)

a babe in a skimpy outfit on just about every cover.

Vol. 1: #1 thru #12 (1939–42) 40.00
Vol. 2: #1 thru #12 (1942–45) 35.00
Vol. 3: #1 thru #12 (1945–48) 25.00
Vol. 4: #1 thru #12 (1948–51) 20.00
Vol. 5: #1 thru #12 (1951–53) 15.00
Vol. 6: #1 thru #11 (1953–55) 10.00

STARTLING STORIES

Vol 1: #1 thru #3 (1939) 50.00
Vol 2 and Vol 3: #1 thru #3 (1939–40) 25.00
Vol 4 thru Vol 9: #1 thru #3 (1940–43) 20.00
Vol 10 thru Vol 14: #1 thru #3 (1943–47) 15.00
Vol 15 thru Vol 19: #1 thru #3 (1947–49) 10.00
Vol 20 thru Vol33: #1 thru #3 (1949–55) 5.00

THRILLING WONDER STORIES

(prev. Wonder Stories)
Vol 8: #1 thru #3 (1936) 100.00
Vol 9: #1 thru #3 (1937) 75.00
Vol 10: #1 thru #3 (1937) 50.00
Vol 11: #1 thru #3 (1938) 40.00
Vol 12: #1 thru #3 (1938) 35.00
Vol 13: #1 thru #3 (1939) 30.00
Vol 14: #1 thru #3 (1939) 25.00
Vol 15: #1 thru #3 (1940) 20.00
Vol 16: #1 thru #3 (1940) 18.00
Vol 17: #1 thru #3 (1940) 18.00
Vol 18: #1 thru #3 (1940) 18.00
Vol 19: #1 thru #3 (1941) 18.00
Vol 20: #1 thru #3 (1941) 18.00
Vol 21: #1 thru #3 (1941–42) .18.00
Vol 22: #1 thru #3 (1942) 17.00
Vol 23: #1 thru #3 (1942–43) .16.00
Vol 24: #1 thru #3 (1943) 15.00
Vol 25: #1 thru #3 (1943–44) .15.00
Vol 26: #1 thru #3 (1944–45) .15.00
Vol 27: #1 thru #3 (1945) 15.00
Vol 28: #1 thru #3 (1946) 12.00
Vol 29: #1 thru #3 (1946–47) .12.00
Vol 30: #1 thru #3 (1947) 12.00

Vol 31: #1 thru #3 (1947–48) .10.00
Vol 32: #1 thru #3 (1948) 10.00
Vol 33: #1 thru #3 (1948–49) .10.00
Vol 34: #1 thru #3 (1949) 10.00
Vol 35: #1 thru #3 (1949–50) .10.00
Vol 36: #1 thru #3 (1950) 10.00
Vol 37: #1 thru #3 (1950–51) .10.00
Vol 38: #1 thru #3 (1951) 10.00
Vol 39: #1 thru #3 (1951–52) .10.00
Vol 40: #1 thru #3 (1952) 10.00
Vol 41: #1 thru #3 (1952–53) .10.00
Vol 42: #1 thru #3 (1953) 10.00
Vol 43: #1 thru #3 (1953–54) .10.00
Vol 44: #1 thru #3 (1954–55) .10.00

TWO COMPLETE SCIENCE-ADVENTURE BOOKS

The gimmick was "$5.00 value for 25¢" and except for issues #6 and #11, one, and sometimes two, good novels appeared in each issue. Of course, they were abridged to fit within the 112 total pages available. By 1953, pulp magazines were dying and Ace Books was producing its famous paperback doubles, although these went for 35¢.

#1: Asimov, Isaac, *Pebble in the Sky* and Hubbard, L. Ron, *The Kingslayer* (Winter 1950) 75.00
#2: Hamilton, Edmond, *The Star Kings* and Clarke, Arthur C. *Seeker of the Sphinx* (Spring 1951) . . .60.00
#3: Blish, James, *Sword of Xota* and Jones, Neil R., *The Citadel in Space* (Summer 1951) 50.00
#4: Wells, H. G., *The Time Machine* and deCamp, L. Sprague, *The Tritonian Ring* (Winter 1951) 50.00
#5: Powell, Anaximander., *The Outcasts of Venus* and Williamson, Jack, *The Humanoids* (Spring 1952) 35.00
#6: Payne, P. L., *The Cructars Are Coming!* and Beyer, W. G., *Minions of the Moon* (Summer 1952) 15.00
#7: Heinlein, Robert A. (as McDonald, Anson), *Beyond This Horizon* and Coppel, Alfred, *The Magellanics* (Winter 1952) 25.00

Two Complete Science-Adventure Books #1 (Winter 1950); Weird Tales (September 1937) Wonder Stories (October 1930)

#8: Blish, James, *Sargasso of Lost Cities* and Fearn, John Russell (as Statten, Vargo) *Survivor of Mars* (Spring 1953) 10.00
#9: Brunner, John (as Brunner, Killian Huston), *The Wanton of Argus* and Berry, B., *Mission to Marakee* (Summer 1953) 10.00
#10: Anderson, Poul, *Silent Victory* and MacDonald, John D., *Ballroom of the Skys* (Winter 1953) 10.00
#11: Wilcox, D., *Tombot!* and Berry, B., *World Held Captive* (Spring 1954) .10.00

UNKNOWN/UNKNOWN WORLDS

Edited by John W. Campbell, Jr. and containing mostly fantasy and science fantasy.

Unknown
Vol 1: #1 thru #6 (1939) 35.00
Vol 2: #1 thru #6 (1939–40) .35.00
Vol 3: #1 thru #6 (1940) 30.00
Vol 4: #1 thru #6 (1940–41) .30.00
becomes: Unknown Worlds (Aug. 1941)
Vol 5: #1 thru #6 (1941–42) .30.00
Vol 6: #1 thru #6 (1942–43) .30.00
Vol 7: #1 thru #3 (1943) 30.00

WEIRD TALES

Weird Tales is much better known for weird, supernatural, horror and heroic fantasy than for science fiction, but it published a lot of the latter over its 279-issue run. It is the most famous of the pulp magazines. As if publishing fiction by H. P. Lovecraft, Clark Ashton Smith, Robert Bloch, Ray Bradbury, C. L. Moore, Robert E. Howard, Edmond Hamilton Robert A. Heinlein and Theodore Sturgeon weren't enough, it has some of the most famous (nude or mostly nude) covers by Margaret Brundage, Virgil Finlay, Hannes Bok and Lee Brown Coye. Farnsworth Wright was the editor from 1924 to 1940 and this was *Weird Tales*' golden age. After 1940, the fiction (and the covers) tapered off.

Vol 1: #1 thru #4 (1923) .1,000.00
Vol 2: #1 thru #4 (1923) .1,000.00

Vol 3: #1 thru #4 (1924) 800.00
Vol 4: #2 thru #4 (1924) 700.00
Vol 5: #1 thru #6 (1925) 250.00
Vol 6: #1 thru #6 (1925) 225.00
Vol 7 and Vol 8: #1 thru #6 (1926) 150.00
Vol 9 and Vol 10: #1 thru #6 (1927) 125.00
Vol 11 and Vol 12: #1 thru #6 (1928) 90.00
Vol 13 and Vol 14: #1 thru #6 (1929) 75.00
Vol 15 and Vol 16: #1 thru #6 (1930) 70.00
Vol 17 thru Vol 22: #1 thru #4 (1931–37) 65.00
Vol 23 thru Vol 25: #1 thru #6 (1934–35) 55.00
Vol 26 thru Vol 28: #1 thru #6 (1935–36) 50.00
Vol 29 and Vol 30: #1 thru #6 (1937) 45.00
Vol 31 and Vol 32: #1 thru #6 (1938) 35.00
Vol 33 thru Vol 34: #1 thru #6 (1939) 30.00
Vol 35 thru Vol 37: #1 thru #10 (1940–44) 25.00
Vol 38: #1 thru #6 (1944–45) .20.00
Vol 39: #1 thru #12 (1945–47) #11 used twice 20.00
Vol 40: #1 thru #6 (1947–48) .15.00
Vol 41: #1 thru #6 (1948–49) .12.00
Vol 42 thru Vol 46: #1 thru #6 (1949–55) 10.00

WONDER STORIES

Air Wonder Stories
Vol 1: #1 thru #11 (1929–30) .35.00

Science Wonder Stories
Vol 1: #1 thru #12 (1929–30) .30.00
combined to form:
Wonder Stories
Vol 2: #1 thru #12 (1930–31) .25.00
Vol 3: #1 thru #12 (1931–2) 20.00
Vol 4 thru Vol 7: #1 thru #12 (1932–36) 17.00
becomes: Thrilling Wonder Stories

Wonder Stories Quarterly
Vol 1: #1 thru #4 (1929–30) 50.00
Vol 2: #1 thru #4 (1930–31) 25.00
Vol 3: #1 thru #4 (1931–2) 25.00
Vol 4: #1 thru #2 (1932–3) 20.00

Avon Fantasty Reader #13 & #16 and Avon Science Fiction Reader #3 (Avon 1950–52)

SF MAGAZINES

Science fiction magazines are still being published and people still read them. There is nothing wrong with them at all, but there are very few collectors. Consequently, back issues are not worth much more than yesterday's newspaper. If you can find a dealer that sells them, he or she will have to get something for them but they do not seem to be worth more than about $1 each if you buy them, and if you try to sell them, forget about it. File them in the circular file where you put your baseball card commons. If enough people do that, the few remaining ones may someday be worth something, but don't hold your breath.

AVON FANTASY READER
AVON SCIENCE FICTION READER
AVON SCIENCE FICTION
AND FANTASY READER

Avon made an early attempt at publishing a digest sized magazine (or magazines). These were mostly saddle-stapled and they reprinted a number of great stories. There are 18 issues of the Avon Fantasy Reader and three of the Avon Science Fiction Reader, all edited by Donald A. Wollheim. Avon followed with two issues of the Avon Science Fiction and Fantasy Reader edited by Sol Cohen. All three make excellent collectibles with good stories and wonderful covers. Its magazine program was discontinued in 1952, but Avon continued to publish science fiction in paperback books.

Avon Fantasy Reader (1947–52)
Digest size, glued binding
#1 featuring *The Power Planet* by Murray Leinster 25.00
#2 featuring *The City of the Living Dead* by Fletcher
    Pratt 20.00
#3 featuring A. Merritt, C.L. Moore and H.P.
    Lovecraft 20.00

#4 featuring *The Arrhenius Horror* by P. Schuyler
    Miller 18.00
Digest size, saddle stapled binding
#5 featuring *Scarlet Dream* by C. L. Moore 20.00
#6 featuring *The Crawling Horror* by Thorp
    McClusky 15.00
#7 featuring *The Curse of a Thousand Kisses* by
    Sax Rohmer 15.00
#8 featuring *Queen of the Black Coast* by Robert E.
    Howard 20.00
#9 featuring *The Flower-Women* by Clarke Ashton
    Smith 20.00
#10 featuring *A Witch Shall Be Born* by Robert E.
    Howard 20.00
#11 featuring *Glamour* by Seabury Quinn 15.00
#12 featuring *The Blonde Goddess of Bal-Sagoth* by
    Robert E. Howard 20.00
#13 featuring *The Love Slave and the Scientists* by
    Frank Belknap Long 15.00
#14 featuring *Temptress of the Tower of Torture and
    Sin* by Robert E. Howard 20.00
#15 featuring *A Man, A Maid, and Saturn's
    Temptation* by Stanley G. Weinbaum 20.00
#16 featuring *The Black Kiss* by Robert Bloch 25.00
#17 featuring *The Sapphire Siren* by Nictzin Dyalhis . .15.00
#18 featuring *The Witch From Hell's Kitchen* by
    Robert E. Howard 20.00
Set: All 18 issues 250.00

Avon Science Fiction Reader (1951–52)
#1 featuring *The War of the Sexes* by Edmond
    Hamilton 20.00
#2 featuring *Priestess of the Flame* by S. P. Wright . . .15.00
#3 featuring *The Robot Empire* by Frank Belknap
    Long 15.00

Avon Science Fiction and Fantasy Reader (1952)
#1 featuring *The Forgotten Enemy* by Arthur C.
    Clarke 15.00
#2 featuring *DP!* by Jack Vance and *The Parasite* by
    Arthur C. Clarke 15.00

COMICS

Humanoid creatures from other planets with strange powers, and humans that develop strange powers from a genetic mutation background or radioactivity or whatever, are perfectly proper themes for science fiction and there are books featuring all of them. However, Superman, the X-Men and Spider-Man didn't start in the science fiction books or pulp magazines. They started as comic books and quickly became their own category — superheroes. There are many interesting aspects to their careers, including how Superman defeated his primary rival in the 1940s, Captain Marvel, in a copyright infringement suit, and how Marvel Comics revived the whole superhero industry in the early 1960s with the invention of Spider-Man and the X-Men. However, superheroes are too big a topic to be included with science fiction in this book. This comics section alone would be 500 pages long instead of less than 50.

Consequently, only hard-core science fiction comics are listed here; no superheroes, no fantasy, no horror. All of the comics based on a particular movie or television series are listed together, so that, for example, *Adventures on the Planet of the Apes* and *Terror on the Planet of the Apes* are both listed under "Planet of the Apes," rather than alphabetically. This works fairly well, except for crossovers such as *Aliens vs. Predator*, which gets its own listing, following "Aliens" but can't be with the other *Predator* comics too. I just hope nobody puts out a comic where Luke Skywalker recruits Flash Gordon to help save Babylon 5 from the Borg. There would be no logical place to list that comic. It might make an interesting story though, now that I think about it. Flash and Vir Cotto become Borg drones, Luke and Dale become romantically involved and Chewbacca and Garibaldi save the station.

Science fiction has a long history in the comic books, but the vast majority of recent titles are adaptations of television shows and movies and naturally *Star Trek* and *Star Wars* dominate these.

STAR TREK

The first *Star Trek* comic adaptations were by Gold Key Comics. The series ran from 1967 to 1979 for a total of 61 issues. There are many logical inconsistencies between the early comics issues and the TV series. The artist was Italian and had only limited information about the TV show, which he had never seen. Many of the Gold Key comics also appeared under the "Whitman" imprint. Some also had variations in cover art. There is no difference in value between the variations for any given issue. These comics are scarce and generally valuable collectibles, sought by both Star Trek and comic book collectors.

Marvel comics got the rights to Star Trek in 1979 and adapted the first and second movies and filled the time in between with new stories. A total of 18 issues were produced. In 1984, DC took over *Star Trek* and its first series spanned the next three movies. With the beginning of *Star Trek, The Next Generation*, DC started over with *Star Trek* comics. DC

Space Adventures #5 (Charlton Comics 1967)
& Flash Gordon #3 (King Comics 1967)

Star Trek #56 (DC Comics 1994)
& Star Trek The Next Generation #63 (DC Comics 1994)

 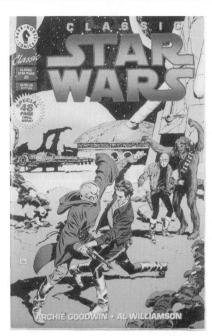 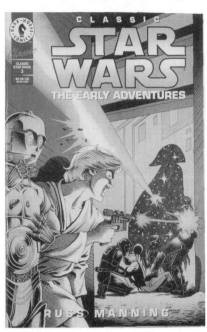

Star Wars #30 (Marvel Comics 1979) Classic Star Wars #20 (Dark Horse Comics 1994)
& Classic Star Wars The Early Adventures #3 (Dark Horse Comics 1994)

kicked off its *Next Generation* comic book series with a six-issue mini-series beginning in February 1988. It also produced an additional second series of comics for the new show. DC reprints some of its comic book stories in trade paperback or graphic novel format. These are distributed by Simon and Schuster and sold in book stores, as well as more traditionally in comic shops.

Malibu got the rights to *Deep Space Nine* and produced a series and several mini series. Marvel bought Malibu and got back into Star Trek in 1996 with series on *The Early Voyages*, *Star Fleet Academy* and *Star Trek Voyager*. The Marvel, DC and Malibu comics have all proved more popular with *Star Trek* collectors than with traditional comic book collectors. Part of the reason is that they are usually assigned to less well-established artists. The big names want to draw Superman and Spider-Man and the X-Men so that they can get even more famous and start their own companies.

STAR WARS

The first *Star Wars* comic appeared just prior to the movie premiere. Marvel adaped it from a rough cut of the movie and so Luke's friend, Biggs Darklighter appears in the early going as well as in the final battle. Since his part was virtually edited out of the movie, he became somewhat of a famous lost character. He made somewhat of a comeback in the Special Edition and now he is even an action figure.

The Marvel series of comics is a popular collectible with *Star Wars* fans, but the Dark Horse comics from the 1990s are much more significant contributions to the *Star Wars* saga. With only a few hours of film available, the careers of the heroes and villains are just barely explored in the movies. The comics (and the novels) continue and fill in their lives and the lives of the dozens of interesting characters from the movies who made only brief appearances. In addition, Lucas Arts has imposed an over-all continuity on the comics and books, so that they do not conflict with each other.

However, Dark Horse Comics' original *Star Wars Dark Empire* series is just about the only one that has done well as a collectible.

OTHER MEDIA ADAPTATIONS

A good number of science fiction movies and television shows have made it into comics. They are generally the same ones that produced action figures and toys and they are discussed in those sections. You are probably already familiar with their names anyway.

You may not be as familiar with all of the science fiction books which have been adapted directly to comics, without having been made into movies first. Edgar Rice Burroughs' other hero, John Carter of Mars, has appeared several times over the years. *Dragonflight* is from the famous Anne McCaffrey *Dragon Riders of Pern* series and *Forever War* is from Joe Haldeman's award-winning book. *A.R.M.* and *Defenseless Dead* comics are from Larry Niven's *Known Space* series stories and *Lucifer's Hammer* is from the Niven and Pournelle novel of the same name. Harry Harrison has had three of his novel series adapted for comics: *Bill the Galactic Hero*, *The Stainless Steel Rat*, and *Deathworld*. *Lensman* comics are from the E.E. "Doc" Smith novels, by way of Japan. In addition, *Retief* is from a Keith Laumer series, *Shadow of the Torturer* from Gene Wolfe's novels and *The Two Faces of Tomorrow* from a fine book by James Hogan. Also, various Harlan Ellison and Ray Bradbury stories have been adapted over the years. All in all, though, there have been relatively few and some of the greatest science fiction has never seen the comic books. Asimov's *Foundation* series and *Robot* series have never been adapted and neither has *Stranger in a Strange Land* or *The Moon is a Harsh Mistress* by Robert Heinlein. Philip José Farmer's *Tier Worlds* and *Riverworld* series would make fine comic books as would *Nine Princes in Amber* by Roger Zelazny and the *Rama* series by Arthur C. Clarke.

*The Adventures of Theown #1
(Pyramid 1986)*

ADVENTURES OF THEOWN
Pyramid 1986
1 thru 3, Limited series . . . .@1.75

ALIEN ENCOUNTERS
Eclipse Comics 1985–87
1 A New Beginning 3.50
2 . . . . .3.00
3 "I Shot the Last Martian" 3.00
4 . . . . .2.00
5 Richard Corben art, "Night of the
   Monkey" 2.00
6 "Now You See It," "Freefall" 2.00
7 . . . . .2.00
8 "Take One Capsule Every Million
   Years," M.Monroe(c) 2.75
9 The Conquered 2.00
10 . . . . .2.00
11 Tim Truman, "Old Soldiers" 2.00
12 "What A Relief," "Eyes of the
   Sibyl" 2.00
13 "The Light at the End" 2.00
14 "Still Born" 2.00

ALIEN NATION
DC 1988
1 movie adaptation 2.50

*Alien Nation: The Spartans #2
(Adventure/Malibu 1990)*

ALIEN NATION
A BREED APART
Adventure Comics (B&W) 1990
1 Friar Kaddish 3.00
2 . . . . .2.50
3 The "Vampires" Busted 2.50
4 Final Issue 2.50

THE FIRSTCOMERS
Adventure Comics (B&W) 1991
1 New Mini-series 2.50
2 Assassin 2.50
3 Search for Saucer 2.50
4 Final Issue 2.50

THE PUBLIC ENEMY
Adventure Comics (B&W) 1991
1 "Before the Fall" 2.50
2 Earth & Wehlnistrata 2.50
3 Killer on the Loose 2.50

THE SKIN TRADE
Adventure Comics (B&W) 1991
1 "Case of the Missing Milksop" . .2.50
2 "To Live And Die in L.A" 2.50
3 A:Dr. Jekyll 2.50
4 D.Methoraphan Exposed 2.50

THE SPARTANS
Adventure Comics (B&W)
1 . . . . .4.00
1a LTD collectors edition 7.00
2 A:Ruth Lawrence 2.50
3 Spartans 2.50
4 conclusion 2.50

ALIENS

ALIENS
Dark Horse (B&W) 1988–89
1 Movie Sequel, R:Hicks, Newt . . .18.00
1a 2nd printing 3.00
1b 3rd printing 2.00
1c 4th printing 1.50
2 Hicks raids Mental Hospital 8.00
2a 2nd printing 2.50
2a 3rd printing 1.50
3 Realize Queen is on Earth 4.00
3a 2nd printing 1.50
4 Queen is freed, Newton on
   Aliens World 3.00
5 All out war on Aliens World 3.00
6 Hicks & Newt return to Earth 3.00
TPB rep.#1–#6 & DHP #24 . . . . . .11.00
HC rep..#1–#6 & DHP #24 (1990) . .25.00

ALIENS (II)
Dark Horse 1989–90
1 Hicks, Newt hijack ship 5.00
1a 2nd Printing 3.00
2 Crazed general trains aliens 3.00
2a 2nd Printing 3.00
3 HicksV:General Spears 3.00
3a 2nd Printing 3.00
4 Heroes reclaim earth from aliens . .3.00
HC, 2,500 made 80.00
HC, 1,000 made 100.00

ALIENS
Dark Horse
1-shot Earth Angel, John Byrne (Aug.
   1994) .3.00
HC rep. Earth Angel 21.00
1-shot Glass Corridor 2.95
1-shot Love Sick (Dec. 1996) 2.95
1-shot Mondo Heat, sequel to Mondo
   Pest (Feb. 1996) 2.50
1-shot Mondo Pest, rep. Dark Horse
   Classics #22–#24 (Apr. 1995) . .2.95
1-shot Purge (Aug. 1997) 2.95
1-shot Pig (Mar. 1997) 2.95
1-shot Sacrifice, rep.Aliens UK (May
   1993) .4.95

Aliens: Purge (Dark Horse 1997)

1-shot Salvation, F:Selkirk (Nov.
   1993) .4.95
1-shot Special (June 1997) 2.50
1-shot Stalker 2.50
1-shot Wraith 2.95
GN Female War, remastered 16.95
GN Genocide, remastered 16.95
GN Labyrinth, remastered 17.95
GN Nightmare Asylum, remaster . .16.95
GN Outbreak, remastered 17.95
GN Rogue, Remastered 16.95

ALCHEMY
Dark Horse 1997
1 (of 3) Richard Corben art 2.95
2 thru 3 . . . .@2.95

BERSERKER
Dark Horse 1995
1 I:Crew of the Nemesis 2.50
2 Terminall 949 . . . . .2.50
3 Traitor 2.50
4 Finale 2.50

COLONIAL MARINES
Dark Horse 1993–94
1 I: Lt. Joseph Henry 3.00
2 I: Pvt. Carmen Vasquez 2.75
3 V:Aliens 2.75
4 F:Lt.Henry 2.75
5 V:Aliens 2.75
6 F:Herk Mondo 2.75
7 A:Beliveau 2.75
8 F:Lt.Joseph Henry 2.75
9 F:Lt.Joseph Henry 2.75
10 final issue 2.50

EARTH WAR
Dark Horse 1990
1 Alien"s War renewed 5.00
1a 2nd Printing 2.50
2 "To trap the Queen" 5.00
3 Stranded on Alien"s planet 4.00
4 Resolution, final 4.00
HC Earth War, rep. #1–#4, signed
   and numbered edition 60.00

GENOCIDE
Dark Horse 1991–92
1 Aliens vs. Aliens 3.50
2 Alien Homeworld 3.00
3 Search for Alien Queen 3.00
4 Conclusion, inc. poster 3.00
TPB Genocide rep. #1–#4 . . . . . . .13.95

HAVOC
Dark Horse 1997
1 (of 2) over 40 creators 2.95
2 . . . . .2.95

HIVE
Dark Horse 1992
1 I:Stanislaw Mayakovsky 4.00
2 A:Norbert 3.50
3 A:Julie, Gill 3.25
4 A:Stan, Final 3.00
TPB Hive rep. #1–#4 . . . . .14.00

KIDNAPPED
Dark Horse 1997–98
1 (of 3) 2.50
2 thru 3 . . . .@2.50

LABYRINTH
Dark Horse 1993–94
1 F:Captured Alien 3.00
2 . . . . .2.50
3 O:Dr.Church 2.50
4 D:Everyone 2.50
TPB rep. #1–#4 . . . . .17.95

MUSIC OF THE SPEARS
Dark Horse 1994
1 I:Damon Eddington 3.00
2 A:Damon Eddington 2.75
3 A:Damon Eddington 2.75
4 last issue 2.75

NEWT'S TALE
Dark Horse
1 How Newt Survived 5.50
2 Newt's point of view on how
   "Aliens" ended 4.95

ALIEN RESURRECTION
Dark Horse 1997
1 (of 2) movie adaptation 2.50
2 Dave McKean(c) 2.50

ALIENS
ROGUE
Dark Horse 1993
1 F:Mr.Kay 3.00
2 thru 4 V:Aliens . . . .@3.00
TPB Nelson cover, rep.#1–#4 . . . . .14.95

STRONGHOLD
Dark Horse 1994
1 thru 4 . . . .@2.50
TPB 16.95

SURVIVAL
Dark Horse 1998
1 (of 3) Tony Harris cover 2.95
2 thru 3 . . . .@2.95

TRIBES
Dark Horse
HC Dave Dorman cover 24.95
TPB 11.95

*Aliens: Colonial Marines #2
(Dark Horse 1993)*

HC 24.95

DARK HORSE PRESENTS
ALIENS
Dark Horse

1 Rep. 4.95
1a Platinum Edition 8.00

BATMAN/ALIENS
Dark Horse/DC 1997

1 (of 2) Berni Wrightson art 4.95
2 conclusion 4.95
TPB 14.95

ALIEN 3
Dark Horse 1992

1 thru 3 Movie Adaptation . . . .@2.50

*Dark Horse Classic: Aliens Versus
Predator #2 (Dark Horse 1997)*

ALIENS VS. PREDATOR
Dark Horse 1990

0 PN, KS, Rep.DHP#34-36, (B&W) .6.00
1 Duel to the Death 4.00
1a 2nd Printing 3.00
2 Dr. Revna missing 3.00
3 Predators attack Aliens 3.00
4 CW, F:Machiko & Predator 3.00
TPB Rep.#1–#4 . . . . .19.95
TPB rep.DHP#34-36 . . . . .19.95
HC rep.DHP#34-36 . . . . .79.95

THE DEADLIEST OF THE SPECIES
Dark Horse 1993–95

1 Chris Claremont story, F:Caryn
    Delacroix 3.75
2 V:Predator 3.00
3 F:Caryn Delacroix 3.00
4 V:Predator 3.00
5 Roadtrip 3.00
6 in Space Station 3.00
7 thru 9 . . . .@2.50
10 Chris Claremont story, Human
    Predators 2.50
11 Chris Claremont, Bolton cover,
    Delacroix vs. DeMatier 2.50
12 Caryn's Fate 2.50
TPB 29.95
Lim. Ed. hc 99.95

BOOTY
Dark Horse 1996

1-shot Rep. Diamond Previews . . .2.50

DUEL
Dark Horse 1995

1 Trap 2.50
2 War 2.50

ETERNAL
Dark Horse 1998

1 (of 4) .2.50
2 thru 4 . . . .@2.50

WAR
Dark Horse 1995

0 Prelude to New Series 2.50
1 Richard Corben(c) F:Machiko 2.50
2 I:Machiko Naguchi 2.50
3 F:Machiko Naguchi 2.50
4 final issue 2.50
TPB 19.95

DARK HORSE CLASSICS:
ALIENS VS. PREDATOR
Dark Horse 1997

1 thru 6 Rep. . . . .@2.95

ALIEN TERROR
Eclipse 1986

3-D #1 "Standard Procedure" 2.00

Alien Worlds #2 (PC Comics)

ALIEN WORLDS
Pacific 1982

1 Al Williamson 4.00
2 . . . . .3.50
3 thru 7 . . . .@3.00
3-D #1 . . . . .5.50

Eclipse 1985

8 Al Williamson 2.50
9 . . . . .2.50

ALL-NEW COMICS
**Family Comics
(Harvey Publ.) 1943–47**

1 A:Steve Case, Johnny Rebel
    I:Detective Shane 2,000.00
2 O:Scarlet Phantom 750.00
3 . . . . .550.00
4 . . . . .550.00
5 Flash Gordon 500.00
6 I:Boy Heroes and Red Blazer . .500.00
7 A:Black Cat & Zebra 500.00
8 A:Shock Gibson 500.00
9 A:Black Cat 500.00
10 A:Zebra 450.00
11 A:Man in Black, Girl
    Commandos 450.00
12 Joe Kubert 450.00
13 Stuntman by Simon & Kirby,
    A:Green Hornet & cover 475.00
14 A:Green Hornet 450.00
15 Smaller size, distributed by mail .400.00

AMERICA'S BEST COMICS
**Nedor/Better/Standard
Publications 1942–49**

1 B:Black Terror, Captain Future,
    The Liberator, Doc Strange .1,700.00
2 O:American Eagle 650.00
3 B:Pyroman 500.00
4 A:Doc Strange, Jimmy Cole . . .400.00
5 A:Lone Eagle, Capt. Future 375.00
6 A:American Crusader 350.00
7 A:Hitler, Hirohito 500.00
8 The Liberator ends 350.00
9 . . . . .425.00
10 . . . . .350.00
11 . . . . .350.00
12 Red Cross cover 350.00
13 . . . . .350.00
14 Last American Eagle app 350.00
15 . . . . .325.00
16 . . . . .335.00
17 Doc Strange carries football . . .325.00
18 Bondage cover 325.00
19 . . . . .325.00
20 vs. the Black Market 325.00
21 Infinity cover 300.00
22 A:Captain Future 300.00
23 B:Miss Masque 350.00
24 Bondage cover 350.00
25 A:Sea Eagle 300.00
26 A:The Phantom Detective 300.00
27 . . . . .300.00
28 A:Commando Cubs, Black
    Terror 300.00
29 A:Doc Strange 300.00
30 . . . . .300.00
31 July, 1949 . . . . .300.00

A.R.M. #1 (Adventure Comics 1990)

A.R.M.
Adventure Comics (B&W) 1990

1 Larry Niven Known Space Tale
    adapt. Death by Ecstasy, pt.1 . .2.50
2 & 2 Death by Ecstasy, pt.2 & 3 . @2.50

AVON ONE-SHOTS
**Avon Periodicals 1949-53
{Listed in Alphabetical Order}**

N# Wally Wood, Attack on Planet
    Mars 550.00
N# Wally Wood, An Earth Man
    on Venus 900.00
1 Wally Wood, Flying Saucers . . .600.00
N# Flying Saucers. 400.00
1 Out of this World 475.00
1 Robotmen of the Lost Planet . . .750.00
N# Wally Wood(c), Rocket to
    the Moon 800.00

*Babylon 5: In Valen's Name #1
(DC 1998)*

BABYLON 5
DC 1995

1 From TV series 16.00
2 From TV series 11.00
3 Mysterious Assassin 8.00
4 V:Mysterious Assassin 8.00
5 Shadows of the Present, pt.1 . . .8.00
6 Shadows of the Present, pt.2 . . .8.00
7 Shadows of the Present, pt.3 . . .7.00
8 Laser-Mirror Starweb, pt.1 . . . . .7.00
9 Laser-Mirror Starweb, pt.2 . . . . .7.00
10 Laser-Mirror-Starweb, pt.3 . . . .7.00
11 final issue 7.00

IN VALEN'S NAME
DC 1998

1 (of 3) Peter David, from TV series .2.50
2 Peter David 2.50
3 Peter David 2.50

BATTLE OF THE PLANETS
Gold Key 1979

1 TV Cartoon 15.00
2 thru 5 . . . .@10.00

Whitman 1980

6 . . . . .7.00
7 thru 10 . . . . .7.00

BATTLESTAR GALACTICA
Marvel 1979–81

1 B:TV Adaptation; Annihilation 3.00
2 Exodus 2.50
3 Deathtrap 2.50
4 Walt Simonson, Dogfight 2.50
5 Walt Simonson, E:TV Adaptation;
    Ambush 2.50
6 Nightmare 2.00
7 Commander Adama Trapped 2.00
8 Last Stand 2.00
9 Space Mimic 2.00
10 This Planet Hungers 2.00
11 Walt Simonson, Starbuck's
    Dilemma 2.00
12 Walt Simonson, Memory Ends . .2.00
13 Walt Simonson, All Out Attack . .2.00
14 Radiation Threat 2.00
15 Ship of Crawling Death 2.00
16 . . . . .2.00
17 Animal on the Loose 2.00
18 Battle For the Forbidden Fruit . . .2.00
19 Starbuck's Back 2.00
20 Duel to the Death 2.00
21 To Slay a Monster..To Deatroy a
    World 2.00
22 Walt Simonson, A Love Story? . .2.00

Battlestar Galactica #9 (Marvel 1980)

23 final issue 2.00

BATTLESTAR GALACTICA
Maximum Press 1995
1 Finds Earth 2.50
2 Council of Twelve 2.50
3 R:Adama 2.50
4 Pyramid Secrets 2.50
TPB series rep. 12.95
Spec. Ed. Painted Book (1997) . . .3.00
Battlestar Galactica: The Compendium #1 rep. Asylum (1997) . . .3.00

APOLLO'S JOURNEY
Maximum Press 1996
1 story by Richard Hatch 2.95
2 . . . . .2.50
3 . . . . .2.50

THE ENEMY WITHIN
Maximum Press 1995–96
1 . . . . .3.00
2 . . . . .2.50
3 . . . . .2.50

JOURNEY'S END
Maximum Press 1996
1 (of 4) Rob Liefeld 3.00
2 Rob Liefeld 3.00
3 Rob Liefeld, the end of Galactica? .3.00
4 Rob Liefeld, conclusion 3.00

*Battlestar Galactica: The Compendium
#1 (Maximum 1997)*

STARBUCK
Maximum Press 1995–96
1 (of 3) Rob Liefeld 2.50
2 Rob Liefeld 2.95
3 Rob Liefeld, the end of Galactica? .2.95

BATTLESTAR GALACTICA
Realm Press 1997
1 by Chris Scalf 3.00
1a variant cover 3.00
2 Law of Volhad 3.00
3 Prison of Souls, pt.1 . . . . .3.00
3a alternate cover 3.00
4 Prison of Souls, pt.2 . . . . .3.00
5 . . . . .3.00
6 A Path of Darkness, pt.1 . . . . . . .3.00
7 A Path of Darkness, pt.2 . . . . . . .3.00
7a photo (c) 3.00
7b signed and numbered 6.00
8 Centurion Prime 3.00
TPB New Beginnings, rep. #1–#4 . .14.00

BETTA: TIME WARRIOR
Immortal Comics 1997
1 (of 3) "Beginnings's End," pt.1 . . . .2.95
2 "The Beginnings's End," pt.2 . . . .2.95

BEYOND MARS
Blackthorne (B&W)
1 thru 5 . . . .@2.00

BILL THE GALACTIC HERO
Topps
1 thru 3 Harry Harrison adapt. . . .@4.95

BLACK HOLE, THE
Whitman 1980
1 & 2 movie adaptation . . . .@1.50
3 & 4 new stories . . . .@1.50

BLADE RUNNER
Marvel 1982
1 Al Williamson, Movie Adaptation . .1.50
2 Al Williamson 1.50

BUCK ROGERS

BUCK ROGERS
Eastern Color Printing 1940–43
1 Partial Painted(c) 2,700.00
2 . . . . .1,000.00
3 Living Corpse from Crimson
   Coffin 850.00
4 One man army of greased
   lightning 800.00
5 Sky Roads 750.00
6 September, 1943 . . . . .750.00

Toby Press 1951
100 Flying Saucers 200.00
101 . . . . .175.00
9 . . . . .175.00

FOUR COLOR
Dell Publishing Co.
[Second Series] 1941–60
733 Buck Rogers (Oct. 1956) 35.00

BUCK ROGERS
Gold Key 1964, 1979–82
1 Painted(c) (Oct. 1964) 55.00
2 Painted(c), movie adaptation 15.00
3 Movie adaptation 15.00
4 Painted(c) 15.00
5 Painted(c) The Missing Element .10.00
6 Painted(c) 10.00

Whitman
7 thru 9 Painted(c) . . . .@8.00

*Buck Rogers in the 25th Century #2
(Gold Key 1979)*

10 and 11 Painted(c) . . . .@4.00
12 and 13 Painted(c) 3.00
14 thru 16 . . . . .3.00

COSMIC HEROES
Eternity
1 Buck Rogers rep. 1.95
2 thru 6 Buck Rogers rep. . . . . . .@1.95
7 thru 9 Buck Rogers rep. . . . . . .@2.25
10 . . . . .3.50
11 . . . . .3.95

BUCK ROGERS
TSR 1990–91
1 thru 3 O:Buck Rogers . . . .@2.95
4 thru 6 Black Barney . . . .@2.95
7 thru 10 The Martian Wars . . . . .@2.95

BUSTER CRABBE
Lev Gleason Pub. 1953
1 Photo(c) 150.00
2 . . . . .150.00
3 . . . . .150.00
4 Flash Gordon(c) 125.00

CHALLENGERS OF THE UNKNOWN
DC 1958–78
1 Jack Kirby, The Man Who
   Tampered With Infinity . . .2,200.00
2 Jack Kirby, The Monster Maker .800.00
3 Jack Kirby, The Secret of the
   Sorcerer's Mirror 700.00
4 Jack Kirby, Wally Wood, The
   Wizard of Time 550.00
5 Jack Kirby, Wally Wood, The
   Riddle of the Star-Stone 550.00
6 Jack Kirby, Wally Wood, Captives
   of the Space Circus 550.00
7 Jack Kirby, Wally Wood, The Isle
   of No Return 550.00
8 Jack Kirby, Wally Wood, The Prisoners of the Robot Planet . .550.00
9 The Plot To Destroy Earth 250.00
10 The Four Faces of Doom 250.00
11 The Creatures From The
   Forbidden World 175.00
12 The Three Clues To Sorcery . . .175.00
13 The Prisoner of the Tiny Space
   Ball 175.00
14 O: Multi Man 175.00
15 Lady Giant and the Beast 175.00
16 Prisoners of the Mirage World .150.00
17 The Secret of the Space
   Capsules 150.00
18 Menace of Mystery Island 150.00
19 The Alien Who Stole a Planet . .150.00

Cosmic Heroes #7 (Eternity 1989)

20 Multi-Man Strikes Back 150.00
21 Weird World That Didn't Exist . .150.00
22 The Thing In Challenger
   Mountain 150.00
23 The Island In The Sky 90.00
24 The Challengers Die At Dawn . .90.00
25 Captives of the Alien Hunter 90.00
26 Death Crowns The Challenge
   King 90.00
27 Master of the Volcano Men 90.00
28 The Riddle of the Faceless Man .90.00
29 Four Roads to Doomsday 90.00
30 Multi-Man...Villain Turned Hero . 90.00
31 O:Challengers 40.00
32 One Challenger Must Die 40.00
33 Challengers Meet Their Master . .40.00
34 Beachhead, USA 40.00
35 War Against The Moon Beast . . .40.00
36 Giant In Challenger Mountain . .40.00
37 Triple Terror of Mr. Dimension . . .40.00
38 Menace the Challengers Made . .40.00
39 Phantom of the Fair 40.00
40 Super-Powers of the Challengers .40.00
41 The Challenger Who Quit 20.00
42 The League of Challenger-
   Haters 20.00
43 New look begins 20.00
44 The Curse of the Evil Eye 20.00
45 Queen of the Challenger-Haters .20.00
46 Strange Schemes of the
   Gargoyle 20.00
47 The Sinister Sponge 20.00
48 A:Doom Patrol 20.00
49 Tyrant Who Owned the World . . .20.00
50 Final Hours for the Challengers .20.00
51 A:Sea Devil 20.00
52 Two Are Dead - Two To Go 20.00
53 Who is the Traitor Among Us? . .20.00
54 War of the Sub-Humans 20.00
55 D:Red Ryan 20.00
56 License To Kill 20.00
57 Kook And The Kilowatt Killer . . .20.00
58 Live Till Tomorrow 20.00
59 Seekeenakee - The Petrified
   Giant 20.00
60 R:Red Ryan 20.00
61 Robot Hounds of Chang 20.00
62 Legion of the Weird 20.00
63 None Shall Escape the
   Walking Evil 20.00
64 Invitation to a Hanging 20.00
65 The Devil's Circus 10.00
66 Rendezvous With Revenge 10.00
67 The Dream Killers 10.00
68 One of Us is a Madman 10.00
69 I:Corinna 10.00
70 Scream of Yesterdays 10.00
71 When Evil Calls 10.00

72 A Plague of Darkness 10.00
73 Curse of the Killer Time Forgot . .10.00
74 A:Deadman 22.00
75 Ultivac Is Loose 7.00
76 The Traitorous Challenger 7.00
77 Menace of the Ancient Vials 7.00
78 The Island of No Return 5.00
79 The Monster Maker 5.00
80 The Day The Earth Blew Up 5.00
81 Multi-Man's Master Plan 5.00
82 Swamp Thing 5.00
83 Seven Doorways to Destiny 5.00
84 To Save A Monster 5.00
85 The Creature From The End
Of Time 5.00
86 The War At Time's End 5.00
87 final issue 5.00

CHALLENGERS OF THE UNKNOWN
DC 1991
1 In The Spotlight 1.75
2 . . . . .1.75
3 Challengers "Split Up" 1.75
4 "Separate Ways" 1.75
5 Moffet 1.75
6 Challengers reunited 1.75
7 June pregnant 1.75
8 final issue 1.75

CHALLENGERS OF THE UNKNOWN
DC 1997–98
1 . . . . .2.25
2 Zombies .2.25
3 Death of Challenger 2.25
4 O:Challengers 2.25
5 V:The Fearslayer 2.25
6 "Convergence,"pt. 3 x-over 2.25
7 "Past Perfect,"pt.1 (of 3) 2.25
8 "Past Perfect,"pt.2 . . . . .2.25
9 "Past Perfect," pt.3 . . . . .2.25
10 F:Brenda Ruskin 2.25
11 in Gothan, pt.1 . . . . .2.25
12 in Gothan, pt.2 . . . . .2.25
13 F:Marlon Corbett 2.25
14 . . . . .2.25
15 Millennium Giants pt. 3, x-over . .2.50
16 original Chalis 2.50
17 disappearances 2.50
18 final issue 2.50

CRUSADER FROM MARS
Approved Publ. (Ziff-Davis) 1952
1 Mission Thru Space, Death in the
Sai 550.00
2 Beachhead on Saturn's Ring,
Bondage(c) 400.00

CYBER 7
Eclipse (B&W) 1989
1 from Japanese 2.50
2 thru 5 . . . .@2.00

Book 2 Rockland 1990
1 thru 7 . . . .@2.00
8 thru 10 . . . .@2.50

DAI KAMIKAZE
Now 1987–88
1 Speed Racer 7.00
1a 2nd printing 1.50
2 . . . . .2.00
3 thru 5 . . . .@1.50
6 thru 12 . . . .@1.75

DEATHWORLD
Adventure Comics (B&W) 1990
1 Harry Harrison adapt. 2.50
2 thru 4 . . . .@2.50

BOOK II 1991
1 Harry Harrison adapt. 2.50
2 thru 4 . . . .@2.50

BOOK III 1991
1 H.Harrison adapt., colonization . .2.50
2 Attack on the Lowlands 2.50
3 Attack on the Lowlands contd. . . .2.50
4 last issue 2.50

DEFENDERS OF THE EARTH
Marvel 1987
1 Flash Gordon & Mandrake 2.00
2 Flash Gordon & Mandrake 2.00
3 O:Phantom 2.00
4 O:Mandrake 2.00

DEFENSELESS DEAD
Adventure Comics (B&W) 1991
1 Larry Niven adapt. A:Gil 2.50
2 A:Organlegger 2.50
3 A:Organlegger 2.50

Doctor Who #20 (Marvel 1986)

DOCTOR WHO
1984–86
1 BBC TV Series, UK reprints,
Return of the Daleks 4.50
2 Star Beast 3.00
3 Transformation 3.00
4 A:K-9, Daleks 3.00
5 V:Time Witch, Colin Baker
interview 3.00
6 B:Ancient Claw saga 3.00
7 . . . . .3.00
8 The Collector 3.00
9 The Life Bringer 3.00
10 This is your Life 3.00
11 The Deal 3.00
12 End of the Line 3.00
13 V:The Cybermen 3.00
14 Clash of the Neutron Knight 3.00
15 B:Peter Davison-Dr. Who 3.00
16 Into the Realm of Satan 3.00
17 Peter Davison Interview 3.00
18 A:Four Dr.Who's 3.00
19 A:The Sontarans 3.00
20 The Stockbridge Horror 3.00
21 The Stockbridge Horror 3.00
22 The Stockbridge Horror 3.00
23 The Unearthly Child 3.00

DRAGONFLIGHT
Eclipse 1991
1 Anne McCaffrey adapt. 4.95
2 novel adapt 4.95
3 novel adapt 4.95

Dune #1 (Marvel 1985)

DUNE
Marvel 1985
1 Movie Adaptation, Rep. Marvel
Super Spec 1.50
2 Movie Adaptation 1.50
3 Movie Adaptation 1.50

EDGAR RICE BURROUGHS' TARZAN: CARSON OF VENUS
Dark Horse 1998
1 (of 4) by Darko Macan and Igor
Kordey, adaptation of novels,
F:Carson Napier 2.95
2 thru 4 . . . .@2.95

ESCAPE VELOCITY
Escape Velocity Press
1 and 2 . . . .@1.50

EXO-SQUAD
Topps 1994
0 . . . . .1.00
1 From Animated Series 2.50
2 F:Nara Burns 2.50
3 V:Neo-Sapiens 2.50

THE FIRST MEN IN THE MOON
Classics Illustrated #144
By H. G. Wells
05/58 **(143)** Original 32.00
11/59 **(153)** rep 6.00
03/61 **(161)** rep 6.00
62/63 **(167)** rep 6.00
12/65 **(167)** rep 6.00
Fl/68 **(166)** 25¢(c) price, Rigid(c);rep .6.00
Wr/69 **(169)** Rigid(c); rep 15.00

MOVIE COMICS
Gold Key/Whitman 1962
First Men of the Moon 30.00

MARVEL CLASSICS COMICS
1976–78
31 The First Men in the Moon 9.00

FLASH GORDON

KING COMICS
David McKay Publications 1936
(all have Popeye covers)
1 Alex Raymond, begin Flash
Gordon; Popeye, Henry,

Mandrake 8,000.00
2 Alex Raymond, Flash Gordon .2,400.00
3 Alex Raymond, Flash Gordon .1,500.00
4 Alex Raymond, Flash Gordon .1,200.00
5 Alex Raymond, Flash Gordon . .800.00
6 Alex Raymond, Flash Gordon . .600.00
7 Alex Raymond, King Royal
Mounties 575.00
8 Alex Raymond, Thanksgiving(c) 550.00
9 Alex Raymond, Christmas(c) . .550.00
10 Alex Raymond, Flash Gordon . .550.00
11 thru 16 Alex Raymond . . . . . .@500.00
17 thru 20 Alex Raymond . . . . . .@475.00
21 thru 25 Alex Raymond . . . . . .@350.00
26 thru 33 Alex Raymond, ...@325.00
34 thru 40 Alex Raymond . . . . . .@275.00
41 thru 51 Alex Raymond . . . . . .@250.00
52 thru 62 Alex Raymond . . . . . .@175.00
63 thru 71 Alex Raymond . . . . . .@150.00
72 thru 75 Alex Raymond . . . . . .@125.00
76 Alex Raymond 135.00
77 thru 81 Alex Raymond . . . . . .@125.00
82 thru 91 Alex Raymond . . . . . .@100.00
92 thru 98 Alex Raymond . . . .@85.00
99 Alex Raymond 100.00
100 . . . . .125.00
101 thru 116 Alex Raymond . . . . .@85.00
117 O:Phantom 75.00
118 Flash Gordon 85.00
119 Flash Gordon 75.00
120 Wimpy(c) 60.00

Flash Gordon #7 (King Comics 1967)

121 thru 140 . . . .@75.00
141 thru 144 Flash Gordon . . . . . .@60.00
145 Prince Valiant 55.00
146 Prince Valiant 55.00
147 Prince Valiant 55.00
148 thru 154 . . . .@45.00
155 End: Flash Gordon 45.00

FOUR COLOR
Dell Publishing Co.
[Second Series] 1941–60
10 Flash Gordon 800.00
84 Flash Gordon 450.00
173 Flash Gordon 150.00
190 Flash Gordon 150.00
204 Flash Gordon 100.00
247 Flash Gordon 125.00
424 Flash Gordon (Sept. 1952) . .150.00
512 Flash Gordon (Nov. 1953) . . .60.00

FLASH GORDON
Harvey Publications 1950–51
1 Alex Raymond, Bondage(c) . . .200.00
2 Alex Raymond 150.00
3 Alex Raymond Bondage(c) 165.00
4 Alex Raymond 150.00

Flash Gordon #1 (Marvel 1995)

MARCH OF COMICS
K.K. Publications/
Western Publ. 1952–56

118 Flash Gordon, Painted(c)	120.00
133 Flash Gordon, Photo(c)	100.00
142 Flash Gordon	80.00

FLASH GORDON
Gold Key 1965

1 . . . . .15.00

FLASH GORDON
King 1966–69

1 Al Williamson, A:Mandrake 35.00
1a Comp. Army giveaway 50.00
2 A:Mandrake, R:Ming 25.00
3 "Lost in the Land of The
  Lizardmen" 30.00
4 Al Williamson, B:Secret Agent
  X-9 . . . . .32.00
5 Al Williamson 32.00
6 On the Lost Continent of Mongo .30.00
7 rep. "In the Human Forest" 30.00
8 . . . . .30.00
9 Alex Raymond, rep 35.00
10 Alex Raymond, rep 35.00
11 . . . . .25.00

Charlton 1969–70

12 . . . . .25.00
13 thru 16 . . . .@20.00
17 Brick Bradford story 20.00
18 "Attack of the Locust Men" 20.00

Gold Key 1975

19 Flash returns to Mongo 6.00
20 thru 30 . . . .@5.00
31 thru 37 Al Williamson movie
  adaptation . . . .@3.00

FLASH GORDON
DC 1988

1 I:New Flash Gordon 2.00
2 A:Lion-Men, Shark-Men 1.75
3 V:Shark-Men 1.50
4 Dale Kidnapped by Voltan 1.50
5 Alliance Against Ming 1.50
6 Arctic City 1.50
7 Alliance vs. Ming 1.50
8 Alliance vs. Ming 1.50
9 V:Ming, final issue 1.50

FLASH GORDON
Marvel 1995

1 R:Flash Gordon 2.00
2 Al Williamson, V:Ming, final issue .2.95

FLYING SAUCERS
Dell 1967

1 . . . . .22.00
2 thru 5 . . . . .15.00

THE FOOD
OF THE GODS
Classics Illustrated #160
By H.G. Wells

01/61 **(159)** Original 40.00
01/61 **(160)** Original;
  Same Except For the HRN# . .35.00
01/64 **(167)** rep 15.00
06/67 **(166)** rep 15.00

MARVEL CLASSICS
COMICS
Marvel 1976–78

22 Food of the Gods 9.00

Forbidden Planet #3 (Innovation 1992)

FORBIDDEN PLANET
Innovation 1992

1 Movie adaptation 2.50
2 thru 4 Movie adaptation, cont. . .@2.50
GN rep.#1–#4 (1997) 8.95

FORBIDDEN WORLDS
American Comics Group 1951

1 Al Williamson, Frank Frazetta .1,000.00
2 . . . . .500.00
3 Al Williamson, Wally Wood, ...500.00
4 Werewolf cover 250.00
5 Al Williamson 400.00
6 Al Williamson, King Kong cover 350.00
7 . . . . .200.00
8 . . . . .200.00
9 Atomic Bomb 225.00
10 . . . . .175.00
11 The Mummy's Treasure 150.00
12 Chest of Death 150.00
13 Invasion from Hades 150.00
14 Million-Year Monster 150.00
15 The Vampire Cat 150.00
16 The Doll 150.00
17 . . . . .150.00
18 The Mummy 150.00
19 Pirate and the Voodoo Queen . .150.00
20 Terror Island 150.00
21 The Ant Master 100.00
22 The Cursed Casket 100.00
23 Nightmare for Two 100.00
24 . . . . .100.00
25 Hallahan's Head 100.00
26 The Champ 100.00
27 Thing with the Golden Hair 100.00
28 Portrait of Carlotta 100.00

Forbidden Worlds #115 (Ace 1963)

29 The Frogman 100.00
30 The Things on the Beach 100.00
31 The Circle of the Doomed 80.00
32 The Invasion of the Dead Things 80.00
33 . . . . .80.00
34 Atomic Bomb 110.00
35 Comics Code 75.00
36 thru 62 . . . .@50.00
63 Al Williamson 75.00
64 thru 68 . . . .@45.00
69 Al Williamson 75.00
70 . . . . .45.00
71 . . . . .45.00
72 I:Herbie 150.00
73 . . . . .45.00
74 . . . . .45.00
75 John Buscema 40.00
76 Al Williamson 60.00
77 . . . . .40.00
78 Al Williamson 60.00
79 thru 85 John Buscema . . . . .@40.00
86 Flying Saucer 50.00
87 thru 93 . . . .@40.00
94 A:Herbie 75.00
95 . . . . .30.00
96 Al Williamson 50.00
97 thru 115 . . . .@30.00
116 A:Herbie 35.00
117 thru 124 . . . .@30.00
125 I:O:Magic Man 35.00
126 thru 132 A:Magic Man . . . . .@25.00
133 I:O:Dragona 25.00
134 A:Magic Man 25.00
135 A:Magic Man 25.00
136 A:Nemesis 25.00
137 thru 39 A:Magic Man . . . . . .@25.00
140 A:Mark Midnight 25.00
141 thru 145 . . . .@15.00

FOREVER WAR, THE
NBM

GN Vol. 1 Joe Haldeman adapt. 8.95
GN Vol. 2 Joe Haldeman adapt. 8.95
GN Vol. 3 Joe Haldeman adapt. 8.95

FROM THE EARTH
TO THE MOON
Classics Illustrated #105
By Jules Verne

03/53 **(106)** AB, P(c), Original 28.00
1954 thru 1971 rep . . . .@5.00

FUTURE WORLD
COMICS
George W. Dougherty 1946

1 . . . . .165.00
2 . . . . .150.00

GALAXION
Helikon (B&W) 1997

1 by Tara Jenkins, science fiction . . .2.75
2 . . . . .2.75
3 . . . . .2.75
4 Choices 2.75
5 . . . . .2.75
6 Communication 2.75
Spec. #1, 16pg. 1.00

GENE RODDENBERRY'S
LOST UNIVERSE
Teckno-Comics 1994

0 I:Sensua 2.50
1 Gene Roddenberry's 2.50
2 Grange Discovered 2.25
3 Secrets Revealed 1.95
4 F:Penultra 1.95
5 I:New Alien Race 1.95
6 Two Doctor Granges 1.95
7 F:Alaa Chi Tskare 1.95

XANDER IN LOST UNIVERSE
Teckno-Comics 1995

1 V:Black Ghost 2.25
2 V:Walker 2.25
3 V:Lady Sensua 2.25
4 thru 7 . . . .@2.25
8 F:Lady Sensua 2.25

[Mini-Series]
Teckno-Comics 1995

1 F:L.Nimoy's Primortals 2.25

HARLAN ELLISON'S
DREAM CORRIDOR
Dark Horse 1995

1 Various stories 2.95
2 Various stories 2.95
3 John Byrne art, "I Have No Mouth
  and I Must Scream"and others .2.95
4 Catman 2.95
5 . . . . .2.95
6 Opposites Attract 2.95
Spec.#1 Various stories 4.95
TPB (1996) 18.95
HC, vol. 1 limited 70.00

DREAM CORRIDOR QUARTERLY
Dark Horse 1996

1 . . . . .5.95
2 . . . . .5.95

HITCHHIKER'S GUIDE
TO THE GALAXY
DC

1 Douglas Adams novel adaptation .7.00
2 Novel Adaptation 6.50
3 Novel Adaptation 6.50
GN from Douglas Adams Novel 14.95

RESTAURANT AT THE END
OF THE UNIVERSE
DC 1994

1 Adapt. 2nd book in Hitchhikers'
  Guide to the Galaxy, I:The
  Restaurant 7.00
2 V:The Meal 7.00
3 Final issue 7.00

LIFE, THE UNIVERSE
AND EVERYTHING
DC 1996

1 thru 3 Doug Adams adaptation. .@6.95

INCREDIBLE
SCIENCE FICTION
E.C. Comics 1955–56

30 . . . . .250.00
31 . . . . .275.00
32 . . . . .275.00
33 . . . . .250.00

Life, The Universe and Everything,
Book 2 (DC 1996)

INDEPENDENCE DAY
Marvel 1996
0 Prequel 1.50
1 Movie adaptation 1.50
2 Movie adaptation 1.50
TPB rep. #0–#2, 96pg 6.95

INVADERS FROM MARS
Eternity (B&W)
1 . . . . .2.50
2 . . . . .2.50
3 . . . . .2.50

BOOK II 1991
1 Sequel to '50s SF classic 2.50
2 Pact of Tsukus/Humans 2.50
3 Last issue 2.50

INVADERS, THE
Gold Key 1967–68
1 Photo(c),TV Show adaptation . .100.00
2 thru 4 Photo(c) . . . .@75.00

THE INVISIBLE MAN
Classics Illustrated #153
By H. G. Wells
11/59 **(153)** Original 45.00
03/61 **(149)** rep 8.00
1963 thru 1971 rep . . . .@6.00

MARVEL CLASSICS
COMICS
Marvel 1976–78
25 The Invisible Man by H.G.Wells . .9.00

IT! TERROR FROM
BEYOND SPACE
Millenium
1 . . . . .2.50
2 . . . . .2.50

ISAAC ASIMOV'S
I-BOTS
Tekno-Comix 1995
1 I:I-Bots 1.95
2 O:I-Bots .1.95
3 V:Black OP 2.25

I-BOTS
Big Comics 1996
1 F:Lady Justice 2.25
2 thru 4 Crackdown, pt.1–pt.3 . . .@2.25
5 Crackdown, pt.4 . . . . .2.25
6 Crackdown, pt.5 . . . . .2.25
7 "Rebirth,"pt.1, triptych (c) 2.25
8 "Rebirth,"pt.2, triptych (c) 2.25

I-Bots, Vol. 2 #7
(Big Entertainment 1996)

9 "Rebirth,"pt.3, Original
   I Bots return, triptych (c) 2.25

JETTA OF THE
21st CENTURY
Standard Comics 1952
5 Teen Stories 150.00
6 . . . . .100.00
7 April, 1953 . . . . .100.00

JOHN CARTER
OF MARS

FUNNIES, THE
(2nd Series)
Dell Publishing Co. 1939–41
30 B:John Carter of Mars 900.00
31 inc. Dick Tracy 550.00
32 . . . . .550.00
33 . . . . .550.00
34 . . . . .550.00
35 John Carter (c) 550.00
36 John Carter (c) 550.00
37 John Carter (c) 550.00
38 Rex King of the Deep (c) 550.00
39 Rex King (c) 550.00
40 John Carter (c) 550.00
41 Sky Ranger (c) 550.00
42 Rex King (c) 550.00
43 Rex King (c) 550.00
44 Rex King (c) 550.00
45 I&O:Phantasmo:Master of the
    World 450.00
46 Phantasmo (c) 450.00
47 Phantasmo (c) 350.00
48 thru 51 Phantasmo (c) . . . . .@325.00
52 thru 55 Phantasmo (c) . . . . .@350.00
56 Phantasmo (c) E:John Carter . .350.00

FOUR COLOR
Dell Publishing Co.
[Second Series] 1941–60
375 John Carter of Mars 275.00
437 John Carter of Mars 175.00
488 John Carter of Mars 175.00

WEIRD WORLDS
DC 1972–74
1 John Carter 30.00
2 Neal Adams, Berni Wrightson . . .25.00
3 Neal Adams 15.00
4 thru 6 Mike Kaluta art . . . .@10.00
7 John Carter ends 10.00

JOHN CARTER,
WARLORD OF MARS
Marvel 1977
1 Gil Kane, O:John Carter, Created
   by Edgar Rice Burroughs 5.00
2 Gil Kane, White Apes of Mars 3.00
3 Gil Kane, Requiem for a Warlord . .3.00
4 Gil Kane, Raiding Party 3.00
5 Gil Kane, Giant Battle Issue 3.00
6 Gil Kane, Alone Against a World . .3.00
7 Gil Kane, Showdown 3.00
8 Gil Kane, Beast With Touch of
   Stone 3.00
9 Gil Kane, Giant Battle Issue 3.00
10 Gil Kane, The Death of Barsoom? 3.00

John Carter, Warlord of Mars #2
(Marvel 1977)

11 O:Dejah Thoris 2.00
12 City of the Dead 2.00
13 March of the Dead 2.00
14 The Day Helium Died 2.00
15 Gil Kane, Prince of Helium
    Returns 2.00
16 John Carters Dilemna 2.00
17 What Price Victory 5.00
18 Tars Tarkas Battles Alone 1.50
19 War With the Wing Men 1.50
20 Battle at the Bottom of the World .1.50
21 The Claws of the Banth 1.50
22 The Canyon of Death 1.50
23 Murder on Mars 1.50
24 Betrayal 1.50
25 Inferno 1.50
26 Death Cries the Guild of
    Assassins 1.50
27 Death Marathon 1.50
28 Guardians of the Lost City Oct.,
    1979 . . . . .2.50
Ann.#1 Gil Kane, Battle story 2.00
Ann.#2 Gil Kane, Outnumbered 2.00
Ann.#3 Gil Kane, Battle story 2.00

TARZAN/JOHN CARTER:
WARLORDS OF MARS
Dark Horse
1 thru 4 E.R.Burroughs adapt. . . .@2.50

JOHN JAKES
MULLKON EMPIRE
Tekno Comix 1995
1 I:Mulkons 2.25
2 O:Mulkons 1.95
3 D:Company Man 1.95
4 Disposal Problems 1.95
5 F:Granny 1.95
6 Where's Karma 2.25

A JOURNEY TO THE
CENTER OF THE EARTH
Classics Illustrated #138
By Jules Verne
05/57 **(136)** NN, P(c), Original 45.00
1958 thru 1963 rep. . . . .@5.00
1964 and 1966 rep. . . . .@8.00

FOUR COLOR
Dell Publishing Co.
[Second Series] 1941–60
1060 Journey to the Center of the Earth,
    P.Boone Photo(c) 125.00

JOURNEY INTO
UNKNOWN WORLDS
Atlas 1950–57
36(1) End of the Earth 1,600.00
37(2) When Worlds Collide 800.00
38(3) Land of Missing Men 600.00
4 Train to Nowhere 375.00
5 Trapped in Space 375.00
6 World Below the Atlantic 375.00
7 House That Wasn't 650.00
8 The Stone Thing 375.00
9 The People Who Couldn't Exist .450.00
10 Undertaker 375.00
11 Frankie Was Afraid 275.00
12 The Last Voice You Hear 275.00
13 The Witch Woman 200.00
14 Condemned Building 500.00
15 They Crawl By Night 500.00
16 Scared to Death 225.00
17 The Ice Monster Cometh 225.00
18 The Broth Needs Somebody . .250.00
19 The Long Wait 250.00
20 The Race That Vanished 200.00
21 thru 25 . . . .@175.00
26 thru 35 . . . .@150.00
36 thru 44 . . . .@125.00
45 Al Williamson 135.00
46 thru 49 . . . .@100.00
50 . . . . .125.00
51 Wally Wood 135.00
52 . . . . .100.00
53 . . . . .125.00
54 . . . . .125.00
55 Al Williamson 125.00
56 . . . . .125.00
57 . . . . .100.00
58 . . . . .100.00
59 Al Williamson, August, 1957 . .125.00
26 Judge Dredd & Gavel? 2.50
27 Cycles, Lunatics & Graffiti
    Guerillas 2.50
28 Cadet Training Mission 2.50
29 "Guinea Pig that changed the

Lensman: The Secret of the Lens #1
(Eternity 1990)

world 2.50
30 Meka-City, V:Robot 2.50
31 Iso-Block 666 . . . . .2.50
32 Missing Game Show Hosts 2.50
33 League of Fatties, final issue 3.00

LARS OF MARS
Ziff-Davis Publishing Co. 1951
10 "Terror from the Sky" 600.00
11 The Terror Weapon 500.00

LARS OF MARS
Eclipse 1987
1 3-D .2.50

LAST STARFIGHTER, THE
Marvel 1984
1 thru 3 Movie adaptation. . . . . . .@1.00

LENSMAN
Eternity (B&W) 1990
1 E.E."Doc"Smith adapt. 2.25
2 thru 6 . . . .@2.25
Collectors Spec #1, 56 pgs. 3.95
TPB Birth of a Lensman, rep. 5.95
TPB Secret of the Lens, rep. 5.95

GALACTIC PATROL
Eternity (B&W) 1990
1 thru 7 E.E. "Doc"Smith adapt. . .@2.25

WAR OF THE GALAXIES
Eternity (B&W) 1990
1 thru 7 . . . .@2.25

LEONARD NIMOY'S PRIMORTALS
Teckno-Comics 1994
1 I:Primortals 5.50
2 Zeerus Reveals Himself 4.00
3 Contact 2.50
4 Message Deciphered 2.25
5 Place & Time Announced 2.25
6 Zeerus Arrives on Earth 2.25
7 Zeerus Received 2.25
8 Hyperspace Escape 2.25
9 Pristar Lands on Earth 1.95
10 V:U.S. Army 1.95
11 V:U.S. Army 1.95
12 V:Zeerus 2.25
13 thru 15 . . . .@2.25

Big Entertainment 1996
0 SEa, MKb 2.25
1 Camera's Eye View 2.25
2 thru 7 . . . .@2.25

Logan's Run #4 (Marvel 1977)

LIGHT FANTASTIC, THE
Innovation 1992
1 Terry Pratchett adapt. 2.50
2 Adaptation continues 2.50
3 Adaptation continues 2.50
4 Adapt.conclusion 2.50

LOGAN'S RUN
Marvel 1977
1 George Perez, From Movie 6.00
2 George Perez, Cathedral Kill 5.00
3 George Perez, Lair of Laser Death 5.00
4 George Perez, Dread Sanctuary . .5.00
5 George Perez, End Run 5.00
6 Mike Zeck, B.U.Thanos/Drax 10.00
7 Cathedral Prime 5.00

LOGAN'S RUN
Adventure Comics (B&W) 1990
1 thru 6 Novel adapt. . . . .@2.50

LOGAN'S WORLD
Adventure Comics (B&W) 1991
1 Seq. to Logan's Run 2.50
2 thru 6 . . . .@2.50

Lost in Space Spec. #1 (Innovation 1991)

SPACE FAMILY ROBINSON
Gold Key 1962–69
1 Dan Spiegle 250.00
2 . . . . .125.00
3 . . . . .75.00
4 . . . . .75.00
5 Mist of Del.. . . . . .75.00
6 B:Captain Venture 75.00
7 thru 10 . . . .@75.00
11 thru 14 . . . .@50.00
Becomes:

SPACE FAMILY ROBINSON LOST IN SPACE
15 thru 20 . . . .@50.00
21 thru 36 . . . .@25.00
Becomes:

SPACE FAMILY ROBINSON LOST IN SPACE ON SPACE STATION ONE 1973–82
37 thru 48 . . . .@7.50
49 thru 59 . . . .@5.00

MARCH OF COMICS
Western Publ.1968–76
(All were Giveaways)
320 Space Family Robinson 100.00

328 Space Family Robinson 55.00
352 Space Family Robinson 75.00
404 Space Family Robinson 40.00
414 Space Family Robinson 35.00

LOST IN SPACE
Innovation 1991–93
(based on TV series)
1 O:Jupiter II Project 3.00
2 "Cavern of Idyllic Summers Lost" .2.75
2a Special Edition 2.50
3 "Do Not Go Gently into that Good Night," Bill Mumy script 2.50
4 "People are Strange" 2.50
5 The Perils of Penelope 2.50
6 Time Warp 2.50
7 thru 9 . . . .@2.50
10 inc.Afterthought 2.50
11 F:Judy Robinson 2.50
12 . . . . .2.95
Project Krell 2.50
Ann.#1 (1991) 2.95
Ann.#2 (1992) 2.95
1Spec.#1 & #2 rep. Seduction of the Innocent . . . .@2.50
GN Strangers among Strangers . . .6.00
1-shot Project Robinson, follows story in issue #12 (1993) 2.50
Becomes

LOST IN SPACE: VOYAGE TO THE BOTTOM OF THE SOUL
Innovation 1993–94
13 . . . . .2.95
14 thru 18 . . . .@2.50

LOST IN SPACE
Dark Horse 1998
1 (of 3) sequel to film 2.95
2 thru 3 . . . .@2.95
TPB rep. series, ...7.95

LOST PLANET
Eclipse 1987–88
1 I:Tyler FLynn 2.00
2 R:Amelia Earhart 1.75
3 . . . . .1.25
4 "Devil's Eye" 1.25
5 A:Amelia Earhart 2.00
6 . . . . .2.00

Lucifer's Hammer #2 (Innovation 1993)

LUCIFER'S HAMMER
Innovation 1993–94
1 thru 6 Larry Niven & Jerry Pournelle novel adaptation . . . .@2.50

MAGNUS: ROBOT FIGHTER
Gold Key 1963
1 I:Magnus, Teeja, A-1, I&B:Capt. Johner & aliens 250.00
2 I:Sen.Zeremiah Clane 125.00
3 I:Xyrkol 125.00
4 I:Mekamn, Elzy 75.00
5 The Immortal One 75.00
6 I:Talpa 70.00
7 I:Malev-6, ViXyrkol 85.00
8 I:Outsiders (Chet, Horio, Toun, Malf) 70.00
9 I:Madmot 70.00
10 Mysterious Octo-Rob 70.00
11 I:Danae, Neo-Animals 50.00
12 The Volcano Makers 50.00
13 I:Dr Lazlo Noel 55.00
14 The Monster Robs 50.00
15 I:Mogul Radur 50.00
16 I:Gophs 50.00
17 I:Zypex 50.00
18 I:V'ril Trent 50.00
19 Fear Unlimited 50.00
20 I:Bunda the Great 50.00
21 Space Spectre 50.00
22 Rep. #1 . . . . .35.00
23 Mission Disaster 35.00
24 Pied Piper of North Am 35.00
25 The Micro Giants 35.00
26 The Venomous Vaper 35.00
27 Panic in Pacifica 35.00
28 Threats from the Depths 35.00
29 thru 46 reprints . . . .@16.00

CAPTAIN JOHNER AND THE ALIENS
Gold Key 1967
1 Rep. Magnus Robot Fighter 12.50

CAPTAIN JOHNER & THE ALIENS
Valiant 1995
1 Rep. Magnus Robot Fighter #1–7 (Gold Key 1963–64) 2.95

MAGNUS: ROBOT FIGHTER
Valiant 1991
0 "Emancipator," with trading card . .7.00
0a no card 3.00
1 B:Steel Nation 4.00
1a no coupon 1.00
2 Steel Nation #2 . . . . .3.00
2a no coupon 1.00
3 Steel Nation #3 . . . . .3.00

Magnus Robot Fighter 4000 A.D. (Gold Key 1964)

*Captain Johner and The Aliens
(Gold Key 1967)*

*Captain Johner and the Aliens #1
(Valiant 1995)*

3a no coupon 1.00
4 E:Steel Nation 3.00
4a no coupon 1.00
5 I:Rai(#1), V:Slagger Flipbook
  format .3.00
5a no coupon 1.00
6 A:Solar, V:Grandmother A:Rai (#2) 2.50
6a no coupon 1.00
7 V:Rai(#3) 2.50
7a no coupon 1.00
8 A:Rai(#4), Solar, X-O
  Armor.E:Flipbooks 2.50
8a no coupon 1.00
9 V:Xyrkol, E-7 . . . . .2.50
10 V:Xyrkol 2.50
11 V:Xyrkol 2.50
12 I:Turok, V:Dr. Noel, I:Asylum,
   40pgs .7.00
13 Asylum Pt 1 . . . . .2.50
14 Asylum Pt 2 . . . . .2.50
15 Unity #4, I:Eternal Warrior of 4001,
   O:Unity 2.50
16 Walt Simonson(c), Unity#12,
   A:Solar, Archer, Armstrong,
   Harbinger, X-O, Rai, Eternal
   Warrior 2.50
17 V:Talpa 2.50
18 R:Mekman, V:E-7 . . . . .2.50
19 V:Mekmen 2.50
20 Tale of Magnus' past 2.50
21 R:Malevalents, Grand-mother . . .3.00
21a Gold Ed. 4.00
22 D:Felina, V:Malevalents,
   Grandmother 2.50
23 V:Malevolents 2.50
24 V:Malevolents 2.50
25 N:Magnus, R:1-A, silver-foil(c) . .3.00
26 I:Young Wolves 2.50
27 V:Dr.Lazlo Noel 2.50
28 V:The Malevs 2.25
29 A:Eternal Warrior 2.25
30 V:The Malevs 2.25
31 V:The Malevs 2.25
32 Battle for South Am 2.25
33 A:Ivar 2.25
34 Captured 2.25
35 V:Mekman 2.25
36 with Valiant Era Card 2.25
37 A:Starwatchers 2.25
38 . . . . .2.25
39 F:Torque 2.25
40 F:Torque, A:Rai 2.25
41 Chaos Effect-Epsilon#4 A:Solar,
   Psi-Lords, Rai 2.50
42 F:Torque, A:Takashi 2.25
43 F:Torque, Immortal E 2.25
44 F:Torque, Stagger 2.25
45 V:Immortal Enemy 2.25

46 V:Immortal Enemy 2.25
47 Cold Blooded, pt.1 . . . . .2.25
48 Cold Blooded, pt.2 . . . . .2.25
49 F:Slagger 2.25
50 V:Invisible Legion 2.25
51 Return of the Robots, pt.1 . . . . . .2.25
52 Return of the Robots, pt.2 . . . . . .2.25
53 Return of the Robots, pt.3 . . . . . .2.25
54 Return of the Robots, pt.4 . . . . . .2.25
55 A:Rai 2.50
56 Magnus in Japan 2.50
57 . . . . .2.50
58 . . . . .2.50
59 V:Rai 2.50
60 R:The Malevs 2.50
61 Secrets of the Malevs 2.50
62 V:Leeja 2.50
63 R:Destroyer 2.50
64 Ultimatum, F:Destroyer 2.50
Yearbook #1 . . . . .3.95
TPB 1-4 . . . . .9.95

MAGNUS (ROBOT FIGHTER)
Acclaim 1997
1 Magnus back from the future 2.50
2 "Tomorrow Never Knows" 2.50
3 "Tomorrow Never Knows" 2.50
4 "Tomorrow Never Knows" 2.50
5 "Tomorrow Never Knows" 2.50
6 A:Janice Whitcraft 2.50
7 "When Titans Clash" 2.50
8 "When Titans Clash" 2.50
9 "See Tirana and Die" 2.50
10 "The Memory" 2.50
11 "Where Angels Fear" 2.50
12 "Showdown" 2.50
13 . . . . .2.50
14 "Wild in the Streets" 2.50
15 Magnus stands alone 2.50
16 "Hart's Home" 2.50
17 "Invasive Procedures" 2.50
18 "Welcome to Salvation" 2.50

ORIGINAL CAPTAIN JOHNAR AND THE ALIENS
Valiant 1995
1 Reprint from Magnus 2.95
2 Russ Manning rep. 2.95

ORIGINAL MAGNUS ROBOT FIGHTER
Valiant 1995
1 Reprint .2.95
2 Russ Manning Art 2.95
3 Russ Manning 2.95

VINTAGE MAGNUS ROBOT FIGHTER
Valiant
1 rep. Gold Key Magnus #22
(which is #1) 6.00
2 rep. Gold Key Magnus #3 . . . . . .4.50
3 rep. Gold Key Magnus #13 . . . . .3.50
4 rep. Gold Key Magnus #15 . . . . .3.50

Mars Attacks #2 (Topps 1994)

MARS ATTACKS
Topps 1994
1 Keith Giffen(s) 6.00
2 thru 6 Keith Giffen(s) . . . . @4.00

[Series 2] 1995–96
1 Counterstrike 3.50
2 Counterstrike, pt.2 . . . . .2.95
3 Counterstrike, pt.3 . . . . .2.95
4 Counterstrike, pt.4 Convictions . .2.95
5 Counterstrike concl. 2.95
6 The Rescue of Janice Brown,pt. 1 .2.95
7 The Rescue of Janice Brown,pt. 2 .2.95
8 . . . . .2.95
Spec. Baseball 3.00

MARS ATTACKS THE SAVAGE DRAGON
Topps 1996–97
1 with bound-in trading card 3.00
2 thru 4 . . . . @3.00

MARS ATTACKS
Image 1996–97
1 Keith Giffen 2.50
2 . . . . .2.50
3 . . . . .2.50
4 End of their world as they knew it .2.50

MARS ATTACKS HIGH SCHOOL
Topps (B&W) 1997
Spec. #1 (of 2) 2.95
Spec. #2 .2.95

MARTIANS!!! IN 3-D
1 . . . . .2.00

MEN FROM EARTH
Future Fun
1 based on Matt Mason toy 6.50

MEN IN BLACK
Aircel (B&W) 1990–91
1 by Lowell Cunningham & Sandy
  Carruthers, basis of Movie 80.00
2 . . . . .60.00

3 F:Jay, Arbiter Doran 60.00
(Book II) 1991
1 . . . . .20.00
2 thru 3 . . . .@10.00

MEN IN BLACK
Marvel 1997
1 Prequel to movie (1997) 4.00
Spec. Movie Adaptation (1997) 4.00
1 Retribution, continuation from
  movie .2.50

MEN IN BLACK: THE ROBORG INCIENT
Castle (B&W)
1 thru 3 . . . .@2.95

MOVIE COMICS
Gold Key/Whitman 1962
Beneath the Planet of the Apes 40.00
Buck Rogers Giant Movie Edition .22.00
Fantastic Voyage 45.00
X, the Man with the X-Ray Eyes . . .70.00

MY FAVORITE MARTIAN
Gold Key 1964–66
1 . . . . .150.00
2 . . . . .75.00
3 thru 9 . . . .@60.00

MYSTERY IN SPACE
DC 1951–81
1 Frank Frazetta, B:Knights of
  the Galaxy, Nine Worlds to
  Conquer 2,800.00
2 A:Knights of the Galaxy, Jesse
  James- Highwayman of
  Space 1,100.00
3 A:Knights of the Galaxy, Duel of
  the Planets 850.00
4 Simon & Kirby, A:Knights of the
  Galaxy, Master of Doom 750.00
5 A:Knights of the Galaxy, Outcast of
  the Lost World 750.00
6 A:Knights of the Galaxy, The Day
  the World Melted 550.00
7 Gil Kane(c), A:Knights of the
  Galaxy, Challenge of the
  Robot Knight 550.00
8 It's a Women's World 550.00
9 The Seven Wonders of Space . .550.00
10 The Last Time I Saw Earth 550.00
11 Unknown Spaceman 400.00
12 The Sword in the Sky 400.00
13 Signboard in Space 400.00

Mystery in Space #107 (DC 1966)

Mystery in Space #51 (DC 1959)

14 Gil Kane(c), Hollywood in Space400.00
15 Doom from Station X 400.00
16 Honeymoon in Space 400.00
17 The Last Mile of Space 400.00
18 Gil Kane, Chain Gang of Space 400.00
19 The Great Space-Train Robbery375.00
20 The Man in the Martian Mask . .350.00
21 Interplanetary Merry-Go-Round 350.00
22 The Square Earth 350.00
23 Monkey-Rocket to Mars 350.00
24 A:Space Cabby, Hitchhiker
    of Space 350.00
25 Station Mars on the Air 325.00
26 Earth is the Target 325.00
27 The Human Fishbowl 325.00
28 The Radio Planet 325.00
29 Space-Enemy Number One . .325.00
30 The Impossible World
    Named Earth 325.00
31 The Day the Earth Split in Two .300.00
32 Riddle of the Vanishing
    Earthmen 300.00
33 The Wooden World War 300.00
34 The Man Who Moved the World 300.00
35 The Counterfeit Earth 300.00
36 Secret of the Moon Sphinx . . .300.00
37 Secret of the Masked Martians .300.00
38 The Canals of Earth 300.00
39 Sorcerers of Space 300.00
40 Riddle of the Runaway Earth . .300.00
41 The Miser of Space 250.00
42 The Secret of the
    Skyscraper Spaceship 250.00
43 Invaders From the
    Space Satellites 250.00
44 Amazing Space Flight
    of North America 250.00
45 Flying Saucers Over Mars . . .250.00
46 Mystery of the Moon Sniper . . .250.00
47 Interplanetary Tug of War 250.00
48 Secret of the Scarecrow World .250.00
49 The Sky-High Man 250.00
50 The Runaway Space-Train 250.00
51 Battle of the Moon Monsters . .250.00
52 Mirror Menace of Mars 250.00
53 Begin Adam Strange stories,
    Menace of the Robot
    Raiders 1,700.00
54 Invaders of the Under-
    ground World 400.00
55 The Beast From the
    Runaway World 300.00
56 Menace of the Super-Atom . . .200.00
57 Mystery of the Giant Footsteps .200.00
58 Chariot in the Sky 200.00
59 Duel of the 2 Adam Stranges . .200.00
60 Attack of the Tentacle World . .200.00
61 Threat of the Tornado Tyrant . .150.00

62 The Beast with the
    Sizzling Blue Eyes 150.00
63 Weapon that Swallowed Men . .150.00
64 The Radioactive Menace 150.00
65 Mechanical Masters of Rann . .150.00
66 Space-Island of Peril 150.00
67 Challenge of the Giant Fireflies .150.00
68 Fadeaway Doom 150.00
69 Menace of the Aqua-Ray
    Weapon 150.00
70 Vengeance of the Dust Devil . .150.00
71 The Challenge of the Crystal
    Conquerors 150.00
72 The Multiple Menace Weapon .100.00
73 The Invisible Invaders of Rann .100.00
74 The Spaceman Who Fought
    Himself 100.00
75 The Planet That Came to a
    Standstill 225.00
76 Challenge of the Rival Starman 100.00
77 Ray-Gun in the Sky 100.00
78 Shadow People of the Eclipse .100.00
79 The Metal Conqueror of Rann .100.00
80 The Deadly Shadows of Adam
    Strange 100.00
81 The Cloud-Creature That Menaced
    Two Worlds 75.00
82 World War on Earth and Rann . .75.00
83 The Emotion-Master of Space . .75.00
84 The Powerless Weapons of
    Adam Strange 75.00
85 Riddle of the Runaway Rockets .75.00
86 Attack of the Underworld Giants .75.00
87 The Super-Brain of Adam
    Strange, B:Hawkman 200.00
88 The Robot Wraith of Rann 175.00
89 Siren of the Space Ark 175.00
90 Planets and Peril, E:Hawkman .175.00
91 Puzzle of the Perilous Prisons . .35.00
92 The Alien Invasion From Earth,
    begin Space Ranger 40.00
93 The Convict Twins of Space 40.00
94 The Adam Strange Story 40.00
95 Hydra-Head From Outer Space .40.00
96 Coins That Doomed Two Planets 40.00
97 Day Adam Strange Vanished . . .40.00
98 The Wizard of the Cosmos 40.00
99 World- Destroyer From Space . .40.00
100 The Death of Alanna 40.00
101 Valley of 1,000 Dooms 40.00
102 Robot World of Rann 40.00
103 The Billion-Dollar Time-
    Capsule(Space Ranger) 40.00
104 thru 109 . . . .@15.00
110 Sept. 1966 . . . . .15.00
111 Sept. 1980 . . . . .15.00
112 thru 117 Joe Kubert(c) . . . . .@15.00

Phoenix #1 (Atlas Comics 1975)

OFF ON A COMET
Classics Illustrated #149
By Jules Verne
03/59 **(149)** GMc, P(c), Original 25.00
1960–66 rep . . . .@6.00
1968 **(166)** 25¢(c) price; rep 20.00

OUT OF THIS WORLD
Charlton Comics 1956–59
1 . . . . .150.00
2 . . . . .75.00
3 thru 7 Steve Ditko . . . .@175.00
8 thru 12 Steve Ditko . . . .@150.00
13 thru 15 . . . .@50.00
16 . . . . .135.00

OUTER LIMITS, THE
Dell Publishing Co. 1964
1 Painted(c) 75.00
2 Painted(c) 50.00
3 thru 10 Painted(c) . . . .@35.00
11 thru 18 Painted(c) 30.00

PHOENIX
Atlas 1975
1 thru 4 . . . .@5.00

PLAN 9 FROM OUTER SPACE
Eternity (B&W)
1 . . . . .2.50
2 and 3 . . . .@2.25

PLANET COMICS
Love Romance Publ.
(Fiction House Magazines) 1940
1 Planet Comics, O:Aura, B:Flint
    Baker, Red Comet, Spurt
    Hammond, Capt. Nelson
    Cole 10,000.00
2 .3,500.00
3 Will Eisner(c) 2,500.00
4 B:Gale Allan and the Girl
    Squad 2,000.00
5 .1,900.00
6 The Ray Pirates of Venus . .2,000.00
7 B:Buzz Crandall Planet
    Payson 1,600.00
8 .1,500.00
9 B:Don Granville Cosmo
    Corrigan 1,500.00
10 . . . . .1,500.00
11 B:Crash Parker 1,500.00
12 B:Star Fighter 1,500.00
13 B:Reef Ryan 1,200.00
14 B:Norge Benson 1,100.00
15 B: Mars, God of War 2,300.00
16 Invasion From The Void 1,100.00
17 Warrior Maid of Mercury 1,100.00
18 Bondage(c) 1,200.00
19 Monsters of the Inner World . .1,100.00
20 Winged Man Eaters of the
    Exile Star 1,100.00
21 B:Lost World Hunt Bowman . .1,200.00
22 Inferno on the Fifth Moon 1,100.00
23 Lizard Tyrant of the Twilight
    World 1,000.00
24 Raiders From The Red Moon 1,000.00
25 B:Norge Benson 1,000.00
26 B:The Space Rangers
    Bondage(c) 1,100.00
27 The Fire Eaters of Asteroid Z . .800.00
28 Bondage (c) 850.00
29 Dragon Raiders of Aztla 800.00
30 City of Lost Souls 800.00
31 Fire Priests of Orbit6X 675.00
32 Slaver's Planetoid 800.00
33 . . . . .675.00
34 Bondage 850.00
35 B:Mysta of The Moon 700.00
36 Collosus of the Blood Moon . . .700.00
37 Behemoths of the Purple Void .700.00

38 . . . . .600.00
39 Death Webs Of Zenith 3 . . . . . .600.00
40 Chameleon Men from Galaxy 9 600.00
41 New O: Auro Bondage (c) . . .650.00
42 E:Gale Allan 600.00
43 Death Rays From the Sun. . . .600.00
44 B:Futura 600.00
45 Her Evilness from Xanado . . .600.00
46 The Mecho-Men From Mars . .600.00
47 The Great Green Spawn 550.00
48 . . . . .550.00
49 Werewolves From Hydra Hell . .550.00
50 The Things of Xeves 550.00
51 Mad Mute X-Adapts 500.00
52 Mystery of the Time Chamber . .500.00
53 Dwarflings From Oceania 500.00
54 Robots From Inferno 500.00
55 Giants of the Golden Atom . . .500.00
56 thru 59 . . . .@450.00
60 Vassals of Volta 450.00
61 The Brute in the Bubble 350.00
62 Musta, Moon Goddess 350.00
63 Paradise or Inferno 350.00
64 Monkeys From the Blue 350.00
65 The Lost World 350.00
66 The Plague of the Locust Men .350.00
67 The Nymphs of Neptune 350.00
68 Synthoids of the 9th Moon . . .350.00
69 The Mentalists of Mars 350.00
70 Cargo For Amazonia 350.00
71 Sandhogs of Mars 250.00
72 Last Ship to Paradise 250.00
73 The Martian Plague,
    Winter 1953 . . . . .250.00

PLANET COMICS
Blackthorne 1988
1 . . . . .2.00
2 and 3 . . . .@2.00

Blackthorne (B&W)
4 and 5 . . . .@2.00

Adventures on the Planet of the Apes #1
(Marvel 1975)

MOVIE COMICS
Gold Key 1970
Beneath the Planet of the Apes, with
    Ape Protest Poster 35.00

PLANET OF THE APES
Marvel 1974–77

(Curtis: black & white magazine)
1 Planet of the Apes movie
    adaptation, pt.1 . . . . .30.00
2 movie adaptation, pt.2 . . . . .20.00
3 movie adaptation, pt.3 . . . . .10.00
4 movie adaptation, pt.4 . . . . .10.00
5 movie adaptation, pt.5 . . . . .10.00

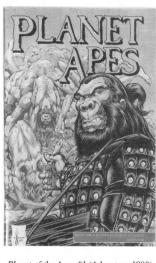

Planet of the Apes #1 (Adventure 1990)

6 movie adaptation, pt.6 . . . . 10.00
7 thru 12 Beneath the Planet of the
  Apes movie adaptation 10.00
13 thru 16 Escape from the Planet of
  the Apes movie adaptation . . @10.00
17 thru 21 Conquest of the Planet of
  the Apes movie adaptation . . @10.00
22 thru 29 . . . . @15.00

ADVENTURES ON THE PLANET OF THE APES
Marvel 1975

1 Planet of the Apes Movie
  Adaptation 2.50
2 Humans Captured 2.50
3 Man Hunt 2.50
4 Trial By Fear 2.50
5 Fury in the Forbidden Zone 2.50
6 The Forbidden Zone, Cont'd 2.50
7 Man Hunt Cont'd 2.50
8 Brent & Nova Enslaved 2.50
9 Mankind's Demise 2.50
10 When Falls the Lawgiver 2.50
11 The Final Chapter; Dec., 1976 . . .2.50

PLANET OF THE APES
Adventure (B&W) 1990–92

1 collect.ed. 7.00
1 2 covers 5.00
1a 2nd printing 2.50
1b 3rd printing 2.25
2 . . . . .3.00
3 . . . . .2.75
4 . . . . .2.75
5 D:Alexander? 2.75
6 Welcome to Ape City 2.75
7 . . . . .2.75
8 Christmas Story 2.50
9 Swamp Ape Village 2.50
10 Swamp Apes in Forbidden City . .2.50
11 Ape War continues 2.50
12 W.Alexander/Coure 2.50
13 Planet of Apes/Alien Nation/ Ape
  City x-over 2.50
14 Countdown to Zero Pt.1 . . . . . . .2.50
15 Countdown to Zero Pt.2 . . . . . . .2.50
16 Countdown to Zero Pt.3 . . . . . . .2.50
17 Countdown to Zero Pt.4 . . . . . . .2.50
18 Ape City (after Ape Nation mini-
  series .2.50
19 1991 "Conquest.."tie-in 2.50
20 Return of the Ape Riders 2.50
21 The Terror Beneath, Pt.1 . . . . . .2.50
22 The Terror Beneath, Pt.2 . . . . . .2.50
23 The Terror Beneath, Pt.3 . . . . . .2.50
Ann #1, "Day on Planet of the Apes" .3.50
Lim.Ed. #1 . . . . .5.00

URCHAKS' FOLLY
Adventure Comics (B&W) 1992

1 . . . . .3.00
2 . . . . .2.50
3 "The Taylorites" 2.50
4 Conclusion 2.50

THE FORBIDDEN ZONE
Adventure (B&W)

1 Battle for the Planet of the Apes &
  Planet of the Apes tie-in 2.50
2 A:Juilus .2.50

SINS OF THE FATHER
Adventure Comics (B&W)

1 Conquest Tie in 2.50

BLOOD OF THE APES
Adventure Comics (B&W)

1 A:Tonus the Butcher 3.00
2 Valia/Taylorite Connection 2.50
3 Ape Army in Phis 2.50
4 . . . . .2.50

TERROR ON THE PLANET OF THE APES
Adventure Comics (B&W) 1991

1 MP, collectors edition 2.50
2 MP, the Forbidden Zone 2.50
3 . . . . .2.50

APE NATION
Adventure Comics 1991

1 Aliens land on Planet of the Apes .3.00
2 General Ollo 3.00
3 V:Gen.Ollo, Danada 2.50
4 D:Danada 2.50

*Predator: Big Game #2
(Dark Horse 1991)*

PREDATOR
Dark Horse 1989–90

1 Mini Series 7.00
1a 2nd Printing 3.00
1b 3rd Printing 2.50
2 . . . . .5.00
2a 2nd Printing 3.00
3 . . . . .4.00
3a 2nd Printing 2.50
4 . . . . .3.00
4a 2nd Printing 2.50
1-shot Predator: Invaders From the
  Fourth Dimension (July 1994) . .3.95
1-shot Predator: Jungle Tales: Rite
  of Passage (March 1995) 2.95
1-shot Dark Horse Classics: Predator:
  Jungle Tales, rep. (May 1996) . .2.95
1-shot Predator: Strange Roux
  (Nov. 1996) 2.95
1-shot Predator: Captive (Apr. 1998) 2.95
TPB series rep. (1990) 13.00

TPB 2nd printing (1995) 12.00
TPB Concrete Jungle 14.95

BAD BLOOD
Dark Horse 1993–94

1 I:John Pulnick 2.75
2 V:Predator 2.75
3 V:Predator, C.I.A. 2.75
4 Last issue 2.50

BIG GAME
Dark Horse 1991

1 Corp.Nakai Meets Predator 3.50
2 Army Base Destroyed, with 2-card
  strip 3.50
3 Corp.Nakai Arrested, with 2-card
  strip 3.50
4 Nakai vs. Predator 3.50
TPB rep. #1–#4 . . . . .13.95
TPB rep. #1–#4, 2nd edition 14.95

BLOODY SANDS OF TIME
Dark Horse 1992

1 Predator in WWI 3.50
2 WWII cont'd. 3.25

COLD WAR
Dark Horse 1991

1 Predator in Siberia 3.50
2 U.S. Elite Squad in Siberia 3.25
3 U.S. vs. USSR commandos 3.25
4 U.S. vs. USSR in Siberia 3.00
TPB 13.95
TPB 2nd printing 13.95

DARK RIVER
Dark Horse 1996

1 thru 4 . . . . @2.95

HELL & HOT WATER
Dark Horse 1997

1 thru 3 . . . . @2.95

HELL COME A WALKIN'
Dark Horse 1998

1 (of 2) by Nancy Collins, Dean
  Ormston 2.95
2 concl. 2.95

KINDRED
Dark Horse 1996–97

1 . . . . .2.50
2 thru 4 . . . . @2.95
TPB Kindred 14.95

NEMESIS
Dark Horse 1997

1 (of 2) 2.95
2 . . . . .2.95

PRIMAL
Dark Horse 1997

1 (of 2) Kevin J. Anderson(s) 2.95
2 (of 2) 2.95

RACE WAR
Dark Horse 1993

0 F:Serial Killer 2.75
1 V:Serial Killer 2.75
2 D:Serial Killer 2.75
3 in Prison 2.75
4 Last Issue 2.75
TPB Race War, serie rep. 17.95

PREDATOR 2
Dark Horse 1991

1 Movie Adapt pt.1 . . . . .3.50
2 Movie Adapt. pt.2 with 2-card strip 3.00

PREDATOR VS. JUDGE DREDD
Dark Horse 1997

1 (of 3) by John Wagner and Enrique
  Alcatena 2.50
2 thru 3 . . . . @2.50

*Predator: Jungle Tales
(Dark Horse 1995)*

PREDATOR VS. MAGNUS ROBOT FIGHTER
Valiant/Dark Horse 1992

1 A:Tekla .3.00
1a Platinum Ed. 5.00
1b Gold Ed. 3.00
2 LW, Magnus Vs. Predator, with 2-
  card strip 3.00
TPB Rep. #1–#2 . . . . .7.95

TARZAN VS. PREDATOR AT THE EARTH'S CORE
Dark Horse 1996

1 Tarzan vs. Predator 2.50
2 V:Predator 2.50
3 Tarzan on the Hunt 2.50
4 . . . . .2.50
TPB series rep. 12.95

BATMAN vs. PREDATOR
DC/Dark Horse 1991–92

1 inc.8 trading cards bound in
  (Prestige) 5.00
1a Newsstand 4.00
2 Inc. pinups (prestige) 4.00
2a Newsstand 3.00
3 conclusion, inc. 8 trading cards
  (Prestige) 4.00
3a Newsstand 3.00
TPB, rep.#1–#3 . . . . .5.95

BLOODMATCH
DC 1994–95

1 R:Predators 2.75
2 A:Huntress 2.50
3 Assassins 2.50
4 V:Head Hunters 2.50
TPB Rep.#1–#4 . . . . .6.95

BLOOD TIES
DC/Dark Horse 1997

1 (of 4) Chuck Dixon vs. pair of
  Predators 2.00
2 Chuck Dixon, pt.2 . . . . .2.00
3 Chuck Dixon, pt.3 . . . . .2.00
4 Chuck Dixon, concl. 2.00
TPB rep. .8.00

QUANTUM LEAP
Innovation 1991–93

(based on TV series)
1 1968 Memphis 3.50
1a Special Edition 2.50
2 Ohio 1962, "Freedom of the Press" 3.00

3 1958 "The $50, 000 Quest" 3.00
4 "Small Miracles" 2.50
5 . . . . .2.50
6 . . . . .2.50
7 Golf Pro, School Bus Driver 2.50
8 1958, Bank Robber 2.50
9 NY 1969, Gay Rights 2.50
10 1960s' Stand-up Comic 2.50
11 1959, Dr.(LSD experiments) 2.50
12 . . . . .2.50
Spec.#1 (#13) Quantum Leap: Time
    and Space 3.00

RACE FOR THE MOON
Harvey Publications 1958
1 . . . . .100.00
2 Jack Kirby & Al Williamson . . .175.00
3 Jack Kirby & Al Williamson, . .175.00

RAY BRADBURY CHRONICLES
Byron Press
1 short stories 10.00
2 short stories 10.00
3 short stories 10.00

RAY BRADBURY COMICS
Topps 1993–94
1 Dinosaurs, with trading cards 3.00
2 with trading cards 3.00
3 Dinosaurs, with trading cards 3.00
4 with trading cards 3.00
5 with trading cards 3.00
Spec.#1 The Illustrated Man 3.00
Spec. Trilogy of Terror 2.50
Spec. The Martian Chronicles 3.00

RETIEF
Adventure (B&W) 1989–90
1 thru 6 Keith Laumer adapt. . . . .@2.00

[New Series] 1990
1 thru 6 . . . .@2.25
Spec.#1 Retief:Garbage Invasion . .2.50
Spec.#1 Retief:The Giant Killer,
    V:Giant Dinosaur (Sept. 1991) . .2.50
Spec.#1 Grime & Punishment, Planet
    Slunch (Nov. 1991) 2.50

RETIEF AND THE WARLORDS
Adventure Comics (B&W) 1991
1 Keith Laumer Novel Adapt. 2.50
2 Haterakans 2.50
3 Retief Arrested for Treason 2.50
4 Final Battle (last issue) 2.50

Retief #2 (Adventure 1990)

RETIEF OF THE CDT
(B&W)
1 Keith Laumer Novel Adapt. 2.00
2 . . . . .2.00

RETIEF: DIPLOMATIC IMMUNITY
Adventure Comics (B&W) 1991
1 Groaci Invasion. 2.50
2 Groaci story cont. 2.50

REX DEXTER OF MARS
Fox Features Syndicate 1940
1 Battle ofKooba 1,500.00

R.O.B.O.T. BATTALION 2050
Eclipse (B&W)
1 . . . . .2.00

Robotech, The Macross Saga #7 (Comico 1985)

MACROSS
Comico 1984
1 . . . . .12.00

Becomes:

ROBOTECH, THE MACROSS SAGA
Comico 1985–89
2 . . . . .5.00
3 . . . . .4.00
4 . . . . .3.00
5 . . . . .2.50
6 J:Rick Hunter 2.50
7 V:Zentraedi 2.00
8 A:Rick Hunter 2.00
9 V:Zentraedi 2.00
10 "Blind Game" 2.00
11 V:Zentraedi 2.00
12 V:Zentraedi 2.00
13 V:Zentraedi 2.00
14 "Gloval's Reports" 2.00
15 V:Zentraedi 2.00
16 V:Zentraedi 2.00
17 V:Zentraedi 2.00
18 D:Roy Fokker 2.00
19 V:Khyron 2.00
20 V:Zentraedi 2.00
21 "A New Dawn" 2.00
22 V:Zentraedi 2.00
23 "Reckless" 2.00
24 V:Zentraedi 2.00
25 "Wedding Bells" 2.00
26 "The Messenger" 2.00
27 "Force of Arms" 2.00
28 "Reconstruction Blues" 2.00

29 "Robotech Masters" 2.00
30 "Viva Miriya" 2.00
31 "Khyron's Revenge" 2.00
32 "Broken Heart" 2.00
33 "A Rainy Night" 2.00
34 "Private Time" 2.00
35 "Season's Greetings" 2.00
36 last issue 2.00
Graphic Novel #1 . . . . .6.00

ROBOTECH: THE NEW GENERATION
Comico 1985–88
1 . . . . .4.00
2 "The Lost City" 3.00
3 V:Yellow Dancer 3.00
4 A:Yellow Dancer 3.00
5 Sam Keith(i), A:Yellow Dancer . . .2.50
6 F:Rook Bartley 2.50
7 "Paper Hero" 2.00
8 . . . . .2.00
9 "The Genesis Pit" 2.00
10 V:The Invid 2.00
11 F:Scott Bernard 2.00
12 V:The Invid 2.00
13 V:The Invid 2.00
14 "Annie's Wedding" 2.00
15 "Seperate Ways" 2.00
16 "Metamorphosis" 2.00
17 "Midnight Sun" 2.00
18 . . . . .2.00
19 . . . . .2.00
20 "Birthday Blues" 2.00
21 "Hired Gun" 2.00
22 "The Big Apple" 2.00
23 Robotech Wars 2.00
24 Robotech Wars 2.00
25 V:Invid, last issue 2.00

ROBOTECH MASTERS
Comico 1985–88
1 . . . . .4.00
2 . . . . .3.00
3 Space Station Liberty 3.00
4 V:Bioroids 2.50
5 V:Flagship 2.50
6 "Prelude to Battle" 2.50
7 "The Trap" 2.50
8 F:Dana Sterling 2.50
9 "Star Dust" 2.50
10 V:Zor .2.50
11 A:De Ja Vu 2.00
12 2OR 2.00
13 . . . . .2.00
14 "Clone Chamber," V:Zor 2.00
15 "Love Song" 2.00
16 V:General Emerson 2.00
17 "Mind Games" 2.00
18 "Dana in Wonderland" 2.00
19 . . . . .2.00
20 A:Zor, Musica 2.00
21 "Final Nightmare" 2.00
22 "The Invid Connection" 2.00
23 "Catastrophe," final issue 2.00

ROBOTECH IN 3-D
Comico 1987
1 . . . . .2.50

ROBOTECH DEFENDERS
DC 1985
1 mini-series 3.50
2 . . . . .3.00

ROBOTECH: GENESIS
The Legend of Zor
Eternity 1992
1 O:Robotech, The Thirsting, with
    trading cards 2.95
1a Limited Edition, extra pages with
    cards #1 & #2 . . . . .5.95
2 The Changing, with cards 2.50

Robotech: The New Generation #2 (Comico 1985)

3 The Immuting, with cards 2.50
4 The Shaping, with cards 2.50
5 with cards 2.50
6 The Avenging, with cards 2.50

ROBOTECH: INVID WAR
Eternity (B&W) 1992–93
1 No Man's Land 2.50
2 V:Defoliators 2.50
3 V:The Invid, Reflex Point 2.50
4 V:The Invid 2.50
5 Moonbase Aluce II 2.50
6 Moonbase-Zentraedi plot 2.50
7 Zentraedi plot contd. 2.50
8 A:Lancer 2.50
9 A:Johnathan Wolfe 2.50
10 . . . . .2.50
11 F:Rand 2.50
12 thru 15 . . . . .2.50

INVID WAR AFTERMATH
Eternity (B&W)
1 thru 6 F:Rand 2.75

ROBOTECH: RETURN TO MACROSS
Eternity (B&W) 1993
1 thru 5 . . . . .2.50

Academy Comics
1 thru 17 Roy Fokker 2.75
18 F:The Faithful 2.75
19 F:Lisa .2.75
20 F:Lisa .2.75
21 V:Killer Robot 2.95
22 War of the Believers 2.95
23 War of the Believers, pt.2 . . . . . .2.95
24 War of the Believers, pt.3 . . . . . .2.95
25 War of the Believers, pt.4 . . . . . .2.95
26 thru 30 . . . .@2.95
31 What is the Federalist Plan? 2.95
32 thru 34 . . . .@2.95
35 Typhoon threatens Macross Island 2.95
36 . . . . .2.95
37 round up of Federalist Agents 2.95

MACROSS II
Viz (B&W) 1992–93
1 Macross Saga sequel 2.75
2 A:Ishtar 2.75
3 F:Reporter Hibiki, Ishtar 2.75
4 V:Feff, The Marduk 2.75
5 . . . . .2.75
6 . . . . .2.75
7 Sylvie Confesses 2.75
8 F:Ishtar 2.75
9 V:Marduk Fleet 2.75

Robotech II: The Sentinels, The Malcontent Uprisings #10 (Eternity 1990)

10 . . . . .2.75

THE MICRON CONSPIRACY
Viz (B&W) 1994
1 Manga 2.75

ROBOTECH
Eternity (B&W)
1-shot Untold Stories 2.50

Academy Comics 1995–96
0 Robotech Information 2.50
Spec. #1 & #2 Robotech The Movie,
  Benny R. Powell & Chi . . . . . .@2.95
1-shot Robotech Romance 2.95
GN The Threadbard Heart 9.95

Antarctic Press 1998
Ann. #1 . . . . .2.95

ROBOTECH SPECIAL DANA'S STORY
Eclipse
1 . . . . .5.00

ROBOTECH
ACADEMY BLUES
Academy Comics (B&W) 1995
0 Classroom Blues 3.50
1 F:Lisa .2.95
2 Bomb at the Academy 2.95
3 Roy's Drinking Buddy 2.95

MECH ANGEL
Academy Comics (B&W) 1995
0 I:Mech Angel 2.95

AFTERMATH
Academy Comics (B&W)
1 thru 10 R:Bruce Lewis . . . . @2.95
11 Zentradi Traitor 2.95
12 and 13 . . . . @2.95

CLONE
Academy Comics (B&W) 1995
1 Dialect of Duality 2.95
2 V:Monte Yarrow 2.95
3 Ressurection 2.95
4 Ressurection 2.95
5 F:Bibi Ava 2.95

MACROSS TEMPEST
Academy Comics (B&W) 1995
1 F:Roy Fokker, Tempest 2.95

MORDECAI
Academy Comics (B&W)
1 . . . . .2.95
2 Annie meets her clone 2.95

SENTINELS STAR RUNNERS: CARPENTER'S JOURNEY
Academy Comics (B&W) 1996
1 . . . . .2.95

WARRIORS
Academy Comics (B&W) 1995
1 F:Breetai 2.95
2 F:Mirya 2.95
3 F:Mirya 2.95
GN The Terror Maker 9.95

THE MISFITS
Academy Comics (B&W)
1 Misfits from Sothern Cross transferred to
  Africa 2.95

ROBOTECH
Antarctic Press 1997
1 by Fred Perry 2.95
2 . . . . .2.95
3 . . . . .2.95
4 Rolling Thunder, pt.1 . . . . .2.95
5 Rolling Thunder, pt.2 . . . . .2.95
6 Rolling Thunder, pt.3 . . . . .2.95
7 Rolling Thunder, pt.4 . . . . .2.95
8 Variants, pt.1 . . . . .2.95
9 Variants, pt.2 . . . . .2.95
TPB Megastorm by Fred Perry & Ben
  Dunn 7.95

VERMILION
Antarctic Press (B&W) 1997
1 (of 4) by Duc Tran 2.95
2 Why did Hiro die? 2.95
3 . . . . .2.95
4 . . . . .2.95

WINGS OF GIBRALTAR
Antarctic Press 1998
1 (of 2) by Lee Duhig 2.95

COVERT OPS
Antarctic Press (B&W) 1998
1 (of 2) by Greg Lane 2.95

ESCAPE
Antarctic Press (B&W) 1998
1 . . . . .2.95

SENTINELS: RUBICON
Antarctic Press (B&W) 1998
1 (of 7) 2.95
2 Shadows of the Past 2.95

ROBOTECH II THE SENTINELS
Eternity (B&W)
1 . . . . .3.50
1a 2nd printing 1.95
2 . . . . .3.00
2a 2nd printing 1.95
3 . . . . .2.00
3a 2nd printing 1.95
4 thru 16 . . . . @1.95

Book 2
1 thru 12 . . . . @2.25
13 thru 20 . . . . @2.25
Wedding Special #1 . . . . .1.95
Wedding Special #2 . . . . .1.95
Robotech II Handbook 2.50

Book Three
1 thru 8 V:Invid 2.50

Book Four
Academy Comics 1995
1 by Jason Waltrip 2.95
2 thru 4 F:Tesla . . . . @2.75
5 interior of Haydon IV 2.95
6 thru 8 . . . . @2.95
9 Breetai, Wolf & Vince return to
  Tirol .2.95
10 Ark Angel attacked by The Black
  Death Destroyers 2.95
11 Tirol, Wolff, Vince & Breetai on

trial for treason 2.95
12 Dr. Lang exposes General
  Edwards' evil designs 2.95
13 F:Tesla 2.75
14 V:Invid 2.75
15 . . . . .2.75
16 . . . . .2.75
17 V:Invid Mechas 2.75
18 F:"HIN" 2.95
19 V:Invid 2.95
20 Final Aplp. Invid Regiss 2.95
21 Predator and Prey 2.95
22 A Clockwork Planet 2.95
Halloween Special JWp, JWt, ...2.95

ROBOTECH II: THE SENTINELS
Eternity
Swimsuit Spec.#1 . . . . .2.95

THE MALCONTENT UPRISING
Eternity (B&W) 1989–90
1 thru 12 . . . . @1.95

CYBERPIRATES
Eternity (B&W) 1991
1 The Hard Wired Coffin 2.25
2 thru 4 . . . . @2.25

ROCKET SHIP X
Fox Features Syndicate 1951
1 . . . . .450.00
2 N# Variant of Original 300.00

ROCKETMAN
Ajax/Farrell Publications 1952
1 Space Stories of the Future 300.00

ROSWELL: LITTLE GREEN MEN
Bongo Comics 1996
1 by Bill Morrison, "The Story of the
  Century" 2.95
2 "The Untold Story" 2.95
3 "The Untold Story,"concl. 2.95
4 V:Mutato 2.95
5 . . . . .2.95
6 time-traveling comic collector 2.95
TPB Roswell Walks Among Us 12.95

SCORCHED EARTH
Tundra 1991
1 Earth 2025, I:Dr.EliotGodwin 3.50
2 Hunt for Eliot 2.95
3 Mystical Transformation 2.95

SHADOW OF THE TORTURER, THE
Innovation 1991
1 thru 6 Gene Wolfe adapt. . . . . . .@1.95

SHATTERED EARTH
Eternity (B&W) 1988–89
1 thru 9 . . . . @1.95

SIX FROM SIRIUS
Marvel Epic 1984
1 Paul Gulacy, limited series 3.00
2 thru 4 . . . . @2.00

SIX FROM SIRIUS II
Marvel Epic 1986
1 Paul Gulacy 1.75

SLIDERS
Valiant 1996
1 and 2 from TV series . . . . @2.50

SLIDERS: DARKEST HOUR
Acclaim 1996
1 .thru 3 . . . . @2.50

Spec. Montezuma IV rules the world .3.95
Spec. #2 "Secrets" 3.95
TPB from TV show 9.00

ULTIMATUM
Valiant 1996
1 and 2 . . . . @2.50

SPACE: ABOVE AND BEYOND
Topps 1995
1 thru 3 TV pilot adaptation . . . . . @2.95

THE GAUNTLET
Topps 1996
1 . . . . .2.95
2 (of 2) 2.95

SPACE ACTION
**Junior Books
(Ace Magazines) 1952**
1 Invaders from a Lost Galaxy . .550.00
2 Silicon Monster from Galaxy X .450.00
3 Attack on Ishtar 450.00

SPACE ADVENTURES
**Capitol Stories/
Charlton Comics 1952–64**
1 . . . . .325.00
2 . . . . .150.00
3 Dick Giordano(c) 135.00
4 Dick Giordano(c) 125.00
5 Stan Campbell(c) 125.00
6 Stan Campbell(c), Two Worlds .100.00
7 Transformation 125.00
8 All For Love 100.00
9 Dick Giordano(c) 100.00
10 Steve Ditko 250.00
11 Steve Ditko 275.00
12 Steve Ditko(c) 275.00
13 A:Blue Beetle 125.00
14 A:Blue Beetle 125.00
15 Photo(c) of Rocky Jones 125.00
16 A:Rocky Jones 150.00
17 A:Rocky Jones 125.00
18 A:Rocky Jones 125.00
19 . . . . .100.00
20 First Trip to the Moon 175.00
21 . . . . .100.00
22 never published
23 Space Trip to the Moon 150.00
24 . . . . .125.00
25 Brontosaurus 125.00
26 Flying Saucers 150.00
27 Flying Saucers 150.00
28 Moon Trap 45.00
29 Captive From Space 45.00
30 Peril in the Sky 45.00

Space Adventures, Vol 3, #13 (Charlton 1979)

31 Enchanted Planet 125.00
32 Last Ship from Earth 125.00
33 Galactic Scourge, I&O:Captain
   Atom 375.00
34 A:Captain Atom 150.00
35 thru 40 A:Captain Atom . . . . .@150.00
41 . . . . .25.00
42 A:Captain Atom 25.00
43 . . . . .25.00
44 A:Mercury Man 25.00
45 A:Mercury Man 25.00
46 thru 59 . . . .@25.00

SPACE ADVENTURES
Charlton 1967–79
Volume 3
1 (#60) O&I:Paul Mann & The
   Saucers From the Future 35.00
2 thru 8 (1968–69) . . . .@20.00
9 thru 13 (1978–79) . . . .@10.00

SPACE BUSTERS
Ziff-Davis Publishing Co. 1952
1 Photo(c), Charge of the Battle
   Women 600.00
2 Bondage Photo(c) 500.00
3 . . . . .450.00

SPACE DETECTIVE
Avon Periodicals 1951
1 Wally Wood, Opium Smugglers
   of Venus 800.00
2 Wally Wood, Batwomen of
   Mercury 500.00
3 Sea Nymphs of Neptune 300.00
4 Flame Women of Vulcan,
   Bondage(c) 325.00

SPACE FAMILY ROBINSON
See: LOST IN SPACE

SPACE GHOST
Gold Key 1967
1 . . . . .150.00

SPACE GHOST
Comico 1987
1 V:Robot Master 6.00

SPACE GIANTS, THE
Pyramid Comics 1997
0 . . . . .1.00
0a deluxe 2.25
1 . . . . .1.00
3 by Jeff Newman 1.00

SPACE MAN
Dell Publishing Co. 1962–72
1 . . . . .75.00
2 . . . . .40.00
3 . . . . .40.00
4 thru 10 . . . .@30.00

SPACEMAN
Atlas 1953–54
1 F:Speed Carter and the Space
   Sentinals 450.00
2 "Trapped in Space" 300.00
3 V:Ice Monster 250.00
4 . . . . .250.00
5 . . . . .250.00
6 "The Thing From Outer Space" .250.00

SPACE: 1999
A Plus Comics
1 John Byrne 2.50

SPACE: 1999
Charlton 1975–76
1 . . . . .10.00

Space: 1999, Vol 2 #3 (Charlton 1976)

2 "Survival" 8.00
3 "Bring Them Back Alive" 7.00
4 John Byrne 7.00
5 John Byrne 7.00
6 John Byrne 7.00
7 . . . . .7.00
8 B&W .7.00

SPACE PATROL
Approved Comics
(Ziff-Davis) 1952
1 Photo(c), The Lady of
   Diamonds 700.00
2 Photo(c), Slave King of Pluto . . .500.00

SPACE PATROL
Adventure (B&W) 1992–93
1 thru 3 . . . . .2.50

SPACE SQUADRON
Atlas 1951
1 F:Capt. Jet Dixon, Blast, Dawn, Revere,
   Rusty Blake 450.00
2 . . . . .400.00
3 "Planet of Madness" 300.00
4 . . . . .300.00
5 . . . . .300.00

Becomes:
SPACE WORLDS
Marvel 1952
6 "Midnight Horror" 300.00

SPACE THRILLERS
Avon Periodicals 1954
N# Contents May Vary 850.00

SPACE WAR
Charlton Comics 1959
1 . . . . .125.00
2 . . . . .65.00
3 . . . . .60.00
4 Steve Ditko 125.00
5 Steve Ditko 125.00
6 Steve Ditko 125.00
7 . . . . .30.00
8 Steve Ditko 125.00
9 . . . . .35.00
10 Steve Ditko 125.00
11 thru 15 . . . .@35.00
16 thru 27 . . . .@30.00

Becomes:
FIGHTIN' FIVE
28 Steve Ditko 35.00
29 Steve Ditko 35.00
30 Steve Ditko 40.00

*Species: Human Race #4
(Dark Horse 1997)*

31 Steve Ditko 40.00
32 . . . . .5.00
33 Steve Ditko 40.00
34 Steve Ditko 40.00

SPECIES
Dark Horse 1995
1 Alien Human Hybrid, movie 2.50
2 thru 4 SIL . . . .@2.50

HUMAN RACE
Dark Horse 1997
1 Phil Hester 2.95
2 . . . . .2.95
3 Steve Bissette 2.95
4 (of 4) .2.95
TPB 11.95

SPIDER KISS
(B&W)
1 Harlan Ellison 3.95

THE STAINLESS STEEL RAT
Eagle 1985–86
1 Harry Harrison adapt. 2.25
2 thru 6 . . . .@1.50

STARBLAZERS
Argo Press 1995
0 Battleship Yamato   2.95
1 F:Dereck Wildstar 2.95
2 After the Comet War 2.95
3 thru 11 . . . .@2.95
12 Nova captured 2.95

STARCHILD MYTHOPOLIS
Coppervale (B&W) 1997
6 (of 14) Fisher King, concl. 2.95

STARCHILD
Taliesin Press (B&W) 1992–97
0 . . . . .35.00
1 . . . . .50.00
1a 2nd printing 4.00
2 . . . . .50.00
2a 2nd printing 4.00
3 . . . . .15.00
4 . . . . .7.00
5 thru 13 . . . .@5.00
14 . . . . .3.00

Coppervale
TPB Coll. Ed. Awakenings, rep.
   #1–#12 . . . . .20.00

HC 35.00

STARCHILD: CROSSROADS
Coppervale (B&W)
1 thru 4, reoffer, by James Owen . .@2.95
TPB Coll. Ed.112 pg. 12.00
HC Coll.Ed. 20.00
Conoisseurs Edition 100.00

STARFORCE SIX SPECIAL
AC Comics
1 . . . . .1.50

*Stargate: One Nation Under Ra #1
(Entity 1997)*

STARGATE
Entity Comics 1996
1 Movie adaptation 2.95
2 thru 4 . . . .@2.95
4a deluxe limited edition 3.50

DOOMSDAY WORLD
Entity Comics 1996
1 new crew explores 2nd StarGate . .2.95
1 prism-foil edition 3.50
2 . . . . .2.95
3 . . . . .2.95
3 deluxe 3.50

THE NEW ADVENTURES COLLECTION
Entity (B&W) 1997
1 rep. Underworld; One Nation Under
   Ra 5.95
1a photo cover 4.95

UNDERWORLD
Entity (B&W) 1997
1 . . . . .2.75
1a deluxe 3.50

ONE NATION UNDER RA
Entity (B&W) 1997
1 . . . . .2.75
1a deluxe 3.50

REBELLION
Entity (B&W) 1997
1 (of 3) from novel, sequel to movie .2.75
1 deluxe 3.50
2 . . . . .2.75
2 deluxe 3.50
3 (of 3) .2.75
3 foil cover 3.50
GN rep. 80 pg. 7.95
GN photo (c) 7.95

Starship Troopers: Brute Creations (Dark Horse 1997)

STARSHIP TROOPERS
Dark Horse 1997
1 (of 2) movie adaptation 2.95
2 movie adaptation, concl. 2.95
TPB rep., inc. Brute Creations, Insect
  Touch, & movie 152 pg. 14.95

BRUTE CREATIONS
Dark Horse 1997
1-shot 2.95

INSECT TOUCH
Dark Horse 1997
1 written by Warren Ellis 2.95
2 and 3 (of 3) . . . .@2.95

DOMINANT SPECIES
Dark Horse 1998
1 (of 4) 2.95

STARTLING COMICS
Better Publ./Nedor Publ. 1940
1 Will Eisner, B&O:Captain Future,
  Mystico, Wonder Man; B:Masked
  Rider 1,700.00
2 Captain Future(c) 700.00
3 Captain Future(c) 550.00
4 Captain Future(c) 450.00
5 Captain Future(c) 350.00
6 Captain Future(c) 325.00
7 Captain Future(c) 325.00
8 . . . . .325.00
9 Bondage(c) 350.00
10 O:Fighting Yank 2,500.00
11 Fighting Yank(c) 775.00
12 Hitler, Mussolini, Tojo cover . . .550.00
13 JBi .450.00
14 JBi .450.00
15 Fighting Yank (c) 450.00
16 Bondage(c), O:FourComrades .500.00
17 Fighting Yank (c), E:Masked
  Rider 325.00
18 B&O:Pyroman 700.00
19 Pyroman(c) 325.00
20 Pyroman(c), B:Oracle 325.00
21 Bondage(c)O:Ape 350.00
22 Fighting Yank(c) 325.00
23 Pyroman(c) 325.00
24 Fighting Yank(c) 325.00
25 Pyroman(c) 325.00
26 Fighting Yank(c) 325.00
27 Pyroman(c) 325.00
28 Fighting Yank(c) 325.00
29 Pyroman(c) 325.00
30 Fighting Yank(c) 325.00
31 Pyroman(c) 325.00
32 Fighting Yank(c) 325.00
33 Pyroman(c) 325.00
34 Fighting Yank(c), O:Scarab 325.00

35 Pyroman(c) 335.00
36 Fighting Yank(c) 300.00
37 Bondage (c) 300.00
38 Bondage(c) 300.00
39 Pyroman(c) 300.00
40 End Captain Future 300.00

STAR TREK

STAR TREK
Gold Key 1967–79
1 Planet of No Return 500.00
2 Devil's Isle of Space 300.00
3 Invasion of City Builders 200.00
4 Peril of Planet Quick Change . . .200.00
5 Ghost Planet 200.00
6 When Planets Collide 165.00
7 Voodoo Planet 175.00
8 Youth Trap 150.00
9 Legacy of Lazarus 150.00
10 Sceptre of the Sun 100.00
11 Brain Shockers 100.00
12 Flight of the Buccaneer 90.00
13 Dark Traveler 80.00
14 Enterprise Mutiny 80.00
15 Museum a/t End of Time 80.00
16 Day of the Inquisitors 80.00
17 Cosmic Cavemen 80.00
18 The Hijacked Planet 80.00
19 The Haunted Asteroid 80.00
20 A World Gone Mad 80.00
21 The Mummies of Heitus VII . . .65.00
22 Siege in Superspace 65.00
23 Child's Play 65.00
24 The Trial of Capt. Kirk 65.00
25 Dwarf Planet 65.00
26 The Perfect Dream 65.00
27 Ice Journey 65.00
28 The Mimicking Menace 65.00
29 rep. Star Trek #1 . . . . .65.00
30 Death of a Star 50.00
31 "The Final Truth". 50.00
32 "The Animal People" 50.00
33 "The Choice" 50.00
34 "The Psychocrystals" 50.00
35 rep. Star Trek #4 . . . . .50.00
36 "A Bomb in Time" 50.00
37 rep. Star Trek #5 . . . . .35.00
38 "One of our Captains is Missing" .35.00
39 "Prophet of Peace" 35.00
40 Furlough to Fury, A: Barbara
  McCoy 35.00
41 The Evictors 35.00
42 "World Against Time" 35.00
43 "World Beneath the Waves" . . .35.00
44 "Prince Traitor" 35.00
45 rep. Star Trek #7 . . . . .35.00

Star Trek #40 (Whitman 1976)

46 "Mr. Oracle" 35.00
47 "This Tree Bears Bitter Fruit" . .35.00
48 Murder on Enterprise 35.00
49 "A Warp in Space" 35.00
50 "The Planet of No Life" 35.00
51 DestinationAnnihilation6 . . . . . .30.00
52 "And A Child Shall Lead Them" .30.00
53 "What Fools..Mortals Be" 30.00
54 "Sport of Knaves" 30.00
55 A World Against Itself 30.00
56 No Time Like The Past,
  A:Guardian of Forever 30.00
57 "Spore of the Devil" 30.00
58 "Brain Damaged Planet" 30.00
59 "To Err is Vulcan" 30.00
60 "The Empire Man" 30.00
61 "Operation Con Game" 30.00
The Enterprise Logs (Vol.1) rep.
  #1–#8 (Golden Press #11185,
  1976) 20.00
The Enterprise Logs, Vol.2 rep.
  #9–#17 (Golden Press #11187,
  1976) 20.00
The Enterprise Logs, Vol.3 rep.
  #18–#26 (Golden Press #11188,
  1977) 20.00
Star Trek, Vol.4, rep. #27, #28,
  #30–#34, #36, #38, (Golden
  Press #11188, 1977) 20.00

STAR TREK
Marvel 1980–82
1 Dave Cockrum, Klaus Janson,
  rep.1st movie Adapt. 8.00
2 rep.1st movie Adapt. 6.00
3 rep.1st movie Adapt. 5.00
4 The Weirdest Voyage 5.00
5 Dr.McCoy..Killer 5.00
6 A:Ambassador Phlu 5.00
7 Kirk/Spock(c) 5.00
8 F:Spock 5.00
9 Trapped in a Web of Ghostly
  Vengeance 5.00
10 Spock the Barbarian 5.00
11 Like A Woman Scorned 5.00
12 Trapped in a Starship Gone Mad .5.00
13 A:Barbara McCoy 5.00
14 We Are Dying, Egypt, Dying 5.00
15 Gil Kane, The Quality of Mercy . .5.00
16 There's no Space like Gnomes . .5.00
17 The Long Nights Dawn 5.00
18 A Thousand Deaths, last issue . . .5.00

STAR TREK
DC 1984–88
[1st Regular Series]
1 Tom Sutton, The Wormhole
  Connection 15.00
2 The Only Good Klingon 8.00
3 Errand of War 7.00
4 Deadly Allies 7.00
5 Mortal Gods 7.00
6 Who is Enigma? 6.00
7 O:Saavik 6.00
8 Blood Fever 6.00
9 Mirror Universe Saga #1 . . . . . .6.00
10 Mirror Universe Saga #2 . . . . . .6.00
11 Mirror Universe Saga #3 . . . . . .6.00
12 Mirror Universe Saga #4 . . . . . .6.00
13 Mirror Universe Saga #5 . . . . . .5.00
14 Mirror Universe Saga #6 . . . . . .5.00
15 Mirror Universe Saga #7 . . . . . .5.00
16 Mirror Universe Saga end 5.00
17 The D'Artagnan Three 5.00
18 Rest & Recreation 5.00
19 W.Koenig story 5.00
20 Girl .5.00
21 Dreamworld 5.00
22 The Wolf #1 . . . . .5.00
23 The Wolf #2 . . . . .4.00
24 Double Blind #1 . . . . .4.00
25 Double Blind #2. . . . . .4.00
26 V:Romulans 4.00
27 Day in the Life 4.00

Star Trek #5 (Marvel 1980)

28 The Last Word 4.00
29 Trouble with Bearclaw 4.00
30 F:Uhura 4.00
31 Maggie's World 4.00
32 Judgment Day 4.00
33 20th Anniv. 4.50
34 V:Romulans 2.50
35 Excelsior 2.50
36 StarTrek IV tie-in 2.50
37 StarTrek IV tie-in 2.50
38 The Argon Affair 2.50
39 A:Harry Mudd 2.50
40 A:Harry Mudd 2.50
41 V:Orions 2.50
42 The Corbomite Effect 2.50
43 Paradise Lost #1 . . . . .2.50
44 Paradise Lost #2 . . . . .2.50
45 Paradise Lost #3 . . . . .2.50
46 Getaway 2.50
47 Idol Threats 2.50
48 The Stars in Secret Influence . . .2.50
49 Aspiring to be Angels 2.50
50 Anniv. 3.50
51 Haunted Honeymoon 2.50
52 "Hell in a Hand Basket" 2.50
53 "You're Dead, Jim" 2.50
54 Old Loyalties 2.50
55 Finnegan's Wake 2.50
56 Took place during 5 year Mission .2.50
Ann.#1 All Those Years Ago (1985) . .4.00
Ann.#2 The Final Voyage (1986) 3.00
Ann.#3 F:Scotty (1988) 3.00
Star Trek III, Movie Special, adapt. . .2.50
Star Trek IV, Movie Special, adapt. . .2.50
StarTrek V, Movie Special, adapt.
  (1989) 2.50

[2nd Regular Series] 1989–96
1 The Return 10.00
2 The Sentence 5.00
3 Death Before Dishonor 4.00
4 Reprocussions 4.00
5 Fast Friends 4.00
6 Cure All 4.00
7 Not Sweeney! 4.00
8 Going, Going 3.50
9 ...Gone 3.50
10 thru 12 Trial of James Kirk 3.50
13 thru 15 Return of Worthy 3.50
16 Worldsinger 3.00
17 Partners? #1 . . . . .3.00
18 Partners? #2 . . . . .3.00
19 Once A Hero 3.00
20 . . . . .3.00
21 Kirk Trapped 3.00
22 A:Harry Mudd 3.00
23 The Nasgul, A:Harry Mudd 3.00
24 25th Anniv., A:Harry Mudd 3.50
25 Starfleet Officers Reunion 2.50

*Star Trek: Early Voyages #5
(Marvel 1997)*

26 Pilkor 3 . . . . .2.50
27 Kirk Betrayed 2.50
28 V:Romulans 2.50
29 Mediators 2.50
30 thru 33 Veritas . . . .@2.50
4 F:Kirk, Spock, McCoy 2.50
35 thru 40 Tabukan Syndrome . . . .@2.50
1 Runaway 2.50
42 Helping Hand 2.50
43 V:Binzalans 2.50
44 Acceptable Risk 2.50
45 V:Trelane 2.50
46 V:Captain Klaa 2.50
47 F:Spock & Saavik 2.50
48 The Neutral Zone 2.50
49 Weapon from Genesis 2.50
50 "The Peacemaker" 4.00
51 "The Price" 2.00
52 V:Klingons 2.00
53 thru 57 Timecrime . . . .@2.00
58 F:Chekov 2.00
59 Uprising 2.00
60 Hostages 2.00
61 On Talos IV 2.25
62 Alone, pt.1, V:aliens 2.25
63 Alone, pt.2 . . . . .2.25
64 Kirk 2.25
65 Kirk in Space 2.25
66 Spock .2.25
67 Ambassador Stonn 2.25
68 . . . . .2.25
69 thru 72 Wolf in Cheap Clothing . .@2.25
73 Star-crossed, pt 1 . . . . .2.50
74 Star-crossed, pt.2 . . . . .2.25
75 Star-crossed, pt.3 . . . . .4.00
76 Tendar .2.25
77 to the Romulan Neutral Zone 2.50
78 thru 80 The Chosen . . . .@2.50
Ann.#1 story by George Takei (Sulu) .4.00
Ann.#2 Kirks 1st Yr At Star Fleet
    Academy 4.00
Ann #3 F:Ambassador Sarek 3.50
Ann.#4 F:Spock on Pike's ship 3.50
Ann.#5 (1994) 3.50
Ann.#6 Convergence, pt.1 . . . . .3.95
Spec.#1 PDd(s), BSz 3.75
Spec.#2 The Defiant 3.95
Spec.#3 V:Orion pirates 3.95
Debt of Honor, AH, CCl(s), HC 27.00
Debt of Honor SC 14.95
Spec. 25th Anniv.. . . . . .6.95
Star Trek VI, movie adapt(direct) . . .5.95
Star Trek VI, movie(newsstand) 2.95
TPB Best of Star Trek reps. 19.95
TPB Who Killed Captain Kirk?,
    rep.Star Trek#49-#55 . . . . .16.95
TPB The Ashes of Eden, Shatner
    novel adapt. (1995) 14.95

TPB Star Trek: Revisitations, rep.
    #22-#24, F:Gary Seven,
    #49-#50, F:Harry Mudd, 176pg 19.95

**THE MODALA IMPERATIVE
DC 1991**
1 Planet Modula 6.00
2 Modula's Rebels 4.50
3 Spock/McCoy rescue Attempt 4.00
4 Rebel Victory 4.00
TPB reprints both minis 19.95

**WHO'S WHO IN STAR TREK
DC 1987**
1 . . . . .6.00
2 . . . . .6.00

**EARLY VOYAGES
Marvel 1996**
1 Dan Abnett, Ian Edginton, Captain
    Pike's crew, double size premier 3.00
2 distress signal 2.00
3 on Rigel 7, prologue to "The Cage" 2.00
4 prologue to "The Cage" 2.00
5 V:Vulcans 2.00
6 Cloak & Dagger concl. 2.00
7 The wrath of Kaaj 2.00
8 F:Dr. Boyce 2.00
9 F:Nano .2.00
10 V:Chakuun, Tholians 2.00
11 The Fallen, pt. 2 . . . . .2.00
12 . . . . .2.00
13 F:Yeoman Colt 2.00
14 Pike vs. Kirk 2.00
15 F:Yeoman Colt 2.00
16 . . . . .2.00
17 Pike & Kaaj 2.00

**STAR TREK
Marvel 1996**
1-shot Star Trek: Mirror, Mirror,
    continuation of famous classic
    episode (Feb. 1997) 3.95
1-shot Operation Assimilation, Borg
    story (Dec. 1996) 2.95
1-shot Star Trek: Telepathy War, pt.4
    x-over, 48pg (Sept. 1997) 3.00
GN Star Trek: First Contact, Movie
    Adapt. (Nov. 1996) 5.95

**STAR TREK: UNLIMITED
Marvel 1996**
1 Al Williamson, Classic series & TNG . .
    3.00
2 . . . . .3.00
3 . . . . .3.00
4 Al Williamson, 2 tales 3.00
5 Al Williamson, 48pg 3.00
6 Telepathy War x-over 2.00
7 F:Q & Trelane 2.00
8 Day of Honor tie-in 2.00
9 V:Klingons 2.00
10 A Piece of the Action, conclusion
    of series. 2.00

**THE UNTOLD VOYAGES
Marvel 1998**
1 (of 5) Star Trek 2nd Five Year
    Mission 2.50
2 Spock, Savik, Dr. McCoy 2.50
3 F:McCoy, McCoy's Daughter 2.50
4 F:Sulu 2.50
5 48pg finale 3.50

**STAR TREK/X-MEN
Marvel**
1-shot, 64pg. 5.00
1a rep. of STAR TREK/X-MEN 4.95

**STARFLEET ACADEMY
Marvel 1996**
1 Cadets vs. Gorns 2.00
2 R&R in Australia 2.00
3 F:Decker 2.00
4 V:Klingon Bird-of-prey 2.00
5 V:Klingons 2.00
6 Funeral of Kamilah Goldstein,

*Star Trek Starfleet Academy #9
(Marvel 1997)*

I:Edam Astrun 2.00
7 F:Edam Astrun, Nog 2.00
8 Return of Charlie X 2.00
9 on Talos, V:Jem'Hadar 2.00
10 F:Captain Pike, Jem'Hadar 2.00
11 F:Christopher Pike 2.00
12 Telepathy War x-over 2.00
13 Parent's Day 2.00
14 T'Priell revealed, pt.1 (of 3) 2.00
15 T'Priell dead?, pt.2 . . . . .2.00
16 T'Priell Revealed, pt3 . . . . .2.00
17 Battle for T'Priell's mind 2.00
18 Entirely in Klingon language 2.00
19 Pava vs. Kovold 2.00

**STAR TREK: THE
NEXT GENERATION
DC 1988
[1st Regular Series]**
1 based on TV series, Where No
    Man Has Gone Before 15.00
2 Spirit in the Sky 10.00
3 Factor Q 8.00
4 Q's Day .8.00
5 Q's Effects 8.00
6 Here Today 8.00

[2nd Regular Series] 1989-95
1 Return to Raimon 16.00
2 Murder Most Foul 9.00
3 Derelict .7.50
4 The Hero Factor 7.50
5 Serafin's Survivors 6.00
6 Shadows in the Garden 6.00
7 The Pilot 5.00
8 The Battle Within 5.00
9 The Pay Off 5.00
10 The Noise of Justice 5.00
11 The Imposter 4.00
12 Whoever Fights Monsters 4.00
13 The Hand of the Assassin 4.00
14 Holiday on Ice 4.00
15 Prisoners of the Ferengi 3.50
16 I Have Heard the Mermaids
    Singing 3.50
17 The Weapon 3.50
18 MM, Forbidden Fruit 3.50
19 The Lesson 3.50
20 Lost Shuttle 3.50
21 Lost Shuttle cont. 3.50
22 Lost Shuttle cont. 3.50
23 Lost Shuttle cont. 3.50
24 Lost Shuttle conc. 3.50
25 Okona S.O.S. 3.50
26 Search for Okona 3.50
27 Worf, Data, Troi, Okona trapped
    on world 3.50
28 Worf/K'Ehleyr story 3.50

29 Rift, pt.1 . . . . .3.50
30 Rift, pt.2 . . . . .3.50
31 Rift conclusion 3.50
32 . . . . .3.50
33 R:Mischievous Q 3.50
34 V:Aliens, F:Mischievous Q 3.50
35 Way of the Warrior 3.50
36 Shore Leave in Shanzibar#1 . . . .3.25
37 Shore Leave in Shanzibar#2 . . . .3.25
38 Shore Leave in Shanzibar#3 . . . .3.25
39 Divergence #1 . . . . .3.25
40 Divergence #2 . . . . .3.25
41 V:Strazzan Warships 3.25
42 V:Strazzans 3.25
43 V:Strazzans 3.25
44 Disrupted Lives 3.25
45 F:Enterprise Surgical Team 3.25
46 Deadly Labyrinth 3.25
47 Worst of Both World's#1 . . . . . . .3.00
48 Worst of Both World's#2 . . . . . . .3.00
49 Worst of Both World's#3 . . . . . . .3.00
50 Double Sized, V:Borg 4.00
51 V:Energy Beings 3.00
52 In the 1940's 3.00
53 F:Picard 3.00
54 F:Picard 3.00
55 Data on Trial 3.00
56 Abduction 3.00
57 Body Switch 3.00
58 Body Switch 3.00
59 B:Children in Chaos 3.00
60 Children in Chaos#2 . . . . .3.00
61 E:Children in Chaos 3.00
62 V:Stalker 3.00
63 A:Romulans 3.00
64 Geordie 3.00
65 Geordie 3.00
66 . . . . .3.00
67 Friends/Strangers 3.00
68 Friends/Strangers, pt.2 . . . . .3.00
69 Friends/Strangers, pt.3 . . . . .3.00
70 Friends/Strangers, pt.4 . . . . .3.00
71 War of Madness, pt.1 . . . . .2.50
72 War of Madness, pt.2 . . . . .2.50
73 War of Madness, pt.3 . . . . .2.50
74 War of Madness, pt.4 . . . . .2.50
75 War of Madness, pt.5 . . . . .4.00
76 F:Geordi 2.50
77 Gateway, pt.1 . . . . .2.50
78 Gateway, pt.2 . . . . .2.50
79 Crew transformed into androids . .2.50
80 Mysterious illness 2.50
Ann.#1 A:Mischievous Q 4.50
Ann.#2 BP, V:Parasitic Creatures . . .4.00
Ann.#3 . . . . .2.50
Ann.#4 MiB(s), F:Dr.Crusher 4.00
Ann.#5 . . . . .4.00
Ann.#6 Convergence, pt.2 . . . . .3.95

*Star Trek, The Next Generation, The
Modala Imperative #4 (DC 1991)*

Star Trek: Deep Space Nine #16 (Malibu 1994)

Star Trek Voyager #8 (Marvel 1997)

Series Finale 4.25
Spec.#1 . . . . .3.75
Spec.#2 CCl(s) 4.00
Spec.#3 . . . . .4.00
Star Trek N.G.:Sparticus 5.00
TPB Beginnings, BSz(c) rep. 19.95

THE NEXT GENERATION/DEEP
SPACE NINE
DC 1994–95
1 Crossover with Malibu 2.50
2 . . . . .2.50

ILL WIND
DC 1995–96
1 Solar-sailing race 2.50
2 Explosion Investigated 2.50
3 A bomb aboard ship 2.50
4 finale 2.50

THE MODALA IMPERATIVE
DC 1991
1 A:Spock, McCoy 6.00
2 Modula Overrun by Ferengi 5.00
3 Picard, Spock, McCoy & Troi
   trapped .4.00
4 final issue 4.00

SHADOWHEART
DC 1994–95
1 thru 3 . . . .@2.25
4 Worf Confront Nikolai 2.25

RIKER SPECIAL
Marvel 1998
1-shot, Dan Abnett, Ian Edginton,
   Riker photo cover 3.50

X-MEN: SECOND CONTACT
Marvel 1998
1-shot, Dan Abnett, Ian Edginton,
   64pg 5.00
1-shot, variant cover (1:5) 5.00

DEEP SPACE NINE
Malibu 1993–96
1 Direct ed. 3.25
1a Photo(c). 3.00
1b Gold foil 5.00
2 w/skycap 3.50
3 Murder on DS9 . . . . .2.75
4 F:Bashir, Dax 2.75
5 V:Slaves .2.75
6 Three Stories 2.75
7 F:Kira 2.75
8 B:Requiem 2.75
9 E:Requiem 2.75
10 Descendants 2.50
11 A Short Fuse 2.75
12 Baby on Board 2.50

13 Problems with Odo 2.75
14 On Bejor 2.75
15 Mythologic Dilemma 2.75
16 Shangheid 2.50
17 Voyager preview 2.50
18 V:Gwyn 2.50
19 Wormhole Mystery 2.50
20 Sisko Injured 2.50
21 Smugglers attack DS9 . . . . .2.50
22 Commander Quark 2.50
23 Secret of the Lost Orb, pt.1 . . . .2.50
24 Secret of the Lost Orb, pt.2 . . . .2.50
25 Secret of the Lost Orb, pt.3 . . . .2.50
26 Mudd's Pets, pt.1 . . . . .2.50
27 Mudd's Pets, pt.2 . . . . .2.50
28 F:Ensign Ro 2.50
29 F:Thomas Riker, Tuvok 2.50
30 F:Thomas Riker 2.50
31 thru 32 . . . .@2.50
Ann.#1 Looking Glass (1995) 3.95
Spec.#1 Collision Course (1995) . . .3.50
Ultimate Ann.#1 (1995) 6.00
Lightstorm #1 Direct ed. (1994) 3.50
Lightstorm 1a, Silver foil 8.00
Spec. Terok Nor, fully painted by
   Goring .2.95

Marvel 1996–98
1 DS9 in the Gamma Quadrant, pt.1
   (of 2) 2.00
2 DS9 in Gamma Quadrant, pt.2 . . .2.00
3 pt.1 (of 2) 2.00
4 pt.2 . . . . .2.00
5 Terrorist Attack 2.00
6 Shirn Sentences Sisko to Death,
   "Risk,"pt.1 . . . . .2.00
7 "Risk,"pt.2 . . . . .2.00
8 V:Maquis & Romulans 2.00
9 V:Maquis & Romulans, pt.2 . . . . .2.00
10 Trapped in the Holosuite 2.00
11 . . . . .2.00
12 Telepathy War x-over 2.00
13 Telepathy War, Jem'Hadar Battle .2.00
14 Why do Klingons Hate Tribbles? .2.00
15 The Tailor's Deeds 2.00

THE CELEBRITY SERIES:
BLOOD AND HONOR
Malibu 1995
1 Mark Lenard(s) 2.95
2 Rules of Diplomacy 2.95

HEARTS AND MINDS
Malibu 1994
1 . . . . .3.00
2 . . . . .2.50
3 Into the Abyss, X-over preview . . .2.50
4 final issue 2.50

THE MAQUIS

Malibu 1995
1 Federation Renegades 2.50
1a Newsstand, photo(c) 2.50
2 Garack 2.50
3 F:Quark, Bashir 2.50

DEEP SPACE NINE/
THE NEXT GENERATION
Malibu 1994
1 Prophet & Losses, pt.2 . . . . .2.50
2 Prophet & Losses, pt.4 . . . . .2.50

STAR TREK: VOYAGER
Marvel 1996
1 F:Neelix & Talaxians, pt.1 . . . . . . .2.00
2 F:Neelix & Talaxians, pt.2 . . . . . . .2.00
3 F:Neelix & Talaxians, pt.3 . . . . . . .2.00
4 "Homeostasis,"pt.1 . . . . .2.00
5 "Homeostasis,"pt.2 . . . . .2.00
6 "Reucquest,"pt.1 . . . . .2.00
7 Ancient Relic 2.00
8 Mysterious Relic encountered 2.00
9 Dan Abnett, Ian Edginton,
   rescue mission 2.00
10 The Borg are back 2.00
11 Zoological Experiment 2.00
12 Zoological Experiment 2.00
13 Crew loses a member 2.00
14 Distress Call 2.00
15 Tuvok Trapped 2.00

Malibu
A V:Maquis 2.75
Aa Newsstand, photo(c) 2.50
B conclusion 2.75
Ba Newsstand, photo(c) 2.50

SPLASHDOWN
Marvel 1998
1 (of 4) Crash landing on water
   planet 2.00
2 The Ship May Sink 2.00
3 Adventure Undersea 2.00
4 Escape from Sea Creatures 2.00

STAR WARS

STAR WARS
Marvel 1977
1 Howard Chaykin, 30 Cent, movie
   adaption. 65.00
1a 35 Cent(square Box). 400.00
1b "Reprint" 7.50
2 movie adaptation 25.00
2b "Reprint" 4.00
3 movie adaptation 25.00
3b "Reprint" 4.00
4 movie adapt.(low dist.) 22.00
4b "Reprint" 4.00
5 movie adaptation 22.00
5b "Reprint" 3.00
6 E:movie adaption 22.00
6b "Reprint" 3.00
7 F:Luke & Chewbacca 20.00
7b "Reprint" 2.50
8 Eight Against a World 20.00
8b "Reprint" 2.50
9 Cloud Riders 20.00
9b "Reprint" 2.50
10 Behemoth from Below 20.00
11 Fate of Luke Skywalker 18.00
12 Doomworld 18.00
13 John Byrne, Deadly Reunion . . .18.00
14 . . . . .18.00
15 V:Crimson Jack 18.00
16 Walt Simonson, V:The Hunter . .18.00
17 Crucible, Low Dist. 18.00
18 Empire Strikes(Low Dist). 18.00
19 Ultimate Gamble(Low Dist) 18.00
20 Death Game(Scarce) 18.00
21 Shadow of a Dark Lord(Scarce) .18.00
22 Han Solo vs.Chewbacca 15.00
23 Flight Into Fury 15.00
24 Ben Kenobi Story 15.00

25 Siege at Yavin 15.00
26 Doom Mission 15.00
27 V:The Hunter 15.00
28 Cavern of the Crawling Death . .15.00
29 Dark Encounter 15.00
30 A Princess Alone 15.00
31 Return to Tatooine 15.00
32 The Jawa Express 15.00
33 V:Baron Tagge 15.00
34 Thunder in the Stars 15.00
35 V:Darth Vader 15.00
36 V:Darth Vader 15.00
37 V:Darth Vader 15.00
38 Riders in the Void 15.00
39 thru 44 Al Williamson, Empire
   Strikes Back adaptation 25.00
45 Death Probe 20.00
46 V:Dreamnaut Devourer 20.00
47 Droid World 20.00
48 Leia vs.Darth Vader 20.00
49 The Last Jedi 20.00
50 Giant Size issue 20.00
51 thru 66 Walt Simonson . . . . . .@15.00
67 . . . . .15.00
68 thru 99 . . . .@20.00
100 Painted(c), double-size 20.00
101 thru 106 . . . .@15.00
107 last issue 50.00
Ann.#1 Walt Simonson(c),
   V:Winged Warlords 10.00
Ann.#2 RN 8.00
Ann.#3 RN, Darth Vader(c) 8.00

RETURN OF THE JEDI
Marvel
1 Al Williamson, movie adapt 3.00
2 Al Williamson, movie adapt 3.00
3 Al Williamson, movie adapt 3.00
4 Al Williamson, movie adapt 3.00

STAR WARS IN 3-D
Blackthorne
1 thru 7 . . . .@2.50

DROIDS
Star 1986
1 . . . . .3.00
2 thru 5 Al Williamson . . . .@3.00
6 thru 8 A:Luke Skywalker . . . . . .@3.00

EWOKS
Star 1985—87
1 Based on TV Series 3.00
2 . . . . .2.50
3 . . . . .2.50
4 A:Foonars 2.50
5 Wicket vs. Ice Demon. 2.50

Star Wars, King Size Annual #1 (Marvel 1979)

Star Wars Droids #3 (Dark Horse 1995)

*Classic Star Wars: The Early Adventures
#9 (Dark Horse 1995)*

*Star Wars: Heir to the Empire #4
(Dark Horse 1996)*

6 Mount Sorrow, A:Teebo 2.50
7 A:Logray, V:Morag 2.50
8 . . . . .2.50
9 Lost in Time 2.50
10 thru 15 . . . .@1.50

STAR WARS:
A NEW HOPE
Dark Horse (B&W) Manga 1998
1 (of 4) by Tamaki Hisao, 96pg. 9.95

SPECIAL EDITION
Dark Horse 1997
1 Al Williamson 2.95
2 thru 4 . . . .@2.95
TPB Rep. #1–#4 Hildebrandt(c) 9.95
Spec. Edition boxed set 30.00

STAR WARS

A NEW HOPE
Dark Horse
1 rep. 4.25
2 rep. 3.95
TPB Rep. #1–#2 . . . . .9.95

THE EMPIRE STRIKES BACK
Dark Horse
1 Movie Adaptation 4.00
2 Movie Adaptation 4.00
TPB Rep.#1–#2 Al Williamson (c) . .9.95
TPB reprint, Hildebrandt(c) 9.95

RETURN OF THE JEDI
Dark Horse
1 Movie Adaptation 4.00
2 Movie Adaptation 3.50
TPB Rep.#1–#2 . . . . .9.95
TPB rep. Hildebrandt(c) 9.95
TPB Return of the Jedi–Special Edition, Hil
  debrandt(c) 9.95

CLASSIC STAR WARS
Dark Horse
1 Al Williamson, newspaper reps. . . .6.00
2 thru 7 Al Williamson, newspaper
  comic strip reps. . . . .@4.00
8 Al Williamson, newspaper reps.
  with trading card 4.00
9 Al Williamson, newspaper reps. . . .3.50
10 Al Williamson, newspaper reps. . . .3.50
11 thru 19 Al Williamson, newspaper
  reps. . . . .@3.00
20 Al Williamson, newspaper strip
  reps., with trading card, final
  issue .4.00
TPB Vol. 1, "In Deadly Pursuit,"
  rep.#1–#7 . . . . .15.99
TPB Vol. 1, rep. 2nd edition 16.95

TPB Vol. 2, "Rebel Storm,"rep.
  #8–#14 . . . . .16.95
TPB Vol. 3, "Escape to Hoth,"rep.
  #15–#20 . . . . .16.95

DEVILWORLDS
Dark Horse 1996
1 (of 2) by Alan Moore 2.50
2 . . . . .2.50

EARLY ADVENTURES
Dark Horse 1994–95
1 Gambler's World 3.00
2 Blackhole 2.50
3 Rebels of Vorzyd-5 . . . . .2.50
3 bagged with trading card DH2 . . .5.00
4 Tatooine 2.50
5 A:Lady Tarkin 2.50
6 Weather Dominator 2.50
7 V:Darth Vader 2.50
8 X-Wing Secrets 2.50
9 A:Boba Fett 2.50
TPB Al Williamson(c) 19.95

HAN SOLO AT STAR'S END
Dark Horse 1997
1 (of 3) by Alfredo Alcala 2.95
2 thru 3 . . . .@2.95
TPB rep. Al Williamson(c) 6.95

STAR WARS
BOBA FETT

Dark Horse 1995
1-shot Bounty on Bar-Kooda, 48pg . .3.95
1-shot When the Fat Lady Swings . . .3.95
1-shot Murder Most Foul 3.95
1-shot Twin Engins of Destruction . .2.95
TPB Death, Lies & Treachery 12.95

CRIMSON EMPIRE
Dark Horse 1997–98
1 thru 5 Dave Dorman(c) . . . . . .@2.95

DARK EMPIRE
Dark Horse 1991–92
1 Destiny of a Jedi 18.00
1a 2nd Printing 5.00
1b Gold Ed. 15.00
2 Destroyer of worlds, very low
  print run 18.00
2a 2nd Printing 5.00
2b Gold Ed. 15.00
3 V:The Emperor 10.00
3a 2nd printing 4.00
3b Gold Ed. 10.00
4 V:The Emperor 7.00
4a Gold Ed. 7.00
5 V:The Emperor 7.00
5a Gold Ed. 10.00

6 V:Emperor, last issue 5.00
6a Gold Ed. 9.00
Gold editions, foil logo set 75.00
Platinum editions, embossed set . .135.00
TPB Preview 32pg. 1.00
TPB rep.#1–#6 . . . . .19.95
TPB 2nd ed. 17.95
HC leather bound 125.00

DARK EMPIRE II
Dark Horse 1994–95
1 2nd chapter 6.00
2 F:Boba Fett 4.00
3 V:Darksiders 4.00
4 Luke Vs. Darksiders 3.50
5 Creatures 3.50
6 Save the Twins 3.50
Platinum editions, set 50.00
TPB rep.#1–#6 . . . . .17.95
HC Leather bound 100.00

DARK HORSE
CLASSICS:
DARK EMPIRE
Dark Horse 1997
1 rep. Dave Dorman(c) 2.95
2 thru 6 rep., Dave Dorman(c) . . .@2.95

DARK FORCE RISING
Dark Horse 1997
1 thru 6 (of 6) . . . .@2.95
TPB series rep 17.95
HC Star Wars: Dark Forces–Rebel
  Agent, by William C. Dietz &
  Dean Williams (March 1998) . .24.95
HC Star Wars: Dark Forces–Soldier
  For the Empire, by William C.
  Dietz and Dean Williams 24.95
TPB Star Wars: Dark Forces–Soldier
  For the Empire 14.95

DROIDS
Dark Horse 1994
1 F:C-3PO, R2-D2 . . . . .3.50
2 V:Thieves 2.75
3 On the Hosk Moon 2.75
4 . . . . .2.75
5 A Meeting 2.50
6 Final issue 2.50
Spec.#1 I:Olag Greck 2.50
TPB The Kalarba Adventures, rep. .17.95

2nd Series
1 Deputized Droids 3.00
2 Marooned on Nar Shaddaa 2.50
3 C-3PO to the Rescue 2.50
4 . . . . .2.50
5 Caretaker Virus 2.50
6 Revolution 2.50
7 & 8 . . . .@2.50
TPB Droids–Rebellion, rep. 17.95

EMPIRE'S END
Dark Horse 1995
1 R:Emperor Palpatine 2.95
2 Conclusion 2.95
TPB rep. .5.95

HEIR TO THE EMPIRE
Dark Horse 1995–96
1 I:Grand Admiral Thrawn 2.95
2 thru 6 . . . . .2.95
TPB from novel by Timothy Zahn . .19.95
HC signed, slipcase 100.00

JABBA THE HUTT—
Dark Horse 1995–96
1-shot The Garr Suppoon Hit 2.50
1-shot Hunger of Princess Nampi . .2.50
1-shot The Dynasty Trap 2.50
1-shot Betrayal 2.50

THE LAST COMMAND
Dark Horse 1997–98
1 thru 6 . . . .@2.95

MARA JADE—
BY THE EMPEROR'S HAND
Dark Horse 1998
1 (of 6) by Timothy Zahn 2.95

ONE-SHOTS
1-shot Star Wars: The Protocol
  Offensive, written by Anthony
  Daniels (Sept. 1997) 4.95
1-shot Star Wars: Shadow Stalker,
  from Galaxy Mag. (Nov. 1997) . .2.95
1-shot Star Wars: Tales From Mos
  Eisley, from Star Wars Galaxy
  Mag. #2–#4 . . . . .2.95
1-shot Classic Star Wars: Vandelhelm
  Mission, F:Han Solo, Lando
  (1995) 3.95
Star Wars: Battle of the Bounty
  Hunters, Pop-up Comic (July
  1996) 17.95

RIVER OF CHAOS
Dark Horse 1995
1 Emperor Sends Spies 2.50
2 Imperial in Allies Clothing 2.50
3 . . . . .2.50
4 F:Ranulf 2.50

SHADOWS OF THE EMPIRE
Dark Horse
1 (of 6) by John Wagner, Kilian
  Plunkett & P. Craig Russell 2.95
2 thru 6 . . . .@2.95
TPB Star Wars: Shadows of the
  Empire 17.95
HC Star Wars: Shadows of the
  Empire 80.00

SHADOWS OF THE EMPIRE —
EVOLUTION
Dark Horse 1998
1 thru 5 . . . .@2.95

SPLINTER OF THE MIND'S EYE
Dark Horse 1995–96
1 thru 4 A.D.Foster novel adapt. . .@2.95
TPB 14.95

STAR WARS:
TALES OF THE JEDI
Dark Horse 1993–94
1 I:Ulic Qel-Droma 6.00
2 A:Ulic Qel-Droma 5.00
3 D:Andur 4.00
4 A:Jabba the Hut 3.50
5 last issue 3.50
TPB 14.95
TPB 2nd printing 14.95

*Classic Star Wars: Return of the Jedi #1
(Dark Horse 1994)*

*Star Wars: X-Wing Rogue Squadron #12
(Dark Horse 1996)*

DARK LORDS OF THE SITH
Dark Horse 1994–95
1 Bagged with card 3.00
2 . . . . .2.50
3 Krath Attack 2.50
4 F:Exar Kun 2.50
5 V:TehKrath 2.50
6 Final battle 2.50
TPB 17.95

THE FREEDON NADD UPRISING
Dark Horse 1997
1 and 2 . . . .@2.75
2 . . . . .2.50
TPB series rep. 5.95

THE SITH WAR
Dark Horse 1995–96
1 F:Exar Kun 2.50
2 F:Ulic Oel-Droma 2.50
3 F:Exar Kun 2.50
4 thru 6 (6 part mini-series) . . . . . .@2.50
TPB 17.95

THE FALL OF THE SITH EMPIRE
Dark Horse 1997
1 (of 5) .2.95
2 thru 5 . . . .@2.95

THE GOLDEN AGE OF THE SITH
Dark Horse 1996–97
1 thru 5 . . . .@2.95
TPB 16.95

THE REDEMPTION OF
ULIC QEL-DROMA
Dark Horse 1998
1 (of 5) by Kevin J. Anderson 2.95
2 . . . . .2.95

STAR WARS: X-WING
ROGUE SQUADRON
Dark Horse 1995
The Rebel Opposition
1 F:Wedge Antilles 4.00
2 . . . . .3.00
3 F:Tycho Clehu 3.00
4 F:Tycho Clehu 3.00
½ Wizard limited exclusive 15.00
The Phantom Affair
5 thru 8 . . . .@3.00
TPB rep. 12.95
Battleground Tatooine
9 thru 12 . . . .@3.00
TPB rep. 12.95
The Warrior Princess
13 thru 16 . . . .@3.00
Requiem for a Rogue
17 thru 20 . . . .@3.00
In the Empire's Service

21 thru 24 . . . .@3.00
Making of Baron Fell
25 . . . . .3.00
Family Ties
26 thru 27 . . . .@3.00
Masquerade
28 thru 31 . . . .@3.00
Mandatory Retirement
32 thru 35 . . . .@2.95

STAR WARS
HANDBOOK
Dark Horse 1998
1 X-Wing Rogue Squadron 2.95

STARWOLVES:
JUPITER RUN
1 . . . . .1.95

STEVE ZODIAC &
THE FIREBALL XL-5
Gold Key 1964
1 . . . . .50.00

STRANGE
ADVENTURES
DC 1950–74
1 Destination Moon movie adapt,
   E.Hamilton's Chris-KL99 . . .2,400.00
2 Simon & Kirby, Doom From
   Planet X 1,100.00
3 Chris KL-99 . . . . .700.00
4 The Invaders From the Nth
   Dimension 700.00
5 Chris KL-99 . . . . .650.00
6 The Confessions of a Martian . .650.00
7 The World of Giant Ants 650.00
8 Evolution Plus 650.00
9 Captain Comet Begins in The
   Origin of Captain Comet . . .1,500.00
10 The Air Bandits From Space . .650.00
11 Day the Past Came Back 450.00
12 Girl From the Diamond Planet .450.00
13 When the Earth was Kidnapped 450.00
14 Destination Doom 450.00
15 Captain Comet-Enemy of Earth .425.00
16 The Ghost of Captain Comet . .425.00
17 Beware the Synthetic Men . . .425.00
18 World of Flying Men 425.00
19 Secret of the Twelve Eternals . .425.00
20 Slaves of the Sea Master 425.00
21 Eyes of the Other Worlds 350.00
22 The Guardians of the Clockwork
   Universe 350.00
23 The Brain Pirates of Planet X . .350.00
24 Doomsday on Earth 350.00
25 The Day That Vanished 350.00

26 Captain Vs. Miss Universe 350.00
27 The Counterfeit Captain Comet 350.00
28 Devil's Island in Space 350.00
29 The Time Capsule From
   1,000,000 B.C. 350.00
30 Menace From the World of
   Make-Believe 325.00
31 Lights Camera Action 325.00
32 Challenge of Man-Ape
   the Mighty 325.00
33 The Human Beehive 325.00
34 . . . . .325.00
35 Cosmic Chessboard 325.00
36 The Grab-Bag Planet 325.00
37 Invaders From the Golden Atom 325.00
38 Seeing-Eye Humans 325.00
39 The Guilty Gorilla 350.00
40 The Mind Monster 300.00
41 The Beast From Out of Time . .300.00
42 Planet of Ancient Children 300.00
43 The Phantom Prize Fighter 300.00
44 The Planet That Plotted Murder 300.00
45 Gorilla World 300.00
46 End Captain Comet Inter-
   planetary War Base 300.00
47 The Man Who Sold the Earth . .300.00
48 Human Phantom 300.00
49 The Invasion from Indiana 300.00
50 The World Wrecker 250.00
51 The Man Who Stole Air 250.00
52 Prisoner of the Parakeets 250.00
53 The Human Icicle 250.00
54 The Electric Man 175.00
55 Gorilla Who Challanged the
   World,pt.I 175.00
56 The Jungle Emperor, pt.II 175.00
57 The Spy from Saturn 175.00
58 I Hunted the Radium Man 175.00
59 The Ark From Planet X 175.00
60 Across the Ages 175.00
61 The Mirages From Space 175.00
62 The Fireproof Man 175.00
63 I Was the Man in the Moon 175.00
64 Gorillas In Space 175.00
65 Prisoner From Pluto 175.00
66 The Human Battery 175.00
67 Martian Masquerader 175.00
68 The Man Who Couldn't Drown .175.00
69 Gorilla Conquest of Earth 175.00
70 Triple Life of Dr. Pluto 175.00
71 Zero Hour For Earth 150.00
72 Skyscraper That Came to Life .150.00
73 Amazing Rain of Gems 150.00
74 Invisible Invader From
   Dimension X 150.00
75 Secret of the Man-Ape 150.00
76 B:Darwin Jones, The Robot
   From Atlantis 150.00

77 A:Darwin Jones, The World
   That Slipped Out of Space . . .150.00
78 Secret of the Tom Thumb
   Spaceman 150.00
79 A:Darwin Jones, Invaders from
   the Ice World 150.00
80 Mind Robbers of Venus 150.00
81 Secret of the Shrinking Twins . .150.00
82 Giants of the Cosmic Ray 125.00
83 Assignment in Eternity 125.00
84 Prisoners of the Atom Universe 125.00
85 The Amazing Human Race 125.00
86 The Dog That Saved the Earth .125.00
87 New Faces For Old 125.00
88 A:Darwin Jones, The Gorilla
   War Against Earth 125.00
89 Earth For Sale 125.00
90 The Day I Became a Martian . .125.00
91 Midget Earthmen of Jupiter 125.00
92 Amazing Ray of Knowledge . . .125.00
93 A:Darwin Jones, Space-Rescue
   By Proxy 125.00
94 Fisherman of Space 125.00
95 The World at my Doorstep 125.00
96 Menace of Saturn's Rings 125.00
97 Secret of the Space-Giant 125.00
98 Attack on Fort Satellite 125.00
99 Big Jump Into Space 125.00
100 Amazing Trial of John (Gorilla)
   Doe 135.00
101 Giant From Beyond 80.00
102 Three Faces of Barry Morrell . .80.00
103 Man Who Harpooned Worlds . .80.00
104 World of Doomed Spacemen . .80.00
105 Fisherman From the Sea 80.00
106 Genie in the Flying Saucer 80.00
107 War of the Jovian Bubble-Men .80.00
108 Human Pet of Gorilla Land . . .80.00
109 Man Who Weighted 100 Tons . .80.00
110 Hand From Beyond 80.00
111 Secret of the Last Earth-Man . .80.00
112 Menace of the Size-Changing
   Spaceman 80.00
113 Deluge From Space 80.00
114 Secret of the Flying Buzz Saw . .80.00
115 Great Space-Tiger Hunt 80.00
116 Invasion of the Water Warriors .80.00
117 I:Atomic Knights 600.00
118 The Turtle-Men of Space 100.00
119 Raiders From the Giant World .100.00
120 Attack of the Oil Demons 250.00
121 Invasion of the Flying Reptiles .65.00
122 David and the Space-Goliath . .65.00
123 Secret of the Rocket-Destroyer100.00
124 The Face-Hunter From Saturn . .75.00
125 The Flying Gorilla Menace 65.00
126 Return of the Neanderthal Man100.00
127 Menace From the Earth-Globe .65.00

Strange Adventures #231 (DC 1968)   *Strange Adventures #243 (DC 1973)*

128 Man With the Electronic Brain . .65.00
129 Giant Who Stole Mountains . ..70.00
130 War With the Giant Frogs 65.00
131 Emperor of the Earth 65.00
132 The Dreams of Doom 70.00
133 The Invisible Dinosaur 65.00
134 Aliens Who Raided New York . .70.00
135 Fishing Hole in the Sky 65.00
136 The Robot Who Lost Its Head . .50.00
137 Parade of the Space-Toys 50.00
138 Secret of the Dinosaur Skeleton 70.00
139 Space-Roots of Evil 50.00
140 Prisoner of the Space-Patch . .50.00
141 Battle Between the Two Earths .65.00
142 Return of the Faceless Creature 50.00
143 Face in the Atom-Bomb Cloud .50.00
144 A:Atomic Knights, When the
      Earth Blacked Out 85.00
145 The Man Who Lived Forever . .50.00
146 Perilous Pet of Space 50.00
147 The Dawn- World Menace 60.00
148 Earth Hero, Number One 50.00
149 Raid of the Rogue Star 50.00
150 When Earth Turned into a
      Comet 55.00
151 Invasion Via Radio-Telescope . .50.00
152 The Martian Emperor of Earth .50.00
153 Threat of the Faceless Creature 50.00
154 Earth's Friendly Invaders . . .50.00
155 Prisoner of the Undersea World 50.00
156 Man With the Head of Saturn . .50.00
157 Plight of the Human Cocoons . .50.00
158 The Mind Masters of Space . . .50.00
159 The Maze of Time 50.00
160 A:Atomic Knights, Here Comes
      the Wild Ones 50.00
161 Earth's Frozen Heat Wave,
      E:Space Museum 35.00
162 Mystery of the 12 O'Clock Man .35.00
163 Creature in the Black Light 35.00
164 I Became a Robot 35.00
165 I Broke the Supernatural Barrier 35.00
166 I Lived in Two Bodies 35.00
167 Team That Conqured Time 35.00
168 I Hunted Toki the Terrible 35.00
169 Prisoner of the Hour Glass . . .35.00
170 Creature From Strange
      Adventures 35.00
171 Diary of the 9-Planet Man? . . .35.00
172 I Became the Juggernaut Man .35.00
173 Secret of the Fantasy Films . . .35.00
174 The Ten Ton Man 35.00
175 Danger: This Town is Shrinking 35.00
176 Case of the Cosmonik Quartet .35.00
177 I Lived a Hundred Lives,
      O:Immortal Man 35.00
178 The Runaway Comet 35.00
179 I Buried Myself Alive 35.00
180 I:Animal Man, "I Was the Man
      With Animal Powers 225.00
181 The Man of Two Worlds 15.00
182 Case of the Blonde Bombshell .15.00
183 The Plot to Destroy the Earth . .15.00
184 A:Animal Man, The Return of the
      Man With Animal Powers 150.00
185 Ilda-Gangsters Inc. 15.00
186 Beware the Gorilla Witch 15.00
187 O:The Enchantress 20.00
188 I Was the Four Seasons 15.00
189 The Way-Out Worlds of Bertram
      Tilley 15.00
190 A:Animal Man, A-Man-the-Hero
      with Animal Powers 150.00
191 Beauty vs. the Beast 15.00
192 Freak Island 15.00
193 The Villian Maker 15.00
194 Menace of the Super-Gloves . .15.00
195 Secret of the Three Earth
      Dooms, A:Animal Man 100.00
196 Mystery of the Orbit Creatures .15.00
197 The Hostile Hamlet 12.00
198 Danger! Earth is Doomed 12.00
199 Robots of the Round Table 12.00

200 . . . . .12.00
201 thru 244 primarily superhero featur-
     ing Deadman, Adam Strange, etc.

STRANGE WORLDS
Avon Periodicals 1950
1 Spider God of Akka 650.00
2 Wally Wood, Dara of the Vikings 600.00
3 Al Williamson & Frank Frazetta,
     Wally Wood 1,200.00
4 Wally Wood, The Enchanted
     Dagger 550.00
5 Wally Wood, Bondage(c); Sirens
     of Space 400.00
6 Wally Wood(c), Maid of the Mist 300.00
7 Sabotage on Space Station 1 . .225.00
8 The Metal Murderer 225.00
9 The Radium Monsters 225.00
18 Joe Kubert 225.00
19 Astounding Super Science
     Fantasies 225.00

The Terminator: Endgame #3
(Dark Horse 1992)

TERMINATOR, THE
Now 1988–90
1 based on movie 10.00
2 . . . . .5.00
3 . . . . .4.00
4 thru 11 . . . .@3.50
12 I:John Connor ($1.75, cov, dbl.sz) 3.50
13 thru 17 . . . .@3.50
Spec. #1 . . . . .3.50
1-shot MW, 3-D const(c2, pop-up
     inside (July 1991) 5.00
Spec. (1998) 2.95

THE BURNING EARTH
Now 1990
1 . . . . .3.00
2 . . . . .3.00
3 thru 5 . . . .@2.50

ALL MY FUTURES PAST
Now 1990
1 Painted Art 3.00
2 Painted Art 3.00

THE TERMINATOR
Dark Horse 1990
1 Tempest 4.00
2 Tempest 3.00
3 . . . . .3.00
4 conclusion 3.00

THE ENEMY WITHIN
Dark Horse 1991–92
1 cont. from Sec.Objectives 4.00
2 C890.L.threat contd. 3.00
3 Secrets of Cyberdyne 3.00

4 Conclusion 3.00
SC rep #1–#4 . . . . .13.95

END GAME
Dark Horse 1992
1 Final *Terminator* series 3.00
2 Cont.last Term.story 2.75
3 (Conclusion of Dark Horse
     Terminator stories) 2.75

SECONDARY OBJECTIVES
Dark Horse 1991
1 cont. 1st DH mini-series 4.00
2 A:New Female Terminator 3.00
3 Terminators in L.A.&Mexico 3.00
4 Terminator vs Terminator concl. . . .3.00

HUNTERS AND KILLERS
Dark Horse 1992
1 V:Russians 3.00
2 V:Russians 2.75
3 V:Russians 2.75

TERMINATOR 2
Marvel 1991
1 movie adaption 1.25
2 movie adaption 1.25
3 movie adaption 1.25
Terminator II (bookshelf format) 4.95
Terminator II (B&W mag. size) 2.25

CYBERNETIC DAWN
Malibu 1995–96
1 thru 4 . . . .@2.50
0 flip-book/T2 Nuclear Twilight 2.50

NUCLEAR TWILIGHT
Malibu 1995–96
1 thru 4 . . . .@2.50
0 flip-book, see above

THING, THE
Dark Horse 1991–92
1 JHi, Movie adaptation 4.00
2 JHi, Movie adaptation 3.50

THING FROM ANOTHER WORLD: CLIMATE OF FEAR
Dark Horse 1992
1 Argentinian Military Base
     (Bahiathetis) 2.75
2 Thing on Base 2.75
3 Thing/takeover 2.75
4 Conclusion 2.75
TPB .15.95

ETERNAL VOWS
Dark Horse 1993–94
1 I:Sgt. Rowan 2.75
2 . . . . .2.75
3 in New Zealand 2.75
4 Last issue 2.75

COLD FEAR
Dark Horse
1 R:Thing 3.00
2 . . . . .2.75

THE TIME MACHINE
Classics Illustrated #133
By H. G. Wells
07/56 **(132)** Painted(c), Original 45.00
1958 thru 1971, rep. . . . .@8.00

FOUR COLOR
Dell Publishing Co.
[Second Series] March 1960
1085 The Time Machine 175.00

MARVEL CLASSICS COMICS
Marvel 1976–78
2 Gil Kane(c), Time Machine 10.00

TIME MACHINE
(B&W)
1 thru 3 . . . .@2.50

TIME TUNNEL, THE
Gold Key 1967
1 from TV show 55.00
2 . . . . .45.00

Time Warp #5 (DC 1980)

TIME WARP
DC 1979–80
1 thru 5 . . . .@2.00

TIME WARRIORS
Fantasy General (B&W)
1 rep.Alpha Track #1 . . . . .1.50
1a Bi-Weekly 75
2 75
3 75

TOM CORBETT SPACE CADET
Dell Publishing Co. 1952
See also Dell Four Color
4 based on TV show 100.00
5 . . . . .75.00
6 . . . . .70.00
7 . . . . .60.00
8 thru 11 . . . .@50.00

FOUR COLOR
Dell Publishing Co.
[Second Series] 1941–60
378 Tom Corbett, Space Cadet . . .200.00
400 Tom Corbett 125.00
421 Tom Corbett 125.00

MARCH OF COMICS
K.K. Publications/
Western Publ. 1946
(All were Giveaways)
102 Tom Corbet, Painted(c) 135.00

TOM CORBETT SPACE CADET
Prize Publications 1955
1 . . . . .200.00
2 . . . . .175.00
3 . . . . .175.00

The Original Tom Corbett #2 Malibu 1990)

The Twilight Zone #78 (Whitman 1977)

The Two Faces of Tomorrow #1 (Dark Horse 1997)

V #11 (DC 1985)

TOM CORBETT SPACE CADET
Eternity (B&W)
1	.2.00
2	.2.00
3	.2.25
4	.2.25

TOM CORBETT II
(B&W)
1 thru 4	@2.25

ORIGINAL TOM CORBET
Eternity (B&W) 1990
1 thru 10 rep. newspaper strips	@2.95

Topps 1993
1 w/Trading Card	.3.25
2 w/Trading Card	.3.25
3 w/Trading Card	.3.25
4 thru 5 w/Trading Card	.3.25

TOTAL RECALL
DC 1990
1 Movie Adaption	.3.00

TWILIGHT ZONE, THE
Gold Key 1961
1 Frank Frazetta, Painted(c) all	.100.00
2	.75.00
3	.55.00
4	.55.00
5 thru 8	@50.00
9	.60.00
10	.50.00
11	.50.00
12 Al Williamson	.50.00
13 Al Williamson	.40.00
14	.40.00
15	.40.00
16 thru 19	@25.00
20	.20.00
21 thru 23	@25.00
24 thru 27	@20.00
28 thru 31	@15.00
32	.20.00
33 thru 39	@15.00
40 thru 42	@12.00
43	.15.00
44 thru 49	@12.00
50 Walt Simonson	.12.00
51 Al Williamson	.15.00
52 thru 58	@12.00
59	.15.00
60 thru 70	@10.00

71 rep	.8.00
72	.10.00
73 rep	.8.00
74 thru 76	@10.00
77	.12.00
78 The Missing Mirage	.12.00
79 rep	.8.00
80	.12.00
81	.10.00
82	.12.00
83 Walt Simonson	.12.00
84	.12.00
85	.10.00
86 rep	.8.00
87 thru 91	@10.00
92 Whitman publ. rep. #1	.2.00

TWILIGHT ZONE
Now 1990
1	.8.00
1a 2nd printing Prestige +Harlan Ellison story	.6.00

[Volume 2]
#1 "The Big Dry"(direct)	.2.50
#1a Newsstand	.1.95
2 "Blind Alley"	.1.95
3 Extraterrestrial	.1.95
4 The Mysterious Biker	.1.95
5 Queen of the Void	.1.95
6 Insecticide	.1.95
7 The Outcasts, Ghost Horse	.1.95
8 Colonists on Alcor	.1.95
9 Dirty Lyle's House of Fun (3-D Holo)	.2.95
10 Stairway to Heaven, Key to Paradise	.1.95
11 Partial Recall	.1.95
3-D Spec.	.2.50
Ann. #1	.2.75

[Volume 3]
1 thru 2	.2.50

THE TWO FACES OF TOMORROW
(Manga B&W)
Dark Horse 1997
1 James P. Hogan novel adaptation, 32pg.	.2.95
2 thru 4	@2.95
5 thru 13	@3.95

2001: A SPACE ODYSSEY
Marvel 1976
1 Based on Movie	.3.00

2001: A SPACE ODYSSEY
Marvel 1976—77
1 Jack Kirby, Based on Movie	.5.00
2 Vira the She-Demon	.3.00
3 Marak the Merciless	.3.00
4 Wheels of Death	.3.00
5 Norton of New York	.3.00
6 Immortality...Death	.3.00
7 The New Seed	.3.00
8 Capture of X-51, I&O:Mr. Machine (Machine-Man)	.4.00
9 A:Mr Machine	.3.00
10 Hotline to Hades, A:Mr Machine	.3.00

2010
Marvel 1985
1 movie adapt	.1.00
2 movie adapt, May, 1985	.1.00

UFO FLYING SAUCERS
Gold Key 1968
1	.25.00
2	.20.00
3 thru 13	@10.00

Becomes:

UFO & OUTER SPACE
Gold Key 1978
14 thru 25	@5.00

UNKNOWN WORLD
Fawcett Publications 1952
1 Will You Venture to Meet the Unknown	.300.00

Becomes:

STRANGE STORIES FROM ANOTHER WORLD
Fawcett 1952–53
2 Will You? Dare You	.325.00
3 The Dark Mirror	.250.00
4 Monsters of the Mind	.250.00
5 Dance of the Doomed	.250.00

UNKNOWN WORLDS OF SCIENCE FICTION
Marvel 1975
(black & white magazine)
1 Al Williamson, Frank Frazetta	.4.00

2 George Perez	.3.25
3 George Perez	.3.25
4 thru 6	@3.25
Spec.#1	.3.50

V
DC 1985–86
1 TV show adaptation	.1.35
2 thru 16	@1.25
17	.1.25
18 End Game	.1.25

MARVEL CLASSICS COMICS
Marvel 1976–78
14 Gil Kane(c), War of the Worlds	.10.00

WAR OF THE WORLDS, THE
Caliber "New Worlds"(B&W) 1996
1 from H.G. Wells	.2.95
1a signed	.2.95
2 war for Kansas City	.2.95
3 Haven & The Hellweed	.2.95
4	.2.95
5	.2.95
TPB rep. #1–#5	.14.95

WAR OF THE WORLDS
Eternity (B&W)
1 TV tie-in	.1.95
2 thru 6	@1.95

WAR OF THE WORLDS: THE MEMPHIS FRONT
Arrow Comics (B&W) 1998
1 (of 5) by Randy Zimmerman & Richard Gulick	.2.95
2	.2.95
3	.2.95

WARP
First 1983–85
1 I:Lord Cumulus & Prince Chaos, play adapt pt.1	.2.00
2 thru 9 play adapt pt.2–9	@1.50
10 Second Saga, I:Outrider	.1.25
11 thru 17 A:Outrider	@1.25
18 A:Outrider&Sargon	.1.25
19 last issue	.1.25
Spec. #1 Howard Chaykin, O:Chaos (July 1983)	.1.50
Spec. #2 V:Ylem (Jan. 1984)	.1.50
Spec. #3 (June 1984)	.1.50

Aliens vs. Predator 12" figures (Hasbro 1996) & Lost in Space: Tybo the Carrot Man (Trendmasters 1998) The fierce and the not-so-fierce

Mars Attacks: Martian Brain Disintegrator (Trendmasters 1996) & Captain Scarlet: Angel Interceptor (Vivid Imaginations 1993)

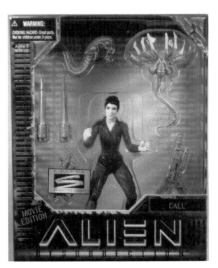

Alien Resurrection: Call & Alien (Hasbro 1997) & Spaceship Troopers: Warrior Bug (Galoob 1997)

The women of Star Trek are popular collectibles: Star Trek The Motion Picture Ilia 12" doll (Mego 1979) Lieutenant Uhura, 9" doll, KayBee special from the classic episode "Mirror, Mirror" (Playmates 1998) & Doctor Beverly Crusher, Starfleet 9" doll (Playmates 1996)

Lieutenant Commander Jadzia Dax, Federation Edition 9" doll (Playmates 1996) Seven of Nine, Warp Factor 4, 9" doll & Counselor Deanna Troi, Star Trek Insurrection 9" doll (Playmates 1998)

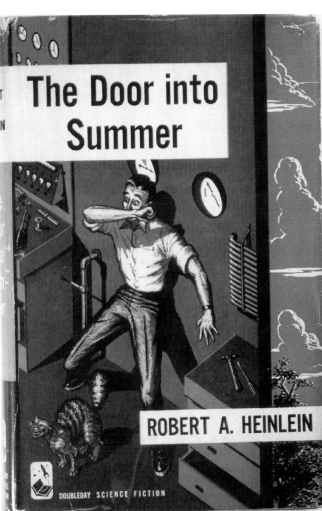

Operation Outer Space by Murray Leinster (Fantasy Press 1954) & The Door Into Summer by Robert A. Heinlein (Doubleday 1957)

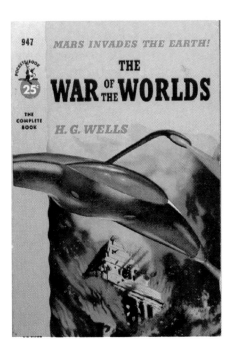

Invasion from Mars edited by Orson Welles, front cover and map back (Dell 1949) & War of the Worlds by H. G. Wells (Pocket 1953)

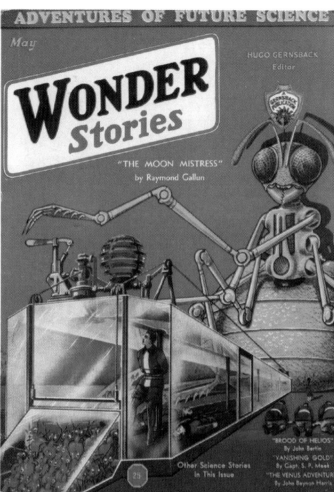

Weird Tales, Dec. 1933 cover by Margaret Brundage & Wonder Stories, May 1932 edited by Hugo Gernsbach

Cover Proof for Blood's A Rover by Harlan Ellison (Ace Books) cover art by Richard Corben. The book was not published

Flash Gordon #18 (Charlton 1970) Buck Rogers in the 25th Century #5 (Gold Key 1979) & Space: 1999 #2 (Charlton 1976)

Space Man (Dell) Space Adventures (Charlton) & The First Men in the Moon (Classic Illustrated #144)

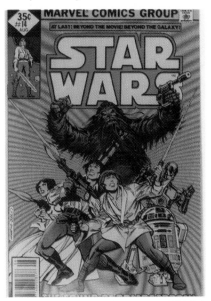

Star Trek The Next Generation, The Modala Imperative #2 (DC 1991) Star Wars #14 (Marvel 1978) & John Carter #21 (Marvel 1979)

2001: A Space Odyssey record (MGM 1968) Logan's Run DVD (MGM 1998) 7 Doctor Who: The Androids of Tara video tape (BBC 1996)

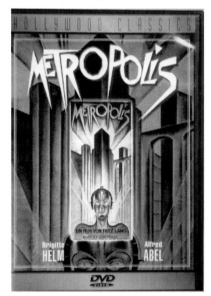  

Metropolis DVD (Madacy 1998) & Close Encounters of the Third Kind record () & Doctor Who: The Invasion (BBC 1993)

 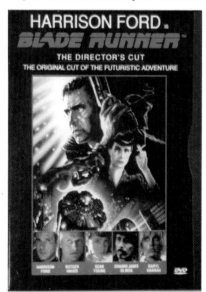 

Doctor Who: The Brain of Morbius video tape (BBC 1996), Blade Runner DVD (Warner 1996)
& Star Wars The Empire Strikes Back record, back (RSO 1980)

Star Wars classic action figures: Star Wars series: Chewbacca & The Empire Strikes Back: Zuckuss (Kenner 1978–81)

Return of the Jedi: See-Threepio (C-3PO) with removable arms & legs; Power of the Force: Princess Leia Organa in Combat Poncho & Tri-Logo: Rebel Commando (Kenner 1983–85)

Star Wars Jabba the Hut cookie jar (Star Jars 1998) & Star Wars MicroMachine Action Fleet KayBee exclusive 2-Pack (Galoob 1996)

Ten figures from the Star Wars Pewter Chess Set (Danbury Mint 1995)

Star Wars Cinema Scenes Cantina Aliens & WalMart exclusive R5-D4 figure (Kenner 1998)

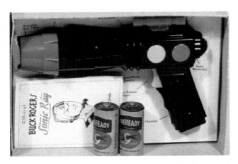
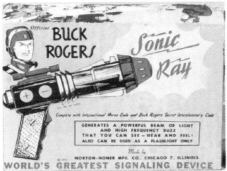

Buck Rogers Sonic Ray Gun (Norton-Honer 1952) & Buck Rogers 25th Century All-Fair card game (E.E. Fairchild 1936)

Buck Rogers Game of the 25th Century, box & game board (Lutz-Shinkman 1934)

Buck Rogers Costume & Rocket Police Patrol ship (Marx 1939)

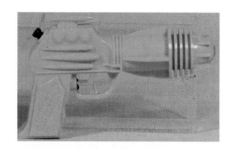

Flash Gordon Water Pistol (Marx 1950s) & Sparkling Rocket Fighter Ship (Marx 1950s)

Flash Gordon Click Ray Pistol (Marx 1950s) & Flash Gordon "City of Sea Caves," part 2 record (Record Guild of America 1960s)

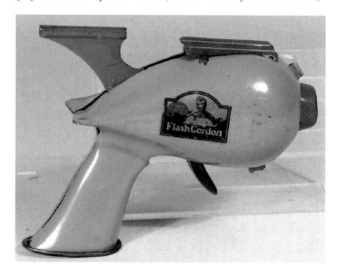

Flash Gordon Wallet (1949) & Flash Gordon Signal Pistol (1950s)

 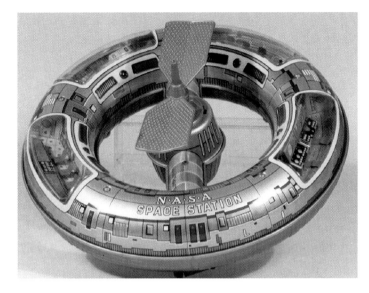

New Space Station, box & station (SH 1960s)

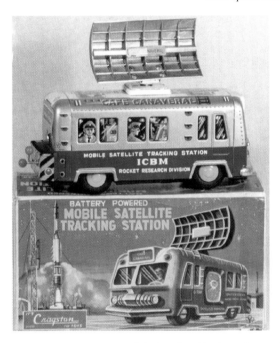 

Mobile Satellite Tracking Station (Cragston 1960s) Moon Explorer (Marken 1960s)

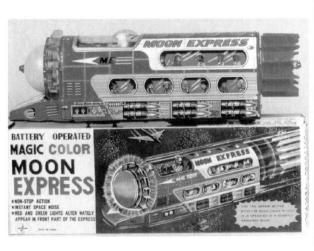  

Magic Color Moon Express (Daysran 1960s) & Space Refuel Station box & toy (Waco 1960s)

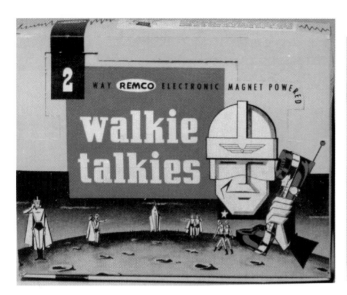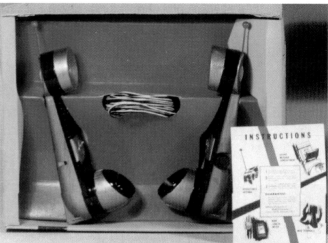

Electronic Walkie Talkies, box and contents (Remco 1960s)

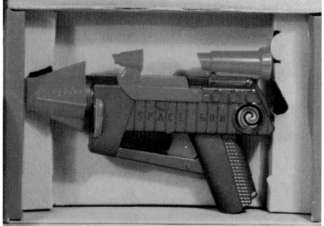

Electronic Space Gun, box & gun (Remco 1960s)

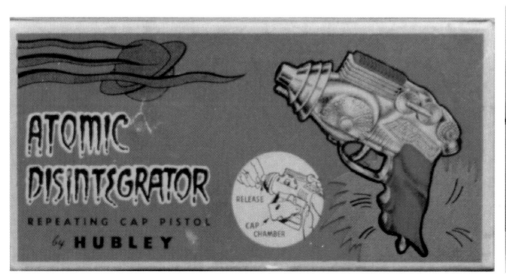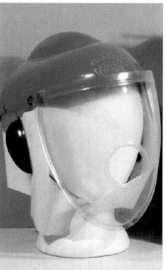

Atomic Disintegrator cap pistol (Hubley 1940s) & Captain Video Space Helmet (Plaxall, Inc. 1950s)

Star Strider AIJI-01 robots, red & blue (Horikawa)

The Hysterical Robot (Straco 1960s) & Space Explorer flying saucer (Baravelli 1960s)

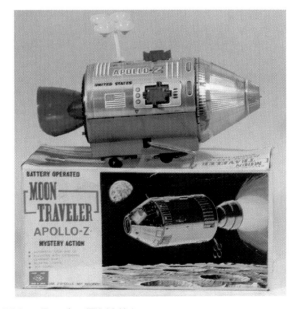

Count Down Playset (Ideal 1950s) & Apollo-Z Moon Traveler (TN 1960s)

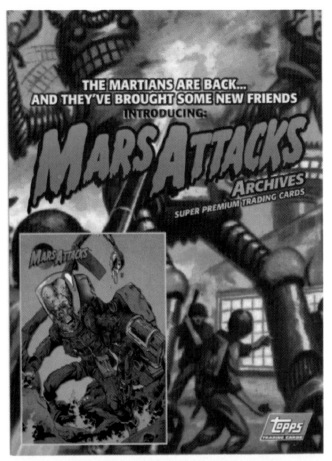

Promo Sheets: Mars Attacks Archives (Topps 1994)
& Aliens Predator Universe (Topps 1993)

Promo Cards: Mars Attacks (Topps 1994),
Roger Dean (FPG 1993), Star Wars Galaxy (Topps 1993),
More Than Battlefield Earth (Comic Images 1994)

Star Trek Episode Video Tape cards: The City on the Edge of Forever & Who Mourns for Adonis? (SkyBox 1993)

Toy Premium cards: Lt. Thomas Riker space cap, Counselor Deanna Troi card & Turtles First Officer Donatello (Playmates 1993–94)

Toy Premium cards: Predator & Luke Skywalker (Kenner Action Masters 1994) & Leia Organa (Topps/Just Toys BendEms 1993)

Colossal Cards #27 Dreamquest by Don Maitz (FPG 1994) & Colossal Cards Series Two #47 Anthology by Tim White (FPG 1995)

Colossal Cards pack (FPG 1994) art by Achilleos & Star Wars MasterVisions #15 (Topps 1995) art by Hugh Fleming

Weird Science #15 (Gemstone 1996)

WEIRD SCIENCE
E.C. Comics May–June
1950–Nov.–Dec. 1953
1 Al Feldstein, Wally Wood	....1,500.00
2 Wally Wood, Flying Saucers(c)	.700.00
3	..650.00
4	..550.00
5 Wally Wood, Atomic Bomb(c)	.400.00
6 Joe Kubert	.350.00
7 Joe Kubert, Classic(c)	.400.00
8 Joe Kubert	.350.00
9 Wally Wood(c), Joe Kubert, Classic(c)	.400.00
10 Wally Wood(c), Joe Kubert, Classic(c)	.400.00
11 Joe Kubert, Space war	.275.00
12 Wally Wood(c), Joe Kubert, Classic(c)	.275.00
13 Wally Wood(c), Joe Kubert	.300.00
14 Wally Wood	.300.00
15 Wally Wood, Al Williamson	.300.00
16 Wally Wood, Al Williamson	.300.00
17 Wally Wood, Al Williamson	.300.00
18 Wally Wood, Al Williamson, Atomic Bomb	.250.00
19 Wally Wood, Al Williamson, Frank Frazetta, Horror(c)	.400.00
20 Wally Wood, Al Williamson, Frank Frazetta	.400.00
21 Wally Wood, Al Williamson, Frank Frazetta	.400.00
22 Wally Wood, Al Williamson, Frank Frazetta	.400.00

Becomes:

WEIRD
SCIENCE FANTASY
March 1954–May–June 1955
23 Wally Wood, Al Williamson	...250.00
24 Wally Wood, Al Williamson, Classic(c)	...225.00
25 Wally Wood, Al Williamson, Classic(c)	...250.00
26 Wally Wood, Flying Saucer(c)	.250.00
27 Wally Wood	.250.00
28 Wally Wood	.250.00
29 Wally Wood, Classic(c)	...450.00

Becomes:

INCREDIBLE SCIENCE
FANTASY
July–Aug. 1955–Jan.–Feb. 1956
30 Wally Wood, Al Williamson	...250.00
31 Wally Wood, Al Williamson	...300.00
32 Wally Wood	.300.00
33 Wally Wood	.300.00

WEIRD SCIENCE
Gladstone 1990–91
1 Rep. #22 + Fantasy #1	..4.00
2 Rep. #16 + Fantasy #17	.3.50
3 Rep. #9 + Fantasy #14	.3.50
4 Rep. #27 + Fantasy #11	.2.00

Russ Cochran/Gemstone 1992
1 thru 21 EC comics reprint	....@2.50

"Annuals"
TPB Vol. #1 rebinding of #1–#5	....8.95
TPB Vol. #2 rebinding of #6–#10	...9.95
TPB Vol. #3 rebinding of #11–#15	..8.95
TPB Vol. #4 rebinding of #16–#18	...9.95
TPB Vol. #5 rebinding of #19–#22	..10.50

WEIRD
SCIENCE–FANTASY
Russ Cochran/Gemstone 1992
1 Rep. W.S.F. #23 (1954)	........2.00
2 Rep. Flying Saucer Invasion	....2.00
3 thru 8 Rep.	...@2.00

Gemstone
"Annuals"
TPB Vol. #1 rebinding of #1–#5	....8.95
TPB Vol. #2 rebinding of #6–#10	...12.95

WEIRD TALES OF
THE FUTURE
S.P.M. Publ./
Aragon Publications 1952–53
1	.600.00
2 Basil Wolverton	.900.00
3 Basil Wolverton	.850.00
4 Basil Wolverton	.600.00
5 Basil Wolverton, Jumpin' Jupiter Lingerie(c)	.850.00
6 Bondage(c)	.350.00
7 Basil Wolverton, Devil(c)	.550.00
8	.450.00

WHITLEY STRIEBER'S
BEYOND COMMUNION
Caliber (B&W) 1997
1 UFO Odyssey	..2.95
1 signed	..2.95
1 special edition, signed by Strieber	6.95
1a 2nd printing	.2.95
2 thru 4	...@2.95

WILLIAM SHATNER'S
TEK WORLD
Marvel 1992–94
1 Lee Sulivan, Novel adapt.	.2.25
2 thru 5 Novel adapt.cont.	@2.00
6 V:TekLords	.2.00
7 E:The Angel	.2.00
8 thru 18	.2.00
19 Sims of the Father #1	.1.75
20 Sims of the Father #2	.1.75
21 Who aren't in Heaven	.1.75
22 Father and Guns	.1.75
23 We'll be Right Back	.2.00
24	.1.75

*William Shatner's Tek World #23
(Marvel Epic 1994)*

WORLDS UNKNOWN
Marvel 1973–74
1 Gil Kane, The Coming of the Martians, Reprints	.15.00
2 Gil Kane, A Gun For A Dinosaur	.10.00
3 The Day the Earth Stood Still	...10.00
4 Arena	.10.00
5 Black Destroyer	.10.00
6 Gil Kane(c), Thing Called It	.10.00
7 Golden Voyage of Sinbad, Pt.1	.10.00
8 Golden Voyage of Sinbad, Pt.2	..10.00

X-FILES
Topps 1995–98
0 adapts pilot episode	..4.00
0a Mulder variant (c)	..7.00
0a Scully variant (c)	..8.00
½ with certificate	..15.00
1 From Fox TV Series	.50.00
1a Newstand	.40.00
1 rep. Hero giveaway (Sept. 1996)	.10.00
2 Aliens Killing Witnesses	.30.00
3 The Return	.20.00
4 Firebird, pt.1	.15.00
5 Firebird, pt.2	.10.00
6 Firebird, pt.3	..8.00
7 Trepanning Opera	.7.00
8 Silent Cities of the Mind, pt.1	..6.00
9 Silent Cities of the Mind, pt.2	...5.00
10 Fealing of Unreality, pt.1	..5.00
11 Fealing of Unreality, pt.2	..5.00
12 Fealing of Unreality, pt.3	..5.00
13 A Boy and His Saucer	..5.00
14	..4.00
15 Home of the Brave	..4.00
16 Home of the Brave, pt.2	..3.50
17	..3.50
18 Night Lights, pt.1	..3.50
19 Night Lights, pt.2	..3.50
20	..3.50
21 Family Portrait, with card	..3.50
22 "The Kanishibari"	.3.00
23 "Donor"	.3.00
24 "Silver Lining"	.3.00
25 "Remote Control,"pt.1	.3.00
26 "Remote Control,"pt.2	.3.00
27 "Remote Control,"pt.3	.3.00
28 "Be Prepared,"pt.1, V:Windigo	..3.00
29 "Be Prepared,"pt.2	.3.00
30 "Surrounded,"pt.1	.3.00
31 "Surrounded,"pt.2 (of 2)	.3.00

32	..3.00
33 widows on San Francisco	..2.95
33 variant photo (c)	..2.95
34 Project HAARP	..2.95
35 Near Death Experience	..2.95
36 Near Death Experience, pt.2	..2.95
37 The Face of Extinction	..2.95
38	..2.95
39 Widow's Peak	..2.95
40 Devil's Advocate	..2.95
40a photo cover	..2.95
Ann.#1 Hollow Eve	..5.00
Ann.#2 E.L.F.S.	..4.50
Spec.#1 rep. #1–#3	..6.00
Spec.#2 rep. #4–#6 Firebird	..5.00
Spec.#3 rep. #7–#9	..5.00
Spec.#4 rep. #10–#12	..5.00
Spec.#5 rep. #13, Ann.#1	..5.00
TPB Vol. 2	..19.95
GN Afterflight	..5.95
GN Official Movie Adapt. (1998)	...5.95

X-FILES DIGEST
Topps 1995
1 All New Series, 96pg.	..3.50
2 and 3	..3.50

GROUND ZERO
Topps 1997
1 (of 4) based on novel by Kevin J. Anderson	..2.95
2 thru 4	...@2.95

The X-Files #20 (Topps 1996)

SEASON ONE
Topps 1997
1 "Deep Throat"	..4.95
N# Deep Throat, variant (c)	...7.50
2 "Squeeze"	..3.95
N# Squeeze	..4.95
3 "Conduit"	..3.95
N# Conduit	..4.95
4 "The Jersey Devil"	..3.95
5 "Shadows"	..3.95
N# Shadows JVF(c)	..4.95
6 "Fire"	..3.95
N# Fire	..4.95
7 "Ice"	..3.95
N# Ice	..4.95
8 "Space"	..3.95
N# Space(c)	..4.95
Spec. Pilot Episode, new JVF(c)	..4.95
Beyond the Sea	..4.95

MODEL KITS, STATUES & REPLICAS

Model kits are popular items and movie and TV spaceships work well as models, probably because they are really just models in the first place. Every new space movie or TV series has a few new ships, so the lines stay fresh. With the advent of syndication and video tapes, television shows can support a model kit line for a long time. Young fans of a popular show will buy action figures when they are young and then graduate to model kits of the same show later when they gain the skill to make them. Creative adults who are still in touch with their inner child will buy expensive vinyl kits of the same shows they watched as kids. All of this keeps popular model kits in production for a long time.

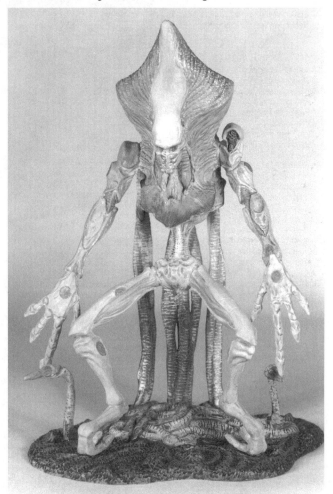

ID4 Independence Day *Alien Exoskeleton model kit*
(Lindberg 1997)

The original legendary model kit company was Aurora and its models are the highest priced in the field. Aurora made famous models for *The Invaders*, *Land of the Giants*, *Lost in Space* and *Star Trek* and when it went out of business, some of its former employees formed Addar and made a number of famous models for *Planet of the Apes*.

Much of the action in new model kits is in expensive vinyl kits. A lot of different ones are being made, so there must be a lot of enthusiasts out there buying them. Production runs are generally not large, even on licensed kits. This also tends to keep kits for older television shows available. Their license fees are a lot less expensive than *Star Trek* or *Star Wars*. In addition, they are not likely to be diligent in checking out every garage-kit company. A really creative sculptor can tackle some of the many characters and aliens from popular science fiction novels.

Just about every model kit collector is also a model kit builder, and this creates a real dilemma in model kit collecting. If you build the model very carefully and skillfully and paint it beautifully, you will still not be able to sell it for what the kit sells for. On the other hand, if you don't build the model, how will you impress your friends? Model kits don't look like much in the box and look like even less if the box is open. Model kits usually come in flimsy boxes that are shrink wrapped. This gives them a strong tendency to buckle over time as the shrink wrap shrinks some more. This, too, can reduce the value of the kit. The best thing to do might be to build the model, put it on display and just collect boxes. You could even re-shrink wrap the box. Of course your collection wouldn't be worth much, but you could pretend.

Statues and other fine replicas can be collected and put on display without losing their value. Of course, there is no creativity involved on the collector's part, only money. There are an increasing number of these available today and many collectors have one as a centerpiece to their collection, but rarely more than a few. They are too expensive for many people to try to collect a whole series. Companies such as The Franklin Mint specialized in these items and advertised them extensively in Sunday newspaper supplements and in magazines and they were limited in production to everyone who ordered one. Essentially, this meant that everyone who wanted one had one and new collectors had little reason to prefer one from a couple of years ago to an equally nice item made recently. By the time there could be collector interest in a 20th anniversary limited-edition replica of the *Millennium Falcon*, there was an equally nice 25th anniversary limited-edition

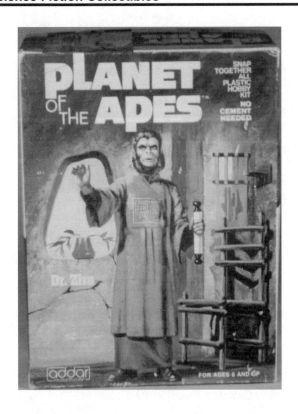

Planet of the Apes: *Dr. Zira model kit (Addar 1975)*

replica available with a better sound chip or whatever. Consequently, price appreciation was slow or non-existent. Your best bet may be to get one of your better funded relatives to buy you one for your birthday.

In the last few years, Icons and a couple of other companies have started making even more elaborate replicas of classic guns, ships, robots and other items. These are expensive, and quite limited in production. Furthermore, it does not look like it will revisit the same item with some slightly different edition. This may make its fine replicas into highly sought collectibles as well, but it is too early to tell.

ALIENS

Model Kits
Alien model kit, 1/10 scale (MPC 1979) 120.00
Alien Jumbo model kit (Tskuda 1979) 150.00
Queen model kit (Kaiyodo 1987) 400.00
Alien Warrior model kit (Kaiyodo 1987) 300.00
Aliens, This Time It's Modeling, 2½" multi-pose polyurethane resin cast figures. Available are Hicks, Drake, Frost, Dietrich, Apone, Vasquez (two different), Hudson, Weirowski, Crowe, Gorman, Ferro, Spunlmeyer, Bishop, Burke, Alien Warrior (4 different), and Ripley (A.E.F. 1988) each 25.00
5" Queen Alien, This Time It's Modeling (A.E.F. 1988) 60.00
Alien Cocoon and Egg Chamber model kit, This Time It's Modeling (A.E.F 1988) 150.00
Powerloader, This Time It's Modeling (A.E.F. 1988) . . .40.00
APC model kit (Halcyon 1987) 35.00
Aliens Armored Personnel Carrier vinyl model kit, 1/35 scale (Halcyon #HAL01, 1992) 30.00

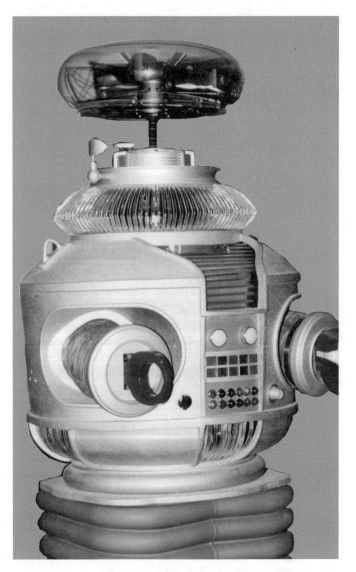

Lost in Space *Robot, life size replica (Icons 1998)*

Aliens Drop Ship vinyl model kit, 1/72 scale (Halcyon #HAL02, 1992) 40.00
Aliens Power Loader with Ripley vinyl model kit, 1/12 scale (Halcyon #HAL03, 1992) 60.00
Alien Warrior vinyl model kit 1/9 scale (Halcyon #HAL004, 1992) 35.00
Narcissus vinyl model kit, 1/144 scale (Halcyon #HAL010, 1992) 36.95
Aliens Sulaco vinyl model kit (Halcyon #HAL12, 1993) 50.00
Alien 3 Queen Chest Burster model kit (Halcyon) 60.00
Dog Burster model kit (Halcyon) 75.00
Chest Burster model kit (Halcyon) 60.00
Attacking Alien model kit (Halcyon) 30.00
Alien Warrior vinyl model kit, 1/5 scale (Horizon #HT-01, 1992) 70.00
Alien Face Hugger vinyl model kit, 1/1 scale (Horizon #HT-02, 1992) 100.00
Nostromo vinyl model kit, 1/960 scale (Horizon #HT-03, 1992) 185.00
Space Jockey vinyl model kit, 1/72 scale (Horizon #HT-04, 1992) 185.00
Alien Queen vinyl model kit (Horizon #HT-05, 1992) . .140.00

Alien Model Kit (MPC)

Alien Chest Burster model kit 1/1 (Horizon) 75.00
Dog Burster vinyl model kit, 1/1 scale (Horizon #HT-
    07, 1992) 99.00
Face Hugger Model (Halcyon 1991) 100.00
Alien 3 cold cast resin (Dark Horse) 200.00
Colonial Marine resin kit, with two heads and two
    weapons 75.00
Alien Warrior model kit, 1/8 scale (Geometric) 60.00
    Base for Alien Warrior, 7" x 7" (Geometric) 20.00
    Deluxe Alien Warrior Base, 14" tall
    (Geometric) 30.00
Ripley model kit, 1/8 scale (Geometric) 50.00
Aliens Customizing Kit, 2 eggs, toolbox and
    facehugger (Geometric) 25.00
Aqua Alien model kit 100.00
Colonial Marine (Vandalay Kits) 60.00

Statues
Alien vs. Predator Statue 150.00

Fine Replicas
M41-A Hero Pulse Rifle, full sized replica, with wall
    mount and plaque (Icons 1998) 1,250.00
M41-A Background Pulse Rifle, full sized replica,
    with wall mount and plaque (Icons 1998) 400.00
    Wall rack 130.00
Queen Alien Skull (Greyzon) 130.00
Face Hugger Alien in Status Tube (Greyzon) 1,000.00

ARMAGEDDON

Model Kit
Russian Space Center (Revell 1998) 20.00

BABYLON 5

Model Kit
Kosh model kit 75.00
Shadows Ship model kit 75.00
Babylon 5 Starfury MK1 model kit, 1/72 scale (Redi
    Monogram #853621) 18.50

Statue
G'Kar Bust, limited to 2,500 (Legends in 3
    Dimensions) 150.00

BARBARELLA

Model Kit
Barbarella, Queen of the Galaxy resin model kit
    (Styrene Studios) 150.00

BATTLE OF THE PLANETS

Model Kit
G-1SP Spaceship model kit (Entex 1978) 15.00

BATTLESTAR GALACTICA

Model Kits
Battlestar Galactica model kit (Monogram 1979) 45.00
Cylon Base Star model kit (Monogram 1979) 45.00
Space Fighter Raider model kit, 1/24 scale
    (Monogram 1979) 30.00
Space Fighter Viper model kit, 1/24 scale
    (Monogram 1979) 30.00
Colonial Viper model kit, 1/24 scale (Monogram
    1978) 25.00
Cylon Raider model kit, 1/48 scale (Monogram 1978) . .35.00
Cylon Raider (Revell 1997) .15.00

Fine Replicas
Battlestar Galactica, limited to 2,500 (Legends in 3
    Dimensions) 150.00
Cylon Baseship, limited to 1,500 (Legends in 3
    Dimensions) 125.00
Colonial Viper replica miniature, with display case
    and plaque signed by Richard Hatch (Icons
    1998) 450.00
Cylon Centurion Helmet, with working red eye and
    plex case (Icons 1998) 500.00
Colonial Warrior Helmet, with illuminated helmet
    piping and plex case (Icons 1998) 500.00

BLACK HOLE

Model Kits
V.I.N.C.E.N.T. model kit, 1/12 scale (MPC 1982) 25.00
Maximillian model kit, 1/12 scale (MPC 1982) 25.00
Cygnus Spaceship model kit, 1/4225 scale (MPC
    1979) 45.00

BLADE RUNNER

Model Kit
Pris, resin kit (Styrene Studios) 90.00
Blade Runner Gun model kit 120.00

Doctor Who, *Mk3 Movie Dalek model kit (Comet)*

BUCK ROGERS

Model Kits
Superdreadnaught model SD51X, 6½" balsa wood
    construction kit (1936) .600.00
Buck Rogers Starfighter model kit, 1/48 scale
    (Monogram 1979) 25.00
Buck Rogers Marauder model kit, 1/48 scale
    (Monogram 1979) 25.00

THE DAY THE EARTH
STOOD STILL

Model Kit
Gort, sculpted by Randy Bowen (Lunar Models) 300.00

DICK TRACY

Model Kit
Dick Tracy Space Coupe model kit, 1/72 scale
    (Aurora 1968) 125.00

DOCTOR WHO

Model Kits
Doctor Who: Tom Baker (M01) 80.00
Doctor Who: Patrick Thoughton (M03) 80.00
MK3 Movie Dalek model kit, 1/8 scale (Comet) 50.00

DUNE

Model Kits
Ornithopter model kit (Revell 1985) 25.00
Sand Crawler model kit (Revell 1985) 25.00
Sandworm model kit (Revell 1985) 30.00
Fayd model kit 90.00

FIFTH ELEMENT

Model Kits
5th Element resin kit (Styrene Studios) 135.00

FIREBALL XL5

Model Kits
Fireball XL5, 36" model kit (ENA Models) 225.00

FLASH GORDON

Model Kits
Flash Gordon (Revell) 100.00
Flash Gordon: Buster Crabbe (TR04) 125.00
Flash Gordon, 1/4 scale (Screamin Products SP-24,
    1993) 40.00

Dune, *Fayd model kit*

Flash Gordon model kit

FORBIDDEN PLANET

Model Kit
Robby The Robot, 22" Battery Operated Model
(Masudaya 1985) 120.00
Robby The Robot, 24½" with voice & lights 250.00
Robby The Robot, 16" with voice & lights 125.00

INDEPENDENCE DAY ID-4

Model Kits
Alien Skull resin (Grey Zon 1997) 110.00
Alien with doctor, resin (Styrene Studios) 185.00
Russell Case's Stearman PT-17 (Lindberg 1997) 15.00
Capt. Steven "Eagle" Hiller's F/A-18 Hornet
(Lindberg 1997) 15.00
Captured Alien Attacker (Lindberg 1997) 15.00
Alien Exoskeleton (Lindberg 1997) 15.00

Statue
Alien Skull (Greyzon) 80.00

Fine Replicas
Alien Attacker miniature replica, 24" across, with
display case and plaque (Icons 1998) 1,000.00

THE INVADERS

Model Kits
U.F.O. from *The Invaders* model kit, including 4
figures, 1/72 scale in 13" x 7" x 2" box (Aurora
#813, 1968) 175.00
Flying Saucer of *The Invaders* model kit, including 8
figures (Aurora #813, 1975) reissue of above . . .90.00
Invaders Flying Saucer model kit (Monogram 1979) . . .45.00

LAND OF THE GIANTS

Model Kits
Land of the Giants (Giant Snake) 1/48 scale in
13" x 7" x 2" box (Aurora #816, 1968) 400.00
Land of the Giants Spaceship, 1/64 scale in
13" x 7" x 2" box (Aurora #830, 1968) 500.00
Rocket Transport Spindrift, from Land of the Giants,
1/64 scale in 13" x 7" x 2" box (Aurora #255,
1975) reissue of above 225.00
Spindrift Interior model kit (Lunar Models 1989) 85.00

LOST IN SPACE

Classic Show, Model Kits
Lost In Space, The Robot, Figure model kit, 1/11
scale in 13" x 5" x 2" box (Aurora #418 1968) . .900.00
Lost In Space model kit, Large Diorama with Chariot,
Cyclops and Robinson Family, 1/32 scale in
12" x 9" x 1½" box (Aurora #420, 1966–68) . .1,500.00
Lost In Space model kit, small diorama with Cyclops,
in 13" x 5" x 2" box (Aurora #419, 1966–68) . .1,000.00
Cyclops, plastic (Polar Lights) 15.00
Robot, plastic (Polar Lights) .15.00
The Jupiter 2 plastic model kit (Polar Lights) 20.00
Lost in Space diorama with cyclops model kit (Polar
Lights) 22.00
Lost in Space Chariot model kit, 1/35 scale (Lunar
Models 1987) 80.00
Jupiter-2 model kit, 24" (Lunar Models 1994) 175.00

ID4 Independence Day, *Captured Alien Attacker model kit*
(Lindberg 1997)

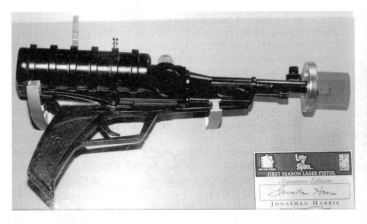

Lost in Space *First Season Jonathan Harris replica gun (Icons 1998)*

Jupiter-2 model kit, 16½" (Lunar Models 1994) 100.00
Jupiter-2 interior kit for 16½" model (Lunar Models
    1994) 150.00
Jupiter-2 model kit, 16" (Lunar Models 1994) 80.00
Jupiter-2 interior kit for 16" model (Lunar Models
    1994) 125.00
Jupiter-2 Fusion Core lighting kit for 16" model
    (Lunar Models 1994) 90.00
Jupiter-2 Accessory set for 16" model (Lunar Models
    1994) 60.00
Robinson Family figures set #1, 1/35 scale (Lunar
    Models 1994) 60.00
Robinson Family figures set #2, 1/35 scale, seated
    to fit in Chariot vehicle (Lunar Models 1994) 50.00
Space Pod model, 3½" high, 1/35 scale (Lunar
    Models 1994) 80.00
Chariot model, 1/35 scale (Lunar Models 1994) 80.00
Cave Diorama model, with Cyclops and three figures
    (Lunar Models 1994) (Lunar Models 1994) 120.00
Spider Diorama model with Spider and Chariot
    (Lunar Models 1994) .110.00
Illusion Machine Diorama with Will, machine and
    three aliens (Lunar Models 1994) 130.00
Launch Site Diorama model with 110 pieces (Lunar
    Models 1994) 175.00
Season One Laser Pistol model, 1/1 scale, with
    electronics (Lunar Models 1994) 115.00
Season Two Laser Pistol model, 1/1 scale, with
    electronics (Lunar Models 1994) 105.00
Jupiter-2 Crash Site Diorama model kit, 1/72 scale
    (Lunar Models 1994) 65.00
Invaders 5th Dimension Space Ship model kit, 1/35
    scale, with two alien figures (Lunar Models
    1994) 60.00
The Derelict Space Ship, with mini Jupiter-2 model
    kit (Lunar Models 1994) 65.00
Penny with alien model kit, 1/8 scale figure (Lunar
    Models 1994) 120.00
John Robinson with laser pistol model kit, 1/8 scale
    figure (Lunar Models 1994) 110.00
Don West with Blawp, model kit, 1/8 scale figure
    (Lunar Models 1994) .120.00
Robot model kit (comic book version) 1/8 scale with
    Mozart figure (Lunar Models 1994) 150.00
Robot model kit, classic version, 10" extra detailed
    (Lunar Models 1994) .150.00
Dr. Smith and Will Robinson model kit, 1/8 scale
    (Lunar Models 1994) .150.00
Deluxe Dr. Smith and Will Robinson model kit, with
    alien creature, 1/8 scale (Lunar Models 1994) . .170.00

Mars Attacks, *Attacking Martian model kit (Screamin' 1997)*

Movie Model Kits
Lost in Space Jupiter 2 (AMT Ertl #8459, 1998) 20.00
Lost in Space Robot (AMT/Ertl #8458, 1998) 17.00

Fine Replicas
First Season Laser Pistol in display case with
    plaque, 2,500 made (Icons 1998) 400.00
    Bill Mumy signature edition, 500 made 525.00
    Jonathan Harris signature edition, 500
    made 525.00
    Mark Goddard signature edition, 500 made 525.00
Deluxe Jupiter 2 miniature, masterpiece series, 18"
    in diameter, in display case, 2,500 made
    (Icons 1998) 500.00
B-9 Robot Replica, life size 7 feet tall, with voice CD
    activated lights, 250 made (Icons 1998) 12,500.00
    Custom CD voice sample, personalized to
    buyer by Dick Tufeld .500.00

MARS ATTACKS

Model Kits
Mars Attacks Bust (Mad Lab) 50.00
Spy Girl, with two heads 120.00
Attacking Martian (Screamin 1997) 75.00
Slaughter in the Streets (Screamin 1997) 75.00
Martian Ambassador Bust, 6" (Jay Jay Productions) . . .95.00

Men in Black Noisy Cricket replica gun (Icons 1998)

MEN IN BLACK

Fine Replicas
Noisy Cricket metal gun replica, with display case
    and plaque (Icons 1998) 300.00
Tri-Barrel Rifle, with display case and plaque (Icons
    1998) 450.00
Neuralizer, with display case and plaque (Icons
    1998) 350.00

MESSAGE FROM SPACE

Model Kit
Galaxy Runner model kit (Entex 1978) 20.00

METROPOLIS

Model Kit
Maria robot (Nostalgic Hero Robots #8542) 60.00
Maria (Masudaya) 100.00

MISCELLANEOUS

Model Kits
Apollo Astronaut on the Moon model kit, 1/10 scale
    (Revell 1970) 50.00
Apollo Lunar Spacecraft model kit, 1/48 scale (Revell
    1970) 125.00
Apollo Spacecraft model kit, 1/96 scale (Revell 1970) .45.00
Apollo-Soyuz model kit, 1/96 scale (Revell 1975) 100.00
Convair Manned Lunar Reconnaissance Vehicle
    model kit (Strombecker 1950s) 200.00
5 Space Ships of the Future model kit (Lindberg
    1958) 750.00
Flying Saucer plastic model kit, 1/48 scale (Lindberg
    1952) 200.00
U.F.O. Unidentified Flying Object model kit, 1/48
    scale (Lindberg 1976) reissue of above 30.00
Interplanetary U.F.O. Mystery Ship model kit, glows

in the dark, 1/635 scale (AMT 1967) 60.00
Invaders From Mars Drone model kit sculpted by
    Randy Bowen (Lunar Models) 225.00
Jupiter "C" model kit (Revell 1950s) 200.00
Jupiter model kit (Revell 1950s) 175.00
Mars Probe Space Station model kit (Lindberg 1969) . .90.00
Mars Probe Communication Satellite model kit
    (Lindberg 1969) 90.00
Mars Probe Landing Module model kit (Lindberg
    1969) 90.00
Moon Ship model kit (Lindberg 1958) 175.00
Moon Ship model kit, 1/96 scale (Revell 1957) 200.00
Pilgrim Observer Space Station model kit, 1/110
    scale (MPC 1970) 35.00
Space Pursuit model kit, 2 rocket ships (Revell 1968) . .35.00
Space Station model kit, 1/96 scale (Lindberg 1958) .300.00
Space Taxi model kit (Monogram 1959) 45.00
Star Probe Space Base model kit, 1/350 scale
    (Lindberg 1976) 25.00
UFO model kit, Glow in the Dark, 1/48 scale
    (Lindberg 1978) 25.00
U.S. Moon Ship model kit, 1/70 scale (Lindberg
    1958) 200.0
U.S. Space Station model kit, 1/350 scale (Lindberg
    1958) 200.00
XSL-01 Manned Space Ship model kit, 1/96 scale
    (Revell 1957) 350.00

THE OUTER LIMITS

Model Kits
Bifrost Alien (Dimensional Designs #OL-01, 1996) 50.00
Ebonite (Dimensional Designs #OL-02, 1996) 50.00
O.B.I.T. (Dimensional Designs #OL-03, 1996) 50.00
Empyrian (Dimensional Designs #OL-04, 1996) 50.00
Luminoid (Dimensional Designs #OL-05, 1996) 50.00
Calco Primative (Dimensional Designs #OL-06, 1997) . .50.00
Zanti Misfit (Dimensional Designs #OL-07, 1997) 50.00
Addro (Dimensional Designs #OL-08, 1997) 50.00
Alien Soldier (Dimensional Designs #OL-09, 1997) 50.00
Sand Shark (Dimensional Designs #OL-10, 1997) 50.00
Box Demon (Dimensional Designs #OL-11, 1997) 60.00
Megazoid (Dimensional Designs #OL-12, 1997) 70.00
Regina Queen Bee (Dimensional Designs #OL-13,
    1997) 50.00
Antheon Creature (Dimensional Designs #OL-14,
    1997) 50.00
Ikar (Dimensional Designs #OL-15, 1997) 50.00
Venusian (Dimensional Designs #OL-16, 1998) 50.00
Chromite (Dimensional Designs #OL-17, 1998) 50.00
Mace Alien (Dimensional Designs #OL-18, 1998) 60.00
Chill Charlie (Dimensional Designs #OL-19, 1998) 60.00
Icthyosaurus (Dimensional Designs #OL-20, 1998) 70.00
Brain Creature (Dimensional Designs #OL-21, 1998) . .50.00
Alien Parasite (Dimensional Designs #OL-22, 1998) . .60.00
Galaxy Being (Dimensional Designs #OL-23, 1998) . . .50.00
Adam Link, Robot (Dimensional Designs #OL-24,
    1998) 50.00
Malignant Plants (Dimensional Designs #OL-25, 1998) .60.00

PLANET OF THE APES

Model Kits
Cornelius model kit, 1/11 scale (Addar 1974) 45.00
Cornfield Roundup model kit, 1/32 scale (Addar
    1975) 65.00
Dr. Zaius model kit, 1/11 scale (Addar 1974) 45.00

General Ursus model kit, 1/11 scale (Addar 1975) 65.00
General Aldo model kit, 1/11 scale (Addar 1975) 45.00
Jail Wagon model kit, 1/55 scale (Addar 1975) 65.00
Dr. Zira model kit, 1/11 scale (Addar 1975) 65.00
Treehouse Bottle scene model kit, 1/32 scale (Addar
    1975) 30.00
Caesar model kit, 1/11 scale (Addar 1974) 45.00
Stallion & Soldier model kit, 1/11 scale (Addar 1974) .125.00
Gorilla (Nagleworks 1998) 90.00

Statues
15" Plaster Statues (Tuscany Statues 1973)
    Zira 75.00
    Dr. Zaius 60.00
    Cornelius 65.00

PREDATOR

Model Kits
Predator model kit, 1/8 scale (Geometric) 75.00
    Customizing kit, helmet head, metal spear,
    wristblades, skull and spinalcord (Geometric) 50.00
    Base, 7" x 9" (Geometric) 25.00
Predator Skull Resin Model Kit, 15" long (Necros
    Studio) 150.00
Predator model kit sculpted by Randy Bowen (Lunar
    Models) 500.00

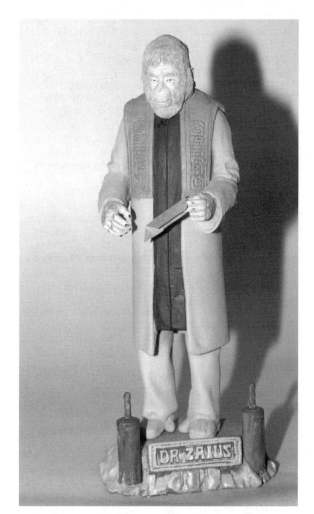

Planet of the Apes, *Dr. Zaius vinyl model kit (1998)*

Predator 2, *Predator Disk replica (Icons 1998)*

Predator cold cast resin assembly kit, limited to
    1,000 (Dark Horse) 300.00
Predator 2 cold cast resin assembly kit, limited to
    1,000 (Dark Horse) 150.00
Predator 2 vinyl kit, limited to 500 (Dark Horse) 125.00

Predator Sculpture
Cinemacast Predator, 14½" cold cast porcelain,
    limited to 5,000 units 200.00
Predator Skull (Greyzon) 135.00

Fine Replicas
Bone Spear/Combi Stick, with wall-mount (Icons
    1998) 400.00
Disc Weapon, with wall-mount (Icons 1998) 400.00
Environment Helmet, with wall-mount trophy rack
    and numbered plaque (Icons 1998) 750.00

ROSWELL

Model Kits
The Roswell Incident 1947–97 model kit (Shadow
    box 1997 . . . . .35.00
Roswell UFO model kit (Testors 1997) 15.00

SPACE: 1999

Model Kits
Space:1999 Alien model kit, 1/25 scale
    (MPC/Fundimensions 1976) 45.00
Eagle Transporter model kit (Imai 1981) 35.00
Hawk Spaceship model kit, 1/72 scale (MPC 1977) . . .60.00
Moonbase Alpha model kit (MPC/Fundimensions
    1976) 75.00
Eagle-1 Transporter model kit, 1/72 scale
    (MPC/Fundimensions 1975) 50.00

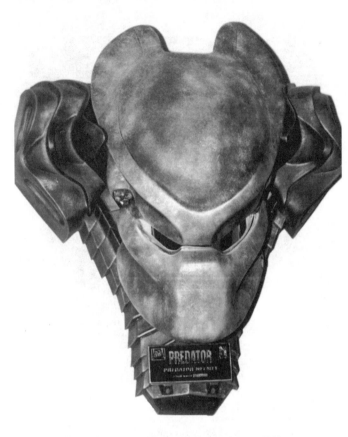

Predator 2, *Predator Mask replica (Icons 1998)*

STARGATE

Model Kits
Ra vinyl model kit (Horizon 1996) 95.00
Horus vinyl model kit (Horizon 1996) 95.00
Anubis vinyl model kit (Horizon 1996) 95.00

STARSHIP TROOPERS

Fine Replicas
Rodger Young Starship miniature maquette, 19½"
    long, with display case and plaque (Icons
    1998) 300.00

STAR TREK

Model Kits
U.S.S. Enterprise space ship model kit, 1/635 scale,
    with lights (AMT 1967) 300.00
Klingon Battle Cruiser with lights model kit, 1/635
    scale (AMT 1967) 300.00
Mr. Spock model kit, 1/12 scale, large box (AMT
    1968) 150.00
Mr. Spock model kit, 1/12 scale, small box (AMT
    1968) 100.00
Star Trek *U.S.S. Enterprise* model kit, 1/635 scale in
    8" x 8" x 4" box (Aurora #921, 1972) from
    1967 AMT 150.00
Mr. Spock of Star Trek (vs. three-headed snake)
    model kit, 1/12 scale in 8" x 8" x 4" box
    (Aurora #922, 1972) .125.00

Klingon Alien Battle Cruiser model kit, 1/635 scale in
    8" x 8" x 4" box (Aurora #923, 1972) from
    1967 AMT 150.00
Exploration Set model kit, 1/2 scale phaser, tricorder
    and communicator, large box (AMT 1974) 125.00
Exploration Set model kit, small box (AMT 1974) 75.00
Romulan Bird of Prey model kit, 1/635 scale, grey
    plastic, 7½" long, with decal in 8½" x 10" box
    (AMT 1974) 100.00
Galileo 7 Shuttlecraft model kit, 1/35 scale, 7¾"
    long with interior seats and navigation
    console (AMT 1974) .100.00
U.S.S. Enterprise Command bridge model kit, 1/32
    scale (AMT 1975) 75.00
K-7 Space Station model kit, 1/7600 scale (AMT
    1976) 75.00
Space Ship Set: *U.S.S. Enterprise*, Klingon D-7 &
    Romulan Bird of Prey model kit, 1/2200 scale
    in 8½" x 10" box (AMT 1976) 25.00
    with revised box (AMT/Ertl 1989) 10.00
Star Trek 3 Piece Adversary Set: Ferengi Marauder,
    Klingon Bird of Prey and Romulan Warbird in
    12" x 17½" box (AMT/Ertl 1989) 20.00
Star Trek 3-Piece *U.S.S.* Enterprise Set in
    12" x 17½" box (AMT/Ertl 1989) 20.00
Star Trek Special Edition 3-Piece *U.S.S. Enterprise*
    Chrome Set in box with 25th Anniversary
    logo (AMT/Ertl 1991) .25.00
Star Trek *U.S.S. Excelsior* 18" plastic model kit, over
    34 parts including display stand, decals and
    instructions (AMT/Ertl #6630, 1994) 17.00
Star Trek Cut-Away *U.S.S. Enterprise NCC 1701*
    (AMT/Ertl #8790, 1996) 20.00
Star Trek The Enterprise Incident Legendary Space
    Encounter, with fiberoptic lights and digital
    sound, three ships with free print (AMT/Ertl
    #8254) 30.00
Star Trek McCoy vinyl model kit, 12" on transporter
    pad base (AMT/Ertl #8774, 1993) 25.00
Star Trek Scotty vinyl model kit, 12" on transporter
    pad base (AMT/Ertl #8777, 1993) 25.00
Star Trek Kirk vinyl model kit, 12" on transporter
    pad base (AMT/Ertl #8773, 1993) 25.00
Starship *Enterprise* Flying Model Rocket kit (Estes) . . .20.00
Klingon Battle Cruiser Flying Model Rocket kit
    (Estes) 5.00
Mr. Spock model kit from *The Devil in the Dark*
    (1997) 120.00
Captain Kirk model kit from *The Trouble with
    Tribbles* (1997) 120.00

Statues & Dioramas
U.S.S. Enterprise NCC-1701, 7¾" cold cast
    sculpture on base (Hamilton Gifts #913235,
    1993) 40.00
"Amok Time" limited edition diorama, 7" cold cast
    resin figure, limited to 2,500 pieces
    (Applause #46142, 1996) 60.00
Swashbuckler Sulu, from "The Naked Time" cold
    cast miniature, 4" resin figure (Applause
    #46158, 1996) 20.00
Star Trek, Arena (Kirk vs. Gorn) cold cast miniature,
    5" resin figure, limited to 7,500 pieces
    (Applause #46157, 1996) 25.00
Star Trek, Space Seed (Kahn and Kirk) limited to
    5,000 pieces (Applause #42699, 1997) 35.00

Star Trek, Uhura, limited to 5,000 pieces (Applause
   #42700, 1997) 35.00
Star Trek, Menagerie (Kirk, Pike and Spock) limited
   to 2,500 pieces (Applause #42701, 1997) 25.00
Star Trek, M-113 Creature (Salt Vampire) limited to
   2,500 pieces (Applause #42738, 1997) 25.00
City on the Edge of Forever statue, showing the
   Guardian of Forever with McCoy leaping
   through into the past and Kirk and Spock
   trying to stop him (Franklin Mint 1994) 200.00
Kirk, 6" Ultra Trek cold-cast resin statue (Playmates
   Aug. 1998) 50.00
Kirk from "Where No Man Has Gone Before,"
   Latinum Edition 12" cold-cast resin statue
   (Playmates Aug. 1998) .85.00
Kirk and Spock from "Mirror, Mirror" Latinum Edition
   Diorama (Playmates 1998) 65.00
Talosian Maquette bust from "The Cage," 15" high . . .180.00
Commander Spock Cold-Cast 3/4 scale bust,
   limited to 7,500 copies (Illusive Originals 1997) .225.00
Crystal *U.S.S. Enterprise NCC-1701*, limited to
   1,200, numbered (Silver Deer) 375.00
U.S.S. Enterprise NCC-1701 Lighted Figurine, with
   lights & voice chip 80.00
Star Trek 30th anniversary pewter scene, "To Boldly
   Go" Spock, Kirk, McCoy, limited to 1,701
   (1996) 95.00

Star Trek, *M-113 Creature diorama, (Applause 1997)*

Ship Replicas

U.S.S. Enterprise NCC 1701, 10" pewter replica with
   red engine highlights and gold antenna, on a
   black base (Franklin Mint 1989) 200.00
Klingon Battle Cruiser, 9" pewter replica on black
   wooden base (Franklin Mint 1990) 200.00
Romulan *Bird of Prey*, pewter replica (Franklin Mint
   1990) 200.00
Three Ships set of the classic *Enterprise*, Romulan
   and Klingon Cruisers, pewter replicas on a
   black base (Franklin Mint 1990) 200.00
Star Trek 25th Anniversary *Enterprise*, pewter,
   white metal with red engine highlights, opens
   to reveal bridge interior (Franklin Mint 1991) . . .300.00
Star Trek *Enterprise* and Shuttlecraft 30th
   Anniversary set, die-cast figurines on base
   with voice-chip (Hallmark 1996) 75.00
Star Trek *U.S.S. Enterprise NCC-1701*, crystal, gold
   and silver sculpture, 13¼" tall (Franklin Mint
   1998) 300.00

Fine Replicas

Star Trek Phaser, limited edition, pewter with silver
   and gold accents, on stand (Franklin Mint
   1996) 200.00
Star Trek Tridimensional Chess Set (Franklin Mint
   1997) 200.00
Klingon Disruptor Prop Weapons set, three scale-
   model replicas, with display case and plaque,
   1966 made (Icons 1998) 1,000.00
Classic D7 Klingon Battle Cruiser model, 28" long,
   with display case and plaque, 950 made
   (Icons 1998) 1,000.00

Star Trek, *Mr. Spock model kit (1998)*

STAR TREK MOVIES

Model Kits
Star Trek, The Motion Picture *Enterprise* model kit
(AMT 1979) 50.00
Star Trek, The Motion Picture Vulcan Shuttle model
kit, grey plastic, 10" long model of the shuttle
Surak, with a detachable sled, in 10" x 12"
box (AMT 1979) 45.00
Star Trek, The Motion Picture Klingon Cruiser
model kit (AMT 1979) 50.00
Star Trek, The Motion Picture Mr. Spock model kit
(AMT 1979) 20.00
Star Trek II *Enterprise* model kit (AMT 1982) 20.00
Star Trek III *Enterprise* model kit (AMT 1984) 15.00
Star Trek IV *Enterprise* model kit (AMT 1986) 10.00
Star Trek V *Enterprise* & Shuttle model kit (AMT
1989) 15.00
U.S.S. Enterprise model kit (AMT 1989) 10.00
Star Trek Generations Klingon Bird of Prey (AMT/Ertl
#8230, 1994) 16.00
Star Trek Generations *U.S.S. Enterprise NCC-1701-
B* (AMT/Ertl 1994) 19.00
Star Trek Generations U.S.S. Enterprise NCC-1701-
D 18" (AMT/Ertl 1994) 15.00
Star Trek VI Klingon Cruiser (AMT/Ertl 1995) 10.00

Statues & Dioramas
Generations Kirk & Picard (on horseback) cold-cast
porcelain figures on base in gift box with
certificate of authenticity, limited to 5,000
hand painted (Applause #45946) 50.00
Borg Queen and Data 6" cold cast diorama
(Playmates #65030, 1997) 100.00
Borg Queen 12" cold cast figurine (Playmates
#65021, 1997) 100.00
Borg Queen, 6" Ultra Trek cold-cast resin statue
(Playmates 1998) 50.00
Locutus, 6" Ultra Trek cold-cast resin statue
(Playmates June 1998) 50.00

Fine Replica
Locutus of Borg, life size replica 4,000.00

STAR TREK,
THE NEXT GENERATION

Spaceship Model Kits
Star Trek The Next Generation *U.S.S. Enterprise*
Starship, 18" model, with 2 display stands
and decals in 12" x 17½" box (AMT/Ertl 1989) ...20.00
Star Trek The Next Generation *U.S.S. Enterprise*
Starship (AMT #6619) 15.00
Star Trek The Next Generation *U.S.S. Enterprise*
with Fiber Optic Lights (AMT/Ertl #8772,
1991) 45.00
Star Trek The Next Generation Klingon Battle
Cruiser 13" with detachable weapons module
(AMT/Ertl #6812, 1991) 20.00

Character Model Kits
Commander Riker vinyl model kit, 1/6 scale, 12"
(GEOmetric 1992–94) 60.00
Lieutenant Commander Geordi La Forge vinyl model
kit, 1/6 scale, 12" (GEOmetric 1992–94) 60.00
Counselor Deanna Troi vinyl model kit, 1/6 scale,
11" (GEOmetric 1992–94) 60.00

Captain Jean-Luc Picard vinyl model kit, 1/6 scale,
12" (GEOmetric 1992–94) 60.00
Lieutenant Commander Data vinyl model kit, 1/6
scale, 12" (GEOmetric 1992–94) 60.00
Lieutenant Worf vinyl model kit, 1/6 scale, 12"
(GEOmetric 1992–94) 60.00

Statues & Dioramas
Darmok with Picard cold cast miniature, 4" resin
figure(s) (Applause #46154, 1996) 25.00
Star Trek: The Next Generation, Q on Throne (in
judges robes) cold cast miniature, 4" resin
figure, limited to 5,000 pieces (Applause
#46155, 1996) 25.00
Star Trek: The Next Generation, Tasha Yar, limited
to 5,000 pieces (Applause #42697, 1996) 25.00
Vulcan Leader, Latinum Edition 12" cold-cast resin
statue (Playmates March 1998) 85.00
Worf from "Rightful Heir," Latinum Edition 12" cold-
cast resin statue (Playmates May 1998) 85.00
Data Bust, limited to 3,000 (Legends in 3
Dimensions) 150.00

Star Trek Generations, *Borg Queen cold cast sculpture
(Playmates 1996)*

Locutus of Borg, limited to 2,500 (Legends in 3
    Dimensions) 150.00
Captain Picard cold cast sculpture, 12" 80.00
Locutus of Borg Sculpture, Sculpted by Greg
    Aronowitz, 10" tall, 5,000 made (Legends in 3
    Dimensions 1997) 150.00
Data cold-cast porcelain bust sculpted by Greg
    Aronowitz (Legends in 3 Dimensions 1997) 150.00
Star Trek 30th anniversary pewter scene, "Engage"
    Picard & Enterprise, limited to 1,701 (1996) 95.00

STAR TREK: DEEP SPACE NINE

Model Kits
Deep Space Nine Runabout *Rio Grande* (AMT/Ertl
    #8741, 1993) 18.00
Deep Space Nine Space Station (AMT/Ertl #8778,
    1994) 17.00
Limited Edition Deep Space Nine Space Station with
    fibre optic lights (AMT/Ertl 1995) 45.00
Star Trek *U.S.S. Reliant* (AMT/Ertl #8766) 16.00

Statues
Star Trek: Deep Space Nine, Odo, limited to 3,000
    pieces (Applause #42693, 1996) 25.00
Star Trek: Deep Space Nine, Sisko, limited to 5,000
    pieces (Applause #42694, 1997) 25.00
Deep Space Nine pewter sculpture, 7¼" diameter
    (Franklin Mint 1997) .200.00

STAR TREK VOYAGER

Model Kits
Star Trek Voyager (Monogram #3604, 1995) 18.00
Maquis Ship (Monogram 1996) 18.00
Kazon Ship (Monogram 1996) 18.00
Kazon Torpedo (Monogram 1996) 16.00
Star Trek Voyager 3 Piece Set (Monogram 1996) 18.00

Statues
Neelix in Kitchen cold cast miniature, 4" resin figure
    (Applause #46163) 20.00

Star Trek, *U.S.S. Enterprise Command Bridge (AMT/Ertl 1990s)*

Janeway with Captain's Chair cold cast miniature, 4"
    resin figure (Applause #46165) 20.00
Star Trek Voyager, Doctor, limited to 5,000 pieces
    (Applause #42702, 1997) 25.00
Star Trek Voyager, Janeway, Chakotay & Tuvok
    from "Caretaker" cole dast resin, diorama,
    2,500 made (Applause 1997) 60.00
Seven of Nine as a Borg, 6" Ultra Trek cold-cast
    resin statue (Playmates Oct. 1998) 50.00
Seven of Nine, Latinum Edition 12" cold-cast resin
    statue (Playmates Nov. 1998) 85.00
Seven of Nine in Isolation Chamber Latinum Edition
    Diorama (Playmates 1998) 65.00

STAR WARS

MPC was Kenner's model kit company. Early kits have its logo. When The Ertl Company bought MPC in about 1990, the logo was changed to MPC/Ertl. Still later, the logo was changed to AMT/Ertl, which is what it is today. The original models have been reissued, and this availability has brought down the collector's price of the originals. The most notable exception is the original *Millennium Falcon*, with lights, since the reissues are unlighted.

Star Wars Characters Model Kits
The Authentic C-3PO (See-Threepio) model kit, 10"
    tall, 1/7 scale (MPC #1913, 1977) 7½" x 10"
    Star Wars box 25.00
    Reissue, 6" x 10" box .20.00
C-3PO model kit (MPC #1935, 1984) *Return of the
    Jedi* box 15.00
The Authentic R2-D2 (Artoo-Detoo) model kit 6" tall,
    1/10 scale (MPC #1912, 1977) *Star Wars*
    box 25.00
    Reissue, 6" x 10" box .20.00
R2-D2 model kit (MPC #1934, 1984) *Return of the
    Jedi* box 15.00
Darth Vader model kit, 11½" tall, 1/7 scale, black full
    figure with glow-in-the-dark lightsaber (MPC
    #1916, 1979) *Star Wars* box 45.00
Darth Vader Bust Action model kit, snap-together,
    1/2 scale (MPC #1921, 1978) illuminated
    eyes and raspy breathing sound, *Star Wars*
    box 60.00
Space Ships
The Authentic Darth Vader TIE Fighter model kit,
    7½" wide, 1/48 scale, with Darth Vader pilot
    figure (MPC #1915, 1977) 14" x 10" *Star Wars*
    box 35.00
    Reissue, 14" x 8" *Star Wars* box 25.00
The Authentic Luke Skywalker X-Wing Fighter model
    kit, 12" long, 10" wingspan, 1/48 scale (MPC
    #1914, 1977) 14" x 10" *Star Wars* box 35.00
    Reissue, 14" x 8" *Star Wars* box 25.00
Han Solo's *Millenium Falcon* model kit, 18" long,
    1/72 scale, with lights (MPC #1925, 1979)
    Star Wars box 120.00

The Empire Strikes Back ships
Star Destroyer model kit (15" long, MPC #1926,
    1980) *The Empire Strikes Back* box 45.00
Luke Skywalker's Snowspeeder model kit, 8" long
    (MPC #1917, 1980) *The Empire Strikes Back*
    box 40.00
AT-AT model kit (MPC #1918, 1980) *The Empire
    Strikes Back* box 40.00

Millennium Falcon model kit, no lights (MPC #1933, 1982) *The Empire Strikes Back* box 40.00
X-Wing Fighter model kit, 12½" (MPC #1930, 1982) *The Empire Strikes Back* box 25.00
Boba Fett's *Slave I* model kit (MPC #1919, 1982) *The Empire Strikes Back* box 35.00

Return of the Jedi ships
AT-AT model kit (MPC #1929, 1983) *Return of the Jedi* box 25.00
Shuttle *Tyderium* model kit, 20" wingspan (MPC #1920, 1983) *Return of the Jedi* box 30.00
Speeder Bike Vehicle model kit, 12" long (MPC #1927, 1983) *Return of the Jedi* box 22.00

Snap Kits
AT-ST model kit, 6" high, scout walker (MPC #1976, 1983) *Return of the Jedi* box 30.00
A-Wing Fighter model kit (MPC #1973, 1983) *Return of the Jedi* box 15.00
B-Wing Fighter model kit (MPC #1974, 1983) *Return of the Jedi* box 15.00
TIE Interceptor model kit (MPC #1972, 1983) *Return of the Jedi* box 20.00
X-Wing Fighter model kit (MPC #1971, 1983) *Return of the Jedi* box 15.00
Y-Wing model kit (MPC #1975, 1983) *Return of the Jedi* box 15.00

Dioramas
Rebel Base Diorama Snap model kit (MPC #1924, 1981) *The Empire Strikes Back* box 45.00
Battle on Ice Planet Hoth model diorama, snap together, 11¾" x 17¾" (MPC #1922, 1981) *The Empire Strikes Back* box 35.00
Encounter With Yoda on Dagobah model kit, snap together, 5¾" x 10" (MPC #1923, 1981) *The Empire Strikes Back* box 35.00
Jabba the Hutt Throne Room model kit, diorama (MPC #1928, 1983) *Return of the Jedi* box 40.00

Mirr-A-Kits
AT-ST model kit (MPC #1105, 1984) *Return of the Jedi* box 15.00
Shuttle *Tyderium* model kit (MPC #1103, 1984) *Return of the Jedi* box 15.00
Speeder Bike (MPC #1106, 1984) *Return of the Jedi* box 15.00
TIE Interceptor model kit (MPC #1102, 1984) *Return of the Jedi* box 15.00
Y-Wing model kit (MPC #1104, 1984) *Return of the Jedi* box 15.00
X-Wing model kit (MPC #1101, 1984) *Return of the Jedi* box 15.00

Structors Action Walking Models, wind-up motor
AT-AT model kit (MPC/Structors #1902, 1984) 30.00
AT-AT (AMT/Ertl #6036, 1998) 10.00
AT-ST model kit, 4½" high (MPC/Structors #1903, 1984) *Return of the Jedi* box 25.00
Scout AT-ST (AMT/Ertl #6029, 1998) 10.00
C-3PO model kit (MPC/Structors #1901, 1984) 25.00

Vans, Snap together, with glow-in-the-dark decals
Artoo-Detoo Van model kit, 1/32 scale (MPC #3211, 1979) 30.00

Darth Vader Van model kit, 1/32 scale (MPC #3209, 1979) 35.00
Luke Skywalker Van model kit, 1/32 scale (MPC #3210, 1979) 35.00

MPC/ERTL and AMT/ERTL (1990–98)
Figures
Darth Vader, stands 12" tall, glow in the dark light saber (#8154, 1992) 14" x 8¼" *Star Wars* box . . .15.00
Reissue: AMT/Ertl 12.50
Darth Vader model kit (AMT/Ertl #8784, 1996) 25.00
Luke Skywalker model kit (AMT/Ertl #8783, 1995) 25.00
Han Solo model kit (AMT/Ertl #8785, 1995) 25.00
Prince Xizor model kit (AMT/Ertl #8256, 1996) in *Shadows of the Empire* box 25.00
Emperor Palpatine (AMT/Ertl #8258, 1996) in *Shadows of the Empire* box 25.00

Scene
Rebel Base Action Scene (MPC/Ertl and AMT/Ertl #8735, 1993) 18¾" x 12¾" *The Empire Strikes Back* box 15.00
Jabba's Throne Room Model (AMT/Ertl #8262, 1996) .13.50
Encounter with Yoda Model (AMT/Ertl #8263, 1996) . . .13.50
Battle on Hoth Action Scene, with 11½" x 17½" vacu-formed base (AMT/Ertl #8743, 1995) 13.50

Flight Display
TIE Fighter Flight Display (AMT/Ertl #8275, 1996) 20.00
Speeder Bike Flight Display (AMT/Ertl #6352, 1997) . .20.00
X-Wing Flight Display (AMT/Ertl #8788, 1995) 19.50

Star Wars, *C-3PO model figure kit (Screamin' 1994)*

Limited Editions

X-Wing Limited Edition (AMT/Ertl #8769, 1995) 31.50

TIE Interceptor Limited Edition (AMT/Ertl #8770, 1995) 31.50

B-Wing Limited Edition Model (AMT/Ertl #8780, 1995) 25.00

Ships

Shuttle *Tyderium* (MPC/Ertl and AMT/Ertl #8733, 1992) 18¾" x 12¾" *Return of the Jedi* box 15.00

Return of the Jedi 3-piece Gift Set: B-Wing Fighter, X-Wing Fighter, TIE Interceptor, snap together (MPC/Ertl and AMT/Ertl #8912, 1992) 14¼" x 10" box 20.00

Speeder Bike (MPC/Ertl and AMT/Ertl #8928, 1990) 14" x 8" *Return of the Jedi* box 10.00

Luke Skywalker's Snowspeeder (MPC/Ertl and AMT/Ertl #8914, 1990) 10" x 7" *The Empire Strikes Back* box 15.00

Star Destroyer (MPC/Ertl and AMT/Ertl #8915, 1990) 20" x 10" *The Empire Strikes Back* box 15.00

Darth Vader TIE Fighter (MPC/Ertl and AMT/Ertl #8916, 1990) 14" x 10¼" *Star Wars* box 12.00

Millennium Falcon (MPC/Ertl and AMT/Ertl #8917, 1990) 19¾" x 14½" *Return of the Jedi* box 20.00

X-Wing Fighter (MPC/Ertl and AMT/Ertl #8918, 1990) 14" x 8" *Return of the Jedi* box 12.00

AT-AT (MPC/Ertl and AMT/Ertl #8919, 1990) 14" x 8" *Return of the Jedi* box 15.00

Star Wars *Shadows of the Empire* Virago Model (AMT/Ertl #8377, 1997) 15.00

TIE Fighter Plus Pack, with glue, paint and paintbrush (AMT/Ertl #8432, 1997) 16.00

Slave I (AMT/Ertl #8768, 1995) 13.50

Fiber Optic Star Destroyer Model (AMT/Ertl #8782, 1995) *The Empire Strikes Back* box 50.00

Millennium Falcon Cutaway Model (AMT/Ertl #8789, 1996) 27.00

Snap Kits

AT-ST, Snap together (AMT/Ertl #8734, 1992) 10" x 7" *Return of the Jedi* box 9.00

TIE Interceptor, snap together (AMT/Ertl #8931, 1990) 10" x 7" *Return of the Jedi* box 10.00

Star Wars, *Slave 1 model kit (AMT/Ertl)*

X-Wing Fighter, snap together (AMT/Ertl #8932, 1990) 10" x 7" *Return of the Jedi* box 11.00

A-Wing Fighter, snap together (AMT/Ertl #8933, 1990) 10" x 7" *Return of the Jedi* box 10.00

Y-Wing Fighter, snap together (AMT/Ertl #8934, 1990) *Return of the Jedi* box 10.00

Vinyl Model Kits

Luke Skywalker pre-painted model, 1/6 scale (Polydata 1995) 35.00

Obi Wan Kenobi pre-painted model, 1/6 scale (Polydata 1995) 35.00

Tusken Raider pre-painted model, 1/6 scale (Polydata 1995) 35.00

Princess Leia pre-painted model, 1/6 scale (Polydata 1995) 35.00

Chewbacca pre-painted model, 1/6 scale (Polydata 1996) 35.00

Lando Calrissian pre-painted model, 1/6 scale (Polydata 1997) 35.00

Boba Fett pre-painted vinyl model kit, 13" tall, 9,000

The Empire Strikes Back, *Star Destroyer model kit (MPC)*

copies, box illustration by Nelson DeCastro
(Polydata 1997) 35.00
Luke Skywalker Vinyl Model, 1/4 scale (Screamin
#3010, 1996) 65.00
Darth Vader Vinyl Model, 1/4 scale (Screamin
#3200, 1992) 65.00
Yoda Vinyl Model, 1/4 scale (Screamin #3300, 1992) . .60.00
Han Solo Vinyl Model, 1/4 scale (Screamin #3400,
1993) 65.00
C-3PO Vinyl Model, 1/4 scale (Screamin #3500,
1993) 65.00
Stormtrooper, 1/4 scale (Screamin #3600, 1993) 65.00
Chewbacca Vinyl Model, 1/4 scale (Screamin #3700,
1994) 68.00
Boba Fett Vinyl Model, 1/4 scale (Screamin #3800,
1994) 70.00
Tusken Raider Vinyl Model, 1/4 scale (Screamin
#3900, 1995) 68.00

Steel Models
Millennium Falcon Star Wars Steel Tec Kit (Remco
#7140, 1995) 25.00
X-Wing Fighter Star Wars Steel Tec Kit (Remco
#7141, 1995) 25.00

Flying Models
Original Rocket Model Kits
R2-D2 Flying Rocket Kit (Estes #1298, 1979) 25.00
T.I.E. Fighter Flying Model Rocket Kit (Estes #1299,
1979) 30.00
X-Wing Fighter Flying Model Rocket Outfit Kit (Estes
#1302, 1979) 30.00
Proton Torpedo Flying Model Rocketry Outfit with
Launching Kit, Darth Vader picture box
(Estes #1420, 1979) 50.00
X-Wing Figther Flying Model Rocket with Launching
Kit (Estes #1422, 1979) 50.00

New Starter Sets
X-wing Flying Model Rocket Starter Set (Estes
#1490, 1996) battery operated 35.00
A-wing Flying Model Rocket Starter Set (Estes
#1491, 1996) battery operated 35.00
Y-wing Flying Model Rocket Starter Set (Estes
#1492, 1996) battery operated 35.00
Death Star Flying Model Rocket Starter Set (Estes
#1493, 1996) battery operated 35.00

Star Wars, *Obi-Wan Kenobi model kit (Polydata 1995)*

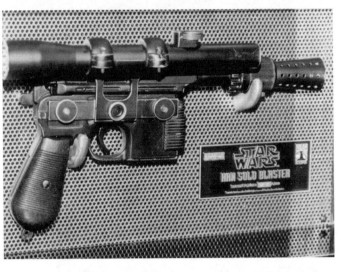

Star Wars, *Han Solo Blaster replica (Icons 1998)*

New Flying Model Rockets
R2-D2 Flying Model Rocket (Estes #2142, 1997) 15.00
Death Star Flying Model Rocket (Estes #2143, 1997) .15.00
Darth Vader's TIE Fighter Flying Model Rocket,
16½" (Estes #2144, 1997) 15.00
Millennium Falcon Flying Model Rocket (Estes
#2146, 1997) 15.00
Star Destroyer Flying Model Rocket (Estes #2147,
1997) 15.00
Shuttle *Tyderium* Flying Model Rocket (Estes #2148,
1997) 15.00

Flying Model Rockets with Recovery Parachute
TIE Fighter Flying Model Rocket with Recovery
Parachute 9" (Estes #2102, 1997) 24.00
X-Wing Flying Model Rocket with Recovery
Parachute 10¾" (Estes #2103, 1997) 18.00
R2-D2 Flying Model Rocket with Recovery
Parachute 9" (Estes #2104, 1997) 29.00

Control Line Aircraft
X-Wing Control Line Fighter kit, with Cox engine
(Estes Cox #9310) 60.00
Darth Vader's TIE Fighter Control Line Fighter kit,
with Cox engine (Estes Cox #9330) 60.00
Snowspeeder Control Line Fighter kit, with Cox
engine (Estes Cox #9320) 60.00
Death Star Battle Station with X-Wing Control Line
Fighter kit, with Cox engine, Radio Controlled
(Estes Cox #9420) 150.00
Landspeeder Radio Control Vehicle kit, with Cox
engine (Estes Cox #9430) 100.00
Star Wars Combat Set, flying 13.6" wingspan X-wing
Fighter and 9.5" wingspan TIE fighter with
motor and control lines (Estes #9410, 1997) . . .100.00
X-Wing Sterling model kit Control Line Fighter, 13"
wingspan (Estes #6760, 1997) requires Cox
engine 25.00
Y-Wing Sterling model kit Control Line Fighter, 10¾"
wingspan (Estes #6761, 1997) requires Cox
engine 25.00

Deluxe
X-Wing Fighter North Coast Rocketry high powered
model rocket, 20" long, 18" wingspan, with
recovery parachute (Estes #3540, 1997) 100.00

Star Wars, *Luke Skywalker lightsaber replica (Icons 1997)*

Statues & Dioramas
Resin Figurines (Applause 1995–97)
Darth Vader Limited Edition Resin Figurine, limited to
5,000 pieces (Applause #46048, Aug. 1995)
light-up base 50.00
Luke Skywalker Limited Edition Resin Figurine,
limited to 5,000 pieces (Applause #46049,
Aug. 1995) light-up base 50.00
Bounty Hunters Resin Diorama, includes Boba Fett,
Bossk and Zuckuss, limited to 5,000 pieces
(#46196, Sept. 1996) 60.00
Jabba and Leia, with Salacious Crumb, limited to
5,000 pieces (#46197, Sept. 1996) 60.00
Darth Vador and Prince Xizor, limited to 5,000
pieces (#46199, Oct. 1996) 60.00
Leia's Rescue Statuette, includes Luke, Leia, Han
and Chewbacca (#42669, 1997) 70.00
Star Wars Rancor Statuette (#42735, 1997) 60.00
Han Solo Release From Carbonite Statue, with built-
in light source, limited to 2,500 copies
(#61064, 1997) Diamond Previews exclusive . . .110.00
Star Wars Sandtrooper on Dewback cold-cast resin
statuette (#42687, 1997) 60.00

Fine Replicas
Darth Vader Lightsaber replica with display case and
plaque (Icons 1997) 350.00
    James Earl Jones Signature Edition 450.00
Skywalker Lightsaber replica with display case and
plaque (Icons 1997) 350.00
    Mark Hamill Signature Edition 450.00
Obi-Wan Kenobi Lightsaber replica with display case
and plaque (Icons 1998) 450.00
Han Solo Blaster replica with display case and
plaque (Icons 1998) 600.00
X-Wing Fighter miniature, 22 in. long with display
case and plaque, 1977 made (Icons 1997) . . .1,500.00
    Mark Hamill Signature Edition, 100 made 1,750.00
Imperial TIE Fighter miniature, 17 in. long with
display case and plaque, 1977 made (Icons
1997) 1,500.00

Statues & Maquettes
Yoda Maquette, 26" mounted on black wood base,
limited to 9,500 (Illusive Originals 1995) 700.00
Boba Fett Maquette, sculpted by Mario Chiodo, 15"
tall, mounted on black wood base, limited to
10,000 (Illusive Originals) 240.00
Admiral Ackbar Maquette, sculpted by Mario Chiodo,
11" tall, mounted on black wood base, limited
to 10,000 (Illusive Originals) 100.00
Jabba the Hutt Maquette, sculpted by Mario Chiodo,
27" long, mounted on black wood base,
limited to 5,000 (Illusive Originals) 240.00
Chewbacca Maquette, sculpted by Mario Chiodo, 17"
tall bust, mounted on black wood base,

Yoda Maquette (Illusive Originals 1995)

limited to 7,500 (Illusive Originals) 200.00
Han Solo in Carbonite Prop Replica, 7' tall, sculpted
by Mario Chiodo, limited to 2,500 (Illusive
Originals) 1,200.00
Darth Vader Reveals Anakin Skywalker Bust, 26"
tall, 40" wide, 17½" deep, 3-piece
mask/helmet, sculpted by Mario Chiodo, plus
stand, limited to 9,500 (Illusive Originals
1998) 1,250.00
Rancor Creature Maquette, 21" x 7" x 24", mounted
on base, limited to 9,500 (Illusive Originals) 600.00
Han Solo Special Edition Statue, Release from
Carbonite, cold-cast resin with built-in light
source, 2,500 pieces (Jan. 1998) 110.00
Boba Fett Bronze Statue, sculpted by Randy Bowen,
12½" tall, mounted on black Spanish marble
(Dark Horse Comics, May 1997) 3,000.00
Rancor Bronze Statue, sculpted by Randy Bowen,
15" tall, mounted on black Spanish marble,
limited edition of 50 (Nov. 1997) 3,000.00

Cold Cast Porcelain Busts
Emperor Palpatine Bust, limited to 3,000 (Legends in
3 Dimensions 1997) 150.00
Greedo Bust, limited to 3,000 (Legends in 3
Dimensions 1997) 160.00
Boba Fett Bust, limited to 5,000 (Legends in 3
Dimensions 1997) 175.00

TERMINATOR 2– JUDGMENT DAY

Model Kits

Cyberdyne Endoskeleton plastic model kit, 1/9 scale
  (Tsukuda #N-012, 1992) 26.95
T-800 Terminator, Schwartzenegger, vinyl model kit,
  1/5 scale (Horizon HM020, 1992) 45.00
T-800 Terminator Endoskeleton, vinyl model kit, 1/5
  scale (Horizon HM021, 1992) 45.00
T-1000 Terminator, vinyl model kit, 1/5 scale
  (Horizon HM022, 1993) 45.00
Sara Connor vinyl model kit, 1/5 scale, sculpted by
  Greg Smith (Horizon HOR046, 1993) 45.00
Aerial Hunter Killer vinyl model kit, 1/35 scale,
  sculpted by John Ferrari (Horizon HOR047,
  1993) 90.00
Hunter Killer Tank vinyl model kit, 1/35 scale,
  sculpted by John M. Eaves (Horizon
  HOR048, 1993) 100.00

Fine Replicas

Endo Skull replica, chrome plated, LED eyes, dental
  acrylic teeth, with display case and plaque
  (Icons 1998) 1,000.00
Endo Arm, with cylindrical display case and plaque
  (Icons 1998) 1,000.00
T-2 Endoskeleton replica, full size 6 foot skeleton,
  LED eyes, chrome plated on base (Icons
  1998) 12,500.00
Endoskeleton, limited to 2,500 (Legends in 3
  Dimensions) 140.00
Flying Hunter Killer, limited to 1,500 (Legends in 3
  Dimensions) 140.00
Hunter Killer Tank, limited to 1,500 (Legends in 3
  Dimensions) 150.00

2001: A SPACE ODYSSEY

Model Kits

Space Shuttle Orion model kit (Airfix 1979) 45.00
The Moon Bus from 2001: A Space Odyssey model
  kit, 1/55 scale in 15" x 10" x 2" box (Aurora
  #828, 1968) 300.00
Pan-Am Space Clipper: 2001 model kit, 1/144 scale
  in 13" x 5" x 1½" box (Aurora #148, 1969) 125.00
Space Shuttle Orion model kit, 1/144 scale in
  13" x 5" x 1½" box (Aurora 1975–77) reissue
  of above 90.00

WALT DISNEY

Model Kits

Disneyland Rocket to the Moon model kit, 1/83 scale
  (Strombecker 1956) .200.00
Disneyland Moon Liner model kit, 1/83 scale
  (Strombecker 1958) re-release of above 225.00
Satellite Launcher model kit, 1/120 scale, from *Man
  in Space* (Strombecker 1958) 150.00
RM-1 Rocket Ship model kit, 1/50 scale, from *Man in
  Space* (Strombecker 1958) 250.00
Space Ship model kit, 1/262 scale, from *Man in
  Space* (Strombecker 1958) 300.00
Space Station model kit, 1/300 scale, from *Man in
  Space* (Strombecker 1958) 400.00

WILLEY LEY SPACE MODELS

Model Kits

Missile Arsenal model kit, with 31 missiles and book
  (Monogram 1959) 200.00
Orbital Rocket model kit, 1/192 scale (Monogram
  1959) 200.00
Passenger Rocket model kit, 1/192 scale (Monogram
  1959) 200.00
The Space Taxi, Transport and Work Ship model kit,
  1/48 scale (Monogram 1959) 200.00

X-FILES

Model Kits

Mulder (Juniper Models) 110.00
Scully (Juniper Models) 110.00

Statues

Mulder bust, 10½" sculpted by Greg Aronowitz in
  collectors box with art by Drew Struzan
  (Legends in 3 Dimensions 1998) 135.00
Scully bust, 10" sculpted by Greg Aronowitz in
  collectors box with art by Drew Struzan
  (Legends in 3 Dimensions 1998) 135.00
Mulder cold cast statue, 12" sculpted by Carl Surges
  (Dark Horse 1998) 175.00
Scully cold cast statue, 12" sculpted by Carl Surges
  (Dark Horse 1998) 200.00
Flukeman cold cast statue, sculpted by Carl Surges
  (Dark Horse 1997) 175.00
Abducted Smoking Alien cold cast statue, sculpted
  by Carl Surges (Dark Horse 1997) 150.00

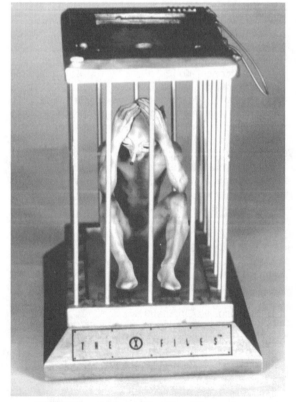

The X-Files, *Abducted Smoking Alien sculpture
(Dark Horse 1997)*

TOYS

This section contains everything that doesn't fall into the other sections, i.e. if it's not an action figure, book, comic, model kit, statue or trading card, it's listed in this section. Most toys and other collectibles are associated with either a movie or a television show and they are listed here by show, but there are also a few special sections for generic Ray Guns, Robots, Spaceships and Miscellaneous Space and Science Fiction — those not associated with any show. In addition, there is a section for Movie Posters from movies that have too few collectibles to get their own sub-section and a UFO section for recent toys with names such as Roswell, Alien or UFO.

Within each sub-section, items are separated into whatever categories seemed best to organize the collectibles. Many items from the shows of the 1940s and 1950s came from food sponsers and fan clubs, while today's licensed dolls and vehicles are available in toy stores, and fan clubs sell to older and more affluent collectors. It's hardly surprising that the products are different.

The number of *Star Trek* and *Star Wars* products that are being produced now is enormous — more than enough of either of them to fill an entire book of this size. Consequently, their coverage here is more selective than in the case of the other movies and shows.

Aliens Power Loader (Kenner 1992)

ALIEN

Alien, the first movie in the series featuring the visual concepts of H.R. Giger. Kenner made only one figure based on this movie. It is poseable, but has only a few points of articulation. It's a famous (and expensive) toy collectible. The clear plastic brain case, which covers the Alien's head, is often missing from loose figures.

FIGURE

Alien 18" Figure (Kenner 1979) boxed $500.00
    Loose, with clear plastic brain case 200.00

ALIENS

FIGURES

Die Cast Figures
Queen Alien Action Master die-cast with card
    (Kenner #62614, 1994) $3.00
Aliens Action Master 4-pack: Classic Alien, Lt. Ellen
    Ripley, Face Hugger Egg, Queen Alien +
    4 trading cards (#62631) 13.00

CLOTHING & ACCESSORIES

Alien, Nostromo Cap (Thinking Cap Co. 1979) 30.00
Alien Chestburster 3D shirt (Distortions Unlimited) . . .250.00
Aliens, Colonial Marines Patches, 4 different, each 8.00
Alien Warrior #1 pin 10.00
Alien Warrior #2 pin 10.00
Alien Queen pin 10.00
Chestburster pin 10.00

GAMES & PUZZLES

Alien Board Game (Kenner Toys 1979) 75.00
Alien Blaster Target Game (H.G. Toys 1979) 250.00
Aliens, This Time It's War, Board Game (Leading
    Edge 1990) 35.00
Aliens, Expansion Set for above game (Leading
    Edge 1990) 20.00
Alien Jigsaw Puzzle, "Giant Poster Size 3 Feet Tall"
    (H.G. Toys 1979) 60.00
Alien Jigsaw Puzzles (H.G. Toys 1979) 4 diff., each 5.00
Nostromo Jigsaw puzzle 20.00
Kane and Egg Jigsaw puzzle 20.00
Egg Jigsaw puzzle 20.00

MICRO MACHINES

1. Nostromo Ship, Alien, Kane, Narcissus (#74850) 5.00
2. USS Sulaco, Dog Burster, Ripley, Drop Ship
    (#74851) 5.00
3. Derelict Ship, Alien Queen, Hicks, Armored
    Personnel Carrier (#74852) 5.00

Aliens Queen Hive playset (Kenner 1993)

Aliens Transforming Action Set, Micro Machines
(Galoob #74815) boxed 15.00

MISCELLANEOUS

Alien Glow Putty (Larami 1979) 15.00
Alien Movie Viewer (Kenner 1979) 100.00
Alien Halloween Costume (Ben Cooper 1979) 85.00
Alien Latex Mask, only 25 cast from original 500.00
Aliens, Rebecca Locator, replica 40.00
Aliens, Miracle Machine, replica 45.00
Aliens, Melter/Welder, replica 125.00
Aliens ministand-up (Comic Images DHM1384, 1994) . .4.00
Aliens soundtrack 25.00
Alien One Sheet Movie Poster 50.00
Aliens Action Figure Collector Case (Tara) 5.00
Alien Queen figural watch (Hope Industries 1993) 15.00

PLAYSET

Queen Hive Playset with Aliens Ooze (Kenner
#65835, 1993) 25.00

ROLE PLAY

Aliens, M41A Pulse Rifle/Grenade Launcher replica . .400.00

VEHICLES

Electronic Hovertread Vehicle (Kenner #65713, 1992) .10.00
Space Marine Power Loader (Kenner #65800, 1992) . .10.00
Space Marine EVAC Fighter (Kenner #65802, 1993) . .20.00
Space Marine Stinger XT-37 (Kenner #65810, 1993) . .10.00

WALL ART

Warrior Poster 7.50
Ripley and Newt poster 10.00
Comic Warrior Poster .20.00
Aliens, Door Poster, 6' tall, full color of Alien Warrior
(GS 1988) 18.00

ARMEGEDDON

DIE-CAST

Action Sites (Micro 1:64) (Mattel 1998)
Space Station (#19418) $10.00
Explosion Zone, with two figures (#19417) 10.00
Drilling Unit, with two figures (#19416) 10.00

Deluxe Vehicles (1:24) (Mattel 1998)
Armadillo Drilling Vehicle, Hot Wheels (#19414) 20.00
Space Shuttle 20.00

FOOD

Candy Asteroid (Nestle 1998) boxed 3.00
Nuclear Candy Bar, with trading card (Nestle 1998) 1.00

BABYLON 5

CD-Rom Book

The Official Guide to J. Michael Straczynski's
Babylon 5, Sierra-on-line, 1997, with bonus
Best of Babylon 5 music CD by Christopher
Franke $20.00

DOLLS & FIGURES

The long-awaited 9" dolls appeared in December 1997. All three were available and none appear to be short-packed. The TV show has a strong following, but very few toy collectibles have been available.

9" Limited Edition dolls (Exclusive Premiere Dec. 1997)
(1 of 12,000) in round tube box with flap
Cpt. John Sheridan (#20000) 15.00
Ambassador Delenn (#20001) 15.00
Ambassador G'Kar (#20002) 15.00

Second Batch (1998)
Vir 15.00
Marcus Cole 15.00
Lennier 15.00

Third Batch (Aug. 1998)
Londo (#20023) 15.00
Garibaldi (#20022) 15.00
Susan Ivanova (#20021) 15.00

RECORDINGS

Babylon 5, Episode music by Christopher Franke,
CD-Rom, Sonic Images 1997:
Severed Dreams 15.00
Z'Ha'Dum 15.00
Shadow Dancing 15.00
Walkabout 15.00
A Late Delivery from Avalon 15.00

*Babylon 5 Ambassador Delenn & Ambassador G'Kar dolls
(Exclusive Premiere 1997)*

BATTLE OF THE PLANETS

Battle of the Planets Lunch Box (King-Seeley
　　Thermos 1979) steel box $25.00
　　thermos, plastic 12.00
Battle of the Planets board game (Milton Bradley
　　1979) 75.00
Battle of the Planets View-Master Reels (GAF BD-
　　185) 15.00

BATTLESTAR: GALACTICA

FIGURES & DOLLS

Stuffed Daggit toy (Mattel 1978) $25.00

GAMES & PUZZLES

Battlestar Galactica, A Game of Starfighter Combat,
　　(FASA) 25.00
Battlestar Galactica board game, 9" x 18" box
　　(Parker Bros. 1978) .25.00
Interstellar Battle Puzzle (Parker Brothers 1978) 15.00
Starbuck Puzzle (Parker Brothers 1978) 15.00
Battlestar Galactica 140 piece jigsaw puzzle,
　　picturing the Fleet (Parker Brothers 1978) 15.00

MISCELLANEOUS

Colorforms Adventure Set (Colorforms 1978) 30.00
Rub 'N Play Magic Transfer Set (Colorforms 1978) . . .25.00
Lunch Box (Aladdin 1979) steel box 35.00
　　thermos, plastic 15.00
Cylon Warrior Costume, with mask (1978) 30.00
Battlestar Galactica Halloween Costume (Universal
　　1978) 25.00
Battlestar Galactica Deluxe Party Mask (General
　　Mills 1978) 20.00
Metal Necklaces (Howard Elton Ltd. 1978)
　　Imperious Leader 8.00
　　Daggit 8.00
　　Ovion 8.00
　　Cylon 8.00
Adama photo Necklace (1978) 10.00
L.E.M. Lander, with pilot, diecast, 4" x 4" (Larami
　　1978) 25.00
Explorer set 10.00
Galactic Cruiser, diecast plane, 3" (Larami 1978)
　　Yellow spoiler & fins .25.00
　　Blue spoiler & fins 25.00
Space Station Kit, 20" x 28" poster, control center
　　replica pieces, cards, patch, etc. (General
　　Mills 1978) 60.00
Big G cereal premiums (General Mills) 5.00
　　Set: 56 different 300.00
Cylon bubble machine 20.00
Cylon inflatable chair 25.00
Vertibird set 40.00
Watch set 15.00

PLAYSET

Viper Launch Station playset (Mattel #2446, 1979) . . .140.00

ROLE PLAY

Battlestar Galactica Lasermatic Pistol (Mattel 1978) . . .50.00
Battlestar Galactica Lasermatic Rifle (Mattel 1978) 75.00
Cylon helmet radio (1979) 40.00

VEHICLES

Colonial Stellar Probe (Mattel 1979) 100.00
　　Original missile firing version 150.00

Battlestar Galactica Colonial Viper (Trendmasters 1997)

Colonial Scarab (Mattel 1979) 100.00
　　Original missile firing version 150.00
Cylon Raider (Mattel 1979) 100.00
　　Original missile firing version 150.00
Colonial Viper (Mattel 1978) 100.00
　　Original missile firing version 150.00
Radio Control Cylon Raider (Mattel 1978) 125.00
Colonial Viper, battery powered (Trendmasters
　　06902, 1997) 13.00
Raider, battery powered (Trendmasters #06901, 1997) .13.00

BIONIC SIX

VEHICLES

Vehicles (LJN 1986)
M.U.L.E.S. Van (boxed) (#3835) $30.00
Dirt Bike (carded) 12.00
Quad Runner 12.00
Electronic Laser Aero Chair (#3815) 12.00
Electronic Flying Laser Throne (boxed) (#3815) 12.00
Secret Headquarters Super Hi-Tech Bionic
　　Laboratory playset (#3840) 40.00

BLADE RUNNER

Blade Runner, DVD Director's Cut, staring Harrison
　　Ford, Rutger Hauer, Sean Young, Daryl
　　Hannah and Edward James Olmos (Warner
　　#12682, 0-7907-2962-8, 1996) $25.00
Blade Runner, Directors cut one sheet movie poster . .25.00

THE BLACK HOLE

CHILDREN'S BOOKS

The Black Hole Press-out book (Whitman) $25.00
Stamp activity book 10.00
Sticker activity book 10.00
Pop-up book 20.00
Poster book 10.00

DOLLS

12½" Figures (Mego 1979)
Captain Dan Holland 55.00

Buck Rogers Puzzles (Puzzle Craft 1945) & Inlaid Puzzle (Milton Bradley 1952)

Dr. Alan Durant 55.00
Dr. Hans Reinhardt 55.00
Captain Harry Booth 55.00
Dr. Kate McCrae 55.00
Pizer 60.00

GAMES & PUZZLES

The Black Hole Space Alert electronic game
    (Mattel 1978) 30.00
Pinball machine 450.00
V.I.N.Cent puzzle (Western Pub. Co.) 10.00
Maximillian & Dr. Reinhardt puzzle (Western Pub. Co.) .10.00
Tray puzzles (Western Pub. Co.) 10.00
The Black Hole Voyage of Fear Game 20.00

MISCELLANEOUS

Space Ship & Logo Button, 3½" (Walt Disney 1979) 5.00
Flasher button, 3" 5.00
Wrist watch (Bradley) 40.00
Black Hole, The (1979) one sheet movie poster 30.00
The Black Hole View-Master Reels (GAF #BK-035) . . .12.00
The Black Hole View-Master Reels (GAF #K35) 15.00

BUCK ROGERS

Buck Rogers actually appeared first in 1928 in *Amazing*, Volume 3 No. 5, a pulp magazine, but he became famous as a comic-strip character in the early 1930s. Of course, he also appeared on the radio and in movie serials. Buck Rogers' products were among the first to be mass-marketed, and there are many famous collectibles from the 1930s and 1940s.

Buck was the first of the great space heroes, and many of his accessories, such as his Rocket Gun and Space Helmet, have become part of the familiar background of all space adventures. Captain Kirk's phaser was a direct continuation of his type of weapon. The audience would have laughed out loud if he carried a mere "gun."

As a 1930s radio character, Buck had a club, the Solar Scouts, which you could join, and there were plenty of premiums for the young fan to acquire. These are all quite valuable today.

CHILDREN'S BOOKS

Big Little Books
Buck Rogers and the Planetoid Plot (1936) $75.00

Buck Rogers and the Super Dwarf of Space 60.00
Buck Rogers and the Overturned World 60.00
Buck Rogers and the Doom Comet (1935) 60.00
Buck Rogers and the Depth Men of Jupiter (1935) . . .80.00
Buck Rogers and the City Below the Sea (1934) 150.00
Adventures of Buck Rogers 70.00
Buck Rogers in the 25th Century A.D. (1938) 100.00
Buck Rogers in the 25th Century A.D. (Cocomalt
    1933) 75.00
*Buck Rogers in the 25th Century A.D. vs. the Fiend
    of Space* 75.00
Buck Rogers in War with the Planet Venus 80.00
Buck Rogers on the Moon of Saturn (1934) 150.00

Little Golden Books
Buck Rogers and the Children of Hopetown, by
    Raven Dwight, ill. by Kurt Schaffenberger (1971) . .7.50
Buck Rogers Paint Book #679 (Whitman 1935) 200.00

Pop-Up/Punch-Out Books
Buck Rogers Pop-Up "A Dangerous Mission" book
    (Blue Ribbon Press 1934) 200.00

CLUBS

Buck Rogers Solar Scouts Radio Club
Solar Scouts Radio Club manual (1936) 400.00
Solar Scouts member badge, gold color (1935) 125.00
Spaceship Commander folder, with Chief Explorer
    application (1936) 150.00
Spaceship Commander banner (1936) 250.00
Spaceship Commander stationery (1936) 150.00
Spaceship Commander whistle badge (1936) 175.00
Wilma handkerchief (1936) .250.00
Chief Explorer badge (1936) 300.00
Chief Explorer folder (1936) 225.00

Rocket Rangers Club
Rocket Rangers enlistment blank (1937) 95.00
Rocket Rangers *Flying Needle* rocket ship plan, red
    on white (1941) 80.00
Confidential Rocker Ranger bulletins 80.00
Rocket Rangers Membership cards 150.00
Rocket Rangers iron-on transfers, set of 3 . . . . .100.00
Rocket Rangers member tab (L. J. Imber 1954) 125.00

Satellite Pioneers Club
Satellite Pioneers pinback, green or blue (Green-
    duck 1958) 40.00

Satellite Pioneers round tab (Greenduck 1958) 90.00
Satellite Pioneers membership card (1958) 50.00
Satellite Pioneers Cadet Commission with auto-
    graphed postcard (1958) 40.00
Satellite Pioneers Starfinder (1958) 40.00
Satellite Pioneers Secret Order #1 (1958) 35.00
Satellite Pioneers Map of the Solar System (1958) 40.00
Confidential Satellite Pioneers Bulletins 20.00

CRAFT & ACTIVITY

Paint by Number set (Craft Master) 20.00
Pencil boxes (American Pencil 1934-38) 160.00
Printing Set, boxed with cartoon sheets
    (Stamperkraft 1930s) 500.00
School crayons ship box and pencils (American
    Pencil 1935) 200.00
Doctor Huer's Invisible Ink Crystals (1936) 170.00
Magic Erasable Dot Pictures (Transogram 1960s) 50.00

LEAD FIGURES & MOLDS

Casting sets with midget, junior and electric caster
    styles, manual and extra 3-figure mold 600.00
Eight extra molds (Rapaport Bros. 1934) each 150.00
Painted lead 2½" figures (Buck, Wilma and Killer
    Kane) in cello bags (Cocomalt 1934) set 350.00
Buck Rogers 1¾" lead figure (1935–36) 75.00
Britains lead figures — Buck, Wilma, Kane, Ardella,
    Doctor Huer and Robot, set of 6 . . . . .2,500.00

FOOD RELATED

Telescope (Popsicle premium) 100.00
Popsicle Pete's Radio Gift News, 15" x 10" 70.00
Punch-O-Bag, balloon with characters in color
    (Morton Salt 1942) 90.00
Ring of Saturn with red stone, glow-in-the-dark white
    plastic formed on crocodile base (Post Corn
    Toasties 1944) 300.00
    Instructions for above 75.00

GAMES & PUZZLES

Game of the 25th Century (Lutz-Shinkman 1934) 500.00
Buck Rogers Interplanetary Games, set of 3 boards
    in illustrated box (John F. Dille 1934) 750.00
    Cocomalt version, plain red box 600.00
Buck Rogers and His Cosmic Rocket Wars Game
    (1934) 350.00

Buck Rogers Siege of Gigantica Game (1934) 600.00
All-Fair card game, "Buck Rogers in the 25th
    Century" 36 cards (E. E. Fairchild 1936) in box .500.00
Combat game, interlocking panels with stand-up
    figures (Warren 1937) 375.00
Buck Rogers Adventures in the 25th Century Game
    (Transogram #3836 1965) 75.00
Target set, 2 styles (Fleetwood) 30.00
Buck Rogers boxed set of 3 inlaid jigsaw puzzles
    (Puzzle Craft 1945) .250.00
Inlaid jigsaw puzzle, space station scene, 14" x 10"
    in paperboard sleeve (Milton Bradley 1952) 20.00

MISCELLANEOUS

Lite-Blaster flashlight (1936) 400.00
Pocket knife (Adolph Kastor 1934) 1,000.00
Pocket watch (E. Ingraham Co. 1935) 100.00
Rocket roller skates (Louis Marx 1935) 3,000.00
Sneakers (U.S. Rubber Co. 1937) 150.00
25th-Century scientific laboratory, with 3 manuals
    (Porter Chemical Co. 1934) 2,000.00
    Instruction envelope 125.00
Buck Rogers Chemistry set, with manual (Grooper
    Co. 1937) simple set 500.00
    Advanced set 700.00
Toyloons (Lee-Tex 1935) 125.00
Rubber balls (Lee-Tex 1935) 75.00
Paddle ball "Comet Socker" (Lee-Tex 1935) 60.00
Rocket football, silver (Edward K. Tryon 1935) 300.00
Wilma pendant, brass color with chain 275.00
Space Ship that flies (Spotswood 1936) 400.00
School kit bag 120.00
Sweater emblem, 3 colors 700.00
Doctor Huer's Invisible Ink Crystals (1936) 170.00
Hearing Aid "Acousticon" Jr. (Dictograph Products
    1937) with large pinback 475.00
Fireworks (National Fireworks Co. 1937)
    Chase of Killer Kane 120.00
    The Sun Gun of Saturn 70.00
    The Battle of Mars 70.00
    Battle Fleet of Rocket Ships 70.00
    Fireless Rocket Ships 70.00
    Catalog of above 125.00
Rubber band gun, 5" x 10" punchout card (Onward
    School Supplies 1940) 50.00

Magic Erasable Dot Pictures (Transogram 1960s) & Space Ranger Kit (Sylvania 1952)

Buck Rogers Uniform (1934)

Strato-kite, 18½" (Aero-Kite Co. 1946) 40.00
Two-way Trans-Ceiver (DA Myco 1948) 90.00
View-Master L-15 series, 3 stereo reels (GAF
      BL015) 15.00

BUCK ROGERS MOVIE SERIALS

Films, set of 6 (Irwin 1936) 250.00
      Movie projector for above, generic 125.00
Buck Rogers on Jupiter 16mm film (1936) 40.00
Universal serial prints 16mm film, 12 b&w chapters
      (Universal 1939) 600.00
Lobby cards for serial (85 different) each 150.00
Posters for serial (1939) 1,200.00
Serial stills (original) (1939) 60.00
Serial press book, 3 versions: Universal Film- craft,
      Planet Outlaws (1939) each 250.00
Strange World Adventures Club pinback, 2 colors
      (Philadelphia 1939) 300.00
Strange World Adventures Club membership card
      (1939) 125.00
Strat-O-Sphere Dispatch balloon with message
      (Thornecraft 1935) 135.00

PAPER

Photo of Twiki, given at Detroit Autorama 7.00
Sticker set, 240 stickers (Panini) 25.00
Large Postcard (Quick Fox) 5.00
Big Thrill Chewing Gum Booklets, in color (Goudey
      1934) set of 6 . . . . .400.00
      #1 *Thwarting Ancient Demons* 60.00
      #2 *A One-Man Army* 60.00
      #3 *An Aerial Derelict* 60.00
      #4 *The Fight Beneath the Sea* 60.00
      #5 *A Handful of Trouble* .60.00
      #6 *Collecting Human Specimens* 60.00
Planet Venus coloring map (1931) 600.00
Newspaper drawings, 8½" x 11" of Buck or Wilma . . .200.00
Buck Rogers origin storybook (Kellogg's 1933) 350.00
Solar System map (Cocomalt 1933) 750.00
Bucktoys cardboard figures (1933):
      #1 Buck Rogers 200.00
      #2 Wilma Deering 250.00
      #3 Killer Kane 200.00
      #4 Ardella 250.00
      #5 Gyrex-Bullet Space Racer 200.00
      #6 Doctor Huer 200.00

Colored face masks of Buck and Wilma (Einson-
      Freeman Co.) each 250.00
Strip cards, #425–#448, "Buck Rogers in the 25th-
      Century" (John F. Dille 1936) each 35.00
      Set of 24, in color 1,000.00
Dandy picture Buck Rogers, 8½" x 5½" (1936) 175.00
Kite folder, #376 (PEP) 50.00
Bird folder, #331 (Corn Flakes) 50.00
Star Explorer chart, unmarked (1936) 75.00
Photograph of Buck and Wilma in Grand Canyon
      (Cocomalt 1934) 125.00
Dixie ice cream cup lid, Matthew Crowley picture
      (1935) 60.00
Breyer's ice cream cup lid, Matthew Crowley picture
      (1935) 60.00
Paperboard spaceship with suction cup (Morton Salt
      1942) 90.00
Blotter with color scene (Chicago Herald American
      1946) 50.00
Comic Traders series A-3 Color cards (1949) Buck
      Rogers 20.00
      Flame D'Amour 20.00
Flying saucer paper plates 75.00
Drawing of Buck, his friends & enemies (Yager 1950s) .50.00
Drawing of Buck, Wilma and Black Barney in space
      (Dworkins 1970s) 16.00
Greeting card (Bantam 1970s) 15.00
Buck Rogers Idea poster (S.D. Warren 1969) 40.00
      Paper Disintegrator noisemaker and postcard
      for above 75.00
Buck Rogers Magic Erasable Dot Pictures Set
      (Transogram 1950s) 90.00
Drawing of Pluton (Yager 1947) 50.00
Space Ranger Kit, 6 punch-out sheets, 11" x 15"
      envelope (Sylvania 1952) 60.00

NEWSPAPER STRIPS

Year	Artist	per/10	per year
1929	Dick Calkins	300.00	1,500.00
1930	Dick Calkins	220.00	1,100.00
1931	Dick Calkins	200.00	1,000.00
1932	Dick Calkins	150.00	750.00
1933	Dick Calkins	125.00	600.00
1934–36	Dick Calkins	100.00	550.00
1937–39	Dick Calkins	90.00	500.00
1940–47	Dick Calkins	50.00	250.00
1949–51	Leon Dworkins	30.00	150.00
1952–58	Leon Dworkins	20.00	100.00
1958–59	Murphy Anderson	22.00	110.00
1959–64	George Tuska	20.00	100.00
1965–67	George Tuska	10.00	50.00
1979–89	Gray Morrow	5.00	25.00
1990–present	Gray Morrow	5.00	25.00

PINS, BADGES

World's Fair, Century of Progress Coin, 1934 "I Was
      There" 200.00
World's Fair pinback, orange & blue (Greenduck
      1934) "I Saw Buck Rogers" 275.00
Buck Rogers pinback (Saturday Chicago American)
      (Greenduck 1934) 150.00
Buck Rogers pinback (Pittsburgh Post Gazette)
      (Bastian Bros. 1934) blue on white 200.00
Buck Rogers pinback (Buffalo Evening News)
      (Bastian Bros. 1934) blue on white 175.00
Buck Rogers in the 25th Century pinback, 3 colors
      on blue (Whitehead & Hoag 1935) 90.00
Buck Rogers & Doctor Huer pinback (1936) 100.00

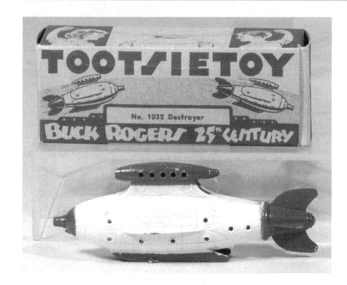 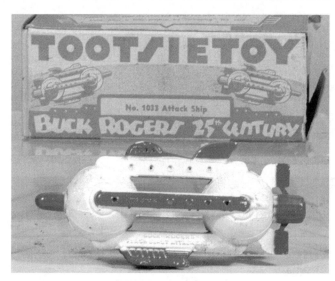

Buck Rogers 25th Century Destroyer (Tootsietoy #1032) & Attack Ship (Tootsietoy #1033)

Buck Rogers pinback, blue on white (1937) 150.00

RINGS

Repeller Ray ring (seal ring) brass color with inset
    green stone 1,500.00
Ring of Saturn with red stone, glow-in-the-dark white
    plastic formed on crocodile base (Post Corn
    Toasties 1944) 300.00
    Instructions for above .75.00
Space Ranger HaloLight ring (Sylvania 1952) 100.00

ROLE PLAY

Ray Guns and Holsters
Rocket Pistol XZ-31, 9½" (Daisy 1934) 250.00
Holster, XZ-33, 9" (Daisy 1934) 200.00
Combat Set, gun and holster, XZ-32 (Daisy 1934) . . .600.00
Buck Rogers 25th Century Rocket Pistol XZ-35, 7¾"
    blued gun steel, nickel plated rocket nozzle
    (Daisy 1935) 300.00
Holster, leather, XZ-36 (Daisy 1935) 100.00
Combat Set, gun and holster, XZ-37 (Daisy 1935) . . .500.00
Disintegrator pistol, XZ-38, gun metal color (Daisy
    1935) 350.00
Holster, XZ-39 (Daisy 1935) 200.00
Combat Set, gun and holster, XZ-40 (Daisy 1935) . . .600.00
Liquid Helium water pistol, XZ-44 (Daisy 1936) with
    red-and-yellow finish .400.00
    with copper finish 225.00
Atomic Pistol, U-235 (Daisy 1945) 200.00
Adventure book folder, b&w, for above 120.00
Atomic Pistol, U-238 (Daisy 1946) 225.00
    Leather holster 60.00
    Colored announcement flyer 40.00
"Sonic Ray" gun, yellow plastic, with code folder
    (Norton-Honer 1952–55) 150.00
Cardboard "Pop" Gun and Helmet, Buck and Wilma
    versions (Einson-Freeman Co. 1933) Cocomalt .350.00

Role Play Equipment
Cloth Helmet, XZ-42 (Daisy 1934) 450.00
Leather Helmet, XZ-34 (Daisy 1935) 750.00
Daisy Equipment catalog of above equipment 350.00
Space Glasses (Norton-Honer 1955) 75.00
Super-Sonic Glasses (1953) 100.00
Super-Scope, 9" plastic telescope, in box (Norton-
    Honer 1955) 75.00

Super-Foto Camera (Norton-Honer 1955) 75.00
Walkie Talkies (Remco 1950s) 125.00
Uniform (Sackman Bros. 1934) 2,000.00
Communications set (H-G Toys) 25.00
Space Communicators (Corgi) 25.00
Two-way Trans-Ceiver (DA Myco 1948) 90.00

SPACESHIPS

Rocket Ship, 12" windup (Marx 1934) 700.00
Rocket Ship motor kit 120.00
Interplanetary Space Fleet Balsa Wood Construction
    Kits (1934):
        #1 Battle Cruiser .500.00
        #2 Martian Police Ship 500.00
        #3 Flash Blast Attack Ship 500.00
        #4 Superdreadnaught 500.00
        #5 Venus Fighting Destroyer 500.00
        #6 Pursuit Ship 500.00
        Fighting Fleet poster (backside of kit construc-
          tion plan (17" x 11") 150.00
Buck Rogers cast-iron rocket (1930s) 200.00
Tootsietoy Rocket Ships with 2 grooved wheels to
    run on string (Dowst Mfg. 1937)
        Buck Rogers Battle Cruiser (#1031) 300.00
        Venus Duo-Destroyer (#1032) 250.00
        Flash Blast Attack Ship 4½" (#1033) 250.00
Tootsietoy Cast figures for above 1¾" (1937)
        Buck, gray 250.00
        Wilma, gold 150.00
        U.S.N. Los Angeles Dirigible 5" 225.00
Whistling rocket ship (Muffets 1939) 225.00
Police Patrol ship, windup (Marx 1939) 750.00

BUCK ROGERS NEW

Buck was revived in the 1970s TV show starring Gil Gerard. TV show collectibles are typical of this era and include an action figure line, a utility belt, Starfighter vehicles, etc. As with most recent toy lines, look for the female figures, Wilma Deering and Ardella.

FIGURES & DOLLS

12½" Dolls, in window box (Mego 1979)
Buck Rogers $65.00

Walking Twiki, 7¼" 60.00
Dr. Huer 65.00
Killer Kane 90.00
Draco 65.00
Tiger Man 90.00
Draconian Guard 65.00
Radio-controlled Twiki, inflatable (Daewoo 1979) 75.00

GAMES & PUZZLES

Buck Rogers board game (Milton Bradley) 30.00
Planet of Zoom video game (Sega) 15.00
Target set, 2 styles (Fleetwood) 30.00
Jigsaw puzzles (Milton Bradley) each 10.00

Role Play Games (TSR 1988-1991)
Buck Rogers Battle for the 25th Century game (TSR
    1988) 45.00
Buck Rogers Martian War game (TSR) 45.00
Poster (TSR) in Dragon Magazine #146 . . . . .10.00
25th Century Wings pin 15.00

HOUSEHOLD

Buck Rogers Lunch Box (Aladdin 1979) Steel box 40.00
    Thermos (plastic) 15.00
Paper plates, 2 sizes (Paper Art 1979) 6.00
Coca-Cola plastic tumblers, 16 oz, each 7.00
    Set, 8 tumblers 45.00
Coca-Cola plastic tumblers, 20 oz, each 8.00
    Set, 5 tumblers 40.00
Video game blue tumbler (Slurpee 1982) 7.00
Video game red tumbler (7-Eleven 1983) 7.00
Coca-Cola glass tumblers:
    Buck Rogers 30.00
    Wilma Deering 30.00
    Twiki 30.00
    Draco 30.00

MISCELLANEOUS

View-Master L-15 series, 3 stereo reels (Showtime) . . .15.00
Communications set (H-G Toys) 20.00
Space Communicators (Corgi) 20.00
Large Postcard (Quick Fox) .5.00
Buck Rogers and the Children of Hopetown Little
    Golden Book 10.00

Buck Rogers lunch box (Aladdin 1979)

Pop-up Buck Rogers (Random House) 10.00
Photo of Twiki, given at Detroit Autorama 7.00
Colorforms Adventure set, vinyl parts and scene
    board (Colorforms 1979) 20.00
Paint by Numer set (Craft Master) 20.00

PLAYSET

Spaceport playset (Mego 1979) 200.00
Galactic playset #892 (H-G Toys) 20.00

ROLE PLAY

Galaxy gun and holster set (Nichols-Kusan 1970s) . . .40.00
Utility belt, including play watch, decoders,
    eyeglasses, and disk-shooting gun (Remco
    1970s) 30.00

SPACESHIPS

Die-cast Starfighter, 6" metal and plastic, with Buck
    and Twiki (Corgi) 30.00
Gas-Powered Flying Starfighter (Cox) 50.00

VEHICLES

Draconian Marauder (Mego #85012) 60.00
Laserscope Fighter (Mego #85014) 40.00
Star Fighter (Mego #85016) .60.00
Land Rover (Mego #85018) 100.00
Star Searcher (Mego #85020) 75.00
Star Fighter Command Center (Mego #85022) 110.00

WATCHES/CLOCKS

Pocket watch (Huckleberry Time 1970s) 200.00
Toy Wrist Watch (GLJ Toys 1978) 20.00
Pendant watch (Huckleberry Time 1970s) 250.00
Wrist watch (Huckleberry Time 1970s) 140.00
Clock (Huckleberry Time 1970s) 50.00

CAPTAIN ACTION

Captain Action was the first action figure, but he was
(and is) really a doll designed to sell to boys. Only a few basic
figures were available. Most of the collecting action is in the
costumes. Most of these were superheroes and are not covered in this book.

DOLLS

12" Captain Action Figures (Ideal 1966–68)
Captain Action in first issue box showing 9 inset
    pictures, with the Lone Ranger shown in a
    red shirt (#3400, 1966) $600.00
Captain Action in second issue box showing the
    Lone Ranger in a blue shirt, including Video-
    Matic ring (1966–67) .750.00
Captain Action in third issue box showing 7 inset
    pictures and "Free! 4 ft. Parachute Inside"
    including Video-Matic ring and parachute
    (1967) 800.00
Captain Action the Super Hero in photo box "enemy
    of the sinister Dr. Evil" (1967–68) 900.00
    Loose figure, including cap, boots, gun and
        gun belt, scabbard and lightning sword 250.00
    Loose ring or parachute, each 35.00

12" Dr. Evil Figures
Dr. Evil, The Sinister Invader of Earth, in photo
    box (1967) 1,000.00
    Loose, with ray gun, gold chain, medallion,
        sandals and face mask 250.00
Dr. Evil with His Disguises and Weapons in window

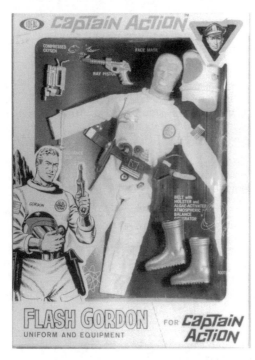 

Captain Action: Flash Gordon Uniform and Equipment Pack (Ideal 1967) & Captain Action and Dr. Evil dolls (Playing Mantis 1998)

box (1968) 2,750.00
Loose, with gold chain, medallion, sandals,
  oriental face mask, bearded face mask and
  lab coat, thought scanner, hypnotic eye,
  laser ray gun, magnifying glass, ionized
  hypo needle and reducing ray 1,500.00

9" Action Boy Figures
Action Boy in photo box (#3420, 1967) 800.00
Loose, with beret, boomerang, knife, belt and
  boots plus Khem, his black panther, with
  collar and leash 400.00
Action Boy, The Bold Adventurer in photo box
  showing space suit (1967–68) 1,100.00
Loose, with space helmet, spack boots,
  gloves, knife, ray gun, belt, black panther
  with collar and leash 500.00

EQUIPMENT

Captain Action Uniform and Equipment Packs (1966)
Flash Gordon costume with face mask, silver astro-
  suit, space helmet, space belt with holster
  and ray pistol, oxygen guidance "Zot" gun
  and silver boots (#3403-3) 525.00

Reissue Uniform and Equipment Packs (1967)
  with "Video-Matic" ring, in window box
Flash Gordon costume with ring (#3403) 700.00

Captain Action Uniform and Equipment Packs (1967)
  with "Video-Matic" ring, in window box
Buck Rogers costume with face mask, space helmet,
  space gun, gloves, space belt and harness,
  twin jet packs, radio microphone with cord,
  canteen, space light, space boots and ring
  (#3416) 1,400.00

ACCESSORIES

Accessories Packs (Ideal 1967)
20-Piece Survival Kit (#3450-4) 300.00

10-Piece Weapons Arsenal (#3451-2) 300.00
Inter-Galactic Jet Mortar (#3452-0) 225.00
4-Foot Working Parachute (#3453-8) 225.00
Inter-Spacial Directional Communicator (#3454-6) . . .225.00
Anti-Gravitational Power Pack (#3455-3) 225.00

VEHICLES & PLAYSETS

Vehicles, Playsets, Carry Cases (Ideal 1967)
Headquarters carry case with **Captain Action** doll in
  Batman costume and ring (Sears exclusive) . . .500.00
Action Cave carry case (Montgomery Ward
  exclusive) 650.00
Quick Change Chamber with **Captain Action** doll
  in Batman costume and ring (Sears exclusive) . .750.00
Silver Streak Amphibian vehicle, 21" long, in box . .1,500.00
Silver Streak Garage (Sears exclusive) 1,200.00
Dr. Evil Sanctuary carry case (Speigel exclusive)
  (#8701) 2,500.00

CAPTAIN ACTION (NEW)

12" Dolls (Playing Mantis 1998)
Captain Action $30.00
Dr. Evil 30.00

CAPTAIN POWER AND THE SOLDIERS OF THE FUTURE

VEHICLES & ACCESSORIES

Vehicles and Accessories (Mattel 1987)
Interlocker Throne/weapon (1987) $12.00
Phantom Striker evil jet (1987) 18.00
Power Base fortress set (1987) 60.00
Power On Energizer with **Capt. Power** figure
  (#4115, 1987) 12.00
Powerjet XT-7 heroic fighter (1987) 20.00
Powerjet XT-7 deluxe with Future Force Training
  Tape 40.00
Dread Stalker vehicle (1988) 12.00

Magna Cycle (1988) 20.00
Trans-Field Base Station (1988) 20.00
Trans-Field Communication Station (1988) 10.00

CAPTAIN SCARLET AND THE MYSTERONS

Captain Scarlet vs. The Mysterons was a 1967 film and British television show done in "Super-Marionation, " i.e. with puppets. The Mysterons are Martian invaders whom the Captain and his Spectrum organization battle to save the world. The series was created by Gerry and Sylvia Anderson.

DOLLS & FIGURES

12" Doll (Pedigree 1967) in window box
Captain Scarlet $210.00
    Loose 100.00

12" Figures (Vivid Imaginations 1993–94)
Captain Scarlet 60.00
Captain Black 60.00

VEHICLES

Vehicles (Vivid Imaginations 1993–94)
Electronic Angel Interceptor .45.00
SPV vehicle 45.00
Captain Scarlet Patrol Car (IB-1204) 9.00
Captain Scarlet Angel Interceptor (IB-1206) 7.00
Captain Scarlet Supersonic Transport Jet (IB-1205) 9.00
Captain Blue figure with transport jet (IB-1209) 1.50
Spectrum Pursuit Vehicle (IB-1713) 24.00
Captain Scarlet Armored Car (IB-2131) 15.00
U.F.O. Shadow Mobile (IB-1242) 8.00

CAPTAIN VIDEO

Captain Video began in 1949 on the Dumont network. It ran until 1955 and in syndication until 1956. Al Hodge played the title role for most of its run. It was the first and longest running of the 1950s television space shows. In its prime it was on live several afternoons a week and even reached the frozen wilds of Minnesota where I watched it. I've been a science fiction fan ever since. *Captain Video's* primary sponser was Powerhouse Candy Bars and for some wrappers and some money you could get various rings and other premiums. The Captain had a teen-age sidekick called the Video Ranger, just like Batman and all heroes of that era, and no one even wondered if there was anything improper in the relationship.

Captain Video game (Milton Bradley 1952)

FIGURES

Plastic Space Men (Post Raisin Bran) each $20.00
Interplanetary Space Men, boxed set of 12 . . . . . . .150.00

GAMES & PUZZLES

Captain Video Space game, 18½" sq. board, fold-
    out instrument panel (Milton Bradley 1952) 200.00
Captain Video inlaid jigsaw puzzle, 10½" x 14½"
    tray (Milton Bradley early '50s) 40.00

MOVIE

Lobby cards 25.00
Serial poster, large 800.00
Serial posters, episodes, each 600.00

PREMIUMS

"Video Ranger" club membership card, oath on
    reverse 60.00
Photo of Captain Video 15.00
Premium photo of Captain Video & Video Ranger
    (Al Hodge & Dan Hastings) 60.00
Photo Ring (Powerhouse Candy 1950) 75.00
Secret Seal Ring "CV" 500.00
Rocket Ring 200.00
Flying Saucer ring with both saucers (Post Toasties) 1,250.00
Captain Video Purity Bread tab badge 30.00
Glo-Photo plastic pendent .120.00
Mysto-Coder with photo 250.00

RECORDINGS

Captain Video and the Captives of Saturn 78 rpm 6
    in 1 record (RCA Victor 1953) 50.00
Captain Video and his Rangers 78 rpm 6 in 1
    record (RCA Victor 1953) 50.00

ROLE PLAY

Captain Video Secret Ray Gun, 3½" battery
    flashlight gun with space map and Luma-Glo
    secret message card (Power House Candy
    premium 1950s) 125.00
Rite-O-Lite flashlight gun kit 150.00
Captain Video Paper Ray gun, perforated paper
    which can be folded and glued (1950s) 50.00
Captain Video Holster, black leather (1950s) 50.00
Official Captain Video Space Helmet, from Post
    Cereals (Plaxall, Inc. 1950s) 150.00
Electronic Video Goggles, in envelope 250.00

SPACE SHIPS

Space vehicles, plastic, boxed set 100.00
Space vehicles, individually boxed
    Troop transport, 4" x 2" box (Lido 1952) 125.00
    Rocket Tank (Lido 1952) 125.00
Captain Video Rocket Launcher (Lido Toy 1950s) . . .100.00
Captain Video Supersonic Space Ships (Lido Toy
    1950s) 100.00
Captain Video pursuit ship (Lido 1950s) 40.00
Space Port (Superior) 800.00
Galaxy Spaceship, ride-on vehicle 800.00
Inflatable rocket ship 200.00

CLOSE ENCOUNTERS

Steven Spielberg's *Close Encounters of the Third Kind* is one of the most popular science fiction movies of all time. The Extraterrestrials didn't appear until the final few minutes of the film and have no lines. Nevertheless, Spielberg's alien design has had great influence—every nut who has seen an

Doctor Who Dalek Robot (Marx 1965) & Doctor Who The Music Record (BBC 1983)

alien in the last 20 years remembers it looking like this one. Of course, this could be because Spielberg based his design on the accounts of actual alien abductees.

FIGURE

Extra Terrestrial bendable figure (Imperial 1977) $30.00

MISCELLANEOUS COLLECTIBLES

Close Encounters of the Third Kind lunch box
    (King-Seeley 1978) steel box 80.00
    thermos (plastic) 35.00
Postcard book (1980) 15.00
Close Encounters buttons "Close Encounters" 3.00
    "I've Seen One" 3.00
    Contact 3.00
    A Close Encounter 3.00
    Watch the Skies 3.00
    We are not alone 3.00
Close Encounters Board Game (Parker Brothers
    1977) 25.00
Close Encounters pinball machine 600.00
UFO Sighting map (Skywatchers Club) premium 10.00
Skywatchers Club newsletter 6.00
Mothership Paperweight, deluxe metal goldtone
    with lights, (O'Quinn Studios) 70.00
Close Encounters of the Third Kind View-Master
    Reels (GAF J47) 15.00
Close Encounters of the Third Kind (1977) one
    sheet movie poster 40.00
Close Encounters of the Third Kind, expanded
    edition (1980) one sheet movie poster 25.00

DEFENDERS OF THE EARTH

VEHICLES & ACCESSORIES

Vehicles and Accessories (Galoob 1985)
Defenders Claw Copter $35.00
Flash Swordship 25.00
Garax Swordship 25.00
Mongor Slithering Evil Serpent (purple) 30.00

DOCTOR WHO

The adventures of the famous Time Lord from Gallifrey began in England in 1963. He roamed the universe and regenerated three times in the 12 years before he and his Tardis

made it across the ocean. He enjoyed a long run in the United States where the best known Doctor was Tom Baker, the fourth. A great deal of the Doctor's exploits are available on video tape.

DOLLS & FIGURES

Dalek Robot, 6.5" tall (Marx 1965) $225.00
Doctor Who doll (Denys Fisher 1976) 200.00
Doctor Who Tardis Play Set (Denys Fisher 1970s) . . .400.00
BBC Talking Dalek, battery-operated, 7" tall (Palitoy
    1975) 95.00
Dalek, Figural Bubble Bath Bottle (Water Margin
    1976) 50.00
Tardis, 6½" tall, with flash light, opening doors,
    carded (Dapol 1994) .35.00

Die-Cast Miniature 25mm Figures
The 5 Doctors (Fasa #9501) 8.00
Companions Set, Sarah Jane, Leela, Adric (#9502) 4.00
Daleks, 2 figures (#9503) 4.00
Cybermen, 3 figures (#9504) 4.00
The Brigadier & U.N.I.T. Troopers, 2 figures (#9505) . . .4.00
U.N.I.T. Troopers, 3 figures (#9506) 4.00
Player Character Time Lords, 3 figures (#9507) 4.00
Temporal Marauders, 3 figures (#9508) 4.00

GAMES

Doctor Who board game (Denys Fisher 1980s) 100.00
War of the Daleks Game (Strawberry Fayre 1975) . . .120.00
Dalek Bagatelle game (Denys Fisher 1976) 150.00
Dalek Shooting Game (Marx 1965) 500.00
Dalek's Oracle Question & Answer game (1965) 250.00
Doctor Who Role Play Game
    Doctor Who (Fasa #9001) 17.00
    The Daleks (Fasa #9101) 11.00
    The Master (Fasa #9102 . . . . .11.00

MISCELLANEOUS

Doctor Who Tardis video tape cabinet, 42" high,
    holds 67 video tapes (1995) 300.00
Tardis Control Console, 6" across, 3¾" high, battery
    powered (1994) 20.00

PAPER

Doctor Who Radio Times 1996 Calendar (Radio
    Times 1995) 20.00
Doctor Who Postcard set, 32 postcards (1995) 25.00

RECORDINGS

Records
Doctor Who, The Music LP record (BBC 1983) 25.00

View-Master
Doctor Who View-Master Reels (GAF BD216) 50.00
Doctor Who View-Master Reels (GAF BD187) 60.00

Video Tapes (Late 1980s and early 1990s)
City of Death (1979) staring Tom Baker (CBS/Fox) 20.00
The Seeds of Doom (Jan. 31–Mar. 6, 1976) staring
    Tom Baker (CBS/Fox 8294) 20.00
Logopolis (1981) staring Tom Baker (CBS/Fox)
    end of Tom Baker era 20.00
The Two Doctors (Feb. 16– Mar. 2, 1985) staring
    Colin Baker & Patrick Throughton (CBS/Fox) 20.00
The Invasion (Nov. 2–Dec. 21, 1968) staring Patrick
    Throughton (CBS/Fox 8251) 20.00
The War Games (Apr. 19–June 21, 1969) staring
    Patrick Throughton (CBS/Fox 3400) two
    tapes 30.00
The Armageddon Factor (Jan. 20—Feb. 24, 1979)
    staring Tom Baker (CBS/Fox 8439) 20.00
Time and the Rani (Sept. 7–28, 1987) staring
    Sylvester McCoy (CBS/Fox 8295) 20.00
Planet of the Spiders (1974) staring Jon Pertwee
    (CBS/Fox 8105) 20.00
Doctor Who and the Silurians (Jan. 31–Mar. 14,
    1970) staring Jon Pertwee (CBS/Fox 8256)
    two tapes 30.00
Ghost Light (Oct. 4–18, 1989) staring Sylvester
    McCoy (CBS/Fox 8369) 20.00
Arc of Infinity (Jan. 3–12, 1983) staring Peter
    Davidson (CBS/Fox 8290) 20.00
The Day of the Daleks (1972) staring Jon Pertwee
    (CBS/Fox 5092) 20.00
The Daemons (1971) staring Jon Pertwee (CBS/Fox) .20.00
The Three Doctors (Dec. 30, 1972–Jan. 20, 1973)
    staring Jon Pertwee, Patrick Throughton and
    William Hartnell (CBS/Fox 3405) 20.00
The Stones of Blood (Oct. 28–Nov. 18, 1978)
    staring Tom Baker (CBS/Fox 8339) 20.00
The Pirate Planet (Sept. 30–Oct. 21 1978) staring

Doctor Who video tapes: The Two Doctors & Time and the Rani
(CBS/Fox)

Tom Baker, written by Douglas Adams
    (CBS/Fox 8437) 20.00
The Caves of Androzani (Mar. 8–16, 1984) staring
    Peter Davidson (CBS/Fox 5733) the end of
    Peter Davidson 20.00
The Curse of Peladon (Jan. 29–Feb. 19, 1972)
    staring Jon Pertwee (CBS/Fox 8291) 20.00
Shada (1979) staring Tom Baker, with added
    naration by Baker covering unfinished
    portions (CBS/Fox 5730) 20.00
The Androids of Tara (Nov. 25–Dec. 16, 1978)
    staring Tom Baker (CBS/Fox 8335) 20.00
The Brain of Morbius, Collector's Edition (Jan. 3–24,
    1976) staring Tom Baker (CBS/Fox 8456) 20.00
Dragon Fire (Nov. 23–Dec. 7, 1987) staring
    Sylvester McCoy (CBS/Fox 8460) 20.00
The Green Death (May 19–June 23, 1973) staring
    Jon Pertwee (CBS/Fox 8457) two tapes 30.00
The Unearthly Child (CBS/Fox 3401) 20.00
The Throughton Years, staring Patrick Throughton
    (CBS/Fox 3402) 20.00
The Hartnell Years, staring William Hartnell (CBS/
    Fox 3403) 20.00
The Curse of Fenric (CBS/Fox 3404) 20.00
The Ark in Space (CBS/Fox 5420) 20.00
The Spearhead From Space (CBS/Fox 5421) 20.00
Terror of the Zygons (CBS/Fox 5422) 20.00
The Time Warrior (CBS/Fox 5423) 20.00
The Brain of Morbius (CBS/Fox 3715) 20.00
The Deadly Assassin (CBS/Fox 5419) 20.00
Death to the Daleks (CBS/Fox 5093) 20.00
The Five Doctors (CBS/Fox 3717) 20.00
Pyramids of Mars (CBS/Fox 3713) 20.00
Revenge of the Cyberman (CBS/Fox 3714) 20.00
The Robots of Death (CBS/Fox 3726) 20.00
Seeds of Death (CBS/Fox 3716) 20.00
The Talons of Weng Chiang (CBS/Fox 5094) 20.00
The Pertwee Years, staring Jon Pertwee (CBS/Fox
    5732) 20.00
The Daleks, 30th Anniversary 1963–1993, featuring
    "The Chase" (6 parts) staring William Hartnell
    and "Remembrance of the Daleks" (4 parts)
    staring Sylvester McCoy (CBS/Fox 4795) 2 tapes .30.00
The Tom Baker Years, staring Tom Baker (CBS/Fox
    3493) two tapes 20.00

Dr. Who and the Daleks (1965 movie) staring Peter
    Cushing (Lumiere/Republic Pictures #8343) 20.00
Dr. Who: Daleks Invasion Earth 2150 A.D. (1968
    movie) staring Peter Cushing (Lumiere/
    Republic Pictures #8333) 20.00

VEHICLE

Tardis (Denys Fisher 1976) 300.00
Tardis (Dapol #W005, 1988?) 25.00

DUNE

CHILDREN'S BOOKS

Activity Book (Grosset & Dunlap 1984) $5.00
Coloring and Activity Book (Grosset & Dunlap 1984) . . .5.00
Dune Storybook 8.00

CLOTHING & ACCESSORIES

Buttons
Film pre-release button (Two Moons) $2.00
Logo button 2.00
Two Moons button 2.00

Dune game (Avalon Hill 1979)

Paul & Feyd button 2.00
Sandworm button 2.00

GAMES

Dune Board Game (Parker Brothers 1984) 15.00
Frank Herbert's Dune Board Game (Avalon Hill 1979) .65.00
    Spice Harvest module for above 20.00
    The Duel module for above 20.00
Dune 2000 Computer Game (Westwood Studios) 40.00

HOUSEHOLD

Dune Lunch Box (Aladdin 1984)
    Lunch box 50.00
    Thermos 20.00

PAPER

Posters
Pre-release movie poster 8.00
Film poster 10.00
"A World Beyond Your Dreams" poster 8.00
Two Moons poster 6.00
Paul & Feyd poster 6.00
Sandworm poster 6.00

Terminology sheet 1.00
Flyer (Novel promotion) 1.00
Paper plates, 2 sizes 5.00
Dune Calendar, 1985 . . . . .12.00
Fan club newsletter 6.00
Book cover 4.00

RECORDING

Dune View-Master Reels (GAF 4058) 15.00

ROLE PLAY

Fremen Tarpel Gun, 8" long, battery operated (LJN
    1984) 75.00

Sardaukar Laser Pistol, 7" long, battery operated
    (LJN 1984) 50.00

VEHICLES

Vehicles (LJN 1984)
Spice Scout 30.00
Sandworm monster 40.00
Sand Roller battery operated vehicle 30.00
Sand Tracker battery operated vehicle 30.00
Sand Crawler battery operated vehicle 30.00

E.T. THE EXTRA-TERRESTRIAL

FIGURES

E.T. 2" with blanket & Speak 'N Spell (LJN 1982) $7.00
E.T. 2" Holding plant (LJN 1982) 7.00
E.T. 2" in costume (LJN 1982) 7.00
E.T. 2" holding beer can (LJN 1982) 7.00
E.T. 2" Reading book (LJN 1982) 7.00
E.T. 2" with phone (LJN 1982) 7.00
E.T. Hugging doll 9.00
E.T. in robe with telephone 9.00
E.T. with sheet over head 9.00
E.T. Lifting potted flower 9.00
E.T. Pointing with right hand .9.00
E.T. with Umbrella & suitcase 9.00
E.T. Puppet Action Toy with glow in-the-dark chest,
    eyes & finger (LJN 1982) 15.00

CLOTHING & ACCESSORIES

E.T. Halloween costume (Collegeville 1982) 25.00
E.T. Keychain 3.00
E.T. Watch, numeral dial 50.00
E.T. Watch, digital 50.00
Melody Glow Alarm Watch 20.00

FAN CLUB

E.T. Fan Club Application 5.00
E.T. Fan Club Membership Certificate 8.00
E.T. Fan Club Membership card 5.00
8" x 10" photo of E.T. & Elliott 5.00

FAST FOOD

E.T. Collector Series Glasses (Pizza Hut 1982) Set
    of 4 . . . . .30.00
    "Be Good" 7.50
    "Home" 7.50
    "I'll Be Right Here" 7.50
    "Phone Home" 7.50
E.T. Glasses (AAFES/Paramount Glasses) ("E.T.
    Phone Home", "To The Space Ship", "I'll Be
    Right Here", or "Be Good") each 8.00

E.T. The Extra-Terrestrial game (Parker Bros. 1982)

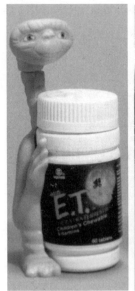

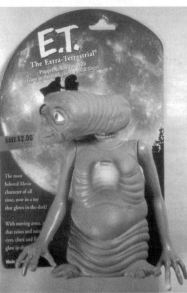

E.T. Multi-Vitiamins (Squibb 1982)
& E.T. Puppet Action Toy (LJN 1982)

E.T. cereal box 30.00
Reese's Pieces box with E.T. walking figure 40.00
Reese's Collector's stickers, sets, each 8.00
Pepsi box with videocassette offer 8.00
Pepsi premium poster 6.00

HOUSEHOLD

E.T., The Extra-Terrestrial metal lunch box (Aladdin 1982)
    lunch box 30.00
    plastic bottle 10.00
E.T. paper cups 4.00
E.T. Message pad 50
Family gift set (Elliott, Gertie, Michael, Mom,
    intruder & E.T.) 60.00
Shrinky Dinks 10.00
Suncatchers, each 4.00
E.T. Finger light 15.00
Puffy stickers 1.00
E.T./Michael Jackson poster 10.00
E.T./Michael Jackson tape .10.00

MISCELLANEOUS

E.T. The Extra-Terrestrial board game (Parker Bros.
    1982) 25.00
Pop-up spaceship 10.00
Stunt spaceship 10.00
E. T. and spaceship launcher 15.00
E.T. premium book 8.00
Spielberg/E.T. postcard 3.00
E.T. Calendar 1983 . . . . .15.00
E.T. photo buttons, each 5.00
E.T. Children's Multi-Vitiamins container (Squibb 1982) 25.00

RECORDINGS

E.T. The Extra-Terrestrial View-Master Reels (GAF N7) 15.00
More Scenes From E.T. The Extra-Terrestrial View-
    Master Reels (GAF 4001) 15.00
E.T. Speaks record 10.00

EXO-SQUAD

VEHICLE

Exocarrier Resolute II (#6372) $27.00

EXO-SQUAD ROBOTECH

VEHICLE

Vehicles (1995) boxed
VeriTech Hover Tank (#6357) $25.00
VeriTech Fighter (#6358) 20.00

FIREBALL XL5

Fireball XL5 Lunch Box (King-Seeley Thermos
    1964-65) steel box $180.00
    thermos (steel/glass) 85.00
Fireball XL5 Game (Milton Bradley 1963) 125.00
Fireball XL5 Magnetic Dart Game (Magic Wand
    1963) 175.00
Fireball XL5 Space City Playset (Multiple Plastic
    Company 1964) 875.00
Fireball XL5 coloring book (Golden 1963) 50.00
Steve Zodiac's Fireball XL5, 20" long plastic rocket
    with 6 figures and 4 missiles (Multiple 1965) . . .150.00
Fireball XL5 Frame tray puzzle (Milton Bradley 1964) . .20.00

FLASH GORDON

Flash Gordon was originally a 1934 comic strip by Alex Raymond which was designed to compete with the highly popular Buck Rogers. His spaceship, ray gun and heroism became necessary components of just about every subsequent science fiction series. There were three black and white serials from the late 1930s starring Buster Crabbe as Flash and Charles Middleton as Ming. These were shown on television in the 1950s, keeping the series alive.

Flash Gordon was created to compete with Buck Rogers. He first appeared in a comic strip in 1934 with some of the best comic art of all time. He had a fan club with many premiums and appeared in several action serials. Unlike most space heroes, Flash lived in the present, not the future. His spaceship, ray gun and heroism became necessary components of just about every subsequent science fiction series.

In many ways, Flash eclipsed Buck Rogers as the prototype space hero. For this young science fiction fan, the reason was Ming the Merciless, as played to perfection by Charles Middleton in the movie serials (later made into TV episodes.) (I was too young to be swayed by any differences in the sex appeal of Dale Arden versus Wilma Deering.) Anyway, you have to like a villain whose goal was to rule both Mongo and Earth (and everything else).

Fireball XL5 Game (Milton Bradley 1963)

Flash Gordon Playset (Mego 1976) Flash Gordon Inlaid Puzzle (Milton Bradley 1951)

CHILDREN'S BOOKS

Big Little Books
Flash Gordon and the Emperor of Mongo (1936) . . .$125.00
Flash Gordon and the Fiery Desert of Mongo (1948) . .50.00
Flash Gordon and the Tournaments of Mongo (1935) . .60.00
Flash Gordon and the Ape Men of Mor 90.00
Flash Gordon and the Tyrant of Mongo 35.00
Flash Gordon and the Monsters of Mongo (1935) 145.00
Flash Gordon and the Red Sword Invaders (1945) . . .115.00
Flash Gordon and the Witch Queen of Mongo (1936) .150.00
Flash Gordon and the Power Men of Mongo 115.00
Flash Gordon in the Ice World of Mongo (1942) 140.00
Flash Gordon in the Forest Kingdom of Mongo 45.00
Flash Gordon in the Jungles of Mongo 35.00
Flash Gordon in the Water World of Mongo (1937) 60.00
Flash Gordon on the Planet Mongo (1934) 190.00

Paint Book
Flash Gordon Mission of Peril (Rand McNally
    #06538, 1979) 15.00

DOLLS & FIGURES

9½" Dolls on header card (Mego 1976)
Flash Gordon (#4400/1) 68.00
Ming the Merciless (#4400/2) 68.00
Dr. Zarkov (#4400/3) 80.00
Dale Arden (#4400/4) 75.00

Syroco Figure
Syroco Wood composition figure of Flash 5" (1944) .1,000.00

PVC Figure
Flash Gordon PVC figure (Comics Spain 1990) 10.00

CLOTHING

Costumes
Space-outfit including belt, goggles and wrist
    compass (Esquire Novelty 1951) 175.00

Accessories
Sun glasses (JA-RU 1981) 5.00
Wallet, with zipper (1949) 30.00

Buttons
Button, Flash and Ming 10.00

Flash Gordon Litho Button (King Features 1934) 50.00
Dale Arden Litho Button (King Features 1934) 60.00

GAMES & PUZZLES

Flash Gordon board game (House of Games 1970s) . .35.00
Three Puzzle boxed set (Milton Bradley 1951) 120.00
Tray puzzle (Milton Bradley 1951) 60.00
Ming punch-out (from Playboy magazine Jan. 1981) . . .3.00

MISCELLANEOUS

Hand Puppet, rubber head (1950s) 30.00
Flash Gordon Pencil box (1951) 60.00
Space Compass on plastic band, carded 50.00
Flash Gordon Kite 50.00
Gordon Bread wrappers 220.00
View-Master packet with 3 reels (1977) 15.00
Medals and insignia (Larami Corp. 1978) 6.00
Flash Gordon Dome Lunchbox (Aladdin 1979)
        Lunchbox 60.00
        Thermos 20.00
Flash Gordeon 2-way telephone, metal (Marx 1940s) . .90.00
Flash Gordon "City of Sea Caves" record
        (Record Guild of America 1960s) 45.00

PAPER COLLECTIBLES

Paper plates (Unique Industries 1978) 6.00
Paper cups (Unique Industries 1978) 6.00
Table cover (Unique Industries 1978) 8.00
Loot bags 4.00
Candy box display 40.00
Candy boxes (Phoenix Candy 1978) 8 different, each .20.00
World Battle Fronts WWII map (1943) 60.00
Buster Crabbe Dixie Ice Cream Lid 25.00
Buster Crabbe Dixie Ice Cream Picture 125.00
Flash Gordon's Trip to Mars (1938) one sheet
        movie poster 1,275.00

NEWSPAPER STRIPS

Year	Artist	per/10	per year
1934	Alex Raymond	.250.00	.1,500.00
1935	Alex Raymond	.200.00	.1,100.00
1936–39	Alex Raymond	.100.00	.550.00
1940–44	Alex Raymond	.60.00	.300.00
1944–48	Austin Briggs	.20.00	.100.00
1948–49	Mac Raboy	.30.00	.150.00
1950–59	Mac Raboy	.15.00	.75.00

1960–67 Mac Raboy	.13.00	.65.00
1967–69 Dan Barry	.10.00	.50.00
1970–79 Dan Barry	.7.50	.37.50
1980–89 Dan Barry	.5.00	.25.00
1990–present Dan Barry	.1.00	.5.00

ROLE PLAY

Space Target	.60.00
3-color Raygun (Nasta 1976)	.30.00
Sparkling Raygun (Nasta 1976)	.30.00
Flash Gordon Water Pistol 7½" plastic (Marx early 1950s)	.150.00
Space Water Pistol (Nasta 1976)	.30.00
Flash Gordon Signal Pistol	.150.00
MIP Soft Target set (King Features 1981)	.40.00
Flash Gordon Radio Repeater gun (Marx 1935)	.500.00
Flash Gordon Click Ray Pistol (Marx 1950s)	.300.00

VEHICLES & PLAYSET

Flash Gordon Starship (Tootsietoy)	.20.00
Ming Starship (Tootsietoy)	.20.00
Ming's Space Shuttle (Mattel 1979)	.30.00
Flash Gordon Large Box, set with 3 figures, 2 ships (Tootsietoy)	.50.00
Flash Gordon Sparkling Rocket Fightership (Marx 1950s)	.300.00
World of Mongo playset (Mego 1977)	.150.00
Flash Gordon Playset (Mego 1976)	.150.00

FLASH GORDON (MOVIE)

Flash Gordon was made into a feature film by Dino de Laurentis in 1980. He also tried his hand at *King Kong* and *Dune*. Collectively, these movies set back science fiction and horror in the cinema for about a decade. *Flash Gordon* at least had good villains. Both Max Van Sydow as Ming and Brian Blessed as Vultan were excellent. Melody Anderson as Dale and future 007 Timothy Dalton as Prince Baron were okay. The same cannot be said for the script, the score or Flash.

BUTTONS

Flash Gordon Movie button (1980)	$5.00
Ming Movie button (1980)	.5.00
Vultan Movie button (1980)	.5.00
Aura Movie button (1980)	.5.00
Barin Movie button (1980)	.5.00

PAPER

Film program (1979)	.10.00
Lobby cards, each	.3.00

SPACESHIP

Flash Gordon Rocketship, 30" inflatable (Mattel #1535, 1979)	.25.00

FLASH GORDON (TV)

Kiddy cartoon version of *Flash Gordon* which made the Dino de Laurentis movie version look like *Hamlet* by comparison.

VEHICLES

Vehicles (Playmates 1996)
Triphibian (#12453)	$16.00
Flash Gordon Rebel AirBike (#12461)	.10.00
Ming's Jaws of Death Throne (#12462)	.10.00

FORBIDDEN PLANET

This classic 1956 film starred Walter Pidgeon as the scientist Morbius, Anne Francis as his daughter Alta and young and handsome Leslie Nielsen and Jack Kelly as the spaceship heroes who battle the invisible monster from the Id. Nielsen gets the girl. The special effects version of the Krell technology is still exciting, but the real star of the movie was Robby the Robot. *Forbidden Planet's* influence can be seen on science fiction movies and television shows all the way into the 1990s. Anne Francis is remembered in one of the songs from The *Rocky Horror Picture Show*. Robby was the prototype for a number of subsequent robots. Recently, the great machine on the planet beneath *Babylon 5* looks a lot like it was built by the Krell.

MOVIE MEMORABILIA

Film poster one sheet, featuring Robby, 41" x 27" (MGM, 1956)	$2,500.00
Lobby cards, 8 different (1956) each	.200.00
Forbidden Planet Record Album, Planet Records (MGM 1956)	.100.00
Forbidden Planet DVD version (#906565)	.25.00

ROBOTS

Robbie Robot (Yonezawa 1950's)	.1,600.00
Robby The Robot, In Space Tank, "V2" space tank, with antenna, Robby type robot in turret, space scene embossed on rear, bump and go action, Robby's face lights up (KO 1950's)	.800.00
Robby The Robot, 5" Wind-Up Robot (Masudaya 1985)	.50.00
Robby The Robot, 5" die-cast Robot (Masudaya #00127, 1997)	.25.00
Robby The Robot, 16" battery powered, talking figure (Masudaya 1980s)	.200.00
Robby The Robot, 22" battery operated model (Masudaya 1985)	.230.00
Robby the Robot Black, red accents, orig. "Mechanized Robot," battery operated (Nomura)	.4,500.00
Robert The Robot, gray plastic, red arms, voice box key wind walking mechanism, Arms swing, appears in movie pressbook (Ideal 1950's)	.345.00

Forbidden Planet Robby The Robot (Masudaya 1980s)

*Land of the Giants Spaceship Spindrift Toothpick Craft
(Remcraft 1968)*

INDEPENDENCE DAY (ID4)

MISCELLANEOUS

Baseball Hat $12.00
T-Shirt 15.00
Coffee Mug 8.00
Hand Held Electronic Game (Tiger #78-624, 1996) . . .19.00

PAPER

Posters, 23" x 35"
City in Peril (#3029) 8.00
Spaceships (#3030) 8.00
Exo-Skeleton/Alien (#3031) 8.00
Lightning/Alien (#3032) 8.00
Earth (#3063) 8.00
Captain Hiller (#3064) 8.00

VEHICLES ACCESSORIES & PLAYSETS

Vehicles
Electronic F/A-18 Hornet fighter jet (#6369) + disk 9 . .18.00
Electronic Alien Attacker ship (#6365) + disk 8 . . . . . . .20.00
Electronic Alien Attack Leader (#7137) 15.00

Accessory
Bio-Containment Chamber (#30750) 5.00

Playsets (Trendmasters 1996)
Area 51 Micro Playset 12.00
Defend New York City Micro Playset 12.00
Los Angeles Invasion Giant Playset 25.00

LAND OF THE GIANTS

Land of the Giants was another late 1960s television show which was sort of a combination of *The Incredible Shrinking Man* and *Gilligan's Island*. Seven Earthlings are lost in a space warp and end up on a planet where everybody is 12 times their size. It featured Gary Conway as Capt. Steve Burton and Don Matheson as Mark Wilson. Every week they tried to fix their ship while avoiding kids, pets, creatures and Inspector Kobrick.

You want to hear a frightening thought? This show was from the same era as *Star Trek*, *Lost in Space* and *Batman*, all of which are still around in the 1990s as movies. Maybe this show will be next!

COSTUMES

Steve Burton Halloween Costume (Ben Cooper 1968) $150.00
Scientist Halloween Costume (Ben Cooper 1968) . . .150.00

CRAFT & ACTIVITY

Land of the Giants Deluxe Pencil Coloring Set
    (Hasbro 1969) 150.00
Colorforms Set (Colorforms 1968) 100.00
Land of the Giants Coloring Book (Whitman 1968) 50.00
Painting Set (Hasbro 1969) 100.00
Land of the Giants Rub-Ons (Hasbro 1969) 75.00

GAMES & PUZZLES

Land of the Giants board game (Ideal 1968) 150.00
Land of the Giants Double Action Bagatelle Game
    (Hasbro 1969) 150.00
Land of the Giants Target Set (Hasbro 1969) 150.00
Land of the Giants Puzzle (Whitman 1968) 75.00

HOUSEHOLD

Land of the Giants metal lunch box (Aladdin 1968)
    Lunch box 225.00
    plastic thermos 40.00

RECORDING

Land of the Giants View-Master set (GAF 1968) 50.00
Movie Viewer (Acme 1968) 70.00

ROLE PLAY

Signal Ray Space Gun (Remco 1968) 175.00
Land of the Giants Walkie Talkies (Remco 1968) 200.00
Wrist Flashlight (Bantam Lite 1968) 75.00
Spaceship Control Panel (Remco 1968) 85.00

SPACE SHIP

Flying Saucer (Remco 1968) 150.00
Land of the Giants Spaceship Spindrift Toothpick
    Craft (Remcraft 1968) 75.00
Motorized Flying Rocket (Remco 1968) 200.00
Space Sled (Remco 1968) .500.00

LOST IN SPACE

Lost in Space was based on the Gold Key comic book series *Space Family Robinson*. It became a television show in 1965. It is remembered fondly by its many fans and was recycled as a movie in early 1998. The original series starred Guy Williams and June Lockhart as the parents, Mark Goddard as Don West, Marta Kristen as Judy Robinson. Much of the action involved Jonathan Harris as Dr. Smith and Bill Mumy as Will Robinson. Just about every week, Smith would sell out to some alien power, Will would get in trouble and The Robot would alert him to the danger. The cliff-hanger endings kept you coming back to the show.

I didn't mind that the show was for kids, but I had a lot of problem with Dr. Smith. I am one of the more forgiving people whom I know and I don't like blood, so the first time he sold out my kids I would have marooned him; the second time I would have shoved him out of an airlock without a space suit. There would have been no third episode.

Official Lost in Space Robot, 10" (AHI #6813 1977)

The late 1960s was also the era of *Batman*, with Adam West and Burt Ward, *The Green Hornet*, with Van Williams and Bruce Lee and, of course, *Star Trek*. Space shows must get into the blood, because you can still see Bill Mumy and Walter Koenig on *Babylon 5*, as Lanier and Bester, respectively.

DOLLS & FIGURES

8" Classic Dolls (Trendmasters 1998–99) in window tube
Major Don West with Laser Assault Rifle (#09503)
    from "The Reluctant Stowaway" $15.00
Will Robinson with B-9 Robot Communicator
    (#09505) from "The Reluctant Stowaway" 15.00
Dr. Zachary Smith .not yet released
Judy Robinson . . . . .not yet released
Tybo the Carrot Man 15.00
Cyclops . . . . .not yet released

GAMES & PUZZLES

Lost in Space Board Game (Milton Bradley 1965) . . .100.00
Lost in Space 3D Action Fun Game, with 4
    spaceman figures (Remco 1966) 250.00
Lost in Space jigsaw puzzle, frame tray, three poses
    (Milton Bradley 1965) 90.00

HOUSEHOLD

Lost in Space Lunch Box (King-Seeley Thermos
    1967-68) steel dome box 500.00
    thermos, steel & glass 70.00

MISCELLANEOUS TOYS

Lost in Space View-Master reels, 3 reels with book
    (GAF B482, 1966) 75.00
Lost in Space Tru-Vue Magic Eyes (GAF 1967) 75.00
Lost in Space Colorforms set (Colorforms 1966) 150.00
Lost in Space Halloween Costume (Ben Cooper
    1966) 250.00
Lost in Space Switch-and-Go Playset (Mattel 1966) 2,000.00

PAPER

Lost in Space 3½" x 5½" fan post card (1966) 30.00
Lost in Space 8" x 10" cast photo (1966) 90.00

ROBOTS

Lost in Space Robot, 10" plastic, battery powered
    (AHI 1977) 300.00
Lost in Space Robot, 12" plastic battery powered
    (Remco 1965) 850.00
Lost in Space YM-3 Robot, 4" wind-up (Masudaya
    #5217, 1985) 30.00
Lost in Space YM-3 Robot, 15" battery operated,
    talking (Masudaya #8501, 1986) 150.00

ROLE PLAY

Lost in Space Walkie-Talkie play set (AHI 1977) 150.00
Lost in Space Saucer Gun (AHI 1977) shoots disks . .100.00
Lost in Space Roto-Jet Gun Set (Mattel 1966) 2,500.00
Lost in Space Helmet and Signal Ray Gun Set
    (Remco 1967) 1,000.00
Laser Water Pistol 65.00

LOST IN SPACE MOVIE

DOLLS & FIGURES

Talking Blawp, with color change skin (#31045,
    1998) $20.00

DIE-CAST

Johnny Lightning Spaceships
Lost in Space Classic Space Pod (#43300) 8.00

MISCELLANEOUS

Keychains
Blawp 4.00
Jupiter 2 . . . . .4.00
Robot 4.00

ROLE PLAY

Transforming Space Blaster (Trendmasters #31011,
    1998) 20.00

VEHICLES

Vehicles (Trendmasters 1998)
Transforming Jupiter 2 with Pop-out Hyperdrive
    Struts and Blasting Missiles (#31110) 30.00
Eagle One Bubble Fighter with Gyro-Swiveling
    Cockpit and Blasting Missiles (#08334) 15.00
Deluxe Bubble Fighter with Gyro-Swiveling Cockpit
    and Blasting Missiles (#31208) 20.00

Lost in Space Transforming Jupiter 2 (Trendmasters 1998)

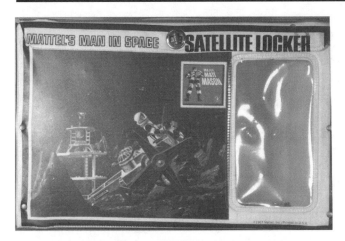

Major Matt Mason Satellite Locker (Mattel 1968)

MAJOR MATT MASON

Mattel's Man in Space was based on the U.S. space program. The figures are "bendies" rather than articulated figures, but this worked well in space suits. A lot of the action was in the outfits and vehicles. Captain Lazer is part of the line, but he is a 12" battery-powered action figure which is way out of scale with the other figures and vehicles. Callisto was an alien "friend," while the first actual villain didn't appear until 1970 in the form of Scorpio. Major Matt Mason is one of the premier collectibles for action figure and space/science fiction fans.

CHILDREN'S BOOK

Major Matt Mason Press-Out Book, 8½" x 11½"
  book (Whitman 1969) $40.00

FIGURES

6" Figures (Mattel 1966–71)
Major Matt Mason with Flight Set (#6300, 1966) $175.00
Major Matt Mason with Moon Suit (#6303, 1967) 190.00
Sgt. Storm (Flight Set) (#6317, 1968) 250.00
Major Matt Mason with Lunar Trac (#6318, 1968) 150.00
Sgt. Storm with Lunar Trac (#6319, 1968) 200.00
Callisto, friend from Jupiter (#6331, 1969)
  Version with big boots, header card green
    behind figure 325.00
  Version with short boots, header card yellow
    behind figure 325.00
Jeff Long with Lunar Trac (#6332, 1969) 400.00
Doug Davis with Lunar Trac (#6333, 1969) 250.00
Major Matt Mason and Space Power Suit (#6336,
  1969) 225.00
Scorpio 7" villain (#6359, 1970) 1,750.00
Talking Major Matt Mason (#6362, 1970) 325.00
Talking, Flying Major Matt Mason (#6378, 1970) 375.00

Multi-Figure Set
Space Mission Team, including **Major Matt Mason**,
  Jeff Long, **Doug Davis** and **Calisto** figures
  (#6337, 1969) 750.00

Large Figure
Captain Lazer, 12" (#6330, 1967) 350.00

FIGURE & ACCESSORY SETS

Space Discovery Set, with **Doug Davis** and **Calisto**
  figures, Space Crawler, Space Bubble and

Space Power Suit (#1910) 600.00
Space Station & Space Crawler Deluxe Action set
  with **Major Matt Mason** (#6310, 1967) 450.00
Space Crawler Action Set with **Major Matt Mason**,
  boxed (#6311, 1967) 220.00
Firebolt Space Cannon Action Set, boxed with
  Capt. Lazer 250.00
Firebolt Space Cannon Super Action Set, boxed with
  Capt. Lazer, **Major Matt Mason**, **Sgt. Storm**,
  Cannon, Space Sled, Jet Pack, Cat Trak 500.00
Orbitor with **Or the Alien** (#6356) . . . . .not seen

VEHICLES & ACCESSORIES

Vehicles & Accessories (Mattel 1967)
Moon Suit Pak, carded (#6301) 75.00
Astro Trac, boxed (#6302) 120.00
Firebolt Space Cannon, boxed (Asst. #6304) 150.00
Space Crawler, boxed (Asst. #6304) 150.00
Rocket Launch Pak, carded (#6305) 75.00
Satellite Launch Pak, carded (#6306) 75.00
Space Probe Pak, carded (#6307) 75.00
Space Station, boxed (#6308) 190.00

Vehicles and Accessories (Mattel 1968)
Major Matt Mason Rocket Ship carrying case (#6316) 160.00
Reconojet Pak, carded (#6320) 75.00
Space Shelter Pak (#6321) 50.00
Satellite Locker carrying case (#6322) 80.00
Uni-Tred & Space Bubble, boxed (#6339) 160.00

Vehicles and Accessories (Mattel 1969)
Talking Command Console, boxed (#5157) 90.00
Gamma Ray-Gard (#6342) 80.00
Supernaut Power-Limbs Pak (#6343) 75.00
Space Power Suit Pak (#6344) 60.00
Space Bubble, boxed (#6345) 60.00
Uni-Tred Space Hauler, boxed (#6346) 130.00
Space Travel Pak (#6347) 60.00
Lunar Base Command Set (#6353) . . . . .unknown
Star Seeker, boxed (#6357) 140.00
Voyage to Galaxy III set (#6380) . . . . .not seen
XRG-1 Reentry Glider 220.00

EXCLUSIVES

Astro Trac, Missile Convoy Set (Sears exclusive)
  40" x 24" with Astro Trac, 3 Mobile Launch
  Pads, Satellite Launcher Space Probe,
  Rocket Launcher 800.00

MARS ATTACKS

RECORDING

Mars Attacks DVD recording (#14480) $25.00

ROLE PLAY

Martian Brain Disintegrator, red pack 25.00
Martian Brain Disintegrator, purple pack 25.00

VEHICLES

Doom Saucer (#6719) 19.00
Martian Flying Saucer (#6996) with mission disk 19.00

THE MARTIAN CHRONICLES

The Martian Chronicles is a collection of short stories by Ray Bradbury. The stories are from the 1940s and were collected into a book in 1950. They are one of the things that made him famous. The stories are about man's first explo-

Mars Attack Martian Flying Saucer (Trendmasters 1997)

ration and colonization of Mars, and encounters with an ancient and enigmatic Martian race. They were made into a television mini series in the 1970s starring Rock Hudson and Darrin McGavin.

The stories and the television adaptation were designed for an older audience, but these Martian figures were made anyway. All three appear on a generic header card, which does not even assign names to them. They have silver masks and white robes, trimmed in different colors. Most of the interest in the figures is from collectors who are familiar with the stories, rather than ones who played with the figures as a child.

FIGURES

8" Figures on generic header card (Larami 1974)
Pink trim $70.00
Blue trim 65.00
Orange trim 65.00

MEN IN BLACK

ALIEN FIGURES

Alien Figures (Galoob 1997)
Elby-17 (#22917) $4.00
Redgick Jr. (#22923) 4.00
Bobo the Squat (#22922) 4.00
Mickey (#22925) 4.00
Mavis 13 . . . . .4.00
Worm Aliens 4.00
Mavis 12 . . . . .4.00
Skulk (#22921) 4.00
Neeble & Gleeble (#22926) 4.00
Sleeble & Mavis 13 (#22915) 4.00

FAST FOOD

Burger King promotion (May 1998) two each week
Squishy Worm Guy 2.00
Squirting Worm Guy 2.00
Split Apart Rotating Zed 2.00
Split Apart Light-Up Zed 2.00
Red Button Building Buster .2.00

Red Button Loop Blaster 2.00
Slimed-Out Kay 2.00
Slimed-Out Jay 2.00
Globe Space Spinner 2.00
Building Space Spinner 2.00
MIB Alien Detector 2.00
MIB Neuralyzer 2.00

VEHICLE

Vehicles (Galoob 1997)
Zap-Em Van (#76232) 10.00

MISCELLANEOUS SPACE & SCIENCE FICTION

Space and science fiction themes were popular in the 1950s and the 1960s and manufacturers cashed in as best they could. The listings below contain generic space theme collectibles, items based loosely on the U.S. space program plus those from movies and television shows which did not generate enough collectibles to have their own listings. Generic ray guns, robots and spaceships each have their own listings. The space vehicles listed in this section include all the space tanks, buses, trains and similar items that do not qualify as Rocketships or Spaceships. Most of them look like their earth-bound counterparts with space decorations, but even the best space heroes need ground transportation occasionally.

COSTUMES

Astronaut Halloween Costume (Collegeville 1962) . . .$50.00
Man From Mars Halloween Costume (Halco 1950's) . .75.00
Man On The Moon Halloween Costume (1970) 35.00

FIGURES

Apollo Astronaut, 5½" tall Hap Hazard figure (Marx 1970) 40.00
Archer Space Men & Robots, 10" x 8" x 4" tall box with 4" tall spacemen, 9 green, 7 purple, 3 brown and 5 robots (1950s) 125.00
Haji Astronaut, mechanical, 6½" tall with tin litho rifle (1950s) 400.00

Apollo Astronaut Hap Hazard figure (Marx 1970)

Men into Space game (Milton Bradley 1960)

Man from Mars Astronaut, 11" mechanical (Irwin
    1950s) 175.00
Mechanical Man From Mars Astronaut (Irwin 1950s) .150.00
Pete the Space Man, 5" tall tin litho and plastic
    (Bandai) 60.00
Space Scout Doll, 7½" tall, 6½" x 10" x 2" window
    box (The House of Dolls 1950s) 60.00
Space Whale PK-3, tin litho, mechanical (KO 1950s) .500.00
Space Men and Robots, 4" tall spacemen: 9 green,
    7 purple, 3 brown and 5 robots (Archer 1950s) .125.00
Space People, 11 space people in 13½x11" box
    (Archer 1950s) 350.00

FOOD

Star Men filled with Candy Moon Rocks (E. Rosen
    1960s) 75.00
Space Gun Pez Dispenser (PEZ 1980's) 50.00
Space Gun Pez Dispenser (PEZ 1950's) 200.00
Space Trooper Pez Dispenser, robot (PEZ) 300.00
Space Trooper Pez Dispenser (PEZ) gold 1,500.00

GAMES & PUZZLES

Games
Astro Launch game (Ohio Art 1963) 75.00
Battling Spaceships Game (Ideal 1977) 50.00
Blast Off! game (Selchow & Righter 1953) 150.00
Countdown: Adventure in Space game (E.S. Lowe
    1967) 100.00
Countdown to Space (Transogram 1960) 75.00
Dragonriders of Pern game (Mayfair Games 1983) . .20.00
Flying Saucers game (Pressman 1950) 75.00
Lay's Lunar Landing game (Milton Bradley 1969) 75.00
Men into Space board game (Milton Bradley 1960) . . .75.00
Mr. Machine Game (Ideal 1961) 80.00
Orbit game (Parker Brothers 1959)
    Small Space Ship 100.00
    Large Space Ship 75.00

Outer Limits game (Milton Bradley 1964) 250.00
Rockets Away Target Game (American Metal
    Specialties 1952) 125.00
Rocket Patrol Magnetic Target Game, 15" x 14" tin
    litho target board and darts (American Toy 1950s) 75.00
Rocket Patrol Magnetic Target Game (American
    Toy Products 1950s) .100.00
Rocket Race to Saturn board game (Lido 1950s) 75.00
Rocket to the Moon game (Hasbro 1959) 100.00
Space Game (Parker Bros. 1953) 125.00
Space Pilot game (Cadaco-Ellis 1951) 150.00
Siren Sparkle Space Target, 19" x 14" x 2" window
    box, with Super Atomic Pistol, darts and
    target board (Knickerbocker #683, 1950s) 75.00
Steve Scott Space Scout board game, 14" square
    board (Transogram 1952) 150.00
Twilight Zone board game (Ideal 1960s) 250.00

Puzzles
Captain Universe frame tray puzzle (1952) 40.00

LAUNCHING PADS, BASES AND TRACKING STATIONS

Astrobase, 20", battery powered, with 8" long scout
    car (Ideal 1960) 75.00
Countdown Rocket Launcher, in 22" x 12" x 3" box
    (Nylint #3500, 1950s) 75.00
Count Down playset, electronic with yellow Atlas
    rocket, space probes and launchpad (Ideal
    1950s) 125.00
Mobile Satellite Tracking Station, Cape Canaveral
    ICBM Rocket Research Division, bus with
    radar antenna (Cragston #30226, 1960s) 75.00
Moon City with Space Shuttle Craft plastic set with 5"
    moon shuttle, 17" x 15" x 3" box (Cragstan 1970) 75.00
Operation Orbit, plastic, battery operated,
    19" x 20" x 10" box (Transogram #3940, 1950s) .75.00
Planetary Cruiser Patrol Space Port, 10" (Pyro 1953) .200.00
Remote Control Satellite (Arnold/Cragstan 1950s) . . .50.00
Rocket Express, 5½" x 5" tin litho, mechanical,
    rockets whirl through tunnel, satellite flys
    overhead (Linemar 1950s) 150.00
Rocket Launching Pad, 4½" x 5" x 8½" (Cragstan
    1950s) 150.00
Satellite Launcher, plastic launcher, 19" x 7" x 6"
    box (Ideal #4874, 1950s) 60.00
Satellite Launching Station, with 22 plastic figures,
    20" x 12" x 5" (Marx #2664, 1958) 150.00
Satellite, remote control, aluminium ball with 3
    yellow plastic antenna and 4 red blades
    (Arnold/Cragston 1950s) 50.00
Space Satellite with Launching Station, tin litho
    (Marx 1950s) 100.00

Steve Scott Space Scout game (Transogram 1952) & The Outer Limits game (Milton Bradley 1964)

The Outer Limits game (Milton Bradley 1964)

Superior Spaceport, tin litho space port and space
    cannon, with spacemen and alien figures (T.
    Cohen 1950s) 350.00
Two Stage Rocket Launching Pad, tin litho rocket
    flies into air, 7" x 4" x 8" box (TN 1950s) 150.00
Voice Control Astronaut Base, 19" x 14" x 8" box
    (Remco 1969) 75.00

LUNCH BOXES

Astronaut Lunch Box (King-Seeley Thermos 1960-66)
    steel dome box (from 1960) 200.00
    thermos (steel/glass) .60.00
Back to the Future Lunch Box (Thermos 1989)
    lunch box 25.00
    thermos 10.00
Captain Astro Lunch Box (Ohio Art 1966-67)
    steel box (no thermos made) 150.00
Moon Landing Lunch Box (Ardee Ind. 1960s) vinyl
    box 45.00
    thermos (plastic) 18.00
Space Explorer Lunch Box (Aladdin 1960) steel box .125.00
    thermos (steel/glass) .50.00
Space Shuttle Orbiter Lunch Box (King-Seeley
    Thermos 1978-79) steel box 45.00
    thermos (plastic) 15.00
UFO Lunch Box (King-Seeley Thermos 1973)
    steel box 90.00
    thermos (plastic) 30.00
U.S. Space Corps Lunch Box (Universal 1961-62)
    steel box 250.00
    thermos (plastic) 95.00

MISCELLANEOUS

Invasion of the Saucer Men, 14" x 11" card (Intl.
    Pictures 1957) 25.00
Space Boy Siren Flashlight, 7" long, tin litho (1950s) . .30.00
Spaceman Modeling Clay, 15" x 11" box (Pressman
    1950s) 75.00
Electronic Walkie Talkies (Remco 1960s) 125.00

Robot Bulldozer (Marusan 1950s)

PLAYSETS

Cape Canaveral playset, 23" x 15" x 4" box (Marx
    #2656, 1960s) 75.00
Captain Solar Space Port playset, tin litho building
    (Marx #7018, 1954) 400.00
Giant Martian Landing Playset, 17" x 8" x 27" (Marx
    1977) 75.00
Hamilton Invaders playset, 8" long beetle, dwarf
    tank and blue defenders in 23" x 9" x 11" box
    (Remco 1960s) 75.00
Martian Landing Playset, plastic in 17" x 8" x 27"
    box (Marx #4306, 1977) 75.00

RAY GUNS, ROBOTS, SPACESHIPS:
SEE SEPARATE HEADINGS BELOW

SPACE VEHICLES & SPACE STATIONS

Aerocar "The Flying Jet" 7½" long (PlasTex #PT560,
    1950s) 40.00
Apollo Moon Orbiter, mechanical wind-up, with
    plastic astronaut on metal rod (Yonezawa 1960s) 50.00
Apollo Space Capsule, NASA, 9" long, tin litho with
    astronauts, battery operated flashing lights
    and rotating antenna (MT 1960s) 50.00
Apollo-Z Moon Traveler, battery operated
    (TN 1960s) 45.00
Explorer Capsule, friction powered (HP #609) 35.00
Flying Air Force Jeep, 7" long with two ½" figures at
    controls, friction powered (Daiya 1950s) 175.00
Friendship 7 Space Capsule, 6" long, tin litho with
    half figure astronaut (NGS/Cragston 1970s) 50.00
Futuristic Car, tin litho with helmeted driver (TKK
    1950s) 200.00
Luna Hovercraft X1, 7½" long, radio controlled,
    battery powered (TPS) 125.00
Magic Color Moon Express, battery powered, with
    lights and noise, (Daysran 1960s) 75.00
Mars Patrol Space Tank, 17" tank (YM 1950s) 85.00
Moon Explorer, battery powered with astronaut pilot
    in front dome (Marken #81237, 1960s) 75.00
New Space Station, battery operated blinking lights
    and space noise, revolving antenna, see
    through rooms (SH 1960s) 150.00
Robot Bulldozer (Marusan 1950's) 265.00
Sea Hawk Future Car, 12" long, tin and plastic, with
    full figure plastic driver (Y) 90.00
Space Bus with Robbie the Robot, 14½" tin litho,
    friction powered (1950s) 225.00
Space Exploration Train, tin litho train with 12
    sections of track and 4 sections of train
    including 6" locomotive, 5" transmitter car, 4"
    radar car and 4" missile carrier (K 1950s) 600.00
Space Refuel Station, battery operated lighted
    windows and revolving antenna, with jet plane
    rocket (Waco 1960s) 95.00
Space Scooter, 7" x 8" box, tin litho, battery pow-
    ered (MT) 75.00
Space Tank X4, 7" long, friction powered, tin litho
    with moveable turret and siren sound (TN
    1950s) 40.00
Supersonic Speedster, 6½" long Rocket Racer with
    tin litho driver's head (MT 1950s) 75.00
The Flying Jet Aerocar, 7½" long (PlasTex 1950s) 35.00
Turbo Jet Car with automatic launching platform, tin
    litho launching platform (Ideal 1950s) 100.00

MOON McDARE

FIGURES

Figure (Gilbert 1966)
Moon McDare $125.00

VEHICLES & ACCESSORIES

Vehicles & Accessories (Gilbert 1966)
Action Communication Set, boxed 50.00
Blinking Light and Battery Pack 50.00
Moon Explorer Set, boxed .75.00
Space Mutt Set, boxed 75.00
Space Suit Outfit, boxed 50.00
Space Gun Set, carded 60.00
Space Accessory Pack, carded 50.00
Spaceman Equipment, binoculars, compass,
    retractable unbilical cord, carded 50.00

MOVIE POSTERS

Every movie produces posters, sometimes many different ones. Posters for really good movies become valuable, as do posters for really bad movies like *Plan 9 From Outer Space*. Science fiction and horror movies are popular with poster collectors, so prices are a little higher than for mundane movies, but posters for recent movies can often be had for $10 to $15. The list below is a sampling of recent prices for posters from movies which are not otherwise listed in this section. They are all reasonably well-known science fiction movies, although some of them are not "space movies."

One Sheet Movie Posters
Amazing Colossal Man, The (1938) $700.00
Back to the Future 25.00
Barbarella (1968) 60.00
Dark Star 25.00
Day of the Triffids, The (1962) 375.00
Day the Earth Stood Still, The (1951) 5,600.00
Destination Moon (1950) .675.00
Fantastic Voyage (1966) 50.00
Incredible Shrinking Man (1957) 425.00
Invaders From Mars (1953) 1,000.00
Invasion of the Body Snatchers (1956) 650.00
It Came From Beneath The Sea (1955) 375.00
It Came From Outer Space (1953) 365.00
King of the Rocket Men (1949) 3,000.00
Logan's Run 45.00
Man From Planet X, The (1951) 2,000.00
Metropolis (1927) 31,000.00
Omega Man, The (1971) 30.00
Outland (1981) 25.00
Plan 9 From Outer Space (1958) 1,250.00
Radar Men From The Moon (1952) 300.00
Rocketship X-M (1950) 300.00
Silent Running (1972) 35.00
Soylent Green (1973) 45.00
Them (1954) 400.00
Thing, The (1951) 350.00
Things to Come (1936) (6-sheet) 15,000.00
This Island Earth (1955) .750.00
THX-1138 (1971) 30.00
Total Recall (1990) 20.00
Total Recall, Advance (1990) 30.00
War of the Worlds, The (1952) 1,750.00
When World's Collide (1951) 600.00

Outer Space Men (Colorforms 1968)

THE OUTER SPACE MEN

This series of bendy-style figures was by Colorforms, of all companies. Prices on these figures are out of this world, as are the figures.

FIGURES

Figures (Colorforms 1968–70)
Alpha 7 (The Man from Mars) $600.00
Astro-Nautilus (The Man from Neptune) 600.00
Colossus Rex (The Man from Jupiter) 750.00
Commander Comet (The Man from Venus) 600.00
Electron (The Man from Pluto) 600.00
Orbitron (The Man from Uranus) 600.00
Xodiac (The Man from Saturn) 600.00

PLANET OF THE APES

The original movie starred Charlton Heston, Roddy McDowell, Kim Hunter and Maurice Evans and was based on a book by Pierre Boulle. Five movies were made in the series from 1968 to 1973. A live-action television show followed in 1974. The movies are still shown regularly on television, but the series has sunk into oblivion.

BANKS

Dr. Zaius, 16" brown plastic (A. J. Renzi 1974) $50.00
Cornelius, 16" brown plastic (A. J. Renzi 1974) 50.00
General Ursus, 16" brown plastic (A. J. Renzi 1974) . .50.00
Dr. Zaius, 11" painted plastic (Play Pal 1974) 35.00
Galen, 11" painted plastic (Play Pal 1974) 35.00

CHILDREN'S BOOKS

Planet of the Apes Cut and Color Book (Artcraft
    1974) 25.00
Planet of the Apes Activity Book (Artcraft 1974) two
    different, each 20.00
Planet of the Apes Coloring Book (Artcraft 1974)

three different, each 20.00
Planet of the Apes Picture Activity Album (Artcraft
  1974) 25.00

CLOTHING & ACCESSORIES

T-Shirts, new, any 20.00

Ties
Alexander Bolo Tie (Lee Belt Co. 1974) 35.00
Cornelius Bolo Tie (Lee Belt Co. 1974) 35.00
Dr. Zaius Bolo Tie (Lee Belt Co. 1974) 35.00
General Ursus Bolo Tie (Lee Belt Co. 1974) 35.00

Belts and Buckles
Alexander Belt & Belt Buckle (Lee Belt Co. 1974) 75.00
Cornelius Belt & Belt Buckle (Lee Belt Co. 1974) 75.00
Dr. Zaius Belt & Belt Buckle (Lee Belt Co. 1974) 75.00
General Ursus Belt & Belt Buckle (Lee Belt Co. 1974) .75.00

CRAFT & ACTIVITY

Mix & Molds (Catalog Shoppe 1974)
Dr. Zaius Mix 'n Mold kit, blue outfit picture 40.00
Dr. Zaius Mix 'n Mold kit, tan outfit picture 45.00
Galen Mix 'n Mold kit 45.00
General Urko Mix 'n Mold kit 45.00
Burke Urko Mix 'n Mold kit .60.00
Virdon Urko Mix 'n Mold kit 60.00

Planet of the Apes Colorforms Adventure Set
  (Colorforms 1974) 35.00
Planet of the Apes Color-Vue Pencil Coloring Set
  (Hasbro 1974) 65.00
Press N' Blow Bubbles (Hot Items Inc.) 65.00
Quick Draw Coloring Set (Pressman) 25.00
Quick Dray Cartoon set (Pressman) 25.00
Planet of the Apes Fun-Doh modeling molds
  (Chemtoy 1974) 15.00

DOLLS & FIGURES

Mego's 1973 figures are based on the movies, while the 1974 figures are from the television show. The show starred James Naughton as Peter Burke, Ron Harper as Alan Verdon, Roddy McDowell as Galen and Mark Lenard as General

Planet of the Apes figures (Mego 1974)

Urko. The 12" Hasbro dolls looked great at Toy Fair but had not yet appeared at press time.

8" Dolls (Mego 1973)
Cornelius, boxed 150.00
  Carded 90.00
Dr. Zaius, boxed 150.00
  Carded 90.00
Zira, boxed 120.00
  Carded 90.00
Soldier Ape, boxed 175.00
  Carded 90.00
Astronaut, boxed 180.00
  Carded 125.00

8" Dolls (Mego 1974)
Galen, boxed 120.00
  Carded 90.00
General Ursus, boxed 200.00
  Carded 90.00
General Urko, boxed 150.00
  Carded 90.00
Peter Burke, boxed 150.00
  Carded 90.00
Alan Verdon, boxed 150.00
  Carded 90.00
Dr. Zaius Sky Diving Parachutist (AHI) 25.00
Galen Sky Diving Parachutist (AHI) 25.00

12" dolls (Hasbro Signature 1998)
Cornelius (#70960) 25.00
Dr. Zaius (#70960) 25.00
General Ursus (#70962) *Beneath The Planet of
  the Apes* 25.00

5" Bend 'n Flex Figures (Mego 1974)
Astronaut Bend 'n Flex figure 50.00
Dr. Zaius Bend 'n Flex figure 35.00
Zira Bend 'n Flex figure 45.00
Galen Bend 'n Flex figure .35.00
Cornelius Bend 'n Flex figure 35.00
Soldier Ape Bend 'n Flex figure 35.00

Plush Figures
Galen Doll, 9" (Well Made Toys 1974) 50.00
Galen Doll, 12" (Well Made Toys 1974) boxed 100.00
Dr. Zaius Doll, 9" (Well Made Toys 1974) 50.00
Dr. Zaius Doll, 12" (Well Made Toys 1974) boxed 100.00
Galen Autograph Doll, 12" (CommonWealth Toy) 75.00
Dr. Zaius Autograph Doll, 12" (CommonWealth Toy) . . .75.00
Dr. Zaius 16" Stuffed Toy (Carnival Toys) 165.00
Galen 16" Stuffed Toy (Carnival Toys) 165.00
Galen Bean Bag Doll (CommonWealth Toy) 50.00
Dr. Zaius Bean Bag Doll (CommonWealth Toy) 50.00

Wind-up figures
Galen Wind-Up on Horse Back (AHI 1974) 85.00
Dr. Zaius Wind-Up on Horse Back (AHI 1974) 85.00
Galen Little Walker Wind-Up (AHI 1974) 85.00
Dr. Zaius Little Walker Wind-Up (AHI 1974) 85.00

Other figures
Galen Jointed Giant wall, 62" (Our Way 1974) 45.00
Dr. Zaius Hand Puppet (CommonWealth 1974) 40.00

FOOD

Planet of the Apes Candy & 2 Prizes (Phoenix 1974)
  Box #1, Gorilla 20.00

Planets of the Apes: Cornelius & Dr. Zaius (Hasbro 1998)

Box #2, Ape Family 20.00
Box #3, Dr. Zaius 20.00
Box #4, ...20.00
Box #5, Galen 20.00
Box #6, Caesar 20.00
Box #7, Lisa 20.00
Box #8, The Lawgiver .20.00

GAMES & PUZZLES

Games
Planet of the Apes board Game (Milton Bradley
    #4426, 1974) 50.00
Playset (Mattel 1974) 300.00
Planet of the Apes Ring Toss (Pressman 1974) 50.00
Planet of the Apes Spin 'N Color game (Pressman
    1973) 50.00
Pop N' Spin Target Set (Larami 1974) 35.00
Planet of the Apes Safety Dart Game (Transogram
    1974) 75.00
Planet of the Apes Target Game (Transogram 1974) . .75.00
Planet of the Apes Target Set (Multiple Toymaker 1974)40.00
Puzzles
Planet of the Apes 96 piece, 10" x 14" jigsaw
    puzzles (H.G. Toys 1974) boxed or canister
    Cornelius, Zira & Lucius 15.00
    General Aldo 15.00
    On Patrol 15.00
Planet of the Apes 500 piece, 16" x 20" jigsaw puzzles
    (H.G. Toys 1974) boxed
    Battle on Planet of the Apes 35.00
    The Chase 35.00
Dr. Zaius Poster-Puzzle, 9 sq. feet (Aurora 1974) 50.00
Galen Poster-Puzzle, 9 sq. feet (Aurora 1974) 50.00

HOUSEHOLD

Plate, Mug, Bowl and Cup set (Deka 1974) 75.00
Planet of the Apes Lunch Box (Aladdin 1974)
    steel lunchbox 125.00
    thermos, plastic 40.00
Wastebasket, short, oval, caged humans pictured
    (Cheinco 1974) 75.00
Wastebasket, tall, round, ape soldier and Statue of
    Liberty pictured (Cheinco 1974) 80.00
Planet of the Apes sleeping bag 100.00

MASKS & COSTUMES

Cornelius Mask (Don Post Studios 1974) 250.00
Dr. Zaius Mask (Don Post Studios 1974) 250.00
Gorilla Warrior Mask (Don Post Studios 1974) 250.00
Zira Mask (Don Post Studios 1974) 300.00
Cornelius Mask (Don Post Studios 1983) 150.00
Dr. Zaius Mask (Don Post Studios 1983) 150.00
General Aldo Mask (Don Post Studios 1983) 200.00
Gorilla Warrior Mask (Don Post Studios 1983) 150.00
Gorilla Mask (Illusive Concepts 1995) 35.00
Gorilla Guard Costume (Illusive Concepts 1995) 35.00

Halloween Costumes
Caesar Costume & Mask (Ben Cooper 1974) 35.00
Dr. Zaius Costume & Mask (Ben Cooper 1974) 35.00
Galen Costume & Mask (Ben Cooper 1974) 35.00
Lisa Costume & Mask (Ben Cooper 1974) 50.00
Warrior Costume (Ben Cooper 1974) 35.00
Dr. Zaius Mask (Ben Cooper 1974) 25.00
Galen Mask (Ben Cooper 1974) 25.00
Lisa Mask (Ben Cooper 1974) 35.00
Warrior Mask (Ben Cooper 1974) 25.00

MISCELLANEOUS

Frisbee (AHI 1974) 75.00
Planet of the Apes Inter-Planetary Ape Phones
    (Larami 1974) 25.00
Ball (Amsco) 45.00
Bike Reflector 25.00
Planet of the Apes Monkey Shines Flashlight
    (Larami 1974) 65.00
Planet of the Apes Periscope (Winner Promotions
    1974) 65.00
Planet of the Apes Chimp-Scope (Larami 1974) 35.00
Rings, Galen, Uirco, Zaius (Zira-Stanto Co. British)
    each 45.00
Silly Soap (Hot Items Inc. 1974) 25.00
Planet of the Apes Helicopter (AHI 1974) 35.00
Planet of the Apes kite (Hi-Flyer 1974) 35.00
Planet of the Apes Monkey Missiles (Larami 1974)
    three different, each 25.00
3-D Wall Plaque (Craft Writing 1974) 50.00

PAPER

Movie Lobby Cards
Planet of the Apes lobby card set of 8 . . . . .150.00
Beneath the Planet of the Apes lobby card set of 8 . .*100.00*
Escape from the Planet of the Apes lobby card set of 8 75.00
Conquest of the Planet of the Apes lobby card set of 8 75.00
Battle for the Planet of the Apes lobby card set of 8 . . .75.00

Movie Posters
Planet of the Apes One Sheet movie poster 150.00
Beneath the Planet of the Apes One Sheet movie
    poster 75.00
Escape from the Planet of the Apes One Sheet
    movie poster 50.00
Conquest of the Planet of the Apes One Sheet
    movie poster 50.00
Battle for the Planet of the Apes One Sheet movie
    poster 50.00

RECORDINGS

Books & Records
Planet of the Apes Book and Record Set, 45 rpm
    (Power Records PR-18, 1974) 25.00
Beneath the Planet of the Apes Book and Record
    Set, 45 rpm (Power Records PR-20, 1974) 25.00

Escape from the Planet of the Apes Book and
Record Set, 45 rpm (Power Records PR-19,
1974) 25.00
Battle for the Planet of the Apes Book and Record
Set, 45 rpm (Power Records PR-21, 1974) 25.00

Records

Planet of the Apes 4 Exciting Stories record, 45 rpm
(Power Records 8147, 1974) four movies 45.00
Planet of the Apes 4 Exciting Stories record, 45 rpm
(Power Records 8148, 1974) "Mountain of
the Delphi" 45.00
Planet of the Apes Mountain of the Death record,
45 rpm (Power Records F1289, 1974) 25.00
Planet of the Apes One Sheet movie sound track
record (Total Sound Stereo 1968) 50.00
Beneath the Planet of the Apes One Sheet movie
sound track record (Amos Records 1970) 75.00

View-Master

Planet of the Apes View-Master Reel set (GAF
1974) 40.00
Planet of the Apes Talking View-Master Reel set
(GAF 1974) 40.00

Film

Charlton Heston in *Planet of the Apes* Super 8 Film
(Ken Films 1974) 45.00
Beneath the Planet of the Apes Super 8 Film (Ken
Films 1974) 25.00
Escape from the Planet of the Apes Super 8 Film
(Ken Films 1974) 25.00
Battle for the Planet of the Apes Super 8 Film (Ken
Films 1974) 25.00
Conquest of the Planet of the Apes Super 8 Film
(Ken Films 1974) 25.00

Video

Movie laser disks (CBS/Fox) each 50.00
Movie video tapes (CBS/Fox) each 15.00

ROLE PLAY

Galen Water Gun (AHI 1974) 85.00
Zaius Water Gun (AHI 1974) 85.00
Fanner Gun (Mattel 1974) 125.00
Rapid Fire Gun with ape mask (Mattel 1974) 200.00
Tommy Burst Sub-Machine Gun with ape mask
(Mattel 1974) 250.00
Automatic Pellet Rifle (Larami 1974) three different
colors, each 75.00
Pellet Shooting Walkie Talkie (Larami 1974) 65.00

VEHICLES AND PLAYSETS

Planet of the Apes Treehouse playset (Mego 1973) . .160.00
Planet of the Apes Village playset (Mego #51925,
1973) 225.00
Planet of the Apes Action Stallion, battery
operated, remote control (Mego #51926, 1973) .125.00
Planet of the Apes Forbidden Zone Trap playset
(Mego 1974) 175.00
Planet of the Apes Fortress (Mego #50916, 1974) . . .200.00
Planet of the Apes Catapult and Wagon (Mego 1975) .45.00
Planet of the Apes Jail (Mego #50913, 1975) 50.00
Planet of the Apes Battering Ram (Mego Asst.
#50905, 1975) 32.00
Planet of the Apes Zaius' Throne (Mego Asst.
#50905, 1975) 35.00
Planet of the Apes Adventure Set, punch out

Predator Blade Fighter (Kenner 1994)

figures and village (Amsco 1974) boxed 150.00
Planet of the Apes mini-playset (Multiple Toymakers
1967) 60.00

PREDATOR

FIGURES

Predator die cast "Action Master" figure with trading
card (Ertl #62613, 1994) $5.00

MICRO MACHINES

1. Stealth Huey, Blain, Invisible Predator, Dutch,
Guerilla Troop Truck (#74853) 6.00
2. Camo Huey, Dillon, Predator, Billy, 4x4 Vehicle
(#74854) 6.00
3. Predator Spaceship, Anna, Predator,
Thermographic Dutch, Guerrilla Truck
(#74855) 6.00
Predator Transforming Action Set, Micro Machines
(Galoob #74817) 15.00

PAPER

Predator ministand-up (Comic Images DHM1385, 1994) 4.00
Predator (1987) one sheet movie poster 15.00

VEHICLE

Predator Blade Fighter in box (Kenner #65719, 1994) .14.00

RAYGUNS & WEAPONS

Let the young G.I. Joes of the world have their rifles and
pistols. Let the junior G-Men shoot it out with gangsters with
their tommy guns. Who cared if the Lone Ranger had two
guns and shot an outlaw's gun out of his hand with silver bul-
lets? With a trusty ray gun at his side, a young space hero
could conquer an entire universe of exotic monsters and
megalomaniac villains! Even better, while young earthbound
heroes could only kill their opponents or take them prisoner,
young space heroes could zap em or fry em or paralyze em
with sparks or colored light rays or sonic booms.

Positive identification of generic ray guns can be tricky.
I have tried to include the words which actually appear on the

Jack Dan Space Gun (Spanish 1960s)

gun, but anyone could use words like "Atomic," "Space," "Rocket," and "Cosmic" and manufacturers were trying to make their product look like other popular guns, so uncertainty can still exist.

Astro Ray Gun (Shudo 1970s) $50.00
Atomic Disintegrator Ray Gun (Hubley 1954) 500.00
Atomic Disintegrator Repeating Cap Pistol, 8", gun
    metal, red plastic handle (Hubley late 1940's) . .300.00
Atomic Flash Gun, blue & yellow tin litho (Chein 1955)125.00
Atomic Gun, tin litho, 9" (Haji 1952) 100.00
Atom Ray Gun, water pistol, red (Hiller 1949) 350.00
Black Ray Gun, plastic, battery powered, light up
    barrel, with holster (Tulio Proni 1970s) 150.00
Cherilea Space Gun, die-cast (Marx) 60.00
Cosmic Ray Gun (Ranger Steel Products 1954) 125.00
Dan Dare & The Aliens Ray Gun 225.00
Dan Dare Sparkling Ray Gun (Mettoy 1950's) 100.00
Dick Tracy Special Ray Gun (Larami 1964) 75.00
Electronic Space Gun (Remco 1960s) 150.00
Flashing Rocket Ship Space Pistol, 7" (Irwin, 1950's) .75.00
Flashy Ray Gun, B.O., 18" (TN 1950's) 125.00
Hamilton's Invaders Cap Firing Pistol, 13" (Remco
    1964) 75.00
Jack Dan Space Gun (Spanish 1960s 50.00
Johnny Apollo Space Pistol, 10" (Marx 1970) 90.00
Ratchet Sound Space Gun (Ideal 1950s) 75.00
Rocket Dart Pistol, tin litho, red body, blue handle
    and barrell tip (Daisy 1940s) 150.00
Space Gun with Boing Sound, 7" (All Nu Metal
    Prod. 1950s) 75.00
Space Navigator Gun, tin (Asahitoy 1953) 100.00
Space Outlaw Ray Gun, die-cast (B.C.M. 1965) 400.00
Space Outlaw Automatic Pistol, Cap Firing, 10"
    (B.C.M. 1950's) 100.00
Space Rocket Gun, 8" (M & L Toy Co. 1950's) 75.00
Space Ship Flashlight Gun (Irwin 1950s) 150.00
Sparking Atom Buster Pistol (Marx) 75.00
Super Site Magic Buller Space Gun, 9" (20th Cent.
    Prod. 1950s) 75.00
Super Sonic Space Gun, silver tin litho with red
    details, astronaut picture on handle (Daiya
    1960s) 75.00
Zooka Pop Pistol (Daisy 1930s) 175.00

Lightsabers (Parks Lightsabers 1997) unlicensed
Rogue Lightsaber 65.00
Shadow Lightsaber 120.00
Magnum Lightsaber 120.00
Alliance Lightsaber 120.00
Abaddon Jedi Knight leather belt 90.00

Blaster (Parks Lightsabers 1997) generic
Sterling Blaster 325.00

REX MARS

MISCELLANEOUS

Rex Mars Planet Patrol Space Cruiser Flag (1952) . .$50.00

ROLE PLAY

Rex Mars Planet Patrol Sparkling Space Gun, 21"
    (Marx 1950's) 2000.00
Rex Mars Planet Patrol Sparkling Pistol, 5" plastic,
    red (Marx 1950's) 125.00
Rex Mars Atomix Pistol Flashlight (Marx 1950s) 100.00
Rex Mars Planet Patrol Machine Gun (Marx 1950s) . .150.00

VEHICLES & PLAYSETS

Rex Mars Planet Patrol playset (Marx #7040) 500.00
Rex Mars Space Drome Patrol playset (Marx
    #7016, 1954) 600.00
Rex Mars Planet Patrol Space Tank (Marx 1950s) . . .150.00
Rex Mars Sparkling Tank, 10" long, tin litho (Marx
    1950s) 250.00

ROBOTECH

DOLLS

11½" Dolls (1986) in window box
Lynn Minmei in Chinese dress $30.00
Lisa Hayes (#5102) in dress uniform 30.00
Dana Sterling in flight uniform 30.00
Rick Hunter in flight uniform 40.00

OUTFITS

Fashion Outfits carded
Exercise Outfit (#5201) 12.00
Star Disguise (#5202) 12.00
Street Clothes (#5203) 12.00
Party Dress (#5204) 12.00
Nightgown (#5205) 12.00
Stage Dress (#5251) 12.00
Fancy Dress Clothes (#5252) male 12.00

Robotech Invid Shock Trooper Battle Pod, back (Matchbox 1986)

Miss Macross Outfit (#5253) 12.00
Evening Gown (#5254) 12.00
Fashion Accessories Pack .12.00

ROLE PLAY
Robotech Water Pistol (Matchhbox 1985) 15.00

VEHICLES & PLAYSETS
Vehicles and Accessories for 12" figure
Dana's Hover Cycle (#5410) 30.00

Vehicles for 3¾" Figures
Armoured Cyclone (#7351) 20.00
Bioroid Hover Craft (#7352) 14.00
Veritech Fighter 40.00
Veritech Hover Tank 32.00
Battle Pods for 3¾" Figures
Tactical Battle Pod (#7254) 30.00
Invid Shock Trooper (#7258?) 30.00
Zentraedi Officer's Battle Pod (#7259) 30.00

Playset for 3¾" Figures
SDF-1 Action Playset 135.00

ROBOTS

The term robot was first used in Karl Capek's play *R.U.R.* with stands for Rossum's Universal Robots. In Fritz Lang's famous science fiction silent movie, *Metropolis*, a robot was changed into a android copy of the heroine, Maria, to lead the workers astray. Robots were popular villains in the science fiction pulp magazines, where a young Isaac Asimov worked out his famous "three rules of robotics" and the implications of trying to program a robot to apply them rigorously. The first two famous movie robots were Gort from *The Day the Earth Stood Still* and Robby, from *Forbidden Planet*.

While all of the above is true, it was actually the tin litho robots from the 1950s which captured the attention of most people. There are hundreds of different ones, mostly Japanese in origin and every child of the 1950s had one. There were no action figures yet and no self respecting boy would have anything to do with dolls, but tin men were obviously not dolls. They walked, they made neat mechanical noises, they shot projectiles and they were colorful. They are still all of the above, plus they are expensive. The prices below are for robots in working condition, with the original box. Most kids then threw away the box and played with their robot until it quit working. Today, many of them are little capitalists and save things like baseball cards in the hopes of making a killing later. They won't, because too many of them are doing it.

Atomic Robot Man, tin litho olive and grey boiler
    plate with gauges and diecast hands
    (Kitahara #81, 1950s) $1,250.00
Attacking Martian Robot, brown tin, red tin feet,
    green plastic designs on chest doors, walks
    with swinging arms, stops as chest doors
    open to reveal lifted and firing guns, action
    repeats, battery operated (S-H Company
    1950s) 450.00
Big Loo Robot (Marx 1962) 2,500.00
Big Max Robot, all plastic, electromagnetic with
    conveyor belt, loads truck with magnetic
    hands, battery operated, remote control

Atomic Robot Man (Kitahara 1950s)

(Remco 1958) 300.00
Billy Blastoff-Space Scout, plastic Robbie robot,
    radioactive retrieval wagon, TV camera, etc,
    Robbie walks, drives and pushes (Eldon
    1960's) 150.00
Blazer-Superhero Robot, tin litho in red, yellow, blue,
    and black, with plastic arms and movable
    heads, wind-up (Bullmark 1960's) 200.00
Blink-A-Gear Robot, black with green blinking eyes,
    clear chest panel reveals multi- colored gears
    which rotate, walks forward with blinking
    lights and machine sound (S-H Co. 1960's) . .1,100.00
Busy Cart Robot, black and yellow with yellow
    hardhat, stop and go action, pushes
    wheelbarrow, raises arms, dump contents,
    then lowers cart and arms. Battery operated
    (Horikawa Company 1960's) 370.00
Captain Astro 85.00
Captain Future Superhero Robot, tin litho with large
    "G" on belt, vinyl cape and extension piece
    on helmet, walks forward with swinging arm
    movement, wind-up (Japan 1960's) 135.00
Chime Trooper Tin litho in grey, red, silver, and
    yellow, white helmet with boy's face, wheels
    forward as music chimes, Keywound (Aoshin) 2,750.00
Chief Robotman (K.O. Company 1950's) 800.00
Colonel Hap Hazard, white NASA suited with
    whirling helicopter blades, walks forward with
    moveable arms, battery operated (Marx 1968) 1,100.00
Combatler-Superhero Robot, tin litho in blue and
    gray with red, yellow and black highlights,
    walks forward with animated arms in unison,
    movable head with horns, wind-up (Bullmark
    1960's) 185.00
Cragstan's Mr. Robot, red and black tin, with
    colorful tin litho chest, spinning lights inside
    clear domed head, bump and go action, with
    free swinging arms, battery operated (Y
    Company 1960's) 850.00

Busy Cart Robot (Horikawa 1960s)

Cragstan Talking Robot, tin litho in red, domed
head with winged ears, broadcasts four
messages as he walks, battery operated (Y
Company 1960's) 900.00
Cragstan Red Astronaut (Daiya) Tin litho, Walks,
stops raises guns and fires, battery operated
(Y Company) 2,900.00
Daiya Astronaut with childs head, similar to red
astronaut, tin litho in blue, red, silver &
cream, battery operated 1,700.00
Dino Robot, black tin plate and plastic, walks
forward head folds down to reveal roaring
dinosaur with lighted mouth (S-H Company
1960's) 1,000.00
Directional Robot, blue/grey finish with swivel head,
"Mystery Action," consists of toy changing
direction on collision (Kitahara #42) 1,000.00
Dux Astroman Green plastic with white head with
red features, transparent green lucite body
reveals mechanism and lights, walks forward,
lifts arms, and bends at waist, remote control,
battery operated (West Germany) 2,400.00
Dynamic Fighter Robot (Junior Toy Company
1960's) 130.00
Electric Robot, black, red and gray skirted plastic,
antenna and control knob, separate controls
for left and right arms, Morse code button,
forward/reverse motion as well as left/right,
head turns and eyes light, sliding tool drawer
compartment in chest (Marx 1950's) 400.00
Engine Robot, grey with clear chest panel revealing
gears, eyes and dome on head light up,
battery operated (Horikawa) 160.00
Excavator Robot (S-H Company 1960's) 160.00
Fighting Robot, dark grey arms and legs, red shoes,
battery operated (S-H Company 1960s) 175.00
Fighting Space Man, dark grey arms and legs, red
feet, yellow light on head, battery operated
(S-H Company 1960s) 175.00
Flashy Jim-The Robot, silver tin with R7 on chest in
red, yellow, and blue, many embossed
details, while walking, mouth and eyes glow

(ACE 1950's) 950.00
Forklift Robot, yellow and red plastic with forklift
platform, walks forward stops, lift up
container and walks, then stops and unloads
his cargo (Horikawa) 2,400.00
Gear Robot, gray tin with red tin feet, gray plastic
arms, tin litho chest plate under clear plastic
shell, yellow and pink gears, walks (Y
Company 1960's) 480.00
Golden Roto Robot, tin litho and plastic, body rotates
360 degrees, shoots, sound, lights, battery
operated (S-H Company 1960's) 265.00
Getter One-Superhero Robot, tin litho in red,
yellow, blue and black, walks forward with
animated arms in unison, head is movable,
wind up (Bullmark 1960's) 185.00
High Bouncer Moon Scout Tin silver astronaut with
American flag litho on chest, walks forward,
chest opens and shoots "High Bouncer" balls,
remote control, battery operated (Marx) 2,400.00
High-Wheel Robot, red tin feet, blue tin body, red
plastic hands, clear plastic chest plate
reveals plastic gears, telescopic antenna, tin
litho oxygen tank and dials (KO 1950's) 475.00
The Hysterical Robot, battery operated (Straco
1960s) 300.00
Interplanetary Space Fighter (Nomura) tin Litho
vehicle with retractable side fins, spaceman
shooting swiveling gun 395.00
Interplanetary Robot (Y Company 1960's) 240.00
Japanese Robot Warrior, plastic, carries weapon in
each hand, attached by chain, walks forward
(ST 1960's) 80.00
Jupiter Robot, orange, lights in transparent lucite
dome, chest with inset stamped lithographed
tubes and circuitry, legs operate indepen-
dently, battery operated (Yonezawea 1950's) .2,750.00
Lavender Robot, tin litho in lavender, machinery
and gauges, lightup eyes and mouth, battery
operated 4,900.00
Lunar Robot 650.00
Lunar Spaceman (1978) 45.00
Magnor (Cragstan 1975) 50.00
Man From Mars, plastic, mechanical shooting
(Irvwin 1960's) 50.00
Mars Explorer Robot (S-H Company 1950's) 450.00
Mars King Robot No. 12101 (S-H Company 1960's) . .490.00
Martian Robot (SJM Company 1970's) 130.00
Mechanic Robot, tin and plastic, stop and go action,
rotating body, blinking gears, sound (space
noise) battery operated (Y Company 1960's) . . .130.00
Mechanical Atom Robot, silver, red, blue, crank lever
operation erratic movements (KO 1950's) 265.00
Mechanical Robot, light blue with red accents, many
embossed details, free swinging arms, coil
antenna, keywound, walks with aid of wire
frame (Kitahara #89) 2,000.00
Mechanical Missile Robot, silver plastic body, walks
forward, two missiles attached to chest can
be fired with lever on back, key wound (TPS
1960's) 95.00
Mechanical Moon Creature (Marx) 250.00
Mechanical Moon Robot, dark grey and red with pink
domed head, containing swirling multi-color
metal ribbons, red spark window, keywound
(Yonezawa) 6,000.00
Mechanical Television Spaceman (ALPS) 100.00

Mighty Robot, red tin with litho gauges, grey plastic head with red features, walks forward and lowers and raises arm as if flexing biceps, key wound (K-O Company 1960's) 505.00

Mighty Robot, grey/blue tin with litho *Mighty Robot* on chest, red plastic arms, clear plastic head with flashing lights, turns in other direction on collision (Yoshiya) 1,750.00

Mighty 8 Robot, grey body with kaleidoscope circular window that lights in many colors as it walks forward (Masudaya) 2,200.00

Missile Man, light grey with dark grey and red highlights, satellite disc antenna, five-missile silo which emerges from a hinged chest panel (Boogaerts, #260) 1,300.00

Mr. Atom The Electronic Walking Robot, large 17" tin body and feet with plastic head and arms, swinging arms, moving head, lights, buzzing noises, "sends" code with signal button, batteries (Advance 1950's) 795.00

Mr. Atomic (Cragstan 1950's) 1,500.00

Mr. Chief Robot (K-O Co. 1950's) 1,200.00

Mr. Hustler Robot (Taiyo Co. 1960's) 300.00

Mr. Machine (Ideal 1960) 265.00

Mr. Mercury, tin body, red feet, grey plastic arms and hands, walks and bends over, raises arms and legs, battery operated, remote control (Linemar 1950's) 875.00

Mr. Robot The Mechanical Brain, silver tin body with dark pink leg markings, pink and black eyes and mouth, lights in hand flash while walking, unusual battery size (Alps 1950's) 1,700.00

Moon Explorer Robot (Bandai 1960's) 1,100.00

Moon Explorer Robot, red and black tin, tin litho face under clear plastic helmet, red "claw" hands, walks with crank action (KO 1950's) 1,500.00

Moon Explorer, red with black accents, Robby style robot, keywound(Yoshiya) 425.00

New Astronaut Robot, brown plastic with orange tinted guns, stop and go action, blinking lights, rotating body, shooting guns with sound battery operated (S-H Company 1970's) 150.00

Non-Stop Robot (see Lavender Robot) 4,900.00

Outer Space Ape Man Robot (Ilco) 30.00

Piston Robot (S-H Company 1960's) 240.00

Planet Robot, mostly tin with red plastic hands, walks, sparks, battery operated (KO 1960's) ...150.00

Planet Robot, black tin, red plastic hands and feet, 12" wind up (KO 1957) 150.00

Planet Robot, light blue with red, metal claws, grid face dome, remote control, battery operated (Yoshiya) 2,750.00

R-35 Robot, litho boiler plate finish with bucket shaped head, moves backwards and forwards, eyes light up, remote control battery box lithographed with various robot figures (M-T Company 1960's) 1,200.00

Radical Robot, blue with white head, maroon arms, light-up eyes, green grid on chest, battery operated (Boogaerts #117) 1,800.00

Radicon Robot, grey textured tin gauge and light inset in chest, light-up eyes, forwards and backwards motion, turning head, Advertised as first and only complete radio remote control robot with a wireless remote control, battery operated (Masudaya) 6,000.00

Radar Robot, grey, carries dish and coil antennas, and wrench, remote control, battery operated (T-N Company 1960's) 2,600.00

Radar Robot (S-H Company 1970's) 145.00

Ranger Robot, plastic with red tin feet, see-through body, gray arms, walks with moving arms, visible gears in chest, smoking action, "voice" sound, clear red battery box (Cragstan 1950's) 580.00

Ranger Robot, clear plastic body with gray arms (in shape of a wrench) tin legs, walks with swinging arms, sound and smoke, battery operated (Daiya Company 1950's) 1,300.00

R-8 Sparking Robot, tin litho in blue with R on one shoulder, 8 on the other, sparking eyes, key wound 795.00

Remote Control Piston Action Robot, Robby style robot, gold upper body, dark blue legs, moveable arms, clear plastic dome battery operated, remote control (Nomura) 2,750.00

Robot (Y Company 1960's) 900.00

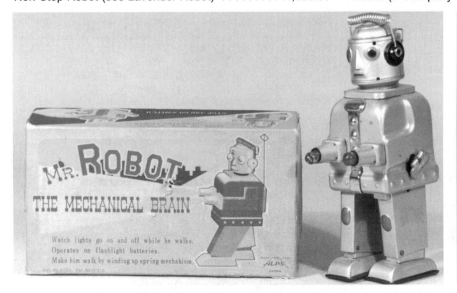

Mr. Robot the Mechanical Brain (Alps 1950s) and Man From Mars (Irwin 1960s)

Robot Commando, molded plastic with "searching eyes", left/right turning action, walks forward, head dome rises, fires rockets and throws balls, battery operated (Ideal 1961) 480.00

Robot 2500, plastic with some steel, blinking lighted eye, flashing chest light, moving arms and legs, battery operated (Durham Ind. 1970's) . . .120.00

Robot ST-1, silver and red simple boiler plate style with coil and diamond shaped antenna, battery operated (Strenco, Germany) 1,250.00

Robot Tank II 325.00

Rock'em-Sock'em Robots (Marx 1961) 185.00

Rocket Man in Space Armor, plastic head opens to reveal astronaut head, with two spring loaded rockets mounted on the back, remote control, battery operated (Rosko Toy by Alps) 3,000.00

Rotate-O-Matic Super Astronaut, tin lithograph with Astronaut face behind plastic visor, stop and go rotating action, chest doors open to reveal blinking, shooting guns, sound, battery operated (SH 1960's) 80.00

Rotate O Matic Robot, colorful tin litho and plastic body, chest doors open to reveal blinking, shooting guns, sound, battery operated (SH 1960's) 80.00

R-1 Robotank, blue-grey tin litho with red eyes and metal hands, swinging arms as it walks forward, two guns come out of body and fire with flash and sound, guns stop firing and retreat back into robot, battery operated (Nomura) 1,100.00

Rudy The Robot, all-plastic orange and yellow with paper decals, walks, moving legs and arms, reverses automatically on collision (Remco 1968) 295.00

Rusher Robot, gray plastic with tin litho, black rubber wheels in chest act as mechanism spin wheels and robot rushes forward, siren sound (SH 1960's) .240.00

Shogun Warrior Robot, tin litho bright colors, plastic head, movable arms and head, wind-up (Tamara 1960's) 150.00

Smoking Robot (M-T Company 1960's) 170.00

Smoking Spaceman, grey tin with red feet, walks forward throwing sparks, pause breathes out smoke and flashes eyes battery operated (Linemar) 2,750.00

Space Commando Robot, 7½" tin litho "boy" with plastic feet, rifle and two tanks on back, walks with swinging arms (TN 1950's) 500.00

Space Dog, tin litho in red or silver, spark window, flapping jaws and ears, spring tail and rolling eyes, friction drive (Yoshiya) 1,100.00

Space Explorer Dark grey or red, square form initially resembles a TV set, raises to reveal head, arms and a 3-D TV screen, battery operated (Yonezawa) 1,100.00

Space Fighter Robot, plastic and tin with tin litho face walks forward with bouncing movement, stops chest doors open to reveal shooting guns with lights and sound (S-H Company 1970's) 145.00

Space Giant Robot, charcoal grey with red accents, head and waist turn, chest doors open to reveal guns (Horikawa) 185.00

Space Patrol Robot, gray & red tin, tin litho astronaut face behind plastic visor, green tinted

Super Astronaut Robot (S-H Company 1960s)

plastic plates on chest, walks with swinging arms, chest opens to reveal firing guns with sound, battery operated (S-H Co. 1950's) 240.00

Space Robot Trooper (K-O Co. 1950's) 795.00

Space Robot X-70 (T-N Co. 1960's) 1,250.00

Spaceman Robot (T-N Company 1950's) 770.00

Spaceman Robot (Linemar 1950's) 555.00

Sparkling Mike the Robot (Ace Company 1950's) . .1,500.00

Sparky Robot, tin litho with red insert plastic chest window for sparks (SY 1950's) 345.00

Star Strider Robot, red with gray highlights, walks forward and stops, chest doors swing open to reveal firing guns with sound (Horikawa) 210.00

Star Strider Robot, blue with gray highlights, walks forward and stops, chest doors swing open to reveal firing guns with sound (Horikawa) 210.00

Super Astronaut Robot, tin body and feet with plastic head and arms, litho on chest, stop and go action, chest doors swing open, blinking, firing guns, realistic sound (S-H Company 1960's) 260.00

Super Giant Robot (S-H Company 1960's) 285.00

Super Hero Robot, tin litho with colorful and movable vinyl head, walks forward with swinging arms (ST 1960's) 135.00

Swil-O-Matic Astronaut Robot (S-H Company 1960's) 185.00

Swinging Baby Robot, tin litho toy with tin litho swinging robot, comes with base and two-sided litho sign to be attached to top of swing (Yonezawa 1950's) 240.00

Target Robot, purple with red target on chest, charges forward shooting darts, striking target causes robot to stop, turn around, robot then reverses and attacks (Masudaya) . .7,000.00

Television Spaceman Gray tin body with white plastic hands, tin litho chest plate, walks forward with swinging arms, space scenes on TV screen in chest, battery operated (Alps 1950's) .370.00

Thunder Robot, brown with red feet, conical shaped body with rotating helicopter blades on head, arms stretch forward to reveal guns as robot walks, blinking eyes, battery operated (Asakusa) 9, 900.00

Tin Man Robot (Remco 1960's) 285.00
Turn Signal Robot (T-N Co. 1960's) 410.00
Train Robot (Also known as Sonic Robot) one of
    "The Gang of Four Robots" comprised of
    Radicon, Target, Train & Lavender, Tin litho
    in red with black head, one red and one
    green eye, walks forward eyes lighting up,
    siren sound (Masadaya) 5,500.00
Tetsuwan Atom (The Mighty Atom or Astro Boy) Tin
    litho body with vinyl head, remote control,
    battery operated 1,750.00
Tremendous Mike The Robot, blue/grey tin plate
    with red arms, blue face plate with red
    features and clear red panel in chest, key
    wound (Aoshin) 1,300.00
Ultra 7-Superhero Robot, tin litho in orange, gray,
    black, and gold, with movable vinyl head,
    walks forward with swinging arms (Bullmark
    19??) 185.00
Uran (younger sister of Tesuwan Atom) Tin litho
    with vinyl head, keywound 1,300.00
Video Robot, tin litho and plastic, walks as scenes
    of the moon appear on chest screen, battery
    operated (S-H Company 1960's) 155.00
Vision Robot (S-H Company 1960's) 330.00
Walking Robot, tin litho in silver with black, white,
    and red highlights, free swinging arms,
    keywound (Linemar 1950's) 480.00
Walking Robot, tin litho in silver with red, black,
    white and yellow highlights, many embossed
    details, free swinging arms, battery operated
    and remote control (Yonezawa 1950's) 555.00
Walking Robot With Spark, colorful tin litho with red
    plastic insert chest window for spark, key
    wound (SY 1950's) 395.00
Wheel-A-Gear Robot, rare version of Blinka Gear
    robot with belt driven gears, large antenna on
    back (Taiyo Co. 1960's) 1,500.00
X-27 Explorer Robot, tin litho in blue and red,
    jointed arms, keywound (Yonezawa) 2,750.00
X-70 Robot, purple tin body with silver highlights,
    red tin feet, Tulip head unfolds to reveal
    yellow and blue interior, walks with flashing
    light and sound (T-N Company 1960's) 2,500.00
Yakkity Yob, turquoise and red plastic, manually
    operated, movable arms, eyes and feet, can
    pick up objects (Eldon 1960's) 320.00
Zerak the Blue Destroyer Zeroid (Ideal 1968) 175.00
Zoomer The Robot, light blue finish with coil
    antenna, retractable backpack antenna, stop
    and go action, clutches wrench in right hand,
    eyes light up (T-N Co. 1950's) 1,100.00

ROCKY JONES, SPACE RANGER

Rockey Jones appeared on television for the 1953–55 seasons. The show was broadcast live and it was, and is, considered inferior to *Captain Video* and *Tom Corbett*.

CHILDREN'S BOOKS

Rocky Jones, Space Ranger coloring book, cockpit
    cover (Whitman 1951) $50.00
Rocky Jones, Space Ranger coloring book, Moon
    scene cover (Whitman 1953) 60.00

ROLE PLAY

Rocky   Jones   Official   Space   Ranger   Wings

(pinback) (Space Ranger Ent. 1950s) 50.00
Rocky Jones Space Ranger Membership pinback
    (Silvercup Bread) 50.00
Rubber Band Gun, cardboard (1954) 50.00
Litho buttons 25.00
Wrist Watch, boxed (1954) .200.00
Space Ranger Inter-Planet Space Wallet set,
    including badge, money and secret code card
    (Space Ranger Ent. 1950s) 100.00

SPACE: 1999

From the syndicated television series starring Martin Landau and Barbara Bain with Barry Morse. The series ran for two years and produced a number of fine collectibles.

DOLLS

9" Dolls (Mattel 1976)
Commander Koenig $70.00
Doctor Russell 70.00
Professor Bergman 70.00
Zython 150.00

CRAFT & ACTIVITY

Space: 1999 Colorforms Adventure set (Colorforms
    1976) 25.00
Space: 1999 Stamping set (1976) 15.00
Cut and Color book (Saalfield 1975) 25.00
Space: 1999 Coloring book #C1881 (Saalfield) 10.00

GAMES & PUZZLES

Space: 1999 board game (Milton Bradley 1975) 25.00
Space: 1999 jigsaw puzzle (H.G. Toys 1976) 20.00

HOUSEHOLD

Space: 1999 Lunch Box (King-Seeley Thermos 1976)
    steel box 35.00
    thermos (plastic) 15.00
Chestpack/AM radio 50.00
Color TV & Stamp set 15.00
Galaxy Time Meter (1976) 15.00

MISCELLANEOUS

Eagle Transport, die-cast metal/plastic red and white
    (Dinky #359, 1975) 100.00

Space: 1999 Lunchbox (King-Seeley Thermos 1976)

Eagle One Transporter with nuclear waste canisters, green & white (Dinky #360, 1975) 150.00
Space: 1999 Adventure Playset, punch-out (Amsco 1976) 65.00
Space: 1999 View-Master Reel set (GAF 1975) 20.00
Space: 1999 Talking View-Master Reel set (GAF 1975) 40.00
Color TV movies 15.00
Film Viewer TV Set (1976) 50.00
Wrist watch/roll viewer with 2 rolls (L-Toys) 15.00

ROLE PLAY

Stun Gun flashlight 30.00
Utility belt with disk shooting stun gun space radiation detector & watch compass (Remco 1976) 80.00
Rocket gun 15.00
Space: 1999 Superscope (1976) 15.00
Space Expedition Dart Set 15.00
Astro Popper Gun (Bradley 1976) carded 25.00

VEHICLES & ACCESSORIES

Moonbase Alpha Control Room & Launch Monitor Center (Mattel 1976) .90.00
Eagle 1 Spaceship with 3" action figures of John Koenig, Dr. Russell and Prof. Bergman (Mattel 1976) 275.00

SPACE PATROL

Space Patrol ran from 1950 to 1955, mostly on ABC. It starred Ed Kemmer as Commander Buzz Corey and Lyn Osborn as Cadet Happy, plus some villains and love interests. It might have been called "Time Patrol" because its heroes made much use of time travel. The early 1950s was also the era of *Captain Video* and *Tom Corbett*, which were slightly better shows, and of *Rocky Jones*, which was a lot worse.

MISCELLANEOUS

Cosmic Cap $300.00
Cosmic Rocket Launcher Set 750.00
Space Patrol Drink Mixer, red and yellow (United Plastics 1950s) 150.00
Space Patrol Handbook 145.00
Interplanetary Space Patrol Credits, each 25.00
Space Patrol Lunar Fleet Base (Ralston Purina premium 1950s) 2,500.00
Man From Mars Totem Head Mask (Ralston Purina premium 1950s) 165.00

Monorail Set (Toys of Tomorrow) 4,000.00
Non-Fall Space Patrol X-16 (Matsudaya) 250.00
Space Patrol Periscope 150.00
Space Patrol Microscope, green/black plastic plus instructions in box (Ralston Purina premium 1950s) 250.00
Space Patrol Terra IV Puzzle, frame tray (Milton Bradley 1950s) 95.00
Space Patrol Coin Album (1950s) 125.00
Space Patrol Stamp, Coin & Ball Point Pen set (1950s) 50.00
Parallo-Ray ring, plastic (Kellogg's cereal premium 1950s) 125.00
Space Patrol Giant Balloon, 36" with picture of space ship (Ralston Purina premium) 75.00
Rocket Port Set (Marx) 300.00
Rocket-Shaped Pen 275.00
Space Patrol Terra V Project-O-Scope, 5½" yellow rocket with blue nose & fins plus film strip (Ralston Purina 1950s) premium 250.00

ROLE PLAY

Ray Guns
Official Space Patrol Atomic Pistol Flashlite, 8" long, gold plastic (Marx 1950s) 200.00
Space Patrol Cosmic Smoke Gun, 5" green, long barrel premium (Ralston Purina premium 1950's) 600.00
Space Patrol Cosmic Smoke Gun, red plastic, short barrel (1950s) 275.00
Hydrogen Ray Gun Ring, glow-in-the-dark (Ralston Purina premium 1950s) 250.00
Official Space Patrol Rocket Gun, red dart gun with 2 darts and Holster set (U.S. Plastic Co. 1951) 450.00
Official Space Patrol Rocket Lite flashlight, 12" tall space ship design (Ray-O-Vac 1950s) boxed . . .350.00
Auto-Sonic rifle 800.00
Official Space Patrol Dart Gun, 10" (U.S. Plastics 1950's) 325.00

Other Role Play items
Space Patrol Outer Space Plastic Helmet, 37" circumfrence (Toys of Tomorrow Ltd. 1952) 350.00
Space Patrol Binoculars, green plastic (Ralston Purina 1950s) store version 275.00
Space Binoculars, black plsatic, 5" long (Ralston Purina premium 1950s) 175.00
Space Patrol Compass (1951) 60.00
Space Patrol Commander Helmet 350.00
Official Space Patrol Jet-Glow Code Belt and

Space Patrol Walkie-Talkie Space-A-Phones (ZVC Co./Ralston Purina premium 1950s)

decoder, 23" long, plastic belt attached to
brass space rocket ship, spinning decoder on
back (Ralston Purina premium 1950s) 275.00
Space Patrol Emergency Kit, includes flashlight . . .1,500.00
Space Patrol Wristwatch 650.00
Space Patrol Space-A-Phones, 4" x 3" x 1" box
(ZVC Co./Ralston Purina premium 1950s) 400.00
Space Patrol Badge, metal oval 500.00
Space Patrol Badge, plastic 175.00
Space Patrol Cadet Membership Card 50.00

SPACE SHIPS

The listing below includes generic rocket ships and
space ships which do not relate to any particular movie or
show. The most popular space ships did belong to shows, so
these are not as highly valued as collectibles. They are not as
valuable as robots from the same era either. In addition to
rocket ships and spaceships, there were a number of other
space vehicles such as space tanks and space trains. These are
listed above under MISCELLANEOUS.

Aero Jet Range Rocket, 11" tall plastic rocket with
energy pellets (Ranger Steel 1950s) $70.00
Astro Sound Rocket Talking Space Toy, plastic,
22" x 10" box (Hasbro 1969) 35.00
Astro Sound Satellite Talking Space Toy, plastic,
22" x 10" box (Hasbro 1969) 35.00
Atomic Rocket X201, with Prop, 7½" tin litho,
frision powered (MT 1960s) 75.00
Dan Dare Space Ship with Jetex Rocket Motor,
wooden ship with plastic and metal parts in
4" x 5" x 20" box (Eagle 1950s) 35.00
Docking Rocket, 16" long, battery operated,
revolving radar antenna (Daiya 1960s) 75.00
Explorer Rocket Ship, friction powered (1950s) 50.00
Fire Rocket X-0077, friction powered (Yonezawa
1950s) 150.00
Flying Saucer Z-101, tin litho in red, yellow and blue,
friction powered (MT 1950s) 75.00
Flying Saucers & Launcher Gun, 5" long (Premiere
1950s) 30.00
Getter One Rocket Ship, 13" long, plastic pilots,
multi-colored tin litho rocket (MT) 75.00
High Speed Rocket "The Moon ZX-8", 9" long,
sparkling, tin litho (Marusan 1950s) 90.00
Interplanetary Rocket, plastic and tin litho, 15" long
(Yonezawa 1960s) 75.00

Atomic Rocket X201 with Prop (MT 1960s)

Space Ship X-8 (Tada 1950s)

Interplanetary Space Fighter V-7 Super Jet, 12" long,
tin litho with antenna, retractable wings, and
astronaut with gun, battery operated (TN 1950s) 225.00
Interplanetary Spaceship Atom Rocket-15, 13"
plastic (Yonezawa) 75.00
Johnny & Jane Apollo Space Expedition, battery
operated space vehicle with Johnny & Jane
inside Space Buggy with meteorite shield,
28" x 8" x 10" box (Marx 1968) 150.00
Jumping Rocket, tin litho, with driver (SY 1950s) 175.00
Jupiter Rocket JP 7A, 9½" long friction powered, tin
litho (Masuda 1950s) 60.00
King "Space Patrol" Flying Saucer X-081, 7½" dia-
meter, tin litho, with lights and sound (KO 1950s)100.00
Lunar-1 Two Stage Moon Rocket Alpha 1, 17" tall
(Scientific Product 1950s) 75.00
Marxman Skyro Space Ship, 8" long (1950s) 25.00
Mechanical Rocket Express, 5½" x 5" (Linemar
1950s) 125.00
Moon Rocket #3, 7" long, friction powered, with
lithoed pilot (MT 1950s) 125.00
NASA Columbia Spacecraft, tin litho and plastic,
13" x 10" box (EGE) 75.00
Non-Fall Moon Rocket, 9" long, tin litho, battery
powered (MT) 90.00
Rocket Fighter, 12" long, tin litho with pilot and gun
(Marx 1950s) 100.00
Rocket Ship Kit, 10" x 13" paper (Hallmark Toy
Card 1950s) 35.00
Round Race Rocket, mechanical, tin litho (Ashitoy
1950s) 110.00
Sky Patrol Flying Saucer, 7" diameter, battery
operated, tin litho with clear plastic dome and
blinking lights (K 1950s) 50.00
Sky Rocket with Tetsujin robot, friction powered,
11" x 22" (Bandai) 225.00
Spacecraft Jupiter with Spark, 4½" diameter,
mechanical wind-up tin litho, with astronaut
under plastic dome (K 1950s) 60.00
Space Explorer flying saucer, with astronaut in
domed cockpit (Baravelli 1960s) 150.00
Space Frontier Rocket, 18" long Saturn 5 rocket,
battery operated, tin litho, astronaut with TV
camera pops up from hatch (KY 1960s) 150.00
Space Patrol 3, 8" diameter, tin litho, with astronaut
(KO 1950s) 60.00
Space Patrol vehicle, 9" long, tin litho, battery
operated (K 1950s) 110.00
Space Rocket Apollo 11, plastic, battery powered
(TN 1960s) 65.00
Space Rocket Ship No. 306, 5" long, tin litho
(Automatic Toy Co. 1950s) 60.00

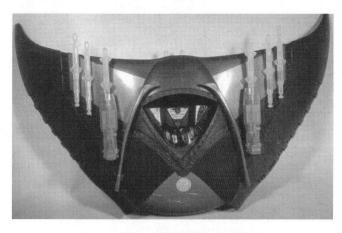

StargateWinged Glider (Hasbro 1994)

Space Ship X-8, 8" long, battery operated, tin litho
    with clear plastic dome and green plastic
    engine cover (Tada 1950s) 90.00
Spacecraft, 6½" long, friction powered (Linemar
    1950s) 60.00
Spacecraft SP-1, 6½" long, with domed top, blue
    tinted windows, three wheels, friction
    powered (Linemar 1950s) 50.00
Sparkling Rocket #3, 7" long tin litho, friction
    powered (MT 1950s) 85.00
Sputnik Space Satellite, 14" long, features rocket &
    satellite with dog circling plastic globe (West
    German 1950s) 100.00
Two Stage Earth Satellite with Launching Station, tin
    litho, rocket blasts off and separates
    (Linemar 1950s) 125.00
UFO-XO5, 7½" diameter battery operated, tin and
    plastic (MT 1950s) 50.00
Winner-23 Rocket, 5½" long, tin litho, battery
    powered (KDP 1950s) 75.00
X-07 Space Surveillant Capsule 9", tin litho (MT
    1950s) 90.00
X-15 Spacecraft, 5" diameter, tin litho with pilot
    under clear plastic dome, friction powered
    (KO 1950s) 50.00
X-2 Space Rocket, 7½" tin litho, friction powered
    (TN 1950s) 40.00
X-326 Space Craft, tin litho with fins and plastic
    saucer (MT 1950s) 40.00
X-40 Space Rocket with Shooting Capsule, 7" long,
    plastic (#232 1960s) 45.00
X-7 Space Explorer Ship, 7" diameter, battery
    operated tin litho, flashing engine lights and
    astronaut under clear plastic dome (MT
    1950s) 65.00

STARGATE

These vehicles are from the movie. If it keeps going,
maybe the *Stargate SG-1* television show will generate a few
collectibles.

VEHICLES

Winged Glider (Alien Attack Craft) (#89026 Hasbro
    1994) $10.00
Mastadge (Beast of Burden) (#89024 Hasbro 1994) 8.00
All-Terrain Cruiser (#89022 Hasbro 1994) 8.00

STARSHIP TROOPERS

The micro creatures and starships listed below are based
on the 1997 movie. The Avalon Hill game comes from the
novel by Robert A. Heinlein, which was the basis for the
movie.

GAME

Starship Troopers game (Avalon Hill 1976) $25.00

MICRO CREATURES

Action Fleet
Hopper Bug vs. Johnny Rico & Zander Barclow
    (#68073) 8.00
Plasma Bug (#68071) 8.00
Retrieval Ship featuring Fleet Pilot & Medic (#68076) ...8.00
Tac Fighter (#68075) 8.00
Tanker Bug (#68072) 8.00
Warrior Bug vs. Corporal Bronski & MI Trooper
    (#68074) 8.00

Battle Packs (Asst. #68050, Oct. 1997)
#1 Warrior Bug vs. Johnny Rico, Ace Levy, MI
    Recruit (#68051) 10.00
#2 Brain Bug vs. Dr. Carl Jenkins, Johnny Rico, MI
    Trooper (#68052) 10.00
#3 Hopper Bug vs. Johnny Rico, Corporal Bronski,
    MI Trooper (#68053) 10.00
#4 MI Pulse Cannon with Zanden Barcalow, MI
    Troopers (2) (#68054) 10.00
#5 Battle-Damaged Warrior Bug vs. Johnny Rico,
    Ace Levy, MI Trooper (#68055) 10.00
#6 Tanker Bug vs. Johnny Rico, Corporal Bronski,
    MI Trooper (#68056) 10.00

REMOTE CONTROL & ELECTRONIC

Remote Control Action Fleet Vehicle & Accessory
Remote Control Drop Ship with Power Cord (#68082) .15.00
Remote Control Hopper Bug (#68081?) 15.00

Electronic Vehicle and Accessory
Electronic Warrior Bug, Movable Jaw with chomping
    sounds, in open box (#22930) 20.00
Electronic Tac Fighter, with Electronic Jet Sounds &
    Lights, in try-me window box (#22927) 20.00

Starship Troopers Drop Ship (Galoob 1998)

STAR TREK

It's been over 30 years since the original 5-year mission began and lots of toys and other collectibles have been produced. The listings below have been separated by show, so that the four different television series, the cartoon series and the movies have their own lists. Generic *Star Trek* items are in the first listing, grouped with the original (now classic) show as are most of the general comments on the categories. This works fairly well for most things, but not for characters such as Worf and O'Brien who were regulars on both *The Next Generation* and *Deep Space Nine*. It also means that you might not find some particular item until you notice that it has a logo for one of the movies on it and look in that section. Of course, if all the listings were organized solely by category, it would be hard to find the movie-related and *Star Trek Voyager* collectibles at all because they would be scattered over many pages.

CERAMICS (CLASSIC SERIES)

First Series Plates (Ernst Enterprises 1983–84)
8½" plates featuring various crew members, each . . .$50.00
Crew on Transporter 50.00
10¼ plate, crew & *Enterprise* 60.00

Plates (Ernst Enterprises) Second Series
The Trouble With Tribbles .45.00
Mirror, Mirror 90.00
A Piece of the Action 45.00
The Devil in the Dark 45.00
Amok Time 45.00
The City on the Edge of Forever 90.00
Journey to Babel 45.00
The Menagerie 45.00
Star Trek V 60.00

Porcelain Plaques 4½" high (Hamilton 1993) with easel
Capt. Kirk (#927228) 12.00
Mr. Spock (#927201) 12.00
Enterprise (#913200) 12.00

Star Trek Porcelain Mini-Plates 4" dia. (Enesco 1993) with Easel
Dr. McCoy (#927082) 7.50
Sulu (#927090) 7.50
Chekov (#927120) 7.50

Scotty (#927104) 7.50
Uhura (#927112) 7.50
U.S.S. Enterprise NCC-1701 (#927848) 7.50
Crew (#927821) 7.50
Capt. Kirk (#927066) 7.50
Mr. Spock (#927074) 7.50

Porcelain Mini Plates with Easel
Captain James T. Kirk and *U.S.S. Enterprise* NCC-1701 4½" in diameter with art by Todd Treadway in *Star Trek The Next Generation* box (Eneasco 109274, 1994) 10.00

Star Trek Enterprise Porcelain Plaque, first in a series of three, by artist Mark Newman, six-sided with gold plated edge, 11" x 10½" x 1½" limited to 9,500 (Willetts #47052) 70.00

Cookie Jars
Ceramic Cookie Jars, 16" high (Star Jars 1998) limited to 1,000 of each:
Enterprise "Space The Final Frontier" 275.00
Spock & Kirk 375.00
Cameos of *Star Trek* cast 375.00
Alien Ships 275.00
Vulcan Hand sign & Insignia 275.00

CLOTHING & ACCESSORIES (CLASSIC SERIES)

Star Trek clothing includes just about anything you can think of to wear with a *Star Trek* patch, logo or saying on it that announces to the world that you are a Trekker. These aren't really collected as much as they are just worn. *Star Trek* uniforms are available for each show, in just about every rank or type of duty, as well as for many of the alien races. Communication, rank and function pins can be added for a really authentic look. Several of the pins are pictured later. Uniforms, too, are mostly bought to be worn to shows and fan club meetings, rather than collected. Used clothing and uniforms are not valuable, unless they still fit you.

Hollywood Pins makes pins for just about any *Star Trek* occasion. Most of these pins are still selling at their original price of around $10. Any given one may be hard to find, but so many different pins are available that prices have not increased. They are essential accessories to your *Star Trek* uniform, since no self-respecting Trekker would appear in public without the correct rank and service branch pins on his

Star Trek Ceramic Plates: Sulu (Ernest 1983) Kirk mini-plate (Enesco 1993) & U.S.S. Enterprise logo cap (Thinking Cap Co. 1980s)

collar and chest. Hollywood Pins eventually made pins for all of the original *Star Trek* TV show episodes as well as many of the episodes from the other shows.

Classic Star Trek (Rubies 1990s)
Star Trek Shirts, Gold, Blue or Red, each $27.00
Star Trek Dresses, Gold, Blue or Red, each 29.00

Ties
Spock 20.00
Mirror, Mirror 20.00
Original *Enterprise* 20.00
Enterprise/Klingon Standoff 20.00
Original Crew 20.00
Captains poly tie 16.00
30th Anniv. Logo tie 25.00

Baseball Caps
Starfleet Academy Baseball Cap embroidered logo . . .12.00
Star Trek Baseball Cap silver embroidered logo 14.00
United Federation of Planets Baseball Cap embroid-
      ered logo (Thinking Cap Company 1982) 14.00
Patches for Hats or uniforms, many different, each 5.00

Wallets
Star Trek zippered wallet (Larami 1977) 35.00

Watches
U.S.S.Enterprise round face (Bradley 1980) 90.00
Kirk & Spock digital (Bradley 1980) 75.00
Spock watch (Bradley 1979) 100.00
Spock/20 years of Star Trek Dimensional Spock &
      Enterprise 40.00
U.S.S.Enterpirse coin watch 90.00
Star Trek 25th anniv. watch (Franklin Mint, 1991) 250.00
Handpainted *Enterprise* 75.00
Klingon Chronometer, digital watch (Timex 1994) 30.00
Rotating U.S.S. Enterprise (Timex 1994) 40.00
Cloaking Romulan Warbird (Timex 1994) 40.00

Totebags
Blue Totebag with United Federation of Planets 12.00
Black totebag with Star Trek logo in silver 12.00

Coin pendants (Rarities Mint 1989) Gold plated 25.00
      Sterling Silver plated 15.00
Coin Keyholder (Rarities Mint 1989) Gold plated 20.00
      Sterling Silver plated 15.00
Enterprise pendant 25.00

Collector's Classic Insignia pins
Limited Edition, The Star Trek Collection, Collectors
      Classics large 5" x 3" pin (Hollywood 1987) 40.00
Communicator pin 12.50
Communicator pin (half size) 10.00
NCC-1701D call letters pin 7.50
Enterprise cut-out pin (TV) 5.00
Star Trek Lives 7.50
Star Trek Forever 7.50
Star Trek Starship *Enterprise* 7.50
Star Trek Twenty Years insignia 7.50
Star Trek theme pin 7.50
Federation Uniform Insignia .29.50
Special UFP-Starfleet Command 7.50
United Federation of Planets Crest 7.50
Star Trek 20th Anniv. 5.00
Starfleet Command symbol 7.50
Klingon symbol, large 7.50

Limited Edition Star Trek Collection Pin, large
(Hollywood Pins 1987)

Romulan Crest, large 7.50

Klingon pins
Klingon symbol, small 5.00
Klingon rank Admiral (2 star) .5.00
Klingon rank Captain (1 large star) 5.00
Klingon rank Flag Admiral 7.50
Klingon rank Admiral 5.00
Klingon rank Commodore 7.50
Klingon rank Captain 7.50

Starfleet Command
Command Division, maroon or white 5.00
Engineering Division, yellow .5.00
Security Division, red 5.00
Medical Division, green 5.00
Science Division, blue 5.00
Executive, black star 5.00
Science, black symbol 5.00
Engineering, black symbol 5.00
Starfleet Branch pins, various branches, each 7.50
S42 *Galileo* Shuttlecraft 5.00
S43 *Galileo* Shuttlecraft w/ship on top 9.00
Caution Force Field pin 5.00
Caution Anti-Matter pin 5.00
Make It So 6.00
Fully Functional 6.00
Borg Ship 6.00
Phaser Gun pin (TV) 7.50
Communicator pin (TV) 7.50

Patches
Kirk Emblem patch (1975) 30.00
Spock Emblem patch (1975) 2 different, each 30.00
Uhura Emblem patch (1975) .30.00
Federation Emblem patch (1975) 30.00
Phaser Emblem patch (1975) 30.00
NCC-1701 Emblem patch (1975) 30.00
Uniform stripe Emblem patch (1975) 30.00
Kirk Emblem patch (1979) 2 different, each 25.00
Spock Emblem patch (1979) 2 different, each 25.00
Kirk & Spock Emblem patch (1979) 25.00
Kirk/Spock/McCoy Emblem patch (1979) 25.00

Episode Pins (Hollywood Pin Company 1990–94)
Star Trek Episodes, title pin .10.00
79 episode pins, each 10.00
Mirror Universe Pin (#350) 6.00

Episode Pins: The City on the Edge of Forever & Mudd's Women
(Hollywood Pins 1990s)

Star Trek Enterprise cut-out cloisonne Pin (#15) 6.00
Star Trek Klingon Symbol cloisonne pin (#151) 8.00
Communicator Sound Board, goes with pins 10.00

Hollywood Pins keychains
The Communicator Pin (#K1022) 7.00
Borg (#K831) 5.00
"Make It So" (K832) 5.00
Star Trek: Original Title (#K834) 6.00
Klingon (#K835) 5.00
Star Trek: The Next Generation (#K836) 5.00
United Fedration of Planets (#K837) 5.00
Star Trek Enterprise cut-out (#K844) 6.00
Starfleet Command Gold Symbol (#K845) 5.00
Star Trek Logo (#K846) 5.95
The Next Generation Logo (#K850) 5.95
Star Trek Theme (#K851) 5.95

Hollywood Pins jewelry
Star Trek charm braclet (#J101) 24.95
Miniature Symbols Earring set (#J150) 17.50

COINS & MEDALLIONS (CLASSIC SERIES)

Coins (Exonumia):
Enterprise coin (1974) 40.00
10th Anniversary coin (1976) .60.00
Silver collector's coins (Rarities Mint 1989) 50.00
Gold collector's coins (Rarities Mint 1989) 350.00

CRAFT & ACTIVITY (CLASSIC SERIES)

Star Trek I rubber stamp 8.00
Star Trek pencil & paint set (Hasbro 1967) 80.00
Colorforms set 30.00
Putty (Larami 1979) 20.00
Mix 'N' Mold casting sets: Kirk, Spock, McCoy, each . .10.00

DIE-CAST AND METAL FIGURES (CLASSIC SERIES)

Ships and crew 25mm Lead Miniatures (FASA)
4 different, each 20–30.00

Other Lead Miniatures (FASA)
Crew figures 25mm (Heritage 1978-79) 10.00
Alien figures 25mm (Heritage 1978-79) 10.00

1/3900 plastic or lead Starline 2200 Miniature ships (FASA)
57 different, each 6.00
Federation Starbase (#7025) .8.00
Klingon B-10 Battleship (#7040) 8.00
Starline 2220 Starships (#7300) boxed sets 13.00

2¼" Pewter Figurines Star Trek (FASA)
Classic crew, 7 different, each 17.50
Classic ships, 5 different, each 17.50
Excelsior (#RF791) 21.00
Enterprise large (#RF1777) 45.00
Kirk 90mm (#RF1774) 35.00

Pewter Spaceships (Rawcliffe 1993–96)
1½" to 2½" high, 1" to 3½" long
    U.S.S. Enterprise NCC-1701 . . . . .16.00
    U.S.S. Enterprise NCC-1701-A 16.00
    U.S.S. Enterprise NCC-1701-D 25.00
    U.S.S. Enterprise NCC-1701, large 45.00
    U.S.S. Enterprise NCC-1701-A, large 55.00
    U.S.S. Enterprise NCC-1701-D with Detach-
       able Saucer 55.00
    U.S.S. Excelsior 20.00
    U.S.S. Grissom 17.00
    U.S.S. Reliant 16.00
    U.S.S. Voyager 35.00
    Borg Ship 70.00
    Ferengi Marauder 35.00
    Deep Space Nine Runabout 25.00
    Klingon Battle Cruiser 16.00
    Klingon Bird of Prey 16.00
    Klingon Bird of Prey, large 65.00
    Regula 1 Space Station 20.00
    Romulan Warbird 25.00
The Women of Star Trek Pewter Figurines (1998)
    Uhura 15.00
    Dr. Beverly Crusher 15.00
    Guinan 15.00
    Daz 15.00
    Kira 15.00
    Deanna Troi 15.00

DOLLS AND FIGURES (CLASSIC SERIES)

The first Star Trek action figures were 8" dolls produced by Mego Corporation in 1974. These earliest figures came on a header card which had only five characters' heads pictured. Dolls on these cards command a premium price. The much

Uhura & Gorn dolls, loose (Mego 1974–75)

more common second version header card adds a picture of Uhura, and her doll made a total of six figures in the first series. Captain Kirk, Mr. Spock and the Klingon were produced in large numbers by Mego, and remaining stocks were being distributed to comic shops as late as 1994.

Later, Mego produced eight aliens, in two series, which were distributed overseas. These are all extremely valuable.

8" Dolls, First Series (Mego 1974)
Capt. Kirk, with phaser, communicator and belt
    (#51200/1, 1974) original header card $110.00
    Reissue on second header card, adding Uhura . .60.00
Mr. Spock, with phaser, communicator, tricorder and
    belt (#51200/2, 1974) original header card 100.00
    Reissue on second header card, adding Uhura . .50.00
Dr. McCoy (*Bones*) with tricorder (#51200/3, 1974)
    original header card 150.00
    Reissue on second header card, adding Uhura .125.00
Lt. Uhura, with tricorder (#51200/4, 1974) 100.00
Mr. Scott (*Scottie*) with phaser, communicator and
    belt (#51200/5, 1974) original header card 160.00
    Reissue on second header card, adding Uhura .130.00
Klingon, with phaser, communicator and belt
    (#51200/7, 1974) original header card 90.00
    Reissue on second header card, adding Uhura . .50.00

Second Series (1975) Foreign issue
Neptunian (#51203/1) 300.00
    Loose figure 125.00
The Keeper (#51203/2) 240.00
    Loose figure 125.00
The Gorn, with phaser (#51203/3) 240.00
    Loose figure 125.00
Cheron (#51203/4) 175.00
    Loose figure 100.00

Third Series (1976) Foreign issue
The Romulan, with helmet and phaser (#51204/1) . .1,000.00
    Loose figure 500.00
Talos, with belt and boots (#51204/2) 500.00
    Loose figure 250.00
Andorian (#51204/3) 750.00
    Loose figure 400.00
Mugato (#51204/4) 600.00
    Loose figure 300.00

COLLECTOR SERIES 9" DOLLS (CLASSIC SERIES)

Just 20 years after Mego introduced the original 8" *Star Trek* dolls, Playmates came out with a 9" series which seemed to out-Mego Mego. The initial three figures were called the "Command Edition" and included the captains of the three television shows then in existence. The Kirk doll is the most valuable figure among the 9" *Star Trek* dolls, all of which have proved highly collectible. Sisko and Picard round out this group, but they are listed under their respective shows. Starfleet and Federation "Editions" followed, but dolls from different shows were grouped together. Movie editions for *Star Trek Generations* and *Star Trek First Contact* and some Alien Editions have also been produced. Currently the dolls are shipped in three-doll "Warp" assortments. Kirk, Aliens, Babes and Store Specials are the most popular. The dolls are listed under their respective shows, with "Editions" noted.

Figures are usually designed to be collectibles, while action figures are designed as toys for kids and just happen to

Command Edition Captain James T. Kirk & Federation Edition Dr. Leonard McCoy (Playmates 199)

be extensively collected. Action figures have several points of articulation, such as the arms, elbows, wrists, knees, hips, waist and neck. If it has only a few points of articulation or none, its a figure, not an action figure. The distinction may be small, but it means that Paramount can license one company to sell action figures and another to sell figures. At the time the Hamilton Gifts figures were produced, there were no action figures being made for any of the TV series. They don't have cloth clothes, or accessories and their investment potential is not as good as the current line of 9" dolls from Playmates. These figures were supposed to be "fully poseable," which in their case meant that just the arms move. The stand has a separate extension to hold the figure at the waist. This series includes the first figures done of Sulu and Chekov.

PVC plastic figures are usually 3½" to 4½" tall and sell for about $3.50 to $4 each. At this size and price you can buy as many as want and put them on your bookshelf or your computer monitor. They fit right in with the superheroes, Looney Tunes and Disney PVC figures. Don't expect to make any money on them.

9" Collector Dolls (Playmates 1994–98)
Captain James T. Kirk (#6068) Command Edition $75.00

Starfleet Edtion
Captain James T. Kirk in Dress Uniform (#6288) 45.00
Lieutenant Uhura (#6294, 1996) 40.00

Federation Edition
Commander Spock (#6291) .35.00
Lt. Commander Montgomery Scott (#6293) 25.00
Chief Medical Officer Dr. Leonard McCoy (#6292) 25.00
Captain Christopher Pike (#16183) 25.00
Lieutenant Hikaru Sulu (#16184) 20.00
Ensign Pavel Chekov (#16185) 20.00

9" Collector Series, Warp Factor 3 (Feb. 1998)
Capt. James Kirk in Casual Attire (#65292) 17.00

Star Trek Federation Edition Captain Christopher Pike doll &
Mister Spock doll ("A Piece of the Action") (Playmates 1996)

Batch III (Aug. 1998)
Talosian 17.00
Garek 17.00
Bele 17.00

Where No Man Has Gone Before, Target Stores Exclusives
    (Playmates 1996)
Captain James T. Kirk (#16096) 35.00
Mr. Spock (#16097) 35.00
Lt. Commander Montgomery Scott (#16098) 35.00
Lieutenant Hikaru Sulu (#16099) 35.00

9" Dolls "A Piece of the Action" Kaybee Exclusives
Captain James T. Kirk (#16091) 100.00
Mister Spock (#16092) 100.00

9" Dolls "City on the Edge of Forever" Kaybee Exclusives (1997)
Captain James Kirk (#65260) .50.00
Spock (#65261) 50.00

9" Dolls "Mirror, Mirror" Kaybee Exclusives (1998)
Kirk (#16091) 40.00
Spock (#16092) 40.00
Dr. McCoy 40.00
Uhura 40.00

12" Doll, Masterpiece Edition, The Captain's Series
    (Nov. 1997) limited to 10,000
Captain James T. Kirk, with book (#65041) 75.00
Pike (July 1998) 55.00

Barbie & Ken
Star Trek Barbie & Ken dolls (Mattel 1996) 25.00

FIGURES (CLASSIC SERIES)

10¾" Vinyl Figures, with base (Hamilton Gifts 1991–92)
Captain Kirk, bagged (1991) .17.50
Mr. Spock, bagged (1991) 17.50
Dr. McCoy (1992) 17.50
Scotty (1992) 17.50
Chekov (1992) 17.50
Sulu (1992) 17.50
Uhuru (1992) 17.50

Andorian, bagged (1992) 17.50
Talosian, bagged (1992) 17.50

Kirk 12" doll, cloth (Knickerbocker 1979) 35.00
Spock 12" doll, cloth (Knickerbocker 1979) 35.00
Kirk porcelain doll (Hamilton) 80.00
Spock porcelain doll (Hamilton) 80.00

Danbury Mint Figurines 5¼" cold-cast porcelain
subscription deal, 1994
Crew, 7 different, each 20.00
Aliens & villains, 5 different, each 20.00
Display Case, 13¼" x 20" x 3¼" . . . . .included

Porcelain Dolls (Earnst 1991) with uniforms and display stand
    Kirk 75.00
    Spock 75.00
    McCoy 75.00
    Scotty 75.00
    Sulu 75.00

PVC
Star Trek 4¼" PVC figures, 7 crew figures
    (Hamilton 1991) each 4.00
Klingon 4¼" PVC figure (Hamilton 1991) 4.00

Aliens Assortment
Mugato 4¼" PVC figure (Hamilton 1992) 5.00
Talosian 4¼" PVC figure (Hamilton 1992) 4.00
Gorn 4¼" PVC figure (Hamilton 1992) 4.00
Tellerite 4¼" PVC figure (Hamilton 1992) 4.00
Andorian 4¼" PVC figure (Hamilton 1992) 4.00

Enterprise (#913022) 4.00

FOOD (CLASSIC SERIES)

Star Trek glasses, candy boxes, cereal boxes and similar
items are much like similar items produced for *Star Wars* and
other movies and television shows. However, *Star Trek* has
also produced some really strange food collectibles. One was
the Federation Science Personal Emergency Rations sold at
the Oregon Museum of Science and Industry, Nationally
Traveling Science Education Exhibit. This whole traveling

Mr. Spock doll ("Mirror Mirror") (Playmates 1998)
Captain Kirk vinyl figure (Hamilton Gifts 1991)

exhibit was on Federation Science. If a kid likes *Star Trek*, he or she should like science! Others included a marshmallow dispenser from Kraft Foods which is listed under the *Star Trek* Movies and *Star Trek Voyager* Popcorn produced by UPN in 1995. You were supposed to pop the popcorn and then watch the premier of the show. Naturally, true collectors bought other popcorn and kept this give-away from the Paramount network. They did, however, watch the show.

```
TV series (Dr. Pepper 1978) glasses, each  . . . . . . .$60.00
     Set, 4 glasses (Kirk, Spock, McCoy Enterprise) .250.00

Candy: Candy Boxes (Phoenix Candy 1976)
     8 different versions, each . . . . . . . . . . . . . . . . . .10.00
General Mills cereal boxes with Star Trek offers:
     Bracelet offer  . . . . . . . . . . . . . . . . . . . . . . .10-30.00
     Iron-on offer, 7 different Starships . . . . . . . . .10-30.00
General Mills iron-on transfers
     Kirk . . . . . . . . . . . . . . . . . . . . . . . . . . . . . .1-3.00
     Spock . . . . . . . . . . . . . . . . . . . . . . . . . . . . .1-3.00
     Kirk and Spock . . . . . . . . . . . . . . . . . . . . . . .1-3.00
     Enterprise  . . . . . . . . . . . . . . . . . . . . . . . . . .1-3.00
General Mills I.D. bracelet . . . . . . . . . . . . . . . . . .5-10.00
Star Trek: Federation Science Personal Emergency
     Rations (American Outdoor Products 1992) in
     silver foil pouch . . . . . . . . . . . . . . . . . . . . . .10–15.00
```

GAMES & PUZZLES (CLASSIC SERIES)

Star Trek has been a popular subject for games for many years. In the 1970s, most of them were traditional board games. Role-playing games became big business in the 1980s, starting with Fasa's basic game set. Fasa also produced close to 100 supplements, extensions, deck plans, etc. The late 1980s brought on a number of computer games and now the rage is *Magic* type customizable card games. Board games are the most popular with traditional game collectors, and have the best investment potential. Scarce cards in the recent card games are also valuable, but their long term potential is unknown.

```
Super Phaser II target game (Mego 1976) . . . . . . . .$70.00
Phaser battle game (Mego) . . . . . . . . . . . . . . . . . .65.00
Fizzbin card game (1976) . . . . . . . . . . . . . . . . . .50.00
Star Trek Game (Hasbro 1976) . . . . . . . . . . . . . . .35.00
```

Star Trek Super Phaser Target Game (Mego 1976)

Star Trek Game (Hasbro 1976)

```
Star Trek Game (Ideal 1966) . . . . . . . . . . . . . . . . .75.00
Star Trek Game "Action and Adventure in Outer
     Space" (Hasbro 1974) . . . . . . . . . . . . . . . . . .60.00
Arcade game, 2 sizes (Sega) . . . . . . . . . . . . . . .1,200.00
Computer game . . . . . . . . . . . . . . . . . . . . . . . . .20.00
Game cloth (Avalon) . . . . . . . . . . . . . . . . . . . . .10-20.00
Trivia game (Golden) . . . . . . . . . . . . . . . . . . . .10-20.00
Star Trek The Final Frontier board game (BMI 1992) . .25.00
Star Trek, The Game (Classic 19231, 1992) 12" x
     19" box featuring Kirk, Spock & Enterprise
     graphics by Keith Birdsong, limited to a mere
     200,000 numbered units . . . . . . . . . . . . . . . . .35.00
Star Trek jigsaw puzzle (H-G 1974-6) each . . . . . . . .15.00
Star Trek Cast 600 Piece Puzzle (#90041) . . . . . . . . .7.50

Role Playing Games
Star Fleet Battles (Task Force)
Star Fleet Battle Manual, game, by Zocchi and
     Kurtick (authors) "Each player captains a
     Starship..." (Game Science Corp. #10305,
     1977) boxed set includes mapsheet,
     counters, etc. . . . . . . . . . . . . . . . . . . . . . . .20–25.00
Star Trek The Role Playing Game (Fasa #2001,
     1983) basic game set including 128-page
     rulebook, deck plans, adventure books,
     counters, dice and hexagonal grid field.
     Cover art by O'Connell. . . . . . . . . . . . . . . . . .50.00
Star Trek The Role Playing Game Klingon D-7 Class
     Battle Cruiser Deck Plans (Fasa #2102,
     1983) six deck plans + booklet. . . . . . . . . . . . .15.00
Pouch game (1st ed.) . . . . . . . . . . . . . . . . . . . . .25.00
Original boxed set . . . . . . . . . . . . . . . . . . . . . . .25.00
Supplement to boxed set
     Volume 1 (1983) . . . . . . . . . . . . . . . . . . . . . .25.00
     Volume 2 (1984) . . . . . . . . . . . . . . . . . . . . . .25.00
     Volume 3 (1985) . . . . . . . . . . . . . . . . . . . . . .25.00
     Federation & Empire (1986) . . . . . . . . . . . . . . .35.00
     Battlecards . . . . . . . . . . . . . . . . . . . . . . . . .10.00
     Terrain maps . . . . . . . . . . . . . . . . . . . . . . . .15.00
     Commander SSD books, #1-9, each . . . . . . . . . . .8.00
     Star Fleet Battle Update #2, #3032 . . . . . . . . . . .9.00
     Megahex #3033  . . . . . . . . . . . . . . . . . . . . . .15.00
     Megahex II, #3034  . . . . . . . . . . . . . . . . . . . . .7.00
     Captain's Log #1, #3004 . . . . . . . . . . . . . . . . . .7.00
     Intro to Star Fleet Battles #3000 . . . . . . . . . . . . .8.00
     Star Fleet Battles Reinforcements #3024 . . . . . . . .8.00
     Captain's Logs #2-4 each . . . . . . . . . . . . . . . . .7.00
     Captain's Log #5, #3026 . . . . . . . . . . . . . . . . . .7.00
     Captain's Log #6, #3027 . . . . . . . . . . . . . . . . . .7.00
     Captain's Log #7, #3028 . . . . . . . . . . . . . . . . . .7.00
     Federation & Empire (2nd Edition 1990) . . . .35.00
```

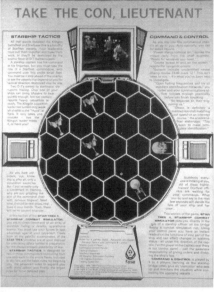

Star Trek The Role Playing Game, box and map (Fasa 1983); Star Fleet Battle Manual (Fasa 1980s)

Federation & Empire conversion 15.00
Task Force game minatures
8 different, each 10.00

Role-Playing games (FASA)
Basic set, original edition 20.00
Basic set, second edition 15.00
Deluxe edition 30.00
USS Enterprise blueprints, set of 9 in box 15.00
Klingon D-7 blueprints, set of 6 in box 15.00
The Triangle 10.00
The Triangle Campaign 10.00
The Vanished 7.00
Witness for the Defense 7.00
Denial of Destiny 7.00
Termination: 1456 . . . . .12.00
Demand of Honor 10.00
The Orion Ruse 7.00
Margin of Profit 7.00
The Outcasts 7.00
A Matter of Priorities 7.00
A Doomsday Like Any Other 8.00
The Mines of Selka 8.00
Graduation Exercise 8.00
Where Has All the Glory Gone? 8.00
Return to Axanar/The Four Years War 12.00
Decision at Midnight 8.00
Imbalance of Power 12.00
A Conflict of Interests/Klingon Intelligence Briefing 12.00
The Dixie Gambit 8.00
The White Flame 8.00
The Strider Incident/Regula I deck plans 12.00
Klingon Ship recognition manual (FASA) 8.00
Federation Ship recognition manual (FASA) 8.00
Romulan Ship recognition manual (FASA) 8.00
Gorn & Minor Races Ship recognition manual (FASA) . .8.00
Trader Captains & Merchant Princes (1st ed.) 12.00
Trader Captains & Merchant Princes (2nd ed.) 18.00
Ship Construction Manual (1st ed.) 12.00
Ship Construction Manual (2nd ed.) 12.00
Starship Combat Hex Grid 8.00
Gamemaster's kit 10.00
Tricorder/Sensors Interactive Display 10.00

Tactical Combat Simulator 20.00
Star Trek III: Starship Combat role-playing game 15.00
Star Trek III Sourcebook .10.00
Star Trek III Sourcebook Update 9.00
Star Trek IV Sourcebook .10.00
The Klingons (1st ed.) 20.00
The Klingons (2nd ed.) 15.00
The Romulans (1st ed.) 15.00
The Romulans (2nd ed.) 12.00
The Orions 15.00
The Federation 14.00
Star Fleet Intelligence Manual 15.00

FASA Star Trek III Starship Combat Game
1/3900 scale Lead Miniatures with plastic base
31 different items, each 5.00
5 different battleships, each 12.00
USS Enterprise Galaxy Class 12.00

Micro Adventure Games
4 different, each 8.00

Role-Playing games (FASA)
First Year Sourcebook 10.00
USS Enterprise blueprints 10.00
Next Generation Officer's Manual 12.00

Star Trek The Card Game (Fleer/Skybox 1996) 15-
    card booster pack 2.75
    65-card starter deck 8.95
Star Trek 25th Anniversary Electronic Game
    (Konami 1991) hand-held with Star Trek
    phrases, blister packed on header card 20.00

HOUSEHOLD (CLASSIC SERIES)

Bowls, Mugs, China and Glassware are grouped here. A number of these items could have all been designed for the same person, at different ages: a 1975 child's bowl, 1976 and 1979 fast food glasses and 1980s and 1990s coffee cups and fine china (listed under *Star Trek* Movies). As *Star Trek* fans have gotten older, the collectibles have grown up, too.

Star Trek Bowl & Mug (Deka 1975)

Hallmark made this first *Star Trek* christmas ornament in 1991 and only its regular keepsake ornament buyers seemed to find out about it before they were all gone. Hallmark completely underestimated the market for this item and so it became an instant high-priced collectible, and still is. Hallmark knew a good thing when it had it and has been producing ornaments every year since. Hallmark has continued to make *Star Trek* spaceship christmas ornaments ever since 1991 and has advertised them on TV during the show. In 1995, Hallmark added Kirk and Picard figures to its annual christmas offering of a *Star Trek* spaceship. These are just hanging figures; they don't light up. They sell for a little over half the cost of the spaceship

Star Trek collectibles that double as useful phone, radio or computer products are fairly popular. They don't cost a lot more than non-collectibles which perform the same function, and they even get discounted after a run on the store shelf. That's the time to buy!

Child's Cereal Bowl, Mug & glass set (Deka 1975) . . .$40.00
Kirk Ceramic stein (Image Products) 50.00
Spock Ceramic stein (Image Products) 50.00
Transporter magic mug 15.00

12 oz. pictoral mugs (Hamilton 1993)
Dr. McCoy (#P7532) 9.00
Sulu (#P7530) 9.00
Chekov (#P7518) 9.00
Scotty (#P7518) 9.00
Uhura (#P7531) 9.00
U.S.S. Enterprise NCC-1701 (#901547) 9.00
Crew (#P7533) 9.00
Capt. Kirk (#P7517) 9.00
Mr. Spock (#P7516) 9.00

Figural Mugs
Kirk Figural Mug (Applause #45846, 1994) 15.00
Spock Figural Mug (Applause #45847, 1994) 15.00
McCoy Figural Mug (Applause #46126, 1995) 15.00
Gorn Figural Mug (Applause #46127, 1995) 15.00
United Federation of Planets Logo Mug (Rawcliffe) . . .13.00
U.S.S. Enterprise/Next Generation Mug (Rawcliffe) . . .10.00
Enterprise Insignia/Star Trek Movie Mug (Rawcliffe) . . .10.00
Warp Speed 16oz commuter mug (Rawcliffe) 16.00

Magic Mugs (image changes with hot liquid)
Kirk, Spock, McCoy magic mug 13.00
Enterprise A/Enterprise B magic mug 13.00
Enterprise Evolution magic mug 13.00

Kirk Commemorative Decal Mug (with Tribbles and
    other images) (Applause #46122) 7.00

Christmas Ornaments
Star Trek *Enterprise* (Original) with blinking lights,
    25th anniversary (Hallmark 1991) 300.00
Shuttlecraft Galileo with voice of Mr. Spock
    (Hallmark 1992) 45.00
Klingon Bird-of-Prey with flickering and glowing
    lights (Hallmark 1994) .35.00
Romulan Warbird (Hallmark 1995) 30.00
Captain James T. Kirk, seated in command chair
    (Hallmark 1995) 30.00
Mr. Spock (Hallmark 1996) .28.00
Dr. McCoy (Hallmark 1997) .18.00

Other Household items
Freezicle set (1975) 45.00
Star Trek Sleeping Bag 30.00
Star Trek Drapes 15.00
Star Trek Beach Towel 15.00
Star Trek TV wastebasket 60.00
Saurian Brandy Bottle (Dickel Whiskey 1968) 100.00
Star Trek metal-dome lunchbox with metal thermos
    (Aladdin 1968) 450.00

Electronic Household Products
Star Trekulator calculator (Mego 1976) 100.00
    with box 150.00
Star Trek Intergalactic Planetarium (Mego 1976) . . .1,500.00
Alarm clock (Zeon 1984) 70.00
Enterprise clock 45.00
Star Trek Spock alarm clock 35.00
Star Trek *Enterprise* wall clock, 12" diameter 33.50
Star Trek *Enterprise* alarm clock 35.00
Star Trek Spock wall clock, 12" diameter 33.50
Star Trek *Enterprise NCC 1701* Telephone
    (TeleMania/KLC Technology 1993) 100.00

HUMOR, PARODY & CROSSOVER
(CLASSIC SERIES)

No set of *Star Trek* collectibles would be complete without a few of the many humorous and parody items that have been created over the years. Even die-hard Trekkers are able to laugh about the show. In fact, one of the very first *Star Trek* collectibles is the *Mad Magazine* parody of the original TV show.

Star Trek Intergalactic Planetarium (Mego 1976)

 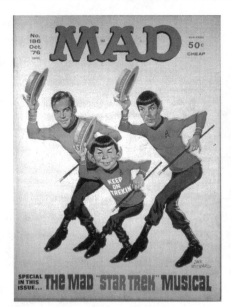 

Star Trek Barbie & Ken collector watch (Mattel 1997) Mad Magazine #186 (Mad 1976)
& Star Trek Communicator #107 (Star Trek Fan Club 1997)

Mad magazine did its first parody of *Star Trek* in November 1966. That's only two months after the TV show began. November magazines are printed in late September to go on sale in early October, so the writers only had a couple of weeks after the show's premier to complete the issue. *Mad* magazine has done at least one parody of each show and movie. Trekkers have a good sense of humor and are not insulted. Collectors love the issues and just add them to their collections.

Cracked magazine did its first parody of *Star Trek* in September 1975 and has done many others since, including parodies of all of the movies and *The Next Generation* show.

Star Trek/Teenage Mutant Ninja Turtle: First Officer
    Donatello, with Classic Subsauce Phaser,
    Classic Sewer Science Tricorder, Pure Logic
    Classic Communicator and Pon Farr Battle
    Bo (Playmates #3454, 1994) carded $15.00
Mad Magazine issue #186 (Mad October 1976)
    Kirk/Spock/Alfred E. Newman cover. 15.00
*All I Really Needed to Know I Learned From
    Watching Star Trek* by Dave Marinaccio
    (Crown 86386-4, 1994) small trade
    paperback first edition, 128 pages 10.00
Starwreck II: The Attack of the Jargonites, by Leah
    Rewolinski, paperback (St. Martins Press
    92737, 1992) "An Unauthorized Parody" 8.00
Star Trek Barbie & Ken wrist watch in collector
    case (Mattel 1997) 15.00

MASKS AND COSTUMES (CLASSIC SERIES)

Costumes & Play Outfits
Mr. Spock (Ben Cooper 1967) 100.00
Kirk (1976) 25.00
Spock (1976) 50.00
Klingon (1976) 50.00

Gorn Head Mask (Don Post 1990) 75.00
Kirk Head Mask (Don Post 1990) 75.00
Mugato Head Mask (Don Post 1990) 75.00
Salt Monster Head Mask (Don Post 1990) 75.00

MICRO

The earliest *Star Trek* Micro Machine packages list only five collections on the back. There was one based on the original series, one based on the movies, two from *Star Trek, The Next Generation* and this one from the *Deep Space Nine* series which had just started its TV run. *Star Trek* Micro Machines are about 2" long and generally come with a display base. There are at least 24 different ones (eight different 3-packs) and many never been available as larger toys or models.

Playmates mini playsets have been a hit with kids, but its too early to tell if they will have much collector value. If they do, it will be because they are cleverly designed to fold up into the shape of spaceships or equipment and can be displayed that way.

1994 packs with 5 listed on back
The Original Star Trek (Collection #1)
    U.S.S. Enterprise NCC-1701; Klingon Battle-
    cruiser; Romulan Bird of Prey (#65881, 1994) . . .$6.00

1995 packs with 8 listed on back
The Original Star Trek (Collection #1)
    Botany Bay; Klingon Battlecruiser; Romulan
    Bird of Prey (#66100?, 1995) 8.00
The Original Star Trek (Collection #2)
    Galileo II; Space Station K-7; *U.S.S.
    Enterprise* NCC-1701 (#, 1995) 8.00

Star Trek Television Series I, 8 ships, pewter color:
    Romulan Bird of Prey, *U.S.S. Enterprise*
    NCC 1701; *U.S.S. Stargazer*; Cardassian
    Galor Warship; Runabout; Botany Bay;
    Klingon Vor'cha Attack Cruiser; Borg Ship
    (#66074, 1995) 20.00
Star Trek Television Series II, 8 ships, pewter color:
    Space Station Deep Space Nine, *U.S.S.
    Enterprise* NCC 1701-C; Space Station K-7;
    Romulan Warbird; Ferengi Marauder;
    Romulan Scoutship; Galileo II; Klingon
    Battlecruiser (#66075, 1995) 20.00

Micro Romulan Warbird & U.S.S. Enterprise (Galoob 1995)

Star Trek Limited Edition Collector Set (16 ships)
   including special edition *U.S.S. Enterprise*
   NCC-1701-A; *U.S.S. Enterprise* NCC 1701;
   Klingon Battle Cruiser; Romulan Bird of Prey;
   U.S.S. Excelsior; Klingon Bird of Prey; *U.S.S.*
   Reliant; Klingon Vor'cha Attack Cruiser;
   U.S.S. Enterprise NCC 1701-D; Romulan
   Warbird; Borg Ship; Ferengi Marauder;
   Shuttlecraft; Space Station Deep Space Nine;
   Cardassian Galor Warship; Runabout
   (#65831) 30.00

MISCELLANEOUS (CLASSIC SERIES)

Kirk 11½" bank, plastic (Playpal 1975) 40.00
Spock 11½" bank, plastic (Playpal 1975) 40.00
Inflatable Spock bop bag (AHI 1975) 60.00
Action Fleet mobile, in envelope 30.00
Star Trek Battle scene string art 15.00
Star Trek stamp book 10.00
   Stamp sets for book 6.00
Tribbles (Mego) each 60.00
   Tribbles, fan created, ...3.00
Star Trek: GAF Viewmaster reel, plus 16 page
   booklet (GAF Viewmaster #21, 1968) cover
   shows *Enterprise NCC 1701* 35.00
Star Trek (Classic) Wood Music Box 7½" long
   (Hamilton #931284, 1993) 65.00
Star Trek Waterball cold cast (Hamilton #913030,
   1993) 8.00
Star Trek: Exhibition Guide, Federation Science
   Oregon Museum of Science and Industry,
   Nationally Traveling Science Education
   Exhibit (Science Network 1992) with 3-D
   stereoscopic pictures and viewer 25–35.00

Flying Toys
Star Trek Sky Diving Parachutist (AHI 1974)
   Captain Kirk 30.00
Mr. Spock 35.00
Star Trek Enterprise Launcher (AHI #6753) 20.00
Star Trek Space Glider (Playco #450, 1977) 50.00
Star Trek Frisbee (Remco 1967) 20.00
Star Trek Frisbees (other manuf.) 10.00
Starship *Enterprise* Flying Model Rocket kit (Estes) . . .20.00
Klingon Battle Cruiser Flying Model Rocket kit
   (Estes) 45.00
Pencil Topper
Star Trek Starships assortment (Enterprise & Klingon
   Battle Cruiser) (Applause #45855, 1994) each 3.00

PAPER (CLASSIC SERIES)

The TV shows and the movies have been covered in just about any magazine you can think of. Any issue with a *Star Trek* cover or article is collectible, although the investment potential is not great. Keep the whole magazine, don't cut out the article or remove the poster. *Starlog* has published official magazines for the three recent shows, usually at the rate of four per season. You can read the articles and find out about recent collectibles from the many ads. Unlike the other three TV shows, the original series never had an official magazine of its own. Walter Irwin and G.B. Lowe's *Trek* magazine is the most famous of the *Star Trek* semi-pro and fan magazines (called fanzines). The original magazine ran 19 issues, from 1975 to 1981. The best material from this magazine has been collected in paperback book form and is listed under BOOKS.

Most maps and blueprints are not good investments because they can be reproduced easily and cheaply. A few early ones from major publishers are the exception.

CINEFANTASTIQUE Magazine
Vol. 12 5/6 double issue featuring *Star Trek II: The*
   Wrath of Khan (1982) $13.00
Oct. 1991 *The Next Generation*, 4th season 8.00
Apr. 1992 *Star Trek VI* 8.00
Oct. 1992 double issue T*he Next Generation* and
   Deep Space Nine 14.00
Apr. 1993 *Deep Space Nine* 8.00
Oct. 1993 double issue *The Next Generation*, sixth
   season 14.00
Dec. 1994 *Generations* 14.00

STAR TREK COMMUNICATOR Magazine
Offical Fan Club Magazine
  1 . . . . .25.00
  2 thru 4 . . . . .20.00
  5 thru 9 . . . . .18.00
 10 thru 19 . . . . .15.00
 20 thru 29 . . . . .12.00
 30 thru 39 . . . . .9.00
 40 thru 49 . . . . .8.00
 50 thru 59 . . . . .7.00
 60 thru 69 . . . . .6.00
 70 thru 79 . . . . .5.00
 80 thru 89 . . . . .5.00
 90 thru 99 . . . . .4.00
100 *Enterprise NCC 1701-D* cover 7.50
101 thru 109 . . . . .3.50
Star Trek magazine (Starlog 1991) 25th Anniversary
   special, $6.95, cover with inset photos of
   Spock, Original Crew & Next Generation crew . . .15.00
Starlog Magazine #1 (O'Quinn Publications, Oct. 1977) .40.00
Trek magazine #1 (New Star Books, Fall 1988)
   originally $3.50, phaser and communicator on
   cover, red, black & white cover 7–10.00

Maps & Blueprints
Star Trek Blueprints in Pouch, by Franz Joseph
   Designs (Ballantine Books 1975) set of
   twelve 9" x 30" blueprints for Constitution
   Class *U.S.S. Enterprise* in vinyl pocket 65.00
Star Trek Maps by New Eye Photography (Bantam
   Books #01202, 1980) four deluxe four-color
   wall maps in pouch, with 32 page Technical
   Manual "*Introduction to Navigation*" 45.00

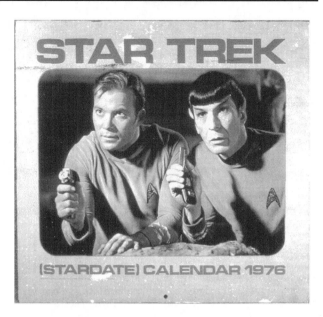

Star Trek Blueprints (Ballantine 1975) & Star Trek Calendar 1976 (Pocket Books 1975)

Starbase 79 Blueprints drawn by Lawrence Miller, 6
    sheets, 17" x 22" originally $12.95 (Lawrence
    Miller Designs 1991) in paper envelope 15.00

Calendars
Star Trek Calendars (Pocket Books)
    1974 to 1979 . . . . .40.00
    1980 to 1985 . . . . .25.00
    1986 to 1990 . . . . .15.00
    1991 to 1999 . . . . .10.00

Greeting cards
Greeting cards (Random House 1976) 24 different
    Small greeting cards, each 5.00
    Medium greeting cards, each 8.00
    Large greeting cards, unpunched, each 10.00
Popshot Pop-Up 3-D Birthday Card, "Birthday
    Greetings From The Starship *Enterprise*"
    (Kirk, Spock, McCoy pop-up in front of
    Enterprise). (PopShots 1993) 5.00

Bumper stickers
Hundreds of regular and fan produced bumper
    stickers are available. If you like the slogan,
    you can buy one for. 2.00

Miscellaneous paper collectibles
Official Star Trek Fan club Membership cards 4.00
Star Trek: Video Tape Club membership cards, Star
    Trek 25th Anniversary (Columbia House
    Video Library 1992) 1.00
Star Trek folio 11" x 14" by Doug Little, Lincoln
    Enterprises 1983, set of 11 . . . . .30.00
Star Trek: Blank Books, Locator Log Book &
    Personal Log (Antioch 1991) 3½" x 6¼" spine
    stapled booklets 2.00

Standees, life size cardboard stand-ups
Kirk (#12) 25.00
Spock (#13) 25.00
McCoy (#14 . . . . .25.00
Kirk, movie uniform 25.00
Spock, movie uniform 25.00

McCoy, movie uniform 25.00
Uhura, movie uniform 25.00
Chekov, movie uniform 25.00
Sulu, movie uniform 25.00
Scotty, movie uniform 25.00
Enterprise, hanging (#9H) .25.00
Enterprise, floor (#9F) 25.00

PHOTOS (CLASSIC SERIES)

You usually pay a lot when you buy a framed photo
that's already signed and you also run the risk of forged signature. It's cheaper and safer to get your own autographs,
instead of buying them. Cast photos are available at any *Star
Trek* collectibles show for a few dollars. If you buy one and
can get the star to sign it and then have it framed, you have
created a very nice collectible. QVC, the Sci-Fi Channel and
others offer photo plaques and similar items from time to
time. Usually they are a lot more expensive than a plain
signed photo available from companies that specialize in such
items.

Autographed Photos
Autographed photo of William Shatner or Leonard
    Nimoy $100.00
Autographed photo of other original cast, each 50.00

Autographed Photo Plaques
Star Trek Original Cast Photo Plaque, signed by
    entire cast 395.00
Star Trek Original Cast photo plaque, signed by
    entire cast (TV offer) 495.00
Star Trek Original Cast Photo Plaque, "Heroes of
    the Final Frontier" signed by entire cast 600.00

PROMOTIONAL MATERIAL (CLASSIC SERIES)

The most collectible posters are those issued by the
movie distributor for promotional use in the theatre lobby.
They are not supposed to be sold, but they get into the hands
of collectors anyway. Even more valuable are the movie press
kits which are given away when the movie opens. However,
the most valuable promotional material of all are the TV show
press kits, which are distributed in much smaller quantities.

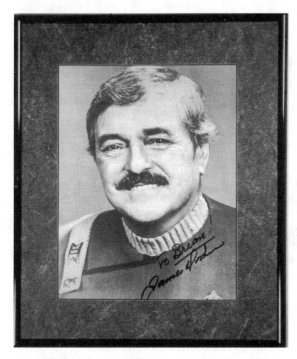

James Doohan (Scotty) autographed photo, framed

Press Kits
Original *Star Trek* TV press kit $90.00

RECORDINGS (CLASSIC SERIES)

Records have long been popular collectibles, but most audio tapes have not been and CDs are only beginning to be collected. The best part about records are their colorful album jackets, but the best part about CDs is that you can play them without any wear, so they remain collectibles. This is the fan/collector's idea of having your cake and eating it too!'

Videotaped episodes have been released periodically since 1985. Each of the seven movies is out on tape individually and you can buy the first six as a set. Most people buy these tapes to watch them, not collect them and their value as an investment is speculative, at best.

Soundtracks (GNP Crescendo Records)
Original TV Soundtrack Pilot Episodes *The Cage* &
    Where No Man Has Gone Before (GNP
    Crescendo Records #GNPC 8006 1985)
    featuring music by Alexander Courage, CD   . . .$20.00
Star Trek TV Soundtrack CD Volume Two (*The
    Doomsday Machine* & *Amok Time*) music by
    Sol Kaplan and Gerald Fried 17.95
Star Trek TV Soundtrack CD Volume Three (*Shore
    Leave* & *The Naked Now*) music by Gerald
    Fried and Alexander Courage 17.95
Boxed set of above three 49.95
*Leonard Nimoy Presents Mr. Spock's Music From
    Outer Space* (Dot Records DLP 25794, 1968)
    12" LP Album with classic Paramount promo
    photo of Mr. Spock holding model of *U.S.S.
    Enterprise NCC 1701* .40.00
Symphonic Star Trek Erich Kunzel & Cincinnati
    Pops Orchestra, Telarc (Digital #80383,
    1996) CD format 20.00

Talking Books (on CD)
Cacophony, A Captain Sulu Adventure, by J.J.
    Molloy, staring the voice of George Takei
    (Simon & Schuster Audio Novel, 1994) on CD . . .15.00

Children's Records
Comic Book & Record *The Crier in Emptiness*
    (Power Records #PR-26, 1975) includes
    7" x 10" 20-page comic by Marvel and 45
    RPM record, originally $1.49, the second of
    three such sets, first release 10.00
The Human Factor (Peter Pan Records #1516,
    1979) 45 RPM record containing "Original
    stories for children inspired by Star Trek,"
    photo cover of Spock & Kirk 5.00
Star Trek: "Four Exciting All-New Action-Adventure
    Stories!" including *Time Stealer* by Cary
    Bates & Neal Adams, *To Starve a Fleaver*,
    The Logistics of Stampede, and *A Mirror for
    Futility*, all three by Alan Dean Foster. TV
    Power Records, division of (Peter Pan
    Records, #8168, 1975) in slipcase with
    cartoon of Kirk, McCoy, Spock and another
    crewman on the bridge of the *Enterprise* 10.00

Video
"The Cage" (Pilot Episode) 73 minutes, color, with
    trading card 15.00
Other episodes, with special trading card, each 13.00
Star Trek Animated Episodes, two episodes per
    tape, each 13.00
Star Trek 25th Anniversary Special, hosted by
    William Shatner & Leonard Nimoy 100 min. 20.00
Star Trek 25th Anniversary CD Collection (Strangers
    from the Sky, Enterprise: The First Adventure,
    Final Frontier) 30.00

FINE COLLECTIBLES (CLASSIC SERIES)

Snow Dome with U.S.S. Enterprise NCC 1701
    inside (Willitts 1992) 65.00
Star Trek 25th Anniversary Tankard, pewter drink-
    ing mug with sculptured panels of the *U.S.S.
    Enterprise* and characters (Franklin Mint 1991) .200.00
Chess Set, figural pieces, Franklin Mint 1,000.00

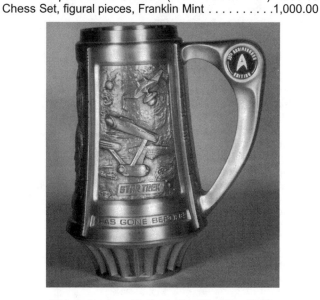

25th Anniversary Tankard (Franklin Mint 1995)

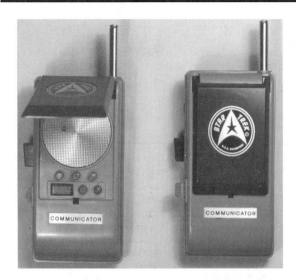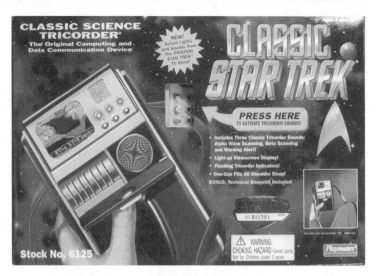

Star Trek Communicators (Mego 1974) Classic Science Tricorder (Playmates 1995)

Star Trek Gold Record, *The Cage* and *Where No*
    Man Has Gone Before, limited edition, (1991) . .250.00
U.S.S. Enterprise NCC-1701 lighted star globe,
    battery powered (1993) 50.00
U.S.S. Enterprise Lasersculpt, 5½" x 7" (1993) 30.00
U.S.S. Enterprise NCC-1701 3-D Space Environ-
    ment, ship hung from 6" x 9" book end (1993) . . .75.00
Starship Enterprise Porcelain Plaque (1993) 60.00
U.S.S. Enterprise NCC-1701 Golden Edition on
    black marble backdrop, book end (1993) 65.00
U.S.S. Enterprise NCC-1701 Sculpture in crystal-
    clear dome, 5½" (Franklin Mint 1997) 37.50

ROLE PLAY (CLASSIC SERIES)

This section covers toys and replicas of the equipment
used on the show — Communicators, Phasers and Tricorders.
This equipment was used in the original show and Paramount
just keeps changing the style for each new movie or series.
Manufacturers have generally tried to make the item do
something like make noises or flash lights. The flip-open
Beam me up Scotty! communicators have frequently been
made into walkie-talkies, while the recent chest-tap models
have mostly become jewelry. There have even been excellent
models of the original communicators which were also working radios, with solid state circuits instead of the older tran-
sistors.

Star Trek Tricorder, two-tone blue with silver and
    black starfleet insignia, with sholder strap,
    blueprint and 30 minute cassette in box
    (Mego #51218, 1976) $150.00
    loose 50.00
Star Trek Communicators Walkie-Talkie set of two,
    two-tone blue with silver and black Starfleet
    insignia (Mego #51214, 1974) 200.00
    loose 75.00
The above two items offered through distributors in
    1994! at prices listed here.
Star Trek Command Communications Console
    (Mego #51230SV, 1976) working base
    control station radio, blue plastic with five
    sound effects and flashing lights, battery
    powered, came in a 13½" x 8" box 175.00
Star Trek Wrist Communicators (Mego 1980) 175.00
Working Comunicators (1989) 50.00

Star Trek Helmet (Enco #6818, 1976) 125.00
Utility Belt, including disk-shooting phaser tricorder
    & communicator, boxed (Remco #203, 1976) . . .150.00
    (Remco #203, 1978) 100.00
Brass belt buckles, many available different designs, .15.00
Leather belt with starships, names and insignia,
    several available 15.00
Binoculars (Larami #9239, 1968) 50.00
Tracer gun 6½" plastic (Ray Plastic 1966) 45.00
Tracer-Scope (Ray Plastic 1966) 125.00
Jet Disks pack (Ray Plastic 1966) 30.00
Star Trek rocket pistol (Remco #870-450, 1967) . . .1,500.00
Ray Gun Flashlight (Larami #9238, 1968) 50.00
Phaser Gun Project-A-Target, 8" plastic, battery
    powered (Remco 1975) 90.00
Phaser Saucer gun (AHI 1975) 50.00
Phaser Ray gun (AHI #6369, 1976) 50.00

USS Enterprise water gun (AHI #6322, 1976) 50.00
Star Trek phaser water gun (AHI #6371, 1976) 30.00

Astro Walkie-Talkies (Remco 1967) 60.00
Classic Star Trek Classic Phaser, battery powered
    with firing sound (Playmates #6118, 1994) 25.00
Star Trek Classic Communicator battery
    powered, belt clip and display base in
    try-me box (Playmates #6117, 1994) 17.95
Classic Star Trek Classic Science Tricorder,
    6" x 3½" battery powered with blueprint in
    10" x 7" x 2½" try-me box (#6125, 1995) 20.00
Classic Star Trek Movie Series Starfleet Wrist
    Communicator (Playmates #16082, 1996) 15.00
Star Trek Talk-Back Communicator, toy on 8" x 10"
    box (Playmates #16065, 1996) working
    recording device, but not a radio 25.00
Star Trek Starfleet Medical Tricorder (Playmates
    #16143) 15.00
Captain Pike's Starfleet Laser Pistol (#16127) 15.00
Klingon D'k Tahg Knife in try-me box (#16142) 15.00

SPACESHIPS, PLAYSETS & VEHICLES
(CLASSIC SERIES)

To toy collectors, a vehicle is anything that an action
figure could use like a playset. The shuttlecrafts and a few of
the alien ships have been made as vehicles over the years, but

the *U.S.S. Enterprise* is too big to be made on a scale that would fit any action figure bigger than a flea. Toy replicas of the *Enterprise* and the alien vessels made to its scale are listed below as Starships. There are a lot of them available, they have excellent detail and most come with sound effects from the show. Many of them are available at your local toy store right now, maybe even at discount.

Playsets are toys designed for your action figures to play with or on. (If they can ride or fly in it, its called a vehicle.) Playsets are generally more expensive than the action figures that use them, so less are produced and sold. If the value of the action figures goes up, so does the value of the playset. Both the Mego action figures from the 1970s and the Playmates action figures from the 1990s have playsets.

Playsets
Star Trek *U.S.S. Enterprise* Action Playset, includes
   bridge and transporter room. Folds up into
   carrying case (Mego #51210, 1975) boxed   . . .$175.00
Star Trek Mission To Gamma VI Playset (Mego
   #51226, 1976) 650.00
Star Trek Telescreen Console playset (Mego
   #51232, 1976) 150.00
Enterprise Transporter Room playset (Mego/Palitoy
   #22608, 1974) 150.00

Ships & Vehicles
Controlled Space Flight *Enterprise* (Remco 1976) 90.00
Star Trek Astro Tank (Remco 1967) 1,250.00
Star Trek Astro Train (Remco 1967) 1,250.00
Star Trek: *Enterprise*, 9" die-cast model, fires plastic
   discs from the saucer (Dinky Toys #358,
   1977) in window box with header flap. 125.00
Star Trek: Klingon Ship, 9" die-cast model, fires
   plastic discs from the saucer (Dinky Toys
   #357, 1977) in window box with header flap 100.00
U.S.S. Enterprise & *Klingon Battle Cruiser* (Dinkey
   #309, 1977) 350.00
Classic Star Trek 30th Anniversary Galileo
   Shuttlecraft with Kirk figure (Playmates
   #16087, 1996) 30.00
Classic Star Trek U.S.S. Enterprise NCC-1701,
   battery powered in 17" x 11¾" x 4" try-me
   box (Playmates #6116, 1995) 50.00

WALL ART (CLASSIC SERIES)

Posters are sold in quantity and do not usually become valuable collector's items. The exception is promotional posters, covered under promotional material. Calendars, however, are a well recognized collecting field and *Star Trek* calendars have been produced every year since the mid 1970s. ChromArt prints are made with a unique graphic process which give them a metallic texture. They are sold shrink wrapped in cardboard matte which brings the total size to 11" x 15" which is suitable for framing. Its hard to decide if they are blueprints or posters. In any event, it has a nice metallic feel to it, much like some chromium trading cards, only larger.

Framed pictures
Star Trek 25th Anniversary Neon framed picture,
   large Next Generation Enterprise with neon
   tubes representing phaser fire (Neonetics) $225.00
Star Trek 25th Anniversary LED framed picture,
   large Next Generation Enterprise with LED
   lights in ports (Neonetics) 140.00

ChromeArt prints
Star Trek Enterprise A Front/Rear, 8" x 10" Chrom-
   Art Blueprint (Zanart 1995) 14.00
Star Trek Enterprise A Side, 8" x 10" ChromArt
   Blueprint (Zanart 1995) 14.00
Star Trek Enterprise A Top, 8" x 10" ChromArt
   Blueprint (Zanart 1995) 14.00

Miscellaneous posters
Blue Print portfolios, not chromium, set of 8 (#ST-BP) .13.00
Star Trek 25th Anniversary Poster of Kirk, Spock,
   McCoy and Uhura (#PTW633) 5.00
Star Trek 25th Anniversary Poster of Star Trek icon
   + Kirk, Spock, McCoy and Scotty (#PTW668) 5.00
Star Trek "All I need to know about life I learned
   from Star Trek" poster (PTW668) 5.00
Star Trek "All I need to know.." mini poster 11¾" x
   36" (#HOT664) 3.50

STAR TREK ANIMATED TV

With all the *Star Trek* movies and other television series, it's easy to overlook the animated show. Most collectors have little or nothing from this show in their collections, and it

Star Trek Action Playset (Mego 1975) Kirk transports to safety from the clutches of an alien female, just in the nick of time!

Star Trek The Motion Picture Captain Kirk doll (Mego 1979) Star Trek Generations Movie Edition Captain Jean-Luc Picard doll (Playmates 1995) & Star Trek First Contact Zephram Cochran doll (Playmates 1996)

does not look as though this will change anytime soon. Fans of animation in general don't collect the show either because they much prefer Disney, Warner Bros., Hanna Barbera or just about anything else. This lack of attention is either sad, or well deserved, depending on your point of view.

ANIMATION CELS & ART WORK

Limited edition cels (Tuttle & Bailey Galleries 1977)
    14" x 18", 25 different, each 100.00
Laser Reproduction cels (Royal Animation Studios
    1990) 24 different, each 100.00
Star Trek crew Seven Star portfolio 12" x 19" by
    Kelly Freas, 1976, set 60.00
Still available thru distributors in 1994 for $70.00
Seri-Cels (1995)
Tribble Trouble 14" x 18" (Royal Animated Art 1995) . .89.95
U.S.S. Enterprise 14" x 18" (Royal Animated Art 1995) .89.95
At The Helm. Enterprise 14" x 18" (Royal Animated
    Art 1995) 89.95

GLASSES, MUGS, PLATES

Cartoon series (Dr. Pepper 1976) glasses, each 40.00
    set, 4 glasses (Kirk, Spock, McCoy
    Enterprise) in box 175.00

STAR TREK MOVIES

CLOTHING & ACCESSORIES

Star Trek The Motion Picture Wallets on card
    (Larami 1979) Kirk & Spock or *Enterprise,* each . .25.00
Star Trek II game watch (Collins 1983) 120.00

Pinback Buttons, Badges & Tabs & Ensignias
Star Trek I buttons (Aviva 1979) each 4.00
Star Trek I metal pins (Aviva 1979) 4.00
Star Trek II buttons (Image Products 1982) 4.00
Star Trek III buttons (Button-Up 1984) 4.00

Star Trek IV The Voyage Home, movie pin, logo in
    circle with two whales (Lincoln Enterprises 1987) .9.00

Collector's Classic pins (Hollywood Pins 1989)
Star Trek V on symbol 7.50
Star Trek V with *Enterprise* in triangle 7.50
Star Trek V with *Enterprise* on top 9.00
Star Trek V with *Galileo* on top 9.00
Star Trek V logo pin 5.00
Star Trek V symbol pin 5.00
Star Trek Generations Communicator Pin
    (Hollywood Pins #1027, 1994). 10.00

DOLLS AND FIGURES (MOVIES)

In 1979, Mego produced seven figures based on the first movie, *Star Trek: The Motion Picture.* They were 12½" dolls. The Arcturian is not from the movie or the television series.

12½" Dolls (Mego 1979)
Capt. Kirk, with phaser (#91210/1) $80.00
Mr. Spock, with phaser (#91210/2) 80.00
Decker, with phaser (#91210/3) 175.00
Ilia, with necklace and white shoes (#91210/4) 100.00
Klingon (#91210/5) 100.00
Arcturian (#91210/6) 100.00

STAR TREK: GENERATIONS, MOVIE EDITION

Only four 9" dolls were released in the Generations series—Kirk, Picard, Data and LaForge. All were regular characters who had been or would be produced as other dolls. Collectors would have liked to see the new characters such as Dr. Soran, B'Etor and Lursa. There were no Space Caps or trading cards with this series.

9" Movie Edition Dolls (1994) with base, no card or cap
Captain Jean-Luc Picard (#6141) $20.00
Captain James T. Kirk (#6142) 60.00
Lieutenant Commander Data (#6143) 30.00
Lieutenant Commander Geordi LaForge (#6144) 30.00

STAR TREK: FIRST CONTACT, MOVIE DOLLS

Collectors would have preferred a figure of Lilly or the Borg Queen, the one who tries to seduce Data, instead of a second Picard figure in this series. At least Playmates made one new 9" figure. For the previous movie there were only four figures, all regular cast members.

9" Movie Figure Dolls (Playmates Nov. 1996) with
    base and mini poster
Captain Jean-Luc Picard (#16131) $17.50
Cmdr. William T. Riker (#16132) 17.50
Lt. Commander Data (#16133) 17.50
Zefram Cochrane (#16134) 20.00
Captain Jean-Luc Picard in 21st-Century Civilian
    Outfit (#16135) 17.50

9" Star Trek Insurrection dolls (Playmates 1998)
Captain Jean-Luc Picard (#65351) 17.50
Counselor Deanna Troi (#65355) 20.00
Lt. Commander Data (#65356) 17.50
Lt. Commander Geordi LaForge (#65354) 17.50

Figures
Star Trek: The Motion Picture: Captain Kirk, 13"
    children's soft doll, Knickerbocker 1979, in
    window box 60.00
Star Trek: The Motion Picture: Mr. Spock, 13"
    children's soft doll, Knickerbocker 1979, in
    window box 60.00

8" Star Trek V: The Final Frontier Figures (Galoob 1989) in
    window box
Captain James T. Kirk 40.00
Mr. Spock 40.00
Dr. Leonard "Bones" McCoy 40.00
Sybok 40.00
Klaa 40.00

10" Vinyl figures
Generations Kirk vinyl doll, 10" (Applause #45949) . . .10.00
Generations Picard vinyl doll, 10" (Applause #45950) . .10.00
Generations Data vinyl doll, 10" (Applause #45952) . . .10.00
Generations Worf vinyl doll, 10" (Applause #45953) . . .10.00

25mm Lead Miniatures (FASA)
Star Trek I 25mm figures (Citidal 1979) 10-20
Star Trek I Kirk 54mm figure (Citidal 1979) 10-20
Star Trek I Spock 54mm figure (Citidal 1979) 10-20
Star Trek I Ilia 54mm figure (Citidal 1979) 10-20
Star Trek I Klingon warrior 54mm (Citidal 1979) 10-20
Star Trek II figures, 17 different, each 2–4.00

PVCs
Star Trek Generations: Captain Kirk, Captain Picard,
    Lt. Commander Data, Lt. Commander Worf,
    Lt. Commander LaForge, Lursa, 4" PVC
    figures (Applause 1995) boxed set 20.00

FOOD (MOVIES)

Food Related Collectibles (McDonald's)
Video Communicator with 5 strips 6.00
Wrist bracelet 8.00
Placemat 10" x 14" 5.00
Enterprise mobile 6.00
Star Trek Happy Meal, Assorted items
Star Trek Navigating Bracelet 12.00
Starfleet Game 12.00

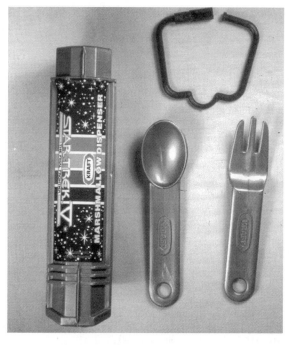

Star Trek V Marshmallow dispenser (Craft 1989)

Captain Kirk Ring w/ secret compartment 12.00
Enterprise Ring w/ secret compartment 12.00
Star Trek Logo Ring w/ secret compartment 12.00
Spock Ring w/ secret compartment 12.00
Iron-On Transfer, 4 different, each 10.00
Happy meal boxes, 6 different, each 7.00

GAMES & PUZZLES (MOVIES)

Star Trek II playing cards 12.50
Star Trek Game (Milton Bradley 1979) 30.00
Star Trek II Starship Combat Simulator (Fasa
    #2003, 1983) with maps, counters, playing pieces 20.00
Star Trek III Starship Combat (FASA 1984) 15.00
Star Trek III Struggle for the Throne, micro
    adventure (Fasa #5004, 1985) with action
    cards, pieces, map, dice & rules. Cover has
    photo of Kruge. 10.00
Star Trek V: The Final Frontier Game (for IBM
    computer) (Midescape, Level Systems 1989) 10.00

Star Trek Frame Tray puzzles (Whitman 1979) each . .10.00
Star Trek I (Milton Bradley 1979)
    Enterprise jigsaw puzzle 10.00
    Faces of the Future jigsaw puzzle 12.50
    Sick Bay jigsaw puzzle .12.50

HOUSEHOLD (MOVIES)

Star Trek: The Motion Picture, Collectible Fast Food
    Glasses (Coca-Cola 1980) glasses, each 30.00
    set, 4 glasses 130.00
Star Trek III (Taco Bell 1984) glasses, each 7.00
    set, 4 glasses (Lord Kruge, Fal-Tor-Pan,
    Enterprise Destroyed, Spock Lives) 30.00
Star Trek VI China, Cup, Saucer and dinner plate,
    stoneware (Pfaltzgraff 1993) with blue & gold
    logo of *U.S.S. Enterprise NCC 1701-A*,
    Boxed set 50.00
Star Trek VI Glassware, fine, large cooler glass &
    small double old fashion glasses (Pfaltzgraff
    1994) with blue & gold logo of *U.S.S.
    Enterprise #1701-A*, boxed set of four 40.00

Star Trek II mugs: Kirk, Spock, Khan, Crew, each 10.00
Star Trek I wastebasket 40.00
Star Trek I bandages (Adam Joseph 1979) 12.50
Star Trek I first aid kit (Adam Joseph 1979) 18.00
Star Trek I beanbag chair, boxed (K-Mart 1979) 40.00
Star Trek V Marshmallow dispenser (Kraft 1989)
    plastic with fork, spoon and belt hook 30.00
Star Trek I metal lunchbox, with thermos (King-
    Seeley 1979) 50.00
U.S.S. Enterprise NCC-1701-E Christmas
    Ornament (Hallmark 1998) 25.00

MASKS AND COSTUMES (MOVIES)

Kirk Halloween Costume (Collegeville Flag 1979) 20.00
Spock Halloween Costume (Collegeville Flag 1979) . . .20.00
Ilia Halloween Costume (Collegeville Flag 1979) 20.00
Klingon Halloween Costume (Collegeville Flag 1979) . .20.00

MICRO (MOVIES)

Star Trek The Movies (Collection #2)
    U.S.S. Excelsior; Klingon Bird of Prey; U.S.S.
    Reliant (#65882, 1994) 6.00
Star Trek The Movies (Collection #3)
    U.S.S. Reliant; Federation Space Dock;
    Klingon Bird of Prey; (#66102, 1995) 6.00
Star Trek The Movies (Collection #4)
    U.S.S. Grissom; U.S.S. Excelsior; Vulcan
    Shuttle Surak (#66103, 1995) 6.00

1995 pack with 8 listed, but different style
Star Trek Generations: *U.S.S. Enterprise* NCC
    1701-B; Klingon Bird of Prey; *U.S.S.
    Enterprise* NCC 1701-D (#65846, 1995?) 6.00

Star Trek Mini Ships (Galoob 1995)
Star Trek The Movies Collectors Edition, 8 ships,
    pewter color: Klingon Bird of Prey; U.S.S.
    Reliant; Federation Space Dock; Vulcan
    Shuttle Surak; U.S.S. Grissom; U.S.S.
    Enterprise NCC 1701-B; U.S.S. Enterprise
    NCC 1701-D; U.S.S. Enterprise NCC 1701-A
    (#66073, 1995) 20.00

MISCELLANEOUS (MOVIES)

Star Trek I kite (Aviva 1979) 25.00
Star Trek III kite (Lando 1984) 30.00
Star Trek: The Motion Picture Cielo Liqueur Bottle,
    figural Mr. Spock bust, silver shirt logo,
    Grenadire 1979, in box 75.00
Star Trek The Motion Picture I.D. set on card
    (Larami 1979) 10.00
Inflatable *Star Trek IV Enterprise* display 30.00
Star Trek: The Motion Picture Matchbook, rainbow
    design in black and yellow (D.D. Bean &
    Sons Co. 1979) 3.00
Star Trek I Lucite keychains, 6 different, each 4.00

PAPER (MOVIES)

Press Kits
Star Trek: The Motion Picture 40.00
Star Trek II: The Wrath of Khan 50.00
Star Trek III: The Search For Spock 40.00
Star Trek IV: The Voyage Home 30.00
Star Trek V: The Final Frontier 20.00

Programs
Star Trek: The Motion Picture 30.00
Star Trek II: The Wrath of Khan 35.00
Star Trek III: The Search For Spock 30.00

Star Trek liquor decanter (Grenadier 1979)

Star Trek IV: The Voyage Home 25.00
Star Trek V: The Final Frontier 20.00

Star Trek I Official Blueprints 14 in pouch (Wallaby
    1979) 8-12.00

Newsletter
Star Trek: The Motion Picture #1 (Paramount,
    Summer 1979). Slick paper, 11" x 17" folded
    in half to form four pages. With color pictures
    of Kirk, Decker, Ilia, Spock and Kirk ad-
    dressing the crew of the *Enterprise* 5.00

Movie Magazines
The Official Star Trek Generations Movie Magazine
    (Starlog 1994) 3-D Lenticular Collectors'
    Edition, with 8 extra pages. 10.00

Magazines, Humor
Mad Magazine Super Special (Mad 1992) *Star Trek
    VI* movie parody. 10.00

PHOTOS (MOVIES)

Autographed Photo Plaques
Star Trek VI William Shatner 160.00
Star Trek VI Leonard Nimoy 160.00
Star Trek VI DeForest Kelly 160.00
Star Trek VI James Doohan 130.00
Star Trek VI Walter Koenig 130.00
Star Trek VI Nichelle Nichols 130.00
Star Trek VI George Takei 130.00

RECORDINGS (MOVIES)

Music
Star Trek II: The Wrath of Khan music by James
    Horner 25.00
Star Trek III: The Search For Spock, music by
    James Horner 25.00
Star Trek VI, The Undiscovered Country, original
    motion picture soundtrack, Music by Cliff

Star Trek Generations Klingon Disruptor (Playmates 1994)

Eidelman, CD format (MCA 1991) 25.00
Star Trek Generations, music by Dennis McCarthy 25.00
Video
Star Trek VI: The Undiscovered Country video tape,
    including two minutes of additional footage 14.95
Video tape of *Star Trek Generations* movie, box
    says "Two Captains, One Destiny"
    (Paramount Home Video 1995) 15.00

ROLE PLAY (MOVIES)

Star Trek I Dual Phaser II set (South Bend 1979) 60.00
Star Trek I Signal gun (Larami #8063-0, 1979) 45.00
Star Trek I water pistol (Aviva 1979) 90.00
Star Trek III phaser (Daisy #39398, 1984) 40.00
Star Trek V Communicator, Proctor & Gamble Crest
    Toothpaste mail-in premium (P. J. McNerney
    & Associates, Model No. 652, 1989) two
    2¾" x 4¼" communicators with flip-up lid and
    telescoping antenna 75.00
Star Trek Generations Klingon Disruptor, 11" x 5"
    battery powered with blueprint, decals and
    poster in 11½" x 6" x 2½" try-me box (#6146,
    1994) 15.00
Classic *Star Trek* Movie Series Starfleet Phaser,
    7½" x 5½" battery powered with two sounds
    plus diagram in 10" x 7" x 2½" try-me box
    (Playmates #16081, 1996) 25.00

SPACESHIPS & PLAYSETS (MOVIES)

U.S.S. Enterprise Bridge (Mego #91233, 1980) 135.00
Star Trek Generations Engineering playset, battery
    powered in box (Playmates #6108, 1994) 35.00

U.S.S. Excelsior NCC-2000, *Star Trek The Movie*
    Collection in 17" x 12" x 3½" try-me box
    (Playmates #6127, 1994) 25.00
Star Trek Generations Starship Enterprise NCC
    1701-D with Blow Apart Battle Damage, mini
    poster, blueprints plus display stand, battery
    powered in 17" x 11¾" x 3½" box (Playmates
    #6171, 1994) 50.00
Star Trek Generations Starship Enterprise NCC
    1701-B battery powered in 17?" x 12?" x
    3½?" try-me box (Playmates #6172, 1994) 50.00
Star Trek Generations Klingon Bird-of-Prey,
    battery powered in 17?" x 12?" x 3½?" try-
    me box (Playmates #6174, 1995) 25.00
Star Trek First Contact Phoenix Warp Drive Ship,
    battery powered in try-me box (Playmates
    #16147, 1996) 27.00
Star Trek First Contact Starship Enterprise NCC
    1701-E, battery powered in try-me box (Play-
    mates #16148, 1996) .27.00

Star Trek First Contact Borg Ship (Playmates
    #16149, 1996) 27.00

Star Trek I Electronic *Enterprise* (Milton
    Bradley/Southbend 1979) 125.00
Star Trek I Small *Enterprise* (Dinky #803, 1979) 75.00
Klingon Battle Cruiser, small (Dinky, #804, 1979) 80.00
Star Trek II Mini *Enterprise* (Corgi 1982) 60.00
Star Trek II Klingon ship (Corgi 1982) 60.00
Star Trek III die cast *Enterprise* (Ertl 1984) 40.00
Star Trek III die cast *Excelsior* (Ertl 1984) 40.00
Star Trek III die cast Klingon *Bird of Prey* (Ertl 1984) . .40.00
Star Trek V Enterprise (Ertl 1989) 20.00
Star Trek V Klingon *Bird of Prey* (Ertl 1989) 20.00

WALL ART (MOVIES)

Star Trek: The Motion Picture poster, rainbow image,
    "There is no comparison" (Paramount 1979) 50.00
Star Trek: The Motion Picture poster, showing
    Enterprise flying at the viewer on its side and
    eight inset photos of the cast (Paramount 1979) .50.00
Star Trek: The Motion Picture, Enterprise Cut-Away
    Poster (Sales Corporation of America 1979)
    22" x 48" 25.00
Star Trek II: The Wrath of Khan film poster 45.00
Star Trek II: The Wrath of Khan movie poster, color
    promo, collage image "At the end of the
    Universe lies the beginning of vengeance."
    (Paramount 1982) 50.00
Star Trek II: The Wrath of Khan poster, 22" x 31"
    (New Eye 1983) 10.00
Star Trek III: The Search For Spock film poster 40.00
Star Trek IV: The Voyage Home film poster 35.00
Star Trek V: The Final Frontier film poster 30.00

Star Trek Movie Enterprise ChromeArt Print (Zanart
    #ST-C, 1995) 15.00
Star Trek The Motion Picture ChromeArt Print
    (Zanart #ST-C2, 1995) 15.00
Star Trek II The Wrath of Khan ChromeArt Print
    (Zanart #ST-C3, 1995) 15.00
Star Trek III The Search For Spock ChromeArt Print
    (Zanart #ST-C4, 1995) 15.00
Star Trek IV The Voyage Home ChromeArt Print
    showing faces and ship over Golden Gate
    Bridge (Zanart 1995). .15.00
Star Trek Generations ChromeArt Print (Zanart
    #STG-C, 1995) 15.00
Generations Klingon Bird of Prey ChromeArt Print
    (Zanart #STG-C2, 1995) 15.00
Generations Enterprise ChromeArt Print (Zanart
    #STG-C3, 1995) 15.00

*Star Trek First Contact Phoenix Warp Drive Ship
(Playmates 1996)*

Star Trek The Next Generation Crew Pin 1988–1989 season, Cast and Crew pin 1990–1991, Encounter at Farpoint Episode pin (Hollywood Pins 1989–91)

STAR TREK, THE NEXT GENERATION

Star Trek, The Next Generation brought Gene Roddenberry's universe back to the small screen in 1987. There were 178 episodes, more than twice as many as the classic series. Worf and O'Brien live on as part of *Deep Space Nine* and everybody came back for the third (if you count *Generations*) movie, which opened in December 1998.

Star Trek, The Next Generation, may live forever in reruns. The original series already has. There are a lot of collectibles from this series, but the classic series still generates as many, if not more. Will *The Next Generation* always be seen as a sequel, or will its fans grow up to drive their own wave of collecting a few years from now? There has never been a situation quite like it. At the moment, new action figures and dolls are being produced based on the classic series and the two ongoing series, but this year's movie did not get any, in part because the figures from *Star Trek First Contact* are still kicking around in toy stores.

CERAMICS

Porcelain Mini Plates 4" dia. (Hamilton 1993) with Easel
U.S.S. Enterprise NCC-1701-D (#913243) $7.50
The Continuing Voyages (Crew) (#913251) 7.50
Lieutenant Worf (#914061) 7.50
Captain Picard (#913278) 7.50
Lt. Commander Data (#914096) 7.50
Counselor Troi (#914088) 7.50

Porcelain Plaques 5½ high (Hamilton 1993) with easel
Lieutenant Worf (#914045) .12.00
Counselor Deanna Troi (#914037) 12.00
Lt. Commander Data (#914039) 12.50
Captain Jean-Luc Picard (#913170) 12.50
U.S.S. Enterprise NCC-1701-D (#913162) 12.50

CLOTHING & ACCESSORIES (NEXT GENERATION)

TNG Adult Uniform Shirt, metal rank pips and communicator pin, in burgundy, gold and blue (Rubies) 50.00
Same, with rank pips & plastic communicator pin:
TNG Deluxe Red Shirt (#15286) 50.00
TNG Deluxe Gold Shirt (#15287) 50.00
TNG Deluxe Teal Shirt (#15288) 50.00

TNG Women's Uniform Jumpsuit, metal rank pips and communicator pin, in burgundy, gold and blue (Rubies #SUF2) 50.00
TNG Deluxe Red Jumpsuit (#15289R) 60.00
TNG Deluxe Gold Jumpsuit (#15289G) 60.00
TNG Deluxe Teal Jumpsuit (#15289B) 60.00
Star Trek, The Next Generation, Mens Jacket (Sichel Personalized Promotional Sportswear 1990–92) black with Star Trek, The Next Generation on front and *U.S.S. Enterprise NCC 1701-D* pictured on back. 125.00

The Next Generation Crew tie 20.00
The Next Generation Baseball Cap embroidered logo .12.00
Star Trek, The Next Generation Belt Bag (Imaginings 3, 1994) 10.00

Star Trek: The Next Generation Chronoscanner, digital watch (Timex 1994) 30.00

The Next Generation Episode Pins
Encounter at Far Point (Hollywood Pins #8501, 1990) 12.00
All Good Things 12.00
Other episode pins, each 8.00

Next Generation Communicator Pin with Sound (Kohn 219817) 13.00
Silver Medallion Pin used on Worf's Sash with moving LCD (Crysalid Group) 20.00
Next Generation Logo cloisonne Pin (#1510) 6.00
Next Generation Enterprise cut-out cloisonne Pin (#1740) 6.00
Next Generation Communicator Pin, full-size (#1022BP) carded 10.00
Next Generation Gold Collar Pip (#PIP1) 4.00
Next Generation Black Collar Pip (#PIP2) 4.00
Next Generation Engage pin (#1039) 8.00
Next Generation Communicator of the Future Pin, full-size (#1024) 15.00
Next Generation "All Good Things" Future Communicator Pin (#1028) 10.00
Next Generation Gold Collar Pin, small (#CPG) 3.00
Next Generation Silver Collar Pin, small (#CPS) 3.00
Next Generation Communicator Pin, ½ size (#1020) . . .6.00

Miniature Communicator Pin #1026 . . . . .5.00
Next Generation "Make it So" pin (#1037) 6.00
United Federation of Planets Logo Pin (#1080) 6.00

Next Generation Klingon Symbol Pin (#152) 8.00
Star Trek, The Next Generation Crew pin, 1988-
    1989 Season tall blue rectangle with logo in
    center (Hollywood Pins 1989) 8.00
Star Trek, The Next Generation: Starfleet Command,
    Fleet Operations Center Sol Sector, insignia
    pin, words in gold onred background, logo at
    top (Hollywood Pins #1806, 1990) 9.00
Star Trek, The Next Generation: Starfleet Com-
    mand, Medical, insignia pins, tall domed
    rectangle with symbol (Hollywood Pins 1986) 9.00
Star Trek, The Next Generation: Starfleet Command,
    Military, insignia pins, tall domed rectangle
    with symbol (Hollywood Pins 1986) 9.00

Collector's Classic pins: Next Generation
S27 United Federation of Planets 5.00
Enterprise cut-out pin 10.00
Next Generation logo pin, blue 5.00
Next Generation logo pin, red 5.00
Make It So pin 5.00

DIE-CAST & METAL (NEXT GENERATION)

2¼" Pewter Figurines Star Trek The Next Generation
Crew, 8 different, each 17.50

Enterprise on black triangular base with pewter
    Federation logo and name plate (#RF797)
    lim. 15,000 copies .100.00
Klingon Bird of Prey (#RF1778) 65.00
Enterprise (#RF794) 26.00
Romulan Warbird (#RF795) 35.00
Ferengi Marauder (#RF796) 35.00

DOLLS AND FIGURES (NEXT GENERATION)

Collector Series 9" Dolls (Playmates 1996–98)
Captain Jean-Luc Picard (#6066) Command Edition . .30.00
Starfleet Edition
Commander Deanna Troi (#6281) 40.00
Doctor Beverly Crusher (#6282) 50.00
Lieutenant Commander Data (#6284) 30.00
Commander William Riker (#6285) 30.00
Lieutenant Commander Geordi LaForge (#6287) 30.00

Star Trek The Next Generation Starfleet Edition 9" dolls, Geordi LaForge & Dr. Beverly Crusher, Data (Playmates 1996–97)

Star Trek The Next Generation 9" doll Data (Playmates 1996) & Data vinyl figure (Enesco 1994)

Captain Jean-Luc Picard in Dress Uniform (#6289) . . .35.00
Guinan (#6283) Federation Edition 40.00

9" Alien Edition Dolls
Lieutenant Worf in Ritual Klingon Attire (#6286) 35.00
Borg (#6069) 50.00
Romulan Commander (#16181, 1996) 15.00
Q (in judges robes) (#16187) painted face 30.00
Q (in judges robes) (#16187) unpainted face 20.00

9" Exclusive Dolls, Spencer Gifts, limited to 15,000
Captain Jean-Luc Picard (#65264) 35.00
Commander William Riker (#65265) 35.00

Vinyl Figures with Starfleet Insignia Base
Data 11½" figure (Hamilton Gifts #911607, 1993) 15.00
Picard 11" figure (Hamilton Gifts #911615, 1993) 15.00
Troi 10¾" figure (Hamilton Gifts #912158, 1993) 15.00

Vinyl Figures, 10½" with stand, in window box
Lt. Commander Geordi LaForge (Enesco 1994) 10.00
Captain Jean-Luc Picard (Enesco 1994) 10.00
Commander William Riker (Enesco 1994) 10.00
Counselor Deanna Troi (Enesco 1994) 15.00
Lt. Commander Data (Enesco 1994) 10.00
Lieutenant Worf (Enesco 1994) 10.00
Ferengi (Enesco 1994) 15.00

PVCs
Star Trek, The Next Generation 6 crew figures
    (Hamilton 1993) each .4.00
Star Trek, The Next Generation 4 aliens (Hamilton
    1993) each 4.00
Enterprise, on stand (Hamilton #913111, 1993) 4.00
Klingon Ship, on stand (Hamilton #771538, 1993) 4.00

Games & Puzzles
Star Trek The Next Generation Game of the
    Galaxies (Cardinal) 25.00
Star Trek The Next Generation Interactive VCR
    Board Game "A Klingon Challenge," includes
    a 60-minute videotape (Decipher 1993) 50.00
Star Trek, The Next Generation hand-held

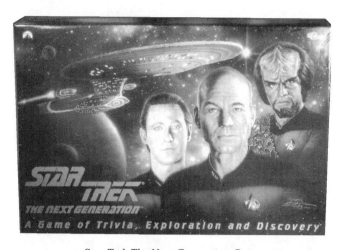

Star Trek The Next Generation Game

computer game (Tiger 1993) 15.00
Star Trek The Next Generation Collage of the
    Enterprise, Romulan Warbird, cast and aliens
    1,000 Piece Puzzle (#90025) 7.50
Star Trek The Next Generation Deluxe Wooden
    Jigsaw Puzzle, designed by J.C. Ayer & Co
    using illustration from the Enterprise Cutaway
    Poster one piece signed & dated 375.00

Playing Cards
U.S.S. Enterprise NCC-1701-D playing cards, in tin
    box (Hamilton #913227, 1993) 8.50
Star Trek Enterprise NCC-1701 playing cards, in tin
    box (Hamilton #913235, 1993) 8.50

HOUSEHOLD (NEXT GENERATION)

Christmas Ornaments
U.S.S. Enterprise (Next Generation) Christmas
    Ornament with blinking light (Hallmark 1993) 60.00
Captain Jean-Luc Picard Christmas Ornament,
    standing in holodeck door (Hallmark 1995) 30.00
Commander William Riker Christmas Ornament
    (Hallmark 1996) 20.00
Commander Data Christmas Ornament (Hallmark
    1997) 25.00

Clocks
Star Trek The Next Generation Crew wall clock, 12"
    diameter 33.50
Star Trek The Next Generation *Enterprise* wall
    clock, 12" diameter 33.50
Star Trek The Next Generation *Enterprise* alarm
    clock 33.50
Star Trek The Next Generation Shuttlecraft Clock
    Radio, replica of the Magellan, collectors
    edition (TeleMania #02322, 1994) 40.00

Lunch Boxes
Next Generation lunch box (Halsey Taylor) 10.00
    bottle for lunch box 4.00
Worf head figural lunch box, speaks when opened . . .25.00
Borg head figural lunch box, speaks when opened . . .25.00
Ferengi head figural lunch box, speaks when opened .25.00

Picture Mugs 11oz ceramic
Lt. Commander Data (#914002) 9.00
Captain Jean-Luc Picard (#914010) 9.00
The Continuing Voyages (Crew) (#913154) 9.00

Counselor Deanna Troi (#913995) 9.00
Lieutenant Worf (#913987) .9.00
U.S.S. Enterprise NCC-1701-D (#913219) 9.00

Star Trek The Next Generation Mugs
Figural Mugs, 6 different (Applause 1994) 15.00
Coffee Mug, blue, yellow lettering, schematic
    drawing of Enterprise "D" (Pfaltzgraff 1994) 15.00
Magic mugs, 8 different, each 13.00
Romulan Warbird logo mug 10.00
Klingon Bird of Prey logo mug 10.00
Enterprise Technical mug 10.00
Ferengis, Klingons and Borgs...Oh My! mug 9.00
Galaxy Class Starship mug 10.00
Picard Commemorative Decal Mug (Generations
    Sailing Ship Captain and other images)
    (Applause #46122) 7.00

MASKS AND COSTUMES (NEXT GENERATION)

Ferengi mask & costume (1987) 15.00

MICRO MACHINE (NEXT GENERATION)

Star Trek: The Next Generation (Collection #3)
    Klingon Vor'cha Attack Cruiser; U.S.S.
    Enterprise NCC-1701-D (Galoob 1994) 6.00
Star Trek: The Next Generation (Collection #4)
    Ferengi Marauder; Borg Ship; Shuttlecraft
    (Galoob 1995) 6.00
Star Trek: The Next Generation (Collection #5)
    Klingon Vor'cha Attack Cruiser; U.S.S.
    Enterprise NCC-1701-D; Romulan Scout Ship
    (Galoob 1995) 6.00
Star Trek: The Next Generation (Collection #6)
    Borg Ship; Ferengi Marauder; U.S.S.
    Enterprise NCC-1701-C (Galoob 1995) 6.00
Star Trek: The Next Generation (Collection #7)
    U.S.S. Stargazer; Romuland Warbird;
    Shuttlecraft; (Galoob 1995) 6.00

STAR TREK INNER SPACE (Playmates 1994)
with 2 tiny figures
Shuttlecraft Goddard mini playset (#6176) 7.00
Borg Ship mini playset (#6177) 7.00
Klingon Bird-of-Prey (#6178) 7.00
Romulan Warbird mini playset (#6179) 7.00

Captain Picard Keepsake Ornament (Hallmark 1995)

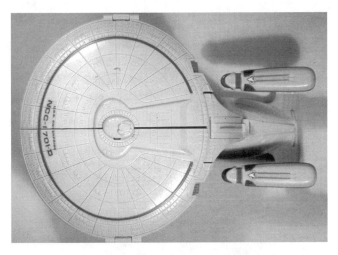

Star Trek Strike Force U.S.S. Enterprise (Playmates 1997)

STAR TREK STRIKE FORCE
Ships with two little figures (Playmates Sept. 1997)
Cardassian Warship with Gul Dukat and Karak
    (#16211) 10.00
U.S.S. Enterprise NCC-1701-D with Captain Picard
    & Commander Riker (#16212) 10.00
Klingon Bird of Prey with Valkris & Commander
    Kruge (#16213) 10.00
Ferengi Marauder with DiaMon Dok and Jason
    Vigo (#16214) 10.00

Mini-Figure Sets (Asst. #16270, Sept. 1997)
Klingon Warriors (#16271) 7.00
Starfleet Away Team (#16272) 7.00
Borg Assimilation Team (#16273) 7.00
Ferengi Commerce Team (#16274) 7.00
Borg Temple with Lt. Cmdr. Data, Lore, Hugh Borg
    and Borg Soldier 10.00
Klingon Great Hall with Lt. Worf, K'mpec, Gowron,
    Karg Pet and Klingon Warrior 10.00

MISCELLANEOUS (NEXT GENERATION)

Ferengi Talking carrying case (#673) 24.95
Borg Talking carrying case (#674) 24.95
Worf Talking carrying case (#675) 24.95
Collector Case (Tara Toys #20910, 1993) plastic
    case for 12 action figures. 15.00

Coin banks in shape of head (Thinkway 1994)
Ferengi Bank 8" (#09835) 15.00
Borg Bank 8" (#09836) 15.00
Klingon Bank 15.00
Electronic Console Bank (#13829) 40.00

Star Trek The Next Generation Yo Yos (#1585)
    Enterprise, Picard, Riker or Worf, each 3.00

Window Cling Decals:
Crew (Image #00077) 5.00
Enterprise, front view (Image #00079) 5.00
Enterprise, side view (Image #00080) 5.00
Worf (Image #00078) 5.00

Star Trek, The Next Generation, Hang Ups! banner,
    28" x 40" (Great Scott Inc. #52008, 1995)
    boxed 15.00
Star Trek, The Next Generation Computer disk
    holder, BrainWorks #10017, 1995, box shown ...12.00

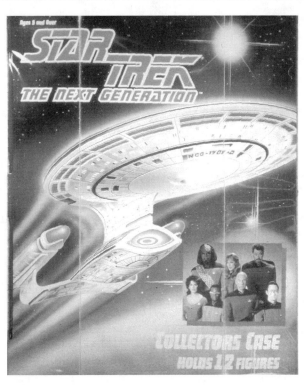

Star Trek The Next Generation Collectors Case (Tara Toys 1993)

Star Trek, The Next Generation Mouse and
    Mousepad, BrainWorks, #10011, 1995,
    boxed 30.00
Star Trek, The Next Generation Phaser Universal
    TV/VCR Remote (TeleMania #02338, 1996)
    in the shape of a Type II Phaser, with Star
    Trek logo, boxed 50.00

Paper
Star Trek The Next Generation press kit 20.00
Star Trek The Next Generation *"All Good Things"*
    Press Kit in box with rubber wrap around
    (Paramount 1994) containing photos and fact
    sheets 250.00
Star Trek, The Next Generation 1994 calendar
    (Pocket Books #86842-X, 1993) 10.00

Star Trek The Next Generation U.S.S. Enterprise
    Business Card Holder (Applause #45862,
    1994) 12.00
Star Trek The Next Generation U.S.S. Enterprise
    Letter Holder (Applause #45863, 1994) 15.00
Star Trek The Next Generation U.S.S. Enterprise
    Pencil Cup (Applause #45864, 1994) 10.00
Star Trek The Next Generation U.S.S. Enterprise
    LCD Alarm Clock (Applause #45866, 1994) 15.00
Star Trek, The Next Generation *U.S.S. Enterprise
    NCC 1701-D* Blueprints by Rick Sternbach
    (Pocket 50093-7, 1996) 13 blueprints plus a
    16 page booklet, shrink wrapped in a book-
    like case. 25.00

The Next Generation Standees
Picard standee (#15) 25.00
Riker standee (#16) 25.00
Data standee (#17) 25.00
Worf standee (#18) 25.00
LaForge standee (#19) 25.00

Troi standee (#20) 25.00
Dr. Crusher standee (#21) 25.00

MAGAZINES (NEXT GENERATION)

STAR TREK THE NEXT GENERATION
1 inverview with Gene Roddenberry 7.00
2 New Enterprise, FX secrets 7.00
3 Frakes, Sirtis & Youngblood 7.00
4 Stewart, Dorn & Wheaton 7.00
5 interviews: Diana Muldaur & Whoopi Goldberg,
   four posters 7.00
6 New bridge sets, four posters 7.00
7 Dorn 7.00
8 Diana Muldaur, Howard Weinstein 7.00
9 Dr. Crusher returns 7.00
10 Wheaton interview 7.00
11 Burton and Frakes 7.00
12 Sirtis, McFadden 7.00
13 Year 4, Burton interview .7.00
14 Trek women 7.00
15 Michael Dorn 7.00
16 thru 30 . . . . .7.00

PHOTOS (NEXT GENERATION)

Cast members from each of the shows appear at *Star Trek* conventions from time to time. If you go to enough shows, you can get autographs from just about all of your favorites. Standing in an autograph line is not a lot of fun. Look for the shorter lines with less famous cast members. You will probably enjoy your autographed photo just as much and you might have time to get another while your friend gets only one in the William Shatner line.

Autographed Photos
Autographed photo of Patrick Stewart $100.00
Autographed photo of other cast members 40.00

Marina Sirtis (Deanna Troi) autographed photo

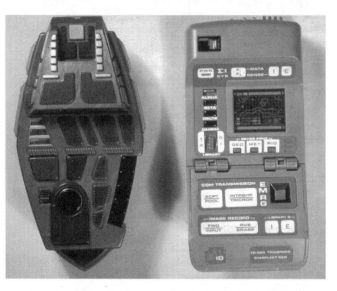
Bajorian & Starfleet Tricorders (Playmates 1993 & 1995)

Autographed Photo Plaques
Nimoy and Spiner Autographed Photo Plaque,
   "Unification" (numbered, limited to 2,500) 270.00
Star Trek William Shatner & Patrick Stewart
   Autographed Photo Plaque, "The Captains"
   (numbered, limited to 2,500) 170.00
Patrick Stewart Autographed Photo Plaque 160.00
John Delancie Autographed Photo Plaque 130.00
Brent Spiner Autographed Photo Plaque 130.00
Michael Dorn Autographed Photo Plaque 130.00
Jonathan Frakes Autographed Photo Plaque 130.00
Marina Sirtis Autographed Photo Plaque 130.00
Wil Wheaton Autographed Photo Plaque 130.00
Gates McFadden Autographed Photo Plaque 130.00

RECORDINGS (NEXT GENERATION)

Encounter at Farpoint video tape, 96 minutes 19.95
Other video tape episodes, each 14.95
Star Trek The Next Generation TV Soundtrack CD
   Volume I (*Encounter at Farpoint*) music by
   Dennis McCarthy 17.95
Star Trek The Next Generation TV Soundtrack CD
   Volume Two (*The Best of Both Worlds I & II*)
   music by Ron Jones 17.95
Star Trek The Next Generation TV Soundtrack CD
   Volume Three (*Yesterday's Enterprise,
   Unification I & II & Hollow Pursuits*) music by
   Dennis McCarthy 17.95
Boxed set of above three 49.95

ROLE PLAY (NEXT GENERATION)

Star Trek, The Next Generation, Phaser weapon,
   on header card, with phaser sound, phaser
   light and intensity control, battery powered
   (Type I) (Galoob 1988) 30.00
Star Trek, The Next Generation (Type II) Phaser, 8"
   long and thin, with grip, no handle; battery
   powered, two sounds & two lights, clips onto
   belt, in a try-me box (Playmates #6151, 1993) . .20.00
Star Trek, The Next Generation (Type I) **Hand
   Phaser**, 5" no handle; battery powered, two
   sounds in a try-me box (Playmates #6159, 1994) 15.00
Star Trek The Next Generation **Bajoran Phaser**,
   7" x 4½" battery powered in 10" x 7" x 2½" try-
   me box (#6271, 1995) 13.00

Star Trek The Next Generation Klingon Disruptor
  (#6129, 1995) 15.00
Star Trek The Next Generation Phaser Rifle, 26",
  battery powered with three sounds and borg
  target in a box (#6110, 1994) 30.00
Star Trek The Next Generation Communicator
  Walkie Talkie, two units with belt clips, clip
  on badges in a 7½" x 12½" x 2¼" box (#6119,
  1993) 30.00
Star Trek The Next Generation Personal
  Communicator, 3¼" x 2¾" in 6½" x 4½" x
  1¾" try-me box, with hanging flap (#6152,
  1992) with sound effects, but no communication .10.00
Star Trek The Next Generation Tricorder, 6" x 3"
  battery powered with blueprint in 10" x 6" x
  2½" try-me box (#6153, 1993) 25.00
Star Trek The Next Generation Bajoran Tricorder,
  6½" x 3" battery powered with diagram in
  10" x 7" x 2½" try-me box (#6273, 1995) 15.00

SPACESHIPS & VEHICLES (NEXT GENERATION)

Galoob's *Enterprise* is made out of metal and is almost
too heavy to be a toy but its a great size for a collector. The
saucer section is detachable. Too bad it didn't come with a
display base.

Star Trek, The Next Generation, Ferengi Fighter
  (Galoob 1989) orange plastic, 4¼" x 6" in
  8¼" x 10¾" box, carries two figures. $50.00
Star Trek, The Next Generation, Shuttlecraft
  Galileo (Galoob #5362, 1988) 8½" x 12" box,
  carries 6 figures, boxed .50.00
Star Trek, The Next Generation *U.S.S. Enterprise*
  Starship (NCC 1701-D) die-cast 4½" x 6"
  (Galoob #5346, 1988) shown loose, from top   . . .35.00
Star Trek, The Next Generation Starship *Enterprise*
  figurine (Enesco 1992) 8" long, box with
  picture of *Enterprise NCC 1701-D* 40.00
Shuttlecraft Goddard vehicle, electronic, dual
  light-up thrusters, two sounds and blueprint,
  battery powered in 16" x 10" x 6" try-me box
  (Playmates #6101, 1992) 35.00
Star Trek: The Next Generation *Enterprise* Bridge
  Playset (Playmates #6103, 1993) 75.00
Star Trek: The Next Generation Transporter
  playset (Playmates #6104, 1993) 60.00
Star Trek The Next Generation Enterprise glider,
  18" foam, with labels (Playmates #6113, 1994) . .15.00
Star Trek The Next Generation Starship Enterprise model, 15" with battery powered dual
  light-up engines, 4 authentic starship sounds
  and blueprint (but no stand) in 17" x 12" x 3½"
  try-me box (Playmates #6102, 1993) 37.00
  Note: Box variation: Small parts warning in one line
  at top (earlier) or two lines bottom left (later).
Star Trek Space Talk Series U.S.S. Enterprise
  NCC 1701-D with over 100 commands and
  sound effects, battery powered with blueprint
  in 17" x 12" x 3½" try-me box (Playmates
  #6106, 1995) 25.00
7th Anniversary Special Collector's Edition gold-
  decorated U.S.S. Enterprise, with base and
  Certificate of Authenticity (50,000 made)
  (Playmates #6112, 1993) 90.00
Star Trek Transwarping Starship *Enterprise NCC*
  1701-D, transforms from two engine nacelles

Star Trek The Next Generation 7th Anniversary U.S.S. Enterprise
(Playmates 1993)

to three (as seen in the *All Good Things*
  episode) (Playmates #16077, 1996) in
  13" x 8¾" x 3½" box 25.00
Star Trek The Next Generation Klingon Bird-of-
  Prey, battery powered with technical
  blueprint in 17" x 12" x 3½" try-me box
  (Playmates #6128, 1995) 25.00
Star Trek The Next Generation Romulan Warbird,
  battery powered with technical blueprint in
  17" x 12" x 3½" try-me box (Playmates
  #6154, 1993) 27.00
Star Trek The Next Generation Klingon Attack
  Cruiser, battery powered with technical
  blueprint in 17" x 12" x 3½" try-me box
  (Playmates #6155, 1993) 27.00
Star Trek The Next Generation Borg Ship, 7½"
  cube plus display stand, battery powered in
  10" x 10" x 7" try-me box (Playmates #6158,
  1994) 25.00
Romulan Bird of Prey (Neutral Zone Incursion
  Craft) battery powered in try me box
  (Playmates #16126, 1997) 27.00

WALL ART (NEXT GENERATION)

Next Generation Enterprise ChromeArt Print
  (Zanart #STN-C, 1995) .15.00
Next Generation Enterprise ChromeArt Print
  (Zanart #STN-C2, 1995) 15.00
Next Generation Klingon Attack Cruiser ChromeArt
  Print (Zanart #STN-C3, 1995) 15.00
Next Generation Romulan Warbird ChromeArt Print
  (Zanart #STN-C4, 1995) 15.00
Next Generation Enterprise A Front/Rear, 8" x 10"
  ChromArt Blueprint (Zanart #STB-C4, 1995) 14.00
Next Generation Enterprise A Side, 8" x 10" Chrom
  Art Blueprint (Zanart #STB-C5, 1995) 14.00
Next Generation Enterprise A Top, 8" x 10" Chrom
  Art Blueprint (Zanart #STB-C6, 1995) 14.00
Next Generation Enterprise cross section poster
  (#PTW715) 5.00
Next Generation Enterprise cut-away poster
  48" x 25½" 25.00

Lifesize Posters
Poster, 26" x 74" 7 different, each 9.00
Next Generation Enterprise 74" x 26" 9.00

U.S.S. Defiant & Quark's Bar pins (Hollywood Pins 1996)

STAR TREK DEEP SPACE NINE

Deep Space Nine has been running since early 1993 and looks like it has several more miles in it. Some of the romantic entanglements seem implausable, but the nightly news on tv reveals even less plausable situations as fact, so why not. In fact, you really have to admire the *Star Trek* characters for trying to establish long term relationships. Kirk couldn't keep a romance going for more than a week. However, he never wrote a book about them. These days, a person who can keep his mouth shut about his sex life seems like a saint. All in all, I'd rather watch *Star Trek* than the news any day.

CLOTHING & ACCESSORIES

DS9 Adult Uniform Shirt plus purple turtleneck, metal rank pips and communicator pin, in Teal, Burgundy & Gold (Rubies #SUF3) $50.00
same as above? with rank pips & plastic communicator pin:
DS9 Deluxe Red Shirt (#15290) 50.00
DS9 Deluxe Gold Shirt (#15291) 50.00
DS9 Deluxe Teal Shirt (#15292) 50.00

Lieutenant Dax Uniform, jumpsuit, with communicator pin (Rubies #SUF4) 50.00
Major Kira Uniform, jumpsuit, with communicator pin (Rubies #SUF5) 50.00
Quark Costume, pants, jacket and insert shirt (Rubies #SUF6) 50.00
Odo Costume, pants, shirt and communicator pin (Rubies #SUF7) .50.00
Deep Space Nine Baseball Cap gold and silver embroidered logo 14.00

Deep Space Nine Title Pin (#DSN05) 8.00
Deep Space Nine Full-Size Bajoran Communicator Pin (#DSN10) 10.00
Deep Space Nine Full-Size Communicator Pin (#DSN10) 10.00
Star Trek: Deep Space Nine *Emissary*, episode pin, depicts station and wormhole (Hollywood Pins 1994) 10.00
   Other Episodes, each 7.50
Star Trek: Deep Space Nine, Cast & Crew pin, 1993-1994, circular, starfield & planet with runabout (Hollywood Pins #DSN94, 1994) 8.00
Deep Space Nine: U.S.S. Defiant insignia pin, cut-out shape of ship (Hollywood Pins #DSN45, 1995) 7.50
Deep Space Nine: Maquis Symbol, insignia pin, (Hollywood Pins #M401, 1995) 7.50
   Deep Space Nine: Quark's Bar insignia pin (Hollywood Pins #DSN51, 1995). 9.00

DOLLS & FIGURES (DEEP SPACE NINE)

Collector Series Dolls (Playmates 1996–98)
Commander Benjamin Sisko (#6067) Command Edition 25.00
Lieutenant Commander Worf in Deep Space Nine Uniform (#6295, 1996) Starfleet Edition 25.00
9" Federation Edition Dolls (1996–97)
Chief Engineer Miles O'Brien (#16182) 15.00
Lieutenant Commander Jadzia Dax (#16186) 30.00
Captain Benjamin Sisko (#16188) 20.00
9" Bajor Edition (Asst. #6280)
Major Kira Nerys (#16189) 25.00
9" Warp Editions
Constable Odo (#65281) Warp 1 . . . . .17.50
Dr. Julian Bashir (#65285) Warp 2 . . . . .17.50
Gul Dukat (#65291) Warp 3 . . . . .17.50
Jem' Hadar Soldier (#65290) Warp 3 . . . . .17.50
Sisko (# 65293) Warp 4 . . . . .17.50
Dax, Warp 4 . . . . .25.00
Elim Garak (#65297) Warp 5 . . . . .17.50

Star Trek Deep Space Nine Vinyl Figures
Sisko vinyl doll (Applause #45856, 1994) 15.00
Kira vinyl doll (Applause #45857, 1994) 15.00
Odo vinyl doll (Applause #45858, 1994) 15.00
Quark vinyl doll (Applause #45859, 1994) 15.00

PVCs
Deep Space Nine, 6 crew figures (Applause #45869, 1994) each 2.50
Star Trek Deep Space Nine: Security Chief Odo, Lieutenant Jadzia Dax, Major Kira Nerys, Chief Miles O'Brien, Proprietor Quark and Command Benjamin Sisko, 4" PVC figures (Applause #45869, 1994) boxed set 20.00

2¼" Pewter Figurine Deep Space Nine
Sisko 90mm (#RF1776) 35.00
Runabout (#RF1779) 35.00

Star Trek Deep Space Nine 9" dolls, Miles O'Brien & Jem'Hadar Soldier (Playmates 1997–98)

HOUSEHOLD (DEEP SPACE NINE)

Star Trek Deep Space Nine Quark Figural Mug
  (Applause #45850, 1994) 15.00
Deep Space Nine magic mug (Rawcliffe #SMG10) 12.50
Sisko Commemorative Decal Mug (DS9 and other
  images) (Applause #46124) 6.00
U.S.S. Defiant Keepsake Magic Ornament, with
  blinking lights (Hallmark 1997) 25.00

MICRO (DEEP SPACE NINE)

Star Trek: Deep Space Nine Micro Machine
  (Collection #5) Cardassian Galor Warship;
  Space Station Deep Space Nine; Runabout
  (Galoob #65885, 1994) 6.00
Star Trek: Deep Space Nine Micro Machine
  (Collection #8) Cardassian Galor Warship;
  Space Station Deep Space Nine; Runabout
  (Galoob #66107, 1995) 6.00

MISCELLANEOUS (DEEP SPACE NINE)

Deep Space Nine Yo Yos: (SpectraStar #1586, 1993)
  Space Station Deep Space Nine 3.00
  Sisko 3.00
  Kira 3.00
  Odo 3.00

Deep Space Nine Armin Shimmerman Autograph-
  ed Photo Plaque 130.00
Deep Space Nine Colm Meaney Autographed
  Photo Plaque 130.00
Deep Space Nine Avery Brooks Autographed Photo
  Plaque 140.00
Deep Space Nine Cirroc Lofton Autographed Photo
  Plaque 130.00

PAPER (DEEP SPACE NINE)

STAR TREK DEEP SPACE NINE Magazine
  1 . . . . .10.00
  2 thru 20 . . . . .7.00
Cracked Magazine (Spaced-Out) Deep Space
  90210 issue. (Globe Communications 1994). 8.00

Deep Space Nine Standees
  Kira (#104) 25.00
  Odo (#105) 25.00
  Sisko (#106) 25.00
  Quark (#107) 25.00
  Dax (#108) 25.00
  Dr. Bashir (#109) 25.00
  O'Brien (#118) 25.00

RECORDINGS (DEEP SPACE NINE)

Star Trek Deep Space Nine Soundtrack CD (*The
  Emissary*) music by Dennis McCarthy 17.95
Star Trek Deep Space Nine Theme CD by Dennis
  McCarthy, single 8.00
Deep Space Nine: Fallen Heroes by Dafyad ab
  Hugh Audio Cassette .16.00

SPACESHIPS & VEHICLES (DEEP SPACE NINE)

Star Trek Deep Space Nine Runabout Orinoco,
  battery powered, holds two figures, with blueprint and Certificate of Authenticity in 16" x
  10½" x 5" try-me box (Playmates #6252, 1994) . .30.00
Star Trek Deep Space Nine Space Station DS9,
  13" diameter, including miniature docking

Starship Enterprise, battery powered with
  rotating display stand, technical blueprint and
  Certificate of Authenticity in 15½" x 13½" x 4"
  try-me box (Playmates #6251, 1994) 27.00
Deep Space Nine *U.S.S. Defiant NX 74205*, in try-
  me box (Playmates #16140) 25.00

WALL ART (DEEP SPACE NINE)

Deep Space Nine Station ChromeArt Print (Zanart
  #DSN-C, 1995) 15.00
Deep Space Nine Cardassian Galor Warship
  ChromeArt Print (Zanart #DSN-C2, 1995) 15.00
Deep Space Nine Station Side, 8" x 10" ChromArt
  Blueprint (Zanart #STB-C7, 1995) 14.00
Deep Space Nine Station Top, 8" x 10" ChromArt
  Blueprint (Zanart #STB-C8, 1995) 14.00
Deep Space Nine Crew poster (#PTW712) 5.00
Deep Space Nine Station Poster (#PTW711) 5.00

STAR TREK VOYAGER

Star Trek Voyager took off in early 1995 and they are still trying to find their way home. The show stars Kate Mulgrew as Captain Janeway, Robert Picardo as the Doctor and other fine characters. If you don't know their names you probably aren't reading this section. Kes is gone but Seven of Nine is a more than ample replacement. In fact, she is about the hotest *Star Trek* item in several years. The shows are still good, but *Star Trek* collecting has slacked off in recent years and this trend is likely to continue due to competition from *Star Wars*.

CLOTHING & ACCESSORIES

Voyager Deluxe Bergundy Shirt (#15445) $50.00
Voyager Deluxe Gold Shirt (#15441) 50.00
Voyager Deluxe Teal Shirt (#15442) 50.00

Voyager Deluxe Bergundy Jumpsuit (#15440) 60.00
Voyager Deluxe Gold Jumpsuit (#15446) 60.00
Voyager poly tie 16.00

Hollywood Pins
Voyager Debut Pin (#V001) 6.00
Voyager Ship Pin (#V020) .6.00

*UPN Popcorn for Voyager premier (1995)
& B'Elanna Torres standee (top half) (1996)*

Star Trek Voyager Spaceship (Playmates 1997)

DOLLS & FIGURES (VOYAGER)

9" Collector Dolls (Playmates 1997–98)
Lt. Tuvok (#65283) Warp 1 . . . . .17.50
Commander Chakotay (#65284) Warp 1 . . . . .17.50
Captain Kathryn Janeway (#65282) Warp 2 . . . . .17.50
Lt. Tom Paris (#65286) Warp 2 . . . . .17.50
Seven of Nine (#65303) Warp 4 . . . . .25.00

HOUSEHOLD (VOYAGER)

U.S.S. Voyager Christmas Ornament (Hallmark 1996) .30.00
Captain Janeway (Hallmark 1998) 15.00

Star Trek Voyager Neelix Figural Mug (Applause
    #46129, 1995) 15.00
Janeway Commemorative Decal Mug (Applause
    #46125) 7.00
Star Trek Voyager UPN popcorn package (UPN
    1995) announcing the 1-16-95 series
    premier. 10.00

PAPER (VOYAGER)

STAR TREK VOYAGER Magazine (April 1995)
1 with crew portrait gallery 7.00
2 . . . . .6.00
3 . . . . .6.00
4 thru 15 . . . . .5.00

Star Trek Voyager Writer Director Guide (QVC
    1995) box cover. 20–40.00
Star Trek Voyager Writers'— Director's Guide, First
    Season Version (Paramount 1995) inside
    xerox papers stapled together plus certificate
    of authenticity. 20.00
Star Trek Voyager, Torres Life-Size Stand-up
    (1995) top half shown .25.00

RECORDINGS (VOYAGER)

Star Trek: Voyager (*Caretaker*) music by Jay
    Chattaway and Jerry Goldsmith 25.00

SPACESHIPS & VEHICLES (VOYAGER)

Star Trek Voyager Starship U.S.S. Voyager NCC-
    74656, battery powered with pivoting engine
    nacelles in 17" x 12" x 3½" try-me box (Play-
    mates #6479, 1996) 35.00

Star Wars Yoda ceramic bank (Sigma 1982)

STAR WARS

Star Wars has been one of the most popular collecting categories for the last 20 years. With a new movie opening in the summer of 1999 and more movies on the horizon, this is almost certain to continue unabated. Licensors have paid huge fees to participate and will have to issue an avalanche of products to have much chance of a profit. A lot of great stuff will probably be produced, but the best buys will come to those who wait for discounts.

Books, posters, comics, games, puzzles and a lot of other stuff appeared before Kenner shipped the first *Star Wars* action figure, but the action figures have been the most significant *Star Wars* collectibles. Kenner has been the name to look for on other items as well. They produced the coins, the die-cast figures, the dolls, the playsets, the weapons and the vehicles and whatever they made, fans collected.

CERAMICS

Ceramic Figural Items (1977–82)
Ceramic Banks, 7"–8" tall, boxed (Roman
    Ceramics 1977) 3 different, each $75.00
Ceramic Banks (Sigma 1982) 3 different, each 45.00
R2-D2 Cookie Jar, 13" tall (Roman Ceramics Corp.
    1977) 150.00
Return of the Jedi, ceramic bisque figures, 7"
    (Sigma 1983) 12 different, each 50.00–65.00
Chewbacca and Darth Vader bookends (Sigma
    1983) 75.00
Luke and Tauntaun teapot set (Sigma 1983) 150.00
R2-D2 and R5-D4 figural salt and pepper shakers
    (Sigma 1983) 125.00
Sy Snootles & Rebo Band music box (Sigma 1983) . . .90.00
Wicket and Kneesa music box (Sigma 1983) 75.00
Other Ceramic figural items (Sigma 1983) 20.00–40.00

Ceramic Cookie Jars, limited editons of 1,000 jars
Obi-Wan Kenobi (Star Jars #026, 1998) 250.00

Klatuu mug (Sigma 1983)

Jabba the Hutt (Star Jars #027, 1998) 250.00
Princess Leia (Star Jars 1998) 250.00
Boba Fett (Star Jars 1998) 250.00

Mugs, Steins & Tankards
Ceramic Figural Drinking Mugs (Sigma 1983) white
    box or *Jedi* box, 7 different, each 30.00
Ceramic Figural Mugs (Rawcliffe 1995) 12 different,
    each 13.00
Ceramic Figural Mugs, 14oz., boxed, with
    certificate (Applause 1995–98) 13 different, each .15.00
Ceramic Decal Mugs, 15" (Applause 1998) 4
    different, each 9.00
Star Wars Trilogy Lidded Steins 6" with pewter lid
    (Metallic Impressions 1995) 3 different, each 34.00
Star Wars Deep Relief Stoneware, boxed (Dram
    Tree 1995) 3 different, each 25.00
Star Wars character Lidded Steins 9½" (Dram Tree
    1997–98) 3 different, each 85.00
Ceramic "Toby" Tankard, boxed (California
    Originals 1977) each 60.00
Collector Plates
Star Wars collector plates, First Series, 8¼"
    (Hamilton Collection 1985–87) 8 different,
    each 50.00
10th Anniversary commemorative plate 60.00
Star Wars Trilogy collector plates, 8¼" art by
    Morgan Weistling (Hamilton Collection 1993)
    3 different, each 40.00
Space Vehicles collector plates, 8¼" with 23K gold
    border, art by Sonia Hillios (Hamilton
    Collection 1995–96) 8 different, each 35.00
Space Vehicles collector plates, 9" with 24K gold
    border, art by Sonia Hillios (Hamilton
    Collection 1997–98) each 35.00
Star Wars Heroes and Villains collector plates, 24K
    gold border, art by Keith Birdsong (Hamilton
    Collection 1997–98) 8 different, each 35.00

CLOTHING & ACCESSORIES

Caps, Hats, Jackets
Logo Caps (Thinking Cap Co. 1980–81) 15.00–20.00
Yoda Ear Cap, cloth ears and artificial hair
    (Thinking Cap Co. 1980–81) 20.00
Character caps (Sales Corp. of America 1983) 15.00

Star Tours caps and hats (Star Tours) 10.00
Poncho and rain jackets (Adam Joseph 1983) 30.00
Star Tours Jackets (Star Tours) each 50.00
Luke Skywalker Bespin Jacket (1997) 80.00
Han Solo Vest (1997) 60.00

Shirts
Light grey T-Shirt (1994) with original 1977 Iron-On
    transfer 20.00
Star Wars Galaxy card image on T-Shirt, American
    Marketing Enterprises (AME 1994) each 19.00
T-Shirts (Changes 1993–1998) each 15.00–19.00
Tie-Dye or Silkscreened T-shirts, each 25.00
Star Tours Polo Shirt, color pocket logo (Star Tours) . . .25.00

Ties
Ties—silk (Ralph Marlin 1995) most 25.00
Star Wars silk tie in tin litho box (Ralph Marlin 1995) . .40.00
Ties—poly (Ralph Marlin 1990s) each 15.00
Star Wars Video Ties (Poly Ties 1996) each 15.00

Suspenders, Belts, Buckles
Suspenders (Lee Co. 1980) 20.00
Elastic Belts (Lee Co. 1983) each 25.00
Leather Belts (Lee Co. 1983) various buckles 30.00
Belt Buckles (Basic Tool & Supply 1977) each 20.00
Belt Buckles (Lee Co. 1979) 15.00
Star Wars belt buckles (Leather Shop 1977) each 20.00

CLOTHING ACCESSORIES

Bags
R2-D2 and C-3PO Duffle Bag (Adam Joseph 1983) . . .30.00
Yoda Duffle Bag, red (Adam Joseph 1983) 30.00
Star Tours Fanny Pack, black with blue/silver "Star
    Tours" logo (Star Tours) 15.00
Star Tours Gym Bag, horizontal design
    withblue/silver "Star Tours" logo (Star Tours) 30.00
Star Tours Toilette Case, black with blue/silver "Star
    Tours" logo (Star Tours) 15.00
Darth Vader and Imperial Guards Tote Bag, red
    canvas (Adam Joseph 1983) 25.00
R2-D2 and C-3PO Tote Bag, blue canvas (Adam
    Joseph 1983) 25.00
Star Tours Tote Bag, black design with blue/silver
    "Star Tours" logo (Star Tours) 20.00

Pins (Hollywood Pins 1994–97)
Movie Theme pins, 3 different, each 13.00
Large Character cut-out pins, each 11.00–13.00
Other pins, many different, each 6.00–10.00

Jewelry
Star Wars head pendants (Weingeroff Ent. 1977)
    boxed, 5 different, each 25.00
Star Wars earrings 5.00–10.00
Charm bracelets 8.00–15.00
The Empire Strikes Back medals (W.Berrie 1980) .4.00–8.00
Return of the Jedi pendants (Adam Joseph 1983) .4.00–8.00
R2-D2 Pendant pin and chain, sterling silver, 1¾"
    tall, with chain 100.00
Wicket the Ewok jewelry (Adam Joseph 1983) 7.50

Wallets
Return of the Jedi Wallets and Coin Holders (Adam
    Joseph 1983) each 15.00
Star Tours Wallet 8.00
Pocket Pals & Coin Holders (Adam Joseph 1983)
    each 10.00

Official Star Wars Watches
Star Wars watches, boxed (Bradley Time 1977–79)
Analog, various styles, each 90.00–125.00
Digital, various styles, each 75.00–125.00
The Empire Strikes Back and *Return of the Jedi*
    watches, boxed (Bradley Time 1980–83)
Analog, various styles, each 65.00–90.00
Digital, various styles, each 50.00–75.00

Plastic Watches (Hope Industries 1990s)
Collector Timepiece Gift Sets, 2 watches and Case
    in window box, each 15.00
Collector Timepiece Gift Set, 3 watches and Case
    in window box, each 20.00
Star Wars Collector Timepiece watch in *Millennium
    Falcon* watch case in window box, each 10.00

Collector Watches (1990s)
Deluxe Collector Watches, analog, limited
    (Fantasma 1993) various styles, each 65.00
Darth Vader Collector's Watches, analog, in Darth
    Vader helmet container (Fossil)
Silver edition, 15,000 copies 85.00
    Gold edition, 1,000 copies 120.00
Boba Fett watch, in tin case with litho image and
    with certificate of authenticity (Fossil)
    Regular edition, 10,000 copies 75.00
    Gold edition, 1,000 pieces, ...120.00

COINS

The Kenner "Power of the Force" coins which came with an action figure related to that figure, except the AT-AT Driver and Nikto had Warok coins. These 35 coins are common, and relatively inexpensive. However, you could also get a coin by mailing in a proof of purchase and then you got a random coin. These coins are scarce and some are very scarce indeed. Collectors who pestered Kenner about the missing coins were eventually given the right to buy a whole set, for $29!. The offer was never made to the public. In addition, there are variations, bringing the total number of coins to several more than the official set total of 62.

Star Wars Coins, Silver Color (Kenner 1985)
    Set of 62...........................$3,000.00
Anakin Skywalker, Jedi 125.00
AT-AT, Star Wars, mail-in, scarce 100.00
Bib Fortuna, Major Domo, mail-in, very scarce 125.00
Boba Fett, Bounty Hunter 200.00
Chief Chirpa, Ewok Leader, mail-in 40.00
Creatures, Star Wars, "at local cantinas" 90.00
    Variation "at local cafes" 150.00
Droids, Star Wars, mail-in, scarce 75.00
Emperor's Royal Guard, Empire, mail-in 75.00
FX-7, Medical Droid, mail-in, very scarce 125.00
Greedo, Bounty Hunter, mail-in, very scarce 125.00
Han Solo, Rebel, variation, "Hans Solo" 75.00
Han Solo, Rebel Hero (Hoth gear) mail-in, scarce 75.00
Hoth Stormtrooper, Empire, mail-in, very scarce 150.00
Imperial Commander, Empire, mail-in, scarce 75.00
Lando Calrissian, Rebel General (with Cloud City)
    mail-in, scarce 60.00
Logray, Ewok, mail-in 40.00
Luke Skywalker, Rebel Leader (on Tauntaun) mail-
    in, scarce 125.00
Luke Skywalker, Jedi Knight (bust, on Dagobah)
    mail-in, very scarce 150.00

Millennium Falcon, Star Wars, mail-in, scarce 120.00
Princess Leia, Boushh, mail-in, very scarce 125.00
Princess Leia, Rebel Leader (head, with R2-D2) 125.00
Sail Skiff, Star Wars, mail-in, very scarce 150.00
    Variation, Does not say "Star Wars" 300.00
Star Destroyer Commander, Empire, mail-in, scarce ..100.00
TIE Fighter Pilot, Empire, mail-in 75.00
Too-One Bee, Medical Droid, mail-in, very scarce ...150.00
Tusken Raider, Sand People, mail-in, very scarce ...150.00
Yak Face, Bounty Hunter 125.00
Zuckuss, Bounty Hunter, mail-in, very scarce 150.00
Others, each 10–25.00

Droids Coins, Gold Color (Kenner 1985)
A-Wing Pilot, Rebel 25.00
Boba Fett, Bounty Hunter 50.00
Others, 12 different, each 5–10.00
Ewoks Coins, Bronze Color (Kenner 1985)
6 different, each 5–8.00
Star Wars 15th Anniversay Silver Coin (Catch a
    Star 1992) limited to 5,000 ....45.00
Millennium Minted Coin, Gold-colored (Kenner
    1998) each 5.00

DIE-CASTS

Ships, carded (Kenner 1978–80)
Land Speeder (#38570) 100.00
Darth Vader TIE Fighter (#39160) 50.00
Rebel Armored Snowspeeder (#39680) 125.00
Slave I (#39670) 90.00
Imperial TIE Fighter (#38590) 40.00
Twin-Pod Cloud Car (#39660) 95.00
X-Wing Fighter (#38680) 75.00

Ships, Boxed (Kenner 1978–80)
Millennium Falcon (#39210) 150.00
Imperial Cruiser (#39230) 200.00
Y-Wing Fighter (#39220) 150.00
    Reissues of above ships, with background 500.00
TIE Bomber (#39260) test market, scarce 800.00

Metal Figurines (Heritage 1977)
Bantha Set, with 2 Sand people 45.00
Characters, 12 different, each 15.00–20.00

Die-Cast Tie Bomber (Kenner 1980)

Star Wars, The Empire Strikes Back 12" dolls Boba Fett & IG-88 (Kenner 1979–80)

Action Master Figures (Kenner 1994–96)
Action Master Die-Cast Figures, with trading
    card, 7 different, each 10.00
Special Edition "Gold" C-3PO mail-in figure 25.00
Collectors Set (4 Pack) with 4 trading cards 30.00
Collectors Set (6 Pack) with 6 trading cards 45.00
Power of the Force 6 Pack set with 6 trading cards . . .45.00

Micro Machine Die-Cast (Galoob 1996–98)
Star Wars Die-Cast MicroMachine Ships (Galoob
    1996–97) on original oval-shaped card, 14
    different, each 6.00
    reissue on rectangular striped card 5.00

Star Wars Characters Pewter Figures (Rawcliffe 1993–95)
Chewbacca (#RF963) 22.00
Obi-Wan Kenobi (#RF961) .22.00
Darth Vader (#RF962) 24.00
Other characters, each 10.00–16.00

Star Wars Pewter Vehicles (Rawcliffe 1993–95)
Star Destroyer (#RF964) 60.00
Other vehicles, each 30.00–36.00

Special Limited Edition Vehicles (Rawcliffe 1993–95)
Death Star 160.00
Millennium Falcon 140.00
TIE Interceptor 76.00
Vader's Custom TIE Fighter 108.00
X-Wing 76.00

DOLLS & FIGURES

Large Figures, *Star Wars* logo (Kenner 1979–80)
Princess Leia Organa (#38070) 11½" tall 225.00
    Loose 125.00
Luke Skywalker (#38080) 11¾" tall 350.00
    Loose 185.00
Chewbacca (#38600) 15" tall 150.00
    Loose 85.00
Darth Vader (#38610) 15" tall 225.00
    Loose 100.00
See-Threepio (C-3PO) (#38620) 12" tall 150.00

    Loose 50.00
Artoo-Detoo (R2-D2) (#38630) 7½" tall 130.00
    Loose 50.00
Han Solo (#39170) 11¾" tall 500.00
    Loose 230.00
Stormtrooper (#39180) 12" tall 300.00
    Loose 130.00
Ben (Obi-Wan) Kenobi (#39340) 12" tall 350.00
    Loose 175.00
Jawa (#39350) 8" tall 175.00
    Loose 75.00
Boba Fett (#39140) 13" tall 375.00
    In *The Empire Strikes Back* box 500.00
    Loose 150.00

Large Figure, *The Empire Strikes Back* logo (1980)
IG-88 (Bounty Hunter) (#39960) 15" tall 750.00
    Loose 300.00

NEW DOLLS—COLLECTOR SERIES

Kenner began issuing "Collector Series" dolls in 1996. The first series of dolls had a dark blue background card inside the package. In December 1996, this was replaced by a light blue card. Obi-Wan Kenobi was almost impossible to find in stores from the very first. Chewbacca, pictured on the back of the first series boxes, did not actually arrive until the fourth series. Lando Calrissian, however, did not sell out and could still be found in many stores well into 1998.

12" Dolls (Kenner 1996) in window box with flap cover
Luke Skywalker, on original dark blue card,
    binoculars on belt, black lightsaber handle $55.00
    Reissue, binoculars on card 35.00
    Reissue, on light blue package card 25.00
    Reissue, black and silver lightsaber handle 20.00
Han Solo, on original dark blue card 35.00
    Reissue, on light blue package card 20.00
Darth Vader, on original dark blue card, black light-
    saber handle 25.00
    Reissue, on light blue package card, black
        lightsaber handle 25.00

Tusken Raider 12" doll (Kenner 1997) & Luke Skywalker, Princess Leia & Han Solo 12" dolls (Kenner 1998)

Reissue, black and silver lightsaber handle 20.00
Obi-Wan Kenobi, on original dark blue card, black
    lightsaber handle and silver belt buckle 60.00
    Reissue, on light blue package card, black or
        black and silver lightsaber handle and
        silver buckle 45.00
    Reissue, with gold buckle 55.00

Second Batch (Kenner Jan. 1997)
Lando Clarissian 18.00
Luke Skywalker in Bespin Fatigues 35.00
Tusken Raider, with Rifle 35.00
Tusken Raider, with Gaderffii Stick 40.00

Third Batch (Kenner July 1997)
Stormtrooper 35.00
Princess Leia 40.00
Luke Skywalker in X-wing Gear 35.00
Boba Fett 50.00

Fourth Batch (Kenner Sept. 1997)
TIE Fighter Pilot 35.00
C-3PO 35.00
Admiral Ackbar 35.00
Chewbacca 75.00

Fifth Batch (Kenner Feb. 1998) box without flap
R2-D2, 6" 15.00
Yoda, 6" 18.00
Jawa, 6" 15.00

Sixth Batch (Kenner April 1998)
Han Solo in Hoth Gear 25.00
Luke Skywalker in Hoth Gear 25.00
AT-AT Driver 25.00
Snowtrooper 25.00

Seventh Batch (Kenner April 1998)
Greedo 25.00

Grand Moff Tarkin with Interrogation Droid 25.00
Sandtrooper with Imperial Droid 30.00
Luke Skywalker in Ceremonial Gear 25.00

Eighth Batch (Kenner October 1998)
Barquin D'an 20.00
Emperor Palpatine 20.00
Luke Skywalker in Jedi Gear 20.00

14" Electronic figure
Darth Vader 40.00

12" Special Dolls/Exclusives (Kenner 1997)
Han Solo & Luke Skywalker in Stormtrooper Gear
    (#27867) KB Limited Edition of 20,000 . . . . . . .175.00
Grand Moff Tarkin & Imperial Gunner with
    Interrogator Droid (#27923) FAO Schwarz 150.00
Luke Skywalker vs. Wampa (#27947) Target stores . .125.00
Han Solo & Tauntaun (#27834) Toys "R" Us, also
    reissued twice in 1998 . . . . .65.00
Cantina Band, WalMart stores
    Doikk Na'ts with Fizzz 45.00
    Figrin D'an with Kloo Horn 50.00
    Ickabel with Fanfar .45.00
    Nalan with Bandfill 45.00
    Tech with Ommni Box 45.00
    Tedn with Fanfar 45.00
Greedo (#27976) J.C. Penney stores 70.00
Sandtrooper (#27928) Comic shops 60.00
AT-AT Driver (#27977) Service Merchandise stores . . .80.00
Jedi Knight Luke Skywalker & Bib Fortuna (#27924) .125.00

12" Special Dolls/Exclusives (Kenner 1998)
Princess Leia in Hoth Gear (#57110) Service
    Merchandise stores 25.00
Luke Skywalker in Tatooine Gear, Princess Leia
    in Boushh Disguise and Han Solo in Bespin
    Gear (#57101) KayBee Stores 100.00
Wedge Antilles and Biggs Darklighter (#57106)

FAO Schwarz 2-pack in window box 75.00
Princess Leia Organa and R2-D2 as Jabba's
    Prisoners (Princess Leia Collection) (#61777)
    FAO Schwarz 2-pack in window box 80.00
Electronic C-3PO and R2-D2 (#57108) Toys "R" Us . . .80.00
Luke Skywalker in Hoth Gear, Han Solo in Hoth
    Gear, Snowtrooper and AT-AT Driver
    (#57109) JC Penny 4-pack in window box 100.00
R5-D4, with retractable leg (#27802) WalMart 15.00
R2-D2, with retractable leg, WalMart 15.00
Wicket the Ewok, WalMart 15.00

BEND-EM FIGURES

Star Wars Galaxy Bend-Ems were originally fairly hot
items with collectors hungry for *Star Wars*-related merchandise. Each figure came with a *Star Wars Galaxy* variant trading card which was also popular. The popularity of Bend-Ems
declined as the action figures appeared. The trading cards are
a separate collectible and are often reported to be selling for
more than the figures with the cards. Go figure!

Bend-Em figures (Just Toys 1993–95) with matching
    Star Wars Galaxy card on 8-back header
    card, 12 different, each $7.00–9.00
    Reissue, no Trading Card, or loose 3.00–4.00
Bend-Em figures (Just Toys 1995) with random Star
    Wars Galaxy I or II card, 8 new figures, each 7.00
    12 reissue figures, each 6.00

Multi-packs
K-Mart exclusive 8-pack (Just Toys #12433) 35.00
4 Piece Gift Set (Just Toys #12492, 1993) no cards . . .10.00
4 Piece Gift Sets, with four trading cards (Just Toys
    1993) three different, each 15.00
Darth Vader bust Collector Case (Just Toys 1994) 15.00
Deluxe Collector Set, all 20 figures in Darth Vader
    bust case (Just Toys #15021, 1995) 70.00
4 Piece Gift Sets, with cards and brass colored coin
    (Just Toys 1995) two different, each 12.00
10 Piece Gift Sets, with cards and brass colored
    coin (Just Toys 1995) two different, each 30.00

PVC FIGURES

Star Wars Classic Collectors Series, 6 PVC figures,
    with Display Platform (Applause #46038,
    1995) 20.00
Star Wars 3½" PVC figures (Applause 1995–98)
    each 3.00–5.00

*Star Wars Bend-Em Stormtrooper (JusToys 1994)
& R2-D2 Plush figure (Kenner 1977)*

Jumbo Dioramas (Jan. 1997)
Han Solo and Jabba the Hutt, 4½" x 6¼" x 4" (#42691) .10.00
R2-D2 and C-3PO, 4¾" x 3½" x 2½" (#42690) 10.00

VINYL FIGURES

Vinyl figures (Suncoast Dolls 1993) 8 different, each . .20.00
Vinyl characters, 9" x 11" loose figures with hanging
    tag (Applause 1995–98) 20 different, each 15.00–20.00
Luke Skywalker, 9" in X-wing Pilot Gear, boxed
    (Applause 1997) 20.00
Darth Vader, 12" boxed (Applause 1997) 25.00

PLUSH FIGURES

Plush
Chewbacca (Regal) 60.00
Chewbacca, 20" tall (Kenner 1977) 35.00
R2-D2, 10" tall (Kenner 1977) 50.00
Ewoks (Kenner 1983)
    18" Zephee 40.00
    14" Wicket 30.00
    14" Princess Kneesa 30.00
    14" Paploo 40.00
    14" Latara 40.00
    8" Woklings, six different, each 15.00
Ewok, 12", light brown with green cowl (Disney) 15.00
Ewok, 8", dark brown with pink cowl (Disney) 12.00

ELECTRONIC AND COMPUTER

Radio-Controled/Remote Controlled
Radio Controlled R2-D2, 8", *Star Wars* logo
    (Kenner #38430, 1979) 125.00
    Loose 65.00
Radio Controlled Imperial Speeder Bike with figure
    (Kenner #27846, 1997) .25.00
Electronic Remote Control R2-D2 (Kenner #27736,
    Sept. 1997) 20.00

Electronic Games
Electronic Battle Command Game (Kenner
    #40370, 1977) 75.00
Electronic Laser Battle Game (Kenner #40090, 1977) 100.00
X-Wing Aces Target Electronic Game, plug-in, *Star
    Wars* logo (Kenner 1978) very rare, offered in
    mini-catalog 1,000.00

Electronic Games (Micro Games of America 1995)
Star Wars Shakin' Pinball 17.00
Star Wars Electronic Game .10.00
The Empire Strikes Back Electronic Game 10.00
Return of the Jedi Electronic Game 10.00
Star Wars Intimidator (INT-200) 10.00

Electronic Games (Tiger Electronics 1997)
Star Wars *Millennium Falcon* Challenge R-Zone
    Headgear 15.00
Star Wars Jedi Adventure R-Zone Xtreme Pocket
    Game 30.00
R-Zone Cartridges, each 10.00
Star Wars Rebel Forces Laser Game 20.00
Star Wars Imperial Assault 3-D Figure Hand Held
    Game 20.00
Millennium Falcon Challenge Electronic LCD Game . . .20.00
Star Wars Electronic Galactic Battle game, includes
    10 different vehicles with sound effects 25.00
Millennium Falcon Sounds of the Force Electronic
    Memory Game 30.00
Star Wars Death Star Escape Game 25.00
Star Wars Quiz Whiz 25.00

Stormtrooper Room Alarm with Laser Target Game,
    13½" figure in window box 25.00
Boba Fett Room Alarm with Laser Target Game,
    13½" figure in window box 25.00
Star Wars Interactive Video Board Game (Parker
    Bros. #40392, 1996) 32.00

Radios and Cassette Players
Luke Skywalker AM Headset Radio, battery
    powered (Kenner #38420, 1979) 40.00
Electronic X-Wing Flight Simulator (Kenner 1997) 23.00
Millennium Falcon Flight Simulator (Kenner 1998) 23.00
Electronic Power F/X Obi-Wan Kenobi vs. Darth
    Vader J.C. Penney stores (Kenner 1997) 100.00

Clocks
R2-D2 and C-3PO Talking Alarm Clock, 9" tall
    (Bradley Time 1980) 90.00
R2-D2 and C-3PO Clock Radio (Bradley Time 1984) .100.00
R2-D2 and C-3PO 3-D Sceni-Clock, 8" tall (Bradley
    Time) 75.00
Ewok Teaching Clock, shaped like Ewok village with
    Wicket on face of clock (Kenner Preschool) 75.00
Star Wars Special Edition Clocks, Drew Struzan
    art, battery powered (1997) each 40.00

Electronic Household Products
Luke Skywalker's Lightsaber Universal (TV) Remote
    Control (Kash 'N' Gold 2366, 1997) boxed 35.00
R2-D2 figural telephone, 12" high (Kash 'N' Gold
    #2363, 1997) boxed 80.00

FOOD COLLECTIBLES

Breakfast Food
General Mills Cereal Boxes, with various premium
    offers, complete box (1978–80) each 25.00–35.00
Kellogg's Cereal Boxes with various premium
    offers, complete boxes (1980s) each 20.00–30.00
C-3PO Cereal (1984) with Mask on Back, six
    different masks, each .30.00
Set, 8 different C-3PO Mask boxes 200.00
C-3PO Cereal (1984) with Rebel Rocket in pack
    plus stickers, each 20.00
Set, 8 different boxes + stickers 200.00

Pizza Hut box (1997)

Empire Strikes Back glasses (Burger King/Coca-Cola 1980)

FAST & JUNK FOOD

The 1970s and 1980s promotions of choice with fast
food restaurants were glasses and plastic cups. The most
famous of these promotions were the Burger King/Coke four-
glass sets sold for each of the three movies. Coke also produced a number of collector plastic cups which were distributed in various fast food chains, both national and regional.

Promotional Glassware (Burger King/Coca-Cola)
Star Wars Glasses (1977) each $15.00
    set of 4 . . . . .60.00
The Empire Strikes Back Glasses (1980) each 12.00
    set of 4 . . . . .50.00
Return of the Jedi Glasses (1983) each 10.00
    set of 4 . . . . .40.00
    Plastic cups, Mass. only, each 12.50
    set of 4 . . . . .50.00

Plastic Coca-Cola Cups 1970s–80s
Star Wars numbered 20-cup set, each 10.00
    Set of 20 . . . . .175.00
Star Wars numbered 8-cup set
    Large, "7–11" or "Coke" each 5.00
    Set of 8 Large cups 30.00
    Small, "Coke" each 5.00
    Set of 8 Small cups 25.00
Star Wars unnumbered 1979 8-cup set, each 5.00
    Set of 8 "Coke" cups 30.00
Return of the Jedi 12-cup set, each 5.00
    Set of 12 "7-11" cups, large or small 50.00
The Empire Strikes Back movie theater plastic cup
    (Coke 1980) depending on size, each 5.00–8.00
Return of the Jedi movie theater plastic cup (Coke
    1983) depending on size, each 4.00–7.00
Star Wars Trilogy Special Edition movie theater
    plastic cup, featuring picture of AT-AT (Pepsi
    1997) 2.00
Star Wars Fast Food Toys (Taco Bell 1996–97) 8
    different, each 2.50
Spirit of Obi-Wan translucent non-action figure, with
    mailer box (Kenner 1997) Frito-Lay mail-in 10.00

Topps Candy Boxes (1980–83)
The Empire Strikes Back figural head candy
    containers (Topps 1980) 18-count box 40.00
    Set of 5 different 12.50
The Empire Strikes Back figural head candy
    containers (Topps 1981) box with 18

containers, New Yoda series 40.00
Set of six different 12.50
Return of the Jedi figural head candy containers
(Topps 1983) box with 18 containers 50.00
Set of six different 15.00

Hersheys 6-pack cartons (1980s) photos on back
Boxes with large C-3PO or Chewbacca photos 15.00
Boxes with smaller Luke on Tauntaun, Boba Fett or
Darth Vader photos 10.00

Star Wars Trilogy Candy Container collection and
card set, 4 head figural candy containders
and 10-card set, on header card (Topps 1997) . . .25.00
Pez Dispensers (1997) bagged or carded, 5
different, each 3.00

GAMES AND PUZZLES

Original Kenner Games (1977–82)
Adventures of R2-D2, board game (1977) 25.00
Destroy Death Star game (1979) 30.00
Escape From Death Star board game (1979) 25.00
Hoth Ice Planet Adventure Board Game (1980) 25.00
Yoda, The Jedi Master board game (1981) 25.00

Parker Bros. (Parker Bros. 1982–98)
Star Wars (1982) 30.00
Wicket the Ewok (1983) 20.00
The Ewoks Save the Trees! (1983) 20.00
Battle at Sarlacc's Pit (1983) 30.00
Return of the Jedi Card Game (1983) 10.00
Ewok Card Games, several different (1984) 15.00

Star Wars Death Star Assault Game, board, X-wing
fighter, 20 TIE fighter pieces (Parker Bros.
#40390, 1995) 13.00
Star Wars Monopoly Classic Trilogy Edition (Parker
Bros #40809, 1997) 35.00

JIGSAW PUZZLES

140-Piece Puzzles 14" x 18" (Kenner 1977–79) each . .10.00
In original blue box, each 15.00
500-Piece Puzzles 15" x 18" (Kenner 1977–79) each . .12.00
In original blue box, each 17.00
1,000-Piece Puzzles (Kenner 1977–79) each 15.00

Star War Jigsaw Puzzle (Kenner 1977)

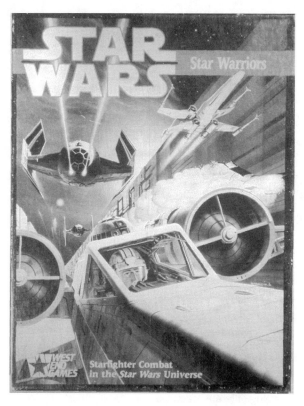

Star Wars: Star Warriors (West End Games 1980s)

1,500-Piece Puzzles (Kenner 1977–79) each 20.00
Return of the Jedi Puzzles (Craft Master 1983)
70 piece puzzles 10.00
170 piece puzzles 12.00
Puzz 3D puzzles (Milton Bradley 1995) each 35.00
Movie Trilogy, 550 piece puzzles (Milton Bradley
1996) each 12.50

ROLE PLAY GAMES

West End Games has been producing role playing games in the *Star Wars* universe since 1987. During much of this period, they were the only company keeping the *Star Wars* saga alive with anything like new *Star Wars* storylines. Role playing games are generally available in book stores and they are almost exclusively bought by fans who want to play the games, not collect them. New and revised editions of rule books are much more useful than original editions. The consequences of this are that most of these items, even in near mint condition, are worth just about the same amount that they originally sold for!

Boxed games (9" x 11½" boxes)
Star Warriors Role-Playing Board Game (West End
Games 1987) $35.00
Assault on Hoth, two person board game (West
End Games 1988) 35.00
Battle for Endor, board game (West End Games
1989) 30.00
Escape From the Death Star, board game (West
End Games 1990) 30.00
Reprints of above (West End Games 1992) 20.00

Basic Game and Sourcebooks (8½" x 11" hardcovers)
Star Wars, The Role-Playing Game, basic rules
book (West End Games 1987) 25.00

Star Wars Customizable Card Game Jabba's Palace
(Decipher 1998)

2nd Edition (West End Games 1993) 25.00
2nd Edition, Revised and Expanded (West
    End Games 1996) 30.00
Sourcebooks (West End Games 1988–98) each 18.00–25.00
Adventure Modules (West End Games 1988–90) each .10.00
Classic Adventures, reprints updated to second
    edition rules (West End Games 1995–96) .18.00–20.00
Galaxy Guide books (West End Games 1989–95)
    12 different, each 13.00–15.00
Other Guide Books (West End Games 1990–98)
    many different, each 13.00–18.00
Other Guide Books, Hard Covers (West End
    Games 1990–98) many different, each . . .25.00–28.00
Supplements (West End Games) each 10.00–15.00
All other books . . . . .cover price

GAMING MINIATURES

West End Games produced 25mm lead miniature figures to accompany its games starting in 1988. They are not
heavily collected by non-gamers, but they were popular with
modelers. There are 14 boxed sets, usually containing 10 figures, which were produced from 1988 to 1991. In 1993, West
End Games began producing three-figure blister packs of figures. It has made over 50 different packs to date, plus several
sets of ships.

Star Wars Miniature Figures, 25mm figures
Boxes with 8 to 10 figures (West End Games
    1988–92) several different, each $20.00–25.00
Blister packs with 3 figures (West End Games
    1993–97) over 50 different, each 5.00–9.00
12-packs (West End Games 1997) 20.00
Ships or vehicles (West End Games 1994–96) . .6.00–10.00
Miniatures Battles, large boxed sets (West End
    Games 1995–97) 35.00

CUSTOMIZABLE CARD GAMES

Customizable Card Games (CCGs) are one of the 1990s
hottest items. Many of the cards are now quite valuable, primarily for their scarcity and play value in the game. Whether
this will translate into long term collector value is anybody's
guess.

STAR WARS LIMITED Decipher Inc. (1995–96)
Complete Set: 324 cards $600.00
Starter Box: 10 starter decks 110.00
Starter Deck: 60 cards 11.00
Booster Pack: 15 cards 4.00

Rarest cards
C-3PO [See-Threepio] (R1) Light 20.00
Darth Vader (R1) Dark 50.00
Devastator (R1) Dark 15.00
Grand Moff Tarkin (R1) Dark 20.00
Han Solo (R1) Light 40.00
Leia Organa (R1) Light 35.00
Luke Skywalker (R1) Light .40.00
Millennium Falcon (R1) Light 30.00
Obi-Wan Kenobi (R1) Light 40.00
Vader's Custom TIE (R1) Dark 15.00

STAR WARS UNLIMITED Decipher Inc. (1996–98)
Complete Set: 324 cards 400.00
Starter Deck: 120 cards 15.00
Starter Deck: 90 cards 9.50
Booster Pack: 15 cards 3.00
Rare and Uncommon cards are worth about 75% of the same
    card in the "Limited Series."

EXPANSION SETS

A NEW HOPE
Complete Set: 162 cards 200.00
Booster Box: 36 pack 95.00
Booster Pack: 15 cards 3.00
Rarest cards
Chewbacca (R2) Light 20.00
Death Star (R2) Dark 15.00
R2-D2 (Artoo-Detoo) (R2) Light 15.00
Wedge Antilles (R1) Light .15.00

THE EMPIRE STRIKES BACK: HOTH
Complete Set: 162 cards 200.00
Booster Box: 36 packs 80.00
Booster Pack: 15 cards 3.00
Rarest cards
Commander Luke Skywalker (R1) Light 30.00
Stalker (R1) Dark 15.00
Tyrant (R1) Dark 15.00

DAGOBAH
Complete Set: 180 cards 200.00
Booster Box: 60 packs 140.00
Booster Pack: 9 cards (inc. 1 rare) 2.50
Rarest cards
Executor (R) Dark 28.00
Son of Skywalker (R) Light 28.00
Yoda (R) Light 35.00

CLOUD CITY
Complete Set: 180 cards 175.00
Booster Box: 60 packs .125.00
Booster Pack: 9 cards (inc. 1 rare) 2.50
Rarest cards
Boba Fett (R) Dark 30.00
Captain Han Solo (R) Light 28.00
Lando Calrissian (R) Dark .20.00
Lando Calrissian (R) Light .20.00
Princess Leia (R) Light 25.00
Slave I (R) Dark 15.00

JABBA'S PALACE
Complete Set: 180 cards 160.00
Booster Box: 36 packs 125.00
Booster Pack: 9 cards (inc. 1 rare) 2.50
Rarest cards
Artoo (R) Light 15.00
Jabba The Hutt (R) Dark 20.00

Star Wars Electric Toothbrush (Kenner 1978)

Princess Leia Organa (R) Light 30.00
Rancor (R) Dark 15.00

HOUSEHOLD—BATHROOM

Bubble Bath
Bubble Bath Character Containers, 4½" x 9½" tall
    (Omni 1981–83) each 15.00
Bubble Bath (Addis 1983) each 15.00
R2-D2 and C-3PO Bubble Bath Gift Set, with 2
    soaps (Addis 1985) 30.00
Ewoks Bubble Bath Gift Set, with soap (Addis 1985) . .25.00

Personal Grooming
Comb and Keeper (Adam Joseph 1983) each . .10.00–15.00
Pop-Up Combs (Adam Joseph 1983) each 15.00
Ewok Personal Care Kit (Adam Joseph 1983) 25.00
Return of the Jedi Toothbrushes, in box, on header
    card (Oral-B 1985) 10.00
Jedi Master Three-pack, shrink wrapped (Oral-B 1985) 30.00
Electric Toothbrush, battery powered (Kenner 1978) . .40.00
The Empire Strikes Back Electric Toothbrush,
    battery powered (Kenner 1980) 30.00
Wicket Electric Toothbrush (1984) 25.00
Shampoo Character Containers (Omni 1981-83) each .15.00
Princess Leia Beauty Bag (Omni 1981) 40.00
Luke Skywalker Belt Kit (Omni 1981) 40.00

Soaps
C-3PO or R2-D2 Soap, 4" (Cliro 1977) each 10.00
Character Soaps (Omni 1981-83) each 10.00
Star Wars Soap Collections, 4 characters (Omni 1981) 30.00

Towels
Bath or Beach towels (1980s) 15.00

HOUSEHOLD—BEDROOM

Bedding
Star Wars sheets (1978–79) 25.00
Star Wars blanket (1978–79) 35.00
Star Wars pillowcase (1978–79) 7.50
Pillowcase (1980–82) 7.00
Curtains (1980–82) 25.00
Blanket (1980–82) 30.00
Sheets, twin (1997) 35.00
Sheets, full (1997) 45.00
Comforter, twin (1997) 50.00
Comforter, full (1997) 60.00
Blanket, twin (1998) 40.00
Blanket, full (1998) 50.00
Pillowcase (1997) 7.00
Star Wars sleeping bag 25.00

Nightlights (Adam Joseph 1983) 5.00

HOUSEHOLD—KITCHEN

Dinnerware
Star Wars China Set (Sigma) 25.00
Return of the Jedi dinnerware set (Deka 1983) 20.00
Wicket the Ewok 3-piece set (Deka 1983) 10.00
Bowls (Deka 1980) 10.00
Cups (Deka 1980) 7.00

Cake Baking items
R2-D2 cake decorating kit (Wilton 1980) 15.00
Darth Vader cake decorating kit (Wilton 1980) 15.00
C-3PO cake pan (Wilton 1980) 10.00
Boba Fett cake pan (Wilton 1980) 25.00

Tissues, cups
Puffs facial tissue boxes (Puffs 1981) 10.00
Star Wars Dixie Cups (Dixie Cups 1978) each box 10.00
The Empire Strikes Back Film Cups (Dixie Cup
    1980) each box 8.00
Return of the Jedi (Dixie Cup 1983) each box 6.00

HOUSEHOLD—OTHER ROOMS

Drapery
Vehicle Diagram Rod Pocket Drape, 84" x 84" (1997) .45.00
Vehicle Diagram Rod Pocket Drape, 84" x 63" (1997) .35.00
Vehicle Diagram Rod Valance 84" x 15" (1997) 20.00
Character Study Rod Pocket Drape, 84" x 84" (1997) . .45.00
Character Study Rod Pocket Drape, 84" x 63" (1997) . .35.00
Character Study Rod Valance 84" x 15" (1997) 20.00

Return of the Jedi Lunch Box (King Seeley 1983)

Furniture (Am. Toy and Furniture 1983)
Return of the Jedi Bookcase 150.00
Ewok and Droid Toy Chest 175.00
Darth Vader Coat Rack 100.00
Desk and Chair 175.00
Return of the Jedi Nightstand 150.00
Picnic Table, 36" long 175.00
Return of the Jedi Table and Chair Set 175.00
R2-D2 Toy Chest, 28" tall .150.00

Switcheroos
The Empire Strikes Back Switcheroos, "light switch
     cover for kids rooms" (Kenner 1980) each 25.00

Wastepaper Baskets (Chein Industries 1983)
Return of the Jedi wastepaper basket 25.00
Ewoks wastepaper basket 20.00

Outdoors
Gym Set (Gym-Dandy 1983) 1,200.00

HOUSEHOLD—LUNCH BOXES

Lunch boxes have their own groups of collectors, making these more valuable than other school related items.

Star Wars, space battle on front & Tatooine scene
     on reverse (King Seeley-Thermos 1977)
     Metal box $55.00
     Droids thermos 20.00
Star Wars, red with Darth and Droids pictured on
     front (King Seeley-Thermos 1978) plastic box . . .35.00
     Droids thermos 15.00
The Empire Strikes Back, Millennium Falcon on
     front & Luke, Yoda and R2-D2 on back
     (King Seeley-Thermos 1980) metal box 45.00
     Yoda thermos 15.00
The Empire Strikes Back, Dagobah scene on lid,
     Hoth battle on back (King Seeley-Thermos
     1980) metal box 45.00
     Yoda thermos 15.00
The Empire Strikes Back, red, Chewbacca, Han,
     Leia and Luke on lid (King Seeley-Thermos
     1980) plastic box 30.00
     Yoda thermos 15.00
The Empire Strikes Back, photo cover with logo
     and inset pictures (King Seeley-Thermos
     1980) plastic box 30.00
     Droids & Logo thermos 15.00
Return of the Jedi, Luke in Jabba's Palace on lid
     and space scene on back (King Seeley-
     Thermos 1983) metal box 40.00
     Ewoks thermos 15.00
Return of the Jedi, red with Wicket and R2-D2 on
     front (King Seeley- Thermos 1983) plastic
     box 25.00
     Ewoks thermos 10.00

HOUSEHOLD—CHRISTMAS ORNAMENTS

Hallmark has made collectible christmas ornaments for many years. It discovered *Star Trek* in 1991 and in 1996 it noticed the marketing hype for the *Star Wars Trilogy Special Edition* movies.

Millennium Falcon ornament (Hallmark 1996) $50.00
Darth Vader hanging ornament (Hallmark 1997) 25.00
Yoda hanging ornament (Hallmark 1997) 30.00
C-3PO and R2-D2 set of ornaments (Hallmark 1997) . .20.00
Luke Skywalker hanging ornament (Hallmark 1997) . . .25.00

Star Wars Darth Vader Keepsake Ornament (Hallmark 1997)

Vehicles of *Star Wars*, 3 miniatures (Hallmark 1997) . .40.00
X-wing Starfighter, light up (Hallmark 1998) 23.95
Boba Fett hanging ornament (Hallmark 1998) 14.95
Princess Leia hanging ornament (Hallmark 1998) 13.95
Ewoks, 3 miniatures (Hallmark 1998) 16.95

MASKS/HELMETS/COSTUMES

Masks (Don Post Studios 1977–98)
C-3PO latex mask (Don Post 1977) 100.00
     reissue (1978) 75.00
     reissue (late 1980s) 50.00
     reissue (1994) 40.00
Cantina Band Member rubber mask (Don Post 1980) . .75.00
     reissue (1990s) 60.00
     reissue, 13" latex (1994) 40.00
Chewbacca rubber mask (Don Post 1977) 250.00
     reissue (1978) 100.00
     reissue (1990) 75.00
     reissue, 11" multicolored hair (1990s) 60.00
Darth Vader Collector Helmet, plastic (1977) 200.00
     reissue (1978–82) 75.00
     reissue (1983) 50.00
     reissue (1994) 60.00
Stormtrooper Collector Helmet, plastic (1977) 90.00
     reissue (1978) 75.00
     reissue (#82002, late 1980s) 60.00
Tusken Raider rubber mask (Don Post late 1970s) 90.00
     reissue (late 1980s) 70.00
     reissue, 11" latex (1995) 30.00
Ugnaught mask (Don Post 1980s) 75.00
Yoda rubber mask (Don Post 1980s) 60.00
     reissue (1990s) 50.00
     reissue, 10" latex with hair (1994) 30.00
Admiral Ackbar rubber mask (Don Post 1983) 75.00
     reissue (1990s) 60.00
     reissue, 13" latex (1994) 40.00
Gammorrean Guard rubber mask (Don Post 1983) . . .75.00
     reissue, 11" (1995) 25.00
Klaatu rubber mask (Don Post 1983) 75.00
     reissue (1990s) 60.00
     reissue, 12" latex with hood (1995) 35.00

Star Wars Micro Collection Bespin World (Kenner 1982)

Nien Nunb rubber mask, 11" (1996) 25.00
Weequay rubber mask (Don Post 1983) 90.00
Wicket W. Warrick rubber mask (Don Post 1983) 90.00
    reissue (1990) 75.00
    reissue, 10" hair and hood (1994) 40.00
Emperor Palpatine rubber mask 80.00
    reissue, 11" latex with hood (1994) 40.00
Greedo, 11" latex (1997) 35.00
Prince Xizor, 12" latex and hair (1994) 35.00

Collector Helmets (Don Post 1996–98)
Boba Fett, 10" plastic with smoked viewplate and
    moveable antenna (#82019, 1996) 80.00
Darth Vader, 13" plastic faceplate and overhelmet,
    with tinted eyepieces (#82001) 50.00
Emperor's Royal Guard, 18" crimson plastic with
    smoked visor (#82020, 1996) 80.00
Stormtrooper, 11" white plastic with simulated
    breathing filters and com-link (#82002) 80.00
TIE Fighter, 11" (#82025, 1997) 90.00
Scout Trooper Helmet, 11" (#82024, 1997) 90.00
X-wing Fighter, 13" (#82026, 1997) 90.00

Classic Action Helmets (Don Post 1997)
Darth Vader Clasic Action Helmet, 15" (#82108) 150.00
Stormtrooper Classic Action Helmet, 13" (#82107) . . .125.00
TIE Fighter Classic Action Helmet, 15" (#82105) 125.00

Riddell Collectible Mini-Helmets, 45% of scale with
    display base, several different 85.00–95.00

Costumes
Costume & Mask *Star Wars* box (Ben Cooper
    1977–79) 9 different, each 35.00
    The Empire Strikes Back or *Return of the Jedi*
    box (Ben Cooper 1980–85) each 20.00
Yoda Costume & Mask (Ben Cooper 1980–85) 30.00
Return of the Jedi characters (Ben Cooper 1983–85) . .25.00

MICRO AND MINI

Kenner's Micro Collection consists of plastic playsets and plastic vehicles for use with 1" die-cast figures. The nine playsets could be bought individually or grouped into three "Worlds."

Action Playsets (Kenner 1982)
Bespin Control Room, with 4 figures $30.00

Bespin Freeze Chamber, with 8 figures 75.00
Bespin Gantry, with 4 figures 30.00
Bespin World: all three above, boxed 125.00
Death Star Compactor, with 8 figures 50.00
Death Star Escape, with 6 figures 50.00
Death Star World: both above, boxed 125.00
Hoth Generator Attack, with 6 figures 25.00
Hoth Ion Cannon, with 8 figures 35.00
Hoth Wampa Cave, with a Wampa and 4 figures 25.00
Hoth World: all three above 100.00
Hoth Turret Defense, with 6 figures 25.00

Vehicles
Imperial TIE Fighter, with pilot 75.00
X-Wing Fighter, with pilot 65.00
Millennium Falcon, with 6 figures, Sears exclusive . . .400.00
Rebel Armored Snowspeeder, with pilot and Har-
    pooner, JC Penny exclusive 200.00

MICROMACHINES

The Galoob *Star Wars* MicroMachines collection debuted in 1994, as part of its "Space" segment. The earliest ones have a 1993 copyright, and only list the first three in the series on the back (3-back). These were reissued, when the next three items were released. They were replaced in 1996 by the *Star Wars* Vehicle Collection, which also said "Space" on its original packages, but had different figures. Packaging was changed in 1997 to a striped design, similar to the stripes on the Action Fleet packages.

Space Series Vehicles (Galoob 1993–94)
#1 to #3 Movie MicroMachine ships on 3-back card
    (Galoob 1993) 3 different, each $15.00
Reissue on 6-back cards (Galoob 1994) each 7.00
#4 to #6 Movie MicroMachine ships on 6-back
    cards (Galoob 1994) each 8.00

Star Wars Vehicle Collection (Galoob 1994–98)
Star Wars MicroMachine Vehicle Collections
    (Galoob 1996–98) various 3-vehicle packs, each . .7.00
Shadows of the Empire MicroMachine Vehicle
    Collections (Galoob 1996) each 6.00
Eight ship boxed sets, pewter finish (Galoob 1995) . . .20.00
Star Wars Collector's Gift Set, 26 items, bronze
    finish (Galoob #64624, 1995) 30.00

*Star Wars Micro Machines Rebel Forces Gift Set, Second Edition
(Galoob 1996)*

Star Wars Action Fleet Ice Planet Hoth playset (Galoob 1997)

Master Collector's Edition, 19 Star Wars vehicles
    (Galoob #64061) 20.00
Star Wars Micro Machine 9-Figure Collections
    (Galoob 1996–98) each 7.00
Droids Collection, 16 droids (Galoob 1997) 17.00

Playsets (Galoob 1994–98)
Playsets, boxed, includes ship and 3 to 5 figures
    (Galoob 1994–98) each 11.00
Transforming Action Sets, Helmet/Head shaped,
    boxed (Galoob 1996–98) each 15.00
Mini-Action Transforming Playsets (Galoob 1997)
    Three heads on a header card, each 6.00
Mini-Action 7-head boxed set (Galoob 1997) 15.00
Adventure Gear playsets (Galoob 1996) each 12.00
Death Star, transforms into planet Tatooine and
    Mos Eisley spaceport, includes *Millennium
    Falcon* and 4 figures (Galoob 1997) 40.00

Exclusive Sets (Galoob 1994–97)
Star Wars Fan Club Star Destroyer vehicle 25.00
Star Wars Fan Club *Millennium Falcon* vehicle 30.00
Star Wars Toy Fair 3-pack, *Millennium Falcon,
    Slave I,* and Death Star, in window box 25.00
Rebel Forces or Imperial Forces Gift Sets, 8 items,
    Target Stores Exclusives, 4 different, each 12.00
Galaxy Battle Collector's Set, 12 items (1994)
    K-Mart exclusive 9.00
Galaxy Battle Collector's Set, Second Edition, 12
    items (1995) K-Mart exclusive 18.00
11 Piece Collector's Gift Set (1994) Kay-Bee exclusive .16.00
Collector's Gift Set, 27 items, bronze color (1995) 40.00
Classic Series I, X-Wing and *Slave I* ships (#67085,
    1996) JC Penny exclusive) 15.00
Classic Series II, Imperial Shuttle and Imperial
    Emblem (1996) FAO Schwarz 15.00
Classic Series III, Darth Vader's TIE Fighter and
    Millennium Falcon (1996) Star Wars catalog 15.00
The Balance Of Power, X-wing Fighter and TIE
    Fighter (1996) 15.00
Rebel Forces vs. Imperial Forces Gift Set, 8 pieces
    (1996) Musicland exclusive 15.00
Millennium Falcon playset, with Y-wing Starfighter
    and 7 figures (#65878) 38.00
    In early box, with 24kt promotion offer 45.00
Master Collector's 19 vehicle set (1994) Toys "R"
    Us exclusive 30.00
Master Collector's 40-vehicle set (1997) Toys "R"
    Us exclusive 40.00

X-Ray Fleet (Galoob 1996–97)
X-Ray Fleet MicroMachine two larger ships per
    pack (Galoob 1996–97) each 7.00
Star Wars Trilogy Gift Set, 10 larger, X-Ray vehicle-
    sized, ships with display stands (#67079, 1996) . .35.00

MICROMACHINE ACTION FLEET

The first 2,500 pieces, from the production run of each of the first batch vehicles, were numbered with a special blue collector's sticker, The Rebel Snowspeeder was short packed in the assortment.

Action Fleet Ships, with 2 figures (Galoob 1996)
Luke's X-Wing Starfighter $12.00
Darth Vader's TIE Fighter 12.00
Imperial AT-AT 12.00
A-Wing Starfighter 12.00
Imperial Shuttle *Tydirium* 12.00
Rebel Snow Speeder 15.00
Any of above, with numbered collector sticker 20.00
Other Action Fleet ships (Galoob 1997–98) each 10.00

Two-Packs
Luke's Landspeeder and Imperial AT-ST, Kay-Bee
    exclusive (Galoob 1995) 20.00
Series Alpha Prototype and Final Design ships,
    with 2 figures (Galoob 1997–98) 7 different, each 15.00
Classic Duels, with 4 figures, Toys "R" Us special
    (Galoob 1997–98) each 20.00

Other MicroMachine Action Fleet items
Flight Controllers (Galoob 1997–98) 4 different, each . .20.00
Battle Packs (Galoob 1996–98) 18 different, each 18.00
Planet Playsets in box with slant side (Galoob
    1997–98) 3 different, each 30.00

PAPER

Calendars were only made for a few years when the movies first appeared. Since 1995, calendars have been sold every year and you can bet this will continue. Calendars appear in about July of the year before the year printed on the calendar, and by December they are available at discount and by January they are discounted heavily. If you intend to collect them, wait to get them at half price and don't unseal them.

Calendars (Ballantine Books)
1978 Star Wars Calendar, sealed $30.00
    Open 15.00
1979 or 1980 Star Wars Calendars), sealed 20.00
    Open 10.00
1981 *The Empire Strikes Back* Calendar), sealed 25.00
    Open 10.00
1984 *Return of the Jedi*, or Ewok Calendar , sealed . . .15.00
    Open 10.00
Star Wars calendars, 1990s
    Sealed . . . . .cover price
    Open . . . . .half cover price

Lobby Cards
Star Wars, Set of eight lobby cards, 11" x 14" (1977) .125.00
Star Wars, Set of eight photo cards, 8" x 10" (1977) . .100.00
The Empire Strikes Back, Set of eight lobby cards,
    11" x 14" (1980) 90.00
The Empire Strikes Back, Set of eight photo cards,
    8" x 10" (1980) 75.00

Return of the Jedi, Set of eight lobby cards, 11" x
  14" (1983) 75.00
Return of the Jedi, Set of eight photo cards, 8" x 10"
  (1983) 60.00

Magazines
Star Wars Galaxy Magazine (Topps 1994–97)
#1 Fall 1994, Star Wars Widevision SWP3 card 7.50
#2 thru #13 bagged with promo card(s) each 5.00
Becomes:
Star Wars Galaxy Collector (Topps 1998)
#1 thru #3 each 5.00

Bantha Tracks
#1 to #4, each 15.00
Combined reissue #1–#4 . . . . .10.00
#5 to #9 . . . . .6.00
#10 to #19 . . . . .5.00
#20 to #33 . . . . .4.00
#34 . . . . .7.50
#35 10th Anniversary, last issue 6.00

Lucas Film Fan Club Magazine (The Fan Club
  1987–94)
1987: #1 Anthony Daniels interview, 14 pgs 10.00
1988: #2 thru #5 14 pages, each 3.00–4.00
1989–94: #6 thru #22 each 4.00–10.00
Becomes:
Star Wars Insider (Star Wars Fan Club 1994–98)
1994–98 #23 thru #39 .5.00–10.00

Star Wars Official Poster Monthly
#1 Stormtrooper cover 10.00
#2 thru 10, each 5.00
#11 thru #18, each 10.00
The Empire Strikes Back, #1 thru #5, each 5.00
Return of the Jedi, #1 thru #4, each 5.00

Star Wars Postage Stamps
Stamps, issued by St. Vincent and the Grenadines
  Metallic Stamp gift pack, folder containing
    9-stamp sheet, plus a souvenir sheet with
    three triangular stamps printed on metallic foil .25.00
  First Day Covers stamp set, 3 covers, boxed,
    with certificate of authenticity 15.00

Return of the Jedi Portfolio (Ballantine 1983)

Portfolios & Blueprints
The Empire Strikes Back promo art portfolio 40.00
Star Wars Intergalactic Passport & Stickers
  (Ballantine 1983) 10.00
Star Wars Blueprints, includes 15 prints, 13" x 19"
  in vinyl pouch (Ballantine 1977) 15.00
  Reprint: (Ballantine 1992) 7.00
Star Wars Portfolio by Ralph McQuarrie, 11" x 14"
  color paintings (Ballantine Books #27382, 1977) . .20.00
The Empire Strikes Back Portfolio by Ralph
  McQuarrie, Ballantine Books (1980) 15.00
Return of the Jedi Portfolio by Ralph McQuarrie,
  Ballantine Books (1983) .15.00
Star Wars Power of the Force Planetary Map, set,
  issued as a mail-in 20.00

Press Kits
Original Star Wars kit (1977) 150.00
Star Wars kit (1978) 100.00
Holiday special kit (1978) .175.00
NPR Presents kit (1979) 35.00
The Empire Strikes Back kit (1980) 60.00
Introducing Yoda kit (1980) .35.00
NPR Playhouse kit (1981) 30.00
Return of the Jedi kit (1983) 30.00

Programs
Star Wars Movie Program (1977) limited quantity
  offered in 1994 . . . . .75.00
The Empire Strikes Back Official Collector's Edition
  (Paradise Press) 8-15.00
The Return of the Jedi Official Collector's Edition
  (Paradise Press) 5-10.00

Standees
Standees (Advance Graphics 1993–98) at least 20
  different, each 20.00–25.00

RECORDINGS & STILLS

Movie Audio Adaptations
Star Wars: The Original Radio Drama, National
  Public Radio (Highbridge #099-4, April 1993)
  6 cassettes 35.00
Star Wars: The Original Radio Drama, National
  Public Radio (Highbridge #005-6, April 1993)
  7 CDs 65.00
The Empire Strikes Back: The Original Radio
  Drama, National Public Radio (Highbridge
  #007-2, Sept. 1993) 5 CDs 55.00
The Empire Strikes Back: The Original Radio
  Drama, National Public Radio (Highbridge
  #000-5, Sept. 1993) 5 cassettes 30.00
Star Wars/The Empire Strikes Back Limited Edition
  set (Highbridge #006-4, Sept. 1993) 12 CDs . . .125.00
Complete *Star Wars/Empire* CD set (Lucasfilm
  #114-1, April 1995) 12 CDs 100.00
Return of the Jedi: The Original Radio Drama,
  National Public Radio (Highbridge #158-3,
  Oct. 1996) 3 CDs 35.00
Return of the Jedi: The Original Radio Drama,
  George Lucas (Highbridge #157-5, Oct.
  1996) 3 cassettes 25.00
Star Wars Complete Trilogy on CD, National Public
  Radio (Highbridge #164-8, Oct. 1996) 15 CDs . .125.00
The *Star Wars* Limited Edition Collector's Trilogy
  CD, National Public Radio (Highbridge #165-6,
  Oct. 1996) deluxe slipcase, only 7,500 made . . .175.00
Star Wars Trilogy CD Set (Highbridge #169-2) 9 CDs . .75.00

Star Wars 3 Position Laser Rifle (Kenner 1978)

Music Soundtrack Albums and CDs
Star Wars LP Soundtrack album, London Symphony Orchestra, two records, with two
sleves, an insert and a poster (20th Century
Records 1977) 30.00
The Empire Strikes Back LP Soundtrack album,
London Symphony Orchestra, two records
with a 12 page color insert (RSO Records
1980) album back features Han and Leia
romantic art 40.00
Return of the Jedi LP Soundtrack album, London
Symphony Orchestra, one record, with 4
page color insert (RSO Records, 1983) 25.00
Star Wars Trilogy Special Edition soundtrack CD
set with Bonus Darth Vader shaped single,
CDs laser engraved with picture, plus 20
pages of liner notes (1997) 110.00

Signed Photos
Harrison Ford 150.00
Other Stars 50.00
Just about anyone else . . . . .under 50.00
Star Wars Movie Photos 5.00
The Empire Strikes Back Movie Photos 4.00
Return of the Jedi Movie Photos 3.00

ROLE PLAY

Classic Lightsabers
Star Wars Light Saber, inflatable (Kenner 1997)
boxed 90.00
Droids Battery Operated Lightsaber (Kenner 1984)
Green 75.00
Red 150.00

Classic Weapons
3 Position Laser Rifle (Kenner 1978) in *Star Wars*
package 225.00
Reissue as Electronic Laser Rifle (1980) in
The Empire Strikes Back package 100.00
Laser Pistol replica of Han Solo's (Kenner 1978)
original *Star Wars* package 125.00
Reissue *The Empire Strikes Back* package 100.00
Reissue *Return of the Jedi* package 75.00
Biker Scout Laser Pistol (Kenner 1983) original
Return of the Jedi package 90.00

New Lightsabers
Luke Skywalker lightsaber (Kenner 1996) 20.00
Electronic Darth Vader Lightsaber (Kenner 1996) 25.00

New Weapons
Chewbacca's Bowcaster (Kenner 1997) 18.00
Electronic Heavy Blaster BlasTech DL-44 (Kenner

1996) 15.00
Electronic Blaster Rifle BlasTech E-11 (Kenner 1996) . .20.00
Electronic Blaster Lazer Rifle (Kenner) 17.00
Endor Blaster Pistol (Kenner 1998) 14.50
Commando Blaster Laser Rifle (Kenner 1998) 20.00
Water Blaster BlasTech DL-44 (Kenner 1997)
Silver color 15.00
Black color 12.00

New Accessories
Luke Skywalker Utility Belt (Kenner 1997) 19.00
Boba Fett Armor Set (Kenner 1998) 16.00
Imperial Walkie-Talkie (Tiger Electronics 1997) 13.00
Darth Vader Voice Changer Walkie Talkies (Tiger
Electronics 1997) 20.00
Rebel Alliance Long Range Walkie Talkies (Tiger
Electronics 1997) reception over 1,500 feet 35.00
Electronic Com-Link Communicators (Kenner 1997) . . .15.00
Darth Vader and Chewbacca Walkie Talkie Masks
(Micro Games of America 1995) 50.00
Darth Vader and Stormtrooper Walkie Talkies
(Micro Games of America 1995) 23.00

**VEHICLES, CREATURES,
PLAYSETS AND ACCESSORIES**

Vehicles are much more important in *Star Wars* than in
most other action figure lines. The 3¾" size of the figures
allowed the production of vehicles which were large enough
to accommodate several figures, and so the larger vehicles
became virtual playsets for the figures. Actual playsets were
also produced and creatures, such as the TaunTaun and
Wampa, and accessories, such as the Mini-Rigs, extended this
playset environment.

Star Wars Vehicles (Kenner 1978–79)
Landspeeder (#38020, 1978) original *Star Wars* box .$75.00
Star Wars Collector's Series Land Speeder
(1983) 35.00
X-Wing Fighter (#38030, 1978) original *Star Wars* box 125.00
Reissue in *The Empire Strikes Back* box 175.00
Imperial TIE Fighter "battle damage" (#38040,
1978) Original *Star Wars* box 135.00
Reissue in *The Empire Strikes Back* box 175.00
Darth Vader TIE Fighter (#39100, 1978) original
Star Wars box 125.00
Original *Star Wars* box with Battle Scene Setting .500.00

Star Wars Land Speeder (Kenner 1978)

Return of the Jedi Y-Wing Fighter (Kenner 1983)

    Star Wars Collector's Series (1983) 60.00
Millenium Falcon Spaceship (#39110, 1979)
    original *Star Wars* box 325.00
    Reissue in *The Empire Strikes Back* box 225.00
    Reissue in *Return of the Jedi* box 150.00
    Star Wars Collector Series Millenium Falcon
      (1983) 125.00
Radio-Controlled Jawa Sandcrawler (#39270,
    1979) original *Star Wars* box 600.00
    Reissue in *The Empire Strikes Back* box 700.00
Imperial Troop Transporter (#39290, 1979) original
    Star Wars box 100.00
    Reissue in *The Empire Strikes Back* box 115.00

Exclusive Vehicles (1979–80)
Sonic-Controlled Land Speeder, J.C. Penny exclus-
    ive (#38540, 1979) original *Star Wars* box 550.00
Imperial Cruiser, Sears exclusive (#93351, 1980) 125.00

The Empire Strikes Back Vehicles (Kenner 1980–82)
Darth Vader's Star Destroyer, 20" long (#39850,
    1980) 135.00
Twin-Pod Cloud Car (#39860, 1980) 80.00
    Reissue with Bespin Security Guard (white)
      figure 125.00
AT-AT All-Terrain Armored Transport (#38810,
    1981) original *The Empire Strikes Back* box 250.00
    Reissue in *Return of the Jedi* box 175.00
Rebel Armored Snowspeeder (#39610, 1982) 90.00
    Reissue with Rebel Soldier (Hoth Battle
      Gear) figure 175.00
Slave I, Boba Fett's Spaceship, including Simulated
    Frozen Han Solo (#39690, 1982) 90.00
    Reissue with Battle Scene Setting 275.00
Rebel Transport (#69740, 1982) 100.00
"Battle Damaged" X-Wing Fighter (#69780, 1981)
    original *The Empire Strikes Back* box 150.00
    Reissue in *Return of the Jedi* box 125.00
Scout Walker (#69800, 1982) original *The Empire
    Strikes Back* box 80.00
    Reissue in *Return of the Jedi* box 60.00
Imperial TIE Fighter (Battle Damaged, blue with
    "damage" decals) (#71490, 1983) original
    The Empire Strikes Back box 150.00
    Reissue in *Return of the Jedi* box 125.00

Return of the Jedi Vehicles (Kenner 1983–84)
Speeder Bike (#70500, 1983) original *Return of the
    Jedi* box 30.00
    Reissue in *Power of the Force* box 20.00
Y-Wing Fighter (#70510, 1983) 100.00

B-Wing Fighter (#71370, 1984) 75.00
TIE Interceptor (#71390, 1984) 90.00
Imperial Shuttle (#93650, 1984) 300.00

Power of the Force Vehicles (Kenner 1984–85)
Tattoine Skiff, 12" long (#71540, 1985) 600.00

Droids Vehicles (Kenner 1985)
A-Wing Fighter, with planetary map (#93700) 600.00
ATL Interceptor (#93900) 35.00
Side Gunner with planetary map (#94010) 50.00

NEW VEHICLES

Power of the Force, red boxes (Kenner 1995–96)
Landspeeder (#69770, 1995) 10.00
TIE Fighter (#69775, 1995) .20.00
Imperial AT-ST (Scout Walker) (#69776, 1995) 25.00
Electronic X-Wing Fighter (#69780, 1995) 30.00
Electronic *Millennium Falcon* (#69785, 1995) 50.00

Power of the Force, green boxes (Kenner 1996–98)
Luke's T-16 Skyhopper (#69663, 1996) 20.00
Cruise Missile Trooper (#69653, 1997) 13.00
Darth Vader's TIE Fighter (#69662, 1997) 20.00
Electronic Rebel Snowspeeder (#69585, 1996) 25.00

Power of the Force with figures (Kenner 1997–98)
A-Wing Fighter with Pilot (#69737, 1997) 25.00
Electronic Imperial AT-AT Walker with Commander
    and Driver (#69733, 1997) [.00] sticker over
    bottom of figures' photo 90.00
    Variation [.01] no sticker, full photo shown 75.00

Shadows of the Empire Vehicles (Kenner 1996–97)
Boba Fett's *Slave I* (#69565, 1996) 30.00
Boba Fett's *Slave I*, including Han Solo in
    Carbonite (#69565) reissue in green box 30.00
Dash Rendar's Outrider (#69593, 1996) 35.00
    Reissue (#69814) green box 20.00

Speeder Bike Vehicles with figures (Kenner 1996–98)
Imperial Speeder Bike with Biker Scout Storm-
    trooper figure (#69765, 1996) 20.00
Swoop vehicle with Swoop Trooper figure
    (#69591, July 1996) 12.00
Speeder Bike with Luke Skywalker (#69651,
    1997) [.00] two white gloves in photo 20.00
    Variation [.01] wearing one black glove 12.00

Star Wars Electronic Millennium Falcon (Kenner 1995)

The Empire Strikes Back Tauntaun (Kenner 1981)

Speeder Bike with Princess Leia Organa (#69727,
    1997) [.00] box 20.00
    Variation [.01] box 15.00
Power Racing Speeder Bike with Scout Trooper
    (#60588, 1998) 12.50

Expanded Universe Vehicles (Kenner 1998)
Cloud Car with Pilot figure (#69786) 15.00
Airspeeder with Pilot figure (#69774) 15.00
Speeder Bike with Rebel Pilot figure (#69772)) 12.50

Electronic Vehicle (Kenner 1998)
Electronic Power F/X Luke Skywalker Red Five X-
    wing Fighter (#69784, 1998) 50.00

SHIPS

Collector Fleet (Kenner 1997–98)
Electronic Blockade Runner (#27844, 1997) 25.00
Electronic Star Destroyer (#27835, 1997) 25.00
Electronic Super Star Destroyer *Executor* (#27914,
    1998) 28.00

CREATURES

Classic Creatures (Kenner 1979–84)
Patrol Dewback (#39240, 1979) in original *Star
    Wars* box 75.00
    Reissue in *The Empire Strikes Back* box 200.00
    Star Wars Collector Series Patrol Dewback
    (1983) 50.00
Tauntaun (#39820, 1980) 75.00
Tauntaun, with Open Belly (#93340, 1982) 75.00
Wampa, Snow Creature (#69560, 1982) original
    The Empire Strikes Back box 60.00
    Reissue as Hoth Wampa 35.00
    Reissue in *Return of the Jedi* box 40.00
Jabba the Hutt Action Playset, including Jabba
    figure, Salacious Crumb molded figure
    (#70490, 1983) original *Return of the Jedi* box . . .60.00
    Reissue in *Return of the Jedi* box (Sears) 40.00
Rancor Monster (1984) original *Return of the Jedi* box .75.00
    Reissue in *Power of the Force* box 60.00

NEW CREATURES

New Creature and figure combos (Kenner 1997–98)
Ronto and Jawa figure (#69728) 15.00
Dewback and Sandtrooper figure (#69743) [.00] 17.00
    Variation [.01] box 15.00
Jabba the Hutt and Han Solo figure (#69742) [.00] . . .25.00

Variation [.01] or [.02] box 15.00
Tauntaun and Luke Skywalker figure (#69729) 15.00
Wampa and Luke Skywalker figure (#69768) 15.00
Tauntaun and Han Solo figure (#64117) 15.00

Deluxe Creatures & Figure (Kenner 1998)
Rancor with Jedi Knight Luke Skywalker figure
    (#69771) 35.00
Bantha with Tusken Raider figure (#69769) 35.00

PLAYSETS

Star Wars Playsets (Kenner 1979)
Death Star Space Station (#38050, 1979) 225.00
Creature Cantina Action Playset (#39120, 1979) 125.00
Land of the Jawas Action Playset (#39130, 1979)
    original *Star Wars* box 150.00
    Reissue in *The Empire Strikes Back* box 200.00
Droid Factory (#39150, 1979) original *Star Wars* box .125.00
    Reissue in *The Empire Strikes Back* box 175.00

The Empire Strikes Back Playsets (Kenner 1980–82)
Imperial Attack Base, Hoth scene (#39830, 1980) . . .125.00
Hoth Ice Planet Adventure Set (1980, 1980) 150.00
    Reissue with Imperial Stromtrooper figure 200.00
Dagobah Action Playset (#38820, 1981) 55.00
Turret & Probot Playset (#38330, 1981) 150.00
Rebel Command Center Adventure Set (#69481,
    1981) 250.00

Return of the Jedi Playset (Kenner 1983)
Ewok Village Action Playset (#70520, 1983) 75.00

Ewok Playset (Kenner 1984)
Ewok Family Hut (Kenner Preschool, 1984) 50.00

Exclusive Playsets
Cantina Adventure Set, Sears promotional (1979) . . .650.00
Cloud City Playset, Sear's exclusive (1981) 375.00
The Jabba the Hutt Dungeon Action Playset
    Variation #1, with Klaatu, Nikto and 8D8,
    red box, Sear's exclusive (1983) 130.00
    Variation #2, with EV-9D9, Amanaman, and
    Barada, green box, Sear's exclusive (1984) .300.00

VEHICLE ACCESSORIES AND MINI-RIGS

Accessories (Kenner 1983–84)
Vehicle Maintenance Energizer (#93430, 1983)
    original *The Empire Strikes Back* box 20.00

Return of the Jedi Ewok Village playset (Kenner 1983)

The Empire Strikes Back MLC-3 (Kenner 1981)

Reissue in *Return of the Jedi* box 15.00
Radar Laser Cannon (#93440, 1983) original *The*
    Empire Strikes Back box 20.00
    Reissue in *Return of the Jedi* box 15.00
Tri-Pod Laser Cannon (#93450, 1983) original *The*
    Empire Strikes Back box 20.00
    Reissue in *Return of the Jedi* box 15.00
Ewok Assault Catapult (#71070, 1984) 18.00
Ewok Combat Glider (#93510, 1984) 18.00
Ewok Battle Wagon with Star Wars Planetary Map
    (#93690, 1984) 100.00
Imperial Sniper Vehicle vehicle (Asst. #93920, 1984) . .80.00
Security Scout vehicle (Asst. #93920, 1984) 250.00
One-Man Sand Skimmer vehicle (Asst. #93920, 1984) .80.00
Ewok Fire Cart (Kenner Preschool, 1984) 40.00
Ewok Woodland Wagon (Kenner Preschool, 1985) 75.00

Mini Rig 1-Figure Vehicles (Kenner 1981-83)
MTV-7 Multi-Terrain Vehicle (#40010, 1981)
    original *The Empire Strikes Back* box 35.00
    Reissue with AT-AT Driver figure 60.00
    Reissue in *Return of the Jedi* box 25.00
MLC-3 Mobile Laser Cannon (#40020, 1981)
    original *The Empire Strikes Back* box 25.00
    Reissue with Rebel Commander figure 60.00
    Reissue in *Return of the Jedi* box 25.00
PDT-8 Personnel Deployment Transport (#40070,
    1981) original *The Empire Strikes Back* box 25.00
    Reissue with 2-1B figure 60.00
    Reissue in *Return of the Jedi* box 15.00
INT-4 Interceptor (#69750, 1982) original *The*
    Empire Strikes Back box 30.00
    Reissue with AT-AT Commander figure 60.00
    Reissue in *Return of the Jedi* box 15.00
CAP-2 Captivator (#69760, 1982) original *The*
    Empire Strikes Back box 30.00
    Reissue with Bossk figure 60.00
    Reissue in *Return of the Jedi* box 15.00
AST-5 Armored Sentinel Transport (#70880, 1983) . . .15.00
ISP-6 (Imperial Shuttle Pod) (#70890, 1983) 20.00
Desert Sail Skiff (#93520, 1984) mini rig 15.00
Endor Forest Ranger (#93610, 1984) mini rig 15.00

NEW ACCESSORIES

New Accessories (Kenner 1996–97)
Detention Block Rescue (#27598, 1996) 15.00
Death Star Escape (#27599, 1996) 15.00

Hoth Battle (#27858, 1997) .18.00
Endor Attack (#27859, 1997) 18.00
Gunner Stations with figure (Kenner 1998)
Han Solo with Falcon Gunner Station 10.00
Luke Skywalker with Falcon Gunner Station 10.00
Darth Vader with TIE Fighter Gunner Station 10.00

VANS AND RACERS

Vans and Racers
Star Wars Duel at Death Star Racing Set
    (Fundimensions 1978) .200.00
Star Wars Van Set, 2 toy vans, plus 12 barrels, 4
    pylons and 2 T-Sticks (Kenner 1978) 150.00
Darth Vader SSP Van (Kenner 1978) 50.00
Star Wars Heroes SSP Van (Kenner 1978) 50.00

WALL ART

SeriCels & ChromArt
SeriCels from the Droids and Ewoks animated TV
    series (Royal Animation 1995–97) each 90.00
ChromArt Prints, 8" x 10" in an 11" x 14" matte
    (Zanart Entertainment) each 12.00
Framed Chromart prints (Zanart 1997) 20.00

Star Wars Theatrical Posters
Advance A One-sheet, "A long time ago in a galaxy
    far far away..." 250.00
Star Wars advance, 2nd version 150.00
Style A One-sheet, Tommy Jung art 175.00
Star Wars advance, style B .150.00
Star Wars, style C 150.00
Style D One-sheet (Circus poster) 325.00
Anniversary One-sheet (1978) theater give-away 600.00
'79 Re-release One-sheet, "It's Back!" 100.00
'81 Re-release One-sheet 60.00
'82 Re-release One-Sheet 50.00

The Empire Strikes Back Theatrical Posters
Advance One-sheet 200.00
Style 'A' One-sheet (Love Story) Rodger Kastel art . . .200.00
Style 'B' One-sheet, Tommy Jung art 75.00
'81 Re-release One-sheet, Tommy Jung art 50.00
'82 Re-release One-sheet, Tommy Jung art 40.00

Revenge of the Jedi
Advance Revenge of the Jedi One-sheet, 41"x27"
    with release date 350.00
Variation, no release date .400.00

Return of the Jedi Theatrical Posters
Style 'A' One-sheet 35.00
Style 'B' One-sheet 40.00
Return of the Jedi, 1985 reissue 35.00

Special Edition Theatrical Posters
Star Wars Trilogy Special Edition Advance One-sheet . .30.00
Version 'B' *Star Wars: A New Hope* One-sheet 30.00
Version 'C' *The Empire Strikes Back* One-sheet 30.00
Version 'D' *Return of the Jedi* One-sheet 30.00

Posters, Commercial
Star Wars 10th Anniversary Poster (1987) 10.00
Star Wars 15th Anniversary poster (1992) 25.00
Other *Star Wars*, *The Empire Strikes Back*, or
    Return of the Jedi Anniversary Posters, each . . .15.00
Star Wars Checklist Poster, 27" x 40" (Killian Enter-
    prises 1995) full color reproductions of all
    movie one-sheet posters and variants 15.00

Thunderbird Puppet

STINGRAY

VEHICLE

Stingray Craft $75.00

TARZAN:
THE EPIC ADVENTURES

FIGURES

4" Two-Pack Bendie Figures
Deja Thoris vs. Nolach the Kaldane (#06017) 6.00
Tarzan of Mars vs. The Plantman (#06018) 6.00
John Carter vs. O Mad Zad (#06019) 6.00

4" Bendie Figures (Kmart exclusives) with badge
Tars Tarkas (#6341) 4.00
Plantman, Vicious Martian Monster (#6343) 4.00

Tarzan: The Epic Adventures (9-pack)
Special Collector Edition of nine 4" figures: Dino-
    Armored Tarzan, Nolach the Kaldane, O Mad
    Zad, The Mahar, The Plantman, King
    Kerchak, Dejah Thoris, John Carter and the
    Leopard Man (#30719, 1996) 24.95

TERMINATOR

PAPER

Terminator, The (1984) one sheet movie poster $35.00
Terminator II (1991) one sheet movie poster 25.00

VEHICLES

Mobile Assault Vehicle (#56450, 1992) 18.00
Heavy Metal Cycle (#56460, 1992) 13.00
Bio-Flesh Regenerator playset (#56470, 1992) 30.00

THUNDERBIRDS

"The Thunderbirds" are based on the most popular of
the Gerry Anderson television programs, which were done in
"Super-Marionation." The original 1967 programs spawned
two feature-length films as well. The 1994 program, which
appeared on FOX, was a redubbed and re-edited rerun of the
1967 show. In the show, Jeff Tracy is the father of the five
Tracy boys: Scott, Virgil, Gordon, Alan and John. The Tracy
clan love their vehicles, the largest of which is Thunderbird 2,
which is 250' long and can fly 5,000 miles per hour, and carries the smaller vehicles on rescue missions. We'd hate to see
their fuel bill. Brains is the genius scientist that builds everything on Tracy Island, while the Hood is the bad guy in the
series. Lady Penelope and her limo driver, Parker, are a pow-
erful international rescue team.

Matchbox and Matchbox UK had their action figure
lines shipping the same figures just a few months apart from
each other. The only really significant difference is in the
header cards. *The Thunderbirds* were a top-selling toy line in
Britain, but in the United States the figures could only be
found here and there. Most collectors were not aware of them
and they have received little coverage in the collector magazines.

British figures get to Canada quickly, and some collectors and dealers have connections in both places.
Consequently, we are not certain if all of the figures and vehicles listed were actually distributed in the United States or
whether some of them are British issue. That wouldn't make
them any less popular or valuable, but we have generally
included only figures distributed in the United States in the
rest of this book. The rarer figures from the series are those of
Lady Penelope and Parker.

FIGURES

4" Figures (Matchbox 1994–95)
Lady Penelope (#41750) $20.00
Scott Tracy (#41751) 5.00
Virgil Tracy (#41752) 5.00
Alan Tracy 5.00
Gordon Tracy 5.00
John Tracy 5.00
Jeff Tracy 5.00
Brains 10.00
Parker 15.00
The Hood 8.00

MISCELLANEOUS

Thunderbirds game (Parker Bros. 1965) 100.00
Thunderbirds Bagatelle pinball set (Marx) 300.00
Thunderbirds Intercom set (Merit) 150.00
Thunderbirds Cap Gun 60.00
Thunderbirds Talking Alarm Clock (Westco 1992) 60.00
Thunderbird 2 Flower Watering Can 200.00

VEHICLES & PLAYSET

Tracy Island Electronic Playset 40.00
Lady Penelope's FAB-1, pink (Dinky #100, 1960s) . . .250.00
Lady Penelope's FAB-1, shocking pink (Dinky #100,
    1960s) 350.00
Thunderbird 2 (Dinky #101) 500.00
Thunderbird 2 (Dinky #106) 175.00
Thunderbird 1, Pilot: Scott Tracy (Matchbox) 10.00

Thunderbird 2 with Thunderbird 4 (Matchbox #41702) .25.00
Thunderbird 3 (Matchbox) 10.00
Thunderbirds Rescue Pack, with all Thunderbird
    vehicles (Matchbox) boxed 40.00
Thunderbird 1, diecast (#36614) 18.00
Thunderbird 2, diecast (#36615) 25.00
Thunderbird 4, diecast (#36837) 18.00
Deluxe Thunderbird 1, diecast (#36333) 38.00
Deluxe Battery operated Jet Mole (#36836) 38.00
Deluxe Thunderbird II (#37072) 88.00
Thunderbird 5 figure set (#37073) 22.00
Thunderbird Mecha Set (#37328) 38.00
Thunderbird VI Skyship (ITB-093) 18.00

TOM CORBETT SPACE CADET

Tom Corbett was created to compete with *Captain Video*. It had a bigger budget and Willie Ley, an actual scientist, as a technical adviser. The series moved around between the major networks and lasted from 1950 to 1955. It was losely based on the novel *Space Cadet* by Robert A. Heinlein. The stories were scientifically better than other shows, but lacked any really great villains. There were a lot of neat collectibles.

CHILDREN'S BOOKS & PUZZLES

Tom Corbett Coloring Book, 10½" x 14", 16 pages
    (Saalfield 1952) $70.00
Tom Corbett Space Cadet Push-Outs book,
    10½" x 14" with 8 pages (Saalfield 1952) 75.00
Picture Puzzles, 10" x 11" cover, three puzzles
    (Saalfield/Rockhill 1952) 35.00
Frame Tray Puzzles (Saalfield 1950s) three
    different, each 45.00
Frame Tray Puzzle, 9" x 12", Tom and crew
    (Saalfield 1952) 25.00
Frame Tray Puzzle, 10" x 11", Tom with Space
    Academy (Rockhill 1952) 25.00

CLOTHING

Tom Corbett Space Cadet girl's costume, with hat . . .125.00
Space Cadet Belt 150.00
Tom Corbett Wristwatch (Ingraham) 650.00
Space Suit Ring 25.00
Rocket Scout Ring 25.00

Tom Corbett Sparkling Space Ship (Marx 1950s)

Official Tom Corbett Space Academy Play Set (Marx 1950s)

Tom Corbett Portrait Ring 50.00

CRAFT & ACTIVITY

Tom Corbett Space Cadet Super Model Craft
    Molding & Coloring Set (Kay Stanley 1952) 250.00
Roger and Astro Model Craft Molding Set (Kay
    Stanley 1952) 150.00

DOLLS & FIGURES

Official Tom Corbett Space Cadet Doll, 7" tall
    plastic (Marcie 1950s) 175.00

HOUSEHOLD

Tom Corbet Space Cadet steel lunchbox (Aladdin 1952)
    lunchbox, paper decal 250.00
    thermos, steel/glass .100.00
Tom Corbet Space Cadet steel lunchbox (Aladdin 1954)
    lunchbox, litho 450.00
    thermos 100.00

MISCELLANEOUS

Official Tom Corbett Space Academy Play Set,
    23" x 15" x 4" (Marx #7012 1950s) 475.00
Signal Siren Flashlight (Usalite) 175.00
Official Space Patrol Rocket Lite, space ship design .400.00
Tom Corbett Space Cadet Pin On Rocket Lites
    (Usalite 1950s) 200.00
Tom Corbett Space Cadet badge, metal (1951) 125.00

RECORDINGS

Tom Corbett "Rescue in Space" 78 RPM record
    (RCA Victor 1952) 50.00
Tom Corbett Space Cadet Song and March record
    (Golden Record 1950s) 50.00
Secret from Space View-Master Set (GAF) 75.00

ROLE PLAY

Ray Guns
Flash X-1 Space Gun 145.00
Official Space Pistol (Marx 1950s) 125.00
Space Cadet Space Gun (Marx 1950s) 200.00
Tom Corbet Space Cadet Atomic Rifle, 24" long,
    grey (Marx 1950s) 250.00
Tom Corbett Space Cadet Sparkling Space Gun
    (Sub-Machine Gun) 22" plastic (Marx, 1950's) . .250.00
Official Space Cadet Atomic Pistol, red plastic
    flashlite pistol, 7½" (Marx early '50's) 150.00

Equipment
Tom Corbett Space Cadet Field Glasses, 3 power
    (Herold 1950s) 150.00

Tom Corbett Space Cadet Electronic Interplanet 2-
    Way Phone (Zimmerman/Rockhill 1951) boxed .125.00
Tom Corbett Space Cadet Medical Kit, 19" x 9" tall,
    11 items (Peerless/Rockhill 1953) boxed 75.00
Tom Corbett Space Cadet Signal Siren Flashlight,
    with planet guide and chart (Usalite) boxed 125.00

SPACE SHIPS

Tom Corbett Space Cadet Polaris Rocket, 12½" tin
    wind-up spaceship (Marx 1952) 500.00
Tom Corbett Sparkling Space Ship, Space Cadet 2
    (Marx 1950s) 600.00

2001: A SPACE ODYSSEY

2001 Jigsaw Puzzle $25.00
2001: A Space Odyssey (1968) one sheet movie
    poster 250.00
2001 A Space Odyssey record (MGM 1968) 25.00
2001 souvenir program 25.00
2010 souvenir program 15.00
Button 25.00

UFO

A number of companies have produced generic alien
figures based on what has become known as the typical
Roswell or UFO type — gray head, large eyes, etc. It's the
same kind the Stephen Spielberg used in *Close Encounters of
the Third Kind*, but that name has to be licensed. "UFO" and
"Roswell" do not. There does not seem to be a whole lot of
collector interest in them at the moment, but I have listed a
few of the more generally available ones. There are also halloween masks, key chains, T-shirts and other stuff available.

CLOTHING

Area 51 cap, red & black (1995) $15.00
Area 51 T-shirt 14.00

FIGURES

UFO Bendies
UFO Files 6-pack (Toy Concepts #6502, 1997) 13.00
Small Aliens, with trading card (Shadowbox Collectibles)
Mother Ship (#55005) 7.00
Other ships, 3 different, each 6.00
Men in Black 5.00
Aliens, 8 different types, each 5.00

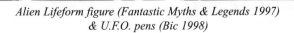

*Alien Lifeform figure (Fantastic Myths & Legends 1997)
& U.F.O. pens (Bic 1998)*

Glow in the Dark four pack (#55280) 10.00
Alien Lifeform (Fantastic Myths & Legends 1997) 15.00

MISCELLANEOUS

Area 51 coffee mug 8.00
Area 51 "No Trespassing" metal sign, 9" x 12" 10.00

V

Based on the popular NBC television mini series and the
unpopular 1984–85 regular television series. Several other
lizard/human-headed figures were planned but only the one
12" figure was produced. Robert Englund played Willie, the
alien Visitor who defected to the human resistance. He went
on to fame as Freddy Krueger.

DOLLS & FIGURES

12" Figure in window box
Enemy Visitor (LJN #4500, 1985) $60.00

HOUSEHOLD

V Lunch Box (Aladdin) box 35.00
        thermos (plastic) 20.00
V Bop bag 20.00

MISCELLANEOUS

V Baseball cap 10.00
V patch 3.00
Visitors Patch 3.00
V & Visitor cloisonne pin, 1", set 11.00
V "To Serve Man" cook book 3.00
The Visitors, A Technical Information Manual 5.00
V The Series, Writers/ Directors Guide 3.00
V 45'er Action Set (Arco) .60.00
200 Piece jigsaw puzzles, 4 diff, each.. . . . . .15.00
Poster 5.00
Poster of Diana, 23" x 35" 20.00
Poster of Diana, 23" x 35" signed by Jane Badler 50.00
Puffy stickers, 3 different, each 1.00

ROLE PLAY

V 45'er Sound Pistol & holster (Arco) 60.00
V M-16 Sound Rifle 90.00
V Walkie Talkies, set of 2 .50.00

X-FILES

CLOTHING & ACCESSORIES

T-Shirts/Sweatshirts/Jackets
Black Sweat-Shirt "The Truth is Out There," front;
    X-Files logo back 44.95
T-shirts, at least 40 different, each 14.95
Spaceship design image on sweatshirt back with
    X-Files pocket logo 29.95
Wool & Leather Jacket with "The Truth is Out
    There" embroidered on back and emblem
    pocket logo, leather arms and wool body 249.95
Lightweight Supplex jacket with pocket logo 99.95

Caps
Green X logo on front of black cap 9.95
Colored logo caps, different styles, each 14.95

Pins
"Trust No One" enamel pin, 1" 5.95
"The Truth is Out There" enamel pin, 1" 5.95

The X-Files: Barbie & Ken dolls (Mattel 1998)

Keychains
X-Files Logo glowing keychain, squeeze to light up 4.45
Binary glowing keychain 4.45
"Trust No One" glowing keychain 4.45
Faces glowing keychain 4.45
Circle X glowing keychain 4.45
"The Truth is Out There" glowing keychain 4.45
X-Files talking keychain, says one of four phrases
        when squeezed 11.45

DOLLS

Barbie & Ken X-Files dolls, original (Mattel 1998) 100.00
        reissue version with shorter hair (Scully) 80.00

HOUSEHOLD

Mugs
Large X-Files logo on 16oz black mug with "The
        Truth is Out There on back 10.95
X-Files logo on 12oz mug, each 7.95
X-Files heat sensitive disappearing Mug, text
        changes from "The Truth is Out There" to
        "Trust No One" with eye icon logo on other
        side 13.95

X-Files Talking Mugs, says one of four phrases when picked
        up: "The Truth is Out There;" "Trust No One;" "Deny
        Everything" and "Apology is Policy"
X-Files logo 15.95
The Lone Gunmen 15.95
Deep Throat & Mr. X 15.95
Eye Image 15.95
Mulder & Scully 15.95
Brush Stroke X 15.95
Comple set of six mugs 86.95

Clocks
X-Files logo wall clock 34.95

MISCELLANEOUS

Mouse Pads
Eye Icon mousepad 10.95

Large X mousepad 10.95
The Scream mousepad 10.95

Photos: 8" x 10" color, authorized, 25 different, each . . .5.00

PAPER

Magazines:
Cinescape Vol. 3, #1 "Special Collectors Issue:"
        The X-Files & conspiracy television, Dec. 1996 . . .9.95
X-Files official magazine, premiere edition, Nov.
        1995, inc. interview with Chris Carter,
        dossiers on David Duchovny and Gillian
        Anderson, 8-page comic story 4.95

Scripts
Fire 13.95
Irresistable 13.95
Deep Throat 13.95
Darkness Falls 13.95
Red Museum 13.95
Complete Set of 5 scripts 64.95

Calendars
1997 X-Files wall Calendar .12.99
The X-Files 1997 desk diary, hardcover 15.00

Phonecard
X-Files prepaid phonecard 10.00

Postcards
Set of 11 X-Files 4" x 6" color picture postcards 8.95

RECORDINGS

Videos (with 2 trading cards)
Pilot & Deepthroat 13.95
Conduit & Ice 13.95
Fallen Angel & Eve 13.95
Darkness Falls & The Erlenmeyer Flask 13.95
Beyond the Sea & E.B.E. 13.95
Squeeze & Tooms 13.95

Audio books
Ground Zero audio tape 17.95
Ruins audio tape 17.95
The Unofficial X-Files Companion, Part 1, audio tape . .10.00
The Unofficial X-Files Companion, Part 2, audio tape . .10.00

35mm Film Cels
Pilot episode 25.00
Squeeze 25.00
Ice 25.00
Erlenmeyer Flask 25.00
Special Agent Fox Mulder 25.00
Special Agent Dana Scully .25.00
Deep Throat 25.00
Four piece collector's boxed set 100.00
22 piece collector's assortment including exclusive
        Cigarette-Smoking Man cel 550.00

WALL ART

Posters
Skully & Mulder half faces with logo, 24" x 36" 7.95
Skully & Mulder, full figure in Doorway, "The Truth is
        Out There" 23" x 35" .7.95
Cathedral with Skully & Mulder faces, 23" x 35" 7.95
Standing Figure, "The Truth is Out There" 23" x 35" 7.95
Trust No One collage, 23" x 35" 7.95

TRADING CARDS

Most of the early science fiction trading cards are based on movies and television series. Topps and now other manufacturers still produce these types of cards today, and just about every movie or television show has its share of cards. For *Star Trek* and *Star Wars*, that's a huge share and it mirrors the share that these two popular marketing properties have in action figures, comics, books and toys.

SCIENCE FICTION AND FANTASY ART

The 1990s did produce one new type of trading card — the science fiction and fantasy artists card. There was great art in the 1930s and 1940s, but it was concentrated in the pulp magazines.

Everybody's pay was low during the Depression and the artists did their best work, happy to have any pay in their chosen field. One might think that it got better in the 1950s and early 1960s, but it did not. Science fiction moved to the mainstream, but science fiction cover art did not. Hardcover publishers could sell science fiction books as literature in book stores and especially to libraries, but they had no budget for, nor interest in, pulp style cover art and they rarely included interior illustrations in their books. Paperbacks were just getting going and while paperback publishers had no prejudice against science fiction art, they had meger budgets for it. In addition, they often kept the originals and frequently didn't credit the artists anywhere in the books.

In order to make a living as a science fiction cover artist in the 1950s and 1960s, you had to be able to work cheaply and produce something quickly. This is not a formula for great art and it is truly sad to think of some of the artists working then who rarely got a chance to show the full extent of their talents.

This changed in the 1960s with Frank Frazetta's covers for Edgar Rice Burroughs books, published by Ace and later for the Conan books from Lancer. His covers sold well and he got decent pay for them. Other publishers had to compete and so quality and pay went up across the industry.

Today, good science fiction or fantasy art on the cover is considered essential for book sales and a number of very fine artists can do their best work and still make a living. Many of them have had their paintings translated into trading cards. The artists generally painted covers for both science fiction and fantasy books and there is no way to separate the two for this listing, so fantasy is included here, even though it is largely excluded elsewhere in this book.

The first two artists to make it to superstar status were Frank Frazetta and Boris Vallejo. Michael Whelan, Rowena Morrill, Don Maitz, The Brothers Hildebrant, Darrell Sweet and many others have followed, including some such as Chris Foss who were best known in England. The cards have usually been taken from the original art, not directly from the book covers and this gives the collector a unique chance to buy a lot of very fine art that he or she would never otherwise be able to see. The only problem with this is size — a standard trading card is just 2½" by 3½". This has been addressed somewhat with the advent of the Colossal Card which is a generous 6" by 10". These are a lot more expensive, but the best way to see the art, short of going to a science fiction convention and seeing the original in the art room.

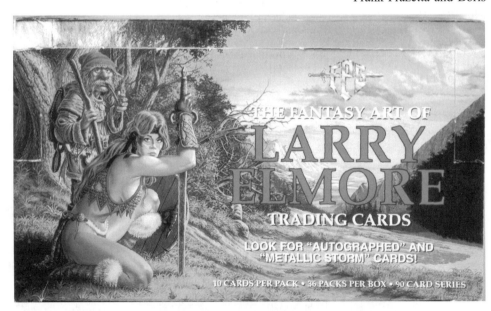

The Fantasy Art of Larry Elmore, trading card box (FPG 1994)

Elmore Colossal Card #48: Transdimensional Critters (FPG 1995)

The two companies issuing art cards are Comic Images and FPG. Comic Images started first and was able to sign up Boris Vallego and Frank Frazetta in 1991. Among their other prominent artists are Greg and Tim Hildebrandt, Richard Corben and Michael Whelan. Their overall science fiction and fantasy production has been less than FPG's because they also produced a number of sets of art by prominent comic book artists.

FPG started in 1992 with Chris Achilleos, an unusual choice because he is best known in England. They have featured more science fiction and fantasy artists than Comic Images, but, on the whole, their artists are less well known. The best known are Joe Jusko, Michael Kaluta, Don Maitz, Rowena Morrill, Barclay Shaw and Darrell Sweet. Between the two companies, just about every prominent artist from the 1980s and 1990s with enough pictures to complete a card set has had one issued. However, there are several who have not, including Ron Walotsky, Victoria, Carl Lundgren, Rick Sternbach, Jill Bauman. While there are many wonderful sets of art cards available, very few have turned out to be particularly expensive. You can still find many of the sets for around $10. They are well worth it. Many of these artists show up at science fiction conventions, so you can get a few cards autographed fairly easily.

CLASSIC PULP COVERS

There have been a handful of card sets which are reproductions of science fiction and fantasy pulp magazine covers from the 1930's, 1940's and 1950's. The 30's and 40's were the era of the bug-eyed monster about to devour the lightly dressed heroine while the hero tries to rescue her with the help of his trusty ray gun. The art is garish, but who cares, because it's great escapist stuff.

Sperry Mini Mags produced Classic Pulps in 1992. Two of the artists who are closely associated with these escapist covers are Earle Bergey and R. G. Jones and both are represented in quantity in this set. The most important artists from the (less garish) late 1940's and 1950's are Frank R. Paul, Ed Emsh(willer), Alex Schomburg, and Frank Kelly Freas. All of them are represented plus one early cover each by Margaret Brundage and J. Allen St. John. Many of the cards in the last half of the set also contain a black & white drawing on the back and most of these are by Virgil Finlay, the undisputed master of this type of illustration.

21st Century Archives produced several sets of classic pulp covers, including one featuring covers from *Astounding* and most significantly one featuring Margaret Brundage and *Weird Tales*. Ms. Brundage was by far the most famous female fantasy artist from the pulp era. She lived in Chicago, and the only magazine published there just happened to be *Weird Tales* which turned out to be the most famous of the pulps, in no small part because of her covers. She started as a fashion illustrator and, when she was hired by *Weird Tales*, she continued to draw women, now scantily clad and menaced by creatures or other nameless horrors. The women were the central figures and they were somehow scared to death and sensous at the same time. Ms. Brundage wasn't the first person to use this formula, just the best. The art was produced with pastel chalks which helped portray the sensousness of the characters, but looks quite different from the oil paint or acrylics used these days. The set contains most, but not all of her covers. The few which don't fit the "Women in Peril" theme seem to have been omitted. When *Weird Tales* was sold to a prudish New York publisher, Ms. Brundage was out of work and out of the fantasy field forever, alas. If you don't own a copy of this set, you should.

EDGAR RICE BURROUGHS

Joe Jusko, well known in the comics field produced two sets of original illustrations for Edgar Rice Burroughs stories. Most of the first set features Tarzan, while the second set concentrates on Burroughs' Mars, Venus and Pellucidar series. The art is great and this alone should be enough to induce you to own the sets. However, there is more. The left half of the backs contain classic ERB cover or interior art by J. Allen St. John, Frank Schoonover, John Coleman Burroughs, Studley O. Burroughs and Rudolph Belarski, comic book art by Morris Gollub and paperback art by Roy G. Krenkel, Frank Frazetta or Richard Hescox. You get a full set of both original and classic art in one card set. What more do you want?!

In the listing that follows, artist cards are listed under the artist's **last** name, except for Boris (Vallejo) and Rowena (Morrill) whose first names are their trademarks. Where the artist has two or more series, they are listed chronologically.

Joe Jusko's Edgar Rice Burroughs Collection II (FPG 1995)

STAR TREK

Star Trek trading cards have been produced for all of the television shows and most of the movies. Card sets before 1990 are not particularly attractive but they are hard to find so they are eagerly sought by collectors and are fairly expensive. Sets produced in the 1990s are very well made and quite beautiful to look at, but they are easy to find so they aren't worth a lot of money. Collectors are mostly interested in the promo and bonus cards. The only recent trading cards that are hard to find today are the ones that came with action figures, food and video tapes.

Leaf made a 72-card set of black and white cards in 1967 while the classic TV show was still on the air. They were not particularly well done and didn't sell all that well at the time, but they are very valuable today. Topps produced one of its typical 88-card, 22-sticker sets in 1976 and another one in 1979 based on the first *Star Trek* motion picture. A variation on these cards was produced for a group of bread companies. There are 33 cards in the set and uncut sheets are reasonably common. The issuing bread company's logo — Rainbo, Kilpatrick or Colonial — is located on the card back. Topps did not continue with the license and sets for movies II through IV appeared from FTCC.

Star Trek cards were modernized when Impel (now SkyBox) produced its 25th Anniversary sets in 1991. Odd numbered cards in the sets were based on the now classic *Star Trek* TV series and even numbered cards were based on *Star Trek, The Next Generation* TV series which was then in its third season. They produced the first chase cards — holograms of the old and the new *Enterprise*. *Star Trek* cards have been produced regularly ever since.

SkyBox recruited prominent science fiction artists for the *Star Trek Master* series, which began in 1993. It produced its first *Deep Space Nine* card set in 1993, and began producing Episode Collections for *Star Trek, The Next Generation* in 1994. In 1995, it started on *Star Trek Voyager*. In 1997, cards featured the TV seasons for the classic series. As with most trading cards in the 1990s, all the action has been in the chase cards, promo cards and sheets.

The current rage in movie cards is 2½" x 4½" cards, printed horizontally. This correspondes with the original aspect ratio of the film and is the best way to produce cards based on a wide-vision movie. SkyBox made a 72-card set for the *Star Trek Generations* movie this way and followed with similar-sized, boxed sets based on the previous six *Star Trek* movies for $25 each. In 1996, it made a 2½" x 4½" card set for the *Star Trek First Contact* movie.

With all these *Star Trek* cards to choose from, it's not surprising that collectors were largely unfamiliar with the trading cards issued with *Star Trek* action figures, video tapes and other products. The action figure cards are variants of the *Star Trek Master Series* cards and came one per action figure. They can be identified by the "Playmates" logo on the back. The first series of *Deep Space Nine* action figures also had premium trading cards. Later series came with Space Caps. In 1995–96, Playmates went back to trading cards. Then it changed to 4" trading cards, half-way between standard size and movie size. The largest series of premium trading cards came with video tapes of the original *Star Trek* episodes which were sold starting in 1993. There were 80 tapes and thus 80 trading cards to collect.

Another interesting trading card set came with Frito-Lay products and was distributed only in Canada. These cards are about one quarter normal size and each originally came in a clear cello bag to protect it from the food contents of the snack product in which it was packaged. Episode cards are actually 16 image fold-outs.

STAR WARS

Topps was the major producer of movie tie-in cards in the 1960s, 1970s and 1980s. The standard that they created and followed with just about every movie set was 66 (or 88) cards plus 11 (or 22) stickers. If the cards were successful, a second series of "all new" cards was produced. The cards and stickers came in colorful wax wrappers, and all three came in boxes of 36 packs. In those days there were no holograms, foils, autographed cards, 3-D redemption cards and not even any promo cards, so collectors had nothing to collect except the cards, stickers, wrappers and boxes.

Star Wars was very successful, so a total of five series of cards and stickers was produced. They are numbered con-

secutively, so as to form one large set of 330 cards and 55 stickers. Stickers came one to a pack, making a sticker set harder to assemble than a card set and making an individual sticker more valuable than a card.

Other early *Star Wars* cards came from Wonder Bread, while General Mills cereals had two series of stickers and Kelloggs had peel-away sticker cards in its cereal. There were also sugar-free bubble gum wrappers, Burger King 3-card strips and Hershey's candy bars 6-packs with a tray card.

There were only three series of *The Empire Strikes Back* cards from Topps, but they contained more actual cards and stickers than for the previous movie. There were only two series of *Return of the Jedi* cards and only about half as many total cards as in the previous two series. In the early 1990s, Topps was forced to upgrade its quality to match the production values of the other card companies.

Star Wars Galaxy cards were the first to use art rather than pictures from the movies. Joe Smith's images from this series have been used extensively. Variant cards came with the Just Toys Bend-ems figures and a number them also made their way onto T-shirts. This first *Star Wars Galaxy* set was also an important element in the *Star Wars* marketing revival. New novels and comics had started in 1991, but very few other collectibles were being produced.

Mars Attacks #59 (Topps 1962)

The second *Star Wars Galaxy* card series continued the fine art work and great overall quality of the first series. As with the first series, most of the collecting has centered around the promo cards and chase cards. Some promo cards, such as those given away at shows, are inevitably difficult to obtain, but the value of other promo cards that came with magazines or comic books, can be misleading. Often these cards can still be found, bagged with the magazine or comic, for a very reasonable price.

With *Star Wars* widevision cards, Topps went back to images from the movies. This time they had high quality and the same aspect ratio as the films (like the letterbox videotape version). The images were transferred directly from the original film master, not a second-generation version. Widevision versions of the other two movies followed and in 1997 the Special Edition was covered in turn.

As with *Star Trek*, several less well known series of cards came with figures. Action Master die-cast figures came with trading cards that were unique to the figures, not promo cards for some card series. Most of JustToys' Bend-em figures came with trading cards from 1993 to 1995. The cards are variant *Star Wars Galaxy* cards, which are lettered on the back instead of numbered. There earliest cards and figures matched, but the later ones were random, making it that much harder to complete a set of cards. Consequently, later cards are worth more than earlier cards. The cards may very well be more collectible (and more valuable) than the figures they came with. For real fans of *Star Wars* art, Topps produced Mastervision cards in 1995. These are large enough to be called wall art and come on premium 24 point stock, UV-coated and foil-stamped. The series features full-bleed artwork by Ralph McQuarrie, Dave Dorman, The Hildebrandts, Boris Vallejo, Ken Steacy, Drew Struzan, Hugh Fleming, Michael Whelan and more.

In the listing that follows, all *Star Trek* or *Star Wars* series are grouped chronologically, not alphabetically, so that, for example, *Deep Space Nine* follows *The Next Generation* and *The Empire Strikes Back* follows *Star Wars*. Listings for things like colossal cards, space caps, album stickers and metal cards follow the listing of trading cards for a series.

Chris Achilleos #60, Medusa (FPG 1992)

Alien #9, Warrant Officer Ripley (Topps 1979)

Alien Nation #9, Cathy Frankel as Terri Treas (FTCC 1990)

Babylon 5 #101, Red Star (Fleer 1995)

ACHILLEOS, CHRIS
FPG Cards (1992) SF art
Set: 90 cards 10.00
Pack: 10 cards 1.25
Box: 36 packs 30.00
Gold Foil stamped cards 2.50
Silver Foil stamped cards 1.00
Autograph card, numbered
    (250 made) 50.00
Original Art bonus card (21 made) . . . . .?
Four card promo sheet 3.00
Binder with card (1994) 20.00

SERIES TWO:
ANGELS AND AMAZONS
FPG (1994) SF art
Set: 90 cards 9.00
Pack: 10 cards 1.25
Box: 36 packs 30.00
Metallic Storm
MS#1 Nuria 7.50
MS#2 Kira 7.50
MS#3 Nikita 7.50
MS#4 Kaisu 7.50
MS#5 Marnie 7.50
Autographed card (1000 made) . . .50.00
Ten card autographed sheet 30.00
?Promo card (1993) 2.50
Promo card (1994), 2 diff., each . . .2.00
P3 promo card 1.50
Two card deluxe promo sheet #16 . . .2.50
Binder with card 20.00

COLOSSAL CARDS
FPG (1996) SF art
Set: 50 .65.00
Single Card 2.00
Box: 60.00
Pack: 5.00
Autograph Card (1:18) 45.00

ACTION MASTERS
Kenner/SkyBox (1994)
Cards come with Die Cast figures
Terminator T-800 . . . . .1.00
Terminator T-1000 . . . . .1.00
Predator .1.00
Alien Queen 1.00
Star Wars
C-3PO 3.00
R2-D2 . . . . .3.00
Darth Vader 3.00
Luke Skywalker 3.00
Chewbacca 3.00
Stormtrooper 3.00
Snowtrooper 3.00
From 6-pack
Darth Vader 3.00

Han Solo .3.00
Stormtrooper 3.00
Luke Skywalker 3.00
Boba Fett 3.00
Chewbacca 3.00
From 4-pack
C-3P0 . . . . .3.00
Princess Leia Organa 3.00
R2-D2 . . . . .3.00
Obi-Wan Kenobi 3.00

ADVENTURES AT
GIANT BAR RANCH
(SPACE)
Zigler (1951)
Set: 26 cards 175.00
Single Card: 5.00

ADVENTURES OF
CAPTAIN CHAPEL TRIP
TO THE MOON
Mister Softee (1962)
Set: 10 cards 30.00
Single Card: 2.50

ALIEN
Topps (1979) Movie
Set: 84 cards/22 stickers 35.00
Pack: 10 cards, 1 sticker 1.50
Box: 36? packs 65.00
Cards #43, #63 and #83 each have two dif-
ferent backs

ALIEN 3
Star Picks (1992) Movie
Set: 80 cards 10.00
Pack: 10 cards 1.00
Box: 36? packs 12.00

ALIENS
Dark Horse (1993) Comic
Set: 5 Comic Book Checklist cards . .5.00

ALIENS/PREDATOR
Dark Horse (1993) Comic
Comic checklist card 1.00

ALIENS/PREDATOR
UNIVERSE
Topps/Dark Horse (1994) Comic
Set: 70 cards + 15 Operation: Aliens 15.00
Pack: 9 cards 1.50
Box: 36? packs 35.00
Topps Finest Chase Cards (1:17)
1 thru 6, each 10.00
Promo card 1.00

One card promo sheet (Previews) . . .1.00
P2 (Adam Hughes art) 1.00
1 of 2 Aliens (Hero master-foil) 1.00
2 of 2 Predator (Hero master-foil) . . .1.00
Two card dealer strip, gold border . .7.50

ALIEN NATION
FTCC (1990) Movie
Set: 60 cards 18.00
Pack: 1.25
Box: 36? packs 30.00

ALL AMERICAN
SPACE FLEET
Skelly Gas (1950s)
Set: 24 cards 300.00
Single Card: unnumbered 15.00

ASTOUNDING STORIES
21st Cent. Archives (1994)
Pulp magazine covers
Set: 55 cards 15.00
Pack: 8 cards 1.00
Box: 36? packs 35.00
Robert Heinlein SculptorCast (1:18)
RH1 . . . . .5.00
RH2 . . . . .5.00
RH3 May 1941–"Universe" 5.00
RH4 . . . . .5.00
RH5 Jan. 1941–"Sixth Column" 5.00
Uncut Sheet 30.00
Factory Set: 55 cards + 1 sculptor . .20.00
Prototype June 1936 cover 1.50

ASTRONAUTS
Topps (1963) Photos
Set: 55 3-D cards 350.00
Card: 7.00
Checklist Card #55 . . . . .35.00
3-D Viewer 20.00

ASTRONAUTS
POPSICLE
SPACE CARDS
Popsicle (1963) Photos
Set: 55 cards 350.00
Card: 6.00

BABYLON 5
Fleer Ultra (1995) TV
Set: 120 cards 100.00
Pack: 8 cards 6.00
Box: 36 packs 175.00
Prismatic Foil Cards (1:4),
    8 different, each 6.00
Space Gallery Set (1:4) 8 diff., each .6.00

Hologram Cards (1:12) 8 diff., each .35.00
Four-card promo sheet (*Combo #9,*
    Collect 10-95; Advance #81;
    Cards Illus.#23) 8.00
Promo, N# 2.00

SERIES TWO
Fleer/Skybox (1996)
Set: 60 cards 17.50
Pack: 8 cards 1.50
Box: 36? packs 70.00
Coming of Shadows (1:10)
    9 different, each 5.00
Creator's Collection (1:10)
    10 different, each 4.00
Babylon 5 Trivia (1:2)
    50 different, each 1.00
Nightwatch Posters (1:5)
    10 different, each 2.00
Laser Cut B5 Logo cards (1:48)
    2 different, each 20.00
Box Topper 5" x 7", 2 diff., each . . .30.00
Straczynski Autograph card (1:576) 300.00

SPECIAL EDITION
Fleer/Skybox (1997) TV
Set: 72 cards 20.00
Pack: 8 cards 2.00
Box: 36? packs 50.00
Trivia Set: 36 cards (1:1) 30.00
Costume cards (1:2)
    18 different, each 2.00
Worlds of Babylon 4 (1:6)
    8 different, each 6.00
Faces of Delenn (1:12)
    4 different, each 10.00
Sculptured Holograms (1:180)
    2 different, each 50.00
Mira Furlan Autograph card (1:720) 300.00
Promo Card 5.00

SEASON FOUR
Fleer/Skybox (1998) TV
Set: 81 cards 20.00
Pack: 2.00
Box: 36? packs 70.00
Parallel Set: 81 cards (1:1) 70.00
Season One Retro Cards (1:4)
    12 different, each 3.00
Starfury Art Cards (1:8) 9 diff., each .4.00
First Ones (1:6) 6 diff., each 6.00
SkyMotion Cards (1:90) 4 diff., each 45.00
TNT Movie Cards (1:36) 2 diff., each 10.00
Autograph Cards (1:90)
Richard Biggs (Dr.) 125.00
Jeff Conaway (Zack Allen) 150.00
Stephen Furst (Vir Cotto) 125.00
Peter Jurasak (Londo) 150.00
Andreas Katsulas (G'Kar) 150.00

*Ken Barr, #59, Terminal Man
(Comic Images 1994)*

*Battlestar Galactica #65, Jane Seymour
as Serina (Topps 1978)*

*Black Hole #30, Holland's Discovery
(Topps 1979)*

*Boris #35, Jade Manikin
(Comic Images 1991)*

Bill Mumy (Lanier) 200.00
Patricia Tallman (Leta Alexander) .125.00
Jeffrey Willerth () 125.00
Jerry Doyle (Garibaldi) 150.00
Bruce Boxleitner (Sheridan) 200.00
Album 20.00

BARLOWE, WAYNE: THE ALIEN WORLD OF
Comic Images (1994) SF art
Set: 90 cards 12.50
Pack: 10 cards 1.00
Box: 48 packs 30.00
Prism cards, (1:18)
P1 thru P6 untitled, each 7.50
Autographed cards (500 made) 50.00
Space Travelers subset (3:case)
1 . . . . .20.00
2 . . . . .20.00
3 . . . . .20.00
Medalion card (2:Case) 25.00
Mini press sheet
Uncut sheet six card subset
    (1:case) 4 different, each 20.00
Promo card 1.50

BARR, KEN: THE BEAST WITHIN
Comic Images (1994) SF art
Set: 90 cards 12.50
Pack: 10 cards 1.00
Box: 48 packs 25.00
Foil cards, (1:16)
F1 thru F6 untitled, each 6.00
Ken Barr's Vampires subset (3:case)
1 Nosferatu Awakens! 12.50
2 Journey Of The Undead! 12.50
3 . . . . .12.50
Autograph card (500 made) 55.00
Medallion card (2:case) 15.00
Mini-Press Sheet 20.00
Six card un-cut sheet (1:case) 20.00
Promo card (Unicorn) 1.00
Promo card (Advance Comics) 1.00

BATTLE BETWEEN TWO PLANETS
Classic/Blackmore (1993)
Set: 45 cards 8.00
Pack: 1.00
Box:

[More Than] BATTLE-FIELD EARTH:
Comic Images (1995) SF art
Set: 90 cards 12.50

Pack: 10 cards 1.00
Box: 48 packs 32.00
Chromium cards (Frazetta art)(1:16)
C1 Man, The Endangered Species . .8.00
C2 The Countess 8.00
C3 Leaping Lizards 8.00
C4 . . . . .8.00
C5 The Lieutenant 8.00
C6 Dreamflight 8.00
Subset: (Jim Warren art) (1:48)
1 . . . . .10.00
2 . . . . .10.00
3 Windsplitter II 10.00
Medallion card (1:144) 20.00
6-card uncut sheet 20.00
Promo card (Frank Frazetta art) . . .2.00

BATTLESTAR GALACTICA
Topps (1978) TV
Set: 132 cards/22 stickers 35.00
Pack: 10 cards, 1 sticker 1.75
Single card 75
Single sticker 1.00

Wonder Bread (1978) TV
Set: 36 .45.00
Single card 1.25

Dart Flipcards (1996) TV
Set: 72 cards 20.00
Pack: 7 cards 1.75
Box: 30 packs 45.00
Gold Foil cards (1:15) 6 diff., each . .8.00
Jumbo Cards, 4 diff., each 10.00
Richard Hatch (1:300) Autograph
    card 100.00
Binder card 10.00
Promo Cards P1, P2, each 2.00
Convention Promos, 3 diff., each . . .5.00
Album, with print 19.00

BEEKMAN, DOUG
Comic Images (1997) SF art
Set: 72 cards, 24pt card stock 12.00
Pack: 8 cards 1.50
Box: 36 packs 25.00
OmniChrome cards (1:12)
    6 different, each 6.00
Autographed card (500 made) 50.00
Promo #1 . . . . .2.00
Promo #2 . . . . .2.00
Binder, with 6-card press sheet . . .20.00

BELL, JULIE
Cardz (1994) Fantasy art
Set: 46 cards + 10 Techchromes . . .27.50
Pack: 7 cards + 1 Techchrome 1.75

Box: 36 packs 35.00
Autographed card (1:576) 2? diff. .50.00
Album 14.00
Promo cards
P1 Demon in the Palace promo 2.00
P2 Beauty and the Steel Beast,
    Tekchrome promo 4.00

JULIE BELL KEEPSAKE
Comic Images (1994, 1995)
Metal Fantasy Set: 8 cards 25.00
Soft as Steel Set: 7 cards 20.00

BERKEY, JOHN
FPG cards (1994) SF art
Set: 90 cards 12.50
Pack: 10 cards 1.50
Box: 36 packs 35.00
Metallic Storm cards
MS1 Nomad II 7.00
MS2 The Foundation 7.00
MS3 Lines Through the Horizon 7.00
MS4 Observation Orb 7.00
MS5 Intrusion, An Unpleasant Visitor 7.00
Boxed Metallic Storm set (1:case) . .35.00
Metallic Storm gold set 65.00
Flying Legs Redemption card . . . .
Autographed card (1000 made) 50.00
Promo cards, 2 diff., each 2.00
Three card promo sheet (Previews) . .3.00
Binder with card 20.00

SERIES TWO
FPG (1996) SF art
Set: 90 cards 15.00
Pack: 10 cards 1.50
Box: 36 packs 40.00
Metallic cards, 5 diff., each 8.00
Autograph Card 55.00

BIG LITTLE BOOK CARDS
(1937)
Flash Gordon, 32 diff., each 75.00
Subset of entire 224 card set

BIONIC WOMAN
Donruss (1976) TV
Set: 44 cards 50.00
Pack: 5 cards 3.00
Box: 90.00
Uncut Sheet 50.00

BLACK HOLE
Topps (1979) TV
Set: 88 cards/22 stickers 20.00
Pack: 10 cards, 1 sticker 1.50
Box 30.00

Box: 36 packs 35.00
Autographed card (1:576) 2? diff. .50.00
Album 14.00
Promo cards
P1 Demon in the Palace promo 2.00
P2 Beauty and the Steel Beast,
    Tekchrome promo 4.00

BORIS
Comic Images (1991) SF/Fantasy
Set: 90 cards 30.00
Pack: 10 cards 1.75
Box: 36? packs 45.00
Autographed card 150.00

BORIS: THE FANTASY CONTINUES
Comic Images (1992) SF art
Set: 90 cards 25.00
Pack: 10 cards 2.00
Box: 36 packs 28.00
Factory Set, with promo 15.00
Prism cards (1:16)
P1 Nomad 9.00
P2 She Vampire 9.00
P3 Mercenary 9.00
P4 Witch and Her Familiar 9.00
P5 Sagittarius, the Archer 9.00
P6 The Magnificent 9.00
Promo card (Pumping Iron) 2.00

BORIS 3
Comic Images (1993) SF art
Set: 72 cards, all-prism 17.50
Pack: 7 prism cards 2.50
Box: 36 packs 35.00
Chromium cards (1:16)
C1 Thytonese 10.00
C2 Phoenix 10.00
C3 Satyr 10.00
C4 Clone 10.00
C5 Private Cosmos 10.00
C6 Sphinx II 10.00
Prism Promo card 5.00

BORIS 4: MAGNIFICENT MYTHS
Comic Images (1994) SF art
Set: 90 cards 17.50
Pack: 10 cards 2.00
Box: 48 packs 45.00
HoloChrome cards (1:16)
H1 Lilith .9.00
H2 Loria .9.00
H3 Nikatjef 9.00
H4 Kamal 9.00
H5 Panty Raid 9.00
H6 Hatch-Mech 9.00
SF Sensations card subset (3:case)
1 Robo Stripper 10.00
2 Floating Island 10.00
3 London 2500 A.D. 10.00
Autograph card (500 made) 90.00
Medallion card (2:case) 25.00
Six-card un-cut sheet (1:case) 15.00
Mini-Press sheet 15.00
Four card promo sheet (D-7 to D-10)

*Boris 4 #32, Space Arachnoid
(Comic Images 1994)*

*Buck Rogers #58, The Princess' Ploy
(Topps 1979)*

*David Cherry #64, Destin-ation: Mutiny
(FPG 1995)*

*Richard Corben #40, Planet Busters
(Comic Images 1993)*

(Previews #61) 2.00
Promo card 2.00

[THE BEST OF] BORIS
Comic Images (1995) SF art
Set: 90 cards, all chromium 45.00
Pack: 7 chromium cards 3.50
Box: 36 packs 75.00
Omnichrome (1:16)
1 thru 6, untitled, each 10.00
Triadmiration (3:case)
 1 thru 3 untitled, each 12.00
Medallion card (4:case) 15.00
Six card un-cut sheet 20.00
Autographed card (500 made) 75.00
Holochrome variation 7.50
Chromium promo card 3.50

BORIS KEEPSAKES
Comic Images (1993)
Boris' Beasts set: 6 beasts on color
6" x 9" cards, 7th card = all 6
images + SpectraScope card . .20.00
Buns Set: 6 buns on color 6" x 9"
cards, 7th card = all 6 images +
Prism card 20.00

BORIS
POSTER CARDS
Kalan (1993)
Set: 12 . . . . .35.00

BORIS WITH JULIE
Comic Images (1996) Fantasy art
Set: 90 cards 40.00
Pack: 7 cards 2.25
Box: 36 packs 70.00
MagnaChrome (1:16) 6 diff., each . . .8.00
Unicorn subset (1:48) 3 diff., each .12.00
Refractors, each 10.00
MagnaChrome Box Card 10.00
Boris Autograph Card (250 made) . .85.00
Julie Autograph Card (250 made) . .85.00
6-card uncut sheet 20.00
Binder 20.00

BROM
FPG (1995) SF art
Set: 90 cards 12.00
Pack: 10 cards 1.50
Box: 36 packs 35.00
Metallics
M1 The Silent Quintet, Part i 8.00
M2 The Silent Quintet, Part ii 8.00
M3 The Silent Quintet, Part iii 8.00
M4 The Silent Quintet, Part iv 8.00
M5 The Silent Quintet, Part v 8.00

Autographed card (1,000 made) . . .50.00
Promo sheet (Previews 3-95) 1.00

BUCK ROGERS
Topps (1979) TV
Set: 88 cards/22 stickers 25.00
Pack: 10 cards, 1 sticker 2.50
Box: 75.00

CALDWELL, CLYDE
FPG (1995) SF art
Set: 90 cards 12.50
Pack: 1.25
Box: 36 packs 40.00
Metallics
M1 Fire from Heaven 10.00
M2 Chrysalis 4 . . . . .10.00
M3 Pot Luck 10.00
M4 Dragon Spell 10.00
M5 Artifact of Evil 10.00
Autograph card (1,000 made) 50.00
Deluxe promo sheet (Previews 1-95) back
promos James Warhola 1.00

CANTY, TOM
FPG (1996) SF art
Set: 90 cards 12.00
Pack: 10 cards 1.25
Box: 36 packs 35.00
Metallic Cards, 5 diff., each 10.00
Autograph Card (1,000 made) 50.00

CHADWICK, PAUL
FPG (1996) SF art
Set: 90 cards 12.00
Pack: 8 cards 1.25
Box: 36 packs 35.00
Metallic Storms
M1 Electronic Thinker 8.00
M2 Protoplasm 8.00
M3 The Button 8.00
M4 Lost Legacy 8.00
M5 Watchers 8.00
Autographed card 40.00
Promo card (Combo #7) 2.00
Promo card (Cards Illus.#21) 2.00

CHERRY, DAVID
FPG (1995) SF art
Set: 90 cards 15.00
Pack: 10 cards 1.50
Box: 36 packs 35.00
Metallics
M1 Cyborg Safari 8.00
M2 Tek Noir 8.00
M3 Out of the Hornet's Nest 8.00

M4 Lady of Light 8.00
M5 Sulcar Keep 8.00
Autographed card (1,000 made) . . .60.00
Promo sheet #27 (Previews 2-95)
back promos Colossal Cards #2 1.00

CHOPPER CHICKS
OF MARS
Studio E (1998)
Set: 60 cards 15.00
Pack: 7 cards 1.50
Box: 36 packs 40.00
Embosses Spaceships, 3 diff., each .5.00
Alien Foil (1:12), 6 diff., each 9.00
Character Cards (1:36) 3 diff., each .15.00
E.T.C. (2:case), 2 diff., each 100.00
Promo Cards, 9 diff., each 2.00

CLASSIC PULPS
Sperry Mini Mags (1992) Covers
Set: 100 cards 15.00
Pack: 7 cards, cello pack 1.00
Box: 20.00
*Set includes duplicate Card #93, w/upside
down back illustration*

CLOSE ENCOUNTERS
OF THE THIRD KIND
Topps (1978) Movie
Set: 66 cards, 11 stickers 30.00
Pack: 1.50
Box: 50.00
Single card 50
Single sticker 1.00

Prime Press (1978) Movie
Set: 65.00
Single card 1.25

Wonder Bread (1977) Movie
Set: 24 cards 9.00
Card: 50

COLOSSAL CARDS
FPG (1994) SF art
Set: 50 cards, 6¾" x 10" 75.00
Pack: 5 cards 7.00
Box: 18 packs 85.00
Single card 3.00
Autographed cards, each 50.00
Three different packages
SERIES TWO
Set: 50 cards 75.00
Pack: 5 cards 7.00
Box: 85.00
Autographed cards, each 50.00

CORBEN, RICHARD
Comic Images (1993) SF art
Set: 90 cards 12.50
Pack: 10 cards 1.00
Box: 48 packs 25.00
Prism cards (1:16)
P1 Blue Dragon 7.00
P2 Snow Monster 7.00
P3 Man versus Robots 7.00
P4 Man in Robot 7.00
P5 Mutant Bear 7.00
P6 Kopok Checks the Prize 7.00
Promo card 2.50

DARK HORSE BATMAN
VERSUS PREDATOR
DC/Dark Horse (1991) Comics
Set: 16 cards 20.00

DEAN, ROGER
FPG cards (1993) SF art
Set: 90 cards 15.00
Pack: 10 cards 1.25
Box: 36 packs 35.00
Metallic Storm foil cards
MS#1 Spaceship Approaching Earth
(Tim White art) 8.00
MS#2 Landed Orange Dawn (Tim
White art) 8.00
MS#3 Head (Tim White art) 8.00
MS#4 Polar Group (Tim White art) . .8.00
MS#5 Coming Ashore (Richard
Clifton-Dey art) 8.00
Boxed Metallic Storm set (1:case) . .35.00
Autographed cards (1000 made)
Promo card, 2 diff., each 2.00
Four card promo sheet (Previews) . . .3.00
Binder with card 20.00

DeVITO, JOE
FPG (1995) SF art
Set: 90 cards 15.00
Pack: 8 cards 1.50
Box: 36 cards 55.00
Metallics
M1 Monsters in Our Midst 7.50
M2 Wetwear 7.50
M3 The Black Hole Affair 7.50
M4 Doomsday Warrior 7.50
M5 Night Strike 7.50
Autograph card (1000 made) 65.00

DiFATE, VINCENT:
BLUEPRINTS OF THE FUTURE
Comic Images (1994) SF art
Set: 90 cards 10.00
Pack: 10 cards 0.75

Vincent DiFate #45, Metal Fingers (Comic Images 1994)

Dr. Who #66, The Fourth Doctor (Cornerstone 1994)

Dune Stickers #6, Feyd Challenges Paul (Fleer 1984)

Chris Foss #19, Easter Island (FPG 1995)

Box: 48 packs 20.00
Omni-Chrome cards (1:16)
1 thru 6, untitled, each 6.00
Larger Than Life subset cards (1:48)
1 . . . . .10.00
2 . . . . .10.00
3 . . . . .10.00
Autographed card 60.00
Medallion Card 20.00
Uncut subset Sheet 25.00
Promo card 1.00

DIMENSION X
Karl Art (1994)
Promo (Roy Krenkel) 1.00

DOCTOR WHO
Cornerstone (1993) TV
Set: 110 cards 10.00
Pack: 10 cards 1.00
Box: 36 packs 35.00
Factory Set: 110 cards with
    extra Dalek prism 20.00
Gold Factory Set, with
    autographed card 80.00
Doctor Prisms (1:18),
    7 different, each 6.00
Autographed cards (1:432)
    7 different, each 50.00
Promo cards
A1 Series Logo 1.00
A2 The Five Doctors 1.00
A3 K9 & companion 1.00
Uncut promo sheet 45.00
Binder .15.00
Box cards, 2 diff., each 2.00

SERIES II (1994)
Set: 110 cards (#111–#220) 15.00
Pack: 10 cards 1.00
Box: 36 packs 35.00
Factory Set 20.00
Cornerstone Premiere (1:2)
    9 different, each 1.00
Enemy foil cards (1:12)
    6 different, each 6.00
Autographed cards (1:510)
    4 different, each 50.00
Promo cards
B1 Series Logo, 2 diff., each 1.50
B2 b&w picture, 2 diff., each 1.50
B3 K9 & Tom Baker, 2 diff., each 1.50
B4, 2 diff., each 1.50
Uncut promo sheet 45.00
Binder .15.00

SERIES THREE
Set: 110 cards (#221–#330?) 15.00
Pack: 10 cards 1.00

Box: 36 packs 32.00
Factory Set 20.00
Foil cards, 7 diff., each 6.00
Premiere Cards, 6 diff., each 1.50
Autograph cards, 5 diff., each 40.00
Promo Cards C1–C3, each 1.50
Promo IT-4 . . . . .10.00
Binder .15.00

SERIES FOUR
Set: 90 cards (#331–#420?) 15.00
Pack: 10 cards 1.25
Box: 36 packs 32.00
Factory Set 20.00
Foil cards (1:9) 7 diff., each 5.00
Autograph cards (1:432), each 60.00
Promo Cards D1–C4, each 2.00
Promo IT-4 . . . . .10.00
Binder .20.00

DUNE
Fleer (1984) Movie
Set: 132 cards 25.00
Sticker Set: 44 stickers 15.00
Pack: 10 cards, 1 sticker 1.50
Box 45.00
Note: 3 different wrappers

[The Fantasy Art of] EASLEY, JEFF
FPG (1995) SF art
Set: 90 cards 12.50
Pack: 10 cards 1.00
Box: 36 packs 35.00
Metallic Storm,
MS1 thru MS5, each 10.00
Autograph card (1,000 made) 50.00
10-card autographed sheet 50.00
Deluxe promo sheet (*Previews* 11-94) .5.00

[The Fantasy Art of] EGGLETON, BOB
FPG (1995) SF art
Set: 90 cards 15.00
Pack: 10 cards 1.00
Box: 36 packs 35.00
Metallic Storm cards (1:12)
M#1 Asimov Chronicles, Vol. 1 . . . . .7.50
M#2 Asimov Chronicles, Vol. 2 . . . . .7.50
M#3 Asimov Chronicles, Vol. 3 . . . . .7.50
M#4 Asimov Chronicles, Vol. 4 . . . . .7.50
M#5 Asimov Chronicles, Vol. 5 . . . . .7.50
M#6 Asimov Chronicles, Vol. 6 . . . . .7.50
Autographed cards (1000 made) 50.00
Autographed 10-up un-cut sheet
    10 different, (1:Case) each 50.00
Deluxe promo sheet (*Previews* 12-94) .5.00
Binder with card 20.00

[The Fantasy Art of] ELMORE, (LARRY)
FPG (1994) SF art
Set: 90 cards 30.00
Pack: 10 cards 1.50
Box: 36 packs 40.00
Metallic Storm cards (1:12)
MS#1 Forging a Magic Blade 10.00
MS#2 A Child of Elvish 10.00
MS#3 Triumph of the Dark Sword . .10.00
MS#4 Artifact 10.00
MS#5 The Conjuring Stone 10.00
Autographed cards (1000 made) . . .75.00
Autographed 10-up un-cut sheet
    10 different, (1:Case) each 30.00
Full un-cut sheet, autographed 50.00
Two card promo sheet (Deluxe Promo #11)
    (*Previews*) 2.00
Binder with card 20.00

COLOSSAL CARDS
FPG (1995) SF art
Set: 50 cards 60.00
Pack: 5 cards 7.50
Box 80.00
Single Card 1.50
Autograph Card 50.00

E.T. THE EXTRA-TERRESTRIAL
Topps (1982) Movie
Set: 87 cards, 12 stickers 35.00
Pack: 10 cards, 1 sticker 1.50
Box 25.00
Stickers (#10–#12), each 3.00

ALBUM STICKERS
Panini (1982)
Set: 120 Album stickers + album . . .20.00
Pack: 1.50
Album 3.00

WIDEVISION
Topps (1996) Movie
Promo Card 2.00
Set not released

FLASH GORDON
Topps (968)
TEST SET
Set: 24 cards 2,800.00
Single cards 100.00

FLASH GORDON SERIAL
Jasinski (1991) Movie Photos
Each series: 5,000 numbered sets
Set #1: 36 cards, B&W 13.00

Set #2: 36 cards (#37-#72) 12.00
Set #3: 36 cards (#73-#108) 11.00

FLASH GORDON CANDY BOX CARDS
Phoenix (1978)
Set: 8 cards 50.00
Card 7.00

FORREST J. ACKER-MAN'S CLASSICARDS!
Dynacomm (1992)
Set #1: 45 color cards 7.50

FOSS, CHRIS
FPG (1996) SF art
Set: 90 cards 10.00
Pack: 8 cards 1.25
Box: 36 packs 30.00
Metallic Storm (1:12?)
M1 thru M5, each 10.00
Autograph Card (1,000 made) 50.00

FRAZETTA
Comic Images (1991) SF art
Set: 90 cards 15.00
Pack: 10 cards 1.25
Box: 48? packs 25.00

FRAZETTA II: THE LEGEND CONTINUES
Comic Images (1993) SF art
Set: 90 cards 12.50
Pack: 10 cards 1.50
Box: 48 packs 25.00
Chromium cards
C1 Las Vegas 6.00
C2 Devil Rider 7.50
C3 Beyond the Grave 6.00
SpectraScope cards
S1 Warrior with Ball and Chain 5.00
S2 Flashman on the Charge 5.00
S3 The Return of the Mucker 5.00
Uncut Sheet 12.00
Promo card 2.00

THE BEST OF FRANK FRAZETTA
Comic Images (1996) SF art
Set: 90 chromium cards 25.00
Pack: 7 chromium cards 3.00
Box: 36 packs 65.00
MagnaChrome Cards (1:16)
    6 different, each 8.00
Comic Covers (1:108) 3 diff., each .12.00
Chromium Card #0 (1:box) 12.00
6-card uncut sheet (1:case) 30.00
Autograph card (500 made) 60.00
Promo Card, N# chromium 3.00

Frazetta II #48, The Secret People
(Comic Images 1993)

Richard Hescox #37, Kioga of the
Unknown Land (FPG 1994)

Bros. Hildebrandt #66
(Comic Images 1994)

Tim Hildebrandt #41, Time
(Comic Images 1994)

FRAZETTA HOLOGRAMS
21st Century Archives (1993)
Series I set: 3 cards in folder 18.00
H1 Dawn Attack 5.00
H2 The Countess 5.00
H3 Dream Flight 5.00
Set: w/gold holograms 40.00
Series II set: 3 cards in folder 18.00
H1 Encounter 5.00
H2 Moonrider 5.00
H3 Man, Endangered Species 5.00
Set: w/gold hologram 40.00

FRAZETTA: THE WONDER YEARS
Comic Images (1995)
Keepsake Collection
Six oversize cards in collectors
envelope plus mini-press card
of all 6 . . . . .20.00

[The Art of]
FREAS, KELLY
FPG (1996) SF art
Set: 90 cards 12.50
Pack: 10 cards 1.50
Box: 48.00
Metallic, 5 diff., each 8.00
Autograph card (1,000 made) 30.00

[The Fantasy Art of]
HESCOX, RICHARD
FPG cards (1994) SF art
Set: 90 cards 12.50
Pack: 10 cards 1.25
Box: 36 packs 35.00
Metallic Storm cards (1:12)
MS#1 Starfarer 7.50
MS#2 Fliers of Antares 7.50
MS#3 Marooned 7.50
MS#4 Werewolves of Kragen 7.50
MS#5 Masks of Scorpio 7.50
Autographed cards (1000 made) . . .65.00
Autographed 10 card Pin-up sheet
10 different (1:Case) each 30.00
Promo cards, 2 diff., each 2.00
Two card promo sheet (Previews) . . .2.00
Binder with card 20.00

HILDEBRANDT, GREG
Comic Images (1992) Fantasy art
Set: 90 cards 10.00
Pack: 10 cards 1.00
Box: 48 packs 40.00
Prism cards (1:16)
P1 Dracula Perishes 9.00
P2 Poe .8.00
P3 The Pied Piper 8.00

P4 Jack the Giant Killer 8.00
P5 Alice Follows the White Rabbit . . .8.00
P6 Alice Falls Down Rabbit-Hole 8.00
Uncut Prism sheet 70.00
Promo card 2.00

HILDEBRANDT:I
30 YEARS OF MAGIC
Comic Images (1993) Fantasy art
Set: 90 cards 10.00
Pack: 10 cards 1.00
Box: 48 packs 28.00
Alice Chromium cards (1:16)
C1 Alice Swims with the Mouse 8.00
C2 Bill the Lizard 8.00
C3 The Puppy 8.00
C4 Alice Meets the Cheshire Cat 8.00
C5 The Pack of Cards 8.00
C6 The Gryphon & The Mock Turtle .8.00
Promo card 2.00

KEEPSAKE
Comic Images (1993)
Dracula Set 20.00
Christmas Fantasy Set: 8 cards 20.00

HILDEBRANDT, TIM
FLIGHTS OF FANTASY
Comic Images (1993) Fantasy art
Set: 90 cards 10.00
Pack: 10 cards 1.00
Box: 48 packs 30.00
Holochrome cards (1:12)
H1 Hippo-Gryph 8.00
H2 Lessa Impresses Ramoth 9.00
H3 Jaxom and Young Ruth 9.00
H4 Blades of the Gods 8.00
H5 The Giant Centaur 8.00
H6 Cold Copper Tears 8.00
Promo card 1.00
Medallion card (2:case) 25.00
Flying Dragon subset cards (3:case)
1 thru 3, each 20.00
Autograph card (500 made) 50.00
Four card promo sheet (D-1 to D-4)
(Previews) 2.50
Mini Press 5" x 7" sheet 20.00

KEEPSAKE
Comic Images (1994)
The Worlds of Dragons Set: 6
dragons on color 6" x 9" cards,
7th card = all 6 images +
Holochrome dragon cardset . . .20.00

HILDEBRANDT, BROS.
Comic Images (1994) Fantasy art
Set: 90 cards 10.00

Pack: 10 cards 1.00
Box: 48 packs 20.00
Foil cards (1:16)
F1 thru F6, untitled, each 7.00
Creatures of Tolkien subset (3:case)
1 Smaug 10.00
2 Balrog 10.00
3 Shelob the Spider 10.00
Autograph card (500 made) 80.00
Medallion card (2:case) 20.00
6-card uncut sheet (1:case) 20.00
Mini-press sheet 15.00
Four card promo sheet (D-11 to D-14)
(Previews #62?) 2.50
Urshurak promo card 2.00

HILDEBRANDT, GREG & TIM
SEPARATE & TOGETHER
Comic Images (1995) Fantasy art
Set: 90 cards 20.00
Pack: 7 cards 2.00
Box: 36 packs 40.00
MagnaChrome (1:16)
1 Dorothy Meets the Scarecrow 8.00
2 Attacked by the Fighting Tree 8.00
3 The Cowardly Lion and the
    Scarecrow 8.00
4 Glenda Ruby's Throne Room 8.00
5 . . . . .8.00
6 The Kalidahs Attack 8.00
Robin Hood subset (1:36)
1 Hand to Hand Fighting 9.00
2 'Tis Our Duty to Help Each Other .9.00
3 Straight Flew his Answering Shot .9.00
Medallion card 20.00
Autograph cards (500 made) 40.00
6-card uncut sheet (1:case) 25.00
Chromium Promo card 2.00

[The Best of the]
HILDEBRANDT BROS.
Comic Images (1996)
Set: 90 cards 30.00
Pack: 7 cards 2.00
Box: 36 packs 60.00
Holochrome set: 90 cards 750.00
Single Hologram card 9.00
MagnaChrome (1:16) 6 diff., each . .8.00
MagnaChrome Subset (1:36)
3 different, each 10.00
Ekedadhim: Magnachrome box card .5.00
Autograph cards (500 made) 70.00
Chromium Promo card N# 3.00
Binder, with 6-card press sheet 20.00

KEEPSAKE SET
Comic Images (1995)
Lord of the Rings Set: 7 cards 20.00

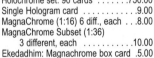

HITCHHIKER'S GUIDE
TO THE GALAXY
Cardz (1994)
Set: 100 cards 12.00
Pack: 8 cards 1.25
Box: 30.00
Holograms, 2 diff., each 6.00
Tekchrome cards, each 6.00
Autographed card 50.00
Promo cards, 3 diff. each. 1.50
Album 15.00

ID4 INDEPENDENCE
DAY (WIDEVISION)
Topps (1996) Movie
Set: 72 cards 15.00
Pack: 6 cards 1.25
Box: 36 packs 35.00
Holofoil cards (1:9) 6 diff. 7.50
P1 Promo card 3.00
Promo cards T1, T2, each 3.00

JETS, ROCKETS,
SPACEMEN
Bowman (1951)
Set: 108 cards 1,500.00
Single Cards #1 or #108 . . . . .20.00
Single Cards #2–#36 . . . . .7.00
Single Cards #37–#72 . . . . .18.00
Single Cards #73–#107 . . . . .12.50
WTW (1985) Reprint Set
Set: 108 cards 55.00

JONES, JEFFREY
FPG (1993) SF art
Set: 90 cards 12.50
Pack: 10 cards 1.25
Box: 36 packs 30.00
3-D Holograms (1:18)
H1 The Red Sky 7.00
H2 Haunted 7.00
H3 The Beast 7.00
Gold holo, set of 3 (1 set:case) 50.00
Autographed card (1000 made) 50.00
Four card promo sheet 3.00
Promo card 1.50
Binder with card 20.00

SERIES 2
FPG (1995) SF art
Set: 90 cards 10.00
Pack: 10 cards 1.50
Box: 36 packs 40.00
Canvas Cards, 5 diff., each 7.00
Autographed card 30.00

Jeff Jones Series 2 #53 The Final Journey (FPG 1993)

Joe Jusko 2, #84, The Captive Princess (FPG 1995)

Tom Kidd #36, Silverhair, The Wanderer (FPG 1995)

Don Maitz #70, Rim Runners (FPG 1994)

JUDGE DREDD
Edge Entertainment (1995) Comics
Set: 90 cards 12.00
Pack: 1.00
Box: 36 packs 30.00
Legends Set, 13 diff., each 4.00
Death Dimensions 1, 4 diff., each . .20.00
Death Dimensions 2, 4 diff., each . .8.00
Sleep fo the Just 9 diff., each 2.00
Movie Preview, 4 diff., each 6.00
Four card promo sheet
  (Previews 2-95) 3.00
Prototypes
Proto1 Judge Dredd 2.00
Proto2 Judge Anderson 2.00
Proto3 Judge Death 2.00
Proto4 Mean Machine 2.00
Proto5 Chopper 2.00
Proto6 Brit-Cit Babes 2.00

JUSKO, JOE
EDGAR RICE BURROUGHS
FPG (1994) Tarzan/Fantasy art
Set: 60 cards 25.00
Pack: 6 cards, thick 1.50
Box: 36 packs 35.00
Metallic: John Carter of Mars six-tych
MS1 The White Ape of Mars 8.00
MS2 Barsoomian Airships 8.00
MS3 The Plant Men of Mars 8.00
MS4 The Banth, A Barsoomian Lion .8.00
MS5 John Carter of Mars and Dejah
  Thoris, Princess of Mars 8.00
MS6 The Thark, Green Men of Mars .8.00
Autographed (1000 made) 50.00
10 card autographed sheet (1:case) 85.00
Promo card, 3 diff., thin, each 2.00
P4 promo, thin 2.00
Promo, thick (*Advance comics*) 2.00
Promo, thick (*Non-Sport Update*) . . .2.00
Promo, thick (*Cards Illustrated*) 1.50
Two card deluxe promo sheet #20 . .10.00
Binder, with card 20.00

EDGAR RICE BURROUGHS II
FPG (1995) SF art
Set: 60 cards 50.00
Pack: 6 cards, thick 1.50
Box: 36 packs 35.00
Metallic Six-tych (1:12)
M1 Thuvia, Maid of Mars, pt. 1 . . . . .9.00
M2 Thuvia, Maid of Mars, pt. 2 . . . . .9.00
M3 Thuvia, Maid of Mars, pt. 3 . . . . .9.00
M4 Thuvia, Maid of Mars, pt. 4 . . . . .9.00
M5 Thuvia, Maid of Mars, pt. 5 . . . . .9.00
M6 Thuvia, Maid of Mars, pt. 6 . . . . .9.00
Autograph card (1,000 made) 50.00

BURROUGHS COLOSSAL CARDS
FPG (1996) SF art
Set: 50 cards 50.00
Pack: 5 cards 7.50
Box: 18 packs 80.00
Autograph card 40.00

COLOSSAL CARDS
FPG (1996) SF art
Set: 50 cards 50.00
Pack: 5 cards 5.00
Box: 18 packs 80.00
Autograph card 40.00

KALUTA, MICHAEL
FPG Cards (1994) SF art
Set: 90 cards 12.50
Pack: 10 cards 1.50
Box: 36 packs 35.00
Metallic Storm (1:12)
MS1 Veep "7" 6.00
MS2 ARIA: Personae 6.00
MS3 ARIA: The Well of the Worlds . .6.00
MS4 Metropolis 6.00
MS5 Paolo and Francesca 6.00
Autographed card (1000 made) 75.00
10-card autographed sheet (1:case) 50.00
P1 promo card 3.00
P2 promo card 3.00
Promo card, *Cards Illustrated* 3.00
Deluxe promo sheet #18 (Previews) .5.00

SERIES II
FPG Cards (1994) SF art
Set: 90 cards 12.50
Pack: 10 cards 1.25
Box: 36 packs 40.00
Metallic Storm (1:12)
M1 Parmeneans 8.00
M2 Order of Hermes 8.00
M3 Verbena 8.00
M4 Celestial Chorus 8.00
M5 Virtual Adepts 8.00
Autograph card 75.00

KELLY, KEN
FPG Cards (1992) SF art
Set: 90 cards 12.50
Pack: 10 cards 1.00
Box: 36 packs 22.50
Holograms
H1 Dungeon of Doom 6.00
H2 Swamp Peril 6.00
H3 Eve of Destruction 6.00
Autographed card (1000 made) 50.00
Four card promo sheet 3.00
Binder with card (1994) 20.00

COLLECTION #2
FPG Cards (1994) SF art
Set: 90 cards 10.00
Pack: 10 cards 75
Box: 36 packs 20.00
Metallic Storm (1:12)
MS#1 The Executioner 7.00
MS#2 The Aggressor 7.00
MS#3 The Defiant 7.00
MS#4 Kreg: The Axeman 7.00
MS#5 Barbarian Zombie 7.00
Autographed card, foil stamped
  (1000 made) 50.00
Original art card (Pencil drawing)
  (1:case) 75.00
Promo cards, 3 diff., each 2.00
Three card deluxe promo sheet #13
  (Previews) 2.00
Binder, with card 20.00
Collection #3 (FPG 1995)
Promo (*Combo #1*) 1.00

COLOSSAL CARDS
FPG (1995) SF art
Set: 50 colossal cards 60.00
Pack: 5 colossal cards 7.50
Box: 18 packs 75.00
Autographed card 35.00

KIDD, TOM
FPG (1995) SF art
Set: 90 cards 15.00
Pack: 10 cards 1.50
Box: 36 packs 35.00
Metallics
M1 Age of Miracles 8.00
M2 Juxtapositions 8.00
M3 Walkaway Clause 8.00
M4 Dying of the Light 8.00
M5 Hunter of Worlds 8.00
Autographed card (1,000 made) . . .50.00

KITCHEN SINK CARDS
Set: 36 cards, oversized 50.00
Card 1.00

LAND OF THE GIANTS
Topps (1968) TV
TEST SET
Set: 55 cards 5,000.00
Card: 90.00

LOST IN SPACE
Topps (1966) TV
Set: 55 cards 750.00
Card #1 or #55, each 25.00
Cards #2–54: 12.00
Pack: .175.00

Reprint Set: 56 cards 25.00
3-card uncut strip, foil 30.00

CLASSIC SERIES
Inkworks (1997) TV
Set: 81 cards 20.00
Pack: 7 cards 2.00
Box: 36 packs 55.00
Robinson Family Set (1:11)
  9 different, each 5.00
Robot Pop-up card 3.00
Weird Aliens (1:17) 6 diff., each 7.50
RoboMetallic Card (1:108) 40.00
Autographed cards (600 made)
  Harris 125.00
  Goddard 125.00
Promos, P1–P3, each 3.00
3-card promo strip (Suncoast) 6.00
Binder .18.00

THE MOVIE
Inkworks (1998) Movie
Set: 81 cards 17.50
Pack: 8 cards 1.75
Box: 50.00
Space Family Robinson (1:11)
  8 different, each 9.00
War of the Robots set (1:24) 90.00
Weird Aliens (1:17) set 75.00
Jupiter 2 . . . . .50.00
Promo card 5.00
Binder .15.00

MAITZ, DON
FPG (1994) SF art
Set: 90 cards 15.00
Pack: 10 cards 1.00
Box: 36 packs 35.00
Metallic Storm (1:12)
MS1 Urine Trouble with the King 8.00
MS2 Grim Reaper in Purgatory 8.00
MS3 Purgatory Zone 8.00
MS4 Spaceman 8.00
MS5 Beneath an Opal Moon 8.00
Autographed card (1,000 made) . . .70.00
10 card autographed sheet 30.00
Four card deluxe promo sheet #14
  (Previews) 2.00

SERIES II
FPG (1996) SF art
Set: 90 cards 15.00
Pack: 10 cards 1.25
Box: 36 packs 35.00
Metallics, 5 diff., each 8.00
Autographed card (1,000 made) . . .70.00
1,995 cases produced.

Mars Attacks #76 (Topps 1996)

David Mattingly #5, Wizard of 4th Street (FPG 1995)

Outer Limits #37, Second Chance (DuoCards 1997)

Keith Parkinson #44, Dolphin Dreams (FPG 1994)

MAN ON THE MOON
Topps (1969–70)
Set: 55 cards (1A-35A,36B-55B) . . .90.00
Card: 1.75
Reissue Set: 99 cards, including
  44 new cards (56C-99C) 175.00
Card: 1.75
Note: Reissue cards say "... of 99 cards"

MARS ATTACKS!
Topps (1962)
Set: 55 cards 2,500.00
Card #1 Invasion Begins 125.00
Card #55, checklist 400.00
Other cards, each 35.00
Renata Galasso (1992) Reprint Set
Set: 56 cards 45.00
B.H.C.R. Reprint Set
Sample Set: 56 cards 125.00
Promos, each 9.00

ARCHIVES
Topps (1994)
Set: 100 cards (#0-#99) 60.00
Pack: 3.00
Box: 36 packs 75.00
ToppsMatrix cards (1:18)
1 Destroying a Dog 15.00
2 Prize Captive 15.00
3 Crushed to Death 15.00
4 Terror in the Railroad 15.00
Super Winner (1:360) 75.00
1st Day prod. cards (1:9?), each 7.50
1st Day set: 55 cards 450.00
Zina Saunders autographed card
  (2000 made) 80.00
Promos (Topps Comics, 1993)
#21 (Norm Saunders) 5.00
#56 (EN) .1.00
A (#21 "Prize Captive") 10.00
B ("Mars Attacks") 10.00
Cards Illustrated scratch off contest 50
Promos (Topps Trading Cards, 1994)
#1 The Invasion Begins 5.00
Mars Attacks Archives 5.00
Non-Sport Update Homage promo . . .3.00
One card promo sheet 3.00
P2 promo 10.00
Philly convention promo (1996) 25.00

WIDEVISION
Topps (1996) Movie
Set: 72 cards 15.00
Pack: 9 cards 2.00
Box: 60.00
Destruct-O-Rama cards, 6 diff., each .9.00
Promos, 2 diff., N# 2.00

MINI COMIC BOOKS
Pocket Comics (1988)
Set: 4 mini-comics 8.00

MATTINGLY, DAVID
FPG (1995) SF art
Set: 90 cards 15.00
Pack: 10 cards 1.50
Box: 36 packs 25.00
Metallic Storm,
M1 The Wizard of Camelot 7.50
M2 The World Next Door 7.50
M3 Dr. Dimension 1 . . . . .7.50
M4 Showboat World 7.50
M5 The Messiah Choice 7.50
Autographed card (1000 made) 75.00
Deluxe promo sheet (*Previews 12-94*) .5.00

MEN IN BLACK
Inkworks (1997) Movie
Set: 90 cards 18.00
Pack: 8 cards 1.75
Box: 36 packs 50.00
Alien Profiles (1:11) 5 diff., each . . .9.00
Techworks (1:24) 5 diff., each 12.00
Cards in Black (1:54) 2 diff., each . . .25.00
Pug Error Card 50.00
Autograph Card 50.00
Promo card 5.00
Binder Album 16.00

MILLER, RON:
FIREBRANDS: HEROINES OF
SCIENCE FICTION & FANTASY
Comic Images (1994) SF art
Set: 90 cards 10.00
Pack: 10 cards 75
Box: 48 packs 20.00
Galaxy cards (1:18)
P1 Alyx #2 . . . . .7.00
P2 Dejah Thoris 7.00
P3 Rifkind 7.00
P4 . . . . .7.00
P5 Bronwyn vs. Spikevass 7.00
P6 Ozma .7.00
Autographed cards (500 made) 45.00
Winged Women subset (3:case)
1 . . . . .10.00
2 . . . . .10.00
3 . . . . .10.00
Medalion card (2:Case) 20.00
Mini press sheet 25.00
Uncut sheet six card subset
  (1:Case) 20.00
Promo card 2.00

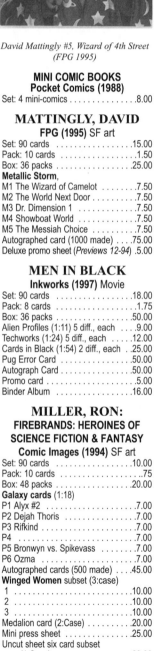

MOEBIUS
Comic Images (1993) art
Set: 90 cards 9.00
Pack: 10 cards 75
Box: 48 packs 20.00
Chromium cards (1:16)
C1 Crystal in the Clouds 7.00
C2 Crystal Transport 7.00
C3 Crystal Performance 7.00
C4 Crystal Companion 7.00
C5 Crystal by the Sea 7.00
C6 Crystal Exhibit 7.00
Signed Uncut Sheet (100 made) . .200.00
Promo card 2.50

MOON-MARS
Space Ventures (1991)
Set: 36 cards, boxed 27.50

MORK & MINDY
Topps (1978) TV
Set: 99 cards, 22 stickers 18.00
Pack: 10 cards, 1 sticker 1.50

[Monsters From]
OUTER LIMITS
Topps/Bubbles Inc. (1964) TV
Set: 50 cards 700.00
Card: 15.00

Reprint Set (1994)
Set: 50 cards 25.00
Promo cards
#1 Man with Super Sight 3.00
#2 Monster from Venus 3.00
#3 The Brain Destroyer 3.00

OUTER LIMITS, THE
Duocards (1997) TV
Set: 81 cards, 24 pt. card stock 20.00
Pack: 7 cards 2.00
Box 45.00
Chromium Rare Art (1:15)
  6 different, each 8.00
Gold Monster Set (2:case), each . . .30.00
6-card uncut sheet (1:case) 60.00
OmniChrome mail-in set: 6 cards . . .20.00
Promos, 2 diff., each 3.00
Binder 15.00

PARKINSON, KEITH
FPG cards (1994) SF art
Set: 90 cards 15.00
Pack: 10 cards 1.25
Box: 36 packs 35.00
Metallic Storm cards (1:12)
MS1 Falkenberg's Legions 8.00

MS2 Lens of the World 8.00
MS3 The Rat Bag-Lady 8.00
MS4 Gateway to Fairy 8.00
MS5 Warworld 8.00
Autographed card (1000 made) 50.00
Autographed 10-up un-cut card sheet
  10 different (1:Case) each 30.00
Full Uncut Autographed shet 25.00
Promo cards, 2 diff., each 2.00
Four card promo sheet (Previews) . .25.00
Binder with card 20.00

COLOSSAL CARDS
FPG (1996) SF art
Set: 50 cards 60.00
Card 1.50
Pack: 5 cards 7.50
Box: 18 packs 85.00
Autographed card 50.00

PLANET OF THE APES
Topps (1969) Movie
Set: 44 cards 125.00
Card: 2.75
Box: 36 packs 500.00
White borders, no actor's names on back

TEST SET
Set: 44 cards 1,600.00
Card: 35.00
Black border, actor's names on back

PLANET OF THE APES
Topps (1975) TV
Set: 66 cards 75.00
Pack: 4.00
Card: 1.50
Box 250.00

PLOOG, MIKE
FPG cards (1994) SF art
Set: 90 cards 12.50
Pack: 10 cards 1.00
Box: 36 packs 30.00
Metallic Storm (1:12)
MS1 The Agawa Chieftain 7.00
MS2 Battle of the Lords 7.00
MS3 The Princess and the Genie . . .7.00
MS4 The Survivor 7.00
MS5 The Path 7.00
Autographed card (1000 made) 50.00
Autographed 10-up un-cut card sheet
  10 different (1:case) each 30.00
Instant Winner orig. comic art
  (50 made) 250.00
Promo cards, 2 diff., each 2.00
Four card deluxe promo sheet #12
  (Previews) 2.50
Binder with card 15.00

Rowena #6, Walking the Dog
(FPG 1993)

Luis Royo #63,
(Comic Images 1993)

Barclay Shaw #72, Rinn's Star
(FPG 1995)

Sliders #59, Mrs. President
(Ink Works 1997)

POTTER, J.K.
FPG (1996) SF art
Set: 90 cards 12.50
Pack: 8 cards 1.50
Box: 36 packs 45.00
Metallics: 6 different, each 8.00
Autographed card 50.00

PREDATOR VS.
MAGNUS ROBOT
FIGHTER
Dark Horse/Valiant (1992) Comic
#1 Predators 3.00
#2 Magnus Robot Fighter 3.00
#3 Promo card (Wizard) (LW &
   Chris Chalenor art) 2.00
#4 Promo card (Wizard) (LW &
   Chris Chalenor art) 2.00

RAY BRADBURY
COMICS
Topps (1993) Comic
Promo: A Sound of Thunder . . .1.50
Promo: Special Horror Issue 1.50
Promo: Tales of the Future 1.50
#1 thru 14, each 50

ROBOTECH: THE
MACROSS SAGA
FTCC (1986)
Set: 60 cards 25.00
Pack: 2.50

ROBOTECH: GENESIS
Eternity Comics (1992) Comic
Set: 10.00
Two card promo sheet 1.00

ROBOT WARS
Fleer (1985)
Set: 66 rub-off game cards,
   33 stickers 40.00
Pack: 3 rub-off cards, 2 stickers 2.00

ROCKETSHIP X-M
FTCC (1979) Movie
Set: 50 cards 25.00
Pack: 6 cards 3.00

ROWENA
FPG Cards (1993) SF art
Set: 90 cards 20.00
Pack: 10 cards 1.25
Box: 36 packs 25.00

Holograms
H1 Golden Devil 7.50
H2 The Magic Carpet 7.50
H3 The Wrong Place to Sit 7.50
Autographed card (1000 made) . . .50.00
Gold Holo set of 3 (1 set:case) 50.00
Four card promo sheet 4.00
Binder with card 20.00

[THE BEST OF] ROWENA
FPG (1996) SF art
Set: 90 cards 30.00
Pack: 7 cards 2.25
Box: 55.00
Holochrome, 6 different, each 9.00

ROYO, LUIS
FROM FANTASY TO REALITY
Comic Images (1993) SF art
Set: 90 cards 15.00
Pack: 10 cards 1.00
Box: 48 packs 35.00
Prism cards (1:16)
P1 The Hormone Jungle 8.00
P2 Cimoc Cover 1985 . . . . .8.00
P3 Conan the Liberator 8.00
P4 Horseclanse #3 . . . . .8.00
P5 Seven of Swords 8.00
P6 The Shooting Robot 8.00
Mini-press sheet 15.00
Promo card 2.50

ROYO2 FORBIDDEN UNIVERSE
Comic Images (1994) SF art
Set: 90 cards 12.50
Pack: 10 cards 1.50
Box: 48 packs 30.00
Prism cards (1:16)
P1 People of the Lakes 7.00
P2 "2041" 7.00
P3 Conan #3 . . . . .7.00
P4 *La Virtical del Sigilo* 7.00
P5 Wolf Dream 7.00
P6 Heavy Metal Cover 7.00
Autographed cards (500 made) 50.00
Warrior Women subset (3:case)
1 . . . . .8.00
2 . . . . .8.00
3 . . . . .8.00
Medalion card (2:Case) 25.00
Mini press sheet 20.00
Uncut sheet six card subset
   (1:Case) 15.00
Promo card 2.00

[The Best Of]
ROYO
Comic Images (1995) SF art
Set: 90 cards, all chromium 20.00

Pack: 7 cards 2.25
Box: 36 packs 60.00
Heavy Metal Magnachrome (1:12)
M1 Heavy Metal cover 1987 . . . . . .7.00
M2 Heavy Metal cover 1994 . . . . . .7.00
M3 Heavy Metal cover 1982 . . . . . .7.00
M4 Heavy Metal cover 19?? 7.00
M5 Heavy Metal cover 19?? 7.00
M6 Heavy Metal cover 1991 . . . . . .7.00
Creature subset (1:36)
1 The Golden Cabala 10.00
2 . . . . .10.00
3 . . . . .10.00
Holochrome Set: 90 cards 650.00
Holochrome single 8.00
Autograph card (500 made) 50.00
6-card uncut sheet 25.00
Album 20.00
Chromium promo card 2.50

ROYO, LUIS: SECRET DESIRES
Comic Images (1997)
Set: 72 heavy stock cards 12.50
Pack: 8 cards 1.50
Box: 45.00
OmniChrome, 6 different, each 8.00
Autographed card (500 made) 50.00
Promo Card, N# 2.00
Binder, with uncut 6 card sheet 20.00

KEEPSAKE
Comic Images (1994)
Set: 6 women on color 6" x 9" cards,
   7th card = all 6 images + Foil
   Card card (5,000 made) 20.00

SANJULIAN
COLLECTION, THE
FPG cards (1994) Fantasy art
Set: 90 cards 12.50
Pack: 10 cards 1.00
Box: 36 packs 25.00
Metallic Storm (1:12)
MS#1 The Choice 7.50
MS#2 Fact or Fiction 7.50
MS#3 Insight 7.50
MS#4 Decisions 7.50
MS#5 Narrow Margin 7.50
Boxed Metallic Storm set (1:case) . .60.00
Autographed card (1000 made) 50.00
Promo cards, 2 different, each 2.00
Four card promo sheet (Previews) . . .3.00
Binder with card 20.00

SAUCER PEOPLE
Kitchen Sink (1992)
Set: 36 cards, boxed, color 12.50
Promo card 10.00

[The Art of]
SHAW, BARCLAY
FPG (1995) SF art
Set: 90 cards 9.00
Pack: 10 cards 1.00
Box: 36 packs 30.00
Metallic Storm
M1 The Complete Asimov, Vol. 1 . . .7.50
M2 Empire of the Atom 7.50
M3 Best of John Brunner 7.50
M4 At the End of Time 7.50
M5 Alternate Warriors 7.50
Autographed card (1000 made) 75.00
10-card autographed sheet 30.00
Promo card, oversized 3.00

SLIDERS
Inkworks (1997) TV
Set: 72 cards 25.00
Pack: 8 cards 2.00
Box: 36? packs 50.00
Embossed (1:11) 9 diff., each 7.50
Foilworks (1:17) 6 diff., each 9.00
Lenticular (1:35) 2 diff., each 25.00
Promo 5.00

SORAYAMA
SEXY ROBOTS AND PINUPS
Comic Images (1993) Robot Art
Set: 90 cards 15.00
Pack: 10 cards 1.00
Box: 48 packs 25.00
Chromium cards (1:16)
C1 Sexy vs. Cute 10.00
C2 Artistic License 10.00
C3 A "Fresh" Look? 10.00
C4 Super-Realism 10.00
C5 Let There Be Light 10.00
C6 Playing Favorites 10.00
Promo card 3.50

SORAYAMA II
CHROMIUM CREATURES
Comic Images (1994) Art
Set: 90 chromium cards, plus variants
   (6,7,8,10,11,36,45,48,61,74) . .30.00
Note: Variant cards are double prints.
All 100 cards have equal frequency.
Pack: 7 chromium cards 1.75
Box: 36 packs 55.00
Foil cards, (1:16)
Foil Stamped Card #1–#6,
   untitled, each 7.00
Surf & Turf subset (3:case)
1 thru 3, each 11.00
Autographed card 50.00
Medallion card (2:case) 15.00

Space: 1999 #62
(Donrus 1976)

StarGate #18, Team Leader
(Collect-A-Card 1994)

Star Trek #2, Toward the Unknown
(Topps 1979)

Star Trek Master #66, The Gorn
(SkyBox 1993)

Chromium Promo card 3.50
D-5 & D-6 promo strip (Previews) . . .2.50
Holochrom variant cards 7.00
MiniPress sheet 15.00
6-card uncut sheet 15.00
6-card uncut sheet (girls) 25.00

SILVER & SATIN
Comic Images (1997)
Set: 72 OmniChrome cards 40.00
Pack: 8 OmniChrome cards 2.00
Box: 65.00
Chromium Cards, (1:12)
  6 different, each 10.00
Autographed card (500) 50.00
Promos
1 of 2 . . . . .1.50
2 of 2 . . . . .1.50

SPACE ART FANTASTIC
World Class Marketing (1993)
Set: 55 cards 10.00
Pack: 9 cards 75
Box: 36 packs 20.00
Promo cards, (from Starlog cards),
  set of 4 . . . . .2.50
Hologram (Space 2000) 7.00
Commemorative Album, with set . .30.00

SPACE CARDS
Topps (1958)
Set: 88 cards 475.00
Card: 6.00
Double print cards 4.00
Same cards as *Target Moon*

SPACE: 1999
Donruss (1976) TV
Set: 66 cards 25.00
Pack: 5 cards 2.00
Box: 40.00

SPACE SHOTS
Space Ventures (1990–91) Photos
Series I, set of 110 cards 50.00
Pack, 12 cards 1.50
Box: 36? packs 50.00
Series II, set of 110 cards 35.00
Commemorative cards 0.15
3-D Moon-Mars cards 0.20
Series II Factory Set: 110 cards
  + Moon-Mars card 35.00
Pack: 12 cards 1.00
Box: 25.00
Series III, set of 110 cards 20.00
Factory Set: 110 cards + holo 35.00
Pack: 8 cards 1.00
Earthrise Hologram 35.00

SPECIES
Comic Images (1995) Movie
Set: 90 cards 10.00
Pack: 10 cards 1.00
Box: 36 packs 35.00
Superstars Chromium cards (1:16)
C1 . . . . .7.50
C2 Michael Madsen 7.50
C3 Alfred Molina 7.50
C4 Forest Whitaker 7.50
C5 Marg Helgenberger 7.50
C6 . . . . .7.50
Sil subset (1:36)
1 . . . . .12.00
2 . . . . .12.00
3 . . . . .12.00
Medallion card (1:3 boxes) Boy Sil .20.00
Uncut sheet, special cards (1:case) 20.00
6-card uncut promo sheet 15.00
Promo card, black with red logo 1.50
Binder 19.95

STARGATE
Collect-A-Card (1994) Movie
Set: 100 cards + 12 game cards . . .10.00
Pack: 7 cards + 1 game card 75
Box: 36 packs 18.00
Adventure foils (1:6) 12 diff., each . .2.50
Video Game tips (1:4) 8 diff., each . .2.00
Characters (1:24), 8 diff., each 6.00
Three card mail-in 20.00
TSM-1 promo (Collect 12-94) 2.00
Prototype 1 Colonel O'Neil 2.00
Prototype 2 Anubis 2.00

STARLOG
World Class Marketing (1993)
Set: 100 cards+6 checklists 12.50
Pack: 9 cards 1.00
(with Space Art promo cards, which see)
Box: 36 packs 15.00
Hologram, Cover #1 . . . . .7.50
Gold Hologram mail-in 5.00
Promos, 5 different, each 1.00

STARSHIP TROOPERS
Inkworks (1997) Movie
Set: 81 cards 15.00
Pack: 8 cards 2.00
Box: 36 packs 60.00
Bug Wars (1:11) 9 diff., each 8.00
Art of Starship troopers (1:17)
  4 different, each 10.00
Starship Gold (1:54) 2 diff., each . .30.00
Promo cards P1–P3, each 2.00
3-card uncut promo strip 3.00
Album binder 16.00

STAR TREK
Leaf (1967) TV
Set: 72 cards (B&W) 3,500.00
Card #1 .250.00
Card #72 . . . . .150.00
Other Cards, each 35.00
REPRINT SET
Set: 72 cards 30.00
A&BC (1969) British
Set: 72 cards 1,800.00
Card #1 .100.00
Card #72 .50.00
Other Cards, each 25.00
Gordon Currie (1968) TV
Set: 8 cards 20.00
Primrose (1971) TV
Set: 12 cards 25.00
Card 2.00
Topps (1976) TV
Set: 88 cards/22 stickers 400.00
Card 3.50
Sticker 52.00
Pack: 20.00
Box: 450.00
Prime Press (1977) TV
Set: 48 cards 95.00
Set, with album 150.00
Card: 2.00

STAR TREK
Impel (1991) TV
25th Anniversary–Odd #'d cards
Next Generation–Even #'d cards
Set: 160 cards 15.00
Pack: 12 cards 75
Box: 36? packs 20.00
Holograms
H1 Enterprise, old 10.00
H2 Enterprise, new 10.00
Four card promo sheet (Diamond) . .25.00
Note: 2 different packs, one each series
STAR TREK II
Impel (1991) TV
25th Anniversary–Odd #'d cards
Next Generation–Even #'d cards
Set: 150 cards (#161-#310) 12.50
Pack: 1.00
Box: 36? packs 25.00
Holograms
H3 Kirk 10.00
H4 Picard 10.00
Star Trek 25th Anniversary Collector's
  set of 310 cards plus all 4

holograms and 2 special cards
  in tin box 90.00
B1 or B2 from tin set, each 15.00

BEHIND THE SCENES
SkyBox (1993)
Set: 39 cards (50,000 made) 8.00

STAR TREK:
MASTER SERIES
SkyBox (1993) SF art
Set: 90 cards 15.00
Pack: 6 cards 1.00
Box: 36 packs 15.00
Spectra cards (1:18) (Gerry Roundtree art)
S-1 Docking at Deep Space Nine . . .8.00
S-2 Romulan Warbird 8.00
S-3 Navagating the Asteroid Field . .8.00
S-4 Enterprise vs. Bird of Prey 8.00
S-5 The Doomsday Machine 8.00
Prototype cards
Excelsior Leaves Spacelock
  (Sonia Hillios art) 4.00
Lieutenant Uhura (Keith Birdsong art) 4.00
Lieutenant Worf (Non-Sport Update) .4.00
Six card promo sheet (National Sports
  Collectors Con. 7,500 made) . .10.00
Album 20.00
Playmates variant cards from action
  figures, each 2.50
Playmates Space Caps, with outer
  card, from action figures, each . .1.50

MASTER 1994
SkyBox (1994) SF Art
Set: 100 cards + survey card 17.50
Pack: 6 cards 1.00
Box: 36 packs 20.00
Crew Triptychs (1:10)
Original Crew (Joe Jusko art)
F1 Checkov & Scotty 9.00
F2 Kirk, McCoy & Spock 9.00
F3 . . . . .9.00
Next Generation (Boris Vallejo art)
F4 . . . . .9.00
F5 Troi & Riker 9.00
F6 . . . . .9.00
Deep Space Nine (Julie Bell art)
F7 . . . . .9.00
F8 Kira, O'Brien & Quark 9.00
F9 . . . . .9.00
Proscenium Holograms Set: 4,
  mail-in 60.00
Promo cards
S1 Argus Array 4.00
S2 (Klingon) promo 4.00
Card Collector's p.g. promo 3.00
Non-Sport update promo 3.00
Collector's Album 20.00

Star Trek The Next Generation: Inagural Edition #023 (Impel 192) Episode Collection #41 (SkyBox 1994) & Season Two #120 (SkyBox 1995)

30 YEARS OF STAR TREK'

PHASE ONE
SkyBox (1995)

Set: 100 cards 20.00
Pack: 8 cards 1.50
Box: 36 packs 30.00
Evolution of Technology (1:12)
E1 Mid-23rd Century Phaser 7.00
E2 Late 23rd Century Phaser 7.00
E3 24th Century Phaser 7.00
E4 Mid-23rd Century Communicator .7.00
E5 Late 23rd Century Communicator .7.00
E6 24th Century Communicator 7.00
E7 Mid-23rd Century Tricorder 7.00
E8 Late 23rd Century Tricorder 7.00
E9 24th Century Tricorder 7.00
Die-Cut Weapons (1:36)
D-1 Klingon Knife 12.00
D-2 Starfleet Phaser 12.00
D-3 Romulan/Klingon Disruptor 12.00
Ship Registry Plaque gold foil (1:72)
R-1 U.S.S. Enterprise 50.00
R-2 NCC 1701-A 50.00
R-3 NCC 1701-B 50.00
R-4 NCC 1701-D 50.00
R-5 U.S.S. Excelsior 50.00
R-6 U.S.S. Stargazer 50.00
R-7 U.S.S. Brattain 50.00
R-8 U.S.S. Sutherland 50.00
R-9 U.S.S. Voyager 50.00
Ship Regestry sheet, mail-in 125.00
SkyMotion exchange card (1:180) .20.00
Enterprise NCC 1701 skymotion . . .65.00
4" x 5½" SkyMotion (5,000 made) . . .40.00
Survey Card 3.00
Ad Card 2.50
Two-card promo sheet 5.00
Album 20.00

PHASE TWO

Set: 100 cards (#101–#200) 20.00
Pack: 8 cards 2.00
Box: 36 packs 40.00
Doppelganger Foils (1:12)
9 different, each 7.00
Dual-Image (1:18) 9 diff., each . . .20.00
Survey Card 2.50
PDE card .2.50
Advertising cards, 2 diff., each 1.00
SkyMotion Exchange (1:180) 25.00
SkyMotion card, Odo 65.00
2-card promo 7.00

PHASE THREE

Set: 100 cards (#201–#300) 20.00
Pack: 8 cards 1.50
Box: 36 packs 40.00
Card Game (1:6) 6 diff., each 2.00
Murals (1:12) 9 diff., each 10.00
3-D Motion (1:18) 3 diff., each 12.00
Blueprints, 9 diff., each 1.00
SkyMotion Exchange (1:180) 25.00
SkyMotion card 60.00
Survey Card 1.50
Ad Card 1.00

First Contact preview card 100.00
2-card promo 9.00

THE ORIGINAL SERIES
SEASON ONE
Fleer/SkyBox (1997) TV

Set: 90 cards 20.00
Pack: 9 cards, including 2 character
log cards and 1 game card . . .2.00
Box: 36 packs, including 1 autograph
card 70.00
Character Log Set: 58 cards 25.00
Character Log singles (2:1) 0.25
Behind the Scenes Set: 58 cards . .50.00
Behind the Scenes singles (1:2) . . .2.00
Character Profile Set: 29 cards . . .70.00
Character Profile singles (1:4) 4.00
Gold Plaque Set: 29 cards 250.00
Gold Plaque singles (1:12) 10.00
Autograph Challenge Set, 11 cards .20.00
I Card (voided) 500.00
I Card (unclaimed) 2,000.00
Autographed cards (26 total, 1:box)
A1 Shatner 500.00
A2 Doohan 200.00
A3 Nichols 125.00
A4 Takei 125.00
A17 Ricardo Montalban 100.00
A23 Joan Collins 350.00
A25 Majel Barrett 350.00
Other cast members, each 50.00

SEASON TWO

Set: 81 cards 20.00
Pack: 5 cards 2.00
Box: 36 packs 90.00
Character Log Set: 52 cards 17.50
Character Log singles (2:1) 50
Behind the Scenes Set: 52 cards . .45.00
Behind the Scenes singles (1:2) . . .1.75
Character Profile Set: 26 cards . . .75.00
Character Profile singles (1:4) 2.50
Gold Plaque Set: 26 cards 240.00
Gold Plaque singles (1:12) 10.00
Autograph Challenge Set, 11 cards .20.00
Autographed cards (1:36) 32 different:
A27 Kelley 300.00
A28 Koenig 100.00
A29 Fontana 50.00
A30 Barrett 100.00
A31 Shatner 400.00
A32 Doohan 150.00
A33 Takai 150.00
A34 Nichols 100.00
A35 Bower 50.00
A36 Andrews 50.00
A37 Forest 50.00
A38 Martel (Arlene) 50.00
A38 Martel (Tasha) 50.00
A39 Windom 50.00
A40 Fiedler 50.00
A41 Macaulay 50.00
A42 Andes 50.00
A43 Luna 50.00
A44 Brill .50.00
A45 Campbell 50.00

A46 Schallert 50.00
A47 O'Connell 50.00
A48 Wheeler 50.00
A49 Kovack 50.00
A50 Ruskin 50.00
A51 Brooks 50.00
A52 Caruso 50.00
A53 Delano 50.00
A54 Bouchet 50.00
A55 Stevens 50.00
A56 Marshall 50.00
A57 Jenson 50.00
A58 Garr 100.00
V card (voided) 30.00
V card (unclaimed) 50.00
Mirror Mirror Set: 7 cards (1:720) 1,500.00
M1 Captain Kirk 500.00
M2 Mr. Spock 500.00
M3 Dr. McCoy 400.00
M4 Scott 400.00
M5 Sulu 300.00
M6 Uhura 300.00
M7 Chekov 400.00

STAR TREK: VIDEO
Paramount/SkyBox (1992–93)
Set: 80 cards 200.00
One card with video tape of TV episode

[STAR TREK]
Personality Comics (1992)
Drawings
Original Crew, 37 card set 5.00
New Crew, 37 card set 5.00

STAR TREK: THE NEXT GENERATION
INAGURAL EDITION
SkyBox (Impel) (1992) TV
Set: 120 cards 18.00
Pack: 10 cards 1.50
Box: 36? packs 16.00
Holograms
01H Klingon Bird-of-Prey 10.00
031 Klingon Bird-of-Prey, error . . .20.00
02H Klingon Vor'cha Cruiser 10.00
033 Klingon Vor'cha Cruiser, error .20.00
03H Romulan Warbird 10.00
034 Romulan Warbird, error 20.00
04H Ferengi Marauder 10.00
036 Ferengi Marauder, error 20.00
05H U.S.S. Enterprise, mail in 10.00
Foreign Language cards
01A Japanese printing 2.00
01B Spanish printing 2.00
01C German printing 2.00
01D French printing 2.00
01E Russian printing 2.00
Sample/Promo cards (Impel Logo)
Series Logo "Coming June 15, 1992" ..75
00A U.S.S. Enterprise NCC-1701-D . .1.00
00B Lieutenant Commander Data . . .1.50
00C Dilithium Crystals 75

EPISODE COLLECTION
SEASON ONE
SkyBox (1994) TV
Set: 108 cards 15.00
Pack: 8 cards 1.25
Box: 36 packs 35.00
Final Episode Tribute card (1:Box) .10.00
Embossed, foil enhanced (1:12)
SP1 Klingon logo 9.00
SP2 Klingon language 9.00
SP3 Klingon language 9.00
SP4 Lieutenant Natasha Yar 9.00
SP5 The "Q" 9.00
SP6 The Traveler 9.00
Animated Hologram (1:180)
HG1 Picard 35.00
HG2 Data 35.00
S1 promo .1.00
S2 Lonely Among Us, prototype 1.00
"The future arrives in 1994"
mail-in card (for future
card info) (2:box) 2.50

SEASON TWO
Skybox (1995) TV
Set: 96 (#109-#204) 15.00
Pack: 8 cards 1.25
Box: 36 packs 35.00
Embossed, foil enhanced (1:12)
S7 Klingon ship plans 9.00
S8 Klingon ? 9.00
S9 Klingon ? 9.00
S10 Guinan 9.00
S11 Doctor Katherine Palaski 9.00
S12 Professor Moriarty 9.00
Animated Hologram (1:180)
HG 3 Counselor Deanna Troi 30.00
HG 4 Commander Riker 30.00
Prototype .1.00
Album 20.00

SEASON THREE
Skybox (1995) TV
Set: 108 cards (#205-#312) 15.00
Pack: 8 cards 1.50
Box: 36 packs 35.00
Embossed, foil enhanced (1:12)
S13 Klingon 9.00
S14 Klingon 9.00
S15 Klingon 9.00
S16 Locutus 9.00
S17 Lal 9.00
S18 K'Ehleyr 9.00
Animated Hologram (1:180)
HG 5 Dr. Beverly Crusher 30.00
HG 6 Lieutenant Worf 30.00
Album 20.00

SEASON 4
SkyBox (1996) TV
Set: 108 cards (#313–#420) 15.00
Pack: 8 cards 1.25
Box: 35.00
Foil Embossed (1:12) 6 diff.
(S19–S24) each 8.00
Holograms (1:180)
HG7 Geordi 50.00

  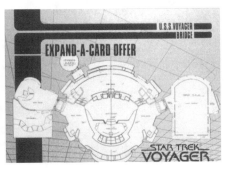

Star Trek The Next Generation Episode Collection Season Three #221 & #309 (SkyBox 1995) & Star Trek Voyager X-2 (SkyBox 1995)

HG8 Wesley 40.00
Survey card 3.50
Ad card 3.00
Promo sheet 10.00
Album .20.00

SEASON 5
SkyBox (1996) TV
Set: 108 cards (#421–#528) 15.00
Pack: 8 cards 1.25
Box: 48 packs 45.00
Foil Embossed (1:12) 6 diff.
    (S25–S30) each 8.00
Holograms (1:180)
HG9 Guinan 45.00
HG10 Ensign Ro 40.00
Survey card 2.00
Ad card 1.50
Album .20.00

SEASON 6
SkyBox (1997) TV
Set: 108 cards (#529–#637) 15.00
Pack: 11 cards 2.00
Box: 24 packs 50.00
Foil Embossed (1:12) 6 diff.
    (S31–S36) each 10.00
Holograms (1:90)
HG11 Chief O'Brien 50.00
HG12 Q 50.00
SkyMotion Card 1:Box 15.00
SkyMotion Card 1:Case 80.00

MAKING OF THE FINAL EPISODE
SkyBox (1994) TV
Set: 100 cards, in numbered box with cer-
    tificate (50,000 of each made):
Platinum Edition with hologram in
    lucite display 75.00
Gold Edition with pin 50.00
Collector's Edition with viewer and
    five 3-D ship model cards 40.00

STAR TREK THE
NEXT GENERATION
Panini (1988)
Set: 240 Album stickers + album . .40.00
Pack 2.00
Album 5.00

Panini (1994)
Set: 240 Album stickers + album . .14.00

STAR TREK
DEEP SPACE NINE
SkyBox (1993) TV
Set: 48 cards, + 2 Spectra cards,
    in factory box 15.00

SkyBox (1994) TV
Set: 100 cards, photos 15.00
Pack: 8 cards 1.00
Box: 36 packs 40.00
Spectra cards (1:18)
SP1 The Planet Bajor 10.00
SP2 Emissary 10.00
SP3 Energy Creature 10.00

SP4 The Mission 10.00
Gold Spectra (1:72)
SPG The Wormhole 16.00
Redemption card (1:180) 45.00
Ten card embossed redemption set .50.00
Sisko promo card 1.00
Dax & Sisko promo card 1.00
S2 "Personal Phasers" prototype 1.00
Playmates variant cards from
    action figures, each 1.50
Playmates Space Caps from
    action figures, each 1.00

PROFILES
SkyBox (1997)
Set: 81 cards 15.00
Pack: 8 cards 1.75
Box: 36? packs 50.00
Quark's Bar (1:3) 9 different, each . . .3.00
Trials and Tribble-ations (:6)
    9 different, each 5.00
Latinum Profiles (1:12) 9 diff., each .12.00
Autograph cards (1:216)
Odo 125.00
Quark .125.00
Dax 125.00

STAR TREK: VOYAGER
SkyBox (1995) TV
Set: 98 cards plus P1 & T1 . . . . . .18.00
Pack: 8 cards 1.00
Jumbo Pack: 15 cards 1.75
Box: 36 packs 30.00
Voyager Crew Spectra cards (1:12)
(1:6.4 jumbo packs)
S1 Captain Kathryn Janeway 10.00
S2 Chakotay 10.00
S3 Tuvok 10.00
S4 Tom Paris 10.00
S5 B'Elanna Torres 10.00
S6 Ensign Harry Kim 10.00
S7 The Doctor 10.00
S8 Neelix 10.00
S9 Kes .10.00
Blueprint Offer (1:18)
X-1 U.S.S. Voyager 8.00
X-2 Bridge 8.00
X-3 Engineering 8.00
Bonus Cards
Emergency Holographic Doctor
    Hologram (1:180) 60.00
SkyMotion Exchange Card (1:180) .55.00
SkyMotion mail-in (5,000 made) . . .40.00
Survey card 4.50
Other cards
P1 "Sneak Peek" Voyager
    Series Two card 3.00
T1 Star Trek: Voyager
    Series One, Title Card 3.00
9-card promo sheet 12.00
Janeway SkyMotion promo 75.00
Promos
N1 cast prototype (*Non-Sport
    Update*) 3.00
C1 ship promo (*Cards Illustrated
    #18*) 3.00

Album .20.00

SERIES 2
SkyBox (1995)
Set: 90 cards + 1 tattoo 20.00
Pack: 8 cards + 1 tattoo 1.50
Box: 36 packs 30.00
Neelix Scratch 'n' Sniff Recipes (1:12)
R-1 Vulcan Plomeek Soup 5.00
R-2 Laurelian Blue Pudding 5.00
R-3 Takar Loggerhead Eggs 5.00
R-4 Proteinaceous Coffee Cocktail .5.00
R-5 Macaroni & Brill Cheese 5.00
R-6 Spinach Shake With Pear 5.00
ZenoBio Spectra Foils (1:12)
S-1 Seska 7.00
S-2 Telek 7.00
S-3 Gathorel Labin 7.00
S-4 Dr. Neria 7.00
S-5 Sulan 7.00
S-6 Jetrel 7.00
S-7 Jabin 7.00
S-8 Lidell 7.00
S-9 Toscat 7.00
Merchandise card (1:18) 3.00
SkyMotion card (1:180) 55.00
SkyMotion mail-in 4" x 5" (5,000) . . .35.00
Survey card 3.50
Ad card .3.00
Six-card promo sheet (mail) 10.00
Album .20.00
#0 Promo 50.00
N# promo 15.00
P1 promo 10.00

SEASON TWO
Set: 100 cards 100.00
Pack: 8 cards 1.50
Box: 50.00
Xeno-Bio Etched Foil (1:12)
    3 different, each 4.00
24th Century Technical (1:12)
    3 different, each 4.00
New World Foils (1:18) 3 diff., each .5.00
Holo-Emiter (1:48) 3 diff., each 15.00
1997 preview card 1.00

STAR TREK:
THE MOTION PICTURE
Topps (1979) Movie
Set: 88 cards/22 stickers 55.00
Pack: 3.00
Card 50
Sticker 75
Box: 85.00

Colonial/Kilpatrick/Rainbo Bread
(1979) Movie
Set: 33 cards 20.00
Uncut sheet, any company 25.00

STAR TREK STICKERS
Burger King (1979)
Set: 4 stickers 15.00

STAR TREK II
THE WRATH OF KAHN
FTCC (1982) Movie
Set: 30 cards (5" x 7") 80.00
Card: 3.00
Box: 100.00

STAR TREK III
FTCC (1984) Movie
Set: 60 cards+20 Spaceship cards .50.00
Card 75
Box: 55.00

STAR TREK IV
THE VOYAGE HOME
FTCC (1986) Movie
Set: 60 cards 35.00
Pack: 1.50
Card: 75
Box: 50.00
Variations of cards #10, 23, 24, 56

STAR TREK
FEATURE FILMS
Paramount/SkyBox (Oct. 1993)
*These cards come from "The Starfleet
Collection" of six movie videos, the six
cards and a watch. 5,000 sets were produced. Cards 1, 4 and 5 are regular cards
and cards 2, 3 and 6 are silver foil holograms.*
1 of 6 Star Trek:
    The Motion Picture 5.00
2 of 6 Star Trek II:
    The Wrath of Kahn 10.00
3 of 6 Star Trek III:
    The Search for Spock 10.00
4 of 6 Star Trek IV:
    The Voyage Home 5.00
5 of 6 Star Trek V:
    The Final Frontier 5.00
6 of 6 Star Trek VI:
    The Undiscovered Country . . .10.00

STAR TREK:
GENERATIONS
SkyBox (1994) Movie
Set: 72 cards + survey & offer 15.00
Pack: 6 tall cards 1.25
Box: 36 packs 30.00
Foil Cards (1:20)
F1 Escaping Reality 6.00
F2 Renegades 6.00
F3 Fragile Alliance 6.00
Spectra-etch cards (1:36)
S1 One Last Time [Kirk] 10.00
S2 The Greatest Legacy 10.00
S3 Legends Meet 10.00
SkyMotion redemption card (1:180) .75.00
SkyMotion mail-in (5,000 made) . . .60.00
Survey card 3.00
Ad Card .2.00
S1 Prototype 1.50
Album .20.00

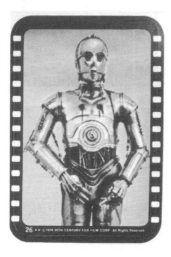

Star Trek IV, The Voyage Home box (SkyBox 1993)

Star Wars Sticker #26 (Topps 1977)

The Empire Strikes Back #59 (Topps 1980)

Return of the Jedi #98, Han Solo's Approach (Topps 1983)

STAR TREK: CINEMA COLLECTION
SkyBox (1995)
Mail-in offer,
Star Trek Generations
Movie 1 Set: 72 cards, tall, boxed . .25.00
Movie 2 Set: 72 cards, tall, boxed . .25.00
Movie 3 Set: 72 cards, tall, boxed . .25.00
Movie 4 Set: 72 cards, tall, boxed . .25.00
Movie 5 Set: 72 cards, tall, boxed . .25.00
Movie 6 Set: 72 cards, tall, boxed . .25.00
Master Set: all 6 movies + mini-sheet &
 6 cards Generations mini-set .125.00
Uncut Promo sheet 25.00

STAR TREK FIRST CONTACT
SkyBox (1996)
Set: 60 tall cards 18.00
Pack: 9 tall cards 2.00
Box: 60.00
Behind the Scenes (1:6)
BS1 Jonathon Frakes the Director . . .3.50
BS2 Directing a Klingon 3.50
BS3 With Friends Like These... . . . .3.50
BS4 On Location 3.50
BS5 Give That Borg a Hand 3.50
BS6 Made for the Job 3.50
BS7 Fit for a Queen 3.50
BS8 It's Easier in Space 3.50
BS9 Lt. Commander Data and
 The Borg Queen 3.50
BS10 A Man Amongst Borg 3.50
Techno-Cell Borg cards (1:8)
B1 Star Trek: The Next Generation Borg
B2 Star Trek: First Contact Borg . .7.00
B3 Locutus 7.00
B4 Klingon Borg 7.00
B5 Bolian Borg 7.00
B6 Cardassian Borg 7.00
B7 Borg Queen 7.00
B8 Borg Alcove 7.00
B9 Borgified Engineering 7.00
B10 Star Trek: First Contact Borg . . .7.00
B11 Star Trek: First Contact Borg . . .7.00
B12 Borg Symbol 7.00

Character Cards (1:9)
C1 Captain Jean-Luc Picard 7.50
C2 Lieutenant Commander Data 7.50
C3 Lieutenant Commander Geordi
 LaForge 7.50
C4 Commander William T. Riker 7.50
C5 Lieutenant Deanna Troi 7.50
C6 Dr. Beverly Crusher 7.50
C7 Lieutenant Commander Worf 7.50
C8 Lieutenant Hawk 7.50
C9 Zefram Cochrane 7.50
C10 Lilly Sloane 7.50

U.S.S. Enterprise NCC-1701-E cards (1:12)
E1 Bridge .7.00
E2 Main Engineering 7.00
E3 Ready Room 7.00
E4 Sickbay 7.00
E5 Evacuation Corridor 7.00
E6 Observation Lounge 7.00
Ships Blueprint Poster card (1:36)
S1 U.S.S. Enterprise 15.00
S2 Borg Cube 15.00
S3 Phoenix 15.00
Autographed (1:3,600)
Autographed Brent Spiner card . . .700.00

STAR WARS
Topps (1977) Movie
Series 1, blue border with stars
Set: 66 cards/11 stickers 100.00
Pack: 7 cards + 1 sticker 7.50
Box: 36 packs 250.00
Box: Empty 15.00
Wrapper: C-3PO, black background .5.00
Series 2, red border
Set: 66 cards (#67–#132) and
 11 stickers (#12–#22) 75.00
Pack: 6.00
Box: 36 packs 150.00
Box: Empty 12.00
Wrapper: Darth Vader,
 yellow background 5.00
Series 3, yellow border
Set: 66 cards (#133–#198) &
 11 stickers (#23–#33) 75.00
Pack: 5.50
Box: 36 packs 130.00
Box: Empty 10.00
Wrapper: R2-D2, purple background .4.00
Series 4, green border
Set: 66 cards (#199–#264) &
 11 stickers (#34–#44) 65.00
Pack: 4.00
Box: 36 packs 110.00
Box: Empty 10.00
Card #207, obscenity 40.00
Wrapper: Obi-Wan & Luke,
 green background 3.00
Series 5, brown/orange
Set: 66 cards (#265–#330) &
 11 stickers (#45–#55) 60.00
Pack: 4.00
Box: 36 packs 110.00
Box: Empty 10.00
Wrapper: X-Wing Fighter,
 purple background 3.00

STAR WARS
Wonder Bread (1977)
Set: 16 cards 25.00

General Mills Cereals (1978–79)
Set: 18 different large cards 50.00
Card: each 3.00
SUGAR FREE GUM WRAPPERS
Topps (1978)
Set: 56 wrappers 75.00
Wrapper: each 1.25
Box: empty 10.00

ALBUM STICKERS
Panini (1977)
Set: 256 stickers with album 35.00
Single sticker 25

STAR WARS & THE EMPIRE STRIKES BACK
"Everybody Wins Trading Cards"
Burger King (1980)
Set: 12 different strips 30.00
Set: 36 cards, cut 25.00
Card: cut .75
(Cards are unnumbered)

THE EMPIRE STRIKES BACK
Topps (1980) Movie
Series 1, grey and red border
Set: 132 cards/33 stickers 80.00
Pack: 12 cards 8.00
Box: 36 packs 90.00
Box: Empty 10.00
Wrapper: .2.50
Series 2, grey and blue border
Set: 132 cards (#133–#264) &
 33 stickers (#34–#66) 65.00
Pack: 12 cards/1 sticker 5.00
Box: 36 packs 70.00
Box: Empty 7.50
Wrapper: "New Series" 2.50
Series 3, green and yellow border
Set: 88 cards (#265–#352 &
 22 stickers (#67–#88) 60.00
Pack: 12 cards/1 sticker 4.50
Box: 36 packs 65.00
Box: Empty 7.50
Wrapper: .2.00

THE EMPIRE STRIKES BACK
Hersey's (1980)
Cards appeared on 6-pack candy
bar trays:
Set: 5 Trays (with uncut cards) 8.00
Set: 5 cards cut from trays 5.00

GIANT PHOTO CARDS
Topps (1980)
Test Issue Set: 60 Giant cards 85.00
Test Issue, single card 2.00
Regular Set: 30 cards 35.00
Regular Set Box: ? packs 50.00
Box: empty 5.00

RETURN OF THE JEDI
Topps (1983) Movie
Series 1, red border
Set: 132 cards/33 stickers 35.00
Pack: 10 cards, 1 sticker 2.50
Box: 36 packs 55.00
Box: Empty 5.00
Wrapper: .1.00
(4 different wrappers: Luke; Jabba; Ewok;
 Darth Vader)
Series Two, blue border
Set: 88 cards (#133–#220) & 22 stickers
 (#33–#55) 25.00
Pack: 10 cards, 1 sticker 2.50
Box: 36 packs 40.00
Box: Empty 5.00
Wrapper: "New Series" 1.00
(4 different wrappers, Leia; Lando;
 C-3PO; Young Ewok; all say "New Series")

ALBUM STICKERS
Topps (1983)
Set: 180 stickers with album 20.00
Single sticker 25
Wax Box .40.00
Album 4.00

STAR WARS GALAXY
Topps (1993) SF/Art
Set: 140 cards 25.00
Pack: 8 cards 2.00
Box: 36 packs 50.00
Millennium Falcon factory set: 140
 cards foil stamped, plus holofoil cards, plus Darth Vader
 3-D hologram & #0 card &
 preview, in plastic ship model 100.00
Millennium Falcon factory set,
 publishers proof, "limited to
 500 sets" on sticker 125.00
Binder, with card SWB1 . . . . .18.00
Etched-Foil cards, untitled, Walt
 Simonson art
1 (Darth Vader) 10.00
2 (Lando Calrissian) 10.00
3 (Luke & R2-D2) 10.00
4 (C-3PO & Chewbacca) 10.00
5 (Yoda & Obi-wan) 10.00
6 (Luke) .10.00
Autographed Cards 35.00

Star Wars Galaxy #76, Even Droids Celebrate (Topps 1993)

Star Wars Galaxy Three #341 (Topps 1995)

Star Wars Galaxy, Bend-Ems #J, Leia Organa (Topps 1993)

Star Wars Finest #16, Winter (Topps 1996)

Six-card uncut-sheet (1:case) 50.00
Promo Cards
Boba Fett & Dengar (Cam Kennedy
   art) from Classic Star Wars #8 .15.00
Jabba the Hutt, Oola and Salacious
   Crumb (Sam Keith art) from
   Starlog #191 and Wizard #20 .10.00
Princess Leia (Brian Stelfreeze art)
   from Non-Sports#2 and shows 10.00
Dewback/Stormtrooper (Al Williamson
   art) from Non-Sports Update
   Vol. 4 #2 . . . . .10.00
Princess Leia & Stormtrooper/
   Dewback promo sheet, from
   Advance Comics #52 . . . . .6.00
Jabba the Hutt/Oola/Salacious Crumb
   promo sheet, from Previews,
   Feb. 1993 and Comics
   Scorecard, Feb. 1993,
   5½" x 7¾" 15.00
SWB1 binder card from Star Wars
   Galaxy Binder 10.00

SERIES TWO
Topps (1994) SF art
Set: 135 cards (#141–#275) 20.00
Pack: 8 cards 1.75
Box: 36 packs 40.00
Factory tin Set, with #00 card, Boris
   Vallejo hologram card and
   Galaxy III promo card 100.00
Etched-Foil cards, untitled (1:18)
   by Walt Simonson
#7 (Grand Moff Tarkin) 9.00
#8 (Imperial Troopers) 9.00
#9 . . . . .9.00
#10 (Boba Fett) 9.00
#11 . . . . .9.00
#12 (Slave 1) 9.00
Uncut Etched-Foil sheet 100.00
Autographed (2000) 50.00
Six-card uncut sheet (1:case) 50.00
Album .16.00
Promo cards
P1 Rancor (Jae Lee art) from
   Cards Illustrated #2 . . . . .15.00
P2 Lightsaber construction (Chris
   Sprouse art) from Non Sports
   Update, Vol. 5 #2 . . . . .15.00
P3 Yoda Shrine, never released, but
   samples exist
   Unknown
P4 Jawas & C-3PO (Dave Gibbons
   art) from Star Wars Galaxy I
   Millennium Falcon Factory set .15.00
P5 Chewbacca and droid (Joe Phillips
   art) from Cards Illustrated #5
   & Just Toys mail-in 15.00
P6 Boba Fett (Tom Taggart art)

from Hero #12 . . . . .15.00
SWG1 promo 10.00
Tusken Raiders (Tim Truman art)
   from Classic Star Wars #20
   or Just Toys mail in 10.00
Biker Scout/Ewok (Jim Starlin art)
   from Triton #3 variant card
   #266, Ewok with knife 20.00
Promo sheet with P1 card from
   Previews Feb. 1994, 5¼" x 7" . .2.00

SERIES THREE
Topps (1995) SF art
Set: 90 cards: #276–#365 +
   #L1–#L12 . . . . .20.00
Pack: 5 cards + 1 1st day issue
   card and 1 insert card 2.00
Box: 36 packs 40.00
First day set: 90 cards 75.00
First day card, each 1.00
Etched Foil Cards untitled (1:12)
   by Walt Simonson
13 Lando Calrissian 9.00
14 Millennium Falcon 9.00
15 Jawas? 9.00
16 Jawas? 9.00
17 Tusken Raiders 9.00
18 Jedi Spirits 9.00
Uncut Etched Foil panorama sheet 100.00
Agents of the Empire Clearzone (1:18)
E1 Brett Booth 10.00
E2 Jeff Scott Campbell 10.00
E3 Jeff Rebner 10.00
E4 Joe Chiodo 10.00
E5 Tom Rainey 10.00
E6 Brian Denham 10.00
Promo Cards
P1 promo, does not seem to exist
P2 Snowtroopers (Chris Moeller art)
   convention give away 18.00
P3 Darth Vader (John Van Fleet
   art) from Non-Sports Update,
   Vol. 6 #4 . . . . .5.00
P4 Luke Skywalker (Arthur Suydam
   art) from Combo #7 . . . . .5.00
P5 Snowspeeder and AT-AT (Steve
   Reiss art) from Advance
   Comics #83 . . . . .5.00
P5 error promo 35.00
P6 cover of Star Wars Galaxy
   Magazine #5 (Bros. Hildebrandt
   art) from Star Wars Galaxy
   Magazine #5 . . . . .5.00
P7 Leia, Solo and twins (Russ Walks
   art) from Wizard #52 . . . . .5.00
P8 Darth Vader and Boba Fett,
   from Cards Illustrated #5 . . . . . .5.00
No# Boba Fett, from Star Wars
   Galaxy II factory set 15.00

#000 Princess Leia promo (Drew
   Struzan art) from Star Wars
   Galaxy Magazine #4 . . . . .5.00
One-Card promo sheet, card #000,
   from Previews Sept. 1995 . . . . .5.00

BEND-EMS (VARIANTS)
Just Toys (1993–95)

Cards come with Bend-Em figures
Mail-Ins
0 Darth Vader (Ken Steacy art) 15.00
00 Darth Vader (Ralph McQuarrie
   art) 15.00
Checklist card, variation of checklist
   card from series, mentions
   Series Two 15.00
Star Wars Galaxy variants
A Darth Vader (Joe Smith) 3.00
B C-3PO (Joe Smith) 3.00
C R2-D2 (Joe Smith) 3.00
D Imperial Troopers (Al Williamson) . .3.00
E Yoda (Joe Smith) 3.00
F Chewbacca (Joe Smith) 3.00
G Luke Skywalker (Joe Smith) 3.00
H Obi-Wan "Ben" Kanobi (Joe Smith) 3.50
I Han Solo 5.00
J Princess Leia (Joe Smith) 2.00
K Emperor Palpatine 5.00
L (Wicket) Ewok (Wm. Stout) 3.00
M Boba Fett (Joe Smith) 3.00
N The Design of Star Wars,
   The Death Star Trench 5.00
O Death Star II, series 2? 5.00
P Lando Calrissian 5.00
Q The Art of Star Wars (Boris Vallejo) 5.00
R X-Wing Pilot 5.00
S Admiral Ackbar (Michael
   Wm. Kaluta) 5.00
T Tusken Raider 5.00
U Emperor's Royal Guard (Jerome
   Moore) 5.00
V Gamorrean Guard 5.00
W Bib Fortuna 5.00
X Darth Vader and Luke 5.00
Star Wars Galaxy Series 2 variants
Y The Merchandising Art of Star Wars5.00
Z Luke & Leia (Zina Saunders) 5.00
AA (Luke, Vader, Han & Leia) 5.00
BB The Illustrators of Star Wars,
   Ken Barr 5.00

STAR WARS
Merlin (1997)
Set: 125 cards 30.00
Pack: 1.50
Box: 45.00
Chase Cards, oversize
  1 thru 3, each 20.00

STAR WARS
MASTERVISION
Topps (1995)
Boxed Set: 36 cards 6¾" x 10¾" . . .40.00
Card: 1.25
Promos
No # Boba Fett and Bounty Hunters
   (Star Wars Galaxy Mag. #2) . . .2.50
P2 Luke and AT-ATs promo (Star
   Wars Galaxy Mag. #5) 2.50

STAR WARS FINEST
Topps (1996) SF art
Set: 90 Chromium cards 60.00
Pack: 5 cards 3.50
Box: 36 packs 75.00
Topps Matrix Chase Cards (1:12)
Han Solo & Chewbacca (Ray Lago) 10.00
Emperor Palpatine (Ray Lago) 10.00
C-3P0 & R2-D2 (John Van Fleet) . . .10.00
Boba Fett (John Van Fleet) 10.00
Embossed Chase Cards (1:9) Dan
   Brereton art
6 different, each 10.00
Topps Matrix six-up chase card
   panel (Dan Brereton art) one
   per case ordered by retailer . . .50.00
Topps Finest Refractor (1:12),
   90 different, each 15.00
Refractor Set: 90 cards 1,100.00
Mastervisions Matrix redemption
   (1:360) 75.00
Mastervision Matrix mail-in 75.00
Album, with card 20.00
Album card 8.00
Promos
SWF1 promo, from Star Wars
   Galaxy Magazine #6 . . . . .4.00
SWF2 promo, from Star Wars
   Galaxy Magazine #7 . . . . .4.00
SWF3 Luke on TaunTaun, from
   Non- Sports Update Vol. 7 #3 . .4.00
Refractor promo 40.00
Oversize Chromium Promo 15.00

STAR WARS: SHADOWS
OF THE EMPIRE
Painted by Greg & Tim Hildebrandt
Topps (1996) SF art
Set: 90 cards (#1 through #72
   and #82 through #100) 15.00
Pack: 9 cards 1.50
Box: 36 packs 50.00
Foil Chase Cards, gold gilt (1:9)
73 Luke Skywalker 7.00
74 Leia & Chewbacca 7.00
75 Lando Calrissian 7.00

Star Wars Widevision #36
Ext. Tatooine—Wasteland (Topps 1995)

Empire Strikes Back Widevision #35,
Ext. Hoth—Battlefield—Ice Plain (Topps 1996)

76 R2-D2 & C-3PO 7.00
77 Dash & Leebo 7.00
78 Prince Xizor 7.00
Embossed Foil Chase Cards (1:18)
79 Guri 10.00
80 Darth Vader 10.00
81 Jix & Big Gizz 10.00
82 Boba Fett 10.00
Redemption card (1:200) 60.00
Autographed Mastervision mail-in
    redemption 50.00
Four different wrappers: Luke, Xizor,
    Darth, Boba Fett
Promo Cards
SOTE1 Prince Xizor (Bros. Hilde-
    brandt art) from Star Wars
    Galaxy Magazine #7 . . . . .3.00
SOTE2 Darth Vader (Bros. Hilde-
    brandt art) from Non-Sports
    Update Vol. 7 #4 . . . . .3.00
SOTE3 Luke and Lightsaber (Bros.
    Hildebrandt art) from Star Wars
    Topps Finest Series One box . . .3.00
SOTE4 Dash Rendar (Bros.
    Hildebrandt art) Star Wars
    Galaxy Magazine #8 . . . . .3.00
SOTE5 Boba Fett (Bros. Hilde-
    brandt art) from QVC and
    convention giveaway 3.00
SOTE6 Guri (Bros. Hildebrandt art)
    from Fan #19 . . . . .3.00
SOTE7 R2-D2 and C-3PO (Bros.
    Hildebrandt art) San Diego
    Con giveaway, Collect
    Vol. 4 #9, Combo #24? 3.00
One card promo sheet, SOTE#3,
    5¼" x 7" 5.00

STAR WARS
WIDEVISION
STAR WARS
Topps (1995) Movie
Set: 120 cards, 4½" 50.00
Pack: 10 cards 5.00
Box: packs 100.00
Topps Finest (1:11) Ralph McQuarrie art
C1 C-3PO and R2-D2 on Tatooine .20.00
C2 Luke watches two suns setting . .20.00
C3 Pulled into the Death Star
    Docking Bay 20.00
C4 On the run within the Death Star 20.00
C5 Darth Vader vs. Luke 20.00
C6 Imperial TIE Fighter chases
    Millennium Falcon 20.00
C7 Rebels approach the Death Star 20.00
C8 TIE Fighter chases X-Wing 20.00
C9 X-Wing in the Death Star trench .20.00
C10 . . . . .20.00
Album, with #00 card 16.00
Promo Cards
SWP0 Han, Luke and Chewie enter
    final ceremony, from Star
    Wars Galaxy II factory set 15.00
SWP1 Stormtroopers stop Luke and
    Ben in landspeeder, from Non-

Sport Update Vol. 5 #6 and
    show giveaway 5.00
SWP2 Interior of Millennium Falcon
    cockpit, from Advance Comics
    #72 .10.00
SWP3 TIE Fighters in Death Star
    trench, from Star Wars Galaxy
    Magazine #1 . . . . .10.00
SWP4 Exterior of Star Destroyer,
    from Wizard #42 . . . . .5.00
SWP5 Darth Vader throttling Rebel,
    from Tuff Stuff Collect
    Jan. 1995 . . . . .10.00
SWP6 Leia & C-3PO in Yavin IV
    control room, from Cards
    Illustrated #14 . . . . .10.00
0 Luke outside X-Wing, from Star
    Wars Widevision binder album .8.00
No# promo sheet Han in gunport,
    from Previews Oct. 1994 . . . . .10.00
Promos from Classic Edition 4-Pack
    action figures
K01 Int. Rebel Blockade
    Runner—Corridor 8.00
K02 Int. Millennium Falcon—Gunport 8.00
K03 Int. Millennium Falcon—Cockpit .8.00
K04 Int. Tatooine—Mos Eisley—
    Cantina 8.00

THE EMPIRE STRIKES BACK
Topps (1995) Movie
Set: 144 cards 45.00
Pack: 9 cards 2.75
2 different packs
Box: 24 packs 80.00
Chromium cards (1:12)
C1 Imperial Probot 13.00
C2 Luke on his Tauntaun 13.00
C3 AT-ATs and Luke on Tauntaun . .13.00
C4 Snowspeeder circles AT-AT 13.00
C5 Yoda and Luke 13.00
C6 Space Slug 13.00
C7 Cloud City of Bespin 13.00
C8 Carbon-freezing Chamber,
    Darth vs. Luke 13.00
C9 Luke dangling 13.00
C10 Droids replace Luke's Hand . . .13.00
Movie Poster Set (1:24)
1 of 6 Advance One-Sheet 8.00
2 of 6 Domestic One-Sheet 8.00
3 of 6 Style B Domestic One-Sheet .8.00
4 of 6 Australian One-Sheet 8.00
5 of 6 German One-Sheet 8.00
6 of 6 Radio Show Poster 8.00
Promos
#0 Darth Vader, from Star Wars
    Galaxy Magazine #3 . . . . .3.00
P1 Han Solo, from Advance Comics
    #79 .10.00
P2 AT-AT, from Non-Sports Update
    Vol. 6 #4 . . . . .10.00
P3 Luke, R2-D2 and Yoda, from Tuff
    Stuff Collect, Aug. 95 and
    Cards Illustrated #20 . . . . .10.00
P4 Luke hanging by hands, from Combo
    #7 and also Combo #12 . . . .12.00

P5 Stormtroopers & Han Solo in Carbonite,
    convention giveaway 30.00
P6 Luke, Leia, C-3PO and R2-D2,
    from Wizard #48 . . . . .10.00
Three-card (P1, P2, P3) promo
    sheet, from Previews May 1995 .4.00

RETURN OF THE JEDI
Topps (1996) Movie
Set: 144 cards 45.00
Pack: 9 cards 2.50
Box: 24 packs 60.00
Topps Finest Chromium (R. McQuarrie)
    (1:12)
C/1 Darth Vader arrives in style 11.00
C/2 Droids held captive 11.00
C/3 Jabba's Palace 11.00
C/4 In the Rancor Pit 11.00
C/5 Escape from the Sail Barge 11.00
C/6 Speeder Bikes 11.00
C/7 . . . . .11.00
C/8 Father vs. Son 11.00
C/9 Emperor and Luke 11.00
C/10 Inside Death Star II 11.00
Mini-Posters (1:box)
1 of 6 Advance One-Sheet 10.00
2 of 6 One-Sheet Style B 10.00
3 of 6 1985 Re-release One-Sheet .10.00
4 of 6 Japanese Poster 10.00
5 of 6 Japanese Poster 10.00
6 of 6 Polish Poster 10.00
3-Di (1:case) Admiral Ackbar 50.00
Redemption card 30.00
Promo Cards
#0 Three dead Jedi Warriors at Ewok
    celebration, from Star Wars
    Galaxy Magazine #6 . . . . .4.00
P1 Han, Luke and Lando, from Star
    Wars Galaxy Magazine #5 . . . . .4.00
P2 Biker Scout and Luke, from
    Advance Comics #83 . . . . .4.00
P3 Stormtroopers, Han and Leia,
    from Non-Sports Update,
    Vol. 7 #1 . . . . .4.00
P4 Emperor Palpatine, from Cards
    Illustrated. #27 . . . . .4.00
P5 Jabba the Hutt and Bib Fortuna,
    from Wizard #54 . . . . .4.00
P6 Han Solo, Luke and Chewbacca,
    from show giveaways 50.00
One-card promo sheet (#0) from
    Previews, Nov. 95 . . . . .5.00

STAR WARS TRILOGY (RETAIL)
Topps (1997) Movies
Set: 72 cards 20.00
Pack: cards 2.00
Box: packs 50.00
Lasercut Set (1:9)
1 of 6 A New Customer Enjoys... . . .9.00
2 of 6 "It's Not My Fault"... . . . . . . .9.00
3 of 6 The Tantive IV Caught... . . . .9.00
4 of 6 Chewbacca Led Away in
    Chains... . . . . .9.00
5 of 6 X-Wings Approach Their
    Target... . . . . .9.00

6 of 6 Imperial View: X-Wing
    Laser Fire... . . . . .9.00
Promos
P0 Lasercut 10.00
P1 Stormtroopers, San Diego Comic
    Con giveaway 5.00
P2 Jabba the Hutt, Star Wars Galaxy
    Magazine #10 . . . . .5.00
P3 X-Wing Fighter Squadron,
    magazines 5.00
P4 Sandcrawler, from Star Wars
    3-D packs 10.00
P5 Luke in Landspeeder, from Star
    Wars 3-D I packs 10.00
P6 Millennium Falcon and Storm-
    troopers, from Star Wars
    3-D I packs 10.00
P7 Landspeeder in Mos Eisley,
    Wizard Sci-Fi Special '97 Star
    Wars Trilogy Special Edition
    promo 5.00
P8 . . . . .5.00

TRILOGY SPECIAL EDITION
Topps (1997) Movies
Set: 72 cards 25.00
Pack: 9 cards 3.00
Box: packs 75.00
Lasercut Set (1:9)
1 of 6 Luke Skywalker is Entranced... 9.00
2 of 6 Han Solo and Co-Pilot
    Chewbacca... . . . . .9.00
3 of 6 Admiral Ozzel feels Darth
    Vader's wrath... . . . . .9.00
4 of 6 A Hologram of Emperor
    Palpatine... . . . . .9.00
5 of 6 A Fate Much Worse... . . . . . .9.00
6 of 6 Emperor Palpatine Unleashes... 9.00
Holograms (1:18) 2 diff. 20.00
Spec. Ed. 3D card (1:Box) X-wings
    Departing 15.00
Galoob MicroMachine Promos
G1 R2-D2 on X-Wing 3.00
G2 TIE Fighter & X-Wing 3.00
G3 Luke in Landspeeder 3.00
G4 Mos Eisley 3.00
G5 Jawa on Ronto 3.00
Hasbro Vehicles Promos
H1 Millennium Falcon 5.00
H2 Massassi outpost 5.00
H3 Han & Jabba 5.00
H4 Droids and Calimari cruiser 5.00

WIDEVISION 3-D
Topps (1997)
Set: 63 cards 90.00
Pack: 3 cards 4.00
Box: 36 packs 120.00
Chase Card (1:36)
1m Death Star 3-D Motion card 30.00
Promos
2m Swoops and Rontos (Star Wars
    Trilogy Special Edition promo .10.00
3Di 1 Darth Vader, Stormtroopers
    and Captain Piett 10.00
3Di 2 Darth and Luke 25.00

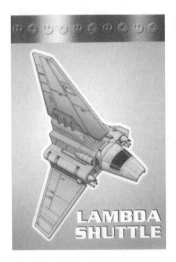

Star Wars Vehicles C4, Lambda Shuttle (Topps 1997)

Star Wars Dark Empire metal cards (Metallic Impressions 1995)

William Stout #80, Rings of Saturn (Comic Images 1993)

Terminator 2 #32, When Cops are Everywhere (Impel 1991)

P1 Darth Vader (Star Wars
    Galaxy #9) 10.00
P2 Luke and Darth Vader (2,500
    made) 50.00
P1 AT-ATs, The Empire Strikes
    Back! promo 20.00
Dm/o Admiral Ackbar Return of
    the Jedi promo 20.00

STAR WARS VEHICLES
Topps (1997)
Set: 72 cards 25.00
Pack: 5 cards 2.00
Box: 36 packs 50.00
Cutaway cards, (1:18) 4 different
C1 . . . . .15.00
C2 . . . . .15.00
C3 . . . . .15.00
C4 Lamda Shuttle 15.00
3-D cards (1:36) Chris Moeller art,
    2 different, each 25.00
Redemption card (1:360) for uncut
    pair of 3-D cards 60.00
Mail-in card 50.00
Promos
P1 Speeder Bikes 50.00
P2 Shuttle Tyderium 85.00
Postcard, 4" x 6" 2.00

OTHER STAR WARS CARDS & STICKERS
Trix Star Wars stickers, each 1.00
set: 4 stickers 5.00
Lucky Charms Star Wars
    stickers, each 1.00
set: 4 stickers 5.00
Monster Cereals Star Wars
    stickers, each 1.00
set: 4 stickers 5.00
Cocoa Puffs Star Wars stickers, each 1.00
set: 4 stickers 5.00
Big G trading cards, with Star Wars
    logo (General Mills 1978) each .1.00
set: 18 photos and wallet 30.00
The Empire Strikes Back Sticker set
    & Album (Burger King) 10.00
3-D Ewok Perk-up sticker sets,
    each 1-5.00
Star Wars Galaxy Magazine
SWGM1 promo (Star Wars Galaxy
    Mag. #1) 4.00
SWGM2 promo (Star Wars Galaxy
    Mag. #2) 4.00
SWGM3 At-At (McQuarrie) (Star
    Wars Galaxy Mag. #3) chromium 5.00
SWGM4 Dagobah swamp (Star Wars
    Galaxy Mag. #4) chromium 5.00

Dark Horse Comics
DH1 Dark Empire II promo, from
    Classic Star Wars: Tales of the
    Jedi: Dark Lords of the Sith #1 .5.00
DH2 Dark Empire II promo, from
    Classic Star Wars The Early
    Adventures #3 . . . . .5.00
DH3 Dark Empire II promo, from
    Classic Star Wars: Return of
    the Jedi #1 . . . . .5.00
Classic Toys Trading Cards
#37 Darth Vader 12" action
    figure (doll) 1.00
#56 C-3PO 12" action figure (doll) . . .1.00

STAR WARS CAPS
Topps
Set: 64 caps + 2 slammers +
    chase caps 15.00
Pack: 3 regular caps + 1 chase cap .1.00
Box: 48 packs 30.00
Promos
0-A R2-D2 and C-3PO box art, from
    Star Wars Galaxy Magazine #3 .2.00
0-B Darth Vader box art, from Star
    Wars Galaxy Magazine #3 . . . .2.00

METAL CARDS
STAR WARS: A NEW HOPE
Metallic Images (1994)
Set: 20 tin cards in tin box with
    certificate (49,900 made) 40.00
Promo P1 . . . . .4.00

THE EMPIRE STRIKES BACK
Metallic Images (1995)
Set: 20 tin cards in tin box with
    certificate (49,900 made) 50.00
Promo P2 . . . . .4.00

SERIES 2
Set: 20 tin cards in tin box with
    certificate (49,900 made) 50.00

RETURN OF THE JEDI
Metallic Images (1995)
Set: 20 tin cards in tin box with
    certificate (49,900 made) 50.00
Promo P3 . . . . .6.00

THE ART OF RALPH MCQUARRIE
Metallic Images (1996)
Set: 20 tin cards in tin box with
    certificate (12,000 made) 60.00

STAR WARS DARK EMPIRE
Metallic Impressions (1995)
Set: 6 metal cards in metal box 15.00
Card, each 3.00

DARK EMPIRE II
Metallic Impressions (1996)
Box with 6 metal cards 15.00
Card, each 3.00

SHADOWS OF THE EMPIRE
Metallic Impressions (1997)
Tin litho box with 6 metal cards 20.00
Card, each 3.00

JEDI KNIGHT
Metallic Impressions (1997)
Box with 6 metal cards 14.00
Card, each 2.50

24K GOLD CARDS
Authentic Images (1997)
Gold Star Wars cards, limited to 1,000 units,
    in acrylic holder, with black vacuum
    formed jewel case:
Series One: A New Hope
Special Edition Ingot 75.00
Han and Jabba 70.00
Luke 70.00
Leia 70.00
Darth Vader 100.00
Obi-Wan Kenobi 70.00
Series Two: The Empire Strikes Back
Luke 75.00
Emperor 75.00
Boba Fett 100.00
Yoda 75.00
Darth Vader 75.00
Series Three: Return of the Jedi
Boba Fett/Luke 75.00
Darth Vader Unmasked 75.00
3 Spirits .75.00
C-3PO and R2-D2 . . . . .75.00
Leia & Jabba 75.00
Gold Gallery Series cards, limited to 500
    units, in acrylic holder, with black vacuum
    formed jewel case:
Gallery Series 1: A New Hope
Jabba & Han 350.00
Darth Vader & Ben Kenobi 550.00
Gallery Series 2: The Empire Strikes Back
Luke and Yoda 325.00
Luke and Darth Vader 400.00
24-karat gold card set, reproduction of 3
    posters, each encased in a lucite block
    in leatherette case, plus three 24" x 36"
    movie posters, JC Penney exclusive,
    only 1,997 sets worldwide 225.00

STERANKO, JIM
FPG (1995) SF art
Set: 78 cards + 12 super girl cards .12.00
Pack: 8 cards 1.50

Box: 36 packs 35.00
Metallics (1:12)
M1 thru M6, each 6.00
Autograph card (1000 made) 80.00

STOUT, WILLIAM
LOST WORLDS
Comic Images (1993) art
Set: 90 cards 10.00
Pack: 10 cards 1.00
Box: 48 packs 20.00
Chromium cards (1:16)
C1 The Emperor 10.00
C2 Weddell Seal, Giant Sponge
    and Starfish 8.00
C3 Gentoo Penguin and Chicks 8.00
C4 Spectacled Porpoise 8.00
C5 Macaroni Penguin and Boiler 8.00
C6 "Fantasia Antartica" 8.00
Promo card 2.00

STOUT, WILLIAM 2
Comic Images (1994) art
Set: 90 cards 9.00
Pack: 10 cards 1.00
Box: 48 packs 18.00
Holochrome cards (1:12)
H1 Heroes of the Universe 7.00
H2 Heroine of the Universe 7.00
H3 Armsman of the Universe 7.00
H4 Demon of the Universe 7.00
H5 Beast of the Universe 7.00
H6 Swordsman of the Universe 7.00
Lower Cretaceous Antarctica (3:case)
1 . . . . .20.00
2 . . . . .20.00
3 . . . . .20.00
Medallion card (2:case) 15.00
Autograph card (500 made) 75.00
Mini-Press sheet 20.00
6-card uncut sheet, 4 diff., each . . .20.00
Promo card 1.50

SAURIANS & SORCERERS
Comic Images (1996) Fantasy art
Set: 90 cards 10.00
Pack: 10 cards 1.00
Box: 48 packs 30.00
Masters of the Universe MagnaChrome,
    (1:16) 6 different, each 5.00
E.C.Comics subset (1:36) 3 diff.,
    each .8.00
6-card mini press sheet (1:Case) . . .3.00
Autographed cards (500 made) 75.00
MagnaChrome box card 5.00
Promo card 1.00

Thunderbirds #024, Virgil The Artist (ProSet 1992)

James Warhola #11, The Four-Armed Joban (FPG 1995)

Jim Warren #34, God's Little Helper (Comic Images 1993)

Waterworld #5, Enola (Fleer Ultra 1995)

ANTARCTIC & AUSTRALIAN DINOSAURS
November 1993 Dinosaur art
Set: 6 dinosaurs on color 6" x 9" cards, 7th card = all 6 images + Dinosaur Opti-prism card 19.99

SUYDAM, ARTHUR
FPG (1995) SF art
Set: 90 cards 12.50
Pack: 10 cards 1.00
Box: 36 cards 30.00
Metallics (1:12)
M1 Humpy Dumper 7.00
M2 The Joker 7.00
M3 The Archer 7.00
M4 Popindink 7.00
M5 The Headache 7.00
Autograph card (1000 made) 50.00

[The Fantasy Art of] SWEET, DARRELL K.
FPG Cards (1994) SF art
Set: 90 cards 25.00
Pack: 10 cards 1.50
Box: 36 packs 30.00
Metallic Storm
MS1 The Dragon's Revenge 7.50
MS2 The Fire Dragon 7.50
MS3 The Forces of Good And Evil ..7.50
MS4 The Warlord 7.50
MS5 Robot's Dilemma 7.50
Autographed card, foil stamped (1000 made) 75.00
Autographed 10-up un-cut card sheet (1:case) 30.00
P1 promo card 1.50
P2 promo card 1.50
One card Deluxe promo sheet #19 ..4.00

TARGET: MOON
Topps (1958)
Set: 88 cards 600.00
Card: 8.00
Double print cards 5.00
Same cards as *Space Cards*

TEK WORLD
Cardz (1993)
(Lee Sullivan art, Ron Goulart text)
Set: 100 cards 10.00
Pack: 8 cards 1.00
Box: 36 packs 35.00
TekChrome cards (LS)
T1 Jake Cardigan 8.00
T2 Sid Gomez 8.00
T3 Dr. Gunsmith 8.00

T4 Beth Kittridge & Jake Cardigan ..8.00
Lee Sullivan autographed card 45.00
William Shatner autographed card ..75.00
Prototypes, 3 diff. (LS), each 2.00
Four card promo sheet (Comicfest '93) 3.00

TERMINATOR 2: Judgment Day
Impel (1991) Movie
Set in collector's box, with 1 special card and 1 hologram 25.00
Set 140 cards, 10 offer cards 10.00
Pack: 12 cards, 1 offer card 50
Box: 36? packs 12.00
Hologram, Schwarzenegger 20.00
Logo promo 1.00

TERMINATOR 2
Topps (1991) Movie
Set: 44 stickers 5.00
Promo sticker 2.00

THERE ARE ALIENS AMONG US!
Fantasma (1993)
Set: 8 holograms, in box 18.00

THUNDERBIRDS
ProSet (1992) TV
Set: 100 cards 30.00
Pack: 6? cards 1.00
Box: 25.00

TOTAL RECALL
Pacific (1990) Movie
Set: 110 cards, ticket, rock Mars money, boxed 20.00

TRON
Donruss (1981) Movie
Set: 66 cards, 8+ stickers (Color) ..15.00
Pack: 8 cards, 1 sticker 1.50
Box: 30.00

URANUS STRIKES
Thing (1986)
Set: 36 cards 40.00

V
Fleer (1984) TV
Set: 66 cards 20.00
Set: 22 stickers, any backs 40.00
Set: 66 stickers, all variations ...75.00
Pack: 10 cards, 1 sticker 2.50
Box: 70.00

No card #28, but two card #30
Three diff. backs for each sticker

[Fantastic Art of] VESS, CHARLES
FPG (1995) SF art
Set: 90 cards 15.00
Pack: 10 cards 1.75
Box: 36 packs 35.00
Metallic cards (1:12) (*2x2 panel from cover of Stardust comic*)
M1 The Fairy Market: A 8.00
M2 The Fairy Market: B 8.00
M3 The Fairy Market: C 8.00
M4 The Fairy Market: D 8.00
Autograph card (1000 made) 50.00

WARHOLA, JAMES
FPG (1995) SF art
Set: 90 cards 15.00
Pack: 10 cards 1.25
Box: 36 packs 35.00
Metallics
M1 The Ole Space Minstrel 8.00
M2 Toxic Rockers 8.00
M3 Cosmic Androgyne 8.00
M4 Skeleton Biker 8.00
M5 Fire Demon 8.00
Autographed cards, 1000 made ...65.00
Deluxe promo sheet (*Previews 1-95*) back promos David Cherry 1.00

WARREN, JIM: BEYOND BIZARRE
Comic Images (1993) Fantasy art
Set: 90 cards 20.00
Pack: 10 cards 1.00
Box: 48 packs 30.00
SpectraScope cards (1:16)
S1 Nuclear Age 8.00
S2 The Pet 8.00
S3 Unknown Soldier 8.00
Opti-Prism cards (1:16)
1 Dracula 8.00
2 Transformation 8.00
3 Ice Cream Dream 8.00
Mini-Press sheet 12.50
Promo card 2.00

MORE BEYOND BIZARRE
Comic Images (1994) Fantasy art
Set: 90 cards 10.00
Pack: 10 cards 1.00
Box: 48 packs 20.00
Prism cards (1:16)
P1 Earth-Love It or Lose It 7.50
P2 Irish Cross 7.50
P3 Pool Shark 7.50

P4 ....7.50
P5 Einstein Sprint 7.50
P6 ....7.50
Evil Eyes subset cards (3:case)
1 ....10.00
2 ....10.00
3 ....10.00
Autograph card (500 made) 65.00
Medallion card (2:case) 25.00
Mini-Press sheet 10.00
6-card uncut sheet (1:case) 4 different, each 20.00
Promo card 2.00

KEEPSAKE
Fanta Sea Set: 6 sea ladies on color 6" x 9" cards, 7th card = all 6 images + bonus Holochrome card 20.00

WATERWORLD
Fleer Ultra (1995) Movie
Set: 150 cards 25.00
Pack: 8 cards 1.25
Box: 36 packs 20.00
Double size cards (1:4) 1.50
Double pack box: 20 packs 20.00
Double Foil cards (1:4)
1 Inhospitable 2.00
2 ....2.00
3 The Rule of Law 2.00
4 Trial by Fire 2.00
5 ....2.00
6 ....2.00
Prismatic Foil cards, (1:6)
1 ....4.00
2 Means of Escape 4.00
3 Home Sweet Home 4.00
4 ....4.00
5 Fire Works 4.00
6 Belly of the Whale 4.00
Hologram cards (1:4),
1 ....2.00
2 Helen 2.00
3 Dolphin Like 2.00
4 Deacon 2.00
5 Cyclops Stare 2.00
6 ....2.00
Four-card promo sheet (*Advance #79; Collect 8-95; Cards Illus. #21*) 2.00

WEIRD TALES WOMEN IN PERIL
21st Century Archives (1993)
Pulp Magazine covers
Set: 55 cards 15.00
Pack: 75

Michael Whelan #35, Pursuit
(Comic Images 1993)

Michael Whelan #17, Monu-ment
(Comic Images 1993)

X-Files #2 (Topps 1995)

X-Files #60, Grotesque Sculpting
(Topps 199)

Box: 15.00
Factory Set: 55 cards +
    sculptorcast 17.50
Sculptor Case, 5 diff., each 5.00
Promos (#SC-1–#SC-5) each 2.00

WHELAN, MICHAEL:
ADVENTURES IN FANTASY
Comic Images (1993) SF art
Set: 90 cards 10.00
Pack: 10 cards 1.00
Box: 48 packs 25.00
Opti-Prism (1:32)
1 The Ultimate Sandbox 9.00
2 Peekaboo Fuzzies 9.00
3 Dragon Lake 9.00
SpectraScope Cards (1:32)
S1 Delirium's Mistress 8.00
S2 Crystal Singer 8.00
S3 Black Sun Rising 8.00
Promo card (Robot) 2.00

OTHER WORLDS
Comic Images (1995) SF art
Set: 90 cards 10.00
Pack: 15 cards 1.00
Box: 36 packs 25.00
Other Worlds Chromium cards (1:16)
1 ....5.00
2 Songs of Distant Earth 5.00
3 2061 ....5.00
4 The Ultimate Enemy 5.00
5 Time and Again 5.00
6 The Ultimate Enemy 5.00
Gunslinger subset (1:36)
1 ....8.00
2 The Temple of the Oracle 8.00
3 The Slow Mutants 8.00
Medallion card (1:3 boxes) 15.00
Autographed card 65.00
6-card uncut sheet 20.00
Promo card 1.50

KEEPSAKE
July 1994
Elric Set: 6 images on color 6" x 9
    cards, 7th card = all 6 images
    (5,000 made) 30.00

WHITE, TIM
FPG (1994) SF art
Set: 90 cards 12.50
Pack: 10 cards 1.25
Box: 36 packs 35.00
Metallic Storm (1:12)
MS1 Out of My Mind 8.00
MS2 Lord of Light 8.00
MS3 Eye of Cat 8.00
MS4 Uriel 8.00
MS5 Too Many Magicians 8.00
Autographed cards (1,000 made) ..65.00
10-card autographed sheet (1:case) 30.00
Four card deluxe promo sheet #15 ..3.00

WURTS, JANNY
FPG (1996) SF art
Set: 60 cards 15.00
Pack: 10 cards 1.50
Box: 36 packs 40.00
Metallics 5 diff., each 8.00
Autographed (1,000) 55.00
1,995 cases produced.

X-FILES, THE
Topps (1995) TV
Set: 72 cards 30.00
Pack: 9 cards 2.00
Box: 36 packs 75.00
Foil singles (1:1) 1.50
Foil Set: 72 cards 70.00
Topps Finest Chromium (1:18)
X1 Agents Mulder and Scully 15.00
X2 The Erlenimeyer Flask 15.00
X3 Fox Mulder 15.00
X4 Dana Scully 15.00
Etched-Foil Inserts (1:8)
i1 Do Not Open Until X-Mas 12.00
i2 A Dismemberance of Things
    Past 12.00
i3 The Return 12.00
i4 Firebird Part One: Khobka's
    Lament 12.00
i5 Firebird Part Two: Cresit Eundo ..12.00
i6 Firebird Part Three: A Brief
    Authority 12.00

#0 (shows) 10.00
P1 promo (comic shops) 25.00
P2 promo (comic shops) 20.00
P3 promo card (comic shops) 10.00
P4 promo card (*Wizard #50*) 10.00
P5 promo card (*Cards Illus.#23*) ..8.00
P6 promo card (*Non-Sport
    Update*) 10.00
One-card (P3) promo sheet 15.00
Binder 18.00

SEASON TWO
Topps (1996) TV
Set: 72 cards 25.00
Pack: 8 cards 1.50
Box: 36 packs 45.00
Foil Singles (1:1) 1.00
Foil Set: 72 cards 65.00
Uncut Foil Sheet 90.00
Etched-Foil Inserts (1:8) 6 diff.,
    each 8.00
Holograms, 4 diff., each 10.00
#0 Promo 3.00
P1 Promo 10.00
P2 Promo 30.00
P3 Promo 10.00
P4 Promo 10.00
P5 Promo 20.00
Oversize Promo 15.00

SEASON THREE
Topps (1996) TV
Set: 72 cards 25.00
Pack: 9 cards 1.25
Box: 36 packs 45.00
Foil card (1:1) 1.00
Foil Set: 72 cards 60.00
Uncut Foil sheet 90.00
3-D Holograms (1:18) 2 diff.,
    each 10.00
Etched Foil (1:12) 6 diff., each ...8.00
Paranormas Finest (1:18)
    2 diff., each 10.00
P1 Promo 3.00
P2 Promo 30.00
P3 Promo 3.00
P4 Promo 3.00
P5 Promo 15.00

X-FILES CONTACT
Intrepid (1997)
Set: 90 cards 40.00
Pack: 1.50
Box: 30.00
Alien Visitations, 9 diff., each 10.00
Clear Cel, 3 diff., each 15.00
Case Card 45.00
Proof Panels Set: 5 ....160.00
Promo card 5.00

X-FILES:
FIGHT THE FUTURE
Topps (1998) Movie
Set: 72 cards 20.00
Pack: 9 cards 2.00
Box: 36 packs 50.00
Mystery (1:12) 6 diff., each 8.00
Autographed cards (1:72) Set of 6 .400.00
William B. Davis (CSM) 100.00
Mitch Pileggi (Skinner) 80.00
John Neville (WGM) 80.00
Dean Haglund (Lone Gunman) 50.00
Tom Braidwood (Lone Gunman) ..50.00
Bruse Harwood (Lone Gunman) ..50.00
Promo 2.00

X-FILES
MASTERVISIONS
Topps (1995)
Set: 30 6½" x 10-1/8" cards on 24
    point card stock 40.00
Card 1.00
Promo XMVI 1.00
Convention promo 15.00

X-FILES SHOWCASE
Topps (1997) TV
Set: 72 cards 30.00
Pack: 9 cards 2.00
Box: 36 packs 60.00
X-Effect (1:8) 6 diff., each 8.00
Laser Cut, 6 diff., each 10.00
P1 Promo 5.00